BUSINESS DICTIONARY

OF

COMPUTERS

BUSINESS DICTIONARY SERIES

DICTIONARY OF BUSINESS AND MANAGEMENT
Jerry M. Rosenberg

DICTIONARY OF BANKING
Jerry M. Rosenberg

DICTIONARY OF INVESTING
Jerry M. Rosenberg

BUSINESS DICTIONARY OF COMPUTERS
Jerry M. Rosenberg

OTHER BOOKS BY THE AUTHOR

Automation, Manpower and Education (Random House)

The Computer Prophets (Macmillan)

The Death of Privacy: Do Government and Industrial Computers Threaten Our Personal Freedom? (Random House)

Inside the Wall Street Journal: The History and Power of Dow Jones & Company and America's Most Influential Newspaper (Macmillan)

Dictionary of Artificial Intelligence and Robotics (John Wiley & Sons, Inc.)

The New Europe: An A to Z Compendium on the European Community (Bureau of National Affairs)

Dictionary of Business Acronyms, Initials, and Abbreviations (McGraw-Hill)

Dictionary of Wall Street Acronyms, Initials, and Abbreviations (McGraw-Hill)

Dictionary of Information Technology and Computer Acronyms, Initials and Abbreviations (McGraw-Hill)

The New American Community: The U.S. Response to the European and Asian Economic Challenge (Praeger)

BUSINESS DICTIONARY
OF
COMPUTERS

Jerry M. Rosenberg

**Professor, Graduate School
of Management, and
School of Business
RUTGERS UNIVERSITY**

Business Dictionary Series

John Wiley & Sons, Inc.

New York • Chichester • Brisbane • Toronto • Singapore

In recognition of the importance of preserving what has been
written, it is a policy of John Wiley & Sons, Inc., to have
books of enduring value published in the United States
printed on acid-free paper, and we exert our best efforts
to that end.

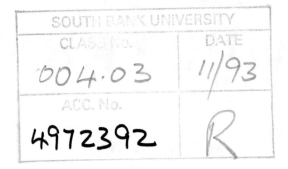
Library of Congress Cataloging-in-Publication Data

Rosenberg, Jerry Martin.
    Business dictionary of computers / Jerry M. Rosenberg.
      p.   cm. — (Business dictionary series)
    Originally published: Dictionary of computers, information
processing, and telecommunications, 1984.
    ISBN 0-471-58575-0 (alk. paper). — ISBN 0-471-58574-2 (pbk.)
    1. Computers—Dictionaries.   2. Electronic data processing—
Dictionaries.   3. Telecommunications—Dictionaries.   I. Rosenberg,
Jerry Martin. Dictionary of computers, information processing, and
telecommunications. II. Title. III. Series.
QA76.15.R66   1993
004'.03—dc20   93-15268

Printed in the United States of America

10 9 8 7 6 5 4 3 2 1

To Elizabeth and to her future

PREFACE

Nine years ago, the *Business Dictionary of Computers,* (then titled the *Dictionary of Computers, Information Processing and Telecommunications*) first appeared. It was expected to be sufficiently current for at least one generation. However, the dramatic explosion in personal computing and research and development accompanied by the increased demand for equipment worldwide has led to a significant growth of terminology. This edition adds the newest terminology in hardware, software, programming concepts and languages, operating systems, electronics, logic circuits, personal computers, supercomputers, networking, windows, desktop, graphics, architecture, microcomputer hardware, and a host of other critical phrases and words.

The result is a totally reworked dictionary, updating and altering older terms, with the most recent entries to be found in any lexicon of computer terminology.

I remain thankful to Stephen Kippur, John Wiley's Senior Vice President and my editor, Karl Weber, Associate Publisher now, but for many years my editor, all retaining the confidence in my work to have launched this new edition. It is Ellen, my wife, daughters Liz and Lauren, son-in-law Bob, who have been and remain the stimuli that inspire me to perpetuate this passion for words. I ask for nothing more.

To my audience and users, I continue to appreciate the time spent communicating with me as to suggestions for new entries and/or corrections of definitions found in this volume.

JERRY M. ROSENBERG

New York, New York

ACKNOWLEDGMENTS

No dictionary can be the exclusive product of one person's effort. Even when written by one individual, such a work requires the tapping of many sources, which is especially true of this book. By the very nature of the fields included, I have had to rely on the able and extensive efforts of others.

When I have quoted a definition from another source, a letter in brackets appears at the end of the definition. This letter indicates the primary reference used in defining the term. The following sources were used:

(A) *American National Dictionary for Information Processing,* Computer and Business Equipment Manufacturers Association, American National Standards Institute.

(B) *Vocabulary of Data Processing,* International Organization for Standardization, International Standards Organization (ISO).

Any apparent similarity to existing, unreleased definitions in those cases where neither designation occurs is purely accidental and the result of the limitations of language.

Much assistance has come indirectly from authors of books, journal articles, and reference materials. They are too numerous to be named here. Various organizations have aided me directly by providing informative source materials. Some government agencies and not-for-profit associations have provided a considerable amount of usable information.

CONTENTS

INTRODUCTION

This dictionary of more than 7,500 entries has been prepared with the hope that awareness of the accepted meanings of terms may enhance the process of sharing information and ideas. Though it cannot eliminate the need for the user to determine how a writer or speaker treats a word, such a dictionary shows what usages exist. It should reduce the arguments about words and assist in stabilizing terminology. Most important, it should aid people in saying and writing just what they intend with greater clarity.

A word can take on different meanings in different contexts. There may be as many meanings as there are areas of specialty. A goal of this dictionary is to be broad and to establish core definitions that represent the variety of individual meanings. My purpose is to enhance parsimony and clearness in the communication process.

Many terms are used in different ways. I have tried to unite them without bias of giving one advantage or dominance over another. Whenever possible (without creating a controversy), I have stated the connection between multiple usages.

Commonly used symbols, acronyms, and abbreviations are given. However, I have avoided, for the most part, including terms of an explicitly commercial nature, unless their use has passed into the generic. Foreign words and phrases are included only if they have become an integral part of our English vocabulary.

This dictionary includes terms from hardware, software, programming concepts and languages, operating systems, electronics, logic circuits, personal computers, supercomputers, networking, windows, desktop, graphics, architecture, microcomputer hardware, and a host of other critical phrases and words.

The entries offer the most recent information taken from contemporary practice.

ORGANIZATION

This is a defining work rather than a compilation of facts. The line is not easy to draw because in the final analysis meanings are based on facts. Consequently, factual information is used where necessary to make a term more easily understood.

All terms are presented in the language of those who use them. Obviously, the level of complexity needed for a definition will vary with the user; one person's complexity is another's precise and parsimonious statement. Several meanings are sometimes given the relatively simple for the layman, the more developed and technical for the specialist.

I have organized the dictionary to provide information easily and rapidly. Keeping in mind two categories of users—the experienced person who demands precise information about a particular word, and the newcomer, support member, teacher, or student who seeks general explanations—I have in most cases supplied both general and specialized entries. This combination of "umbrella" entries and specialized definitions should make this dictionary an unusually useful reference source.

ALPHABETIZATION

Alphabetization. Words are presented alphabetically. Compound terms are placed where the reader is most likely to look for them. They are entered under their most distinctive component, usually nouns, which tend to be more distinctive than adjectives. Should you fail to locate a word where you initially look for it, turn to a variant spelling, a synonym or another, different word of the compound term.

Entries containing mutual concepts are usually grouped for comparison. They are then given in inverted order; that is, the expected order of words is reversed to allow the major word of the phrase to appear at the beginning of the term. These entries precede those that are given in the expected order. The terms are alphabetized up to the first comma and then by words following the comma, thus establishing clusters of related terms.

Headings.   The currently popular term is usually given as the principal entry, with other terms cross referenced to it. Some terms have been included for historical significance, even though they are not presently in common usage.

Cross References.   The rule followed for cross references calls for going from the general to the specific. Occasionally, **see** references from the specific to the general are used to inform the user of words related to particular entries. **See** references to presently accepted terminology are made wherever possible. The use of **Cf.** suggests words to be compared with the original entry. **Deprecated term** indicates that the term should not be used and that there is a preferred word or phrase.

Synonyms.   The words **synonymous with** or **synonym for** following a definition does not imply that the term is exactly equivalent to the principal entry under which it appears. Usually the term only approximates the primary sense of the original entry.

Disciplines.   Many words are given multiple definitions based on their utilization in various fields of activity. The definition with the widest application is then given first, with the remaining definitions listed by area of specialty (identified in boldface italic type). Since the areas may overlap, the reader should examine all multiple definitions of a term.

A:
- (1) see *adder.*
- (2) see *analog.*
- (3) see *asynchronous.*
- (4) see *attribute.*

A and I: abstracting and indexing.

abbreviated combined relation condition: in COBOL, the combined condition that results from the explicit omission of a common subject or a common subject and common relational operator in a consecutive sequence of relation conditions.

ABEND: see *abnormal end of task.*

abend: synonymous with *blow up.*

aberration: an error condition, usually in the cathode ray tube of a terminal.

able: the digit in a hexadecimal numbering system that is equal in value to 10. It is written as X'A'.

abnormal end of task (ABEND): termination of a task prior to its completion because of an error condition that cannot be resolved by recovery facilities while the task is executing.

abort: to terminate, in a controlled manner, a program or processing activity in a computer system because it is impossible or undesirable for the activity to proceed.

abort timer: a device which stops dial up data transmission if no data are sent within a predetermined time period.

ABSLDR: see *absolute loader.*

absolute address:
- (1) an address in a computer language that identifies a storage location or a device without the use of any intermediate reference. (B)
- (2) an address that is permanently assigned by the machine designer to a storage location.
- (3) synonymous with *explicit address, machine address, specific address.* (A)

absolute addressing: a method of addressing in which the address part of an instruction contains an absolute address. (A) (B)

absolute assembler: an assembly-language program designed to yield binary programs only with absolute addresses and address references.

absolute code: coding designed so that all instructions are described in basic machine language. Synonymous with *specific code.*

absolute coding: coding that uses computer instructions with absolute address. Synonymous with *specific coding.* (A)

absolute data: in computer graphics, values in a computer program that specify the actual coordinates in a display space or image space. Cf. *relative data.*

absolute error:
- (1) the algebraic result of subtracting a true, specified, or theoretically correct

value from the value computed, observed, measured, or achieved. (B)

(2) the amount of error expressed in the same units as the quantity holding the error.

(3) loosely, the absolute value of the error, that is, the magnitude of the error without regard for its algebraic sign. (A)

absolute expression: in assembler language, an assembly-time expression whose value is not affected by program relocation. An absolute expression can represent an absolute address.

absolute instruction: a computer instruction in its final, executable form. (A)

absolute loader (ABSLDR): a routine that reads a computer program into main storage, beginning at the assembled origin. (A)

absolute term: a term whose value is not affected by relocation.

absolute value: a quantity, the magnitude of which is known by the computer, but the algebraic sign is not relevant.

absolute-value computer: a computer for processing all data using full values of all variables at all times.

abstract: a shortened representation of the contents of a document.

abstract symbol:

(1) a symbol whose meaning and use have not been determined by a general agreement but have to be defined for each application of the symbol. (B)

(2) in optical character recognition, a symbol whose form does not suggest its meaning and use; these should be defined for each specified set of applications. (A)

A-bus: the major internal bus within a microprocessor.

AC: see *acoustic coupler.*

ACC:

(1) see *accumulate.*

(2) see *accumulator.*

acceleration period: the period in which a card reader and/or punch actually move(s) the card into position where data can be read.

acceleration time: that part of accesstime required to bring an auxiliary storage

device, typically a tape drive, to the speed at which data can be read or written.

accent: a mark placed above or below a character; frequently to show its pronunciation.

acceptance test: actions made to prove that a system fulfills agreed upon criteria; for example, that the processing of specified input yielded expected results.

access: the manner in which files or data sets are referred to by the computer. See *direct access, direct-access storage, immediate-access storage, random access, remote access, serial access.*

access arm: a part of a disk storage unit that is used to hold one or more reading and writing heads. (A)

access authority: an authority that relates to a request for a type of access to data sets. The access authorities are NONE, READ access, UPDATE access, CONTROL access, and ALTER access.

access button: synonymous with *skip key.*

access environment: a description of the current user including current connect group, user attributes, group authorities. An access environment is constructed during user identification and verification.

access level: see *physical-access level.*

access mechanism: a group of access arms that move together as a unit.

access method: a technique for moving data between main storage and input/output devices. See also *access method routines, basic access method, basic direct access method, basic indexed sequential access method, basic partitioned access method, basic sequential access method, queued indexed sequential access method, queued sequential access method.*

access method routines: routines that move data between main storage and input/output devices.

access mode: a technique that is used to obtain a specific logical record from or to place a specific logical record into a file assigned to a mass storage device. (A)

accessory: a basic part, subassembly, or assembly used with another assembly, unit, or set.

access privilege: the ability to see folders, see files, or make changes to a shared disk or folder. Access privilege is granted by the owner of the shared item and are used to determine what other network users can do with the disk or folder and its contents.

access scan: a procedure for receiving data from files by searching every data item until the required one is obtained.

access time:
(1) the time interval between the instant at which an instruction control unit initiates a call for data and the instant at which delivery of the data is completed. Access time equals latency plus transfer time. (A) (B)
(2) the time interval between the instant at which data are requested to be stored and the instant at which storage is started.
(3) deprecated term for *cycle time*. (A) (B)
(4) see also *latency, seek time*.

accounting machine:
(1) a keyboard-actuated machine that prepares accounting records.
(2) a machine that reads data from external storage media, such as cards or tapes, and automatically produces accounting records or tabulations, usually on continuous forms.
(3) see *electrical accounting machine*. (A)

ACCUM: see *accumulator*.

accumulate (ACC): to enter the result of an operation in an accumulator.

accumulating reproducer: equipment that reproduces punched cards and possesses limited additional capabilities of adding, subtracting, and summary punching.

accumulator (ACC) (ACCUM):
(1) a device in which the result of an arithmetic or logical operation is determined.
(2) a register that stores a quantity. When a second quantity is entered, it arithmetically combines the quantity and stores the result in the location of the register.

accumulator address: an address used when the operand is in an accumulator.

accumulator register: synonymous with *accumulator*.

accumulator shift instruction: a computer instruction causing the contents of a register to be displaced by a specific number of digit positions left or right.

accuracy:
(1) a quality held by that which is free of error. (B)
(2) a qualitative assessment of freedom from error, a high assessment corresponding to a small error. (B)
(3) a quantitative measure of the magnitude of error, preferably expressed as a function of the relative error, a high value of this measure corresponding to a small error. (A) (B) Cf. *precision*.

accuracy control character: a control character used to indicate whether the data with which it is associated are in error, or are to be disregarded, or cannot be represented on a particular device. Synonymous with *error-control character*. (A)

accuracy control system: a system of error detection and control.

achromatic color: in computer graphics, one that is found along the gray scale from white to black.

ACK: affirmative acknowledgment; used in block transmission, indicates that the previous transmission block was accepted by the receiver and that it is ready to accept the next block of the transmission.

ACL: audit command language; a high level programming language.

ACM: Association for Computer Machinery; a major professional society devoted to the consistent advancement of the science and art of computer technology.

A-conversion: a FORTRAN instruction to transmit alphanumeric data to and from variables within storage.

acoustic coupler (AC): a type of telecommunication equipment that permits use of a telephone network for data transmission by means of sound transducers.

acoustic coupling: a method of coupling a data terminal equipment or similar device to a telephone line by means of transducers that utilize sound waves to or from a telephone handset or equivalent.

ACR: see *alternate recovery*.

acronym: any word formed from the first, or first few letters of each of a group of words; that is, BASIC for Beginner's All-Purpose Symbolic Instruction Code.

action: activity or processing activity steps, operations, etc.

action cycle: any total operation performed on data.

action entry: one of four sections of a decision logic table; specifies what actions should be taken.

action message: a message issued because of a condition that requires an operator response.

action paper: paper that makes a carbon of whatever is typed. Used to analyze the number of errors, retypings, and half-done pages that crop up before a final perfect page emerges.

action specification: in a PL/1 ON statement, the on unit or the single keyword SYSTEM, either of which specifies the action to be taken whenever an interruption results from raising of the named on condition. The action specification can also include the keyword SNAP.

action stub: one of four sections of a decision logic table; describes possible actions applicable to the problem to be solved.

activate (a block): in PL/1, to initiate the execution of a block. A procedure block is activated when it is invoked at any of its entry points; a begin block is activated when it is encountered in a normal flow of control, including a branch.

activation: in a network, the process by which a component of a node is made ready to perform the functions for which it was designed.

active:

(1) operational.

(2) pertaining to a node or device that is connected or is available for connection to another node or device. Cf. *inactive.*

active file: a permanent file or a temporary file, having an expiration date that is later than the job date.

active link: a link that is currently available for transmission of data. Cf. *inactive link.*

active master file: a master file holding relatively active items.

active master item: the most active items on a master file measured by usage of the data.

active memory: synonymous with *associative memory.*

active program: any program that is loaded and ready to be executed.

active storage: see *main storage.*

active window: In Macintosh and Microsoft windows environments, the window with solid lines running across its title bar; belongs to the program in use. See *active program.*

activity: the percentage of records in a file that are processed in a run. See also *volatility.*

activity level: the value taken by a structural variable in an intermediate or final solution to a programming problem.

activity loading: a method of storing records on a file in which the most frequently processed records can be located with the least number of reads.

activity ratio: the ratio of the number of records in a file that are in use to the total number of records in that file.

actual address: synonymous with *absolute address.*

actual code: synonymous with *absolute code.*

actual data transfer rate: the average number of bits, characters, or blocks per unit of time transferred from a data source and received by a data sink.

actual decimal point: in COBOL the physical representation, using either of the decimal point characters (. or ,), of the decimal point position in a data item. When specified, it will appear in a printed report, and it requires an actual space in storage.

actual instruction: deprecated term for *effective instruction.* (A) (B)

actual key: in COBOL, a key that directly expresses the physical location of a logical record on a mass storage medium. (A)

actual parameter: a variable or expression contained in a procedure or function call and passed to that procedure or function.

actual time: the performance of computing during the specific time where the related process, event, problem, or communication takes place.

actuating signal: an input impulse in the control circuitry of computers.

actuator: a mechanical unit making something occur. Used most often with disk drives where an actuator moves the read/write head to a desired position over the disk surface.

A/D: analog-to-digital; indicating a conversion from analog information to digital form.

ADA: a high-level language for real time processing problems. Developed in 1983 by computer scientists at New York University, it is the first successful version of a key program for the U.S. Defense Department to develop a standard computer language for the military. It is named after Augusta Ada Byron, Lord Byron's daughter, who is considered the world's first programmer.

ADAPSO: association of the U.S. and Canadian data-processing service organizations including a software developer and marketing units.

adapter: a mechanism for attaching parts, for example, parts having different diameters. See *channel-to-channel adapter, line adapter.*

ADC: see *analog-to-digital converter.*

add: the procedure of increasing or decreasing a number utilizing an arithmetic operation involving a second number.

added entry: in cataloguing, a secondary entry, that is, any entry other than the main entry.

addend: in an addition operation, a number or quantity added to the augend. (A) (B)

adder (A) (ADDR):
(1) a device whose output data are a representation of the sum of the numbers represented by its input data. (B)
(2) a device whose output is a representation of the sum of the quantities represented by its inputs.
(3) see *serial adder.* (A)

adder subtracter: a device that acts as an adder or subtracter depending upon the control signal received. The adder subtracter may be constructed so as to yield the sum and the difference at the same time. (A) (B)

add file: a file to which records are being added.

add-in: an electronic component placed on a printed circuit board (already installed into a computer) to increase capability. In PCs, these can be expansion boards, cartridges, or chips.

addition: in data processing, combining quantities according to various circuitry designs, machine rules regarding changes in values, and types of carry-over operations. See *parallel addition, serial addition.*

additional character: synonymous with *special character.*

addition record: a record which results in the creation of a new record in the master file being updated.

addition table: the area of main storage holding a table of numbers used during the table-scan concept of addition.

additive attributes: in PL/1, attributes for which there are no defaults and which, if required, must always be added to the list of specified attributes or be implied.

add-on: circuitry or system that is attached to a computer to increase memory or performance. See *add-in.*

add operation:
(1) a disk or diskette operation that adds records to an existing file.
(2) an operation caused by an add instruction.

ADDR:
(1) see *adder.*
(2) see *address.*
(3) see *addressing.*
(4) see *address register.*

address (ADDR) (ADRS):
(1) a character or group of characters that identifies a *register,* a particular part of memory, or some other data source or destination. (A) (B)
(2) to refer to a device or an item of data by its address. (A) (B)
(3) in word processing, the location, identified by an address code, of a

specific section of the recording medium or storage.

(4) digital information (a combination of bits) that identifies a location in a storage device or equipment unit.

(5) see also *absolute address, base address, direct address, effective address, four-address, four-plus-one address, generated address, immediate address, indexed address, indirect address, instruction address, machine address, multiaddress, multilevel address, n-level address, one-level address, real address, relative address, relocatable address, return address, self-relative address, single address, specific address, symbolic address, two-level address, virtual address, zero-level address.*

addressability:

(1) in micrographics, the number of addressable positions within a specified film frame, as follows: number of addressable horizontal positions by number of addressable vertical positions. (A)

(2) in computer graphics, the number of addressable points within a specified display space or image space.

addressable: the storage location within main memory that is directly accessed through an instruction.

addressable cursor: a cursor moved at will, by either software or by keyboard controls, to any position on a screen.

addressable horizontal positions:

(1) in micrographics, the number of positions within a specified film frame at which a vertical line can be placed. (A)

(2) in computer graphics, the number of positions within a specified raster, at which a full length vertical line can be placed. Synonymous with *display line.*

addressable register: a temporary storage location with a fixed location and address number.

addressable unit: a computer-attached unit capable of being addressed.

addressable vertical positions:

(1) in micrographics, the number of positions within a specified film frame at which a horizontal line can be placed. (A)

(2) in computer graphics, the number of positions, within a specified raster, at which a full length horizontal line can be placed. Synonymous with *display column.*

address code: in word processing, a program instruction that identifies an address.

address comparator: a unit that verifies that the correct address is being read. The comparison is made between the address read and the specified address.

address computation: computer operations which create or modify the address portion of instructions.

address constant: a value, or an expression representing a value, used in the calculation of storage address.

addressed memory: memory units that hold each individual register.

addressee: the intended recipient of a message.

address effective: any modified address; an address actually considered for use in a particular execution of a computer instruction.

addresses: see *decoding.*

addresses of address: programming technique used primarily with subroutines.

address field: that part of a computer word containing either the address of the operand or the information needed to derive that address.

address format:

(1) the arrangement of the address parts of an instruction. The expression "plus-one" is frequently used to indicate that one of the addresses specifies the location of the next instruction to be executed, such as one-plus-one, two-plus-one, three-plus-one, four-plus-one.

(2) the arrangement of the parts of a single address, such as those required for identifying a channel, module, or track on magnetic disk. (A)

addressing (ADDR):

(1) the assignment of addresses to the instructions of a program.

(2) see *absolute addressing, deferred addressing, implied addressing, indirect addressing, one-ahead addressing, relative addressing, repetitive addressing, self-relative addressing, symbolic addressing.* See also *polling.*

addressing characters: identifying characters sent by the computer over a line that cause a particular station (or component).

addressing mode: a means of storing and retrieving data in main memory.

addressless instruction format: an instruction format containing no address part, used either when no address is needed, or when the address is in some way implicit.

address mapping: conversion of data showing the physical location of records with assignment of these records to storage locations; for example, the translation of a virtual address to an absolute address.

address mark: a byte of data on a disk or diskette, used to identify the data field and ID field in the record.

address modification: any arithmetic, logic, or syntactic operation performed on an address. (A)

address part: a part of an instruction that usually contains only an address or part of an address. (A) (B)

address reference: synonym for *address* (2).

address register (ADDR): a register in which an address is stored. See also *base address register, instruction address register.* (A)

address size: the maximum number of binary digits in an instruction used in directly addressing memory.

address space: the complete range of addresses that is available to a programmer.

address space identifier (ASID): a unique, system-assigned identifier for an address space.

address stop: a capability to specify at the system console an address which when encountered causes a halt in processing. See also *breakpoint, instruction address stop.*

address track: a track that contains addresses used to locate data on other tracks of the same device. (B)

address translation:

(1) the process of changing the address of an item of data or an instruction to the address in main storage at which it is to be loaded or relocated.

(2) in virtual storage systems, the process of changing the address of an item of data or an instruction from its virtual storage address to its real storage address.

add-subtract time: time needed to perform one addition or subtraction, exclusive of the read or write time.

add time: the time required for one addition, not including the time required to get the quantities from storage and return them to storage.

add to storage: the process that instantly enters the final sum of the accumulator into the computer memory.

ADI: American Documentation Institute, now, American Society for Information Science (ASIS).

adjacency: in character recognition, a condition in which the character spacing reference lines of two consecutively printed characters on the same line are separated by less than a specified distance. (A)

adjacent: in a network, pertaining to devices, programs, or domains that are connected by a data link or that share common control.

adjacent domains:

(1) domains that are connected by a direct data link.

(2) domains sharing a common subarea node (e.g., a communication controller) or two domains connected by a cross-domain subarea link with no intervening domains.

adjoint (system): computational method based on the reciprocal relations between a system of ordinary linear differential equations and its adjoint.

adjustable extent: in PL/1, a bound (of an array), length (of a string), or size (of an area) that may be different for different generations of the associated variable. Adjustable bounds, lengths, and sizes are specified as expressions or asterisks (or by REFER options for based variables), which are evaluated separately for each generation. They cannot be used for static variables.

adjust text mode: in word processing, a mode that reformats text to accommodate specified line lengths and page sizes and to help the operator to adjust line endings using word-processing control functions.

ADMIN: see *administrator.*

administrative data processing: automatic data processing used in accounting or in management. Synonymous with *business data processing.* (A) (B)

administrative operator: see *control operator.*

Administrative Support System: a word processing system used primarily by business managers.

administrator (ADMIN): see *system administrator.*

ADP: see *automatic data processing.* (A)

ADPE: abbreviation for *automatic data processing equipment.*

ADPS: abbreviation for *Automatic Data Processing System.*

ADP system: synonymous with *computer system.*

ADR: see *address.*

ADRS: see *address.*

advanced optical character reader (AOCR): optical character reader capable of storing approximately 90 fonts to typewritten addresses.

affinity: the relationship among data-processing elements where there is an inherent likeness or agreement.

AFIPS: American Federation of Information Processing Societies.

AFR: automatic field/format recognition; a computer input facility.

agenda: set of control-language statements prescribing a solution path or run procedure; an ordered listing of major operations as part of a procedure for a solution or computer run.

aggregate expression: in PL/1, an array expression or a structure expression.

aggregate function: in database terminology, a function that computes a single value on the collective values of a single column or field in all records of the database. For example, should a database have 100 records, an aggregate function can utilize the value in the third field of each of the 100 records to determine a result.

aggregate motion printer: a printing unit where the mechanism does not return to an "at rest" position between characters.

AI: see *artificial intelligence.*

airline reservation system: an on-line application in which a computing system is used to keep track of seat inventories, flight schedules, and other information required to run an airline. The reservation system is designed to maintain up-to-date files and to respond, within seconds or less, to inquiries from ticket agents at locations remote from the computing system.

AL: see *assembler language.*

ALD: see *automated logic diagram.*

alert box: a box appearing on the screen to give a warning or other message, sometimes accompanied by an alert sound.

algebraic language: an algorithmic language many of whose statements are structured to resemble the structure of algebraic expressions, for example, ALGOL, FORTRAN. (A)

algebraic sign conventions: the rules of algebra that determine whether a result is positive or negative when numbers are added, subtracted, multiplied, or divided.

ALGOL (algorithmic language): a language primarily used to express computer programs by algorithms. (A)

algorithm: a finite set of well-defined rules for the solution of a problem in a finite number of steps; for example, a full statement of an arithmetic procedure for evaluating sin x to a stated precision. Cf. *heuristic.* (A) (B)

algorithmic language: an artificial language established for expressing algorithms.

algorithmic routine: a program or routine that directs a computer specifically toward a solution of a problem in a finite number of distinct and discrete steps as contrasted to trial-and-error methods, that is, heuristic methods or routines.

alias:

(1) an alternate label. For example, a label and one or more aliases may be used to refer to the same data element or point in a computer program. (A)

(2) an alternate name for a member of a partitioned data set.

(3) a file that stands for and points to a file, folder, or disk that can be used as if it were the original.

aliasing: removing the jagged line, or "step edge" effect on graphic displays.

alias name: an alternate name.

alignment: the storing of data in relation to certain machine-dependent boundaries. See *boundary alignment.*

all-caps mode: found on most computer keyboards, a mode that is like the shift lock on a standard typewriter, except that only alphabetic letters are shifted to upper case.

all-in-one microcomputer: a computer system consisting of major system components—the central processing unit, memory, circuitry, disk drives, input/output interfaces, cathode-ray tube screen, and keyboard—all contained within one housing.

ALLOC: see *allocation.*

allocate: to assign a resource, such as a disk or a diskette file, to a specific task.

allocated storage: see *storage.*

allocation: see *dynamic storage allocation, resource allocation, storage allocation.*

allowance: the downward adjustment in the selling price of merchandise because of damage, trade-in, or promotion.

all-purpose computer: a computer combining the benefits previously assigned solely to general-purpose or special-purpose computers. Synonymous with *general-purpose computer.*

alphabet:

(1) an ordered set of all the letters used in a language, including letters with diacritical signs where appropriate, but not including punctuation marks. (B)

(2) an ordered set of symbols used in a language, for example, the Morse code alphabet, the 128 ASCII characters. (A)

alphabetic character: a letter or other symbol, excluding digits, used in a language.

alphabetic character set: a character set that contains letters and may contain control characters, special characters, and the space character, but not digits. (A) (B)

alphabetic character subset: a character subset that contains letters and may contain control characters, special characters, and the space character, but not digits. (A) (B)

alphabetic code: a code according to which data is represented using an alphabetic character set. (A) (B)

alphabetic-coded character set: a coded character set whose character set is an alphabetic character set. (A) (B)

alphabetic shift: a control for selecting the alphabetic character set in an alphanumeric keyboard printer.

alphabetic string:

(1) a string consisting solely of letters from the same alphabet. (B)

(2) a character string consisting solely of letters and associated special characters from the same alphabet. (A)

alphabetic word:

(1) a word consisting solely of letters from the same alphabet. (B)

(2) a word consisting of letters and associated special characters, but not digits. (A)

alphameric: synonymous with *alphanumeric.* (A)

alphamosaic: a means for generating videotex images on a screen. Displays are made using a mosaic of dots.

ALPHANUM: see *alphanumeric.*

alphanumeric (ALPHANUM): pertaining to a character set that contains letters, digits, and usually other characters, such as punctuation marks. Synonymous with *alphameric.* (A)

alphanumeric character set: a character set that contains both letters and digits and may contain control characters, special characters, and the space character. (A) (B)

alphanumeric character subset: a character subset that contains both letters and digits and may contain control characters, special characters, and the space character. (A) (B)

alphanumeric code: a code according to which data is represented using an alphanumeric character set. (A) (B)

alphanumeric-coded character set: a coded character set whose character set is an alphanumeric character set. (A) (B)

alphanumeric data: data represented by letters and digits, perhaps with special characters and the space character. (A) (B)

alphanumeric display device: synonymous with *character display device.*

alphanumeric edited character: in COBOL, a character within an alphanumeric character string that contains at least one B or O.

alphanumeric field: a field that can contain any alphabetic, numeric, or special character.

alphanumeric instruction: the name given to instruction that can be used equally well with alphabetic or numeric kinds of data.

alphanumeric keyboard: a keyboard used to enter letters, numbers, and special characters into a display station buffer; it is also used to perform special functions such as backspacing and to produce special control signals.

alphanumeric sort: process in which a word processor puts a list into alphabetical or numerical order, or both.

alpha test: the first stress test of a new product under laboratory conditions. See also *beta testing.*

alpha testing: trying out a new product where it was manufactured. The next step, beta testing, involves trying out a product at a place other than the site of manufacture. Cf. *beta testing.*

ALT: see *alternate key.*

alterable memory: a storage medium that can be written into.

alteration switch: a manual switch on the computer console or a program-simulated switch that can be set on or off to control machine instructions.

altering: any operation for inserting, deleting, or changing information.

alter mode: a program condition that allows changing or updating data in storage.

alternate character sets: different typefaces found in some printers.

alternate key (ALT): On PC keyboards, a special key that is pressed before another key to indicate an alternate use of the second key. At times the alternate meaning will be printed on the front of letter and number keys.

alternate path retry (APR): a facility that allows an input/output operation that has failed to be retrieved on another channel assigned to the device performing the input/output operation. It also provides the capability to establish other paths to an on-line or off-line device.

alternate recovery (ACR): a facility that attempts system recovery when a processing unit fails by transferring work to another processing unit.

alternate route: a secondary or backup route that is used if normal routing is not possible.

alternation: synonymous with *OR operation.*

alternative attribute: an attribute that may be chosen from a group of two or more alternatives. If none is specified, one of the alternatives is assumed.

alternative denial: synonymous with *NOT-AND operation.*

ALU: see *arithmetic and logic unit.* See also *arithmetic unit, logic unit.*

ambiguity error: an error resulting from an incorrect choice when there are two possible readings of a digitized number.

ambiguous name: the unspecified name, usually of a file. Cf. *unambiguous name.*

ambiguous reference: in PL/1, a reference that is not sufficiently qualified to identify one and only one name known at point of reference.

amendment record: synonymous with *change record.*

American National Standard control characters: control characters defined by American National Standard FORTRAN.

American National Standard Labels (ANL): magnetic tape labels that conform to the conventions established by the American National Standards Institute.

American National Standards Institute (ANSI): an organization for the purpose of establishing voluntary industry standards.

American Standard Code for Information Interchange: see *ASCII*.

amount field: the field where a clerk manually inserts the amount of a check; used in the processing of bank checks.

ampersand: the symbol "&."

amphibolous: relating to an ambiguity; an uncertainty; doubtfulness.

A/N: see *alphanumeric*.

analog (A): pertaining to data in the form of continuously variable physical quantities. See *network analog*. Cf. *digital*.

analog adder: a device where analog output variable is equal to the sum, or a weighted sum, of two or more analog input variables. Synonymous with *summer*. (B)

analog computer:
(1) a computer in which analog representation of data is mainly used.
(2) a computer that operates on analog data by performing physical processes on these data.
(3) see also *digital computer, hybrid computer*.

analog data: data represented by physical quantity that is considered to be continuously variable and whose magnitude is made directly proportional to the data or to a suitable function of the data. (A) (B)

analog-digital conversion: the process of converting a continuous measurement to digital form. Often accomplished by sampling a continuous signal at discrete intervals of time and specifying the value of the signal in digital form.

analog/digital converter (A/D): a converter able to change analog representation of some physical quantity into a form suitable for digital computer processing.

analog divider: a device whose analog output variable is proportional to the quotient of two analog input variables. (B)

analog input module: devices that convert analog input signals from process instrumentation into a digit code for transmission to the computer.

analog integration: integration of an analog computer, performed by means of an operational amplifier with a capacitor instead of a resistor in the feedback loop.

analog monitor: a monitor compatible with analog signalling, such as the conventional CRT monitor. Cf. *digital monitor*.

analog multiplier: a device whose analog output variable is proportional to the quotient of two analog input variables. (B)

analog representation: a representation of the value of a variable by a physical quantity that is considered to be continuously variable, the magnitude of the physical quantity being made directly proportional to the variable or to a suitable function of the variable. (A) (B)

analog scaling: considering the limited range of values obtainable on the computer.

analog simulation: the use of an electrical system to represent any physical system.

analog-to-digital converter (A/D):
(1) a functional unit that converts analog signals to digital date. (B)
(2) a device that senses an analog signal and converts it to a proportional representation in digital form.

analogue: see *analog*.

analog unit: a unit that generates, responds to, or acts upon analog data.

analysis: the methodical investigation of a problem, and the separation of the problem into smaller related units for further detailed study. See *flow analysis, numerical analysis*. (A)

analysis block: relocatable portion of the computer storage where program testing or statistical data are kept which can later be used to analyze the performance of the system.

analysis mode: a mode of operation where special programs monitor the performance of the system for subsequent analysts.

analyst: a person who defines problems and develops algorithms and procedures for their solution. (A)

analytical engine: one of Charles Babbage's earliest computer machines. Developed in 1833, it was the first general-purpose automatic digital computer.

analytic relationship: the relationship existing between concepts and corresponding terms, by virtue of their definition and inherent scope of meaning.

analyzer: see *differential analyzer, digital differential analyzer, network analyzer.*

ancestral task: in PL/1, the attaching task or any of the tasks in a direct line from the given task to, and including, the major task.

ancillary equipment: synonym for *auxiliary equipment.*

AND: logic operator having the property that if P is a statement, Q is a statement, R is a statement, . . . , then the AND of P,Q,R, . . . is true if all statements are true, false if any statement is false. Synonymous with *logical multiply.* (A) (B)

AND circuit: synonymous with *AND element.*

AND element: logical element that performs the boolean operation of conjunction. (B) Synonymous with *AND circuit* and *AND gate.*

AND gate: see *AND element.*

AND-not operation: deprecated term for *exclusion.* (A) (B)

AND operation: see *conjunction.* (A) (B)

angle brackets: slang; the characters < and > .

annex memory: a small memory unit used as a go-between for the input and output units and main memory. Synonymous with *buffer.*

annotation: an added descriptive comment or explanatory note. (A)

annotation symbol: a symbol used to add messages or notes to a flowchart.

ANSI: see *American National Standards Institute.*

ANSI BASIC: a programming language that has a universally accepted set of standard rules. See *BASIC.*

anthropomorphic image: a means of describing computers, computer procedures, and objects controlled by computers as though the computer were a person.

anti-aliasing: in computer graphics, a filtering technique to give the appearance of smooth lines and edges in a raster image. The technique involves the use of intermediate intensities between neigh-

boring pixels to soften the "stairstep effect" of sloped lines.

anticipation mode: a visual way of representing binary data, represented by a line, or lack of line.

anticipatory buffering: a technique by which data are stored in a buffer before they are needed. (A)

antistatic mat: a floor mat before a unit such as a tape drive that is sensitive to static, preventing shocks that could cause loss of data during human handling of the unit.

any mode:
(1) the form of a RECEIVE request that obtains input from any one (unspecified) session.
(2) the form of an accept request that completes the establishment of a session by accepting any one (unspecified) queued CINIT request.

any sequence queue: a collection of items in the system that are waiting for the processor's attention; organized so that items can be removed from the collection without regard to the sequence in which they entered it.

AOCR: see *advanced optical character reader.*

AP:
(1) see *application program.*
(2) see *attached processor.*

aperture:
(1) one or more adjacent characters in a mask that cause retention of the corresponding characters. (B)
(2) an opening in a data medium or device such as a card or magnetic core; for example, the aperture card combining a microfilm with a punched card, or in a multiple aperture core.
(3) a part of a mask that permits retention of the corresponding portions of data.
(4) see *multiple-aperture core.* (A)

aperture card: a processible card of standard dimensions in which microfilm frames can be inserted. (A)

aperture core: see *multiple-aperture core.* (A)

aperture time: time needed to make a measurement or conversion with an A/D converter; is considered to be a time uncertainty or amplitude uncertainty. The aperture and amplitude uncertainty are related by the time rate of change of the signal.

APF: see *authorized program facility.*

"A" pins: module pins used for interconnecting purposes, with the physical circuit of a single substrate.

API: see *application program interface.*

APL (a programming language):

(1) a programming language with an unusual syntax and character set, primarily designed for mathematical applications, particularly those involving numeric on literal arrays.

(2) a general-purpose language for diverse applications such as commercial data processing, system design, mathematical and scientific computation, database applications, and the teaching of subjects such as mathematics.

append: adding to the end of a structure, as in appending a character to a character string or an item to a list.

appendage: see *I/O appendage.*

application: the use to which a dataprocessing system is put; for example, a payroll application, a network application, a word processing application.

application code: programs that perform a specific data-processing activity for users.

application developer: an individual responsible for tailoring the basic capabilities of the information system into a form suitable for end-users, mainly through the design and implementation of application programs.

application layer: in open systems architecture, the highest layer explicitly defined by end-users, that provides all the functions needed to execute their application programs or processes. Deprecated term for *end-user.*

application level: a protocol governing the way movement occurs through a network.

application-level timer: a computer-furnished timer set used by an application program. The program sets the timer and proceeds with other activi-

ties until the timer interrupts it, at which time the program commences a time-dependent action.

application note: provided by a vendor or manufacturer, lists instructions or recommendations for utilizing a particular device in a specific fashion or for a specific activity.

application-oriented language:

(1) a programming language that has facilities or notations useful for solving problems in one or more specific classes of applications, such as numerical scientific, business data processing, civil engineering, simulation; for example, FORTRAN, COBOL, COGO, SIMSCRIPT. Synonymous with *problem-oriented language.*

(2) a problem-oriented language whose statements contain or resemble the terminology of the occupation or profession of the user, for example, a report program generator.

application package: a series of interrelated routines and subroutines designed to perform a specified task.

application program (AP):

(1) a program written for or by a user that applies to the user's work.

(2) a program used to connect and communicate with stations in a network, enabling users to perform application-oriented activities.

(3) a program that is used for doing work on the computer, such as word processing, database management, graphics, etc.

application-required language: a problem-oriented language whose statements contain or resemble the terminology of the occupation or profession of the user; for example, a report program generator. (A)

applications package: a package designed for an application.

applications program: a program created to solve a specific problem for an application, such as a payroll program.

application program interface (API): a language used between programs. For example, application programs must communicate with the operation system, database management system, and other control programs. An API is composed of a set of codes and commands used to interrupt the computer, get the attention of the other program and pass messages back and forth between them.

applications programmer: an individual who writes programs for the solution of any application.

applications software (ASW): programs and packages designed to satisfy applications. Cf. *systems software.*

application study: determining the system and set of procedures for using a computer in a specific application.

application system: a related group of application programs.

application trace: produced by a computer, a report showing every step a machine takes in running a program. Used often in troubleshooting and debugging programs.

apply button: applies the current settings in a dialog box without closing the box.

APR: see *alternate path retry.*

arbitrary access: equal access time to all memory locations, independent of the location of the previous memory reference.

arbitrary sequence computer: a computer in which each instrument explicitly determines the location of the next instruction to be executed. (A) (B)

arbitration: management of competing claims of multiple systems or processes for a limited resource.

architecture: a specification which determines how something is constructed, defining functional modularity as well as the protocols and interfaces which allow communication and cooperation among modules. See *computer architecture, net work architecture, open architecture, closed architecture.*

archival: the process of placing computer-stored information within an archive.

archival storage: see *backing storage.*

archive: used as a verb or noun, showing the process of storing data files in a retrieval form or the data files so stored. See *backup.*

archive diskette: synonymous with *diskette* and *floppy disk.*

ARCNET: the first local area network technology that interconnect a wide variety of personal computers and workstations via coaxial cable. It can transmit at 2.5 megabits per second.

area: in PL/1, a declared portion of contiguous internal storage identified by an area variable and reserved, on allocation of based variables. See *clear area, image area, input area, output area, save area.*

area search: in information retrieval, a search of items within a database which make up a single group or category.

area variable: in PL/1, a variable with the AREA attribute; its values may only be areas.

ARG: see *argument.*

argument (ARG):
(1) an independent variable. (A) (B)
(2) any value of an independent variable. (A) (B)
(3) a parameter passed between a calling and a called program.
(4) in FORTRAN, a parameter passed between a calling program and a subprogram or statement function.
(5) in PL/1, an expression and argument list that is part of a procedure reference.

argument addresses: a single instruction to resolve any number of argument addresses, storing the results in the stack for use by the subroutines needed.

argument list:
(1) a string of arguments.
(2) in PL/1, a parenthesized list of one or more arguments, separated by commas, following an entry-name constant, an entry-name variable, a generic name, or a built-in function name. The list is passed to the parameters of the entry point.

arithmetical instruction: synonym for *arithmetic instruction.* (A) (B)

arithmetic and logic unit (ALU): a part of a computer that performs arithmetic operations, logic operations, and related operations. (A) (B)

arithmetic check: synonym for *mathematical check.* (A)

arithmetic constant: in PL/1, a fixed-point constant or a floating-point constant. Although most arithmetic constants can be signed, the sign is not part of the constant.

arithmetic conversion: the transformation of a value from one arithmetic representation to another.

arithmetic data: in PL/1, data that has the characteristics of base, scale, mode, and precision. It includes coded arithmetic data, pictured numeric character data, and pictured numeric bit data.

arithmetic exception: an overflow, underflow, or divide check exception.

arithmetic expression:

(1) in assembler programming, a conditional assembly expression that is a combination of arithmetic terms, arithmetic operators, and paired parentheses.

(2) in COBOL, a statement containing any combination of data names, numeric literals, and figurative constants, joined together by one or more arithmetic operators in such a way that the statement as a whole can be reduced to a single numeric value.

(3) in FORTRAN, a combination of arithmetic operators and arithmetic primaries.

arithmetic instruction: an instruction in which the operation part specifies an arithmetic operation. Synonymous with *arithmetical instruction.* (A) (B)

arithmetic logic unit: the element able to perform basic data manipulations in the central processor; usually the unit can add, subtract, complement, negate, rotate, AND and OR.

arithmetic operation: an operation that follows the rules of arithmetic. (B) See *binary arithmetic operation.* (A)

arithmetic operator:

(1) in assembler programming, an operator that can be used in an absolute or relocatable expression, or in an arithmetic expression to indicate the actions to be performed on the terms in the expression. The arithmetic operators allowed are: +, −, *, /. See *binary operator, unary operator.*

(2) in COBOL and FORTRAN, a symbol that directs the system to perform an arithmetic operation. The arithmetic operators are:

Meaning	Symbol
addition	+
subtraction	−
multiplication	*
division	/
exponentiation	**

arithmetic overflow:

(1) that portion of a numeric word expressing the result of an arithmetic operation by which its word length exceeds the word length provided for the number representation. Synonymous with *overflow.* (B)

(2) that portion of a word expressing the result of an operation by which its word length exceeds the storage capacity of the intended storage device. (A) (B)

arithmetic picture data: decimal picture data or binary picture data.

arithmetic primary: in FORTRAN, an irreducible arithmetic unit; a single constant, variable, array element, function reference, or arithmetic expression enclosed in parentheses.

arithmetic progression: the sequence of numbers where the difference between two adjacent numbers is constant (e.g., 5, 10, 15, 20 . . .).

arithmetic register: a register that holds the operands or the results of operations such as arithmetic operations, logic operations, and shifts. (A) (B)

arithmetic relation: two arithmetic expressions separated by a relational operator.

arithmetic section: that part of the hardware of a computer where arithmetic and logical operations are performed.

arithmetic shift: a shift, applied to the representation of a number in a fixed-radix numeration system and in a fixed-point representation system, in which only the characters representing the absolute value of the number are moved. An arithmetic shift is usually equivalent to multiplying the number by a positive or a negative integral power of the radix except for the effect of any rounding. (A) (B)

arithmetic statement: any instruction specifying an arithmetic operation.

arithmetic term: a term that can be used only in an arithmetic expression.

arithmetic underflow: in an arithmetic operation, a result whose absolute value is too small to be represented within the range of the numeration system in use. For example, the condition existing, particularly when a floating-point representation system is used, when the result is smaller than the nonzero quantity that can be represented; the result may underflow because of the generation of a negative exponent that is outside the permissible range. (A) (B)

arithmetic unit (AU): a part of a computer that performs arithmetic operations, and related operations. (A) (B)

arithmetic variable name: in BASIC, a variable name consists of a single letter A through Z or a letter followed by a digit, O through 9. Thus, Q and D7 are variable names.

arm: see *access arm.*

armed interrupt: accepts and holds the interruption signal; it may be enabled or disabled. An interrupt signal for an enabled condition causes certain hardware processing to take place; a disabled interrupt is held waiting for enablement.

array:
(1) an arrangement of elements in one or more dimensions. (A)
(2) in assembler programming, a series of one or more values represented by a SET symbol.
(3) in FORTRAN, an ordered set of data items identified by a single name.
(4) in PL/1, a named, ordered collection of data elements, all of which have identical attributes. An array has dimensions specified by the dimension attribute, and its individual elements are referred to by subscripts. An array can also be an ordered collection of identical structures.
(5) in APL, BASIC, and RPGII, a systematic arrangement of elements in a table format.

array declarator: in FORTRAN, the part of a statement that describes an array used in a program unit. It indicates the name of the array, the number of dimensions it contains, and the size of each dimension. An array declarator may appear in a DIMENSION, COMMON, or explicit specification.

array element: in FORTRAN, a data item in an array, identified by the array name followed by a subscript indicating its position in the array.

array expression: in PL/1, an expression whose evaluation yields an array value.

array index number: a number identifying a particular element within an array.

array name: the name of an ordered set of data items.

array of structures: in PL/1, an ordered collection of identical structures specified by giving the dimension attribute to a structure name.

array pitch: synonym for *row pitch.* (A)

array variable: a symbol that can be used to represent groups of similar data items.

arrival rate: the number of characters, messages, or other measurable entities arriving at a communications medium per unit of time.

arrow: a key with an arrow on it.

artificial cognition: a machine's ability to sense a character by optical means, and subsequently to determine its nature by comparing it with a set of standard characters.

artificial intelligence (AI): the capability of a device to perform functions that are normally associated with human intelligence, such as reasoning, learning, and self-improvement. See also *machine learning.* (A)

artificial language: a language whose rules are explicitly established prior to its usage. Cf. *natural language.* (A) (B)

AS: see *auxiliary storage.*

ASA: American Standards Association; former name of the American National Standards Institute. See *American National Standards Institute.*

ASA control characters: see *American National Standard control characters.*

ASA label: see *American National Standard label.*

ASAP: as soon as possible.

ascender: the part of a lowercase letter, such as "b," that extends above the main part of the character. See also *descender*.

ascending key: in COBOL, a key upon the values of which data is ordered starting with the lowest value of key up to the highest value of key in accordance with the rules for comparing data items.

ascending sort: a sort where the final sequence of records is such that successive keys compare "greater than or equal to."

ASCII: American Standard Code for Information Interchange. The standard code, using a coded character set consisting of seven-bit coded characters (eight bits including parity check), used for information interchange among data-processing systems, data-communication systems, and associated equipment. The ASCII set consists of control characters and graphic characters. Word processing files stored in the ASCII format are called ASCII files. (A)

ASCII control characters: deprecated term for *American National Standard control characters*.

ASCII-8: an eight-bit version of the *ASCII*.

ASCII keyboard: a keyboard including keys for all of the characters of the ASCII character set. Usually includes three cases for each alpha character: upper case, lower case and control.

ASCII label: deprecated term for *American National Standard label*.

ASID: see *address space identifier*.

ASIS: see *ADI*.

ASM: see *assembler*.

ASP: see *attached support processor*.

aspect: in information retrieval, those features of the contents of documents which are represented by index term, descriptors, and so on.

aspect card: a card with numbers which record the location of documents used in an information retrieval system.

aspect ratio: in computer graphics, the ratio of the horizontal to vertical dimensions of a frame or image. Critical in the transfer and reproduction of an image on various types of display or in printed material.

assemble:
(1) to translate a program expressed in an assembly language into a computer language and perhaps to link subroutines. Assembling is usually accomplished by substituting the computer language operation code for the assembly-language operation code and by substituting absolute addresses, immediate addresses, relocatable addresses, or virtual addresses for symbolic addresses. (B)
(2) to prepare a machine-language program from a symbolic language program by substituting absolute operation codes for symbolic operation codes and in absolute or relocatable addresses for symbolic addresses. (A) (B) Cf. *disassemble*.

assemble-and-go: an operating technique in which there are no stops between the assembling, loading, and execution of a computer program. (A)

assembled origin:
(1) the computer program origin assigned by an assembly program, a compiler, or linkage editor.
(2) the address of the initial storage location assigned to a computer program by an assembler, a compiler, or a linkage editor. (A)

assemble duration: synonym for *assembling time*. (A) (B)

assembler (ASM): a computer program used to assemble. Synonymous with *assembly program*. (A) (B)

assembler directives: controls or directs the assembly processor as operation codes control or direct the central computer. These directives are represented by mnemonics.

assembler language (AL): a source language that includes symbolic machine language statements in which there is a one-to-one correspondence with the instruction formats and data formats of the computer.

assembler program: a computer program that takes nonmachine-language instructions prepared by a programmer and converts them into a form that may be used by the computer.

assembling: composing or integrating instructions into subroutines or main routines for acceptance and use by computing units.

assembling phase: synonym for *assembly phase.* (A) (B)

assembling time: the elapsed time taken for the execution of an assembler. Synonymous with *assemble duration.* (A) (B)

assembly: utilizing an assembler to produce a machine-language program.

assembly language:

(1) a computer-oriented language whose instructions are usually in one-to-one correspondence with computer instructions and that may provide facilities such as the use of macroinstructions. (B)

(2) a computer programming language whose statements may be instructions or declarations. The instructions usually have a one-to-one correspondence with machine instructions.

(3) synonymous with *computer-dependent language, computer-oriented language.* (A)

assembly language instruction: the instruction written in assembly language consisting of an optional label, an OP code, and an operand.

assembly listing: the output of an assembler.

assembly phase: in a run, the logical subdivision that includes the execution of the assembler. Synonymous with *assembling phase.* (A) (B)

assembly process: the translation step that reduces a symbolic language to a machine language. The process converts symbolic addresses to absolute addresses, converts symbolic operation codes to machine instruction codes, and often provides other translation features.

assembly program: synonym for *assembler.* (A) (B)

assembly routine:

(1) a procedure that directs the conversion of a program written in relative or symbolic form into a machine-language program, most often on an instruction-by-instruction design.

(2) a computer program operating on symbolic input data to produce from such data-machine instructions.

assembly time: the time at which an assembler translates the symbolic machine-language statements into their object code form (machine instructions). See also *pre-assembly time.*

assignment indexing: a form of automatic indexing where extracted terms are used in conjunction with some form of thesaurus to yield a list of index terms chosen from a controlled vocabulary list. The index terms are assigned.

assignment statement:

(1) in a high-level language, a statement used to bind variables.

(2) an instruction used to express a sequence of operations, or used to assign operands to specified variables, or symbols, or both.

(3) in COBOL, a statement used to associate a file with the symbolic name of a device. (A)

(4) in FORTRAN, an arithmetic or logical variable or array element, followed by an equal sign ($=$), followed by an arithmetic or logical expression.

assisted panel: in an interactive system, a screen explaining a question the computer has requested, with available alternatives, format expected, and so on. Assisted panels are often associated with user-friendliness.

ASSM: see *assembler.*

Association for Computer Machinery: see *ACM.*

associative memory: a type of parallelism which can immensely speed up certain computing tasks, such as retrieving information from data-bases, by eliminating the role of the central processor in searching through memory. In essence, each piece of data would be stored with its own tiny processor, smart enough to respond when a centralized computer calls for that item. Synonymous with *active memory.*

associative storage: a storage device whose storage locations are identified by their contents, or by part of their contents, rather than by their names or positions. Synonymous with *content-addressed storage.* (A) (B)

assumed decimal point: in COBOL, a decimal point position that does not involve the existence of an actual character in a data item. It does not occupy an actual space in storage.

asterisk protection: inserting a series of asterisks on the left of the most important digit.

ASW: see *applications software.*

asymmetrical: a network considered asymmetrical when there is no easy movement from one computer program to another, or when one person can enter a system, but another cannot enter his or hers.

asymmetric devices: in multiprocessing, devices that have only one path to or from a multiprocessor. They are physically attached to only one processing unit.

asymmetric I/O: I/O devices physically attached to only one processing unit, that are available to jobs executing on another processing unit.

ASYNCH: see *asynchronous.*

asynchronous (A) (ASYNCH): without regular time relationship; unexpected or unpredictable with respect to the execution of a program's instructions.

asynchronous computer: a computer in which each event or the performance of each operation starts as a result of a signal generated by the completion of the previous event or operation, or on the availability of the parts of the computer required by the next event or operation. (B) Cf. *synchronous computer.* (A)

asynchronous data transfer: a physical transfer of data to or from a device that occurs without a regular or predictable time relationship following the execution of an I/O request.

asynchronous device: a device having an operating speed not related to any specific frequency of the system to which it is connected.

asynchronous operation:

(1) an operation that occurs without a regular or predictable time relationship to a specified event; for example, the calling of an error diagnostic routine that may receive control at any time during the execution of a computer program.

(2) a sequence of operations in which operations are executed out of time coincidence with any event. (A)

(3) synonymous with *asynchronous working.*

(4) cf. *synchronous operation.*

asynchronous working: synonym for *asynchronous operation.* (A)

at end condition: in COBOL, a condition caused during the execution of a READ statement for a sequentially accessed file; during the execution of a RETURN statement, when no next logical record exists for the associated sort or merge file; and during the execution of a SEARCH statement, when the search operation terminates without satisfying the condition specified in any of the associated WHEN phrases.

ATLAS: Automatic Tabulating, Listing and Sorting System; a software package used for the purposes indicated.

ATM: automated teller machine. A communication unit, under computer direction, enabling the customer to make bank deposits, withdrawals, and so on, free of human intervention.

atom: the basic element in a list. With list processing languages, one item in a list.

atomic symbol: see *atom.*

ATR: see *attribute.*

attach: in programming, to create a task that can be executed asynchronously with the execution of the mainline code.

attached processing: where an arbitrary number of compact, inexpensive computers are linked together to form a large-scale computing facility.

attached processor (AP): a processor affixed to a central processor, often sharing its memory.

attached support processor (ASP): using multiple computers, usually two, connected via channel-to-channel adaptors, to increase the efficiency in processing many short duration jobs.

attention (ATTN): an occurrence, external to an operation, that could cause an interruption of the operation.

attention interruption: an I/O interruption caused by a terminal user pressing an attention key, or its equivalent. See *simulated attention.*

attention key: a function key on terminals that, when pressed, causes an I/O interruption in the processing unit.

ATTN: see *attention.*

attribute (A) (ATR):

(1) a property or characteristic of one or more entities, for example, color, weight, sex.

(2) in PL/1, a descriptive property associated with a name to describe a characteristic of items that the name may represent, or a descriptive property used to describe a characteristic of the result of evaluation of an expression.

(3) see *data attribute.*

A-type address constant: in the assembler language, an address constant used for branching within a module or for retrieving data. See also *V-type address constant.*

AU: see *arithmetic unit.*

audible alarm: an alarm that is activated when predetermined events occur that require operator attention or intervention for system operation.

audible feedback: a clicker or beeper that sounds whenever a key is depressed on a keyboard.

audio input systems: data entered into a computer system and responses received through human voice audio transmissions.

audio inquiry: keying or dialing data into a computer that has an audio response unit attached to provide an audible response.

audio monitor: a speaker in a modem permitting the user to hear the modem making a phone connection with another modem.

audio response: a form of output that uses verbal replies to inquiries. The computer is programmed to seek answers to inquiries made on a time-shared on-line system and then to utilize a special audio response unit which elicits the appropriate prerecorded response to the inquiry.

audio response message: an audible response generated by an audio response unit from output accepted from a computer.

audiotape storage unit: a device able to store computer programs and/or data on ordinary audio cassette tape; audio tones are utilized to represent binary data.

audio terminal: a unit of equipment associated with an audio response unit at which keyed or dialed data is entered for transmission to the computer; an associated audio response unit produces an audible response.

audit command language: see *ACL.*

audit in depth: the detailed examination of all manipulations performed on a single transaction or piece of information.

auditing: processing, employing techniques and information sources, by which source data, methodology, and report conclusions and sums are checked for accuracy and validity as well as credibility.

audit programming: application of a program designed to enable use of the computer as an auditing tool.

audit total: the sum of a known quantity, used for verifying data. Such totals are often checked to assure that all records are present.

audit trail: a manual or computerized means for tracing the transactions affecting the contents of a record.

augend: in an addition operation, a number or quantity to which numbers or quantities are added. (A) (B)

augment: increasing a quantity to bring it to its full value.

augmenter: the quantity added to another to bring it to its full value. Usually positive, however, when an augmenter is added, a negative quantity is also called an *augmenter.*

authoring language: a computer language or application development system designed primarily for creating databases, programs, and materials for computer-aided instruction. See *authoring system; Hypertext.*

authoring system: a combination of hardware and software designed to ease the tasks involved in producing interactive programs. See *authoring language; Hypertext.*

authority: see *access authority.*

authority file: a set of records identifying a standard for established forms of headings, index terms, or other items, that are used for information retrieval. An authority file may also contain established cross-references, that is, a thesaurus.

authorization code: a code made up of user identification and password, used to protect against unauthorized access to data and system facilities.

authorized library: a library that can contain authorized programs.

authorized program: a system program or user program that is allowed to use restricted functions.

authorized program facility: a facility that permits the identification of programs that are authorized to use restricted functions.

authorized stated: a condition in which a problem program has access to resources that would otherwise not be available.

auto-abstract:
(1) pertaining to the material abstracted from a document by machine methods.
(2) to select keywords from a document by machine methods.

auto backup: a function that makes sure that when a text from the file is removed, there is still a backup version retained.

auto bypass: a capability that allows continuous operation of downstream terminals when another terminal in the daisy chain is powered down.

auto-index: to prepare an index by a machine method.

automate: to convert a process or equipment to automatic operations.

automated bibliography: a bibliography stored within a computer file.

automated data medium: synonym for *machine-readable medium.* (A)

automated dictionary: an automated lexicon used in machine-aided translation systems, listing roots. Cf. *automated glossary.*

automated glossary: an automated lexicon used in machine-aided translation systems, containing entire words and thus presents numerous variations of a generic root. Cf. *automated dictionary.*

automated lexicon: the generic term for all forms of automated dictionary and automated glossary. These lexicons constitute the primary component within a machine-aided translation system.

automated logic diagram (ALD): a computer generated diagram that represents functioning circuitry in terms of logic blocks, interconnecting conductor networks, and input-output terminals.

automated management: types of management completed with the assistance of data-processing equipment.

automated office: a general term that refers to the merger of computers, office electronic devices, and telecommunications technology in an office environment.

automated operator user-exit routine: a user-exit routine that is passed a copy of system messages destined for the master terminal, operator-entered commands, and command responses. The user-exit routine may examine the commands and command responses and write a message to any terminal or to a queue for processing by an application program.

automated production management: management with the aid of under the control of data-processing equipment relating to production planning, scheduling, design or change, and control of output.

automated stock control: using software on a computer to check on receipt and delivery of items, including keeping accounts and forecasting demand.

automated teller machine: see *ATM.*

automated thesaurus: a computer-based thesaurus used along with an automated lexicon within a machine-aided translation system.

automatic abstract: synonymous with *auto-abstract.*

automatic abstracting: seeking the criteria by which people judge what should be abstracted from a document, as programmed.

automatic carriage: a control mechanism for a typewriter or other listing device that can automatically control the feeding, spacing, skipping, and ejecting of paper and preprinted forms. (A)

automatic check: a check performed by equipment built in specifically for checking purposes. Synonymous with *built-in check, hardware check.* Cf. *programmed check.* (A)

automatic control engineering: that branch of science and technology which deals with the design and use of automatic control devices and systems. (B)

automatic data processing (ADP):
(1) data processing performed by computer systems.
(2) data processing largely performed by automatic means. (B)
(3) the branch of science and technology concerned with methods and techniques relating to data processing largely performed by automatic means. (B)
(4) pertaining to data-processing equipment such as electrical accounting machines and electronic data-processing equipment.
(5) data processing by means of one or more devices that: (a) use common storage for all or part of a program and also for all or part of the data necessary for execution of the program, (b) execute user-written or user-designated programs, (c) perform user-designated symbol manipulation such as arithmetic operations, logic operations, or character-string manipulations, and (d) can execute programs that can modify themselves during their execution.

automatic data-processing system: an interacting assembly of procedures, processes, methods, personnel, and automatic data-processing equipment to perform a series of data-processing operations. See *automatic data processing.*

automatic dictionary: the component of a language-translating machine that provides a word-for-word substitution from one language to another.

automatic error correction: a technique applying error-detecting codes and error-correcting codes.

automatic-feed punch: a keypunch that automatically moves punch cards from a card hopper, along a card path, and to a card stacker. (A)

automatic field duplication: a data-file utility feature that allows one or more fields to be copied from one record to another.

automatic indexing: an automatic production of an index for document in any database.

automatic interrupt: see *interrupt.*

automatic library call: the process whereby control sections are processed by the linking editor or loader to resolve references to members of partitioned data sets.

automatic logon (log on): a facility of intelligent terminals used for on-line searching where passwords and addresses needed are stored at the terminal so that the log on process is carried out with one, or a few, key strokes.

automatic pagination: in word processing, automatically printing page numbers at the bottom, top, left, or right side of each page. Like most features, it can be switched off so that no page numbers appear.

automatic paper carriage: a unit for holding paper prior to printing. The carriage feeds sheets, or continuous paper, to the writing heads.

automatic polling: see *autopoll.*

automatic programming: the process of using a computer to perform some stages of the work involved in preparing a computer program. (A)

automatic programming language: see *APL.*

automatic punch: synonym for *card punch.* (A)

automatic recovery program: a program enabling a system to remain functioning while equipment has failed. The automatic recovery program activates duplex circuitry, a standby computer, or switches to a mode of degraded operation.

automatic restart: a restart that takes place during the current run, that is, without resubmitting the job. An automatic restart can occur within a job step or at the beginning of a job step. Cf. *deferred restart.*

automatic routine: a routine that is independently executed of manual operations, but only if specific conditions occur within a program or record, or during some other process.

automatic sequencing: the ability of equipment to put information in order or in a connected series without human intervention.

automatic sequential operation: to develop a series or family of solutions from a set of equations, various initial conditions are recalculated with other parameters.

automatic shutdown: the ability of a system's software to cease a network or system in an orderly way. Such shutdowns occur when unacceptable conditions exist (i.e., excessive errors, hardware malfunctions, etc.).

automatic stop: a halt programmed to take place when an error is detected by an automated check.

automatic switchover: an operating system that has a standby machine that detects when the on-line machine is faulty and once this determination is made, switches this operation to itself.

automatic time stamp: a feature in some modems that puts a time and date on any message sent or received.

automatic variable: in PL/1, a variable that is allocated at the activation of a block and released at the termination of that block. Cf. *controlled variable.*

automatic volume recognition (AVR): a feature that allows the operator to mount labeled volumes on available I/O devices before the volumes are needed by a job step.

automation:
(1) the implementation of processes by automatic means. (B)
(2) the conversion of a procedure, a process, or equipment to automatic operation. (B)
(3) the theory, art, or technique of making a process more automatic.
(4) the investigation, design, development, and application of methods of rendering processes automatic, self-moving, or self-controlling. (A)

automaton: a machine designed to simulate the operations of living things, or to respond automatically to predesigned programs, stimuli, or signals.

automonitor: see *monitor.*

automonitor routine: an executive program or routine that develops a selective record of a computer's execution of another program to be completed.

autonomous working: the initiation and execution of a part of a computer or automation system independent and separate from other operations being performed on other parts of the system.

autopiler: a specific automatic compiler.

autoplotter: a system designed to permit the user to automatically generate a variety of plotted data with a minimum of control in a wide variety of input and output formats. It plots paragraphs, histograms, point and line graphs, and so on.

autopoll: a machine feature of a transmission control unit that permits it to handle negative responses to polling without interrupting the processing unit.

auto save: a function by which a program automatically saves data files at intervals.

autoscore: the automatic underlining of text.

auxiliary console: a console other than the main console.

auxiliary data: data related to other data, but not part of it (i.e., back-up data).

auxiliary equipment: equipment not under direct control of the processing unit. Synonymous with *ancillary equipment.*

auxiliary memory: see *auxiliary storage.*

auxiliary operation: an off-line operation performed by equipment not under control of the processing unit. (A)

auxiliary routine: a routine designed to assist in the operation of the computer, and in debugging other routines.

auxiliary storage (AS):
(1) a storage device that is not main storage. (B)
(2) storage that supplements another storage. (A)
(3) data storage other than main storage; for example, storage on magnetic tape or

direct-access devices. Synonymous with *external storage, secondary storage.* (4) cf. *main storage.*

auxiliary store: synonymous with *backing store.*

availability: the degree to which a system or resource is ready when needed to process data.

availability ratio: the percentage indicating the amount of time a system was actually available for use compared to the amount of time it should have been available.

available machine time: the elapsed time when a computer is in operating condition, whether or not it is in use.

available time: the time during which a functional unit can be used. Synonymous with *up time.* (B) Cf. *maintenance time.* (A)

average access time: the average time between the instant of request and the delivery from a storage device.

average conditional information content: synonym for *conditional entropy.* (A) (B)

average edge line: an imaginary line, in OCR, that traces and smoothes the form of the printed or handwritten character to better convey the intended form.

average effectiveness level: the percentage calculated by subtracting the total computer down time from the total performance hours and dividing the difference by the total performance period hours.

average information content: synonym for *entropy.* (A) (B)

average information rate: in information theory, the mean entropy per character per time unit. The average information rate may be expressed in a unit such as Shannon per second. (A) (B)

average transfer rate: the transfer of blocks of data over a lengthy time period to include gaps between the blocks, words, or records. Regeneration time and other items not part of program control are included. Programmed control items such as starting and searching are not included.

average transinformation content: synonym for *mean transinformation content.* (A) (B)

AVR: see *automatic volume recognition.*

awareness network: the condition where the central processor is cognizant of the status of the network.

axes: in a two-dimensional coordinate system, lines used as references for horizontal (x) and vertical (y) measurement in graphic representation.

B:
(1) see *base.*
(2) see *batch.*
(3) see *binary.*
(4) see *bit.*
(5) see *block.*
(6) see *boolean.*
(7) see *bus.*
(8) see *byte.*

back-end processing: the further processing of data after the primary work has been completed.

back-end processor: a small CPU serving as an interface between a large CPU and a large data base stored on direct access storage device.

background (BG) (BKGRD):
(1) pertaining to a low-priority job that the computer works on when it is not occupied by more pressing matters.
(2) in multiprogramming or multitasking, the conditions under which low-priority programs are executed. See *program level.* Cf. *foreground.*

background display image: synonym for *static display image.*

backgrounding: synonymous with *background processing.*

background ink: in optical character recognition, a type of ink with high reflective characteristics that is not detected by the scan head, and thus is used for print location guides, logotypes, instructions, and any other desired preprinting that would otherwise interfere with reading.

background job: a low-priority job, usually a batched or noninteractive job.

background noise:
(1) extra bits or words ignored or removed from the data at the time it is used.
(2) errors introduced into the data in a system.
(3) any disturbance tending to interfere with the normal operation of a system or unit.

background partition: in a multiprogramming system, a partition holding a lower-priority program that is executed only when high-priority programs are not using the system.

background printing: see *simultaneous input-output.*

background processing:
(1) the execution of lower-priority computer programs when higher-priority programs are not using the system resources. (A) (B)
(2) in word processing, the execution of an operator's request such as printing a document while the operator is performing other tasks.
(3) cf. *foreground processing.*
(4) synonym for *backgrounding.*

background program: in multiprogramming, the program with the lowest priority. Background programs are executed from batched or stacked job input.

background reader: a system task started by the operator to process foreground-initiated background jobs.

background region: a region to which a background job is assigned.

backing storage: synonymous with *backing store.*

backing store: a storage that supports the main memory. Backing store has greater capacity than memory and is less expensive, but has slower access time. Synonymous with *auxiliary store, backing storage, bulk storage, bulk store, secondary store.*

backout: procedures in written form detailing how to remove a change.

back panel: the back of the computer, where the power switch and ports for attaching external devices can be found. Synonymous with *connector panel.*

back plane: the area where the boards of a system are plugged. Synonymous with *motherboard.*

backspace:
(1) to move back the reading or display position according to a prescribed format.
(2) to move a data carrier backward a specific distance usually deleting the preceding character(s). (B)

backspace character (BS): a format effector that causes the print or display position to move one position backward along the line without producing the printing or display of any graphic. (A) (B) See also *numeric backspace character, unit backspace character.*

backtracking: processing a list of names, addresses, and so on, in reverse order.

backup (BAK):
(1) pertaining to a system, device, file, or facility that can be used in the event of a malfunction or loss of data.
(2) to make a copy of a disk or of a file on a disk. Backing up files and disks ensures that information won't be lost if the original is lost or damaged.

backup copy: a copy of a file or data set that is kept for reference in case the original file or data set is destroyed.

backup diskette: a diskette that contains information that was copied from another diskette or the disk. It is used in case the original information is unintentionally altered or destroyed.

backup file: a complete or partial copy of a file made for possible later reconstruction of the file. Synonymous with *job-recovery control file.*

Backus Naur form (BNF): a meta-language used to specify or describe the syntax of a language in which each symbol, by itself, represents a set of strings of symbols. Synonymous with *Backus normal form.* (A)

Backus normal form (BNO): Synonym for *Backus Naur form.* (A)

backward compatability: a property of hardware or software revisions where earlier protocols, formats, and layouts are discarded in favor of improved and newer protocols, formats, and layouts. When the change is so drastic that all the formats are not retained in the new version, it is said to be backward compatable.

backward compatable: see *backward compatability.*

backward file recovery: the return of a file to a previous state by using data that have been recorded in a journal. Cf. *forward file recovery.*

backward recovery: see *backward file recovery.*

backward supervision: the use of supervisory sequences sent from the slave to the master station. Cf. *forward supervision.*

bad branch: a program error where execution jumps to the wrong place, resulting in an unexpected outcome. Bad branches are usually the result of errors made in the writing of a program.

bad sector: a segment of disk storage that cannot be read or written because of some physical flaw in the disk. Bad sectors on hard drives are marked by the operating system and then ignored. If data is recorded in a sector that becomes bad, it is usually not recoverable by normal procedures. Special hardware and software must be employed to recover valuable data in bad sectors.

bagbiter: slang; programs or equipment that fail intermittently.

BAK: see *backup.*

BAL: basic assembly language, a simplified form of an assembly language.

balanced error:
(1) an error relating to a range having a balance of zero, or a mean value of zero.
(2) a set of errors, the distribution of which has the mean value zero. (A) (B)

balanced merge: an external sort that places strings created by an internal sort phase on half of the available storage devices and then merges strings by moving them back and forth between an equal number of devices until the merging process is complete. (A)

balanced merge sort: a merge sort, which is an external sort, such that the sorted subsets created by the internal sorts are equally distributed among half of the available auxiliary storage devices.

The subsets are merged onto the other half of the auxiliary storage devices and the process is repeated until all items are in one sorted set. Cf. *unbalanced merge sort.* (A)

balanced sorting: a technique used in a sort program to merge strings of sequenced data.

balanced system: a computer system where the quantity of computations to be carried out by the CPU is equal to the number of input-output operations being performed.

balloons: small boxes containing text identifying objects on the screen and explaining usage.

BAM: see *basic access method.*

band:
(1) a group of tracks on a magnetic drum or on one side of a magnetic disk. (B)
(2) in data communication, the frequency spectrum between two defined limits. (A)

band printer: see *chain printer.*

bandwidth: the maximum number of data units that can be transferred along a channel per second. Expressed digitally in bits/bytes per second (bps), or in cycles per second, Hertz (Hz) for analog devices.

bank: in automatic switching, a bank is an assemblage of fixed contacts used to establish electrical connections. See *data bank.*

banking: in optical character recognition, a misalignment of the first character of a line with respect to the left margin.

bank on-line teller system: transactions handled in real time by an on-line bank teller system. Teller consoles at office windows can be linked to the computer and the on-line central file.

banks: synonymous with *electronic information services* and *on-line data bases.*

bank select: turning internal system components on and off with electronic control signals. Synonymous with *bankswitching.*

bankswitching: synonymous with *bank select.*

banner word: in a file record, the first word.

BAR: see *base address register.*

bar: see *type bar.*

bar-code: a code on labels to be read by a wand or bar-code scanner. See *bar-code scanner.*

bar-code scanner: an optical device that reads data from documents having characters recorded in the form of parallel bars. The characters are translated into digital signals for storage or processing.

bar printer: an impact printer in which the type slugs are carred on a type bar. (A)

barrel printer: see *drum printer.*

base (B):
(1) in the numeration system commonly used in scientific papers, the number that is raised to the power denoted by the exponent and then multiplied by the mantissa to determine the real number represented. (B)
(2) a number that is multiplied by itself as many times as indicated by an exponent.
(3) a reference value. (A)
(4) the number system in terms of which an arithmetic value is represented.
(5) see *complement base, data base, floating-point base.* Cf. *radix.*

base address:
(1) a numeric value that is used as a reference in the calculation of addresses in the execution of a computer program. (B)
(2) a given address from which an absolute address is derived by combination with a relative address. (A)

base address register (BAR): a register that holds a base address. Synonymous with *base register.* (A) (B)

based storage allocation: in PL/1, the allocation of storage for based variables.

based variable: in PL/1, a variable whose generations are identified by locator variables. A based variable can be used to refer to values of variables of any storage class; it can also be allocated and freed explicitly by use of the ALLOCATE and FREE statements.

base element: in PL/1, the name of a structure member that is not a minor structure.

base item: in PL/1, the automatic, controlled, or static variable or the parameter upon which a defined variable is defined. The name may be qualified, subscripted, or both.

base mass storage volume: see *base volume.*

base notation:
(1) a notation consisting of a decimal number, in parenthesis, written as a subscript suffix to a number, its decimal value indicating the radix of the number.
(2) a number written without its radix notation is assumed in the radix of ten.

base number: a quantity that specifies a system of representation for numbers. See *radix numeration system.*

base point: see *radix point.*

base register (BR): synonym for *base address register.*

base type: the set of allowable values that a variable may take.

base volume: a mass storage volume that can have copies or duplicates.

BASIC (beginner's all-purpose symbolic instruction code): a programming language with a small repertoire of commands and a simple syntax, primarily designed for numerical application.

basic access method (BAM): any access method in which input-output statement causes a corresponding machine input/output operation to occur. Cf. *queued access method.*

basic assembly language: see *BAL.*

basic code: synonymous with *absolute code.*

basic controller: the part of a communication controller that performs arithmetic and logic functions.

basic direct access method (BDAM): an access method used to directly retrieve or update particular blocks of a data set on a direct access device.

basic exchange format: a format for exchanging data on diskettes between systems or devices.

basic indexed sequential access method (BISAM): an access method used in one form to directly retrieve or update particular blocks of a data set on a direct access device, using an index to locate data set. The index is stored in direct access storage along with the data set. Other forms of this method can be used to store or retrieve, in a continuous sequence, blocks of the same set.

basic input-output system (BIOS): part of the operating system consisting of drivers and other software to control peripheral units such as keyboards, disk drives, etc. Needs to be modified each time a peripheral unit is altered. See also *NETBIOS*.

basic instruction: in program modification, the instruction that is modified to obtain the instruction that is to be followed. Synonymous with *presumptive instruction, unmodified instruction.*

basic linkage: a linkage used repeatedly in one routine, program, or system and that follows the same set of rules every time. See also *linkage.*

basic partitioned access method (BPAM): an access method that can be applied to create program libraries, in direct-access storage, for convenient storage and retrieval of programs.

basic real constant: in FORTRAN, a string of decimal digits containing a decimal point.

basic sequential access method (BSAM): an access method for storing or retrieving data blocks in continuous sequences, using either a sequential-access or a direct-access device.

basis weight: the weight in pounds of a ream (500 sheets) of paper cut to a given standard size for that grade. The basis weight of continuous forms for computer output is based on the size for bond papers.

BAT: see *batch.*

batch (B) (BAT):
(1) an accumulation of data to be processed.
(2) a group of records or data-processing jobs brought together for processing or transmission.

batch compiler: a compiler that can translate all statements in a program at the same time, rather than line by line. Cf. *interactive compiler.*

batch file: a set of operating system commands that is executed as if each command were interactively entered one at a time. Synonymous with *BAT file.*

batched communication: the sending of a large body of data from one station to another station in a network, without intervening responses from the receiving unit.

batched job:
(1) a job that is grouped with other jobs as input to a computing system.
(2) a job whose job control statements are grouped with job control statements of other jobs as input to a computing system. Synonymous with *stacked job.*

batch partition: partition in which batch processing takes place.

batch processing (BP):
(1) the processing of data or the accomplishment of jobs accumulated in advance in such a manner that each accumulation thus formed is processed or accomplished in the same run. (B)
(2) the processing of data accumulated over a period of time.
(3) loosely, the execution of computer programs serially.
(4) pertaining to the technique of executing a set of computer programs such that each is completed before the next program of the set is started.
(5) pertaining to the sequential input of computer programs or data. (A)
(6) in real-time systems the processing of related transactions that have been grouped together.
(7) see *remote batch processing, sequential batch processing.* See also *stacked job processing.*

batch-processing interrupt: a major feature of a real-time system made possible through a unique feature permitting remote external units with information of high precedence to interrupt computer processing.

batch region: in a multiprogramming environment, one of several regions controlled by the operating system where batch processing can be performed. There may be several batch regions, which normally run at low priority compared to interactive regions.

batch save/restore: an optional facility of a partitioned outline batch system. It allows a real-time job to preempt on the basis of assigned priorities, a partition being used for batch processing. Upon preemption, the batch program is saved on direct-access storage and when the real-time program is completed, the batch program is loaded into storage and execution is resumed.

batch/sequential processing: a method of processing data in which data items are collected and forwarded to the computer in a group; normally uses punched cards or magnetic tape for generating periodic output (e.g., payroll).

batch session: a session established between a communication controller and the host system for the purpose of transmitting batches of records or messages.

batch systems: any data-processing system utilizing batch-processing techniques.

batch terminal: a terminal that handles a large number of off-line users via high-speed input/output units, typically card readers and line printers.

batch terminal simulation (BTS): a means for testing communications programs without having actual terminals functioning. With BTS a batch program generates messages and passes them to the communications program so it is actually interacting with a terminal.

batch ticket: a control document that summarizes the control totals and identifies the appropriate group of source documents.

batch total:
(1) the sum of certain quantities pertaining to batches of unit records, used to verify accuracy of operations on a particular batch of records.
(2) each or any of a number of sums that can be calculated from a series of records which are intended to serve as aids to verify the accuracy of computer activities.

batch transaction files: transactions accumulated as a batch ready for processing against the master file.

BAT file: see *batch file.*

batten system: synonymous with *Cordonnier system.*

baud:
(1) a unit of signaling speed equal to the number of discrete conditions or signal events per second. For example, one baud equals one-half dot cycle per second in Morse code, one bit per second in a train of binary signals, and one three-bit value

per second in a train of signals each of which can assume one of eight different states. (A)
(2) in asynchronous transmission, the unit of modulation rate corresponding to one unit interval per second; that is, if the duration of the unit interval is 20 milliseconds, the modulation rate is 50 baud. (A)

baud rate: the speed at which data is transmitted from a source to a destination, usually from one computer to another through a modem.

bay: a shelf, cabinet or other structure where electronic devices are mounted.

BBS: bulletin board system.

BCC: see *block-check character.*

BCD:
(1) see *binary-coded decimal notation.*
(2) see *four-bit binary coded decimal.*

BCDIC: see *extended binary-coded decimal interchange code.*

BCH: see *block control header.*

BCO: see *binary-control octal.*

BCP: byte control protocol.

BDAM: see *basic direct access method.*

BDRY: see *boundary.*

beam deflection: on a CRT display device, the process of changing the orientation of the electron beam.

beat: a fundamental state of the control unit of the computer or the duration of such a state.

begin: a procedure delimiter in the ALGOL language.

begin block: in PL/1, a collection of statements headed by a BEGIN statement and ended by an END statement that is a part of a program that delimits the scope of names and that is activated by normal sequential flow of control, including any branch resulting from a GO TO statement.

Beginner's All-Purpose Symbolic Instruction Code: see *BASIC.*

beginning of a file label: the record at the beginning of a file which shows information about the file's content and boundaries.

beginning of information marker (BIM): a reflective spot on the rear of a magnetic tape, 10 feet from the physical beginning of the tape, that is sensed photoelectrically to show the point on tape at which recording begins.

beginning-of-tape mark: a mark on a magnetic tape used to indicate the beginning of the permissible recording area; for example, a photoreflective strip, a transparent section of tape. (B) Cf. *end-of-tape mark*. (A)

Bell-compatible: modems able to communicate with Bell Telephone modems, which are presently the standard within the industry.

bells and whistles: slang; unnecessary but useful or amusing features of a program.

benchmark (BM): a point of reference from which measurements can be made.

benchmark problem:
(1) a problem used to evaluate the performance of hardware or software or both.
(2) a problem used to evaluate the performance of several computers relative to each other, or a single computer relative to system specifications. (A)

benchmark program: a standardized computer program for testing the processing power of a computer in comparison with other computers.

benchmark routine: a set of routines or problems that help determine the performance of a given piece of equipment.

Bernoulli box: a removable disk system that connects to personal computers through a small computer systems interface.

beta testing: putting a new product into operation in an environment other than the manufacturer's; the initial test in a consumer environment. Cf. *alpha testing*.

bezel: the frame holding a faceplate.

BF: see *blocking factor*.

BG: see *background*.

BI: see *input blocking factor*.

bias:
(1) a systematic deviation of a value from a reference value. (B)
(2) the amount by which the average of a set of values departs from a reference value. (A)
(3) see *ordering bias*.

biased data: distribution of file records which is nonrandom with respect to the sequencing or sorting criteria. Biased data impacts on sorting time, depending on the approach used during the first pass on the data.

bias testing: see *marginal check*.

bibliographic(al): relating to the description of documents.

biconditional operation: synonymous with *equivalence operation, exclusive-NOR*.

bid: in the contention form of invitation or selection, an attempt by the computer or by a station to gain control of the line so that it can transmit data.

bidirectional: able to operate in two directions, that is, toward the input and output.

bidirectional printing: alternately printing in either direction. A line printed left-to-right is followed by a line printed right-to-left thereby avoiding usual carriage return delays, greatly increasing throughput.

bifurcation: a logic condition where only two states are possible. This is the basic logic pattern of binary digital computers.

big bang implementation: where new programs and peripheral units are placed into operation at the same time. Synonymous with *lightning cut-over*.

Big Blue: slang name for International Business Machines Corporation (IBM).

billi-: prefix denoting 10^9, as in billibit, synonymous with *giga-*.

billisecond: see *nanosecond*.

BIM: see *beginning of information marker*.

bimap:
(1) a set of bits that represents a graphic image.
(2) a dot-by-dot representation of a text character or graphic image.

BIN: see *binary*.

binary (B) (BIN):
(1) pertaining to a selection, choice, or condition that has two possible values or states. (B)
(2) pertaining to a fixed-radix numeration system having a radix of two. (B)
(3) countable using two digits, zeros and ones. The basic requirement of a computer is its ability to represent numbers and to perform operations on the numbers represented; and since any number can be rep-

resented by an ordered arrangement of ones and zeros; most computers use this system of counting.

(4) see *Chinese binary, column binary, row binary.* (A)

binary arithmetic operation: an arithmetic operation in which the operands and the result are represented in the pure binary numeration system. (B) Synonym for *dyadic operation.* (A)

binary boolean operation: deprecated term for *dyadic boolean operation.* (A) (B)

binary card: a card containing data in column binary or row binary form. (A)

binary cell: a storage cell that holds one binary character. (A) (B)

binary chain: a series of binary circuits arranged so that each chain will impact on the following circuit.

binary chop: a means of searching a table ordered in a known sequence by comparing the required key with a key midway in the table. Synonymous with *binary search, dichotomizing search.*

binary code: a code that makes use of exactly two distinct characters, usually 0 and 1. (A) See also *gray code.*

binary-coded decimal character code: a character set containing 64 6-bit characters. See also *extended binary-coded decimal interchange code.*

binary-coded decimal code: synonym for *binary-coded decimal notation.* (A)

binary-coded decimal interchange code (BCDIC): see *extended binary-coded decimal interchange code.* (A)

binary-coded decimal notation (BCD): a binary-coded notation in which each of the decimal digits is represented by a binary numeral; for example, in binary-coded decimal notation that uses the weights 8-4-2-1, the number "23" is represented by 00100011 (compare its representation 10111 in the pure binary numeration system). Synonymous with *binary-coded decimal code, binary-coded decimal representation, coded decimal notation.* (A) (B)

binary-coded decimal representation: synonym for *binary-coded decimal notation.* (A)

binary-coded notation: a binary-coded notation in which each of the decimal digits is represented by a binary numeral. (A) (B)

binary-control octal (BCO): a system where binary numbers are used to represent the octal digits of an octal number.

binary counter: a counter that counts according to the binary number system.

binary digit (BIT): in binary notation, either of the characters 0 or 1. (A) (B) See *equivalent-binary-digit factor.* Synonymous with *bit.*

binary digit characters: in PL/1, the picture specification characters 1, 2, and 3.

binary dump: that portion of a program permitting printing, displaying, or punching of a binary copy of a part of memory.

binary element: a constituent element of data that takes either of two values or states. The term *bit,* originally the abbreviation for the term *binary digit,* is misused in the sense of binary element or in the sense of Shannon. (A) (B)

binary element string: a string consisting solely of binary elements. (A) (B)

binary file: a software program in machine language form that can be directly executed by the computer.

binary format:

(1) numbers stored in pure binary form in contrast with binary coded decimal form.

(2) any information representation stored in a binary coded form, such as data, text, images, voice, and video.

binary half-adder: a half-adder with digits representing binary signals that receives two inputs and delivers two outputs.

binary incremental representation: incremental representation in which the value of an increment is rounded to one of the two values of plus or minus one quantum and is represented by one binary digit. (B)

binary loader: a unit for loading a binary format such as that needed by a binary dump program, link editor, or assembler.

binary notation:

(1) any notation that uses two different characters, usually the binary digits 0

and 1, for example, the gray code. The gray code is a binary notation but not a pure binary numeration system. (B)

(2) fixed-radix notation where the radix is two. For example, in binary notation the numerical 110.01 represents the number 1×2 squared plus 1×2 to the first power plus 1×2 to the minus 2 power, that is, $6\frac{1}{4}$.

(3) a binary number. Loosely, a binary numeral. (A)

binary number: a component of computer language, which usually contains more than one figure. The numbers allowed are 0 and 1. See *binary numeral.*

binary numeral:
(1) a numeral in the pure binary numeration system; for example, the binary numeral 101 is equivalent to the Roman numeral V. (B)
(2) a binary representation of a number. (A)

binary numeration system: synonym for *pure binary numeration system.* (A)

binary operation: deprecated term for *binary arithmetic operation, boolean operation.* (A) (B)

binary operator: an arithmetic operator having two terms. The binary operators that can be used in absolute or relocatable expressions and arithmetic expressions are: addition ($+$), subtraction ($-$), multiplication (*), and division (/). Synonym for *dyadic operator.* (A) Cf. *unary operator.*

binary pair: a circuit having two states, each needing an appropriate trigger for excitation and transition from one state to the other. Synonymous with *R-S-T flip-flop, stable trigger, trigger pair.*

binary picture data: in PL/1, arithmetic picture data specified by picture specifications containing the following types of picture specification characters: binary digit characters; the virtual point picture character; the exponent character, K; and the sign character, S.

binary point: the point in a binary number separating the integral from the fractional part.

binary representation: using a two-state, or binary, system to represent data; as in

setting and resetting the states of a magnetic core.

binary row: a means of representing binary numbers on a punched card using rows instead of columns.

binary search: a dichotomizing search in which, at each step of the search, the set of items is partitioned into two equal parts, some appropriate action being taken in the case of an odd number of items. (A) (B) Synonymous with *binary chop.*

binary symmetric channel: a channel designed to convey messages consisting of binary characters and that has the property that the conditional probabilities of changing any one character to the other character are equal. (A) (B)

binary synchronous communication (BSC):
(1) communication using binary synchronous line discipline.
(2) a uniform procedure, using a standardized set of control characters and control character sequences, for synchronous transmission of binary-coded data between stations.

binary system: a system of numbers having two as its base and utilizing only combinations of the digits zero and one. This system is based on the addition of progressive powers of two. These two states—zero and one—are signified by the two states in computer circuitry—on and off—indicated by the presence or absence of voltage.

binary-to-decimal conversion: conversion of a binary number to the equivalent decimal number, that is, a base-two number to a base-ten number.

binary-to-hexadecimal conversion: the method of converting a binary (base 2) number to an equivalent hexadecimal (base 16) number.

binary-to-octal conversion: the method for converting a binary (base 2) number to an equivalent octal (base 8) number.

binary tree: a data structure where the first node (record) is identified as the root: all subsequent nodes branch to the right when their key is less than that of a previous node and to the left when it is greater. The record is stored with the keys of those records to its right and with those to its left in order that the record can be determined by following the keys from the root through subsequent nodes.

binary variable: a variable that assumes one of two values (e.g., true or false, 1 or 0).

bind:
(1) to assign a value to a variable; in particular, to assign a value to a parameter. (A) (B)
(2) to associate an absolute address, virtual address, or device identifier with a symbolic address or label in a computer program. (B)

binder-hole card: a card that contains one or more holes for binding. (A)

binding time: the instant when an expression or a symbol has been translated into machine code and given an address of a storage location in its main memory.

bionics: a branch of technology relating the functions, characteristics, and phenomena of living systems to the development of mechanical systems. (A)

BIOS: see *basic input-output system.*

biquinary code: a notation in which a decimal digit n is represented by a pair of numerals, a being 0 or 1, b being 0, 1, 2, 3, or 4, and $(5a + b)$ being equal to n. The two digits are often represented by a series of two binary numerals. (A) (B)

BIS: see *business information system.*

BISAM: see *basic indexed sequential access method.*

bistable circuit: a trigger circuit that has two stable states. (A) (B) Synonymous with *bistable trigger circuit, flip-flop.*

bistable device: a device, such as a switch, that assumes only one of two possible states, such as on or off. The use of bistable devices suggests the use of a binary number system, which also requires only two values, 0 and 1, for arithmetic and data-processing operations.

bistable multivibrator: synonymous with *flip-flop.*

bistable trigger circuit: synonym for *bistable circuit.* (A)

bisync: acronym for binary synchronous. See *binary synchronous communication.*

bisynchronous: the continuous exchange of synchronization signals between communications units.

bit (B):
(1) in the pure binary numeration system, either of the digits 0 and 1. Synonymous with *binary digit.* (B)
(2) the smallest possible unit of information. One bit is enough to tell the difference between two opposites such as yes or no.
(3) deprecated term for *binary element, Shannon.* (A) (B)
(4) see *check bit, information bits, redundancy check bit, sign bit.*

bit-bender: slang, an individual whose hobby is working with computers.

bit bucket: a container that catches the pieces punched out of cards in card-punching devices.

bit bumming: attempting to squeeze the required software into the minimum amount of memory in a microcomputer system.

bit check: the manual or machine-conducted examination of a word or bit group for verifying presence of a parity bit in its prescribed position.

bit density: a measure of the number of bits received per unit of length or area.

bite: alternate spelling of *byte.*

bit errors: intermittent errors which cause bits to be received incorrectly.

bit-flipping: synonymous with *bit manipulation.*

bit grinding: slang, the processing of data-processing instructions.

bit location: a storage position located on a record capable of storing one bit.

bit manipulation: turning bits on and off to impact on the way a program functions. Synonymous with *bit-flipping.*

bit mapped: a method for displaying text and images on a screen that produces much finer definition than conventional displays.

bitmapped character: a character in a font that's rendered as a bitmap and drawn as a pixel pattern on the screen.

bitmapped font: a font in a single point size made up of bitmapped characters. Synonymous with *fixed-size font.*

bit-oriented protocol (BOP): a protocol using a unique bit pattern representing a flag character to separate distinct groups of data bits.

bit pattern: a combination of n binary digits representing 2 to the n (2^n) possible choices; for example, a three-bit pattern represents eight possible combinations.

bit position: a character position in a word in a binary notation. (A) (B)

bit sign: the value of a binary digit for indicating the polarity of data representing a number or quantity such as an angle.

bit slice microprocessor: microprocessors; for example, of two- or four-bit word length, chained together and microprogrammed to form processors of long word length. Each bit slice performs a unique function within the chain.

bit-slicing processing: microprocessors that permit large scale parallel data processing, that is, allowing many jobs to be done at the same time.

bits per inch: the number of characters recorded per linear inch on magnetic tape.

bit stream: a binary signal without regard to group by character.

bit string: a string consisting solely of bits. (A) (B)

bit-string operators: in PL/1, the logical operators—(not), & (and), and / (or).

bit stuffing: in time division multiplexed systems, entails the insertion of redundant bits into an incoming bit stream to increase its rate. The presence of the stuffed bits is signaled to the receiver so that they can be removed to restore the original data. See *time shifting.* Synonymous with *digital filling.*

bit test: the check performed by software to determine if a particular bit is on (1) or off (0).

bit track: a track on a magnetic drum or disk where bits are recorded or read by a read/write head. Cf. *logical track.*

bit twiddler: slang, an operator of computer equipment.

BKGRD: see *background.*

black box approach: acceptance of computed results without questioning the method of working of the computer.

blank:
(1) a part of a data medium in which no characters are recorded. (A)
(2) in computer graphics, to suppress the display of all or part of a display image.

blank character: a graphic representation of the space character. (A)

blank coil: a tape (for perforation) with only the feed holes punched.

blank common: in FORTRAN, an unlabeled (unnamed) common block.

blank deleter: a device that eliminates the receiving of blanks in perforated paper tape.

blank diskette: see *unformatted diskette.*

blank instruction: synonymous with *do-nothing operation.*

blank medium: various types or blank forms of media.

blank transmission: a feature permitting the checking of the data field for all blank positions.

blast: to release internal or external memory area under dynamic storage allocation. Synonymous with *blow.*

bleed: in optical character recognition, spreading of ink beyond the edges of a printed character.

blind: to make a device nonreceptive to unwanted data, through recognition of field definition characters in the received data. See also *lockout, polling, selection.*

blind keyboard:
(1) a keyboard that does not produce a visual display.
(2) hardcopy of data entered through a keyboard.

blink rate: the number of times per second that a cursor or text on a video display blinks.

blip: synonym for *document mark.* (A) (B)

blip counting: a position-sensing approach based on adding or deleting one from a location register, based on the direction in which each position mark (blip) passes a sensor.

BLK: see *block.*

block (B) (BLK):
(1) a string of records, a string of words, or a character string formed for technical or logic reasons to be treated as an entity. (B)
(2) a set of things, such as words, characters, or digits, handled as a unit.
(3) a collection of contiguous records recorded as a unit. Blocks are separated by interblock gaps and each block may contain one or more records.
(4) a group of bits, or n-ary digits, transmitted as a unit. An encoding procedure is generally applied to the group of bits or n-ary digits for error-control purposes. (A)
(5) in PL/1, a begin block or procedure block.
(6) to record data in a block.
(7) see *program block, record blocking.*

block cancel character: a cancel character used to indicate that the preceding portion of the block, back to the most recently occurring block mark, is to be disregarded. Synonymous with *block ignore character.* (A) (B)

block character: see *end-of-transmission-block character.* (A)

block check: that part of the error-control procedure used for determining that a data block is structured according to given rules.

block-check character (BCC): in longitudinal redundancy checking and cyclic redundancy checking, a character that is transmitted by the sender after each message block and is compared with a block-check character computed by the receiver to determine if the transmission was successful.

block control: a storage location holding information in condensed, formalized form needed for the control of a task, function, operation, or quantity of information.

block copy: to copy a file, from one medium to another, without altering its contents. See *block transfer.*

block diagram: a diagram of a system, a computer, or a device, in which the principal parts are represented by suitably annotated geometrical figures to show both the basic functions of the parts and their functional relationships. (B) Cf. *flowchart.*

blocked records: records grouped on magnetic tape or magnetic disk to reduce the number of interrecord gaps and more fully utilize the storage medium.

blockette: a subdivision of a block which is input and output as a single unit or block in its own right.

block gap: deprecated term for *interblock gap (2).*

block header: data appearing at the beginning of a block that describes the organization of the file and relationship between blocks.

block heading statement: in PL/1, the PROCEDURE or BEGIN statement that heads a block of statements.

block ignore character: synonym for *block cancel character.* (A)

blocking: the process of combining two or more records into one block.

blocking factor (BF): the number of logical records in each block. See also *input blocking factor, output blocking factor.* (B)

blocking of records: synonymous with *grouping of records.*

block input: a group of words transferred from external storage to internal storage. Cf. *block output.*

block length:
(1) the number of records, words, or characters in a block. (B)
(2) a measure of the size of a block, usually specified in units such as records, words, computer words, or characters. (A)
(3) synonymous with *block size.*

block list: a printout of a file's content where records are listed in the sequence in which they appear.

block loading: bringing the control sections of a load module into adjoining positions of main storage. Cf. *scatter loading.*

block output: a group of words transferred from internal storage to external destination. Cf. *block input.*

block paging: paging of multiple pages simultaneously to or from real or external storage.

block parity system: a system using an additional bit to a block of information to find single-bit errors in the entire block.

block prefix: an optional, variable length field that may precede unblocked records or blocks of records recorded in American National Standard Code for Information Interchange (ASCII) on magnetic tapes.

block record: a specific storage area of a fixed size containing a main memory or file storage, set into standard blocks to permit more flexibility in storage allocation and control.

block search: scanning through data to find a particular word or character.

block size: synonymous with *block length*.

block sort: a sort that separates a file into segments, using the highest-order portion of the key, orders the segments separately, and then joins them.

block structure: a hierarchy of program blocks. (A)

block transfer: the process, initiated by a single action, of transferring one or more blocks of data. (A) (B)

blow: pertaining to the writing into a programmable read-only memory (PROM), or variants, such as EPROM. Cf. *zap*. Synonymous with *blast, burn*.

blowing: programming read only memory (ROM) utilizing special devices; as in PROM blowing.

blow up: program termination due to poor data. Synonymous with *abend*.

BLP: see *bypass label processing*.

BLT: see *block transfer*.

blue ribbon program: a program that runs effectively upon first try. Synonymous with *star program*.

BM:
(1) see *benchmark*.
(2) see *business machine*.

BNF:
(1) see *Backus Naur form*.
(2) see *Backus normal form*. (A)
(3) see *normal form Backus*.

BNO: see *Backus normal form*.

Bo: see *output blocking factor*.

board: an electrical panel that can be changed with an addition or deletion

of external wiring. Synonym for *panel, plugboard, wire board*.

board tester: a unit, usually computer controlled, which performs electronic tests on printed circuit boards.

body group: in COBOL, generic name for a report of TYPE DETAIL, CONTROL HEADING or CONTROL FOOTING.

bogus: nonfunctional, false.

boilerplate: previously stored words, phrases, or paragraphs, such as stock contractual terms, or form letters.

bold: a text that has been printed extra dark.

boldface: in word processing, typing each character twice, but the second impression is slightly to one side of the first.

bomb: deprecated term for when a program fails spectacularly.

book: a group of source statements written in the assembler or COBOL language.

book message: a message to be sent to two or more destinations.

BOOL: see *boolean*.

boolean (B) (BOOL):
(1) pertaining to the processes used in the algebra formulated by George Boole. (A)
(2) a value of 0 or 1 represented internally in binary notation. See also *boolean algebra*.

boolean ADD: synonym for *OR*(3). (A)

boolean algebra: a mathematical system relating logical functions instead of numbers. Boolean operatives such as "AND," "OR," and "NOR" are used to compare one expression to another. In computers, logical operations utilizing Boolean Algebra result in conditions serving as input into branching functions in programs.

boolean complementation: deprecated term for *negation*. (A)

boolean function: a switching function in which the number of possible values of the function and each of its independent variables is two. (A)(B)

boolean operation:
(1) any operation in which each of the operands and the result take one of two values. (B)
(2) an operation that follows the rules of boolean algebra. (B)

(3) see *dyadic boolean operation, n-adic boolean operation, n-ary boolean operation.* (A)

boolean operation table: an operation table in which each of the operands and the result take one of two values. (A) (B)

boolean operator: an operator, each of the operands of which and the result of which take one of two values. (B) See *dyadic operator, monadic operator.* (A)

BOOT: see *bootstrap.*

booting: see *bootstrap.*

bootleg program: a conventional routine or stop-gap program that begins, captures, and processes information in a specifically prescribed form, usually to start or initiate the reading of a program by means of its own action.

bootstrap (BOOT):
(1) a technique or device designed to bring itself into a desired state by means of its own action; for example, a machine routine whose first few instructions are sufficient to bring the rest of itself into the computer from an input device usually applied to the loading of the operating system, starting the computer.
(2) an existing version, perhaps a primitive version, of a computer program that is used to establish another version of the program. (B)
(3) that part of a computer program used to establish another version of the computer program.
(4) to use a bootstrap. (B)
(5) see also *bootstrap loader, boot-up, initial program loader.* (A)

bootstrap loader: an input routine in which simple present computer operations are used to load instructions which in turn cause further instructions to be loaded until the complete computer program is in storage. (B) See also *bootstrap, initial program loader.* (A)

bootstrap memory: a time-saving unit built into the main computer.

boot-up: start the computer. The word is derived from bootstraps, which aids a person in getting on boots. Booting or booting up helps the computer get its first instruction. A cold boot is when the computer is first turned on. A warm boot is when the computer is already on and is being reset. See *bootstrap.*

BOP: see *bit-oriented protocol.*

borrow: an arithmetically negative carry. See *end-around borrow.* (A)

borrow digit: a digit that is generated when a difference in a digit place is arithmetically negative and that is transferred for processing elsewhere. In a positional representation system, a borrow digit is transferred to the digit place with the next higher weight for processing them. (A) (B)

BOT: beginning of tape.

both-way communication: synonym for *two-way simultaneous communication.*

both-way operation: synonym for *duplex operation.*

bottleneck analysis: a description of a computer system's configuration indicating where bottlenecks occur.

bottom: the end of a file.

bottom-up method: the usual approach in writing a program where each step along the way is completed before the next step is written.

bounceless contact: a mechanical contact conditioned by means of a flip-flop or a device with only one stable state to eliminate all noise during contact.

bound: in PL/1, the upper or lower limit of an array dimension.

boundary (BDRY): see *character boundary, integral boundary.*

boundary alignment: the positioning in main storage of a fixed-length field, such as a half-word or double-word, on an integral boundary for that unit of information.

bounds register: a nonaddressable register holding the upper and lower address bounds that a program can reference.

box:
(1) a symbol used in flow charting indicating a choice or branch in the path of the flow.
(2) a block or enclosed area used to represent a function, circuit, stage, or element graphically.

BP: see *batch processing.*

BPAM: see *basic partitioned access method.*
BPI: bytes per inch.
bpi: bits per inch.
"B" pins: module pins used only for stacking purposes and located in the top substrate.
BPS:
(1) bits per second. In serial transmission, the instantaneous bit speed with which a device or channel transmits a character.
(2) bytes per second.
BR: see *base register.*
branch:
(1) a set of instructions that are executed between two successive branch instructions. (A)
(2) loosely, a conditional jump. (A)
(3) in the execution of a computer program, to select one from a number of alternative sets of instructions. (A) (B)
(4) to select a branch as in (1). (A)
(5) deprecated term for *jump.* (A) (B)
branch and link: an instruction used to call a subroutine.
branching: a computer operation, like switching where a selection is made between two or more possible courses of action depending upon some related fact or condition.
branch instruction: an instruction that controls branching. Synonymous with *decision instruction.* Deprecated term for *jump instruction.* (A) (B)
branch-on condition: see *conditional jump instruction.*
branchpoint:
(1) a point in a computer program at which branching occurs, in particular the address or the label of an instruction. (B)
(2) a place in a routine where a branch is selected. (A)
branch statement: a statement that alters the sequential execution of instructions in a program by directing that the next step in the calculation be determined by and dependent upon a previously calculated quantity.
branch table: a table of arguments and related addresses to which control can be passed on the basis of tests.

breakpoint:
(1) a place in a computer program, usually specified by an instruction, where its execution may be interrupted by external intervention or by a monitor program. (A) (B)
(2) an instruction address stop that can be established by command. See *instruction address stop.*
breakpoint halt: a closed loop consisting of a single jump instruction that effects a jump to itself, often used to achieve a breakpoint. Synonymous with *breakpoint instruction, dynamic stop.* (A) (B)
breakpoint instruction: synonym for *breakpoint halt.* (A) (B)
breakpoint switch: a manually operated switch that controls conditional operations at breakpoints; used primarily in debugging.
bridgeware: hardware or software, used to transcribe data files or programs written for one type of computer into a format that can be used with another type of computer.
bridging: in optical character recognition, a combination of peaks and smudges that may close or partially close a loop of a character.
briefcase computer: a computer housed in a box appearing like a briefcase made possible by having a flat panel liquid crystal display to replace the larger cathode-ray tube display. Cf. *portable computer.*
brightness ratio: a measure of contrast; the ratio between the brightest and darkest parts of a printed paper sheet.
broadband transmission: a high frequency mode of transmission used with local area networks, utilizing coaxial cable and permitting longer transmission distance than possible with baseband transmission.
broadcast: the dissemination of information to several receivers simultaneously, usually via electromagnetic signals.
broken: not working properly.
broket: a broken bracket; either of the characters $<$ and $>$.
brush: an electrical apparatus for reading information from a punched card.

brute-force approach: an attempt to comprehend with existing equipment the size of problems that do not use precise computation or logical manipulations.

BS: see *backspace character.* (A)

BSAM: see *basic sequential access method.*

BSC: see *binary synchronous communication.*

BSC or SS line: a line that uses binary synchronous or start-stop protocols.

BTS: see *batch terminal simulation.*

bubble: the magnetic domain of a bubble memory.

bubble memory: a memory device placed on a chip. The bubbles are microscopically small, magnetized domains that can be moved across a thin magnetic film by a magnetic field. Magnetic-bubble chips that store a million bits of information have been fabricated. Magnetic bubble memory is not as fast as RAM or ROM, but many times faster than mass memory devices such as tapes and disks.

bubble sort: an exchange sort in which the sequence of examination of pairs of items is reversed whenever an exchange is made. Synonymous with *sifting sort.* (A)

bucket: in random-access memory, a unit or place of storage.

bucket brigade: the continued shifting of data bits in a stated direction.

BUF: see *buffer.*

buffer (BUF):
(1) to allocate and schedule the use of buffers. (A)
(2) an area of storage that is temporarily reserved for use in performing an input/output operation, into which data is read or from which data is written. Synonymous with *I/O area.*
(3) a portion of storage for temporarily holding input or output data.
(4) In DOS Systems, actually a *disk buffer* that holds data read from a disk. Each DOS buffer is 528 bytes.

buffer channel: a means of interfacing devices with a computer, which contains memory addressing potential and an ability to transfer words.

buffered computer: a computer system with a storage unit that allows for input and output data to be stored temporarily in order to match the slow speed of input-output devices with the higher speeds of the computer.

buffered device: a device that has I/O elements queued to a direct access device before being written.

buffer management: a portion of the network control program supervisor that controls buffer chains, senses critical storage usage requirements, and initiates recovery procedures.

buffer output: a buffer developed to receive and store data being transmitted into a computer, and that usually includes instructions.

buffer pad characters: a sequence of characters that the network control program sends to an access method buffer preceding message data, to allow space for the host access method to insert message prefixes.

buffer pool: an area of storage in which all buffers of a program are kept.

buffer storage:
(1) a storage device that is used to compensate for differences in the rate of flow of data between components of an automatic data-processing system, or for the time of occurrence of events in the components. (A) (B)
(2) in word processing, a temporary storage in which text is held for processing or communication.

buffer store: see *buffer storage.*

bug:
(1) a mistake or malfunction. (A)
(2) an error in a program.

bug patch: a temporary circumvention of a program element or automatic routine via manual control.

building block: a self-contained element serving as a stage or subsystem by interconnection with other such elements to provide an approach to system and hardware design permitting expansion of a system using a modular technique.

built-in adapter: deprecated term for *integrated adapter.*

built-in check: synonym for *automatic check.* (A)

built-in function: a function that is supplied by a language. Synonymous with *standard function.*

built-virtual-machine: a modeling procedure where a machine program duplicates an actual defined system configuration.

bulk storage: deprecated term for *mass storage.* (B)

bulk store: synonymous with *backing store.*

bulletin board: see *electronic bulletin board.*

bum: slang, to make highly efficient in time or space, often with loss of clarity.

bundled: the practice whereby the cost of a computer system may include not only the CPU but also an operating system, peripheral devices, maintenance agreements, and so on; has largely been dropped as a result of litigation.

bundled software: the software programs that are included with the computer and its peripherals when purchased.

bundling: forcing a buyer to purchase products in combination. *Memory bundling* requires the purchase of a certain amount of extra computer memory along with the computer or other components purchases. *Software bundling* requires the purchase of certain software along with other components.

burn: synonymous with *blow.*

burn-in: the phase of component testing where basic flaws or early failures are screened out by running the circuit for a specified length of time, such as a week, generally at increased temperatures in some sort of oven.

burst: to separate continuous-form paper into discrete sheets. See *error burst.* (A)

burster: a mechanical unit that bursts printouts.

bus (B):
(1) one or more conductors used for transmitting signals or power. (A)
(2) circuits inside the computer that transmit information from one part of a computer system to another. In PCs, these connect all the system components. The width of the bus, say 16-bit v. 32-bit, determines the amount of data that can be transmitted. Every bus has a clock speed in terms of MHz.

bus bar: deprecated term for *bus.*

bus cable: a cable that connects to a bus and extends it outside the computer unit, or to a differing physical bus within the same computer.

bus extender: a device permitting additional cards to be plugged into a computer's bus.

business data processing: data processing for business purposes, for example, recording and summarizing the financial transactions of a business. Synonym for *administrative data processing.* (A) (B)

business graphics: in computer graphics, bar charts, pie charts, graphs and other visual representations of the operational or strategic aspects of a business (i.e., market share, sales vs. costs, comparative product performance, etc.). Synonymous with *management graphics.*

business information system (BIS): a combination of people, data processing equipment, input/output devices, and communications facilities. The system must accept information at the point where it is generated, transport it to the point where it is processed, process it, and finally deliver the information to the point where it is to be used.

business machine (BM): a machine designed to facilitate clerical operations in commercial or scientific activities.

business machine clocking: a time-base oscillator supplied by the business machine for regulating the bit rate of transmission. Synonymous with *nondata-set clocking.* Cf. *data-set clocking.*

bus wire: a group of wires that permits the memory, the CPU, and the input-output devices to exchange words.

button: an image, sometimes resembling a pushbutton, that clicks to designate, confirm, or cancel and action.

bypass action: approaches taken to get around a problem and accomplish some task until the problem has been corrected.

bypass label processing (BLP): disabling a system feature that reads and writes a tape label.

bypass procedure: a procedure used to get the most information into the main computer when the line control computer fails.

byproduct: data developed without further effort from a unit whose basic purpose is to perform some other operation.

byte (B):

(1) a binary character operated upon as a unit and usually shorter than a computer word. (A)

(2) the representation of a character.

(3) a unit of information consisting of a fixed number of bits. One byte usually consists of a series of eight bits. See *kilobytes, megabyte, n-bit byte.*

byte-addressable: designating a computer wherein each byte has a different address that can be used to access data in a program. Cf. *word-addressable.*

byte count-oriented protocol: a protocol using a unique character indicating the beginning of a message containing a count of the number of data characters in addition to the actual data. Once transmitted, special characters follow verifying that the correct number of data characters has been sent.

byte manipulation: manipulating, as individual instructions, groups of bits, such as characters.

byte mode: synonym for *multiplex mode.*

byte multiplexing: the process where time slots on a channel are delegated to individual slow input-output devices so that bytes from one after another can be interlaced on the channel to or from main memory.

bytewide memory: a byte-addressable main memory.

C:

(1) see *capacitor.*

(2) see *carry.*

(3) see *centi.*

(4) see *clear.*

(5) see *clock.*

(6) see *computer.*

(7) see *constant.*

(8) see *control.*

(9) see *controller.*

(10) see *counter.*

(11) a high-level programming language for writing systems software. The UNIX, ATT operating system was written using the C language. C language aids in reducing program length and increases efficiency.

C++: a high-level programming language that modifies the C language with object-oriented features. See also *object oriented.*

CA: see *control area.*

cache: in a processing unit, a high-speed buffer storage that is continually updated to contain recently accessed contents of main storage. Its purpose is to reduce access time.

cache memory: a reserved section of main memory or a special bank of high-speed memory that is used to improve computer performance. A main cache memory holds instructions and data that are transferred to and from a disk when the disk is read, a large block of data is copied into the cache.

CAD: see *computer-aided design.*

CAD/CAM: an acronym for computer-aided design/computer-aided manufacturing. CAD permits the design and testing of a product on a computer screen in simulation. CAM permits a computer to direct the manufacture and assembly of a product.

CAE: see *computer-aided engineering.*

CAFS: content-addressable file store. A computer storage device, using hard disks, that includes special hardware for searching for information in the store.

CAI:

(1) see *computer-aided instruction.*

(2) see *computer-assisted instruction.*

CAL: see *Conversational Algebraic Language.*

calculate: the arithmetic and/or logical manipulation of data.

calculating punch: a calculator with a card reader and a card punch that reads the data on a punched card, performs some arithmetic operations or logic operations on the data, and punches the results on the same or another punched card. Synonymous with *multiplying punch.* (A) (B)

calculator: a device that is especially suitable for performing arithmetic operations, but that requires human intervention to alter its stored program, if any, and to initiate each operation or sequence of operations.

calculator chip: a chip with a micro-processor that has a built-in microprogram to solve arithmetic functions.

call:
(1) the action of bringing a computer program, a routine, or a subroutine into effect, usually by specifying the entry conditions and jumping to an entry point. (B)
(2) in computer programming, to execute a call. (A) (B)
(3) in data communication, the action performed by the calling party, or the operations necessary in making a call, or the effective use made of a connection between two stations.
(4) to transfer control to a specified closed subroutine. (A)
(5) see *subroutine call.* (A)
(6) synonymous with *cue.* (A)

call by reference: a subroutine or procedure call where the addresses of the parameter's storage locations are passed to the subroutine.

call by value: a subroutine or procedure call in where the actual values of the parameters are passed to the subroutine.

calligraphic plotter: in computer graphics, a plotter that draws an image on a CRT consisting of lines alone.

calling statement: in BASIC, any statement that accesses a library function, a user-defined function, or a subroutine.

call instruction: an instruction which, after diverting execution to a new sequence of instructions, allows a return to the program's original sequence.

call number: a group of characters identifying a subroutine.

call processing system: in a digital exchange, a subsystem used to control the progress of each call on the basis of instruction received from users.

call processor (CP): a subsystem consisting of a microcomputer, a synchronizer, and a random access memory. Contains sufficient memory to accommodate the call-processing program and its data base.

CAM:
(1) content addressed memory; maintains a capability to retrieve data identified by content rather than by a numbered location or an identifiable data pattern.
(2) computer-aided manufacturing. See *CAD/CAM.*

CAN: see *cancel character.* (A)

cancel (CNCL): when used cancels the execution of the current job in the partition in which the command was given.

cancel character (CAN):
(1) a control character used by some convention to indicate that the data with which they are associated are in error or are to be disregarded. Synonymous with *ignore character.* (B)
(2) an accuracy control character used to indicate that the data with which it is associated are in error or are to be disregarded.
(3) see *block cancel character.* (A)

cancellation error: a loss in accuracy during addition or subtraction of numbers of widely differing sizes, due to limits of precision. See *representational error.*

CANCL: the status word indicating that the remote system has deleted information transmitted earlier.

canned paragraphs: in word processing, describes pre-recorded paragraphs in frequent usage, and combined in various ways.

canned programs: programs prepared by an outside supplier and provided to a user in a machine-readable form.

canned routine: a prewritten program for use with a specific computer that performs one or more generalized functions, such as sorting, standard mathematical calculations, or payroll.

canned software: synonymous with *package.*

CAP: see *capacity.*

capacitor (C): an electronic unit with the properties of capacitance.

capacitor storage: a storage device that uses the capacitive properties of certain materials. (A) (B)

capacity (CAP): see *channel capacity, storage capacity.* (A)

caps mode: see *all-caps mode.*

capture: in optical character readers, to gather picture data from a field on an input document, using a special scan. Saving information on a display screen to a file is called screen capture.

card (CD): see *aperture card, binary card, binder-hold card, check card, double card, circuit board edge-coated card, edge-notched card, edge-punched card, expansion card, flash card, header card, Hollerith card, laced card, magnetic card, mark-sensing card, punch card, punched card, scored card, short card, source data card, stub card, trailer card.* (A)

card cage: a chassis or frame that holds a central processor, memory cards and interfaces. Synonymous with *card chassis.*

card chassis: synonymous with *card cage.*

card checking: checking the validity of a card image transfer.

card code: the combinations of punched holes that represent characters (e.g., letters, digits) in a punched card.

card column:
(1) a line of punch positions parallel to the storage edges of a punch card. (B)
(2) a line of punch positions parallel to the Y datum in line of a punch card. (A)

card cycle: time needed to read and/or punch a card.

card deck: a group of punched cards. Synonymous with *card pack.* (B)

card field: a specific combination of punch positions, mark-sensing positions, or both, on a card. (A)

card form: see *printed card form.* (A)

card format: pertaining to the columns and fields of data in a punched card.

card guide: the U-shaped slot that contains the edge of a printed circuit board within a card cage.

card hopper: the part of a card-processing device that holds the cards to be processed and makes them available to a card-feed mechanism. (B) Cf. *card stacker.* (A)

card image: a one-to-one representation of the hole patterns of a punched card; for example, a matrix in which a 1 represents a punch and a 0 represents the absence of a punch. (A)

cardinality: in PASCAL, the number of values contained in an ordinal type.

card input: the introduction of information to a processing unit with punched cards. The data channel used to feed card information into a device.

card jam: a malfunction of a card-processing device in which cards become jammed. (A)

card loader: a routine used to load a program from punched cards into store.

card pack: synonym for *card deck.*

card path: the part of a card-processing device that moves and guides the card through the device. (B)

card-programmed computer: either a mini-sized computer or an older computer, limited in input operation in gathering information from punched, wired, or magnetic cards or as preprogrammed computers.

card punch (CP):
(1) a computer-actuated punch that punches holes in a punch card or punched card. (B)
(2) a device that punches holes in a card to represent data. (A)
(3) synonymous with *automatic punch.*
(4) deprecated term for *keypunch.* (B)

card random access memory (or method): see *CRAM.*

card reader (CDR) (CR):
(1) a device that reads or senses the holes in a punched card, transforming the data from hole patterns to electrical signals. (B)
(2) an input device that senses hole patterns in a punched card and translates them into machine language. Synonymous with *punched card reader.* (A)

card reproducer: a device that reproduces a punch card by punching another similar card.

card row:
   (1) a line of punch positions parallel to the longer edges of a punch card. (B)
   (2) a line of punch positions parallel to the X datum line of a punch card. (A)

cards: see *continuous-form cards.* (A)

card set: cards and forms, bound in a manner that provides multiple copies of source data. (A)

card sorter: a device that deposits punched cards in pockets selected according to the hole patterns in the cards. (B)

card stacker: the part of the card-processing device that receives the cards after they have been processed. (B) Cf. *card hopper.* (A)

card-to-disk (or tape) converter: a program that can copy the data stored on a punch card onto a disk or tape.

card-to-tape: pertaining to equipment that transfers information directly from punched cards to punched or magnetic tape.

card track: the part of a card-processing device that moves and guides the card through the device. (A)

card verification: see *key verification.*

card verifying: a way of checking the accuracy of key punching and is a duplication check. A second operator verifies the original punching by depressing the keys of a verifier while reading the identical source data, and the machine compares the key depressed with the hole already punched in the card.

card whalloper: a device that punches, reads, or in some fashion manipulates punched cards.

caret: a symbol (^) used to indicate the location of a decimal point.

carousel: the rotary device that shows a data medium such as micro-film at an identified position for reading or recording.

carriage: see *automatic carriage.* (A)

carriage control character: the first character of an output record (line) that is to be printed; it determines how many lines should be skipped before the next line is printed.

carriage control tape:
   (1) a tape that is used to control vertical tabulation of printing positions or display positions.
   (2) a tape that contains line-feed control data for a printing device. (A)

carriage return (CR): the operation that prepares for the next character to be printed or displayed at the specified first position on the same line. (A) Synonymous with *ENTER.*

carriage return character (CR):
   (1) a format effector that causes the print or display position to move to the first position on the same line. (A) (B).
   (2) a format effector that causes the location of the printing or display position to be moved to the first space on the same printing or display line.
   (3) cf. *carrier return character, new-line character.*

carrier holes: the holes in the side margins on continuous forms paper. When placed on the tractor pins, the holes maintain printer alignment and registration and control movement of the paper. Synonymous with *tractor holes.*

carrier return character (CRC): a word-processing formatting control that moves the printing or display point to the first position on the next line. Carrier return may be ignored during text adjust mode operations. Synonymous with *new-line character.* See *required carrier-return character.* Cf. *carriage return character.*

carry (C) (CY):
   (1) the action of transferring a carry digit. (B)
   (2) one or more digits, produced in connection with an arithmetic operation on one digit place of two or more numerals in positional notation, that are forwarded to another digit place for processing there.
   (3) the number represented by the digit or digits in (2).
   (4) most commonly, a digit as defined in (2), that arises when the sum or product of two or more digits equals or exceeds the radix of the number representation system.
   (5) less commonly, a borrow.
   (6) the command directing that a carry be forwarded.

(7) to transfer a carry digit.

(8) to forward a carry.

(9) see *cascaded carry, complete carry, end-around carry, high-speed carry, partial carry, standing-on-nines carry.* (A)

carry digit: a digit that is generated when a sum or a product in a digit place exceeds the largest number that can be represented in that digit place and that is transferred for processing elsewhere. In a positional representation system, a carry digit is transferred to the digit place with the next higher weight for processing there. (A) (B)

carry flag: an indicator signaling when a register overflow or underflow condition exists during mathematical operations with an accumulator.

carry/link bit: on some systems, a bit set if a carry from the most significant bit occurs during an add, a complement-and-add, or a decimal-add instruction. The bit is included in the shift right with link and the rotate right with link instructions.

carry time: time needed for transferring all the carry digits to higher columns and adding them for all digits in the number.

cartridge: a portable memory container that can be inserted into the slot of a computer or printer. These can be comprised of magnetic tape, a magnetic disk, or a chip.

cartridge disk: a type of hard disk that can be removed from its drive.

cartridge drive: a unit to read and write cartridges.

cascade control: a system of organizing control units in sequence so that each unit controls the function of its successor and is in turn regulated by its predecessor.

cascaded carry: in parallel addition, a procedure in which the addition results in a partial sum numeral and a carry numeral which are in turn added; this process is repeated until a zero carry is generated. (B) Cf. *high-speed carry.* (A)

cascade menu: an additional menu that opens when a cascade item is chosen from a menu. Cascade items on a menu are marked with a right-facing arrow.

case statement: in PASCAL, a selection control structure that provides for multi-way selection of different courses of action; a generalization of the IF statement equivalent to nested IF-THEN-ELSE statements.

cashlike document: a document such as a check, gift, or certificate that is used in the same manner as cash, for payment of merchandise. Synonymous with *cashlike tender.*

cashlike tender: synonym for *cashlike document.*

casting-out-nines: utilizing a remainder from the operand by dividing by nine and carrying out the same operations on the remainders as are performed on the operands.

CAT: computer aided testing.

catalanguage: synonymous with *object language.*

catalog (CATLG):

(1) a directory of locations of files and libraries. (B)

(2) an ordered compilation of item descriptions and sufficient information to afford access to the items. (A)

(3) the collection of all data set indexes that are used by the control program to locate a volume containing a specific data set.

(4) to enter information about a file or a library into a catalog. (B)

(5) to include the volume identification of a data set in the catalog.

catalog directory: a table in a catalog that identifies items in the catalog.

cataloged data set: a data set that is represented in an index, or hierarchy of indexes, in the system catalog; the indexes provide the means for locating the data set.

cataloged procedure: a set of control statements that has been placed in a library and can be retrieved by name.

catalogue: see *catalog.*

catastrophic errors: in a situation where so many errors have occurred, no more useful diagnostic information can be produced and the compilation is ended.

catena: a series of items linked in a chained list; specifically, a string of characters in a word.

catenate: pertaining to the arrangement of a series of items in a catena. Synonymous with *concatenate.*

cathode-ray storage: an electrostatic storage that uses a cathode-ray beam for access to data. (A) (B)

cathode-ray tube (CRT): a vacuum tube display in which a beam of electrons can be controlled to form alphanumeric characters or symbols on a luminescent screen, for example, by use of a dot matrix. Synonymous with *video display terminal.*

cathode-ray tube display (CRT display):
(1) a device that presents data in visual form by means of controlled electron beams.
(2) the data display produced by the device as in (1). (A)

CATLG: see *catalog.*

caveman: slang, referring to an antiquated computer; any obsolete data-processing equipment.

CAW: see *channel address word.*

CBA: see *computer-based automation.*

CBASIC: a compiler version of the BASIC programming language for use with some microprocessors.

CBBS: computerized bulletin board service. See *electronic bulletin board.*

CBEMA: Computer and Business Equipment Manufacturers Association.

CC:
(1) see *cluster controller.*
(2) see *command chain.*
(3) see *communication controller.*
(4) see *control counter.*

CCD: see *charge couple device.*

CCHS: see *cylinder-cylinder-head-sector.*

CCP: see *certificate in computer programming.*

CCU: see *central control unit.*

CCW: see *channel command word.*

CCW translation: see *channel program translation.*

CD: see *card.*

CDF: see *combined distribution frame.*

CD-I (Compact Disc Interactive): a compact disk standard that includes CD audio static data (CD ROM), still video pictures and animated graphics. Holds up to

550 megabytes of data and provides multiple levels of audio and video format. It allows users access to large texts or picture databases. Cf. *CD-ROM.*

CDP: see *certificate in data processing.*

CDR: see *card reader.*

CD-ROM (Compact Disc Read Only Memory): a computer storage disk in the same physical form as a CD audio disk, holding 550 megabytes of digital data. Used for such things as encyclopedias, dictionaries, and large reference works. Cf. *CD-I.*

C-drives: synonymous with *E-disks.*

cell: In spreadsheets, a cell is a box containing a single unit of data. See *binary cell, data cell, magnetic cell, storage cell.* See also *circuit unit assembly.*

center line: see *stroke center line.* (A)

centi (C): hundred or one hundredth.

centimeter (CM): one hundredth of a meter; 0.39 inch.

centisecond: one-hundredth of a second.

central computer: deprecated term for *host computer.*

central control unit (CCU): the communication controller hardware unit that contains the circuits and data flow paths needed to execute instructions and to control its storage and the attached adapters.

centralization: concentration of problem solving within an organization structure; often takes place to make optimum use of a computer-based information system. Centralization enables management to weigh all the relevant data, whereas a fragmented system cannot.

centralized data processing: data processing performed at a single, central location on data from several regional locations or managerial levels.

central processing unit (CPU): a unit of a computer that includes circuits controlling the interpretation and execution of instructions. Synonymous with *central processor, main frame.* See also *microprocessor.*

central processing unit loop: the main routine of a control program and that which is associated with the control of the internal status of the processing unit.

central processor (CP): synonymous with *central processing unit.*

central scanning loop: a loop of instructions that determine which task is to be performed next.

central station: deprecated term for *control station.*

ceramic dual-in-line package: see *cer-DIP.*

cer-DIP: ceramic dual-in-line package. A package offering higher performance than conventional ceramic units.

certificate in computer programming (CCP): certification indicating experience and professional competence at the senior programmer level.

certificate in data processing (CDP): a certificate awarded by the ICCP to qualified candidates who have successfully passed an examination consisting of five sections—data-processing equipment, computer programming and software, principles of management, quantitative methods, and systems analysis and design.

certified tape: computer tape that is machine-verified on all tracks throughout each roll and certified by the supplier to have less than a specific total number of errors or to have no errors.

CESD: see *composite external symbol dictionary.*

CFIA: see *component failure impact analysis.*

CGA: color/graphics adapter. This was the first color graphics system for the IBM-PC.

CH: see *channel.*

chad:
(1) the material separated from a data carrier when forming a hole.
(2) the residue separated from the carrier holes in continuous forms paper.
(3) synonymous with *chip.*

chadded: pertaining to the punching of tape in which chad results.

chadless tape: punched tape that has been punched in such a way that chad is not formed. (A)

chain: see *Markov chain.* See also *chained list.*

chain additions program: an instruction set that will permit new records to be added to a file.

chain code: an arrangement in a cyclic sequence of some or all of the possible different n-bit words, in which adjacent words are related such that each is derivable from its neighbor by displacing the bits on digit position to the left, or right, dropping the leading bit and inserting a bit at the end. The value of the inserted bit needs only to meet the requirement that a word must not recur before the cycle is complete, for example, 000 001 010 101 011 111 110 100 000 . . . (A)

chained file: a computer file arranged so that each data item or key in a record in a chain has the address of another record with the same data or key.

chained list: a list in which the items may be dispersed but in which each item contains an identifier for locating the next item. (A) (B)

chained record: a record in a chained file.

chained sector: a storage method permitting one logical unit to be spread across different areas on disk, as contrasted to being stored as one contiguous area.

chaining: a method of storing records in which each record belongs to a list or group of records and has a linking field for tracing the chain.

chaining overflow: on a direct-access storage device, the writing of overflow records on the next higher available track; each track contains a record that provides a link between the home track and the overflow track. Cf. *progressive overflow.*

chaining search: a search in which each item contains the means for locating the next item to be considered in the search. (A) (B)

chain links:
(1) various series of linked data items.
(2) in sequential processing, successive program segments, each of which relies on the previous segment for its input.

chain maintenance program: an instruction set permitting the deletion of records from a file.

chain pointer: information that indicates where to find the next item in a chained list.

chain printer: an impact printer in which the type slugs are carried by the links of a revolving chain. (A) (B)

chance failure: synonymous with *random failure.*

change case: a function in which the processor automatically changes text from lowercase to uppercase, or vice versa.

change character: see *font change character.* (A)

change dump: a selective dump of those storage locations whose contents have changed. (A) (B)

change file: a file of transactions forming change records; used to update a master file during batch processing. Synonymous with *detail file, transaction file.*

change record: a record which results in the modification of some of the information in the corresponding master file record.

change tape: synonymous with *transaction tape.*

channel (CH) (CHNL):
(1) in information theory, that part of a communication system that connects the message source with the message sink. Mathematically, this part can be characterized by the set of conditional probabilities of occurrence of all the possible messages received at the message sink when a given message emanates from the message source. (B)
(2) the portion of a storage medium that is accessible to a given reading or writing station, for example, track, band. (A)
(3) see *binary symmetric channel, data channel, forward channel, information channel, input channel, input/output channel, output channel.*

channel address word (CAW): an area in storage that specifies the location in main storage at which a channel program begins.

channel capacity: in information theory, the measure of the ability of a given channel subject to specific constraints to transmit messages from a specified message source expressed as either the maximum possible mean transinformation content per character, or the maximum possible average transinformation rate. (A) (B)

channel command: an instruction that directs a data channel, control unit, or device to perform an operation or set of operations.

channel command word (CCW): a double-word at the location in main storage specified by the channel address word. One or more CCWs make up the channel program that directs data-channel operations.

channel configuration: the types and numbers of units connected to each channel on a computer.

channel controller (CC): provides an independent data path to storage and assures multiprocessor systems maximum availability, permitting each processing unit access to each channel within the system.

channel director: a specialized computer located within a larger computer that controls the activities of several channels.

channelize: a procedure employed to divide a communications circuit into a number of channels.

channel overload: a state in which data transfer to or from the processor and I/O devices reaches a rate that approaches the capacity of the data channel.

channel program: one or more channel command words that control a specific sequence of data-channel operations. Execution of the specific sequence is initiated by a single start I/O instruction.

channel program translation: in a channel program for a virtual storage system, replacement by software of virtual storage addresses with real addresses.

channel queue: a queue of data or requests waiting to be processed on a channel.

channel reliability: the percentage of time the channels meet all arbitrary standards.

channel set: a collection of channels that can be concurrently addressed by a processor.

channel skip: a carriage control character indicating to the printer to carry out a vertical tab or to skip to the top of the following page.

channel status word (CSW): an area in storage that provides information about the termination of input-output operations.

channel synchronizer: a unit providing the proper interface between the central computer and peripheral devices.

channel-to-channel adapter (CTCA): a hardware device that can be used to connect two channels on the same computing system or on different systems.

chapter: deprecated term for *segment*. (A)

CHAR: see *character*.

character (CHAR) (CHR):
(1) a member of a set of elements upon which agreement has been reached and that is used for the organization, control, or representation of data. Characters may be letters, digits, punctuation marks, or other symbols, often represented in the form of a spatial arrangement of adjacent or connected strokes or in the form of other physical conditions in data media. (A) (B)
(2) a letter, digit, or other symbol that is used as part of the organization, control, or representation of data. A character is often in the form of a spatial arrangement of adjacent or connected strokes. (A)
(3) see *accuracy control character, alphanumeric character set, backspace character, blank character, block cancel character, cancel character, carriage return character, carrier return character, check character, code extension character, control character, cyclic redundancy check character, data-link escape character, delete character, device control character, end-of-medium character, end-of-text character, enquiry character, erase character, escape character, font-change character, form feed character, gap character, graphic character, horizontal tabulation character, illegal character, indent tab character, index character, index return character, line feed character, longitudinal redundancy check character, negative acknowledge character, new-line character, null character, numeric backspace character, numeric space character, print control character, redundancy check character,*
repeat character, required carrier-return character, required hyphen character, required page-end character, required space character, shift-in-character, space character, special character, start-of-heading character, start-of-text character, start-stop character, stop character, substitute character, superscript character, switch character, syllable hyphen character, synchronous idle character, unit backspace character, vertical tabulation character, word underscore character.

character-addressable: see *byte-addressable*.

character-addressable storage device: computer memory where each character has one specific location with its own address. Synonymous with *variable word length storage*.

character addressing: the process of gaining access to a character position by using an address.

character arrangement: an arrangement composed of graphic characters from one or more modified or unmodified character sets.

character assembly: the process by which bits are put together to form characters as the bits arrive on a data link. In the communication controller, character assembly is performed either by the control program or by the communication scanner, depending on the type of scanner installed. Cf. *character disassembly*.

character-at-a-time printer: synonym for *character printer*. (A)

character average information content: synonym for *character mean entropy*. (A)

character based: describes programs that can display on screen only ASCII characters.

character blink: part of a terminal device that permits one or more characters to blink together with the main cursor or out of synchronization with the main cursor.

character boundary: in character recognition, the largest rectangle, with a side parallel to the document reference edge, each of whose sides is tangential to a given character outline. (A)

character cell: the maximum physical boundary of a single character.

character check: a check that verifies the observance of rules for the formation of characters. (A)

character code: in a data communications code, a pattern of bits representing a numeric or alphabetic character, or a punctuation mark or special symbol.

character crowding: the reduction of the appropriate interval between characters on a magnetic medium. See *pack.*

character-deletion character: a character within a line of terminal input specifying that it and the immediately preceding character are to be removed from the line.

character density: a measure of the horizontal spacing of characters.

character device control: a control character used to control devices associated with computing or telecommunication systems; for example, the switching on or off of these devices.

character disassembly: the process by which characters are broken down into bits for transmission over a data link. In the communication controller, character disassembly is performed either by the control program or by the communication scanner, depending on the type of scanner installed. Cf. *character assembly.*

character display device: a display device that gives a representation of data only in the form of characters. (A) (B) Synonymous with *alphanumeric display device, readout device.*

character edge: in optical character recognition, the imaginary edge running along the optical discontinuity between the printed area and the unprinted area of a printed symbol or character.

character element: a basic information element as transmitted, printed, displayed, and so forth, or used to control communications, when used as a code.

character expression: in assembler programming, a character string enclosed by apostrophes. It can be used only in conditional assembly instructions. The enclosing apostrophes are not part of the value represented. Cf. *quoted string.*

character fill: to insert as often as necessary into a storage medium the representation of a specified character that does not itself convey data but may delete unwanted data. (A) (B)

character format memory: memory-storing approach for storing one character in each addressable location.

character generator:
(1) In computer graphics, a functional unit that converts the coded representation of a graphic character into the shape of the character for display. See also *stroke character generator.*
(2) in word processing, the means within equipment for generating visual characters or symbols from coded data.

character information rate: synonym for *character mean entropy.* (A)

characteristic:
(1) in a floating-point representation, the numeral that represents the exponent.
(2) the integer part, which may be positive or negative, of the representation of a logarithm. (A) (B)
(3) Cf. *mantissa.*

character manipulation: the operations and techniques for handling strings of alphanumeric information, including searching, sorting, and reorganization of names, words, phrases, and textual information.

character mean entropy: in information theory, the mean per character of the entropy for all possible messages from a stationary message source. Synonymous with *character average information content, character mean information content, character information rate.* (A) (B)

character mean information content: synonym for *character mean entropy.* (A) (B)

character mode: a program mode determining a lower level of display resolution.

character modifier: a constant utilized in address modification to reference the location of the character.

character oriented: pertaining to a computer where character locations rather than words are addressed.

character-oriented protocol: a protocol using specific characters showing the beginning of a message and the end of a block of data.

character-oriented word-processing programs: programs that display the words in the order, but not necessarily the format, in which they will be printed.

character outline: the graphic pattern established by the stroke edges of a character. (A)

character parity: see *vertical redundancy check.*

character pitch: the number of characters per inch found in a line of text.

character pitch display: the capability of a printer to output characters in a number of different pitches (sizes) requested by the software.

character printer (CP): a device that prints a single character at a time, for example, a typewriter. Synonymous with *character-at-a-time printer, serial printer.* Cf. *line printer.* (A)

character reader: an input unit that performs character recognition. (A) (B)

character recognition:
(1) the identification of characters by automatic means. See *magnetic ink character recognition, optical character recognition.* (B)
(2) the identification of geographic, phonic, or other characters by various means including magnetic, optical, or mechanical. (A)

character relation: in assembler programming, two character strings separated by a relational operator.

character repertoire: the set of characters available in a specific code.

character row: synonym for *display line.*

character set:
(1) a finite set of different characters upon which agreement has been reached and that is considered complete for some purpose. (B)
(2) a set of unique representations called characters; for example, the 26 letters of the English alphabet, 0 and 1 of the boolean alphabet, the set of signals in the Morse code alphabet, and the 128 ASCII characters. (A)
(3) a defined collection of characters.

(4) see *alphabetic character set, alphabetic-coded character set, alphanumeric character set, alphanumeric-coded character set, coded character set, numeric character set, numeric-coded character set.*

character size: the number of binary digits in a single character in the storage unit.

character size control: the capability for viewing a full page of data at a regular character size or one-half page at double size.

character skew: in optical character recognition, the angular rotation of a character relative to its intended or ideal placement.

character spacing reference line: in character recognition, a vertical line that is used to evaluate the horizontal spacing of characters. It may be a line that equally divides the distance between the sides of a character boundary or that coincides with the center line of a vertical stroke. (A)

character string:
(1) a string consisting solely of characters. (A) (B)
(2) a connected sequence of characters.

character string literals: a group of letters, numbers, or special characters assigned when a program is written (i.e., not calculated by a program) that are to be printed exactly as is on the output page.

character stroke: OCR lines, points, arcs, and other marks used as parts or portions of graphic characters. The dot over the letter *i* or the cross of a *t* is a stroke.

character style: in OCR, a distinctive construction, with no restriction as to size that is common to a group of characters.

character subset: a selection of characters from a character set, comprising all characters that have a specified common feature; for example, in each of the character sets of International Standards Organization (ISO) Recommendation R646 "6- and 7-bit coded character sets for information processing interchange," the digits 0 and 9 may constitute a character subset. (B) See *alphabetic character sub-*

set, *alphanumeric character subset, numeric character subset.* (A)

charge couple device (CCD): a memory unit with high packing density and low power consumption. Synonymous with *image sensor.*

chart: see *data flowchart, flowchart, plugboard chart.* (A)

chassis: the frame on which boards are mounted. See *hot chassis.*

check (CHK): a process for determining accuracy. (A) See *automatic check, character check, cyclic redundancy check, duplication check, expiration check, longitudinal parity check, marginal check, mathematical check, parity check, programmed check, redundancy check, selection check, sight check, summation check, transfer check.* See also *check digit, machine check interruption.*

check bit: a binary check digit; for example, a parity bit. See *redundancy check bit.* (A)

check box:
(1) a small box associated with an option in a window.
(2) a small square box used to turn options on and off in menus and in dialog boxes. Clock a check box to turn it alternately on or off. The check box darkens when it is on. It can be turned on or off independently from other check boxes.

check card:
(1) a punched card suitable for use as a bank check.
(2) a punch card used for checking. (A)

check character: a character used for the purpose of performing a check. (A)

check code: to isolate and remove mistakes from any routine.

check diagnostic: a routine designed to locate a malfunction or error in a computer.

check digit: a digit used for the purpose of performing a check. (A)

check indicator: a device that can display or announce when an error has been made or a malfunction has occurred.

checking program: a computer program that examines other computer programs or sets of data for mistakes of syntax. (A)

check number: synonymous with *check digit.*

check out: synonym for *debug.*

check-out routine: various routines assisting programmers in the debugging of routines.

checkpoint (CHKPT):
(1) a place in a computer program at which a check is made, or at which a recording of data is made for restart purposes. (A) (B)
(2) a point at which information about the status of a job and the system can be recorded so that the job step can be later restarted.
(3) to record such information.

checkpoint and restart: a program-verifying method permitting processing to continue from the last checkpoint instead of from the beginning of the run after an error detection or other form of interrupt.

checkpoint data set: a data set that contains checkpoint records.

checkpoint dump: recording data at a checkpoint.

checkpoint records: records that contain the status of a job and the system at the time the records are written by the checkpoint routine. These records provide the information necessary for restarting a job without having to return to the beginning of the job. See also *control record.*

checkpoint restart: the process of resuming a job at a checkpoint within the job step that caused abnormal termination. The restart may be automatic or deferred, where deferred restart involves resubmitting the job. See also *automatic restart, deferred restart.* Cf. *step restart.*

checkpoint routine: a series of instructions that generate information for future verification.

checkpoint sorting: the point at which a restart, or rerun can be initiated. Memory, registers, and the position of tapes are recorded at this point.

check register: a register where data is stored temporarily prior to making a comparison with the same data input at a differing time or by a differing path.

check reset key: a push button that shows an error and resets the error detection mechanism indicated by the check light; required to restart a program following the making of an error found in a batch mode.

check solution: the solution to a problem drawn by independent means to verify a computer solution.

check total: one of a large number of totals or sums that can be correlated as a check for the consistency of reconciliation in a set of calculations.

check word: the machine word used to represent a check symbol and is affixed and printed to the block thereby signifying the check.

chief programmer team (CPT): a method of organization used in the management of system projects where a chief programmer supervises the programming and testing of system modules. Programmer productivity and system reliability are increased.

child: a data record that can be created only from the contents of one or more other records already in existence. These latter records are referred to as parents. See *parent.*

child segment: in a data base, a segment immediately below another segment in a hierarchy. A child segment has only one parent segment. See also *parent segment.*

Chinese binary: synonym for *column binary.* (A)

chip: the typical PC is made up of several chips connected to circuit boards. For types of PC chips. See DIP, PGA, SIMM.
(1) a minute piece of semiconductive material used in the manufacture of electronic components. (A)
(2) an integral circuit on a piece of semiconductive material. (A)
(3) in micrographics, a piece of microform that contains both microimages and coded identification.
(4) synonym for *chad.* See *steppers.*

chip microprocessor: LSI circuits residing on a single silicon chip, able to perform the necessary activities of a computer; popularly called "computer on a chip."

chip processes: processes involved in producing integrated circuits.

chip register architecture: the arrangement of registers on a chip, including the number and function of on-chip registers, the type and depth of the stack register, interrupt capability, and the direct-memory-access feature.

CHK: see *check.*

CHKPT: see *checkpoint.*

CHNL: see *channel.*

choice device: in computer graphics, an input device that provides integers specifying alternatives. See also *locator device, pick device, valuator device.*

choose: to give a command by dragging through a menu and releasing a mouse button when the command is highlighted.

chooser:
(1) a program that permits the designation of devices, such as printers and shared disks on a network.
(2) a desk accessory that permits printing from any attached printer with printer software on the startup disk. The chooser can designate the port to which a printer is attached.

CHR: see *character.*

CICS: see *customer information control system.*

CIF: computer-integrated factory.

CIM: see *computer input microfilm.*

cine-oriented image: in micrographics, an image appearing on a roll of microfilm in such a manner that the top edge of the image is perpendicular to the long edge of the film. Cf. *comic-strip oriented image.* (A)

ciphertext: synonym for *encryption.*

CIR: see *current instruction register.*

circuit: in data communications, a means of two-way communication between two data terminal installations.

circuit analyzer: apparatus consisting of one or several test instruments that are controlled by a microprocessor and used for measuring one or more quantities or to verify performance of a circuit.

circuit board: a board to which is affixed the circuitry of a microprocessor. Synonymous with *card, circuit card.*

circuit card: synonymous with *circuit board.*

circuit hold: the component mounting hole appearing within or partially within the conductive lines of a printed circuit board.

circuit unit assembly (CUA): a subassembly within an equipment cabinet. Synonymous with *cell*.

circular list: a chained list, which, following the processing of all items from any starting place, permits a return to the item preceding the starting point.

circular polling: where the host computer passes through a list of nodes and solicits a response from every station once during each pass. Cf. *priority polling*.

circular shift: synonym for *end-around shift*. (A)

circulating register: a shift register in which data moved out of one end of the register are reentered into the other end as in a closed loop. (A)

circulating storage: dynamic storage involving a closed loop. Synonymous with *cyclic storage*. (A)

circumvention: see *bypass action*.

CISC: see *complex instruction-set computing*.

citation: a statement of reference relating to other sources of data or special notes concerning the data found on punched cards.

CIU: see *computer interface unit*.

CKD: see *county-key-data device*.

CL: see *command language*.

class: a means of grouping jobs that require the same set of resources for their execution. There are two classes: input class and output class.

class condition: in COBOL, a statement that the content of an item is wholly alphabetic or wholly numeric. It may be true or false.

classification: the arrangement of data in classes or groups; needed to produce summary reports.

classify: the arrangement of data into classes or groups according to a definite plan or method.

clause: in COBOL, a set of consecutive words whose purpose is to specify an attribute of an entry. There are three types of clauses: data, environment, and file.

clean and certify: a housekeeping procedure where a magnetic tape is run through a machine that cleans it, writes a data test pattern on it, and checks for errors caused by damage.

clear (C) (CLR):
(1) to put one or more storage locations or registers into a prescribed state, usually that denoting zero. (B)
(2) to cause one or more storage locations to be in a prescribed state, usually that corresponding to zero or that corresponding to the space character. (A) (B)
(3) a command that removes selected material.

clear area: in character recognition, a specified area that is to be kept free of printing or any other markings not related to machine reading. (A)

clear band: in optical character recognition, the area on a document that must be kept free of printing. Synonymous with *clear area*.

cleared condition: synonymous with *zero condition*.

clear data: data that is not enciphered. Synonymous with *plaintext*.

clear memory: deprecated term for *clear storage*.

click: to position the mouse pointer over an object or at a specific location and quickly press and release the mouse button. Clicking usually selects an object or places a cursor at the location indicated by the pointer.

clipboard: an area in the computer's memory that functions as a holding place for what was last cut or copied. Word processing programs use these to cut and paste text.

clipping: synonym for *scissoring*.

CLK: see *clock*.

clobber: writing new data over good data within a file, thus making the file useless.

clock (C) (CLK):
(1) a device that regulates the performance speed of computer components.
(2) a register whose content changes at regular intervals in such a way as to measure time. (A)
(3) deprecated term for *timer*. (A) (B)

clock counter: a memory location that records real-time progress, or its approximation, by accumulating counts produced by a clock count pulse interrupt.

clock frequency: see *clock speed.*

clocking: in binary synchronous communication, the use of clock pulses to control synchronization of data and control characters.

clock pulse: a synchronization signal provided by a clock. Synonym for *clock tick.* (A) (B)

clock speed: the time rate at which pulses, or ticks, are emitted from the clock; determines the rate at which logical or arithmetic gating is performed with a synchronous computer. The CPUs of PCs require a fixed number of ticks for each instruction. Speed is expressed in megahertz (MHZ).

clock tick: the output of a device that generates periodic signals used for synchronization. Synonymous with *clock pulse.* (A) (B)

clock time: see *cycle time.*

clock track: a track on which a pattern of signals is recorded to provide a timing reference. (B)

clone: describes IBM-compatible PCs manufactured by non-IBM companies.

close: to call a subroutine to terminate the reading from or writing to a file by a program.

close classification: the arrangement of subjects into a classification system involving small subdivisions.

closed architecture: a proprietary system whose detailed, technical specifications are not made available to the public. Cf. *open architecture.*

closed array: an array that cannot be extended at either end.

closed loop: a loop that has no exit and whose execution can be interrupted only by intervention from outside the computer program in which the look is included. (A) (B)

closed loop (control) system: a control system with feedback characteristics.

closedown: the deactivation of a device, program, or system.

closed routine: a routine that is not inserted as a block of instructions within a main routine, but is instead entered by basic linkage from the main routine.

closed shop: pertaining to the operation of a computer facility in which most productive problem programming is performed by a group of programming specialists rather than by the problem originators. The use of the computer itself may also be described as closed shop if full-time trained operators, rather than user/programmers, serve as the operators. Cf. *open shop.* (A)

closed subroutine: a subroutine of which one replica suffices for the subroutine to be linked by calling sequences for use at more than one place in a computer program. (B) Cf. *open subroutine.* (A)

closing a terminal: performing the store and equipment procedures necessary to shut down the point of sale terminal at the close of a sales period or at the close of a particular program. See also *opening a terminal.*

closing of a file: the disassociation of a file from a data set.

CLP: see *current line pointer.*

CLR: see *clear.*

cluster controller: a device that can control the input-output operations of more than one device connected to it. A cluster controller may be controlled by a program stored and executed in the unit. See *cluster controller node.* Synonymous with *cluster control unit.*

cluster controller node: a peripheral node that can control a variety of devices.

cluster control unit: synonym for *cluster controller.*

clustered units: terminals, that is, CRTs and printers, connected to a common controller.

CM:
(1) centimeter.
(2) corrective maintenance.

CMI: computer-managed instruction. Similar to CAI, except that the computer is the major teacher and the student requires assistance only via tutoring and guidance.

CMND: see *command.*

CMOS: complementary metal-oxide semiconductor; chips that use far less electricity than other types where circuits are relatively immune to electrical interference and operate in a wide range of temperatures. In PCs, battery-powered CMOSs store date, time, and setup data.

CNC: computer numerical control.

CNCL: see *cancel.*

CNOP: conditional nonoperation. An assembly language instruction causing the assembler to generate NOP (do-nothing) machine instructions as a filler until the next full-word boundary is reached.

CNT: see *count.*

CNTL: see *control.*

CNTR: see *counter.*

CNTRL: see *control.*

coalesce:

(1) to combine two or more sets of items into one set of any form. (B)

(2) to combine two or more files into one file. (A)

coarse-grained parallel computers: a confederation of a few large, sophisticated von Neumann processors which can work together on a problem to solve it faster than a single processor. See also *fine-grained architectures, intermediate-grained computer architectures.*

coated card: see *edge-coated card.* (A)

COBOL:

(1) common business-oriented language. An English-like programming language designed for business data processing applications.

(2) a general purpose (machine) language designed for commercial data utilizing a standard form. It is a language that can present any business program to any suitable computer and also act as a means of communicating these procedures among people.

COBOL character: any of the 51 valid characters in the COBOL character set.

CODASYL: Conference on Data Systems Languages. A U.S. Department of Defense Committee which identifies specifications for standards such as the language COBOL, and so on.

code:

(1) a set of unambiguous rules specifying the manner in which data may be represented in a discrete form. Synonymous with *coding scheme.* (B)

(2) a set of items, such as abbreviations, representing the members of another set.

(3) to represent data or a computer program in a symbolic form that can be accepted by a data processor.

(4) to write a routine. (A)

(5) loosely, one or more computer programs, or part of a computer program.

(6) synonym for *coded character set, coded representation.*

(7) deprecated term for *coded representation, code set.* (B)

(8) see *alphabetic code, alphanumeric code, binary code, biquinary code, chain code, computer instruction code, data code, error detecting code, excess-three code, gray code, hamming code, inline code, interpretive code, minimum distance code, numeric code, object code, operation code, perforated tape code, pseudocode, retrieval code, return code, skeletal code, two-out-of-five code.*

Code and Go FORTRAN: a version of FORTRAN IV for rapid compilation and execution of programs.

code area: in micrographics, a part of the film frame reserved for retrieval code. (A)

codec:

(1) an assembly comprising an encoder and a decoder in the same equipment.

(2) a device that performs the dual function of encoding two-way analog data into digital data and two-way digital data into analog data.

code chain: an arrangement in a cyclic sequence of some or all of the possible different N-bit words in which adjacent words are linked by the relation that each word is derived from its neighbors by displacing the bits one digit position to the left or right, dropping the leading bit, and inserting the bit at the end.

code check: to isolate and remove errors from a routine.

code conversion: a process for changing the bit grouping for a character in one code into the corresponding bit grouping for a character in a second code. Synonymous with *code translation.*

code converter: a data converter that changes the representation of data, using one code in the place of another or one coded character set in the place of another. (A) (B)

coded: see *binary-coded decimal notation.*

coded arithmetic data: arithmetic data that is stored in a form that is acceptable, without conversion, for arithmetic calculations.

coded character set: a set of unambiguous rules that establish a character set and the one-to-one relationships between the characters of the set and their coded representations. Synonymous with *code (6).* (B) See *alphabetic-coded character set, alphanumeric-coded character set, numeric-coded character set.* (A)

coded decimal notation: synonym for *binary-coded decimal notation.* (A)

coded-image space: synonymous with *image storage space.*

coded program: a program expressed in the language or code of a specific machine or programming system.

coded representation: the representation of an item of data established by a code or the representation of a character established by a coded character set; for example, "ORY" as the representation of Paris (Orly) in the code for three-letter identification for airports; the seven binary elements representing the delete character in the ISO seven-bit coded character set. Synonymous with *code value.* (A) (B)

coded stop: synonymous with *program halt.*

code element: synonym for *coded representation.* (A)

code error: illegal control code on a binary card.

code extension character: any control character used to indicate that one or more of the succeeding coded representations are to be interpreted according to a different code or according to a different coded character set. (A) (B)

code frame: a set of characters that recur cyclically.

code holes: the information holes in perforated tape, as opposed to the feed or other holes.

code key: in word processing, a key, which when operated in conjunction with another key, gives an alternate meaning to the key, such as to initiate a program or execute a function.

code level: the number of bits used to represent a character.

code line: the written form of a program instruction.

code line index: in micrographics, a visual index consisting of an optical pattern of clear and opaque bars parallel to the long edge of the role of microfilm and located between the images. (A)

code position: synonym for *punch position.* (A) (B)

coder: a person who writes but does not usually design computer programs. (A) (B)

code set: the complete set of representations defined by a code, or by a coded character set; for example, all of the three-letter international identifications for airports. Synonymous with *code (6).* (A) (B)

code translation: synonymous with *code conversion.*

code value: one element of a code set; for example, the eight-binary digit code value for the delete character. Synonym for *coded representation.* (B)

coding: see *relative coding, straight line coding, symbolic coding.* (A)

coding check: a test used to determine that a program is error free.

coding form: a form marked with rows and columns for which a program is written.

coding scheme: synonym for *code (1).* (A)

coding sheet: a pre-printed form on which program instructions are written.

coefficient unit: a functional unit whose output variable equals the input variable multiplied by a constant. (B)

coincidence circuit: synonymous with *AND element.*

coincidence element: synonymous with *AND element.*

coincidence error: the error caused by a time difference in switching different integrators to the computer mode or to the holding mode. (B)

coincidence gate: synonymous with *AND element.*

coincident-current selection: in an array of magnetic storage cells, the selective switching of one cell in the array by the simultaneous application of two or more currents such that the resultant magnetomotive force exceeds a threshold value only in the selected cell. (B)

COL: see *column.*

cold boot: see *boot-up.*

cold fault: a computer fault determined at the time the machine is turned on.

cold restart: synonym for *initial program load.* See also *checkpoint restart, system restart.*

COLL: see *collator.*

collate: to alter the arrangement of a set of items from two or more ordered subsets to one or more other subsets each containing a number of items, commonly one, from each of the original subsets in a specified order that is not necessarily the order of any of the original subsets (B). See also *merge.* (A)

collating sequence:
(1) a specified arrangement used in sequencing. Synonymous with *sequence.*
(2) an ordering assigned to a set of items, such that any two sets in that assigned order can be collated.
(3) deprecated term for *order (1).* (A) (B)

collating sorting: a sort that utilizes the technique of continuous merging of data until one sequence is developed. See *collating sequence.*

collator (COLL): a device that collates, merges, or matches sets of punched cards or other documents. (A) (B)

collect: to gather data from various sources and assemble it at one location.

color: in optical character recognition, the spectral appearance of the image dependent upon the spectral reflectance of the image, the spectral response of the observer, and the spectral composition of incident light. (A)

color circle: synonymous with *hue circle.*

color graphics: the ability of a system to use colors to draw pictures, generate graphics, and so on.

color map: in computer graphics, a table storing the definitions of the red, green, and blue components of colors to be displayed.

color solid: see *color space.*

color space: in computer graphics, the type of three-dimensional coordinate system that defines a model showing colors organized in space by attributes such as hue, lightness, and saturation. A physical model of a color space is called a *color solid.*

color television receiver: a television receiver where there are three guns corresponding to red, green, and blue outputs from a color television signal.

color wheel: synonymous with *hue circle.*

column (COL): a vertical arrangement of characters or other expressions. See *card column, mark-sensing column, punch column.* Cf. *row.* (A)

column binary: pertaining to the binary representation of data on cards in which the weights of punch positions are assigned along card columns. For example, each column in a 12-row card may be used to represent 12 consecutive bits. Synonymous with *Chinese binary.* Cf. *row binary.* (A)

column matrix: a matrix of one column and n rows. Synonym for *column vector.*

column move: in word processing, a process in which a vertical column of text or numbers is moved from one part of a document to another, or from one document to another.

column split: the capability of a card-processing device to read or punch two parts of a card column independently.

column vector: synonym for *column matrix.*

COM:
(1) see *computer output microfilm.*
(2) see *computer output microfilmer.* (A)

COM file: a DOS command file with the .COM filename extension.

COMB: see *combination.*

comb: a unit supporting the access arms on a disk drive. These arms are supported in a single column and look similar to the teeth on a comb.

combination (COMB): a given number of different elements selected from a set without regard to the order in which the selected elements are arranged (B). See *forbidden combination.* Cf. *permutation.* (A)

combinational circuit: a logic device whose output values, at any given instant, depend only upon the input values at that time. A combinational circuit is a special case of a sequential circuit that does not have a storage capability. Synonymous with *combinatorial circuit.* (A) (B)

combinational logic element: a device having at least one output channel and zero or more input channels, all characterized by discrete states, such that any instant the state of each output channel is completely determined by the states of the input channels at the same instant. Cf. *sequential logic element.* (A)

combinatorial circuit: synonymous with *combinational circuit.* (A)

combined condition: in COBOL, a condition that is the result of connecting two or more conditions with the 'AND' or the 'OR' logical operator.

combined distribution frame (CDF): a distribution frame combining the functions of the main distribution frame and intermediate distribution frame.

combined head: synonym for *read/write head.* (A) (B)

combined read/write head: synonym for *read/write head.*

combiner: a functional block that groups several inputs that are separated by space to form a single output.

come down gracefully: when a system shuts down without losing data.

comic-strip oriented image: in micrographics, an image appearing on roll microfilm in such a manner that the top edge of the image is parallel to the long edge of the film. Cf. *cine-oriented image.* (A)

command (CMND):
(1) a control signal.
(2) loosely, a mathematical or logic operator; an instruction. (A)
(3) a request from a terminal for the performance of an operation or the execution of a particular program.

(4) a character string from a source external to a system that represents a request for system action.
(5) deprecated term for *instruction.* (A)
(6) see *channel command, operator command, subcommand.*

command chain (CC): the sequence of input-output instructions that can be executed independently of the process of which they form a part.

command control program: a program that handles all commands addressed to the system from the user-consoles.

command double-word: a double-word containing detailed information concerning a part of an input-output operation.

command driven: programs that accept commands in the form of coded words or characters. Cf. *menu driven.*

command functions: instructions used by the CPU to govern the circuitry to carry out a specific action.

command language (CL): a source language consisting primarily of procedural operators, each capable of invoking a function to be executed. (A) Synonymous with *query language and search language.*

command level: the ability to control any system with commands.

command list: a sequence of steps, generated by the central processing unit, pertaining to the performance of an I/O operation.

command mode: a mode of operation of a terminal where different commands are entered as required to place the terminal in edit mode or input mode, or to perform other functions such as storing a file.

command name: the first term in a command, usually followed by operands.

command pointer: a specific multiple-bit register that shows the memory location being accessed in the control store.

command processing: the reading, analyzing, and performing of commands issued via a console or through an input system.

command processor (COMPROC) (CP):
(1) a problem program executed to perform an operation specified by a command.
(2) the portion of an operating system that executes commands.

command retry: a channel and control unit procedure that causes a command to be retried without requiring an I/O interruption.

command statement: a job control statement that is used to issue commands to the system through the input stream.

comment:

(1) a description, reference, or explanation, added to or interspersed among the statements of the source language, that has no effect in the target language. (A) (B) Synonymous with *computer program annotation*.

(2) a statement used to document a source program. Comments include information that may be helpful in running a job or reviewing an output listing. Synonymous with *remark*.

comment-entry: in COBOL, an entry in the Identification Division that may be any combination of characters from the computer character set.

comment field: the field within an instruction, used for explanations and remarks, which are ignored by the compiler or the assembler.

comment statement: a source language statement that has no effect other than to cause itself to be reproduced on an output listing.

commercial character: in PL/1, the following picture specification characters: 1) CR (credit), (2) DB (debit), (3) T, I, and R, the overpunched-sign characters, which indicate that the associated position in the data item contains or may contain a digit with an overpunched sign and that this overpunched sign is to be considered in the character string value of the data item.

commercial instruction set: a combination of instructions of the standard instruction set and the decimal feature.

COMMON: the area within memory shared by two or more programs used to pass information.

commonality: the way two devices or systems work together in harmony, or the ease with which one can replace another.

common area: a control section used to reserve a main storage area that can be referred to by other modules.

common block: in FORTRAN, a storage area that may be referred to by a calling program and one or more subprograms.

Common Business-Oriented Language: see *COBOL*.

common command language: a command language created for the searching of more than one host, where the searcher can easily switch from host to host during a search.

common error: the maximum size of common was not specified in the first loaded program.

common field: a field that can be accessed by two or more independent routines. (A)

common language: a language in a machine-sensible form that is common to a group of computers and associated equipment.

common language code: codes used to ensure uniform abbreviation of equipment and facility names, place names, and so forth.

common memory: the shared storage medium that a microcomputer may have access to.

common program: a program that solves a frequently found problem such as determining the square root of a number, and usually stored in a library where it can be used with different programs.

common segment: in an overlay structure, an overlay segment upon which two exclusive segments are dependent.

common software: computer programs and routines in a language common to a number of computers and users.

common storage: see *common area*.

common storage area: synonymous with *common area*.

common target machine: see *target computer*.

communality: that proportion of one correlated variance held in common with other measures in the same set.

communicate: a step in the output phase of data flow. To transfer information in intelligible form to a user.

communication controller (CC): a type of communication control unit whose operations are controlled by one or more programs stored and executed in the unit.

communications software: a program for sending information to or receiving information from another device; works in conjunction with special hardware such as modems, telling the computer what to do with them.

COMP: see *compatible.*

compact disk: a computer data storage device. A single disk, 4.7 inches in diameter, can hold 550 million bytes or characters, the equivalent of more than 100,000 typewritten pages.

compaction: techniques for reducing space, bandwidth, costs, transmission, and data storage. Such techniques often eliminate repetitions and remove irrelevant operations and steps in coding data. Synonymous with *squish.*

compaction of file records: the reduction of space required for records by compressing or compacting them by means of specialized coding and formatting under a programmed routine.

companding: compressing and expanding.

companion store backup: see *backup.*

comparator:
(1) a functional unit that compares several items of data and indicates the result of that comparison. (B)
(2) a device for determining the dissimilarity of two items, such as two pulse patterns or words. (A)

compare: to examine two items to discover their relative magnitudes, their relative positions in an order or in a sequence, or whether they are identical in given characteristics. (A) (B)

comparing unit: synonymous with *comparator.*

comparison: the process of examining two or more items for identity, similarity, equality, relative magnitude, or for order in a sequence. See *logical comparison.*

comparison operator: see *relational operator.*

compatibility test: tests conducted to check acceptability of both software and hardware as a system, that is, to test component workability.

compatible (COMP): pertaining to computers on which the same computer programs can be run without appreciable alteration. See also *upward compatibility.*

compatible software:
(1) software capable of being run on different computers without modification.
(2) a feature enabling different application software programs to share common conventions and rules so they can be utilized together.

compatibility: the ability of hardware or software to work with other hardware or software of different manufacturers.

compilation: the activity of a compiler.

compilation time: the time needed for compiling or translating a program.

compile:
(1) to translate a computer program expressed in a problem-oriented language into a computer-oriented language. (B)
(2) to prepare a machine language program from a computer program written in another programming language by making use of the overall logic structure of the program, or generating more than one computer instruction for each symbolic statement, or both, as well as performing the function of an assembler.

compile and go: an operating technique in which there are no stops between the compiling, loading, and execution of a computer program. (A)

compile duration: synonym for *compiling time.* (A) (B)

compile phase: the logical subdivision of a run that includes the execution of the compiler. Synonymous with *compiling phase.* (A) (B)

compiler: a program that decodes instructions written as pseudocodes and produces a machine language program to be executed at a later time. Synonymous with *compiling program.* (B)

compiler-compiler: a machine-independent language that generates compilers for any specific machine.

compiler directing statement: synonym for *compiler directive.*

compiler directive:
  (1) a nonexecutable statement that supplies information to a compiler to affect its action but which usually does not directly result in executable code; for example, all declarations, symbols used to indicate a macrocall, symbols used to indicate a comment.
  (2) in COBOL, a statement that causes the compiler to take a specific action at compile time, rather than causing the object program to take a particular action at execution time.
  (3) synonymous with *compiler directing statement.*

compiler generator: a translator or an interpreter that is used to construct compilers. (A) (B)

compiler interface: functions carried out by an operating system to provide supporting capability for a compiler.

compiler language: a high-level language needing a compiler to translate it into machine language.

compiler listing: the report generated by a compiler with an annotated listing of the source program, along with other useful information.

compiler manager: software, often part of an operating system, that controls the process of compiling.

compiler options: key words that can be specified to control certain aspects of compilation. Compiler options can control the nature of the load module generated by the compiler, the types of printed output to be produced, the efficient use of the compiler, and the destination of error messages.

compiler program: the translator program for a high-level language such as FORTRAN or COBOL; translates source-program statements into machine-executable code.

compiler toggle: the parameter passed to a compiler for turning on some unique feature or for controlling the way in which it functions.

compile time: see *compiling time.*

compile-time statement: see *pre-processor statement.*

compiling: the process whereby a digital computer translates the instructions of a program written in a high-level language into their machine language equivalents.

compiling duration: time needed to translate one computer program into an acceptable language for another computer, or to translate to an assembly program, or to generate and diagnose programs.

compiling phase: synonym for *compile phase.* (A) (B)

compiling program: synonym for *compiler.* (A) (B)

compiling routine: a routine used to computer-construct a program.

compiling time: the elapsed time taken for the execution of a compiler. Synonymous with *compile duration.* (A) (B)

complement:
  (1) in a fixed-radix numeration system, a numeral that can be derived from a given numeral by operations that include subtracting each digit of the digital representation of the given number from the corresponding digit of the digital representation of a specified number. (B)
  (2) a number that can be derived from a specified number by subtracting it from a second specified number. For example, in radix notation, the specified number may be a given power of the radix or one less than a given power of the radix. The negative of a number is often represented by its complement.
  (3) see *diminished radix complement, nines complement, ones complement, radix complement, tens complement, twos complement.* (A)

complementary metal-oxide semiconductor: see *C MOS.*

complementary operation: in a boolean operation, another boolean operation whose result, when it is performed on the same operands as the first boolean operation, is the negation of the result of the first boolean operation. (A) (B)

complementary operator: the logic operator whose result is the NOT of a given logic operator. (A)

complementation: an operation resulting in the reverse significance in each digit position in a series of digits.

complement base: in a fixed-radix numeration system, the specified number whose digital representation contains the digits from which the corresponding digits of the given number are subtracted in obtaining a complement of the given number. (A) (B)

complementer: a device whose output data are a representation of the complements of the numbers represented by its input data. (A) (B)

complement form: the representation of the negative of a number as the complement of the number; usually stored in memory in complement form. See *twos complement.* Cf. *true form.*

complementing: pertaining to the carrying out of a complementary operation.

complement-on-nine: synonym for *nines complement.* (A) (B)

complement-on-one: synonym for *ones complement.* (A) (B)

complement-on-ten: synonym for *tens complement.* (A) (B)

complement-on-two: synonym for *twos complement.* (A) (B)

complement procedure: a means for relating the base and the system in obtaining the complement.

complete carry: in parallel addition, a procedure in which each of the carriers is immediately transferred. (B) Cf. *partial carry.* (A)

complete operation: implementation of an instruction that includes the getting of the instruction, interpreting it, finding the needed operands, executing the instruction, and placing the results in store.

complete routine: a routine that does not require modification before it is used. Such routines are usually found in company libraries.

completion code: a code communicated to the job stream processor by batch programs to influence the execution of succeeding steps in a job in the input stream. See also *return code (2).*

complex condition: in COBOL, a condition in which one or more logical operators act upon one or more conditions. See *combined condition, negated combined condition, negated simple condition.*

complex constant: in FORTRAN, an ordered pair of real constants separated by a comma and enclosed in parentheses. The first real constant represents the real part of the complex number; the second represents the imaginary part.

complex data: arithmetic data, each item of which consists of a real part and an imaginary part.

complex decision-making simulation: a process allowing people to make certain decisions which are difficult to define sufficiently rigorous for incorporation into the computer-based portion of the model.

complex instruction-set computing (CISC): CISC approaches dates from the earliest days of digital computers. It feeds instructions to a computer's brain in clusters of related operations.

complex number: a number consisting of an ordered pair of real numbers, expressible in the form $a + bi$, where a and b are area numbers and i squared equals minus one. (A) (B)

complex relocatable expression: in assembler programming, a relocatable expression that contains two or more unpaired relocatable terms or an unpaired relocatable term preceded by a minus sign, after all unary operators have been resolved. A complex relocatable expression is not fully evaluated until program fetch time.

component: a functional part of an operating system; for example, the scheduler or supervisor. See *solid state component, terminal component.*

component address: the fixed address of a terminal component, as opposed to the address of the terminal itself.

component failure impact analysis (CFIA): an account management technique that determines the impact of a critical system component failure.

composite console: a console consisting of two different physical devices that are considered as one unit. One device is used for input and the other for output, such as a reader and printer.

composite external symbol dictionary (CESD): control information associated with a load module that identifies the external symbols in the module.

composite module data set: a disk-resident or diskette-resident data set that contains composite modules.

composite modules: object modules (programs) structured into a resident segment and optional overlay segments. A composite module is in relocatable format; that is, its address constants can be modified to compensate for a change in its origin.

composite operator: an operator composed of two operator symbols; for example, ->.

composite video signal: a signal including video information, plus the synchronization pulses for controlling the positions of the raster in a television receiver or monitor for playing back a video message. Cf. *RGB video.*

composition coding: a means for displaying character sets for languages encompassing diacritical marks, such as accents in Latin-based language forms. Cf. *dynamically redefinable character set.*

composition file: the filing of records within a storage unit.

compound condition: in COBOL, a statement that tests two or more relational expressions. It may be true or false.

compound logical element: computer circuitry that provides an output resulting from multiple inputs.

comprehensive distribution channels: authorized dealers, company-owned product centers, direct sales forces, and value-added resellers used to sell systems. See also *value-added firms.*

compression: see *data compression.*

COMPROC: see *command processor.*

CompuServe: a large on-line data service, with a variety of features, including electronic mail.

computational stability: the degree to which a computational process remains valid when subjected to effects such as errors, mistakes, or malfunctions. (A)

computations: instructions that perform arithmetic operations such as addition, subtraction, multiplication, division, and exponentiation.

compute-bound: a computer system or program that performs more computations that input-output operations. Cf. *I/O bound.*

computed GO TO statement: a multibranch conditional transfer statement used when a decision has more than two possible outcomes.

compute limited: a restriction found in computing units limiting the output because operations are delayed awaiting completion of a computation operation.

compute mode: an operating mode of an analog computer during which the dynamic solution is in progress. Synonymous with *operate mode.* (B)

computer (C): a functional unit that can perform substantial computation, including numerous arithmetic operations or logic operations, without intervention by a human operator during a run. See *analog computer, arbitrary sequence computer, asynchronous computer, consecutive sequence computer, digital computer, general-purpose computer, hybrid computer, parallel computer, self-adapting computer, self-organizing computer, sequential computer, serial computer, simultaneous computer, special-purpose computer, stored program computer, synchronous computer.* See also *computer system.*

computer administrative records: records showing the source of statistics that tell how the computer use is distributed, that is, by department, by programmer, by application, and by time.

computer-aided design (CAD): a system where engineers create a design and see the proposed product in front of them on a graphics screen or in the form of a computer printout. See also *CAD/CAM.*

computer-aided engineering (CAE): essentially computer software purporting to use the computer to predict how the part, machine or manufacturing process can perform.

computer-aided instruction (CAI): educational process utilizing computers, including tutorials and automated worksheets. Synonymous with *computer-assisted instruction.*

computer-aided manufacture (CAM): see *CAD/CAM*.

computer architecture: the specification of the relationships between the parts of a computer system. (A)

computer-assisted instruction: synonymous with *computer-aided instruction*.

computer-assisted management: management performed with the aid of automatic data processing. (A) (B)

computer-based automation (CBA): concept describing the potential speed and accuracy of an adequately programmed digital computer to accomplish automated operating objectives in place of noncomputerized methods.

computer bureau: an agency which runs other people's work on its own computer and often provides other consulting and assistance services.

computer capacity: the span, dimension, or range of values that a number (variable) can assume in a computer, frequently expressed within beginning and ending limits of using N, when such limits are unknown.

computer center: an office or establishment providing computer services.

computer code: synonymous with *machine code*.

computer conferencing: the interchange of messages on a specific topic via a computer network.

computer configuration: equipment connected to form a single computer center or system for various computer runs.

computer console: a part of a computer used for communication between operator or maintenance engineer and the computer.

computer control: a computer designed so that inputs from and outputs to a process directly control the operation of elements in that process.

computer-dependent language: synonym for *assembly language*. (A)

computer duplex: a pair of usually identical computers that operate so that if and when one is shut down for maintenance, checkouts, and so forth, the other can operate without a reduction in capability of the total system.

computer equation: an equation derived from a mathematical model for more convenient use on a computer. Synonymous with *machine equation*.

computerese: slang, language used by computer specialists.

computer family: all the models of a single type of computer, sharing the same logical design.

computer-generated map: a map constructed through mathematical projections using a computer.

computer generations: see *first-generation computer, fourth-generation computer, second-generation computer, third-generation computer*.

computer-independent language: a programming language that is not a computer language, but instead one requiring translation or compiling to any one of a variety of computer languages. The language which is a particular language of that machine or one which has compilers for translating to its own machine language.

computer input microfilm (CIM): a system utilizing microfilm technology instead of printing on paper.

computer instruction: an instruction that can be recognized by the processing unit of the computer for which it is designed. Synonymous with *machine instruction*. (A) (B)

computer instruction code: a code used to represent the instructions in an instruction set. (B) Synonymous with *machine code, instruction code*. Synonym for *operation code*. (A)

computer instruction set: a complete set of the operators of the instructions of a computer together with a description of types of meanings that can be attributed to their operands. Synonymous with *machine instruction set*. (A)

computer interface unit (CIU): a device which interfaces with the central processing unit and peripheral devices such as disks or printers.

computerization: a computer's application to any activity formerly done either by hand or without computers.

computerize:
(1) equipping an office or plant with computers to facilitate or automate procedures.
(2) converting a manual function into one that is performed by a computer.

computerized bulletin board service (CBBS): see *electronic bulletin board.*

computerized foreman: computers used to minimize inventory and production bottlenecks on the factory floor. If orders or materials change, or if machines break down, these systems will automatically change the schedule.

computerized hyphenation: in word processing, a feature that allows units to use standard rules of grammar to automatically hyphenate most words at the end of a typing line.

computer language: a computer-oriented language whose instructions consist only of computer instructions. Synonymous with *machine language.* Deprecated term for *computer-oriented language.* (A) (B)

computer language symbols: prescribed graphical special meanings or functions in any computer program.

computer learning:
(1) the process by which a computer modified program according to its own memory or experience, that is, changes of logic paths, or parameters values. An example is a chess-playing computer.
(2) in process control, an analog computer is able to change its parameters by a continuous process according to temperatures, or other gauge reports it receives.

computer letter: a letter of standard form into which personal information, that is, names and addresses, are inserted using word processing software.

computer-limited: on buffered computers, a section of a routine in which the time required for computation exceeds the time required to read and write to or from input-output devices.

computer literacy: knowledge of and fluency in computer usage and terminology.

computer-managed instruction: see *CMI.*

computer network: a complex consisting of two or more interconnected computing units. (A)

computer numerical control: a state in which a number of numerical control devices are linked together via a data transmission network and brought under the control of a single numerical control machine. See also *direct numerical control.*

computer operation: one of the elementary operations which a computer is designed to perform. Synonymous with *machine operation.* (A)

computer operator: data-processing operations personnel whose duties include setting up a processor and related equipment, starting the program run, checking to insure proper operation, and unloading equipment at the end of a run.

computer-oriented language:
(1) a programming language that reflects the structure of a given computer or that of a given class of computers. (B)
(2) a programming language whose words and syntax are designed for use on a specific class of computers. Synonymous with *machine-oriented language.*
(3) see also *computer language.* (A)

computer output microfilm (COM): microfilm that contains data that are recorded directly from computer-generated signals. (B)

computer output microfilm system: see *COM system.*

computer output microfilmer (COM): a recording device that produces computer output microfilm. (A)

computer peripherals: the auxiliary devices under control of a central computer, such as card punches and readers, high-speed printers, magnetic tape units, and optical character readers.

computer processor: the part of the computer that actually processes signals sent to it, performing calculations and sending information to other devices.

computer program: a sequence of instructions suitable for processing by a computer.

computer program annotation: synonym for *comment.* (A) (B)

computer programming: the process of planning a sequence of instructions for a computer to perform.

computer program origin: the address assigned to the initial storage location of a computer program in main storage. (A)

computer run: the processing of a batch of transactions, or the performance of one or several routines that are linked, forming an operating unit.

computer sciences (CS): the branch of science and technology that is concerned with methods and techniques relating to data processing performed by automatic means.

computer simulator: a computer program that translates computer programs prepared for a computer of one model for execution on a computer of a different model. (A) (B)

computer store: a retail store that sells computers and is structured to appeal to the small businessperson or personal user.

computer system: a functional unit, consisting of one or more computers and associated software, that uses common storage for all or part of a program and also for all or part of the data necessary for execution of the program; executes user-written or user-designated programs; performs user-designated data manipulation, including arithmetic operations and logic operations; and that can execute programs that modify themselves during their execution. Synonymous with *ADP system, computing system.*

computer time: in simulation, the time required to process the data that represents a process or that represents a part of a process. (A)

computer word: a word stored in one computer location and capable of being treated as a unit. Synonymous with *machine word.* (B) See also *half-word.* (A)

computing: performing activities on data in order to obtain a desired objective.

computing element: a computer component that performs the mathematical operations required for problem solutions.

computing power: the speed with complex operations can be performed in a computing system. See also *supercomputer.*

computing system: synonym for *computer system.*

COM system: a computer output microfilm system that is part of a line printer.

concatenate: to connect in a series. Synonymous with *catenate.*

concatenated data strings: a group of logically connected data that are treated as one data set for the duration of a job step.

concatenation: in PL/1, the operation that joins two strings in the order specified, thus forming one string whose length is equal to the sum of the lengths of the two strings. It is specified by the operator.

concatenation character: in assembler programming, the period (.) that is used to separate character strings that are to be joined together in conditional assembly processing.

concatenation operation: a symbol in a programming language used for joining two character strings. Using vertical bars | ; for example if A is a character string equaling "WHY" and B equals "NOT." than A | B equals "WHYNOT."

concordance: an alphabetic list of words appearing in a document, with an indication of the place where they appear.

concordant: an arrangement of information or data into fixed or harmonious locations on particular documents.

concurrent: pertaining to the occurrence of two or more activities within a given interval of time. (B) Cf. *consecutive, sequential, simultaneous.* (A)

concurrent execution: synonymous with *multiprogramming.*

concurrent operation: a mode of operations which includes the performance of two or more operations within a given interval of time. (A)

concurrent peripheral operations (CPO): synonym for *spooling.*

concurrent printing: the ability to enter and edit one document while printing out another document at the same time.

concurrent processing:
(1) the ability to carry out more than one program at a time.
(2) the processing of more than one independent task simultaneously by a single computing system involving interlaced timesharing of at least one section of

hardware, usually the control unit and memory-address register or the multiplexing unit, for selecting individual control units and memory-address registers for each task.

concurrent processor: a unit that operates on more than one program at a time.

concurrent word and data processing: the ability to do both word and data processing on the same computer at the same time.

COND: see *condition.*

condenser storage: a storage unit utilizing the capacitance of the medium for storing information.

condensing routine: a routine that converts machine language, that is, the one-instruction-per-card output format, from an assembly program or system into several instructions per card.

condition (COND):
(1) one of a set of specified values a data item can assume.
(2) in COBOL, a simple conditional expression: relation condition, class condition, condition-name condition, sign condition, switch-name condition, switch-status condition, NOT condition.
(3) see *on condition, restart condition.*

conditional assembly: an assembler facility for altering at preassembly time the content and sequence of source statements that are to be assembled.

conditional assembly expression: an expression that an assembler evaluates at preassembly time.

conditional assembly instruction: an assembler instruction that performs a conditional assembly operation. Conditional assembly instructions are processed at preassembly time.

conditional branch instruction: deprecated term for *conditional jump instruction.* (A) (B)

conditional breakpoint: a breakpoint where the setting of certain conditions permit variation in the particular program sequence.

conditional breakpoint instruction: an instruction at a breakpoint that serves as a conditional branch instruction following

the intervention resulting in the breakpoint has occurred.

conditional code: used to define a group of program instructions such as carry, borrow, and overflow. Usually the code is listed in a condition code register.

conditional control transfer instruction: deprecated term for *conditional jump instruction.* (A) (B)

conditional entropy: in information theory, the mean of the measure of information conveyed by the occurrence of any one of a finite set of mutually exclusive and jointly exhaustive events of definite conditional probabilities, given the occurrence of events of another set of mutually exclusive events. Synonymous with *average conditional information content, mean conditional information content.* (A) (B)

conditional expression: in COBOL, an expression having the particular characteristic that, taken as a whole, it may be either true or false, in accordance with the rules.

conditional implication operation: synonym for *implication.* (A) (B)

conditional information content: in information theory, a measure of information conveyed by the occurrence of an event of a definite conditional probability, given the occurrence of another event. (B) See *average conditional information content, mean conditional information content.* (A)

conditional jump: a jump that takes place only when the instruction that specifies it is executed and specified conditions are satisfied. (A) (B)

conditional jump instruction: an instruction that specifies a conditional jump and the conditions that have to be satisfied for the conditional jump to occur. (A) (B)

conditional nonoperation: see *CNOP.*

conditional operator: a logical operator used in a conditional statement, such as IF-THEN or IF-THEN-ELSE.

conditional statement:
(1) a statement that permits the execution of one of a number of possible operations, with or without a transfer of control; for example, a case statement, a

computer GOTO in FORTRAN, an IF statement.

(2) a statement used to express an assignment or branch, based on specified criteria; for example, an IF-THEN statement. (A)

(3) in COBOL, a statement made up of data names, literals, figurative constants, logical operators, or a combination of such operators, so constructed that it tests a truth value. The subsequent action of the object program is dependent on this truth value.

conditional stop instruction: an instruction that causes a program to be halted on the detection of a condition such as the setting of a console switch by the operator.

conditional transfer: a transfer of control to other statements in the program based on the evaluation of a mathematical expression.

conditional transfer instruction: deprecated term for *conditional jump instruction, jump instruction*. (A) (B)

conditional variable: in COBOL, a data item that can assume more than one value; one or more of the values it assumes has a condition name assigned to it.

condition code: a code that reflects the result of a previous input-output, arithmetic, or logical operation.

condition list: in PL/1, a list of one or more condition prefixes.

condition name:

(1) in COBOL, the name assigned to a specific value, set of values, or range of values, that a data item may assume.

(2) in PL/1, a language key word (or CONDITION followed by a parenthesized programmer-defined name) that denotes an on condition that might arise within a task.

condition-name condition: in COBOL, a statement that the value of a conditional variable is one of a set (or range) of values of a data item identified by a condition name. The statement may be true or false.

condition prefix: in PL/1, a parenthesized list of one or more language condition names, prefixed to a statement. It specifies whether the named on conditions are to be enabled.

conditions: see *entry conditions*. (A)

conference control: synonym for *sensitivity control.*

Conference on Data Systems Languages: see CODASYL.

confidence level: a degree of probability and/or of certainty that can be expressed as a percentage.

configuration:

(1) the arrangement of a computer system or network as defined by the nature, number, and the chief characteristics of its functional units. More specifically, the term *configuration* may refer to a hardware configuration or a software configuration.

(2) the devices and programs that make up a system, subsystem, or network.

configuration file: the file that executes a system's configuration. In DOS, the file is CONFIG.SYS.

configuration section: a section of the environment division of a COBOL program. It describes the overall specification of computers.

configure: to plan the needed component parts of a computer system to fulfill the requirements of a specified application or group of applications.

conjunction: the boolean operation whose result has the boolean value 1 if and only if each operand has the boolean value 1. Synonymous with *AND operation, intersection, logical product*. (B) Cf. *nonconjunction*. (A)

connected reference: in PL/1, a reference to connected storage; it must be apparent, prior to execution of the program, that the storage is connected.

connected storage: in PI/1, internal storage of an interrupted linear sequence of items that can be referred to by a single name.

connection: an association established between functional units for conveying information.

connective: in COBOL, in word or a punctuation character that associated a data name or paragraph name with its qualifier, links two or more operands in a series, or forms a condition expression.

connector: the end of a cable that plugs into a port, connecting two devices.

connector block: a larger barrier strip.

connector panel: synonymous with *back panel.*

connect time: time that elapses while the user of a remote terminal is connected to a time-shared system; measured by the duration between sign-on and sign-off.

CONS: see *console.*

consecutive: pertaining to the occurrence of two sequential events without the intervention of any other such event. (B) Cf. *sequential.* See also *concurrent, simultaneous.* (A)

consecutive operation: synonym for *sequential operation.* (A)

consecutive sequence computer: a computer in which instructions are executed in an implicitly defined sequence unless a jump instruction specifies the storage location of the next instruction to be executed. (A) (B)

console (CONS):

(1) a part of a computer used for communication between the operator or maintenance engineer and the computer. (A) See *terminal.*

(2) a COBOL mnemonic name associated with the console typewriter.

(3) see *operator console.* (A)

CONST: see *constant.*

constant (C) (CONST): a fixed or invariable value or data item. See *figurative constant, hexadecimal constant, logical constant.*

constant area: an area of store allocated by a program, used to hold constants.

constant instruction: an instruction not intended to be executed as an instruction, written in the form of a constant.

constant length field: an entry on a document or card requiring a fixed number of alphanumeric characters.

constant ratio code: a code in which all characters are represented by combinations having a fixed ratio of ones to zeros.

constant storage: a part of storage designated to store the invariable quantities needed for processing.

constant words: descriptive data that is fixed and does not generally appear as an element of input.

construct: the means of organizing the logic of a computer program.

constructing: synonym for *blocking.*

constructs: construction drawings generated by a patented process using a computer and a plotter.

CONT: see *controller.*

contained text: in PL/1, all text in a procedure except its entry names and condition prefixes of the PROCEDURE statement; all text in a begin block except labels and conditions prefixes of the BEGIN statement that heads the block. Internal blocks are contained in the external procedure.

contamination: placing data within memory in the wrong place, resulting in unexpected or error filled information.

content: see *conditional information content, decision content, information content, joint information content, mean transinformation content, transinformation content.* (A)

Content-Addressable File Store: see *CAFS.*

Content-Addressed Memory: see *CAM.*

content-addressed storage: synonym for *associative storage.* (A)

context: words of text that occur prior to and following a particular group of words.

context editing: a method of editing a line without using line numbers. To refer to a particular line, all or part of the contents of that line are specified.

contextual declaration: in PL/1, the appearance of an identifier that has not been explicitly declared, in a context that allows the association of specific attributes with the identifier.

contiguous: touching or joining at the edge or boundary; adjacent. For example; an unbroken consecutive series of storage locations.

contiguous items: in COBOL, items that are described by consecutive entries in the data division, and that bear a definite hierarchic relationship to each other.

continuation card: a punched card that holds data that has been started on a previous card. This is permitted in many compilers such as FORTRAN.

continuation line: a line of a source statement into which characters are entered when the source statement cannot be contained on the preceding line or lines.

continuous data: data assuming an indefinite number of values, as in recording temperature. Cf. *discrete data.*

continuous error: an error occurring often, needing manual intervention or correction to restore normal functioning.

continuous-form cards: special cards attached together in continuous strips to facilitate printing. They can be separated into individual punched cards. (A)

continuous forms: a series of connected paper forms that feed continuously through a printing device. The connection between the forms is perforated to allow the user to tear them apart. Prior to printing, the forms are folded in a stacked arrangement, with the folds along the perforations. Cf. *cut form.*

continuous forms paper: a continuous length of single-ply, fan-folded paper with both edges punched for tractor feeding and with perforation between pages. There are various sizes and basis weights.

continuous items: in COBOL, consecutive elementary or group items in the data division that have a definite relationship with each other.

continuous processing: the processing of data on a continuous basis.

contract programmers: programmers who are not employees of the organization using their services.

contrast:
(1) in optical character recognition, the difference between color or shading of the printed material on a document and the background on which it is printed. See *print contrast ratio.* (A)
(2) in computer graphics, the difference in brightness or color between a display image and the area in which it is displayed.

control (C) (CNTL) (CNTRL) (CTRL): the determination of the time and order

in which the different parts of a data processing system and the devices that contain those parts perform the input, processing, storage, and output functions. See *loop control, numerical control, real-time control, sequential control.*

control area (CA): see *control block.*

control block: a storage area used by a computer program to hold control information. Synonymous with *control area.* (B)

control break:
(1) a program utilized to print out various items of intermediate information, such as subtotals and headings, when a change occurs in a field.
(2) such a change in a field.

control break level: in COBOL, the relative position within a control hierarchy at which the most major control break occurred.

control bus: control lines (paths) usually from 10 to 100, with a function to carry the synchronization and control information needed to the computer system.

control button: the control button appears in the upper left-hand corner of a window. Clicking it brings up the control menu that permits the user to maximize, minimize, restore, and close the window. Double-clicking it closes the window.

control bytes: bytes associated with a physical record that serve to identify the record and indicate characteristics such as its length and blocking factor.

control card: a punched card containing input data or parameters for initiating or modifying a program.

control character:
(1) in IBM PC systems, any character pressed with the CTRL key.
(2) a character whose occurrence in a particular context initiates, modifies, or stops a control operation. See *accuracy control character, device control character, print control character, transmission control character.*

control clerk: a worker responsible for the integrity of the data received, processed, and dispatched from the data-processing department.

control code: information sent to a unit to create an action, rather than as data.

control computer: a computer which, by means of inputs from and outputs to a process, directly control the operation of elements in that process.

control console: a console enabling an operator to control and monitor all processing functions from a central location, having a typewriter or other keyboard input for communicating with a processor.

control counter (CC): synonym for *instruction address register.* (B)

control cycle: a specific cycle of a punch card machine's main shaft during which the feeding is stopped due to a control change.

control data: items of data, used to select, execute, identify, or modify another routine, record, file, operation, or data value.

control data name: in COBOL, a data name that appears in a CONTROL clause and refers to a control data item.

control dictionary: the external symbol dictionary and the relocation dictionary, collectively, of an object or load module. See also *dictionary.*

control engineering: see *automatic control engineering.* (A)

control field:
(1) a field that is compared with other fields to determine the record sequence in the output file.
(2) a field in a record that identifies the relationship of the record to other records (such as a part number in an inventory record). Control fields determine when certain operations are to be performed.
(3) in sorting or merging records, a group of contiguous bits in a control word used in determining sequence.

control footing: in COBOL, a report group that is presented at the end of the control group of which it is a member.

control format item: in PL/1, a specification used in edit-directed transmission to specify positioning of a data item within the stream or printed page.

control function: synonym for *control operation.* (A)

control group: in COBOL, a set of body groups that is presented for a given value of a control data item or of FINAL. Each control group may begin with a CONTROL HEADING, end with a CONTROL FOOTING, and contain DETAIL report groups.

control heading: a title or short definition of a control group of records which appear in front of each such group.

control hierarchy: in COBOL, a designated sequence of report subdivisions defined by the positional order of FINAL and the data names within a CONTROL clause.

control hole: synonym for *designation hole.* (A) (B)

control instruction: instruction used to manipulate data within the main memory and the control unit, to ready main memory storage areas for the processing of data fields and to control the sequential selection and interpretation of instructions in the stored program.

control instruction register: deprecated term for instruction address register. (A) (B)

control key: a key on an IBM PC keyboard labelled CTRL that controls some cursor or program activity.

control language: see *job control language.* (A)

control lead: a character or sequence of characters sent to a unit alerting it that the information following is a control code and not data.

controlled parameter: in PL/1, a parameter for which the CONTROLLED attribute is specified; it can be associated only with arguments that have the CONTROLLED attribute.

controlled storage allocation: the allocation of storage for controlled variables.

controlled variable: in PL/1, a variable whose allocation and release are controlled by the ALLOCATE and FREE statements, with access to only the current generation. Cf. *automatic variable.*

controlled vocabulary: a fixed listing of terms used to index records for storage and retrieval, usually required in on-line searching.

controller: a device that directs the transmission of data over the data links of a network; its operation may be controlled by a program executed in a processor to which the controller is connected or they may be controlled by a program executed within the device. See *communication controller, input-output controller, store controller, subsystem controller.*

controller functions: an action or series of actions built into a controller and taken by the controller in response to a request from a terminal, another controller function, or a host system.

control line: the randomly timed cycle control that tells each terminal in a reel when to begin transmitting.

control logic: steps needed to perform a specific function.

control loop: synonymous with *control tape.*

control mark: synonymous with *tape mark.*

control memory: memory in a control unit for storing microinstructions.

control-message display: a machine that displays information in plain language; for example, a display on the screen of a terminal.

control number: the quantity or number (value) that is the result of a process or problem needed to prove the accuracy of a process or problem.

control operation: an action that affects the recording, processing, transmission, or interpretation of data; for example, starting or stopping a process, carriage return, font change, rewind, and end of transmission. Synonymous with *control function.* (A) (B)

control operator: the person who generally performs special administrative, control, and testing functions.

control panel: a part of a computer console that contains manual controls. Synonym for *plugboard.* See *operator control panel.*

control printing: a list of the control group for purposes of identification without the list of the detail records.

control program (CP): a computer program designed to schedule and to supervise the execution of programs of a computer system.

control punch: synonym for *designation hole.* (A) (B)

control read-only memory: see *CROM.*

control record: a checkpoint record that contains data used to initiate, modify, or stop a control operation, or to determine the manner in which data is processed.

control register: deprecated term for *instruction address register.* (A) (B)

control routine:

(1) a routine that controls loading and relocation of routines and can make use of instructions that are unknown to the general programmer.

(2) a set of coded instructions designed to process and control other sets of coded instructions.

(3) a set of coded instructions used in realizing automatic coding.

control section (CSECT): that part of a program specified by the programmer to be a relocatable unit, all elements of which are to be loaded into adjoining main storage locations.

control sequence: the usual order in which instructions are executed.

control stack: a number of storage locations for providing control in the dynamic allocation of work space.

control statement:

(1) a statement that controls or affects the execution of a program in a data processing system.

(2) in programming languages, a statement that is used to alter the continuous sequential execution of statements; a control statement may be a conditional statement such as IF, or an imperative statement such as STOP.

(3) see *job control statement, linkage editor.*

control station: in basic mode link control the data station in a multipoint connection or a point-to-point connection that nominates the master station and supervises polling, selecting, interrogating, and recovery procedures.

control storage: a portion of storage that contains microcode.

control storage save: the automatic writing of critical areas of store controller storage onto areas of the integrated disk unit when a power failure is detected or when certain machine errors occur.

control store: an address register permitting the user to monitor the program point at which a program operation is ceased.

control structure: a construct that determines the flow of control in part of a program (usually represented by a statement), with the basic types being the sequence, selection, and loop.

control system: a system of the closed-loop type in which the computer is used to govern external processes.

control tape: see *carriage control tape.* (A)

control terminal: any active terminal at which the user is authorized to enter commands affecting system operation.

control total: a sum, resulting from the addition of a specified field from each record in a group of records, that is used for checking machine, program, and data reliability. Synonymous with *hash total.*

control unit (CU): a device that controls input-output operations at one or more devices. See *device control unit, instruction control unit, main control unit, peripheral control unit.*

control variable: in PL/1, a variable used to control the iterative execution of a group. See *loop-control variable.*

control volume: a volume that contains one or more indexes of the catalog.

control word (CW): all control fields used to sort or merge a particular group of records; the major field appears first and other fields follow in descending order of importance.

CONV: see *conversion.*

convention: specific standard and accepted procedures in programs and systems analysis; the abbreviations, symbols, and their meanings as developed for particular systems and programs.

convention equipment: devices considered to be part of the computer system but which are not specifically part of the computer itself.

conventional memory: in DOS systems, the part of memory available for conventional programs.

conversation: a dialog between a user and an interactive data-processing system.

conversational: pertaining to a program or a system that carries on a dialog with a terminal user, alternately accepting input and then responding to the input quickly enough for the user to maintain his train of thought. See also *interactive.*

Conversational Algebraic Language (CAL): a general purpose language designed to be used extensively in time sharing; developed at the University of California; similar in usage to BASIC.

conversational language: a language using a near-English character set which aids communication between user and the computer.

conversational remote job entry (CRJE): an operating system facility for entering job control language statements from a remote terminal, and causing the scheduling and execution of the jobs described in the statements. The terminal user is prompted for missing operands or corrections.

conversion (CONV):

(1) the process of changing from one method of data processing to another or from one data-processing system to another.

(2) the process of changing from one form of representation to another; for example, to change from decimal representation to binary representation. See also *translation.*

conversion costs: one-time expenses, which are incurred when an organization installs a computer for the first time or when it applies an existing system to a new application area.

conversion device: a piece of peripheral equipment that converts data from one form into another form or medium, without changing the date, content, or information.

conversion routine: a flexible program that is used by a programmer to alter the presentation of data from one form to another, such as from card to disk.

conversion table: the table indicating various characters in one code and their corresponding representation in another.

convert: to change the representation of data from one form to another, without changing the information they convey; for example, radix conversion, code conversion,

conversion from punched cards to magnetic tape, analog to digital conversion. (B) Synonymous with *transform*. See also *copy, duplicate.* (A)

converter: a device capable of converting impulses from one mode to another, such as analog to digital, or parallel to serial, or from one code to another. See *code converter, data converter, disk converter.*

converting: transferring data from one form to a different one.

convex programming: in operations research, a particular case of nonlinear programming in which the function to be maximized or minimized and the constraints are appropriately convex or concave functions of the controllable variables. (B) Cf. *dynamic programming, integer programming, linear programming, mathematical programming, nonlinear programming, quadratic programming.* (A)

cookbook: slang, the document indicating how to install and utilize software and/or accomplish tasks.

coordinate data: data that specifies a location within a display space or an image space. See also *absolute data, relative data.*

coordinate indexing: an indexing means where all descriptors are correlated and combined indicating interrelationships.

coordinate paper: a continuous-feed graph paper used for printouts produced on a plotting unit, such as a flat-bed plotter.

coprocessor: an auxiliary processor designed to relieve the demand on the main processor by performing a few specific tasks. Generally, coprocessors handle tasks that would be performed more slowly by the main processor. Math coprocessors are common in IBM PC and compatible systems.

copy:

(1) to read data from a source, leaving the source data unchanged, and to write the same data elsewhere in a physical form that may differ from that of the source; for example, to copy a deck of punched cards onto magnetic tape. The degree of editing that may be carried out at the same time

depends upon the circumstances in which the copying is performed. (A) (B)

(2) in word processing the reproduction of selected recorded text from storage or from a recording medium to another recording medium.

(3) see *hard copy, soft copy.*

copy holder: a device for holding paper to be more easily read by a user while typing on the keyboard. Synonymous with *data holder.*

copying disks: taking text from one magnetic disk and putting it on another disk, without erasing the first one.

copy-protect: to make a disk difficult if not impossible to copy. Software publishers sometimes copy-protect their disks to prevent them from being illegally duplicated.

CORAL: Computer On-Line Real-Time Applications Language, a high-level language designed for real-time applications.

Cordonnier system: an information-retrieval system using peek-a-boo cards; that is, cards with small holes drilled at intersections of coordinates (column and row designations) to represent document numbers. Synonymous with *batten system.*

core:

(1) deprecated term for *tape spool.* (A)

(2) deprecated term for *main storage.*

(3) see *magnetic core, multiple aperture core, switch core.*

core dump: a listing of the selected parts or contents of a storage device. Synonymous with *memory dump, memory printout.*

core image: the form in which a computer program and related data exist at the time they reside in main storage. (B)

core image library: a library of phases that have been produced as output from link editing. The phases in the core image library are in a format that is executable either directly or after processing by the relocating loader in the supervisor.

core memory (CM): a storage device consisting of ferromagnetic cores, or an apertured ferrite plate, through which sense windings and select lines are threaded.

co-resident: pertaining to the condition in which two or more modules are located in main storage at the same time.

core storage:
(1) a magnetic storage in which the magnetic medium consists of magnetic cores. (A)
(2) deprecated term for *main storage*.
(3) see *magnetic core storage*.

corner cut: a corner removed from a card for orientation purposes.

Corporation for Open Systems: see *COS*.

correct and copy: a designated record is copied from one tape to another with specified corrections. In manipulating magnetic tapes, either a record-counting method or a file-identification method is used. The file option provides further convenience in that it allows operation over an entire tape or file, rather than over a specified number of records.

correct bit: a bit of information correctly received over a circuit, as opposed to an error bit in which the significance of the bit has been reversed, that is, a 0 becomes a 1 or a 1 becomes a 0.

correction: a quantity (equal in absolute value to the error) that is added to a calculated or observed value to obtain the true value.

correction program: a routine used following a failure or error. The routine is inserted at a point before the error, during a run or rerun of the program.

corrective maintenance: maintenance specifically intended to eliminate an existing fault. Cf. *preventive maintenance*. (A)

corrective maintenance time: time, either scheduled or unscheduled, used to perform corrective maintenance. (A)

correspondence printer: a printer yielding typewriter-like copy. Synonymous with *letter-perfect printer, letter-quality printer*.

corruption: the mutilation of code or data caused by hardware or software failure.

COS: Corporation for Open Systems. An organization that creates and promotes a standard set of software rules that enables different brands of computers to communicate.

cost-center accounting: financial accounting where charges are recorded, keypunched, edited, sorted, and posted.

This information is then used as input to the computer to post the required formal ledgers.

count (CNT): the cumulative total of the number of times a specific event occurs, kept as a factual record.

counter (C) (CNTR) (CT) (CTR): a device whose state represents a number and that, on receipt of an appropriate signal, causes the number represented to be increased by unity or by an arbitrary constant; the device is usually capable of bringing the number represented to a specified value, for example, zero. (A) (B) See *instruction counter, reversible counter*.

counter inhibit: the bit, in the program status double-word, that shows whether (if one) or not (if zero) all (clock) count zero interrupts are inhibited.

count-key-data (CKD) device: a disk storage device that stores data in the format count field, usually followed by a key field, followed by the actual data of a record. The count field contains, among others, the address of the record in the format CCHHR (CC = cylinder number, HH = head number, R = record number) and the length of the data; the key field contains the record's key (search argument).

count modulo-N: when a number in a counter reverts to zero in the counting sequence after reaching a maximum value of (N-1), the counter is said to count modulo-N.

coupled systems: two or more computers attached to each other electronically. See *tightly coupled*.

coupler: interconnecting unit.

courseware: computer programs utilized in teaching activities.

coursework: computer programs used in teaching environments.

CP: see *call processor, card punch, central processor, character printer, command processor, control program*. **CPI:** characters per inch.

CPM: see *critical path method*.

CP/M: abbreviation for control program for microprocessor; a once common disk operating system used by many microcomputers.

CPO: see *concurrent peripheral operations.* Synonym for *spooling.*

CPS: characters per second.

CPT: see *chief programmer team.*

CPU: see *central processing unit.* (B)

CPU bound: a program performing a significant amount of calculation such that the limiting factor of performance is determined by the speed of the CPU and its memory.

CPU handshaking: the interaction between a CPU and peripheral units, or, at times, between the CPU and users.

CPUID: the identification number indicating that the CPU is in a machine-readable format on demand by a program.

CPU time: the amount of time needed to execute a set of instructions in the CPU; excluded waiting time for input-output operations. Differs from time between the star and end of execution. Cf. *real time.*

CR: see *card reader, carriage return.*

CRAM: card random access memory (or method). The trademark for a direct access storage device composed of removable cartridges, each containing several hundred magnetic cards that can individually be selected from the cartridge and wrapped around a rotating drum to access the stored data.

crash: a computer system is said to "crash" when it stops working for some reason and must be restarted by the operator.

crashing: when two or more processors battle to use the same section of memory at the same time. See also *crashless supercomputer.*

crashless supercomputer: a computer that is engineered to avoid crashing by leapfrogging the fastest machine now available by at least 10 times or more. The key is a unique memory architecture that is totally random. Data are not stored in specified memory locations. Instead, they get slapped into the first available spot the computer finds, along with a tag that describes the contents. If there is a traffic jam in one part of the memory, the computer simply skips to someplace else. See also *crashing.*

CRC: see *carrier return character, cyclic redundancy check.*

create a document: to make a place on a disk for a new document and to begin entering text.

crippled leapfrog: a variation of the leapfrog tests for uncovering computer malfunctions or errors. These tests are done from a fixed set of locations rather than using shifting locations as in the leapfrog tests. See *leapfrog test.*

critical path method (CPM): a technique defining a project by component events. By ordering these events and demonstrating their interdependency, this approach permits a user to isolate critical events, whose delay could delay overall completion of a project. Such events are said to lie on the critical path. A map shows the paths along a time scale to identify the critical path of those functions which, if delayed, would postpone the entire activity.

CRJE: see *conversational remote job entry.*

crock: slang, a feature or programming technique that needs to be made cleaner.

CROM: control read-only memory. The storage area in the CPU set aside for micro instructions which, when put together, establish procedures such as branch, add, and so on.

cross assembler: a program run on one computer for the purpose of translating instructions for a different computer.

cross check: checking the result of a calculation by obtaining a solution by a different method and comparing the results.

cross compiler: a compiler that yields object code suitable for a different computer from the one on which the compiler is used.

cross-domain communication: synonym for *networking.*

cross-domain sub-area link: a link between two sub-area nodes in different domains.

crossfoot: to add across several domains of numerical information.

cross-reference listing (XREF): a document from a compiler or assembler indicating the names of symbolic variables within a program and the memory addresses assigned to them.

cross-reference table: a table produced by a language processor containing each variable and constant used in a program, its corresponding value, and instructions in which it is used.

cross-sectional testing: a series of tests required to obtain a representative sampling of system performance.

cross section of an array: in PL/1, the elements represented by the extent of at least one dimension (but not all dimensions) of an array. An asterisk in the place of a subscript in an array reference indicates the entire extent of that dimension.

cross software: software allowing users to develop programs for a target computer on a host computer.

crosstalk: the unwanted energy transferred from one circuit, called the disturbing circuitry, to another circuit, called the disturbed circuit. (A)

cross tracking: a specific crosslike array of bright dots on the cathode-ray tube display used for locating points and lines or for drawing curves.

crowding: in optical character recognition, the insufficient horizontal spacing between characters.

CRT: see *cathode-ray tube.*

CRT display:
(1) cathode-ray tube display. (A)
(2) a display device that uses a cathode-ray tube.

CRT display device: a display device in which display images are produced on a cathode-ray tube.

crufty: slang, poorly constructed, possibly overly complex.

crunch: slang, to process, usually in a time-consuming or complicated fashion.

cryogenics: the study and use of devices utilizing properties of materials near absolute zero in temperature. (A)

cryogenic storage: a storage device that uses the superconductive and magnetic properties of certain materials at very low temperatures. Synonymous with *cryogenic store.* (A) (B)

cryogenic store: synonym for *cryogenic storage.* (B)

cryostat: a device designed to use evaporative and condensing cycles to achieve extremely low temperatures, and often used to liquify gases.

cryotron: a device that makes use of the effects of low temperatures on conductive materials such that small magnetic field changes can control large current changes. (A)

cryptographic: pertaining to the transformation of data to conceal its meaning. See also *decipher, encrypt.*

cryptographic algorithm: a set of rules that specify the mathematical steps required to encipher and decipher data.

cryptography: the transformation of data to conceal its meaning.

CS: see *computer sciences.*

CSECT: see *control section.*

CSW: see *channel status word.*

CT: see *counter.*

CTCA: see *channel-to-channel adapter.*

CTR: see *counter.*

CTRL: see *control.*

CTY: the terminal physically associated with a computer's operating console.

CU: see *control unit.*

CUA: see *circuit unit assembly.*

cue: synonym for *call.* (A)

cumulative index: an index showing all items appearing in a number of separate indexes.

currency symbol: a graphic character used to designate monetary quantities; for example, $.

current address register: see *program counter.*

current attenuation: the loss of current in apparatus or circuit, or along a line; expressed as the ratio of output to input current in decibels.

current beam position: on a CRT display device, the coordinates on the display surface at which the electron beam is aimed. Synonymous with *starting point.*

current connect group: the group to which a user is associated during a terminal session or batch job.

current generation: in PL/1, that generation of an automatic on or controlled variable currently available by reference to the name of the variable.

current instruction: an instruction currently being executed.

current instruction register (CIR): the control section register which contains the instruction currently being executed after it is brought to the control section from memory. Synonymous with *instruction register.*

current line pointer (CLP): in systems with time sharing, a pointer that indicates the display line on which operations are being performed.

current record: the record pointed to by the current line pointer.

current record pointer: in COBOL, a conceptual entity that is used in the selection of the next record.

current startup disk: the disk containing the system files the computer is currently using.

cursor:

(1) in computer graphics, a movable marker that is used to indicate a position on a display space.

(2) a movable spot of light on the screen of a display device, usually indicating where the next character is to be entered, replaced, or deleted.

(3) a marker displayed on the screen that indicates the place where the next action will take place, often where the next character typed on the keyboard will appear. A cursor may be a blinking vertical line, a solid block, or some other signal. The mouse pointer is sometimes referred to as a cursor. Cf. *pointer.*

cursor arrows: arrows marked on the buttons of a CRT keyboard that control the cursor's movement.

cursor positioning: the action of moving a cursor in different directions—up, down, right, left, home (upper left corner of the screen), bottom of screen, and so on.

cursor tracking: controlling the cursor on a graphics display by moving a stylus on a graphics table connected to a terminal.

curtate: a group of adjacent card rows. See *lower curtate, upper curtate.* (A)

curve follower: an input unit that reads data represented by a curve. (A) (B)

cushion: a contiguous address space in dynamic storage that is held in reserve and not normally used to satisfy a request for storage until such requests cannot be satisfied from other areas of dynamic storage.

customer access area: a specifically designated area of a machine or system to which the customer has access to connect, install, and maintain signals, control, power, or other utilities.

customer information control system (CICS): a program product that enables transactions entered at remote terminals to be processed concurrently by user-written application programs. It also includes facilities for building, using, and maintaining data bases.

customer reference number: a reference number unique for each user of a service that enables user charges and utilization statistics to be attributed to particular users.

customization: the process of designing a data-processing installation or network to meet the requirements of particular users.

custom software: programs created for a special order to fulfill a user's particular needs. Such custom work tends to be more expensive than traditionally packaged software.

cut and paste: to move text, graphics, or other material from one place in a document to another place in the same or a different document.

cut form: a single form, not connected to other forms. The form may have more than one part; that is, it may have an original and one or more copies. Cf. *continuous forms.*

cut-forms mode: a mode in which a printer produces one form at a time.

cutoff: the point of degradation, due to attenuation or distortion, at which a signal becomes unusable.

cutout: a part of a form that has been eliminated or perforated for subsequent removal.

cutover:

(1) as a noun: the point when testing terminates and day-to-day usage begins.

(2) as a verb: to place into active use.

cut-sheet printer: a printer for producing output on separate pieces of paper instead of on fan-fold paper. See *fan-fold paper.*

cut sheets: separate sheets of paper, thought of as a cut apart when compared to the continuous roll or folded sheet of conventional computer paper.

cut-to-tie ratio: the length of the cut and the tie associated with perforations. If the length of the cut is less than the length of the tie, it is reasonable to assume that the perforation has greater strength than a perforation with the opposite case. See also *perforation, tie.*

CV: constant value.

CW:

(1) *clockwise.*

(2) see *control word.*

CXR: abbreviation for *carrier.*

CY: see *carry.*

cybernation: automation through the use of computers. See also *cybernetics.*

cybernetics: the branch of learning that brings together theories and studies on communication and control in living organisms and in machines. See also *cybernation.* (A) (B)

cycle:

(1) an interval of space or time in which one set of events or phenomena is completed.

(2) any set of operations that is repeated regularly in the same sequence. The operations may be subject to variations on each repetition. (A)

(3) see display cycle, search cycle.

cycle bound: similar to CPU bound, except that the work load exceeded the capability of the present computer to process it all. See also *CPU bound.*

cycle count: the number of times a cycle has been performed.

cycled interrupt: the change of control to a given operation in a predetermined fashion, such as a particular sequence or operation cycle.

cycle index: the number of times a cycle of instructions has been or remains to be completed.

cycle reset: the setting of a cycle index or cycle count to its initial value or to another specified value.

cycle sharing: the process by which a device utilizes machine cycles of another device or processing unit. Synonymous with *cycle stealing.*

cycle shift: a nonarithmetic shift where digits are removed from one end of a word and shifted to the other end.

cycle steal: a hardware function that allows I/O devices to access storage directly.

cycle stealing: synonym for *cycle sharing.*

cycle time: the minimum time interval between the starts of successive read write cycles of a storage device. See *display cycle time, read/write cycle time.*

cyclical parity: see *cyclic redundancy check.*

cyclic redundancy check (CRC):

(1) a redundancy check in which the check key is generated by a cyclic algorithm.

(2) a system or error checking performed at both the sending and receiving station after a block check character has been accumulated. See also *longitudinal redundancy check, vertical redundancy check.*

cyclic redundancy check character: a character used in a modified cyclic code for error detection and correction. (A)

cyclic shift: synonym for *end-around shift.*

cyclic storage: synonym for *circulating storage.* (A)

cyclic storage access: a storage device allowing access only during specific, equally spaced intervals; found in magnetic drums.

cycling: the periodic change permitted on a variable or function by a control system or controller.

CYL: see *cylinder.*

cylinder (CUL):

(1) in a disk pack, particularly on a hard disk, the set of all tracks with the same nominal distance from the axis about which the disk pact rotates. (B)

(2) the tracks of a disk storage device that can be accessed without repositioning the access mechanism.

cylinder concept: a concept that data on all tracks above and below the one currently in use is available by merely switching read/write heads. Permits access to large amount of information with no extra movement of the access unit.

cylinder-cylinder-head-sector (CCHS): the representation of the address of a data field on a disk.

cylinder scanning: scanning used in facsimile transmission, where the object image is wrapped around a rotating cylinder that can be scanned by a photosensitive unit. Synonymous with *drum scanning*.

D:
(1) see *data*.
(2) deci. Ten or tenth part.
(3) see *decimal*.
(4) see *destination*.
(5) see *digit*.
(6) see *digital*.
(7) see *displacement*.
(8) see *domain*.

DA:
(1) see *data administrator*.
(2) see *deka*.

D/A: see *digital to analog*.

DAC: see *digital-to-analog converter*.

daemon: slang, a program not used explicitly which lies dormant waiting the occurrence of some condition(s).

dagger operation: synonymous with *NOR operation*.

daisy print wheel: a plastic or metal print wheel found in word-processing printers that makes the typing impression on paper. Its unique circular design allows these units to print up to 540 words per minute.

daisy wheel (DW): a serrated plastic disk around which is arranged a set of print characters.

daisywheel printers: like typewriters, they offer letter-quality text output. They are not as fast as dot matrix printers and laser printers.

damaged pack: a disk drive made partially unusable by a scratch on its recording surface or by a significant software error causing control information on the disk to be unreadable.

DASD: see *direct-access storage device*.

DASD queue: a queue that resides on a direct-access storage device.

DASM: see *direct access storage media*.

DAT: see *digital audio tape, dynamic address translation*.

data (D):
(1) a representation of facts, concepts, or instructions in a formalized manner suitable for communication, interpretation, or processing by human or automatic means. (B)
(2) any representations such as characters or analog quantities to which meaning is, or might be, assigned. (A)
(3) see *absolute data, alphanumeric data, analog data, digital data, discrete data, input data, numeric data, output data, relative data, test data*.

data access register: a register for RAM stacking address arithmetic.

data acquisition: the process of identifying, isolating, and gathering source data to be centrally processed. See also *data collection*.

data acquisition and control: a system for collecting data and preparing it for additional processing. Includes transducers, transducer amplifiers, multiplexers, and data converters in addition to logging devices, such as disk printers, plotters, and paper tape units.

data adapter unit (DAU): a unit that allows the central processor to be connected to a number of data-communications channels.

data administrator (DA):
(1) a control element from a data-base management system.
(2) an individual responsible for data definition and control of the data-base management system.

data area: a storage area used by a program to hold information.

data attribute: a characteristic of a unit of data such as length, value, or method of representation. (A)

data bank:

(1) a set of libraries of data. (B)

(2) a comprehensive collection of libraries of data. For example, one line of an invoice may form an item, a complete invoice may form a record, a complete set of such records may form a file, the collection of inventory control files may form a library, and the libraries used by an organization are known as its data bank. (A)

data base (DB):

(1) a collection of data fundamental to a system.

(2) a collection of data fundamental to an enterprise. (A)

(3) a set of data that is sufficient for a given purpose or for one or several given data-processing systems.

(4) a collection of interrelated or independent data items stored together without unnecessary redundancy, to serve one or more applications.

(5) see *relational database.*

database administration: establishing data bases by a data administration.

database administrator (DBA):

an individual responsible for the design, development, operations, safeguarding, maintenance, and use of a database.

(2) a person who is responsible for a database system, particularly for defining the rules by which data is accessed and stored. The database administrator is usually responsible also for database integrity, security, performance, and recovery.

database analyst: a key person in the analysis, design, and implementation of data structures in a database environment.

database management system (DBMS): a software system facilitating the creation and maintenance of a database and the execution of computer programs using the database.

data block: see *block.*

data break: synonymous with *direct memory access.*

data buffering: reading data into a separate storage unit normally contained in the control unit of the input-output subsystem.

data buffer register: a temporary storage register in a CPU or a peripheral unit able to receive or transmit data at varying input and output rates.

data bus (DB): see *bus.*

data capture: the act of collecting data into a form that can be directly processed by a computer system. Some electronic funds transfer systems are designed to capture transaction data at the precise time and place the transaction is consummated.

data card: see *source data card.* (A)

data cell: a direct-access storage volume containing strips of tape on which data is stored.

data center: the computer room and its support facilities.

data chain: the combination of two or more data elements in a sequence providing meaningful information.

data chaining: storing parts of records in areas that are not contiguous and are referenced as a whole by each record with the ability to call the next.

data channel (DC) (DCH): a device that connects a processor and main storage with I/O control units. Synonymous with *input-output channel.*

data-channel multiplexor: a multiplexor that services communications channels operating at high speeds to service these channels successively, a character at a time. See *multiplexer.*

data check: a data read error caused by a flaw on the recording surface of a medium such as magnetic tape or disk. The error cannot be corrected at that place and that portion of the recording surface is unusable.

data circuit: associated transmit and receive channels that provide a means of two-way data communications. Synonym for *link connection.*

data clause: in COBOL, a clause that appears in a data description entry in the data division and provides information describing a particular attribute of a data item.

data code (DC):
(1) a structured set of characters used to represent the data items; for example, the codes 01, 02, . . . 12 may be used to represent the months January, February, . . . December of the data element months of the year. (A)
(2) in data communications, a set of rules and conventions according to which the signals representing data should be formed, transmitted, received, and processed. (B)
(3) deprecated term for *code set.* (A) (B)
(4) see *numeric code.* (A)

data collection:
(1) a facility for gathering small quantities of data from a nominated group of addresses, assembling them within the network into a single message for delivery to another nominated address.
(2) an application in which data from several locations is accumulated at one location (in a queue or on a file) before processing. See also *data acquisition.*

data-collection station: synonym for *data-input station.* (A) (B)

DATACOM: see *data communication.*

data communication (DATACOM) (DC):
(1) the transmission and reception of data.
(2) the transmission, reception, and validation of data. (A)
(3) data transfer between data source and data sink via one or more data links according to appropriate protocols.

data compaction: any method for encoding data to reduce the storage it requires.

data compression: a technique that saves storage space by eliminating gaps, empty fields, redundancies, or unnecessary data to shorten the length of records or blocks.

data constant: see *figurative constant.*

data contamination: synonym for *data corruption.*

data control: the organization of data entering or leaving the system.

data control block (DCB): a control block used by access method routines in storing and retrieving data.

data conversion: the process of changing data from one form or representation to another.

data conversion line: the channel utilized in transferring data elements between data banks.

data converter: a device whose purpose is to convert data. (A) (B)

data corruption: a deliberate or accidental violation of data integrity. Synonymous with *data contamination.* (E)

data definition (DD): a program statement that describes the features of, specifies relationships of, or establishes context of data. (A)

data-definition name (ddname): the name of a data-definition (DD) statement that corresponds to a data-control block that contains the same name.

data-definition (DD) statement: a job control statement that describes a data set associated with a particular job step.

data delay: measured time concerned in the waiting period for information before another process can be performed.

data delimiter: synonymous with *delimiter.*

data-description entry: in COBOL, an entry in the data division that is used to describe the characteristics of a data item. It consists of a level number, followed by an optional data name, followed by data clauses that fully describe the format the data will take. An elementary data-description entry (or item) cannot logically be subdivided further. A group data-description entry (or item) is made up of a number of related group items, elementary items, or both.

data descriptor: in an assembly language program, the programming statement for defining constants or reserve storage locations in main memory.

data design: a layout or format of computer storage or machine storage allocation, that is, for input and output.

data dictionary (DD): a centralized repository of information about data such as meaning, relationships to other data, origin, usage, and format. It assists company management, data base administrators, systems analysts, and application programmers in effectively planning, controlling, and evaluating the collection, storage, and use of data. See also *dictionary*.

data-directed transmission: in PL/1, the type of stream-oriented transmission in which data is transmitted as a group, comprising one or more items separated by commas, terminated by a semicolon, where each is of the form name = *constant*. The name can be qualified, subscripted, or both.

data display unit: synonymous with *terminal*.

data division (DD): one of the four main component parts of a COBOL program. The data division describes the files to be used in the program and the records contained within the files. It also describes any internal working-storage records that will be needed. Synonym for *data item*.

data element: a set of data items to be considered in a given situation as a unit. Synonym for *data item*.

data-element chain: an ordered set of two or more data elements used as one data element. Synonymous with *macroelement*.

data-encrypting key: a key used to encipher and decipher data transmitted in a session that uses cryptography. Cf. *key-encrypting key*.

data entry (DE):
(1) a catalog entry that describes a cluster's or catalog's data component. A data entry contains the data component's attributes, allocation and extent information, and statistics. A data entry for a cluster's or catalog's data component can also contain the data component's passwords and protection attributes.
(2) the method of entering data into a computer system for processing, usually via terminal applications.
(3) the entry of data into a computer by an operator from a single data device, such as a card reader, badge reader, keyboard, or rotary switch.

data-entry mode: see *input mode*.

data-entry operator: data-processing operations personnel whose job includes transcribing data into a form suitable for computer processing, for example, by keypunching.

data-entry terminal: a terminal enabling data to be collected and readied for transmission over a circuit.

data error: a deviation from correctness in data, often an error, which occurred before the processing of the data.

data evaluation: the review and analysis of data so as to make an assessment of its inherent meaning, probable accuracy, relevancy, and relation to given situations.

data-examination clerk: the individual who is responsible for maintaining accuracy, correctness, and appropriateness of input-output data.

data-extent block (DEB): an extension of the data-control block that contains information about the physical status of the data set being processed.

data field (DF): any designated portion of a data-base segment. A segment may contain one or more data fields.

data file: a collection of related data records organized in a specific manner; for example, a payroll file (one record for each employee, showing such information as rate of pay and deductions) or an inventory file (one record for each inventory item, showing such information as cost, selling price, and number in stock). See also *data set (1), file, logical file*.

data flowchart: a flowchart that represents the path of data in the solving of a problem, and that defines the major phases of the processing as well as the various data media used. Synonymous with *data-flow diagram*. (A) (B)

data-flow control (DFC): the layer within a half-session that controls whether the half-session can send, receive, or concurrently send and receive, request units (RUs); group related RUs into RU chains; delimits transactions via the bracket protocol; controls the interlocking of requests and responses in accordance with control modes specified at session activation; generates sequence numbers; and correlates requests and responses.

data-flow diagram: synonym for *data flowchart*. (A) (B)

data format: procedures and rules that describe the way data is retained in a file or record, whether in character form, as binary numbers, and so forth.

data-format item: in PL/1, a specification used in edit-directed transmission to describe the representation of a data item in the stream.

data gathering: see *data acquisition, data collection.*

data generator: a data-set utility program that creates multiple data sets within one job for the sequential and partitioned access methods.

data handling:
(1) the production of records and reports.
(2) the performance of data-processing activities, that is, sorting, input-output operations, and report generation.

data hierarchy: a data structure consisting of sets and subsets such that every subset of a set is of lower rank than the data of the set. (A)

data highway: an often used term for *network.*

data holder: synonymous with *copy holder.*

data host: a host that is dedicated to processing applications and does not control network resources, except its locally attached devices.

data independence:
(1) the property of a data-base management system that enables data to be processed independently of access mode, storage method, or arrangement of data.
(2) the definition of logical and physical data so that application programs do not depend on where physical units of data are stored; data independence reduces the need to modify application programs when data storage and access methods are modified.

data input: data ready for processing, such as coding, sorting, computing, summarizing, and reporting, recording, and communication.

data-input station: a user terminal primarily for the insertion of data into a data-processing system. Synonymous with *data-collection station.* (A) (B)

data integrity:
(1) the quality of data that exists as long as accidental or malicious destruction, alteration, or loss of data are prevented.
(2) preservation of data for its intended purpose.

data item:
(1) the smallest unit of named data that has meaning in the schema or subschema. Synonymous with *data element.*
(2) in COBOL, a unit of recorded information that can be identified by a symbolic name or by a combination of names and subscripts. Elementary data items cannot logically be subdivided. A group data item is made up of logically related group items, elementary items, or both, and can be a logical group within a record or can itself be a complete record.
(3) in FORTRAN, a constant, variable, or array element.
(4) in PL/1, a single unit of data. Synonymous with *element.*

data level: the position of a data element in relation to other elements specified as part of the same record in a source language.

data library: a collection of related files; for example, in stock control, a collection of inventory control files. (A) (B)

data link (DL):
(1) the physical means of connecting one location to another for the purpose of transmitting and receiving data. (A)
(2) the interconnecting data circuit between two or more equipments operating in accordance with a link protocol; it does not include the data source and the data sink.

data-link escape character (DLE): a transmission control character that changes the meaning of a limited number of contiguously following characters or coded representations and that is used exclusively to provide supplementary transmission control characters. (A) (B)

data list (DL): in PL/1, a parenthesized list of expressions or repetitive specifications, separated by commas, used in a stream-oriented input or output specifications that represent storage locations to which data items are to be assigned during input, or values which are to be obtained for output.

data logging: the recording of data about events that occur in time sequence. (A)

data management (DM):
(1) the function of controlling the acquisition, analysis, storage, retrieval, and distribution of data.
(2) in an operating system, the computer programs that provide access to data, perform or monitor storage of data, and control input-output devices. (A)

data-management programming system: programs designed to provide an operator with the capability for querying, augmenting, and manipulating large computer-stored data bases in a natural language.

data manipulation: defining operations needed by users in processing data followed by carrying out the operations.

datamation: a shortened term for automatic data processing; taken from *data* and *automation.* See both terms.

data migration: the moving of data from an on-line device to an off-line or low-priority device, as determined by the system or as requested by the user. Cf. *staging.*

data mode: a move mode in which the data portions of all segments of a spanned record are accessed.

data name (DN):
(1) a character or group of characters used to identify an item of data. (A) (B)
(2) in COBOL, a name assigned by the programmer to a data item in a program. It must contain at least one alphabetic character.

data organization: see *data-set organization.*

data origination: the translation of information from its original form into a machine-readable form or directly into electrical signals.

data output: data obtained from a unit, such as a logic element, or the output channel of a logic element.

data plotter: a unit providing a visual display in the form of a graph on paper.

data pointer: a specific register holding the memory address of the data to be utilized by the instruction. The register "points" to the memory location of the data.

data preparation: pertaining to the conversion to machine-readable form data.

data printer: any terminal utilized for printing as hard copy information received over a communications network.

data processing (DP): the systematic performance of operations upon data, for example, handling, merging, sorting, computing. Synonymous with *information processing.* See *administrative data processing, automatic data processing, business data processing, distributed data processing, electronic data processing, integrated data processing, remote-access data processing.*

data-processing center: see *computer center.*

data-processing cycle: the sequence of operations associated with data processing, from the collection of data to displaying and storing the results of all machine activities.

data-processing machine: a generic name for a device that can store and process numeric and alphabetic information.

data-processing system (DPS): a system, including computer systems and associated personnel, that performs input, processing, storage, output, and control functions to accomplish a sequence of operations on data. See also *computer, computer system.*

data-processing system security: all of the technological and managerial safeguards established and applied to a data-processing system to protect hardware, software, and data from accidental or malicious modifications, destruction, or disclosure.

data processor (DP): a device capable of performing data processing, such as a desk calculator, a punched card machine, or a computer. (B) See *processor.*

data protection: a safeguard against the loss or destruction of data. See also *data integrity, security.*

data purification: validating and correcting data to reduce errors entering a data-processing system.

data record: a record containing data to be processed by a program.

data reduction: the transformation of raw data into a more useful form, for example, smoothing to reduce noise. (A)

data registers: registers found in many microprocessors for the temporary storage of data.

data reliability: the ratio that relates the extent to which data meet a given standard, usually concerning the accuracy of data, or the degree to which data is error free.

data representation: the machine-readable from in which data is recorded, such as the Hollerith code on punch cards.

data retrieval: the return of data by selecting, searching, or retransmission of information from a file data bank, or storage unit.

data scaling: see *scaling*.

data security: the protection of data against unauthorized disclosure, whether accidental or intentional. See also *data-processing system security*.

data set (DS):
(1) the major unit of data storage and retrieval, consisting of a collection of data in one of several prescribed arrangements and described by control information to which the system has access. See *direct data set, partitioned data set, sequential data set*.
(2) deprecated term for *modem*.
(3) see also *file*.

data set adapter: a unit for interfacing a computer and a modem by breaking down bytes from the computer into bits for serial transmission. For received signals the process is reversed.

data-set clocking: a time-base oscillator supplied by the data set for regulating the bit rate of transmission. Cf. *business machine clocking*.

data-set control block (DSCB): a data set label for a data set in direct-access storage.

data-set definition table (DSD table): a table that contains parameters for data sets.

data-set label:
(1) a collection of information that describes the attributes of a data set and is

normally stored on the same volume as the data set.
(2) a general term for data-set control blocks and tape data-set labels.

data-set name (DSN) (DSNAME): the term or phrase used to identify a data set. See also *qualified name*.

data-set organization (DSORG): the arrangement of information in a data set; for example, sequential organization or partitioned organization.

data-set reference number: in FORTRAN, a constant or variable in an input-output statement, which specifies the data set that is to be operated upon. Synonymous with *external-unit identifier*.

data-set security: see *data security*.

data-set utility programs: programs that can be used to update, maintain, edit, and transcribe data sets.

data sheet: see *source document*.

data signaling rate: the aggregate signaling rate in the transmission path of a data-transmission system, expressed in normalized form in binary digits (bits) per second. Cf. *actual data transfer rate*.

data signaling rate transparency: the ability of a network to provide compatibility between terminals operating at different data rates.

data sink: that part of data terminal equipment (DTE) that receives data from a data link. Cf. *data source*.

data source: that part of data terminal equipment (DTE) that enters data into a data link. Cf. *data sink*.

data specification: in PL/1, the portion of a stream-oriented data transmission statement that specifies the mode of transmission (DATA, LIST, or EDIT) and includes the data list (or lists) and, for edit-directed mode, the format list (or lists).

data storage: the use of any medium for storing data.

data stream:
(1) all data transmitted through a data channel in a single read or write operation.
(2) a continuous stream of data elements being transmitted, or intended for transmission, in character or binary-digit form, using a defined format.

data structure: the syntactic structure of symbolic expressions and their storage allocation characteristics.

data system: synonymous with *information system.*

data tablet: a unit with which to input graphics, making it possible to draw images directly into the computer. See *graphics tablet.*

data terminal (DT): a device, associated with a computer system for data input and output, that may be at a location remote from the computer system, thus requiring data transmission. See *terminal.* See also *station, work station.*

data time: the unit of time needed to fulfill a single instruction.

data transfer: the movement, or copying, of data from one location and the storage of the data at another location.

data-transfer rate: the average number of bits, characters, or blocks per unit of time transferred from a data source to a data sink. The rate is usually expressed as bits, characters, or blocks per second, minute, or hour. See *actual data-transfer rate.* Synonymous with *data-signaling rate.*

data-transfer register: a temporary storage unit that eases the shifting of data within the computer.

data transmission: synonym for *transmission.* (A)

data-transmission system: different pieces of hardware and software for transmitting data from one location to another.

data-transmission utilization measure: the ratio of useful data output of a data-transmission system, to the total data input.

data-transmission video display unit: input-output device with a special feature of displaying information on a screen, usually a cathode-ray tube.

data unit: a group of characters related so that they form a whole.

data validation: reviewing data for compliance with requirements.

data verification: determining if data has been accurately collected and recorded as carried out by visual and other checks such as record counts and limit checks.

data word: a unit of data stored in a single word of a storage medium.

dating routine: a routine which computes and/or stores, where needed, a date such as current day's date, expiration date of a tape, and so forth.

datum: the singular form of "data."

datum line: see *X-datum line, Y-datum line.* (A)

DAU: see *data adapter unit.*

DB:
(1) see *data base.*
(2) see *data bus.*

DBA:
(1) adjusted decibels.
(2) see *database administrator.*

dBm: decibel based on one milliwatt.

DBMS: see *data-base management system.*

DC:
(1) see *data channel.*
(2) see *data code.*
(3) see *data communication.*
(4) see *direct current.*

DCB: see *data-control block.*

DCC: device cluster controller.

DCH: see *data channel.*

DCL: see *declaration.*

DC1, DC2, DC3, DC4: see *device control character.* (A)

DD:
(1) see *data definition.*
(2) see *data dictionary.*
(3) see *data division.*

DDA: see *digital differential analyzer.* (A)

DDC: see *direct digital control.*

ddname: see *data-definition name.*

DDP: see *distributed data processing.*

DDR: see *dynamic device reconfiguration.*

DD statement: see *data-definition statement.*

DE: see *data entry.*

deactivated: in PL/1, the state in which a preprocessor variable or entry name is said to be when its value cannot replace the corresponding identifier in source program text.

dead file: any file that is not in current use but which is kept.

dead halt: see *drop-dead halt.*

deadlock:
(1) unresolved contention for the use of a resource.

(2) an error condition in which processing cannot continue because each of two elements of the process is waiting for an action by or a response from the other.

deadly embrace: synonymous with *deadlock.*

dead key: a key for typing something without advancing, so a second character on top of the first can be typed.

dead time:

(1) any definite delay deliberately placed between two related actions in order to avoid overlap that can confuse or permit a particular different event, such as a control decision, switching event, or similar action, to take place.

(2) the delay between two related actions, measured in units of time for efficiency study.

dead zone unit: a functional unit whose output variable is constant over a particular range of the input variable. (B)

deallocate: to release a resource that is assigned to a specific task.

DEB: see *data-extent block.*

deblock: to separate the parts of a block, for example, to select records from a block. (A)

debug: to detect, to trace, and to eliminate mistakes in computer programs or in other software. Synonymous with *check out.* (A) (B)

debug aids: prewritten sets of computerized routines for providing information in assisting a programmer or computer technician in the tracing of bugs.

debugger: an essential program purporting to aid software debugging, providing breakpoints, dump facilities, register and memory examine/modify, usually in symbolic form.

debugging aid routine: a routine used for testing programs.

debugging suppression: suppression of printing repetitions of the same bug within a program. Only the first occurrence of a bug within a loop can be printed out for examination.

debug macros: aids within a program added by the applications programmer in addition to those supplied by the supervisory program: a form of unit testing.

debug statements: in FORTRAN, the statements DEBUG, AT, TRACE ON, and TRACE OFF.

DEC:

(1) see *decimal.*

(2) see *decoder.*

(3) see *decrement.*

deca: see *deka.*

decade: a group of ten items; for example, a group of ten storage locations.

decade counter: a counter advancing in increments of ten.

decay: the dissipation of static electricity representing bits in memory which, if allowed to exist, would result in loss of data.

decentralized information system: two or more sets of information-processing equipment operated by the same enterprise to perform processing, but without any implied cooperation among the sets.

decentralized processing: the processing of data by individual subdivisions of an organization at different locations.

deci: tenth part.

decimal (D) (DEC):

(1) pertaining to a selection, choice, or condition that has ten possible different values or states. (B)

(2) pertaining to a fixed-radix numeration system having a radix of ten. (B)

(3) see *binary-coded decimal notation.* (A)

decimal arithmetic operation: a type of arithmetic operation whereby data enters and leaves the system as zoned decimal and is processed as packed decimal.

decimal digit: in decimal notation, or in the decimal numeration system, one of the digits 0 to 9. (A) (B)

decimal notation: a notation that uses ten different characters, usually the decimal digits, for example, the character string 196912312359, construed to represent the date and time one minute before the start of the year 1970; the representation used in the Universal Decimal Classification (UDC). (B) Cf. *decimal numeration system.* (A)

decimal number: see *decimal numeral.*

decimal number system: the base 10 number system representing a decimal number as the sum of successive powers of 10; for example, the decimal number 5647 can be expressed as $(5 \times 10^3) + (6 \times 10^2) + (4 \times 10^1) + (7 \times 10^0)$, where $10^0 = 1$.

decimal numeral: a numeral in the decimal numeration system. (A)

decimal numeration system: the fixed-radix numeration system that uses the decimal digits and the radix 10 and in which the lowest integral weight is 1. (B) Cf. *decimal notation.* (A)

decimal picture data: in PL/1, arithmetic picture data specified by picture specifications containing the following types of picture specification characters: decimal digit characters, the virtual point picture character, zero-suppression characters, sign and currency symbol characters, insertion characters, commercial characters, and exponent characters.

decimal point: the radix point in the decimal numeration system. The decimal point may be represented, according to various conventions, by a comma, by a period, or by a point at mid-height of the digits. (A) (B)

decimal symbol: a graphic symbol, usually a period or comma, used to separate the fractional part of a decimal number from the whole part of a decimal number.

decimal to binary conversion: converting a number written to the base of ten, or decimal, into the equivalent number written to the base of two, or binary.

decimeter (DM): one tenth of a meter; 3.94 inches.

decipher: see *decryption.*

decision: see *leading decision, trailing decision.* (A)

decision box: in flowcharting, a symbol used to indicate a choice of branching in the information-processing path.

decision content: in information theory, a logarithmic measure of the number of decisions needed to select a given event among a finite number of mutually exclusive events; in mathematic notation, this measure is $H = \log_2 n$, where n is the number of events. In information theory, the term *event* is to be understood

as used in the theory of probability. For instance, an event may be the presence of a given element of a set, the occurrence of a specified character or of a specified word in a given position of a message. (A) (B)

decision element: synonymous with *threshold element.*

decision feedback system: a system based on the error control principles of automatic repeat request.

decision instruction: deprecated term for *discrimination instruction.* Synonym for *branch instruction.* (A) (B)

decision integrator: in incremental computers, a digital integrator that provides an increment that is maximum positive, maximum negative, or zero, based on input values.

decision logic: a decision made in a computing system as a result of the internal organization of that system, where one of the binary, or yes or no type, and basically relating to questions of equality, inequality, or relative magnitude, is the result of a particular computation less than, equal to, or greater than some reference point or number.

decision logic table (DLT): a standardized table that organizes relevant facts in a clear and concise manner to aid in the decision-making process.

decision mechanism: the component part of a character reader, in character recognition, that receives the finalized version of the input character, and makes a determination as to its probable identity.

decision rules: the programmed criteria which an on-line, real-time system uses to make operating decisions.

decision support system (DSS): the interrelated system of computer programs and data designed to aid managers in making informed decisions.

decision symbol: a flow charting symbol used to indicate where in a program alternatives are to be considered. A diamond-shaped figure is used for the decision symbol.

decision table (DETAB):
(1) a presentation in either matrix or

tabular form of a set of conditions and their corresponding actions. (A)

(2) a table of all contingencies that are to be considered in the description of a problem, together with the actions to be taken for each set of contingencies.

decision theory: the formal specifications and analysis of choice situations in terms of the alternative actions available to the decision maker, the likely outcomes, and the preference ordering of all possible consequences.

decision tree: a pictorial description of available alternatives in a process.

DECK: see *deque.*

deck: see *card deck.* (A)

declaration (DCL):

(1) in a programming language, a meaningful expression that affects the interpretation of other expressions in that language. Synonymous with *directive.* (A) (B)

(2) in PL/1, the establishment of an identifier as a name and the construction of a set of attributes (partial or complete) for it. Also, a source of attributes of a particular name.

(3) a nonexecutable statement that supplies information about data or about particular aspects of a computer program. Synonymous with *declarative statement.*

declaration section: the part(s) of a Pascal program where identifiers to be used in a procedure or program are specified.

declaration time: time that elapses between finishing the reading or writing of a tape record and the time when the tape stops moving. Synonymous with *stop time.*

declarative: deprecated term for *declaration.* (B)

declaratives: a set of one or more compiler-directing sections written at the beginning of the procedure division of a COBOL program. The first section is preceded by the header DECLARATIVES. The last section is followed by the header END DECLARATIVES.

declarative statement: synonym for *declaration.*

declare: in assembler-language programming, to identify the variable symbols to

be used by the assembler at preassembly time.

decliter (dl): one tenth of a liter; 0.21 pints.

decode:

(1) to convert data by reversing the effect of some previous encoding. (B)

(2) to interpret a code. See *decoding.*

(3) Cf. *encode.* (A)

decoder (DEC):

(1) a device that decodes data. (B)

(2) a device that has a number of input lines of which any number may carry signals and a number of output lines of which not more than one may carry a signal, there being a one-to-one correspondence between the output and the combinations of the input signals. (B)

(3) cf. *encoder.*

(4) see *operation decoder.* (A)

decoding:

(1) internal hardware operations by which the computer determines the meaning of the operation code of an instruction; also sometimes applied to *addresses.*

(2) in interpretive routines, some subroutines, and elsewhere, an operation by which a routine determines the meaning of parameters. See also *decode.*

decollate: to separate the plies of a multipart form or paper stock. Synonymous with *deleave.* (A)

decollator: a device that combines the removal of carbon paper and separation of various copies of a standard multipart continuous form.

DECR: see *decrement.*

decrement (DEC) (DECR):

(1) the quantity by which a variable is decreased.

(2) in some computers, a specific part of an instruction word.

(3) to decrease the value of a number.

decrypt: decode data.

decryption: the decoding of data made inaccessible by *encryption.*

decurl: in a printer, to remove abnormal curving of the paper.

dedicated: machines, programs, or devices designed or set apart for one usage.

dedicated device: a device that cannot be shared among users.

dedicated port: the access point to a communication channel used only for one specific type of traffic.

dedicated register: a register used to contain a specific item.

dedicated word processor: a computer designed first and foremost to do word processing. May also indicate that the system is limited to word processing.

dedicated server: a computer in a network that manages key functions of the network.

dedication: pertaining to the assignment of a system resource—an I/O device, a program, or a whole system—to one application or purpose.

DEF: see *definition*.

default:

(1) a value, action, or setting that a computer system assumes, unless given a different instruction.

(2) a present response to a question or prompt. The default is automatically used by the computer if a different response is not given. Default values prevent a program from stalling or crashing if no value is supplied by the user.

(3) synonymous with *preset*.

default button: the default button in a dialog box is marked with a double border to indicate that it is the safest or most logical choice.

default group: the group to which a user is associated when a group name is not specified on the TSO LOGON command or batch JOB statement.

default option: the implicit option that is assumed when no option is explicitly stated. (A)

default parameters: parameter values supplied by a computer system when no explicit values are provided by a program.

default value: the choice among exclusive alternatives made by the system when no explicit choice is specified by the user.

deferred addressing: a method of addressing in which one indirect address is replaced by another to which it refers a predetermined number of times or until the process is terminated by an indicator. (A) (B)

deferred entry: an entry into a subroutine that occurs as a result of a deferred exit from the program that passed control to it.

deferred maintenance: maintenance specifically intended to eliminate an existing fault that did not prevent continued successful operation of the device or computer program. (A)

deferred maintenance time: time, usually unscheduled, used to perform deferred maintenance. (A)

deferred processing: processing that can be delayed or considered low priority and is completed when computer time is at nonpeak periods.

deferred restart: a restart performed by the system on resubmission of a job by the programmer. The operator submits the restart deck to the subsystem through a system input reader. Cf. *automatic restart*.

define: establishing a value for a variable or symbol or establishing what the variable represents.

defined item: in PL/1, a variable declared to represent part or all of the same storage as that assigned to another variable known as the base item.

definition (DEF): see *data definition, macrodefinition*. (A)

definition mode: when a programming language is used in this mode, a series of instructions is entered into memory, and the entire program is executed on command from the programmer.

DEF statement: the BASIC statement form that allows the user to define his or her own functions. The function itself may be single or multiline.

degeneracy: the condition created by negative feedback.

degradation factor: a measure of the loss in performance that results from the reconfiguration of data-processing system; for example, a slowdown in run time due to a reduction in the number of processing units.

degraded mode: the condition of a system resulting from degradation.

degree of multiprogramming: the number of transactions handled in parallel by the systems involved in a multiprogram.

deinstall: removing a software or hardware feature from active use.

deka (DA): ten.

dekaliter (dal): ten liters; 2.64 gallons.

dekameter (dam): ten meters; 32.81 feet.

DEL:

(1) see *delete.*

(2) see *delete character.* (A)

delay: the amount of time by which an event is retarded. (A)

delay counter: a counter for inserting a deliberate time delay allowing an operation external to the program to occur.

delay line:

(1) a line or network designed to introduce a desired delay in the transmission of a signal, usually without appreciable distortion. (B)

(2) a sequential logic element with one input channel and in which an output channel state at any one instant, T, is the same as the input channel state at the instant T-N, where N is a constant interval of time for a given output channel; for example, an element in which the input sequence undergoes a delay of N time units.

(3) see *electromagnetic delay line.*

delay line storage: a storage device that uses delay lines. (A) (B)

delay programming: see *minimum delay programming.*

delay time: the amount of elapsed time between the end of one event and the beginning of the next sequential event.

delay unit: a device that yields, after a given time interval, an output signal essentially similar to a previously introduced input signal. (A) (B)

deleave: synonym for *decollate.* (A)

delete (DEL):

(1) to remove or eliminate an item, record, or group of records from a file.

(2) to erase a program from memory.

delete character (DEL): a control character used primarily to obliterate an erroneous or unwanted character; on perforated tape, this character consists of a car hole in each punch position. Synonymous with *erase character.* (A) (B)

delete key: in word processing, a control that enables text already recorded on the recording medium or in storage to be deleted.

deletion of an I/O device: removal of the I/O unit from the supervisor configuration tables.

deletion record: a new record that replaces or removes an existing record of a master file.

delimiter:

(1) a flag that separates and organizes items of data. Synonymous with *punctuation symbol, separator.* (A)

(2) a string of one or more characters used to separate or organize elements of computer programs or data; for example, parentheses, blank character, arithmetic operator, if, "BEGIN."

(3) a character that groups or separates words or values in a line of input.

(4) in PL/1, all operators, comments, and the following characters: percent, parentheses, comma, period, semicolon, assignment symbol, and blank; they define the limits of identifiers, constants, picture specifications, and key words.

delimiter statement: a job control statement used to mark the end of data.

delivery confirmation: the notification passed to a data terminal using a delayed delivery facility, confirming that the network has delivered the message to a destination terminal.

delta clock: a clock for timing subroutine operations; used to restart a computer using an interrupt following a fault, forcing the machine into a closed programming loop.

delta noise: the difference between the 1-state and the 0-state half-selected noise.

demand: an input-output coding technique in which a read or write order is initiated as the need to read a new block or write a new block of data occurs. Operations do not take place in parallel.

demand fetching: a memory multiplexing design in which segments are kept on a backing storage and only placed in an internal storage when computations refer to them.

demand processing: the processing of data as rapidly as it becomes available or ready.

This is real time and avoids the need for storage of any appreciable amount of unprocessed data.

demand staging: moving data from disk to main memory when requested by an applications program and not before, as opposed to anticipatory staging.

demarc: short for *demarcation.*

demarcation: a point defining the boundary of responsibility.

demarcation strip: usually a terminal board acting as a physical interface between the business machine and the common carrier. See also *interface.*

demented: slang, a program that functions as designed, but where the design is poor.

demon: slang, a portion of a program that is not invoked explicitly, but lies dormant awaiting the occurrence of some condition(s).

demount: to remove a volume from a tape unit or a direct-access device.

demountable pack: a type of disk drive where the pack, or physical storage medium, is removed and replaced with another by the computer operator.

demultiplexer (demux): a unit for connecting a single input line to any of several output lines. Cf. *multiplexer.*

demultiplexing: dividing one or more information streams into a larger number of streams.

demux: short for *demultiplexer.*

denary: synonym for *decimal (2).* (A) (B)

dense binary code: a binary code where all possible bit patterns are used to represent characters, as opposed to one in which some patterns have no meaning.

dense list: a list of the contents of contiguous storage areas. Synonymous with *linear list.*

density: the closeness of space distribution on a storage medium, particularly a tape or disk.

dependency: a sequence of program execution where one job has to have been completed before another one can begin.

dependent segment:

(1) in a tree structure, a segment that relies on at least the root segment and possibly other dependent segments for its full meaning.

(2) in a database, a segment that relies on a higher level segment for its full hierarchical meaning.

deposit: synonymous with *dump.*

depth queuing: a technique for enhancing the three-dimensional appearance of a two-dimensional subject.

DEQ: see *dequeue.*

deque (DECK): a list permitting insertions and deletions at both ends. The deque is input-restricted when insertions are made at only one end and deletions are made at either end. The deque is output-restricted when deletions are made at only one end and insertions are made at either end.

dequeue (DEQ): to remove items from a queue. Cf. *enqueue.*

derail: an instruction to go to a subroutine.

derivative action: a type of response in control systems, the output response of which is the derivative of the input.

descender: the part of a letter, such as "j" or "y," that extends below the main body of a character; easier to read on some printers than others. See also *ascender.*

descending key: in COBOL, a key upon the values of which data is ordered starting with the highest value of key down to the lowest value of key, in accordance with the rules for comparing data items.

descending sort: a sort in which the final sequence of records is such that all successive keys compare "less than" or "equal to."

description: see *problem description.*

description list: a list of data elements and their attributes.

descriptor: in information retrieval, a word used to categorize or index information. Synonymous with *key word.* (A) See *parameter descriptor.*

deselect: to change a selected item so that it is no longer selected.

deserialize: to change from serial-by-bit to parallel-by-byte. Cf. *serialize.*

deserializer: synonym for *serial-to-parallel converter.*

design: see *functional design, logic design.*

design aids: special hardware or software elements intended to aid in implementation of a data-processing system.

designating device: a unit on some tabulators that permits the first item of a series of similar data to be printed, and inhibits some or all printing of the rest of the series.

designation hole: a hole punched in a punch card to indicate the nature of the data on the card, or the functions that a machine is to perform. (B) Synonymous with *control hole, control punch, function hole.*

designator: any part that classifies.

desktop computer:
(1) another name for microcomputer.
(2) a computer's working environment, for example a menu bar. A number of documents on the desktop can appear at the same time.

desktop publishing: the use of personal computers and page printers to compose and print documents.

despatch: to allocate time of a CPU to a specific job.

despooler: software that reads information awaiting printing from a spool file and routes it to a printer.

DEST: see *destination.*

destination (D) (DEST):
(1) in a network, any point or location, for example, a node, a station, or a terminal, to which data is to be sent.
(2) the disk or folder that receives a copied or translated file.

destination address field: a field of information within a frame that identifies the address of the station to which a particular packet or frame of data has been routed.

destination field (DF): a field in a message header that contains the destination code.

destructive addition: addition after which the sum appears in the location previously occupied by an operand, usually the augend; thus destroying the operand.

destructive cursor: on a CRT display device, a cursor that erases any character through which it passes as it is advanced, backspaced, or otherwise moved. Cf. *nondestructive cursor.*

destructive read: reading that erases the data in the source location. (A) (B)

destructive storage: a storage unit where read operations are destructive and the contents must be regenerated after being read if they are required at the same location following a read operation. See *destructive read.*

DETAB: see *decision table.*

detached keyboard: a keyboard connected to the video screen by a cable— not molded to it; permits moving around more.

detail card: synonym for *trailer card.*

detail diagram: describing the specific function performed or data items used in a module.

detail file: synonym for *transaction file.* (A) (B)

detail flowchart: depicts the processing steps required within a particular program.

deterministic simulation: simulation where a given input always yields the same output.

development system: a computer system with needed facilities for appropriate software and hardware application development.

development time: that part of operating time used for debugging new routines or hardware. See *program development time.* Cf. *makeup time.* (A)

development tools: hardware and software aids used in evolving programs and/or electronic systems.

deviation from linearity: concerns the maximum deviation of output from the most favorable straight line that can be drawn through the input-output curve. The method of determining the most favorable line has to be given, to be expressed in percent of output full scale.

device (DVC): a mechanical, electrical, or electronic contrivance with a specific purpose. Typical PC devices include printers, keyboards, modems, etc. See *character display device, choice device, display device, locator device, logic device, mass storage device, pick device, raster display device, storage device, valuator device.* See also *device type, end-user device.*

device address: see *logical device address.*

device backup: pertaining to the assignment of alternate devices.

device cluster: devices, usually terminals, that share a controller.

device control character: a control character used for the control of ancillary devices associated with a data-processing system or data-communication system; for example, for switching such devices on or off. (A) (B)

device control codes (DC1, DC2, DC3, and DC4): codes occurring within the character set of standard data communication codes that are used for representing instructions to activate specified functions on a terminal unit.

device controller: a hardware unit that electronically supervises one or more peripheral devices. It acts as the link between the CPU and the I/O devices.

device control unit: a hardware device that controls the reading, writing, or displaying of data at one or more input-output devices or terminals.

device coordinate: in computer graphics, a coordinate specified in a coordinate system that is device dependent.

device-dependent: pertaining to an application program that is responsible for controlling the terminal to which it is connected. The application program is not responsible for controlling the use of the line by which the terminal is attached.

device-dependent program: a program that must consider the characteristics of a specific type of I/O device when processing an I/O request.

device driver: see *driver.*

device end pending: a hardware error where a peripheral fails to respond when addressed by the CPU.

device flag (DF): a register with one bit for recording the status of a peripheral unit.

device independence (DI): the capability to write application programs so that they do not depend on the physical characteristics of devices.

device-independent: pertaining to the ability to request I/O operations without regard for the characteristics of specific types of input-output devices. See also *symbolic I/O assignment.*

device-independent program: a program that does not consider the characteristics of a specific type of input-output device when processing an input-output request.

device line: synonym for *display line.*

device media control language: a language for specifying the physical implementation of the database logical data structure.

device name: the logical name assigned to a device.

device name assignment: utilizing a symbolic name instead of an address to refer to a peripheral unit.

device number: the reference number assigned to any external device.

device queue: a queue of requests to use a unit.

device selection check: a check verifying that the correct unit was chosen during a program instruction.

device status word: a word in which the condition of the bits indicates the status of peripheral units. See *device flag.*

device type: the general name for a kind of device; for example, 2311, 2400, 2400-1. See also *group name, unit address.*

DF:
   (1) see *data field.*
   (2) see *destination field.*
   (3) see *device flag.*

DFC: see *data-flow control.*

D flip-flop: a flip-flop with a delayed reaction where the output is conditioned by previous input.

DFT: see *diagnostic function test.*

DI: see *device independence.*

diablo: slang, any letter-quality printing device.

diad: synonymous with *doublet.*

diadic boolean operation: synonymous with *binary boolean operation.*

diagnosis: locating and explaining detectable errors in a computer routine or hardware component.

diagnostic: pertaining to the detection and isolation of a malfunction or mistake. (A)

diagnostic check: a specific routine designed to locate a malfunction in a computer.

diagnostic function test (DFT): a program to test overall system reliability.

diagnostic message: a computer-generated message to the programmer informing him of one or more grammatical errors in the program. See also *error message.*

diagnostic program: a computer program that recognizes, locates, and explains either a fault in equipment or a mistake in a computer program. (A) (B)

diagnostic routine: a routine designed to locate a malfunction, either in other routines or in the computer hardware.

diagnostics: mechanisms built into hardware and software to inform users that an error has prevented the program from running properly. Systems which locate malfunctioning sections of a computer.

diagnostic test: the running of a machine program or routine for the purpose of discovering a failure or potential failure of a machine element, and to determine its location or its potential location.

diagnostic trace: a program for performing diagnostic checks on other programs.

diagram: see *block diagram, functional diagram, logic diagram, setup diagram, Veitch diagram, Venn diagram.* (A)

dialect: a version of a programming language that closely resembles other versions, but also differs in other respects.

dialectic sensors: an approach used in reading data from paper tape by a special sensor.

dialog box: a box containing a message requesting more information. At times the message warns that the computer is being asked to do something it can't do or that some information is about to be destroyed. In such cases, the message is often accompanied by a beep. See *directory dialog box.*

dibit: a group of two bits. In four-phase modulation, each possible dibit is encoded as one of four unique carrier phase shifts. The four possible states for a dibit are 00, 01, 10, and 11.

DIBOL: Digital Business Oriented Language.

dichotomizing search: a search in which an ordered set of items is partitioned into two parts, one of which is rejected, the process being repeated on the accepted part until the search is completed. See also *binary search.* (A) (B)

dichotomy: a division into subordinate units or classes, that is, all white and all nonwhite, or all zero and all nonzero.

DICT: see *dictionary.*

dictionary (DICT): synonym for *proofreader, spell check, table.* See *composite external symbol dictionary, data dictionary, external symbol dictionary, relocation dictionary.*

DIFF: see *difference.*

difference (DIFF): in a subtraction operation, the number or quantity that is the result of subtracting the subtrahend from the minuend. (A) (B)

difference engine: a forerunner to the computer, it is the machine designed and developed by Charles Babbage to solve polynominal expressions or equations by the difference method.

difference report: a report showing resultant changes from an original computer program and a program change.

differential analyzer: an analog computer using interconnected integrators to solve differential equations. (B) See *digital differential analyzer.* (A)

differential gear: in analog computers, a mechanism that relates the angles of rotation of three shafts, usually designed so that the algebraic sum of the rotation of two shafts is equal to twice the rotation of the third. A differential gear can be used for addition or subtraction. (A)

differentiator: a device whose output function is proportional to the derivative of the input function with respect to one or more variables; for example, a resistance-capacitance network used to select the leading and trailing edges of a pulse signal. (A)

diffusion: a semiconductor production, introducing small quantities of impurity into a substrate material, such as silicon, permitting the impurity to spread into the substrate.

DIG: see *digit.*

digit (D) (DIG):
(1) a graphic character that represents an integer; for example, one of the characters 0 to 9. (B)
(2) a symbol that represents one of the nonnegative integers smaller than the radix; for example, in decimal notation, a digit is one of the characters from 0 to 9.
(3) synonymous with *numeric character*.
(4) see *binary digit, borrow digit, carry digit, check digit, decimal digit, sign digit, significant digit*. (A)

digital (D): pertaining to data in the form of digits. Cf. *analog*.

digital adder: see *adder*.

digital/analog conversion: the process by which a series of numbers is converted into a continuous signal or measurement.

digital audio tape (DAT): high-performance memory storage typically in a cartridge.

digital block: a set of multiplexed equipment that includes one or more data channels and associated circuitry. Digital blocks are usually designated in terms of signaling speed.

digital carrier system: a common carrier communication system that handles digital data.

digital circuit: a communications channel that carries data in a digital format. These circuits do not have modems, but usually have a unit for converting digital pulses into a bipolar format.

digital clock: a system clock in a digital mode that yields precisely timed voltage pulses of fixed duration.

digital computer:
(1) a computer that operates on discrete data by performing arithmetic and logic processes on these data. (A)
(2) a computer that consists of one or more associated processing units and peripheral equipment and that is controlled by internally stored programs.
(3) see also *analog computer, hybrid computer*.

digital connection: the digital path between two terminals operating at a stated bit rate and utilizing a switched connection through a digital switch.

digital control: synonymous with *direct digital control (DDC)*.

digital data: data represented by digits, perhaps with special characters and the space characters. (A) (B)

digital data link: resources utilized for transmission of information recorded in digital form at a given bit rate between two locations.

digital differential analyzer (DDA):
(1) an incremental computer in which the principal type of computer unit is a digital integrator whose operation is similar to the operation of an integrating mechanism. (B)
(2) a differential analyzer that uses digital representations for the analog quantities. (A)

digital filling: synonymous with *bit stuffing*.

digital filter: a filtering process performed on a digitized signal by a general- or special-purpose computer.

digital incremental plotter: an output unit that accepts digital signals from the CPU and uses them to activate a plotting pen and paper-carrying drum.

digital monitor: a monitor that is compatible with digital signaling. Cf. *analog monitor*.

digital read-out: an immediate display of data in digital form.

digital recorder: a peripheral device that records data as discrete numerically defined points.

digital representation: a discrete representation of a quantized value of variable, that is, the representation of a number of digits, perhaps with special characters and the space character. (A) (B)

digital signal: a discrete or discontinuous signal; one whose various states are discrete intervals apart.

digital signal processing (DSP): the art of using computer methods to enhance, analyze, or otherwise manipulate images, sounds, radar pulses, and other real-world signals. It runs a digitized signal through a series of mathematical procedures or algorithms repeatedly.

digital signature: a numerical representation of a set of logic states, typically used to describe the logic-state history at one output of the unit under test during the complete test program.

digital sort: an ordering or sorting first according to the least significant, followed by a resort on each next higher order digit until all the items are completely sorted; most often used in punched card sorting.

digital subject: data in a specific format that is set by control information to which the system has access.

digital-to-analog (D/A): the process of converting digital electrical signals from a computer into analog signals such as voltage to drive external units requiring analog input.

digital-to-analog converter (DAC):
(1) a functional unit that converts digital data to analog signals. (B)
(2) a device that converts a digital value to a proportional analog signal.

digital traffic: information transmitted over a circuit where every message is transferred as a digital signal rather than an analog signal.

digit arithmetic: see *significant digit arithmetic.*

digit compression: a technique for increasing the number of digits stored in a storage area, thereby decreasing the size of a file.

digit delay elements: a logic device for introducing a delay element of one digit period.

digit emitter: a character emitter limited to the 12 rows of a punched card.

digitization: converting analog signals to digital signals, creating steps at distinct levels of the analog signal.

digitize: to express or represent in a digital form data that are not discrete data; for example, to obtain a digital representation of the magnitude of a physical quantity from an analog representation of that magnitude. (A) (B)

digitizer:
(1) a unit that converts an analog measurement to digital form.
(2) an electronic cursor or pen such as an optical scanner together with a tablet, which transmits drawings into data.

digitizing pad: a flat bed where a piece of paper is placed. A special pen traces lines

or plots separate points on the paper yielding digital data that are input to a computer.

digit period: the time interval for the single digital signal in a series, determined by the pulse repetition frequency of the computer. Synonymous with *digit time.*

digit place: in a positional representation system, each site that may be occupied by a character and that may be identified by an ordinal number or by an equivalent identifier. Synonymous with *digit position, symbol rank.* (A) (B)

digit position: synonym for *digit place.* (A) (B)

digit pulse: the pulse corresponding to a particular digit position in a transmission sequence, representing a binary number or a particular time slot.

digit punch: a punch in rows 1, 2 . . . 9 of a punched card. See also *eleven punch, twelve punch.* Cf. *zone punch.* (A)

digit rate: the number of digits transferred in a specified time interval.

digit rows: the lower ten rows (numbers 0 through 9) that are found on an 80-column punched card.

digit time: synonymous with *digit period.*

dike: slang, to remove or disable a module.

dimension: in assembler-language programming, the maximum number of values that can be assigned to a SET symbol representing an array.

dimensionality: in PL/1, the number of bound specifications in an array declaration.

diminished radix complement: a complement obtained by subtracting each digit of the given number from the number that is one less than the radix of that digit place. Synonymous with *radix-minus-one complement.* (A) (B)

dimmed: buttons and menu items that appear in gray instead of black and cannot be chosen. There are some options and menu items that are not available until the user first performs some other action.

DIM statement: a statement used to alert the computer that a list or array is to be assigned to a variable name.

dingbat: a small graphical element used for decorative purposes in a document. Some fonts, for example, Zapf Dingbat, are designed to present sets of dingbats.

DIP: see *dual in-line package.*

DIP switches: a small series of on-off switches on a dual-in-line package, providing user selection of options on a circuit board without hardware alteration.

DIR: see *directory.*

direct access: the facility to obtain data from a storage device, or to enter data into a storage device in such a way that the process depends only on the location of that data and not on a reference to data previously accessed. (B) Cf. *serial access.* (A)

direct-access hash: pertaining to indexing, a hash algorithm that precludes collision, where no two elements have the same hash indices.

direct-access inquiry: a storage approach allowing direct information inquiry from temporary or permanent storage devices.

direct-access storage:
(1) a storage device in which the access time is in effect independent of the location of the data. (A)
(2) a storage device that provides direct access to data.
(3) see also *immediate-access storage.*

direct-access storage device (DASD): a device in which the access time is effectively independent of the location of the data.

direct-access storage media (DASM): media capable of storing programs and data so that the time needed to access specific elements is quick and independent both of their location, and of the location of the last data element accessed. See *memory.*

direct address: an address that designates the storage location of an item of data to be treated as an operand. Synonymous with *one-level address.* (B) Cf. *indirect address.* (A)

direct addressing: a method of addressing in which the address part of an instruction contains a direct address. (B) Cf. *indirect addressing.* (A)

direct code: synonymous with *absolute code.*

direct coding: instructions written in absolute code.

direct-coupled flip-flop: a flip-flop composed of electronic circuits in which the active elements are coupled with transistors. See also *flip-flop.*

direct current (DC): a unidirectional current of effectively constant value.

direct data organization: the organization of records in a nonsequential order. Each record is located at an address which is computed by a randomizing process.

direct data set: a data set whose records are in random order on a direct-access volume. Each record is stored or retrieved according to its actual address or its address relative to the beginning of the data set. Cf. *sequential data set.*

direct digital control (DDC): a computer-control technique where a time-shared digital computer is substituted for a portion of or all of the analog simulator, thereby lowering capital investment and permitting greater facility in transferring a program from one system to another. Synonymous with *digital control.*

directed-beam scan: in computer graphics, a technique of generating or recording the display elements of a display image in any sequence. Synonymous with *directed scan, random scan.*

directed scan: synonym for *directed-beam scan.*

direct file: a file whose records are stored in random order on a direct access storage unit, thereby permitting them to be retrieved in any order.

direct insert routine: synonym for *open routine.*

direct insert subroutine: synonym for *open subroutine.* (A) (B)

direct instruction: an instruction that contains the direct address of an operand for the operation specified. (A) (B)

directive: synonym for *declaration.* (A) (B)

directive commands: in an assembler, a command permitting the user to produce data words and values for stated conditions in assembly time.

directive statements: statements for defining the program structure, that is, ORIGIN STATEMENT, END STATEMENT. Such statements do not produce executable code.

direct memory access (DMA): high-speed data transfer direct between an input/output channel and memory. Synonymous with *cycle stealing, data break.*

direct memory access channel (DMAC): an input-output channel for transferring data between main memory and high-speed peripheral units.

direct numerical control: a situation where a number of numerical control units are connected via a data transmission network. They can be under the direct control of a central computer, with or without the aid of an operator. In the latter situation, the system is referred to as *computer numerical control.*

directory (DIR):
(1) a table of identifiers and references to the corresponding items of data. (A) (B)
(2) an index that is used by a control program to locate more blocks of data that are stored in separate areas of a data set in direct-access storage.
(3) a listing of files and subdirectories that are stored together. Directories help to organize files to create a different directory to hold each group of related files.

directory devices: a unit that contains a table of contents with critical information about the files on that machine. Besides the filename and data of creation or modification, the directory has the size and address of the file on the device, although the directory listing on the terminal may not show all of this information.

directory dialog box: a dialog box that presents the contents of disks and folders so that a document can be saved in a particular folder or disk, or open a document that's in a particular folder or disk. See *dialog box.*

direct read after write: see *DRAW.*

direct reference address: a virtual address not modified by indirect addressing; can be modified by indexing.

direct view storage tube (DVST): in computer graphics, a type of graphic display device in which the display does not need to be refreshed, because low level electron flood guns sustain the illumination of the phosphors activated by the directed beam.

direct voice input: input of information into a unit directly using the human voice, without an intermediate stage of keyboarding.

DIS: see *disconnect.*

disabled:
(1) pertaining to a state of a processing unit that prevents the occurrence of certain types of interruptions. Synonymous with *masked.*
(2) pertaining to the state in which a transmission control unit or audio response unit cannot accept incoming calls on a line.
(3) not selectable.
(4) in PL/1, the state in which a particular on condition does not result in an interrupt.

disabled module: a module that cannot be interrupted during its execution. It must be executed from beginning to end once it has gained control. Cf. *enabled module.*

disarm: to disallow an interrupt.

disassemble: translating a program from machine language into assembly language for easier comprehension. Cf. *assemble.*

disassembler: a program that translates from machine language to assembly language, often to decipher existing machine language programs by generating symbolic code listings.

disaster dump: a dump made when a nonrecoverable computer program error occurs.

disc (DSK): alternate spelling for disk. (A) See *magnetic disk.*

disconnect (DIS): to disengage the apparatus used in a connection and to restore it to its ready condition when not in use. Synonymous with *release.*

disconnect timeout: an indication that a station has gone on-hook.

discrete: pertaining to data in the form of distinct elements such as characters, or to physical quantities having distinctly recognizable values. Cf. *analog.*

discrete data: data represented by characters. (A) (B)

discrete programming: synonym for *integer programming.* (A)

discrete representation: a representation of data by characters, each character or a group of characters designating one of a number of alternatives. (A) (B)

discrete simulation: simulation where all major components and events are identified individually and used at irregular intervals. Synonymous with *event-oriented simulation.*

discretionary hyphen: in word processing, a hyphen inserted by an operator to divide a word when there is insufficient space to produce the whole of that word at the end of a line. Synonymous with *syllable hyphen character.* See also *required hyphen character.*

discrimination: skipping of various instructions as developed in a predetermined set of conditions as programmed.

discrimination instruction: an instruction of the class of instructions that comprises branch instructions and conditional jump instructions. (A) (B)

disjunction: the boolean operation whose result has the boolean value 0 if and only if each operand has the boolean value 0. Synonymous with *inclusive-OR operation, logical ADD, OR operation.* (B) Cf. *non-disjunction.* (A)

disk:

(1) any circular object with a magnetic surface that is used to store files (programs and documents) on a computer. The files are stored as magnetic signals. See *cartridge, CD-ROM erasable optical disk, floppy disk, hard disk.*

(2) loosely, a magnetic disk unit. See *integrated disk, magnetic disk.*

disk accessing: the process used in transferring data to and from a disk file.

disk-based operating system: a system where software is held on one or more magnetic disks.

disk buffer: a small amount of memory set aside for the objective of storing data read from, or about to be written to, a disk. When the program contains information to store, it writes it into the disk buffer area in memory. When the buffer has been filled up, the entire contents of the buffer are written to disk in one operation.

disk cache: a portion of the computer's random access memory (RAM) that is set aside for programs to store frequently used instructions. See *cache memory, SRAM.*

disk capacity: the maximum amount of data a disk can hold, usually measured in megabytes or kilobytes.

disk controller card: a printed-circuit board which interfaces disk storage hardware to the CPU of a computer.

disk converter: a machine or a process that takes the material on one disk—with the standards and protocols of one vendor—and translates that into code that is understandable. The disk isn't converted, the material is. See *conversion.*

disk crash: the failure of a disk causing a system to malfunction. This breakdown is usually a result of destructive contact between the read/write head of the disk drive and the surface of the disk.

disk drive: a mechanism for moving a disk pack or a magnetic disk and controlling its movements: a device that reads and writes data to and from a disk.

diskette: see *floppy disk.*

diskette 1: any diskette that is the medium used to record single-density information on one side.

diskette 2: any diskette that is the medium used to record single-density information on both sides.

diskette 2D: any diskette that is the physical medium used to record double-density information on both sides.

diskette drive: see *disk drive.*

diskette-formatted tape: a tape that is formatted so that it can be read by a data converter unit, which transfers the data written on it to a diskette.

diskette hard-holes: small mylar doughnuts affixed to the center hole of a diskette for additional protection.

diskette-only feature: a special feature or a specific feature that, through macroinstructions or microinstructions on diskette, either: (1) activates, suppresses, or adapts product application functions; or (2) simulates functions to enhance the capability, storage capacity, or performance of the product. For example, a feature on diskette that enables a processor to execute the instructions of some other machine.

diskette storage: storage on magnetic diskettes.

diskette storage device: a direct-access storage device that uses diskettes as the storage medium.

diskette storage drive: a device that rotates diskette disks in a diskette storage device. Deprecated term for *diskette storage device*.

disk file: an associated set of records of the same format, identified by a unique label.

disk file controller: a unit that controls the transfer of data between a number of magnetic disk units and main memory.

diskless disk: see *E-disks*.

disk operating system: see *DOS*.

disk overlay: deprecated term for *overlay*.

disk pack:
(1) a removable assembly of magnetic disks. (B)
(2) a portable set of flat, circular recording surfaces used in a disk storage device. (A)

disk sector: a 512-byte area of disk storage. Each disk sector contains two 256-5 byte disk data blocks.

disk sorting: a sort program that utilizes disk-type memory for auxiliary storage during sorting.

disk storage device: see *disk drive*.

disk storage drive: see *disk drive*.

disk storage module: a nonremovable assembly of magnetic disks serviced by two access mechanisms.

disk system: all components needed for disk storage, including the disk, disk drive, read/write heads, control electronics, and software.

disk unit: see *magnetic disk unit*. (B)

disk volume: a disk pack or part of a disk storage module.

dismount: deprecated term for *demount*.

disorderly closedown: ceasing a system because of device error when it is not possible to shut down in an orderly fashion.

disperse: pertaining to the distribution of items from an input record to locations in one or more output records.

dispersed intelligence: synonymous with *distributed intelligence*.

dispersion: synonymous with *NOT-AND operation*.

DISP:
(1) see *displacement*.
(2) see *display*.

displacement (D) (DISP): the distance from the beginning of a record, block, or segment to the beginning of a particular field. Synonym for *relative address*.

display (DISP) (DSPL):
(1) a visual presentation of data. (A) (B)
(2) in word processing, a device for visual presentation of information on any temporary character-imaging device.
(3) loosely, a display device. (B)
(4) see *cathode-ray tube display*.
(5) see also *display device, raster display device*.

display background: see *static display image*.

display-based word-processing equipment: word-processing equipment that can electronically display text and other graphics, using, for example, a cathode ray tube (CRT), light emitting diode (LED), or gas plasma display. Cf. *non-display-based word-processing equipment*.

display buffer memory: the number of characters held in storage for immediate display on a screen.

display center: the position on a display screen for duplicating data or information to an advantage.

display character generator: on a CRT display device, a hardware unit that converts the digital code for a character into signals that cause the electron beam to create the character on the screen.

display column: in computer graphics, all display positions that constitute a full-length vertical line on the display surface. Synonymous with *addressable vertical positions*. Cf. *display line*.

display cycle time: in computer graphics, the minimum time interval between the starts of successive display cycles.

display device:
(1) an output unit that gives a visual representation of data. (A) (B)

(2) in computer graphics, a device capable of presenting display elements on a display surface; for example, a cathode ray tube, plotter, microfilm viewer, printer.

(3) see *character display device, raster display device.*

display drum: a magnetic, digital, data buffer storage drum that stores data to be used for display on a visual unit.

display element: in computer graphics, a basic graphic element that can be used to construct a display image; for example, a dot, a line segment, a character. Synonymous with *graphic primitive, output primitive.*

display foreground: see *dynamic display image.*

display frame:

(1) in computer graphics, an area in storage in which a display image can be recorded.

(2) in computer micrographics, an area on a microform in which a display image can be recorded.

display image: in computer graphics, a collection of display elements or display groups that are represented together at any one time in a display space. See *dynamic display image, static display image.* See also *screen image.*

display line: in computer graphics, all display positions that constitute a full-length horizontal line on a display surface. Synonymous with *addressable horizontal positions.* Cf. *display column.*

display panel: synonymous for *panel.*

display RAM: the RAM are of memory (separate from main memory), which stores information later shown on a video display. The information is not kept in memory once the power has been turned off.

display register: a register with corresponding indicators on a display panel; used for displaying the contents of the register chosen by the display switch.

display screen: the visual portion of a monitor.

display space: in computer graphics, that portion of a display surface available for a display image. The display space may be all or part of the display surface. Synonymous with *operating space.* See also *image storage space.*

display station: a device for indicating alphanumeric information in a communications or computer system.

display tube: a tube, usually a cathode-ray tube, used to display data.

disposition: the status of a file after being closed by a program.

dissector: synonymous with *image dissector.*

distributed database (DBM): a database whose data is stored in various computer systems.

distributed (data) processing (DDP): data processing in which some or all of the processing, storage, and control functions, in addition to input-output functions, are situated in different places and connected by transmission facilities, i.e., in two or more computers. See also *local area networks, parallel processing, remote-access data processing.*

distributed function:

(1) the use of programmable terminals, controllers, and other devices to perform operations that were previously done by the processing unit, such as managing data links, controlling devices, and formatting data.

(2) functions, such as network management, processing, and error recovery operations, that are dispersed among the nodes of a network, as opposed to functions that are concentrated at a central location.

distributed intelligence: deprecated term for *distributed data processing, distributed function.*

distributed intelligence microcomputer system: a multiprocessing technique where tasks assigned to the distribution system remain fixed.

distributed logic: systems where logic, or intelligence, is distributed within the system instead of being located centrally, that is, word processing systems linking intelligent terminals to make shared use of other resources, such as storage, printer.

distributed processing: a technique for implementing a set of information processing functions within multiple physically separate physical devices.

distributed system: see *distributed data processing, distributed function.*

dithering:
(1) in a color display, a combination of juxtaposed different-colored dots that creates an illusion of still another single color.
(2) in a black and white display, juxtaposing black and white dots in varying ratios so that groups of these dots create an illusion of a gray scale tone.

divided slit scan: a device, in OCR, that scans an input character at given intervals to obtain its horizontal and vertical components; consists of a narrow column of photoelectric cells.

division: the parts into which a COBOL program is organized; identification division provides information to identify the source and object programs.

division header: the COBOL words that indicate the beginning of a particular division of a COBOL program. The four division headers are: identification division, environment division, data division, and procedure division.

divisor (DR): in a division operation, the number or quantity by which the dividend is divided. (A) (B)

DL:
(1) see *data link.*
(2) see *data list.*

DLE: see *data-link escape character.* (A)

DLT: see *decision logic table.*

DM:
(1) see *data management.*
(2) see *decimeter.*

dm: see *decimeter.*

DMA: see *direct memory access.*

DMAC (DEE mack): see *direct memory access channel.*

DMP: see *dump.*

DN: see *data name.*

DO: a programming word in high-level languages preceding a statement(s) to be executed when a particular condition is met.

document:
(1) a data medium and the data recorded on it, that generally has permanence and that can be read by man or machine. (A)
(2) a unified collection of information pertaining to a specific subject or related subjects.
(3) in word processing, a collection of one or more lines of text that can be named and stored as a separate entity.

documentation:
(1) the management of documents, which may include the actions of identifying, acquiring, processing, storing, and disseminating them. (B)
(2) a collection of documents on a given subject. (A) (B)

document fulfillment agency: an agency providing copies of documents ordered by users. Requests are generated following an on-line search and transmitted to the agency via a computer network.

document handling: a procedure system or process for loading, feeding, transporting, and unloading a cut-form document submitted for character recognition.

document leading edge: the edge which is first encountered during the reading process in character recognition, and whose relative position shows the direction of travel.

document mark: in micrographics, an optical mark, within the recording area and outside the image on a roll of microfilm, used for counting images or film frames automatically. Synonymous with *blip.* (A)

document reader: apparatus for sensing and interpreting the codes found in punched cards or printed materials.

document reference edge: in character recognition, a specified document edge with respect to which the alignment of characters is defined. (A)

document retrieval: a system for indexing, searching and identifying documents, from which information is requested.

docuterm: a word or phrase used to describe the contents within a document and can be used in future retrieval as a data name.

dog: a digit in the hexadecimal numbering system that is equivalent in value to 13; written as X'D'.

DO group: in PL/1, a sequence of statements headed by a DO statement and ended by its corresponding END statement, used for control purposes.

DO loop: in FORTRAN, repetitive execution of the same statement or statements by use of a DO statement.

domain (D):
(1) in a network, the resources that are under the control of one or more associated host processors.
(2) the network resources that are under the control of a particular system services control point (SSCP).

domain tip: a memory device using thin films for creating magnetic domains for storing digital data.

donor: an element introduced in small quantities as an impurity to a semi-conducting material.

do-nothing operation: synonym for *no-operation instruction.* (A) (B)

dopant: a chemical impurity added to a semiconductor material to change its electrical characteristics.

doped: subjected to *dopant.*

do protocol: slang, to perform an interaction with something or someone that evolves from a clearly defined procedure.

dorfed up: slang, damage to a file rendering its contents useless or questionable. Synonymous with *hosed up.*

DOS (disk operating system): a program that controls the computer's transfer of data to and from a hard or floppy disk. Frequently combined with the main operating system. Most commonly used to refer to the various versions of PC-DOS and MS-DOS, which are almost identical. PC-DOS is used exclusively by the IBM PC, where MS-DOS is available for any IBM-PC compatible.

DO statement: a statement used to group a number of statements in a procedure.

dot addressable: the capability on a video display screen or a dot matrix printer to specify individual dots that form character images.

dot chart: synonymous with *scatter plot.*

dot command: a command for defining the format of a line.

dot graphics: nonalphanumeric information, such as pictures, formed from closely packed visual dots on a CRT screen or a dot matrix printer.

dot leaders: a string of periods.

dot matrix:
(1) in computer graphics, a two-dimensional pattern of dots used for constructing a display image. This type of matrix can be used to represent characters by dots.
(2) in word processing, a pattern of dots used to form characters. This term normally refers to a small section of the set of addressable points; for example, a representation of characters by dots.
(3) in micrographics, a method of generating characters using a matrix of dots so that the combination of energized dots produces a human-readable character. (B)

dot matrix character formation: a means for forming character images by the use of dots.

dot matrix printer: synonymous with *wire matrix printer.*

dot printer: synonym for *matrix printer.* (A)

dots per inch: see *dpi.*

double buffering: where two buffers hold data being transferred from one unit to another.

double card: a special card that is approximately twice the length of a general-purpose paper card. A double card usually consists of two separable general-purpose paper cards. (A)

double-check: to position the pointer over an object or at a specific location and then click twice rapidly. Double-clicking with the left mouse button opens a file or a directory, or starts an application.

double-click: a means to position the pointer on an object, and then to press and release a button twice in succession without moving the button.

double-dabble: a means for converting binary numbers to their decimal equivalents by doubling the bit to the far left, adding the next bit, doubling the sum, and so on until the sum contains the rightmost bit.

double-density: an approach used to increase bit density on a magnetic storage medium to twice the amount so additional information may be stored in the same amount of area.

double-ended queue: a list of variable length, whose content may be changed by adding or removing items at either end. (A)

double-entry card: a particular punched card designed to hold data for entry into two different accounts, that is, a card containing both payroll and labor distribution information.

double-length register: two registers that function as a single register. Each register may be individually accessed. For example, a double-length register may be used in exact multiplication for storing the result, in exact division for storing the partial quotient and remainder, in character manipulation for shifting character strings, and for accessing the left or right portion. Synonymous with *double register.* (A) (B)

double precision: pertaining to the use of two computer words to represent a number in accordance with the required precision. (A) (B)

double-precision arithmetic: computations made within a computer that utilize twice as many bits as normal calculations for ensuring a greater degree of accuracy.

double-pulse recording: phase modulation recording magnetized in opposite polarity with unmagnetized regions on each end. A zero may be represented by a cell composed of a negative region followed by a positive region, and a one by a positive region followed by a negative region, or vice versa. (A) (B)

double punch: more than one numeric punch in any one column of a punched card.

doubler: an internal component that doubles a given digit and is used in the multiplication routine.

double-rail logic: pertaining to self-timing asynchronous circuits in which each logic variable is represented by two electrical lines which together can take on three meaningful states: zero, one, and undecided. (A)

double register: synonym for *double-length register.* (A) (B)

double-sided disk: a disk with both surfaces available for the storage of data.

double-sided media: storage media that hold data on both surfaces.

double strike: in word processing, typing each character twice, which gives a darker, more solid impression. It is useful for preparing copy that will be printed.

doublet: a byte composed of two binary elements. Synonymous with *two-bit byte.* (A) (B)

double-word (DW): a contiguous sequence of bits or characters that comprises two computer words and is capable of being addressed as a unit. (A)

DO variable: in FORTRAN, a variable, specified in a DO statement, which is initialized or incremented prior to each execution of the statement or statements within a DO loop. It is used to control the number of times the statements within the DO loop are executed.

DO-WHILE: a programming statement in a high-level language that aids the instructions in a loop to perform while a specific condition exists, as while variable x is less than 10.

down: a computer is "down" when it is not running. It may be shut down for maintenance, there may be a hardware failure, or the operating system may have been disarranged by a runaway program.

downconverter: a type of converter which is characterized by the frequency of the output signal being lower than the frequency of the input signal. It is the converse of an "up" converter.

down-line loading: when a computer automatically updates a file on another computer using data communications.

down loaded: a programming method in which the program to be used in a remote terminal is sent down the line from central location to that terminal and stored there for local use.

download: to transfer files or information from one computer to another, or from a computer to a peripheral device such as a printer.

downtime: the time interval during which a functional unit is inoperable due to a fault. (A)

downward compatibility: the capability of an advanced system to interact with a lesser advanced one.

downward reference: in an overlay structure, a reference made from a segment to a segment lower in the path, that is, farther from the root segment.

DP:

(1) see *data processing*.

(2) see *data processor*.

DPC: data-processing center. See *computer center*.

dpi (dots per inch): a unit used to measure the resolution of a printer. The more dots per inch, the better the resolution.

DR: see *divisor*.

draft copy: in word processing, a printout prepared for approval or editing. See also *edited copy, final copy*.

drag: to position a pointer on something, press and hold a button, move the button, and release the button. When released, the button will confirm a selection or move an object to a new location.

dragon: slang, a program that is not invoked but instead used by the system to perform various secondary tasks.

DRAM: see *dynamic random access memory*.

DRAW: direct read after write. The operation where data recorded on a video disk is read immediately after being recorded so as to detect errors. These errors cannot be erased or written over on this disk, but are made at a new location. The computer is then directed to the new location so that the section with the error is bypassed.

DRCS: see *dynamically redefinable character set*.

drift: a change in the output of a circuit that occurs slowly.

drift error: in analog computers, an error caused by a drift.

drifting characters: see *sign and currency symbol characters*.

drive: the turntable that drives magnetic disks around and around, while the information on them is read. See *disk storage drive, tape drive*.

driver:

(1) a program that controls a peripheral unit connected on line.

(2) a program that the computer uses to direct the operation of a peripheral device, such as a printer or scanner.

drop-dead halt: a machine halt from which there is no recovery.

drop folder: a shared folder with access privileges that doesn't permit network users to open it but does allow network users to place files or folders into it.

drop-in:

(1) the reading of a spurious signal whose amplitude is greater than a predetermined percentage of the nominal signal. (A)

(2) an error in the storage into or in the retrieval from a magnetic storage device, revealed by the reading of a binary character not previously recorded. Drop-ins are usually caused by defects in, or the presence of particles on the magnetic surface layer.

drop out:

(1) in magnetic tape a recorded signal whose amplitude is less than a predetermined percentage of a reference signal.

(2) in data communication, a momentary loss in signal, usually due to the effect of noise or system malfunction.

(3) a failure to read a bit from magnetic storage. (A)

drum drive: a mechanism for moving a magnetic drum and controlling its movement. (B)

drum printer: a line printer in which the type is mounted on a rotating drum that contains a full character set for each printing position. (A)

drum scanning: in facsimile transmission, scanning where the object to be imaged, is wrapped around a drum, which then rotates past an optical sensing unit. Synonymous with *cylinder scanning*.

dry running: the examination of the logic and coding of a program from a flowchart and written instructions, and record the results of each step of the operation before running the program on the computer.

DS: see *data set (2)*.

DSCB: see *data-set control block*.

DSDD: double-sided double-density.

DSDT: see *data-set definition table*.

DSD table: see *data-set definition table*.

DSECT: see *dummy control section*.

DSK: see *disc*.

DSN: see *data-set name*.

DSNAME: see *data-set name*.

DSP: see *digital signal processing*.

DSPL: see *display*.

DSS:

(1) see *decision support system*.

(2) see *dynamic support system*.

DSSD: double-sided single-density.

DT: see *data terminal*.

dual channel controller: controller enabling reading from, and writing to, a unit to occur simultaneously.

dual density: a feature that allows a program to use a tape unit in 800- or 1600-byte-per-inch recording.

dual disk drive: a floppy disk system with two drive mechanisms and recording heads, permitting additional storage capacity and disk-to-disk data transfer and back-up.

dual in-line package (DIP): a standard integrated circuit or chip, enclosed in a molded plastic unit. Consists of two parallel rows of pins connected to the circuit board. Such circuits are the foundation of integrated circuit boards.

dual intensity: printers or display units that can produce symbols in regular and bold-faced formats.

dual operation: of a boolean operation, another boolean operation whose result, when it is performed on operands that are the negation of the operands of the first boolean operation, is the negation of the result of the first boolean operation. For example, disjunction is the dual operation of conjunction. (A) (B)

dual port memory: a memory unit having dual data and address connections suitable for low-level communication.

dual processor system: a configuration including two central processors, each

receiving the same input and executing the same routines. Synonymous with *dual system*.

dual system: synonymous with *dual processor system*.

ducol-punched card: a punched card with 12 rows of punching positions in each column, that is, zero through 9, an X and Y, representing numerals zero to 99 using multiple punching in each column and using a punch or no punch in the X and Y positions, lower-value digit positions are the ten digit, higher positions, the units.

dumb terminal: a terminal with no independent processing ability of its own which can only carry out operations when connected to a computer.

dummy: pertaining to the characteristic of having the appearance of a specified thing but not having the capacity to function as such: for example, a dummy character, a dummy plug, or a dummy statement. (A)

dummy address: an artificial address used for illustration or instruction purposes.

dummy argument:

(1) in FORTRAN, a variable within a FUNCTION or SUBROUTINE statement or statement function definition, with which actual arguments from the calling program or function references are associated.

(2) in PL/1, temporary storage that is created automatically to hold the value of an argument that is constant, an operational expression, a variable whose attributes differ from those specified for the corresponding parameter in a known declaration, or an argument enclosed in parentheses.

dummy check: a check consisting of adding all the digits during dumping, and verifying the sum when retransferring.

dummy control section (DSECT): a control section that an assembler can use to format an area of storage without producing any object code. Synonymous with *dummy section*.

dummy data set:

(1) a data set for which operations such as disposition processing, input-output operations, and allocation are bypassed.

(2) data sets, created by the programmer and used during the testing phase of program validation services, that represent the data sets that the program would use during normal execution.

dummy file: a nonexistent file to which a program "thinks" it is writing output data. Synonymous with *null file.*

dummy instruction: an item of data in the form of an instruction that is inserted in a set of instructions, but is not intended to be executed. (A) (B)

dummy load: transferring to storage of a program without execution so as to determine if all specifications and requirements were met.

dummy parameter: a parameter meaning nothing, but included in a command or instruction because the system expects it. Synonymous with *null parameter.*

dummy record: meaningless information.

dummy section: synonym for *dummy control section.*

dummy variable: a symbol inserted at definition time, which will be replaced at a future time by the actual variable.

dump (DMP):
(1) data that have been dumped. (B)
(2) to write the contents of a storage, or of part of a storage, usually from an internal storage to an external medium, for a specific purpose such as to allow other use of the storage as a safeguard against faults or errors, or in connection with debugging. (B)
(3) see *change dump, disaster dump, dynamic dump, postmortem dump, selective dump, snapshot dump, static dump.* (A)

dump and restart: approaches used to ensure that a run is satisfactorily restarted following a dump.

dump check: a check used to ensure that a dump has been correctly made or properly restarted.

dump point: that step in a program at which a dump is started.

dump program: a printout that lists the contents of registers and main storage locations.

dump routine: a utility routine that dumps. (A) (B)

duodecimal:
(1) characterized by a selection, choice, or condition that has 12 possible different values or states. (B)
(2) pertaining to a fixed-radix numeration system having a radix of 12. (A) (B)

DUP: see *duplicate.*

duplex: in data communication, pertaining to a simultaneous two-way independent transmission in both directions. Synonymous with *full duplex.* (A) See also *duplex transmission.* Cf. *half-duplex.*

duplex console: a switchover console connecting two or more computers for on-line control.

duplexed system: a system with two distinct and separate sets of facilities, each of which is capable of assuming the system function while the other assumes a standby status. Usually, the sets are identical.

duplex operation: a mode of operation of a data link in which data may be transmitted simultaneously in both directions over two channels. Synonymous with *both-way operation, full-duplex operation.*

duplex transmission: data transmission in both directions at the same time.

duplicate (DUP): to copy from a source to a destination that has the same physical form as the source; for example, to punch new punched cards with the same pattern of holes as an original punched card. Synonymous with *reproduce.* (A) (B)

duplicate mass storage volume: see *duplicate volume.*

duplicate volume: an inactive mass storage volume that has the same identification as another mass storage volume and is not a copy.

duplication check: a check based on the consistency of two independent performances of the same task. (A)

duplication factor: in assembler programming, a value that indicates the number of times that the data specified immediately following the duplication factor is to be generated.

duplicator: a machine that uses direct litho duplicating, offset litho duplicating, spirit (or other fluid) duplicating, or stencil duplicating to produce multiple copies from a master. See also *duplicator with semiautomatic master change.*

duplicator with semiautomatic master change: a duplicator in which masters are fed individually by hand into a loading device, are then introduced automatically to the attachment device, and are finally removed, either automatically or by hand.

duration: see *assemble duration, compile duration, run duration, translate duration.*

DVC: see *device.*

DVST: see *direct view storage tube.*

DW:
(1) see *daisy wheel.*
(2) see *double-word.*

dwell: a programmed time delay of variable duration.

DWIM: do what I mean. Slang, being able to guess, sometimes correctly, what result was intended when given bogus input.

dyadic boolean operation: a boolean operation on two and only two operands. (A) Synonymous with *binary boolean operation.*

dyadic operation: an operation on two and only two operands. (A) (B)

dyadic operator: an operator that represents an operation on two and only two operands. The dyadic operators are AND, equivalence, exclusion, exclusive OR, inclusion, NAND, NOR, OR. Synonymous with *binary operator.* (A) (B)

dynamic: occurring at the time of execution.

dynamic accuracy: accuracy determined with a time-varying output.

dynamic address translation (DAT): a computer's ability to convert a relative address into an absolute address within memory during the running of a program.

dynamic address translator: a hardware unit for converting a virtual address into a real address.

dynamic allocation:
(1) an allocation technique in which the resources assigned for the execution of computer programs are determined

by criteria applied at the moment of need.
(2) assignment of system resources to a program at the time the program is executed rather than at the time it is loaded into main storage. See also *dynamic storage allocation.*

dynamically redefinable character set (DRCS): a method allowing a terminal to be used alternately to display different character sets, such as English, German, French. See also *composition coding.*

dynamic buffer allocation: synonym for *dynamic buffering.*

dynamic buffering:
(1) a dynamic allocation of buffer storage.
(2) allocating storage for buffers as they are needed for incoming data during program execution.

dynamic check: a test of a process conducted by subjecting the apparatus, process, or function to the rigors of its anticipated operational environment.

dynamic data set definition: the process of defining a data set and allocating auxiliary storage space for it during job-step execution rather than before job-step execution.

dynamic data structure: a data structure that may expand and contract during runtime.

dynamic debug: debug programs designed for interactive debugging of user-written programs.

dynamic device reconfiguration (DDR): a facility that allows a demountable volume to be moved, and repositioned if necessary, without abnormally terminating the job or repeating the initial program load procedure.

dynamic display image: in computer graphics, that part of a display image that can be frequently changed by the user during a particular application. Synonymous with *foreground display image.* Cf. *static display image.*

dynamic dump: dumping performed during the execution of a computer program, usually under the control of that computer program. (A) (B)

dynamic instructions: the sequence of machine steps performed by the computer in real-time or simulated environment.

dynamicizer: synonym for *parallel-to-serial converter, serializer.* (A) (B)

dynamic loading: the loading of routines into main storage as needed by an executing program. Dynamically loaded routines are not part of the executing program's load module.

dynamic memory: synonymous with *dynamic storage.*

dynamic memory allocation: the time-varying allocation of a limited main memory among competing processes according to some system-dependent strategy.

dynamic parameter: synonym for *program-generated parameter.* (A) (B)

dynamic port allocation: any device able to allocate access ports to incoming channels automatically in response to operating conditions.

dynamic printout: a printout of data occurring as one of the sequential operations during the machine run.

dynamic programming: in operations research, a procedure for optimization of a multistage problem solution wherein a number of decisions are available at each stage of the process. (B) Cf. *convex programming, integer programming, linear programming, mathematical programming, nonlinear programming, quadratic programming.* (A)

dynamic RAM: see *dynamic random access memory.*

dynamic random access memory (DRAM): developed in 1986 in Belgium, high-performance, premium chips that boost what can be crammed onto tiny microchips, thus increasing their potential and opening the way to a new generation of super powerful computers. Cf. *static RAM.*

dynamic relocation: a process that assigns new absolute addresses to a computer program during execution so that the program may be executed from a different area of main storage. (A)

dynamic response: the behavior of the output of a device as a function of the input, with respect to time.

dynamic scheduling: scheduling that changes with the different demands that are made on the system rather than being fixed as in conventional applications.

dynamic stop: synonym for *breakpoint halt.* (A) (B)

dynamic storage:
(1) a device storing data in a manner that permits the data to move or vary with time such that the specified data are not always available for recovery. Magnetic drum and disk storage are dynamic non-volatile storage. An acoustic delay line is a dynamic volatile storage. (A)
(2) the available storage left within the partition after the task set is loaded.
(3) synonymous with *dynamic memory.*

dynamic storage allocation (DYSTAL): a storage allocation technique in which the storage assigned to computer programs and data is determined by criteria applied at the moment of need. (A) (B)

dynamic subroutine: a subroutine in skeletal form with regard to certain features, such as the number of repetitions, decimal point position, or item size, that are selected or adjusted in accordance with the data-processing requirements. (A)

dynamic support system (DSS): an interactive debugging facility that allows authorized maintenance personnel to monitor and analyze events and alter data.

dynamic test set: an item of test equipment used for testing the performance of modems and other line equipment, permitting the operator to create a wide range of operating conditions to test the efficiency of the equipment at different operating speeds and for various activities.

dynaturtle: in logo language, a dynamic cursor instead of a static one. The cursor is called a turtle, which is used to produce graphics. Commands to the dynaturtle specify a change in velocity and acceleration during the creation of a drawing. The path of the turtle becomes a line of the drawing. See also *turtle.*

DYSTAL: see *dynamic storage allocation.*

E:

(1) see *error*.

(2) see *execute*.

(3) see *execution*.

(4) see *exponent*.

(5) see *expression*.

EA: see *effective address*.

EAE: see *extended arithmetic element*.

EAM: see *electrical accounting machine*. (A)

EAROM: electrically alterable read-only memory. A type of ROM that is easily erased and reprogrammed without having to be removed from the circuit board.

easy: the digit found in the hexadecimal numbering system that is equivalent in value to 14. Usually written as X'E'.

easy access: a control panel that is used to adjust the keyboard so that the pointer can be controlled from a numeric keypad, to type keyboard shortcuts without having to press the keys at the same time, and to type very slowly.

EBCDIC: extended binary-coded decimal interchange code. A coded character set consisting of eight-bit coded characters.

EBR: see *electron-beam recording*. (A)

ECB: see *event-control block*.

ECC: see *error checking and correction*.

Eccles-Jordan trigger: a bistable multivibrator where the output of one section is coupled into the input of the other section, making it capable of storing one bit of information.

echoplex: low-speed data transmission usually used between a keyboard unit and the computer. When the key is struck on the keyboard, a character is sent over the line and echoed back to the sending unit, where it is shown on a screen or printed.

ECMA: European Computer Manufacturer's Association.

EC pads: the plated areas around a chip site that are in series with I/O circuits of the chips. Each pad provides a wiring function where two discrete wires may be bonded, plus a delete area for repairs, ECs, and test probing.

ED: see *editor*.

edge: see *document reference edge, reference edge, stroke edge*. (A)

edge card connector: a device that connects printed circuit cards to a motherboard or other units, such as an input-output device hooked up through cables.

edge-coated card: a card that has been strengthened by treating one or more edges. (A)

edge-notched card: a card in which notches representing data are punched around the edges. Usually long needles are used to select a specified set. (B)

edge-punched card: a card that is punched with hole patterns in tracks along the edges. Usually the hole patterns are in punch tape code. Synonymous with *verge-punched card*. (A)

EDI: see *editor*.

E-disks: emulated disk. Software packages, often accompanied by a random-access memory expansion board. A diskless disk whose primary function is to modify certain aspects of the operating system (the DOS program that actually runs the computer), telling it when and how to print something, what to display on the screen, and how to deal with its disk drives. Synonymous with *C-drives, hyperdrives, memory disks, pseudodrives, RAM disks*.

edit:

(1) to prepare data for a later operation. Editing may include the rearrangement or the addition of data, the deletion of unwanted data, format control, code conversion, and the application of standard processes such as zero suppression. (A) (B)

(2) to enter, modify, or delete data.

edit-directed transmission: in PL/1, the type of stream-oriented transmission in which data appears as a continuous stream of characters and for which a format list is required to specify the editing desired for the associated data list.

edited copy: in word processing, a draft copy marked up with corrections or amendments. See also *final copy*.

editing character: in COBOL, a single character or a fixed two-character combination used to create proper formats for output reports.

editing sessions: a period of time beginning when the editor is invoked and ending when the editor has completed processing.

editing symbol: in micrographics, a symbol on microfilm that is readable without magnification and that provides cutting, loading, and other preparation instructions. (A)

editing terminal: a terminal for preparing text and graphics by an information provider.

edit menu: a menu that is available in most programs and lists editing commands.

edit mode: in systems with time sharing, an entry mode in which a user may issue subcommands to enter, modify, delete, or rearrange data.

editor (ED) (EDI) (EDT): see *linkage editor.* (A)

editor program:
(1) a computer program designed to perform such functions as the rearrangement, modification, and deletion of data in accordance with prescribed rules. Cf. *linkage editor.* (A)
(2) a program designed to create and modify text files.

EDP: see *electronic data processing.*

EDPM: electronic data-processing machine.

EDSAC: electronic delay storage automatic computer; the first "stored-program computer."

EDT: see *editor.*

edulcorate:
(1) to improve by eliminating worthless information.
(2) to weed out.

EEPROM: electrically erasable, programmable read-only memory. Synonymous with *E²-PROM.* See *erasable programmable read-only memory.*

effective address (EA):
(1) the contents of the address part of an effective instruction. (B)
(2) the address that is derived by applying any specified indexing or indirect addressing rules to the specified address and that is actually used to identify the current operand. (A)

effective byte: the byte actually accessed in an operation on a single byte or byte string.

effective double-word: the double-word accessed in a double-word operation.

effective half-word: the half-word accessed in a half-word operation.

effective instruction: an instruction that may be executed without modification. (A) (B)

effective operand address: an address obtained at the time of execution by a computer giving the actual operand address.

effective speed: speed (less than rated) that can be sustained over a significant span of time and that reflects slowing effects such as those caused by control codes, timing codes, error detection, retransmission, tabbing, or hand keying.

effective transmission speed: the rate at which information is processed by a transmission facility, expressed as the average rate over a significant time interval; expressed as average characters per unit of time, or average bits per unit of time.

effective word: the word accessed in an operation on a single word.

effective word location: the storage location pointed to by the effective virtual address of a word-addressing instruction.

effector: apparatus used to produce a desired response, from a shift in its input, upon another unit where the end result is needed.

EFTS: see *electronic funds transfer system(s).*

EGA: see *enhanced graphics adapter.*

egoless programming: a structured formula-oriented approach in program writing; used to standardize programs.

EIA: Electronic Industries Association. An association of electronic manufacturers that maintains standards in electronic product areas.

EIA interface: see *RS-232C.*

eight bit: word size.

eight-bit byte: synonym for *octet.* (A) (B)

80 column display standard: a terminal and associated transmission system permitting a display of information containing 80 columns of characters for each page.

EISA: Extended Industry Standard Architecture, a bus architecture for advanced IBM PCs and compatibles.

EITHER/OR: synonymous with *OR ELSE*.

either-or operation: deprecated term for *disjunction*. (A) (B)

either-way communication: synonymous with *two-way alternate communication*.

eject: to remove a disk from a disk drive.

elastic buffer (store): a buffer store holding a variable amount of data.

electrical accounting machine: pertaining to data-processing equipment that is predominantly electromechanical such as a keypunch, mechanical sorter, collator, and tabulator.

electrical interface: the electrical requirements for communicating between two units and encompassing the signals that must pass between the units for transferring control or message information.

electrically alterable memory: a memory unit whose contents are revised with electrical signals.

electrically erasable read-only memory: see *EAROM*.

electrical schematic: a diagram representing all the circuit elements, utilizing symbols and interconnecting lines.

electroluminescent display (ELD): the flat-panel screen display used in laptop computers.

electromagnetic delay line: a delay line whose operation is based on the time or propagation of electromagnetic waves through distributed or lumped capacitance and inductance. (A)

electromechanical one-shot: synonymous with *Kipp relay*.

electron-beam recording (EBR): in micrographics, a specific method of computer output microfilming in which a beam of electrons is directed onto an energy-sensitive microfilm. (A)

electronic: any circuit or network using solid state or vacuum tube active units.

electronic accounting machines: synonymous with *tabulating equipment.*

electronic beam recording: using an electron beam for storing and reading information on a target.

electronic bulletin board: an electronic call-up service that allows users to compose and store messages to be retrieved by other users later.

electronic cash register: a cash register in which electronic circuitry replaces electromechanical parts.

electronic control: utilizing electronic units for industrial and consumer control applications.

electronic crosspoint: a microelectronic unit used in electronic exchanges for handling voice and data traffic.

electronic data processing (EDP): data processing largely performed by electronic devices.

electronic data-processing system: a machine system that receives, stores, operates on, and records data without the intermediate use of tabulating cards, and which possesses an ability to store internally at least some instructions for data-processing functions, and the means for locating and controlling access to data stored internally.

electronic delay storage automatic computer: see *EDSAC*.

electronic digital computer: a device using electronic circuitry for performing arithmetic and logic operations by means of an internally or externally stored program of machine instructions.

electronic filing: in word processing, the way processors store information electronically on disks, cards, or tapes.

electronic funds transfer system(s) (EFTSs): a loose description of computerized systems that process financial transactions or process information about financial transactions, or effect an exchange of value between two parties.

Electronic Industries Association: see *EIA*.

electronic information services: accessing bibliographic, full text, or numerical information on hundreds of subjects. Synonymous with *banks* and *on-line databases.*

electronic mail (E-mail): messages sent by a user and retrieved by another through an electronic service system, most often via telephone lines or radio transmission. Each user needs to know the other's identification number.

electronic mail box: a system allowing messages to be placed into a storage medium, such as a digital computer, enabling a specific subscriber to retrieve the message when he or she next logs onto the system.

electronic mailing: in word processing, the ability of processors to transmit documents over cables or phone lines.

electronic message system: communication via terminals in a communications network.

electronic multiplier: an all-electronic device for yielding the product of two variables.

electronic numerical integrator and calculator: see *ENIAC.*

electronic pen: synonymous with *light pen.*

electronic phone: an instrument that uses microprocessors, either in the unit itself or in the PBX, to allow use of advanced features.

electronic printer: any computer printer; a printer for units which hold a magnetic tape record of the text and reproduces it via digitized fonts.

electronic scales: microcomputer-based units with electronic weighing indicators that can handle numerous operations involved in static weighing and simple batching.

electronic spreadsheet: software that simulates a business or scientific worksheet where a user indicates data relationships. When data are altered, the program has the ability to instantly redetermine any related factors and to save all the information within memory.

electronic statistical machine: a sorter that can print and add data while storing.

electronic stylus: an input unit permitting images to be drawn, having the form of a light pen or a purely electronic unit used in conjunction with, for example, a graphics tablet.

electronic tutor: a teaching unit making use of instructions within the computer to help students achieve goals; with each student communicating directly with the computer via a terminal.

electronic whiteboards: devices enabling users to draw characters and graphics onto a board and print a copy (or multiple copies) of what has been written using optical sensors that transform the written data into printable image form.

electrosensitive printer: see *electrostatic printer.*

electrostatic printer: a unit for printing an optical image on paper, where dark and light areas of the original are represented by electrostatically charged and uncharged areas on the paper.

electrostatic storage: a storage device that uses electrically charged areas on a dielectric surface layer. (A) (B)

electrothermal printer: see *thermal printer.*

elegant: any efficiently written program utilizing the least possible amounts of main memory by decreasing the number of instructions needed to accomplish a variety of tasks.

ELEM: see *element.*

element (ELEM) (ELT):
(1) in a set, an object, entity, or concept having the properties that define a set. Synonymous with *member.* (A) (B)
(2) in PL/1, a single item of data as opposed to a collection of data items such as an array; a scalar item.
(3) the particular resource within a subarea that is identified by an element address.
(4) see *AND element, binary element, combination logic element, display element, exclusive -OR element, identity element, IF-AND-ONLY-IF element, IF-THEN element, inclusive-OR element, logic element, majority element, NAND element, NOR element, NOT element, NOT-IF-THEN element, picture element, sequential logic element.*

elementary gate: see *gate.*

elementary item: in COBOL, a data item that cannot logically be subdivided.

element expression: in PL/1, an expression whose evaluation yields an element value.

element string: see *binary element string.* (A)

element variable: in PL/1, a variable that represents an element; a scalar variable.

eleven punch: a punch in the second row from the top, on a Hollerith card. Synonymous with *X punch.* (A)

elimination factor: in information retrieval, the ratio obtained by dividing the number of documents that have not been retrieved by the total number of documents held within the file.

ELSE clause: that part of an IF statement used to specify the action to be performed if the comparison of operands on the IF statement is false.

ELT: see *element.*

EM: see *end-of-medium character.*

E-mail: see *electronic mail.*

embedded command: in word processing, one or more characters inserted in the text which do not print but, instead, instruct either the printer or the word processing program to perform a task.

embossment:

(1) a distortion of the surface of a document.

(2) in character recognition, the distance between the undistorted surface of a document and a specified part of a printed character. (A)

EMC: electromagnetic compatibility.

emergency maintenance: maintenance specifically intended to eliminate an existing fault, which makes continued production work unachievable. (A)

emergency maintenance time: time, usually unscheduled, used to perform emergency maintenance. (A)

emitter: a unit, used on punched card machines, giving timed pulses at regular intervals during a machine cycle.

empty medium: a data medium that does not contain data other than a frame of reference; for example, a preprinted form, tape punched only with feed holes, a magnetic tape that has been erased. (B)

empty set: a set that has no elements. Synonymous with *null set.* (A) (B)

empty shell: a room designed for a computer system.

empty statement: an allowable Pascal syntax, implying no action, that is created when two statement separators (such as a semicolon and END) are used consecutively. Sometimes needed when no action is required after a case label list.

empty string: synonymous with *numeric string.*

emulate: to imitate one system with another, primarily by hardware, so that the imitating system accepts the same data, executes the same computer programs, and achieves the same results as the imitated system. Cf. *simulate.* (A)

emulated disk: see *E-disks.*

emulation:

(1) the imitation of all or part of one computer system by another, primarily by hardware, so that the imitating computer system accepts the same data, executes the same programs, and achieves the same results as the imitated computer system.

(2) the use of programming techniques and special machine features to permit a computing system to execute programs written for another system.

(3) cf. *simulation.*

emulator:

(1) a device or computer program that emulates. (A)

(2) the combination of programming techniques and special machine features that permits a given computing system to execute programs written for another system. See also *integrated emulator.*

emulator generation: the process of assembling and link editing an emulator program into an operating system during system generation.

emulsion laser storage: a storage system using a controlled laser beam for exposing small units of a photosensitive area.

enable: restoration of a suppressed interrupt feature.

enabled:
(1) pertaining to a state of the processing unit that allows the occurrence of certain types of interruptions. Synonymous with *interruptible*.
(2) in PL/1, that state in which a particular on condition will result in a program interrupt.

enabled module: a module that can be interrupted at any time during its execution. When the interruption occurs, the enabled module waits for the external routine that interrupted it to complete its processing and then continues. Cf. *disabled module*.

enabled page fault: a page fault that occurs when I/O and external interruptions are allowed by the processing unit.

enabling signal: a signal that permits the occurrence of an event. (A)

encode:
(1) to convert data by the use of a code or a coded character set in such a manner that reconversion to the original form is possible. Encode is sometimes loosely used when complete reconversion is not possible. (B)
(2) cf. *decode*. (A) (B)
(3) see also *encrypt*.
(4) synonymous with *code*.

encoded point: in computer graphics, an addressable point in an image space.

encoded question: a question set up and encoded in an appropriate format for operating, programming, or conditioning a searching unit.

encoder:
(1) a device that encodes data. (B)
(2) a device that has a number of input lines of which not more than one at a time may carry a signal and a number of output lines of which any number may carry signals, there being a one-to-one correspondence between the combinations of output signals and input signals. (B)
(3) cf. *decoder*. (A) (B)

encoding law: regulations set for defining quantization levels and their relative values, in the process of pulse code modulation.

encrypt:
(1) to scramble data or convert it, prior to transmission, to a secret code that masks the meaning of the data to any unauthorized recipient. See also *encode*.
(2) to convert plaintext into ciphertext.

encryption: the process of concealing data from unauthorized users.

END: statement showing the end of a program.

end-around borrow: the action of transferring a borrow digit from the most significant digit place to the least significant digit place. (A) (B)

end-around carry: the action of transferring a carry digit from the most significant digit place to the least significant digit place. An end-around carry may be necessary when adding two negative numbers that are represented by their diminished radix complements. (A) (B)

end-around shift: a shift in which the data moved out of one end of the storing register are reentered into the other end. Synonymous with *circular shift*. (A)

end-data symbol: the representation showing that no more data will follow this symbol.

endless loop: the endless repetition of a series of instructions resulting from programming error, with no exit from the loop possible. An endless loop can only be stopped by canceling the program or resetting the computer system.

end mark: a signal or code showing termination of a unit of information.

end of address (EOA): one or more control characters transmitted on a line to indicate the end of nontext characters (for example, addressing characters).

end of block (EOB): a code that marks the end of a block of data.

end-of-data indicator: a code that signals that the last record of a consecutive data set has been read.

end-of-file mark (EOF): a code which signals that the last record of a file has been read.

end of form: the last print position, left or right side at the bottom of a form.

end-of-line marker (EOLM): the mechanism for indicating the end of a line. PASCAL returns a blank when this marker is read.

end-of-medium character (EM): a control character that may be used to identify the physical end of the data medium, the end of the used portion of the medium, or the end of the wanted portion of the data recorded on the medium. (A) (B)

end-of-message code (EOM): the specific character or sequence of characters that indicates the end of a message or record.

end-of-page indicator: a feature that halts the printer at the end of each completed page of output, permitting a user to handle paper, ribbon, or font changes manually.

end-of-procedure division: in COBOL, the physical position in a COBOL source program after which no further procedures appear.

end-of-record mark: the character that signifies the end of a record of a file; that is, a carriage return.

end-of-record word: the final word of a record on tape; having a unique bit configuration and used to define the end of a record in memory.

end-of-run: a routine for housekeeping just before a run is ended; may be used for rewinding tapes or printing out totals.

end-of-tape arrangement: a programmed routine used during the processing of the final tape in a multireel program.

end-of-tape mark (EOT): a mark on a magnetic tape used to indicate the end of the permissible recording area; for example, a photoreflective strip, a particular bit pattern. (A)

end-of-tape warning: a visible magnetic strip on magnetic tape indicating that a few feet, often five, of the tape remain available.

end-of-text character (ETX): a transmission control character used to terminate text. (A)

end-of-transmission-block character (ETB): a transmission control character used to indicate the end of a transmission block of data when data are divided into such blocks for transmission purposes. (B)

end-of-transmission character (EOT): a transmission control character used to indicate the conclusion of a transmission, which may have included one or more texts and any associated message headings. (A) (B)

end-of-transmission code: the specific character, or sequence of characters, that indicates termination of sending.

endorser: a feature on most magnetic-ink character readers (MICRs) that is an endorsement record for a bank after the document has been read.

end point: on a display device, the coordinate on the display surface to which a display writer is to be moved.

end sentinel: the character that signifies the end of a message or record.

END statement: a statement used to indicate the end of a procedure or the end of one or more DO loops

end-use device: a device, such as a printer, that provides the final output of an operation without further processing.

end user (EU):
(1) the ultimate source or destination of information flowing through a system.
(2) a person, process, program, device, or system that employs a user-application network for the purpose of data processing and information exchange.

end-user device: a device such as a printer that provides the final output of an operation without further processing.

end value: a value used for comparison with a count, index, and so on, to determine if a certain condition has been met.

engineering improvement time: machine time set aside for installing and testing modifications to a system.

ENGLISH: the source code of a program found at times in any language, as opposed to BINARY.

enhanced function: hardware and software that have been upgraded and which can now perform at a more sophisticated level than earlier.

enhanced graphics adapter (EGA): a video display board capable of producing a high resolution monochrome or color display.

enhanced keyboard: the current IBM-PC keyboard, with 12 function keys.

enhancement: any improvement in hardware and/or software.

ENIAC: electronic numerical integrator and calculator; the first "electronic digital computer."

enlarger printer: apparatus that projects an enlarged image from microfilm, and develops and fixes the image on hardcopy medium.

ENQ: see *enquiry character.* (A)

enqueue: to place items on a queue. Cf. *dequeue.*

enquiry character (ENQ): a transmission control character used as a request for a response from the station with which the connection has been set up; the response may include station identification, the type of equipment in service, and the status of the remote station. (A) (B)

ENTER: synonymous with *carriage return.*

enter: to place on the line a message to be transmitted from a terminal to the computer.

enter/inquiry mode: the use of a terminal to enter data, to request the system to provide information, or for a combination of these operations. Cf. *rerun mode.*

enter key: synonymous with *start key.*

entity: an object or an event about which information is stored in a data base; for example, a person, or a train departure time.

entrance: synonym for *entry point.* (A) (B)

entropy: in information theory, the mean value of the measure of information conveyed by the occurrence of any one of a finite number of mutually exclusive and jointly exhaustive events of definite probabilities. Synonymous with *average information content, mean information content, negentropy.* See *character mean entropy, conditional entropy.* (A) (B)

entry:

(1) any consecutive set of descriptive clauses terminated by a period, written in the identification, environment, or procedure divisions of a COBOL program.

(2) an element of information in a table, list, queue, or other organized structure of data or control information.

(3) a single input operation on a terminal.

(4) synonym for *entry point.* (A) (B)

entry block: a block of main-memory storage assigned on receipt of every entry into a system and associated with that entry throughout its life within the system.

entry conditions:

(1) the conditions to be specified on entering a computer program, a routine, or a subroutine. For example, the address of those locations from which the program, routine, or subroutine will take its operands and of those locations with which its entry points and exits will be linked. (B)

(2) the initial data and control conditions to be satisfied for successful execution of a given routine. (A)

entry constant: in PL/1, an entry name.

entry expression: in PL/1, an expression whose evaluation yields an entry value.

entry instruction: the first instruction to be executed in a subroutine, that is, it may have several different entry points, each of which corresponds to a differing activity of the subroutine.

entry name:

(1) a name within a control section that defines an entry point and can be referred to by any control section.

(2) a programmer-specified name that establishes an entry point in a COBOL subprogram.

(3) in PL/1, an identifier that is explicitly or contextually declared to have the ENTRY attribute (unless the VARIABLE attribute is given) or has an implied ENTRY attribute; the value of an entry variable.

entry point:

(1) the address or the label of the first instruction executed upon entering a computer program, a routine, or a subroutine. A computer program, a routine, or a subroutine may have a number of different entry points, each perhaps corresponding to a different function or purpose. Synonymous with *entrance, entry.* (B)

(2) in a routine, any place to which control can be passed. (A)

(3) in PL/1, a point in a procedure at which it may be invoked. See *primary entry point* and *secondary entry point.*

entry symbol: an ordinary symbol that represents an entry name or control section name. See also *external symbol.*

entry time: the time when control is transferred from the supervisory to the application program.

entry value: in PL/1, the entry point represented by an entry constant; the value includes activation information that is associated with the entry constant.

entry variable: in PL/1, a variable that can represent entry values.

envelope: a group of binary digits formed by a byte augmented by a number of additional bits which are required for the operation of the data network.

envelope detection: a process by which an original message signal is derived from a modulated carrier wave.

environment:

(1) the physical conditions surrounding a computer installation, including heat, pressure, pollution, vibration, and so forth.

(2) the status of the computer as determined by the hardware, programs, and/or operating system being used, e.g., the windows environment or the UNIX environment.

environment clause: in COBOL, a clause that appears as part of an environment division entry.

environment division: one of the four main component parts of a COBOL program. The environment division describes the computers upon which the source program is compiled and those on which the object program is executed, and provides a linkage between the logical concept of files and their records, and the physical aspects of the devices on which files are stored.

environment (of activation): in PL/1, information associated with the invocation of a block that is used in the interpretation of references, within the invoked block, to data declared outside the block. This information includes generations of automatic variables, extents of defined variables, and generations of parameters.

environment (of a label constant): in PL/1, identity of the particular activation of a block to which a reference to a statement-label constant applies. This information is determined at the time a statement-label constant is passed as an argument or is assigned to a statement-label variable, and it is passed or assigned along with the constant.

EOA: see *end of address.*

EOB: see *end of block.*

EOJ: see *end of job.*

EOLM: see *end-of-line marker.*

EOM: see *end-of-message code.*

EOR: end of record.

EOT:

(1) see *end-of-tape mark.*

(2) see *end-of-transmission character.* (A)

epilog: in PL/1, those processes that occur automatically at the termination of a block or task.

EPROM: erasable, programmable, read only memory. Has permanent data electrically recorded or programmed into it until exposure to ultraviolet light. See *PROM.*

EPROM programmer: a special unit used to program EPROM chips.

equality: synonymous with *exclusive-NOR.*

equation: an arithmetic statement consisting of two expressions, connected by an equal sign (=), having equality.

equation solver: an analog unit for solving systems of equations.

equation statements: statements used in high-level languages that appear as mathematical equations, but may not have any mathematical validity.

equipment clock: a clock which satisfies the particular needs of equipment and in some cases may control the flow of data at the equipment interface.

equipment compatibility: the characteristics of some computers where one system accepts and processes data prepared by another computer without conversion or code modification.

equipment failure: a fault in equipment, excluding all external factors, that prevents the accomplishment of a scheduled job.

equipment side: that portion of a device that looks toward the in-station equipment.

equivalence: a logic operator having the property that if P is a statement, Q is a statement, R is a statement, then the equivalence of P, Q, R, . . . , is true if and only if all statements are true or all statements are false. (A)

equivalence gate: see *exclusive-NOR.*

equivalence operation: the dyadic boolean operation whose result has the boolean value 1 if and only if the operands have the same boolean value. Synonymous with *IF-AND-ONLY-IF operations.* (A) (B)

equivalent-binary-digit factor: the average number of binary digits required to express one radix digit in a nonbinary numeration system. For example, approximately $3\frac{1}{3}$ times the number of decimal digits is required to express a decimal numeral as a binary numeral. (A)

equivalent bit rate: the number of binary digits transmitted over a circuit in a stated time interval, and related to the information content of a signal instead of to the control information needed to handle the signal on the particular transmission path.

equivocation: in information theory, the conditional entropy of the occurrence of specific messages at the message source, given the occurrence of specific messages at a message sink connected to the message source by a specified channel. The equivocation is the mean additional information content that must be supplied per message at the message sink to correct the received messages affected by a noisy channel. (A) (B)

ER: see *error.*

erasable optical disk: an optical disk on which data can be moved, changed, and erased just as it can on magnetic disks.

erasable programmable read-only memory: see *EPROM.*

erasable storage: a storage device whose contents can be modified. (B) Cf. *read-only storage.* (A)

erase:
(1) to remove data from a data medium, leaving the medium available for recording new data. (B)
(2) to remove all previous data from magnetic storage by changing it to a specified condition; that may be an unmagnetized state or a predetermined magnetized state.

erase character: deprecated term for *delete character.* (A) (B)

erase head: a device on a magnetic tape drive whose sole function is to erase previous information before new information is written.

Eratosthenes' sieve: a means of calculating prime numbers; useful for comparing the execution speeds of differing computers or programming languages.

EREP: the environmental recording, editing, and printing program. Keeps records of hardware error problems and determinations.

ergonomics: the technology that studies the biological and engineering problems of the man-machine relationship.

ERP: see *error recovery procedures.*

ERR: see *error.*

error (E) (ER) (ERR):
(1) a discrepancy between a computed, observed, or measured value or condition and the true, specified, or theoretically correct value or condition. (B)
(2) deprecated term for *mistake.* (B)
(3) cf. *fault, malfunction, mistake.* (A)
(4) see *absolute error, balanced error, inherited error, relative error, rounding error, truncation error.*
(5) see also *error condition.*

error ambiguity: a gross error occurring in the reading of some digital codes as the parameters represented by the codes change.

error bit: a binary digit of information incorrectly received.

error blocks: blocks of data where errors are detected; for example, by means of a cyclic redundancy check.

error burst: in data communication, a sequence of signals containing one or more errors but counted as only one unit in accordance with some specific criterion or measure. An example of a criterion is that if three consecutive correct bits follow an erroneous bit, then an error burst is terminated. (A)

error character: synonymous with *ignore character.*

error checking and correction (ECC): the detection, in the processing unit, and correction of all single-bit errors, plus the detection of double-bit and some multiple-bit errors.

error-checking code: a general term for all error-correcting codes and all error-detecting codes. See *error code.*

error code: the marking of a specific error with a character or code. The code is usually printed out to show that an error has taken place, or can be associated on a storage device with an item of data that is in error so that the item can be corrected or ignored when the data is later processed.

error condition: the state that results from an attempt to execute instructions in a computer program that are invalid or that operate on invalid data.

error-control character: synonym for *accuracy control character.* (A)

error-correction routine: a routine for the detection and correction of errors on data files.

error-correction submode: a mode of operation that provides the ability to go back in a program to a point where the environment was saved, thereby permitting correction of a previously entered field.

error-detecting code: a code in which each element representation conforms to specific rules of construction so that if certain errors occur, the resulting representation will not conform to the rules, thereby indicating the presence of errors. Synonymous with *self-checking code.*

error detection: in data transmission, the detection of lost or inverted bits by automatic means.

error diagnostics: verifying source language statements for errors during compilation, and the printing of error messages showing all found errors.

error dump: dumping of a program into a medium so that the cause of an error interrupt can be studied.

error file: a file established during execution of a program to store records having errors as found by the program. Usually, this file is printed so that the records can be visually scanned for the errors.

error handling: the capability of software for dealing automatically with data errors.

error interrupts: an interrupt that occurs when a program or hardware malfunctions.

error list: produced by a compiler that shows incorrect or invalid instructions in a source program.

error message: an indication that an error has been detected. (A)

error peak: a time period during the day when the frequency of error bits is at its highest.

error protocol: a portion of a protocol dealing with the detection and correction of errors.

error range: the set of values that an error may take. Deprecated term for *error span.* (A) (B)

error rate: a measure of the quality of a circuit or system; the number of erroneous bits or characters in a sample, frequently taken per 100,000 characters.

error ratio: the ratio of the number of data units in error to the total number of data units. (A)

error record: a record that indicates the occurrence of errors.

error-recovery procedures (ERP): procedures designed to help isolate and, where possible, to recover from errors in equipment. The procedures are often used in conjunction with programs that record the statistics of machine malfunctions.

error report:

(1) a printout of records holding data on malfunctions that have occurred in a computer system. The data is recorded on disk as malfunctions occur, and the report is produced for use by individuals responsible for maintenance.

(2) a printout of records in a file found, during the execution of a program, to contain an error.

error routine: a routine entered on the detection of an error. This routine may output an error message, correct the error, duplicate the process that caused the error, or perform any other specified action.

error span: the difference between the highest and the lowest error values. (A) (B)

error tape: magnetic tape containing errors for later listing and analysis.

ESC: see *escape character.* (A)

escape: the departure from one code or language to another code or language, that is, the removal from existing pattern.

escape character (ESC): a code extension character used, in some cases, with one or more succeeding characters to indicate by some convention or agreement that the coded representations following the character or the group of characters are to be interpreted according to a different code or according to a different coded character set. (B) See *data-link escape character.* (A)

escape code: a code used with text input to show that the next character (or characters) will represent a function code.

ESCAPE key: the button found on a keyboard for generating the ESCAPE character.

ESCAPE sequence: a series of control characters beginning with ESCAPE; used for display control functions such as cursor addressing, and so on.

ESD: see *external symbol dictionary.*

esoteric name: the name for a group of units within the computer system.

ETB: see *end-of-transmission-block character.* (A)

Ethernet: one of the first products in local area networks, providing up to 1,024 stations, at a data rate of 10 million bits per second.

E-time: execution time.

E²-PROM: synonymous with *EEPROM.*

ETX: see *end-of-text character.* (A)

EU: see *end user.*

EUROMICRO: European Association for Microprocessing and Microprogramming.

evaluation: in PL/1, reduction of an expression to a single value (which may be an array or structure value).

even parity check: a parity check where the number of ones (or zeroes) in a group of binary digits is expected to be even. Cf. *odd parity check.*

event:
(1) an occurrence or happening.
(2) an occurrence of significance to a task; typically, the completion of an asynchronous operation, such as an input-output operation.
(3) in PL/1, an activity in a program whose status and completion can be determined from an associated event variable.

event chain: a series of actions resulting from an initial event.

event-control block (ECB): a control block used to represent the status of an event.

event-drive monitor: a monitor that counts each event performed by the system, reporting system activity more accurately than a statistical monitor.

event-oriented simulation: synonymous with *discrete simulation.*

event posting: the saving of a computer program and data context of a task and establishing the program and data of another task to which control is to be passed, based on an event such as completion of loading of data into main storage. (A)

event variable: in PL/1, a variable with the EVENT attribute, which may be associated with an event; its value indicates whether the action has been completed and the status of the completion.

even-word boundary: a memory address that is an even multiple of the word length of a computer.

everyone: a category of users for whom access privileges can be made to shared folders and disks. The category refers to anyone who is connected to a computer as a guest or registered user.

evoke module: a module with hard-wired circuits that is used for dedicated automatic control systems. These modules are used where changes to the program are not expected.

EX: see *execute.*

exceed capacity: the generating of a word, the magnitude or length of which is too great or too small to be represented by a computer, such as in an attempt to divide by zero.

except gate: synonymous with *exclusive-OR element.*

exception: an abnormal condition such as an I/O error encountered in processing a data set or a file. See *overflow exception.*

exception-handling: in BASIC, a sequence of statements that help the program to handle gracefully problems that would otherwise lead to a premature stop.

exception reporting: a record containing only specific types of results, such as changes, values that do not match preset criteria, or values that exceed earlier indicated limits.

except operation: deprecated term for *exclusion.* (A) (B)

excess fifty: a binary code where the number n is represented by the binary equivalent of $n + 50$.

excess-*n* notation: a notation where a binary number, x, is represented as $x + n$.

excess 64 binary notation: in assembler programming, a binary notation in which each component of a floating-point number E is represented by the binary equivalent of E plus 64.

excess-three code: the binary-coded decimal notation in which a decimal digit n is represented by the binary numeral that represents $(n + 3)$. (A) (B)

exchangeable disk storage (EDS): a backing store device using magnetic disks loaded in a disk drive; the operator can replace capsules of, for example, six disks during operation.

exchange buffering: a technique using data chaining to avoid moving data in main storage, in which control of buffer segments and user program work areas is passed between data management and the user program.

exchange instruction: an instruction to replace the contents of one register (or registers) with the contents of another, and vice versa.

exchange sort: a sort in which succeeding pairs of items in a set are examined; if the items in a pair are out of sequence according to the specified criteria, the positions

of the items are exchanged; for example, a bubble sort. This process is repeated until all items are sorted. (A)

exclusion:
(1) the dyadic boolean operation whose result has the boolean value if and only if the first operand has the boolean value 1 and the second has the boolean value 0. (B)
(2) a logic operator having the property that if P is a statement and Q is a statement, then P exclusion Q is true if P is true and Q is false, false if P is false, and false if both statements are true. P exclusion Q is often represented by a combination of "AND" and "NOT" symbols, such as PôQ. (A)
(3) synonymous with *NOT-IF-THEN, NOT-IF-THEN operation.*

exclusive-NOR: a boolean operation on two operands (p and q), the result (r) being as follows:

Operands		Result
p	q	r
0	0	0
1	0	1
0	1	1
1	1	0

Synonymous with *biconditional operation, equality, nonequivalence.*

exclusive-OR: a logic operator having the property that if P is a statement and Q is a statement, then P exclusive-OR Q is true if either but not both statements are true, false if both are true or both are false. Cf. OR. (A)

exclusive-OR element: a logic element that performs the boolean nonequivalence operation. Synonymous with *exclusive-OR gate.* (A) (B)

exclusive-OR gate: synonym for *exclusive-OR element.* (A) (B)

exclusive reference: a reference from a segment in storage to an external symbol in a segment that will cause overlaying of the calling segment.

exclusive segments: segments in the same region of an overlay program, neither of which is in the path of the other. They cannot be in main storage simultaneously.

EXEC: see *execute*.

exec statements: a console-entered statement which initiates the program from the library for processing.

executable file: a file having been either written in, or translated by a language processor into, machine language, and that is now ready for computer execution. In DOS systems, these files have a .COM or .EXE filename extension.

executable program: a program that has been link edited and is therefore capable of being run in a processor.

executable statement:
(1) a statement that specifies one or more actions to be taken by a computer program at execution time; for example, instructions for calculations to be performed, conditions to be tested, flow of control to be altered.
(2) in FORTRAN, a statement that specifies action to be taken by the program; for example, calculations to be performed, conditions to be tested, flow of control to be altered.

execute (E) (EX) (EXEC):
(1) to perform the execution of an instruction or of a computer program. (A)
(2) in programming, to change the state of a computer in accordance with the rules of the operations it recognizes. (B)

execute cycle: the period during execution of one machine language instruction when the CPU converts the instruction into electronic signals. See also *instruction cycle*.

execute key: synonymous with *start key*.

execute phase: the logical subdivision of a run that includes the execution of the target program. Synonymous with *executing phase*. (A) (B)

execute (EXEC) statement: a job control language (JCL) statement that marks the beginning of a job step and identifies the program to be executed or the catalogued or in-stream procedure to be used.

executing phase: synonym for *execute phase*. (A) (B)

execution (E):
(1) the process of carrying out an instruction by a computer. (A) (B)

(2) in programming, the process by which a computer program or subroutine changes the state of a computer in accordance with the rules of the operations that a computer recognizes. (B)
(3) the process of carrying out the instructions of a computer program by a computer. (B)

execution cycle: that part of a machine cycle during which the actual execution of the instruction occurs.

execution-error detection: detection concerned with errors found during the execution of the user's program.

execution mode: when a programming language is used in this mode, the terminal can be used much like a desk calculator.

execution path: the major course or line of direction taken by a computer in the execution of a routine, directed by the logic of the program and the nature of the data.

execution time (E-time):
(1) the time during which an instruction is decoded and performed. See also *instruction time*.
(2) in COBOL, the time at which an object program performs the instructions coded in the procedure division, using the data provided.

executive: a program, routine, or system having supervisory control over others.

executive cycle: synonymous with *execute phase*.

executive program: synonym for *supervisory program*. (A) (B)

executive routine: synonym for *supervisory routine*. (A) (B)

executive supervisor: the executive-system component that controls the sequencing, setup, and execution of all runs entering the computer.

executive system: an integrated collection of service routines for supervising the sequencing of programs by a computer.

executive termination: the normal or abnormal termination of an operating program and its return of assigned facilities to an available status.

exerciser: a test or program to find malfunctions in a memory, disk, or tape unit prior to use.

EXF: see *external function.*

exhaustivity: the number of keywords assigned to a record in a file with any information retrieval system.

exit: any instruction in a computer program, in a routine, or in a subroutine after the execution of which control is no longer exercised by that computer program, that routine, or that subroutine. (A) (B)

exit macroinstruction: a supervisory program macroinstruction that is the last instruction in an application program, showing that processing is over.

exit point: the instruction that transfers control from a main routine to a subroutine. See *exit routine.*

exit routine:
(1) a routine that receives control when a specified event occurs, such as an error.
(2) any of several types of user-written routines.

EXP:
(1) see *exponent.*
(2) see *expression.*

expandable: a computer capable of having its storage capacity increased with the addition of further main memory and/or disk drives.

expanded memory specification (EMS): a system to free extra RAM in DOS-systems. Expanded memory manager programs allow the use of more than the 1 MB of memory that DOS usually supports.

expander boards: boards that interface with the system permitting the user to add more circuitry for system expansion.

expansion board: a printed-circuit board which accommodates additional components or cards for expanding a computer.

expansion card: a removable circuit board that plugs into one of the expansion slots in some computers. This card enables the computer to use a special device or to perform an additional function. See *expansion slot.*

expansion cascading: shifting from a fine level of detail to increasingly broader levels.

expansion interface: a device to expand the functional capacity of a computer by containing additional memory or controlling more peripherals.

expansion slot: a long, rectangular socket on the main circuit board of some computers into which an expansion card can be installed giving the computer additional capabilities. See *expansion card.*

expert programs: computers acting as intelligent assistants, providing advice and making judgments in specialized areas of expertise.

expert systems: programs aiming to endow computers with the ability to imitate the thought processes of human experts.

expiration check: a comparison of a given date with an expiration date associated with a transaction, record, or file. Synonymous with *retention period check.*

expiration date: the date set at which a file is no longer protected from automatic deletion by the system.

explicit address: synonym for *absolute address.* (A) (B)

explicit declaration: in PL/1, the appearance of an identifier in a DECLARE statement, as a label prefix, or in a parameter list.

explicit specification statement: an INTEGER, REAL, DOUBLE PRECISION, or LOGICAL statement, which specifies data type.

exponent (EX):
(1) in a floating-point representation, the numeral denotes the power to which the implicit floating-point base is raised before being multiplied by the fixed-point part to determine the real number represented; for example, a floating-point representation of the number 0.0001234 is 0.1234-3, where 0.1234 is the fixed-point part and -3 is the exponent. (A) (B)
(2) a number indicating how many times another number (the base) is to be repeated as a factor. Positive exponents denote multiplication, negative exponents denote division, fractional exponents denote a root of a quantity. In COBOL, exponentiation is indicated with the symbol **, followed by the exponent.

exponent characters: in PL/1, the following picture specification characters, (1) K and E, which are used in floating-point picture specifications to indicate the beginning of the exponent field; (2) F, the scaling-factor character, specified with an integer constant which indicates the number of decimal positions the decimal point is to be moved from its assumed position to the right (if the constant is positive) or to the left (if the constant is negative).

exponential growth: a mathematical concept that states that the increase in a variable is directly proportional to the variable.

export: format and send data to another processing application.

EXPR: see *expression*.

expression (E) (EX) (EXPR):
(1) a configuration of signs. (A)
(2) a source-language combination of one or more operations.
(3) in assembler programming, one or more operations represented by a combination of terms and paired parentheses.
(4) a notation, within a program, that represents a value; a constant or a reference appearing alone, or combination of constants and references with operators.
(5) see *absolute expression, arithmetic expression, character expression, complex relocatable expression, relocatable expression*.

express menu: the menu that permits quick switching between running applications, start any application, or exit to DOS.

extended addressing: an addressing mode created to reach almost anywhere in the memory system.

extended arithmetic element (EAE): a central processor element implemented with hardware for multiplying, dividing, and normalizing functions.

extended binary-coded decimal interchange code (EBCDIC): see *EBCDIC*. See also *binary-coded decimal character code*.

extended floating-point numbers: floating-point operand fractions extended for greater precision.

extended format diskette: a diskette in 256-byte format.

extended memory: memory beyond the 1 MB of memory that DOS systems usually support. Unlike expanded memory, which uses a memory manager, extended memory is not configured in any particular way, and can't be used by most applications.

extended mnemonic: an operation code that is an extension to an instruction.

extended-precision floating point: a feature that permits floating-point operand fractions to be 112 bits long for greater precision than in short or long floating-point arithmetic.

extended punched-card code: see *Hollerith code*.

extended range (of a DO statement): in FORTRAN, those statements that are executed between the transfer out of the innermost DO of a completely nested group of DO statements and the transfer back into the range of the innermost DO.

extended-time scale: the time scale used in data processing when the time-scale factor is greater than one. Synonymous with *slow time scale*. Cf. *fast-time scale*. (A)

extension: letters at the end of a filename, usually following a period, as in config.sys.

extension character: see *code extension character*. (A)

extension register: a register that provides expansion for the accumulator register or the quotient register.

extent:
(1) a continuous space on a direct-access storage volume, occupied by or reserved for a particular data set, data space, or file.
(2) in PL/1, the range indicated by the bounds of an array dimension, the range indicated by the length of a string, or the range indicated by the size of an area.
(3) see also *primary space allocation*.

exterior label: a label affixed to the outside of a reel. Cf. *interior label*.

external clocking: synchronization signals for a device supplied by a different device so that the two units operate at the same rate of speed. Cf. *internal clocking*.

EXTERNAL declaration: a declaration in a programming language for identifying a symbolic name used in this program as being defined in a differing program.

external delays: time lost due to circumstances beyond the control of the operator or maintenance engineer; for example, failure of external power source. (A)

external device address: specifies which external device a particular instruction is referring to.

external error: pertaining to a specific file mark that has been incorrectly read or an end of tape that has been sensed during a loading operation.

external event module: a module for detecting power failure and control interrupts, and processor startup and half functions where the module implements the system priority scheme in the event of a power loss.

external file: a permanently stored file separate from the executing program.

external function (EXF): in FORTRAN, a function whose definition is external to the program unit that refers to it.

external-interrupt inhibit: the bit, in the program status double-word, that shows whether (if 1) or not (if 0) all external interrupts are inhibited.

external-interrupt status word: a status word accompanied by an external-interrupt signal; where the signal informs the computer that the word on the data lines is a status word, and the computer puts the word into main memory.

externally stored programs: programs with instruction routines set up in wiring boards or plugboards for manual insertion in older models or small-scale processors.

external memory: synonymous with *external storage.*

external merge: a sorting technique that reduces sequences of records or keys to one sequence, usually following one or more internal sorts.

external modem: synonym for *stand-alone modem.* Cf. *integrated modem.*

external name:
(1) a name that can be referred to by any control section or separately assembled or compiled module; that is, a control section name or any entry name in another module.
(2) in PL/1, a name (with the EXTERNAL attribute) whose scope is not necessarily confined only to one block and its contained blocks.

external number: a number by which a party is called through an external line.

external-page address: an address that identifies the location of a page in a page data set.

external procedure:
(1) a procedure that is not contained in any other procedure.
(2) in FORTRAN, a procedure subprogram or a procedure defined by means other than FORTRAN statements.

external-program parameter: in a computer program, a parameter than must be bound during the calling of the computer program. (A) (B)

external reference (EXTRN):
(1) a reference to a symbol that is defined as an external name in another module.
(2) an external symbol that is defined in another module; that which is defined in the assembler language by an EXTRN statement or by a V-type address constant, and is resolved during linkage editing. See also *weak external reference.*

external registers: registers referenced by the program, but located in control store as specific addresses. Synonymous with *location registers.*

external sort:
(1) a sort that requires the use of auxiliary storage because the set of items to be sorted cannot be held in the available internal storage at one time.
(2) a sort program, or a sort phase of a multipass sort, that merges strings of items, using auxiliary storage, until one string is formed. (A)
(3) when building an alternate index, the sorting of the alternate keys into ascending sequence by using work files.
(4) see also *internal sort.*

external storage:
(1) storage that is accessible by a computer only through input-output channels. (B)

(2) in a hierarchy of storage devices of a data-processing system, any storage device that is not internal storage. External storage and internal storage are terms which take on precise meanings only with reference to a particular configuration.

external symbol:

(1) a control section name, entry point name, or external reference that is defined or referred to in a particular module.

(2) in assembler programming, an ordinary symbol that represents an external reference.

(3) a symbol in the external symbol dictionary.

(4) see also *entry symbol.*

external symbol dictionary (ESD): control information, associated with an object or load module, that identifies the external symbols in the module.

external-unit identifier: synonym for *data-set reference number.*

extracode: machine instructions used for providing extra capability for machine storage.

extract:

(1) to select and remove from a set of items those items that meet some criteria; for example, to obtain certain specified digits from a computer word as controlled by an instruction or mask. (A) (B)

(2) to separate specific parts of a word from the whole word.

(3) to remove specific items from a file.

extract instruction: an instruction that requests the formation of a new expression from selected parts of given expressions. (A)

extraction: the reading of only selected parts of a record into storage.

extractor: see *filter.*

extraneous ink: ink deposited on a computer printout that is not confined to the printed characters themselves.

extremity routine: a routine used when initiating a new tape or when reaching the end of reel of a multireel file. The routine need not be included in memory if all tapes are set up or initiated automatically by the system supervisor and the open or close macros are not used. The primary value of this routine is that it performs needed tape housekeeping, checks on the operator, and provides needed information concerning the program being run.

extrinsic function: a function, not internal to the system, defined by a programmer in a program. See *intrinsic function.*

EXTRN: see *external reference.*

F:

(1) see *fetch.*

(2) see *file.*

(3) see *fixed.*

(4) see *flag.*

(5) see *function.*

FAC: see *facsimile.*

FACE: field-alterable control element. A chip found in some systems permitting a user to write microprograms.

face: in OCR, a character style with given relative dimension and line thicknesses.

face-change character: synonym for *font-change character.* (A) (B)

facility:

(1) an operational capability, or the means for providing such a capability.

(2) a service provided by an operating system, for a particular purpose; for example, the checkpoint/restart facility.

(3) a measure of how easy it is to use a data-processing system.

facsimile (FAC) (FAX):

(1) an exact copy or likeness.

(2) a system for the transmission of images by digitizing them. Personal computers that use FAX modems can send or receive such images.

fact correlation: a process that is an integral part of linguistic analysis and adaptive learning that employs techniques of manipulating and recognizing data elements, items, or codes to examine and determine explicit and implicit relations of data in files; for example, for fact retrieval in place of document retrieval.

factor: in a multiplication operation, any of the numbers of quantities that are the operands. (A) (B) See *equivalent-binary-digit factor, multiplier factor, relocation factor, scale factor, time scale factor.*

factorial: the product of positive integers from 1 up to and including a given integer; for example, factorial 5 is the product of $1 \times 2 \times 3 \times 4 \times 5$, or 120. (A) (B)

factoring: in PL/1, the application of one or more attributes or of a level number to a parenthesized list of names. See *level number.*

fail safe: descriptive of a system which is able to close down in a controlled fashion during a serious failure, although some deterioration in performance can be expected. Synonymous with *fail soft.*

fail soft: synonymous with *fail safe.*

failure: the termination of the capability of a functional unit to perform its required function. A failure is the effect of a fault. (B) Cf. *error, fault, mistake.* (A)

failure analysis: laboratory or on-the-spot analysis and study of a failure to identify the exact cause of the failure.

failure logging: the automatic listing of failures that can be detected by a program, permitting corrective procedures to be attempted.

failure prediction: techniques used for determining when failures are most likely to occur in particular parts and equipment; attempts to permit a schedule for replacement parts prior to the failure occurring.

failure rate: a measure of the number of a specified type or class of failures over a stated time frame.

failure recovery: resumption of a system following a failure.

fallback:
(1) the use of a backup module in a redundant system during degraded operation.
(2) a condition in processing when special computer or manual functions are employed as either complete or partial substitutes for malfunctioning systems.

fallout: the failure of components experienced during the burn-in of new equipment.

fallthrough: a software step resulting in machine cycling to the operation represented by the next lower block on a flowchart.

false add: to form a partial sum, that is, to add without carries. (A)

false code: a code producing an illegal character.

false colors: synonymous with *pseudo-colors.*

false drop: synonymous with *false retrievals.*

false error: the signaling of an error when no error exists.

false retrievals: library references that are not pertinent to, but are vaguely related to, the subject of the library search, and are sometimes obtained by automatic search methods. Synonymous with *false drop.*

fan-fold paper: continuous sheets of paper joined along perforations and folded in a zigzag manner. Usually used with printers as it can be continuously fed and folded without ongoing operator participation. Synonymous with Z-*fold.*

fast-access storage: the section of the storage from which data is obtained most rapidly.

fast-time scale: the time scale used in data processing when the time-scale factor is less than one. Cf. *extended-time scale.* (A)

FAT: see file allocation table.

fatal error: an unplanned condition resulting from the execution of a program which precludes additional running of a program.

father file: see *generation data set.*

fault: an accidental condition that causes a functional unit to fail to perform in a required manner. (B) Cf. *error, failure, mistake.* See *pattern-sensitive fault, program-sensitive fault.* (A)

fault defect: an anomaly preventing the correct operation of a unit.

fault diagnosis: determining the specific reasons for errors or interruptions to a communication service.

fault dictionary: a set of fault signatures, each indicating the probable faults causing the error message from matching the signature.

fault-location: a program for identification or information dealing with the failure of equipment.

fault report point: the location or organizational entity to which faults within a system are to be notified.

fault signature: an output response or set of responses generated when a test program is executed on a unit having a fault.

fault time: synonymous with *downtime*.

fault-tolerant: a program or system that continues to function properly in spite of a fault or faults.

FAX: see *facsimile*.

FB: see *fixed block*.

FBA: see *fixed-block architecture device*.

FC:
(1) see *font-change character*.
(2) see *function code*.

F-conversion: one of the three types of FORMAT specification in FORTRAN; used to convert floating-point data for input-output operations.

FCS: see *frame check sequence*.

FCT: see *function*.

FD:
(1) see *file description*.
(2) see *flexible disk*.
(3) full duplex. See *duplex*.

FDC: see *floppy disk controller*.

FDX: full duplex. See *duplex*.

FE: see *format effector character*. (A)

feasibility study: a preliminary investigation to determine the overall soundness of applying electronic computers to potential applications.

feature:
(1) a surprising, occasionally documented, property of a program.
(2) slang, a well-known and friendly property; a facility.

feed:
(1) to cause data to be entered into a computer system, employing punched cards, paper tape, or other medium instead of by direct data entry.
(2) a device for causing data to be entered.

feedback: the return of part of the output of a machine, process, or system to the computer as input for another phase, especially for self-correcting or control purposes.

feedback loop: the components and processes involved in correcting and/or controlling a system by using part of the output as input. (A)

feedback system: see *information feedback system*. (A)

feedforward: a control action where conditions that disrupt the control variable are reduced or converted into corrective actions.

feed hole:
(1) a hole punched in a data medium to enable it to be moved or synchronized. (A) (B)
(2) a hole punched in a data carrier to enable it to be positioned.
(3) synonymous with *sprocket hole*. (A)

feeding: a system used by character readers in character recognition, where each input document is issued to the document transport at a predetermined and fixed rate.

feed pitch: the distance between corresponding points of adjacent feed holes along the feed track. (A)

feed punch: see *automatic-feed punch*. (A)

feed reel: a specific reel from which tape is unwound throughout the processing.

feed track: the track of a data carrier that contains the feed holes. Synonymous with *sprocket track*.

feep: slang, the soft bell of a display terminal.

FEFO: see *first-ended, first-out*.

ferrite: an iron compound frequently used in the construction of magnetic cores. (A)

ferroelectric: found in certain materials exhibiting spontaneous electric polarization along with dielectric hysteresis.

ferromagnetic: the capability of some materials to be highly magnetized and to exhibit hysteresis; that is, iron and nickel.

ferrous oxide: a medium for containing encoded information on magnetic tape.

fetch (F):
(1) to locate and load a quantity of data from storage. (A)
(2) in virtual storage systems, to bring load modules or program phases from auxiliary storage into virtual storage.

(3) a control program routine that accomplishes (1) or (2).

(4) the name of the macro instruction (FETCH) used to accomplish (1) or (2).

(5) see also *loader*.

(6) synonymous with *retrieve*.

fetch-ahead: fetching an instruction before the last instruction is finished executing.

fetch cycle: the time phase that a CPU needs to read the following machine instruction before acting on it during program execution. See *execute cycle*.

fetch data: a command specifying the unit and file to which access is desired.

fetch instruction: the instruction for locating and returning instructions that have been entered in the instruction register.

fetch phase: an alternate part of the cycle of the computer activity wherein the instruction is brought from memory into the program register.

fetch process: addressing the memory and reading into the CPU the information word or byte stored at the addressed location.

fetch protection: a storage protection feature that determines right of access to main storage by matching a protection key, associated with a fetch reference to main storage, with a storage key, associated with each block of main storage. See also *store protection*.

FF:

(1) see *flip-flop*.

(2) see *form feed character*. (A)

F format: a data-set format in which logical records are the same length.

FG: see *foreground*.

Fibonacci number: an integer in the Fibonacci series. (A)

Fibonacci search: a dichotomizing search in which the number of items in the set is equal to a Fibonacci number or is assumed to be equal to the next higher Fibonacci number and then at each step in the search a division is made in accordance with the Fibonacci series.

Fibonacci series: a series of integers in which each integer is equal to the sum of the two preceding integers in the series.

fiche: see *microfiche*. (A)

FICON: see *file conversion*.

field (FLD):

(1) in a record, a specified area used for a particular category of data; for example, a group of card columns in which a wage rate is recorded. (B)

(2) a group of adjacent card columns on a punch card. (A)

(3) in a database, the smallest unit of data that can be referred to. See also *data field*.

(4) see *card field, common field*.

field-alterable control element: see *FACE*.

field checking: on some terminals, the numeric-only and alpha-only field checks that are dynamically performed to find errors as they occur.

field data code: a standardized military data transmission code consisting of 7 data bits plus 1 parity bit.

field designator: a unique character found at the start of a field for identifying the nature of the data contained within the field. Usually used when data are not rigidly formatted.

field-developed program: a licensed program that performs a function for the user. It may interact with program products, system control programming, or currently available type 1, type 2, or type 3 programs, or it may be a standalone program.

field (in a data stream): in PL/1, that portion of the data stream whose width, in number of characters, is defined by a single data or spacing format item.

field flyback: the interval in a scanning function of a television picture, where the electron beam is blocked off and the raster is repositioned to commence a new scanning operation.

field frequency: a frequency with which a complete sequence of scanning operations occurs in the establishment of a television picture.

field identifier: the name of a component in a record.

field length (FL): the number of characters or words in a field or a fixed-length record.

field (of a picture specification): in PL/1, any character-string picture specification or that portion (or all) of a numeric-character of numeric-bit picture specification that describes a fixed-point number.

field mark: the symbol used to show the beginning or the end of a set of data, that is, group, file, block.

field name: the symbolic name a programmer gives to a specific field of data.

field programmable logic array: see *FPLA*.

field-protected: a display field where the user is not permitted to enter, modify, or erase data from a keyboard.

field replaceable unit (FRU): an assembly that is replaced in its entirety when any one of its components fails. In some cases a field replaceable unit may contain other field replaceable units; for example, a brush and a brush block that can be replaced individually or as a single unit.

field scan: the vertical movement of a raster during the scanning function to establish a television picture.

field selection: the ability of computers to isolate a specific data field within one computer word or words, without isolating the entire word.

field shifting: the process of adjustment for the address of a field to realign the item of data.

field upgrading: upgrading of devices by the insertion of functional logic boards such as expanded memory and I/O device controllers, with utilization of the appropriate program.

field utilization: using fields, or groups of computer characters as a single data item.

fieldwidth specification: in PASCAL, a colon and integer value following a parameter in a WRITE statement, specifying the number of columns in which that parameter will be printed and right-justified.

FIFO (first-in, first-out): a queuing technique in which the next item to be retrieved is the item that has been in the queue for the longest time. (A)

FIFO buffering: a means for handling communications messages in the order of arrival.

FIFO queue: a first-in-first-out waiting line where the most recent arrival is placed at the end of the line and the item waiting the longest receives service first. Synonymous with *push-up list.*

FIFO storage: a storage system using the FIFO method.

15-supergroup: an assembly of devices carrying fifteen separate supergroups in a frequency division multiplexing system and providing the means of transmission for up to 900 separate speech channels along a single coaxial tube. Synonymous with *hypergroup.*

fifth-generation computers: a new family of computers to appear in the 1990s designed especially for artificial intelligence applications. The effort includes both computer hardware design and advanced computer programs. See also *artificial intelligence.*

figurative constant:

(1) a data name that is reserved for a specified constant in a specified programming language. (A) (B)

(2) in COBOL, a reserved word that represents a numeric value, a character, or a string of repeated values or characters. The word can be written in a COBOL program to represent the values or characters without being defined in the data division.

(3) deprecated term for *literal.* (A) (B)

file (F):

(1) any named, ordered collection of information stored on a disk. Applications programs and operating systems are made of files. A file is made when you create text or graphics, give the material a name, and save it on a disk.

(2) a set of related records treated as a unit; for example, in stock control, a file could consist of a set of invoices. (A) (B) See *backup file, detail file, inverted file, master file, transaction file.* See also *data set, file cleanup.*

file activity ratio: the ratio of the number of records or other file elements for which a transaction occurs during a given number of runs to the number of records or other file elements within the file.

file-address checking system: a program that checks addresses when macros instruct to write on the file, to see that the program is not writing on the incorrect area.

file allocation table: in DOS systems, a table in a hidden file that the operating system uses to locate stored files.

file attribute: any of the attributes that describe the characteristics of a file.

file buffer: see *file buffer variable.*

file buffer variable: in PASCAL, a variable of the same type as the components of the file with which it is associated, and used as a "window" through which we can read or write file components.

file clause: in COBOL, a clause that appears as part of either of the following data division entries: file description (FD) or sort-merge file description (SD).

file cleanup: the removal of superfluous data from a file. Synonymous with *file tidying.*

file composition: filing of records within a storage unit.

file constant: in PL/1, a name declared for a file and for which a complete set of file attributes exists during the time that the file is open.

file control: in COBOL, the name and header of an environment division paragraph in which the data files for a given source program are named and assigned to specific input/output devices.

file control system: a system created to assist in the storage and retrieval of data without restricting the type of input/output device.

file conversion (FICON): the transformation of parts of records from their original documents into magnetic files by a computer.

file description (FD):
(1) a part of a file where file and field attributes are described.
(2) in COBOL, an entry in the file section of the data division that provides information about the identification and physical structure of a file.

file directory: see *catalog.*

file event: a single file access, either reading or writing.

file expression: in PL/1, an expression whose evaluation yields a filename.

file extent: an area with a file made up of contiguous tracks on a file storage medium.

file feed: an extension unit that increases the punch card capacity of the feed hopper peripheral units.

file gap: an area on a data medium intended to be used to indicate the end of a file and, possibly, the start of another. A file gap is frequently used for other purposes, in particular, as a flag to indicate the end or beginning of some other group of data. (A)

file-handling routine: the portion of a computer program for reading data from, and/or writing data to, a file.

file insertion: in word processing, allows the user to add the contents of files B, C, and D to file A, just by pushing a few buttons, creating files of frequently used paragraphs or phrases, and adding them to letters or contracts in seconds.

file interrogation program: a program purporting to examine the contents of a computer file.

file label: a form of file identification; the initial record or block in a file is a set of characters unique to the file.

file layout: the arrangement and structure of data or words in a file, including the order and size of the components of the file. (A) (B)

file length: in word processing, determines the amount of text the word-processor file can contain; usually measured in kilobytes. See *kilobytes.*

file list: a scrollable list that permits a user to open directories and files.

file maintenance: the activity of keeping a file up to date by adding, changing, or deleting data. (A) (B)

file management: supervision and optimization of on-going work on a computer.

file management program: computer program which assigns, or recognizes, labels showing at data files, and facilitates their being called from storage when needed.

filemark: an identification mark showing that the last record in a file has been reached.

file menu: a menu that lists commands that affect whole documents and other files.

file merge: in word processing, the creating of form letters. One file contains the base document, the other the names and addresses to be plugged into specified areas in the base document. Synonymous with *mail merge.*

filename:

(1) a name assigned to a set of input data or output data. In COBOL, a filename must include at least one alphabetic character.

(2) a name declared for a file.

filename extension: a code, usually of three letters, that forms the second part of a filename and which is separated from the filename by a period; used to aid in differentiating related files.

file organization: a procedure designed for organizing different information files; these files are usually random-access files to evolve maximum use of storage and swift retrieval for processing.

file-oriented programming: when I/O coding is simplified with the general file and record control program, programming is file-oriented rather than device-oriented and information is requested in device-independent fashion.

file packing density: the ratio of available file- or data-storing space to the total amount of data kept within the file.

file processing: operations connected with the evolution and utilization of files.

file protected: pertaining to a tape reel with the write-enable ring removed.

file protection: prevention of the destruction of data recorded on a volume by disabling the write head of a unit.

file protect ring: a plastic ring on the back side of a magnetic tape when data is recorded. When not in place, the tape drive senses the ring's absence and will not write on the tape, thereby protecting it against accidental or unauthorized writing.

file purging: the erasing of the contents within a file.

file reconstitution: the recreation of a file which has been corrupted during system failure, or other cause.

file recovery: see *backward file recovery, forward file recovery.*

file reel: a magnetic tape reel that feeds toward the rewrite head.

file section: in COBOL, a section of the data division that contains descriptions of all externally stored data (or files) used in a program. Such information is given in one or more file description entries.

file security: limiting access to computer systems by approved operators only. Passwords are frequently used in file security.

file separator character (FS): the information separator intended to identify a logical boundary between items called files. (A) (B)

file server: a computer with special software that allows network users to store and retrieve files on the hard disks or other storage devices attached to it.

file set: a collection of files forming a unit and stored consecutively on a magnetic disk unit.

file sharing: the capability of sharing files among computers on a network.

file store: the files of an operating system, usually kept on a backing store.

file structure: see *data structure.*

file tidying: synonym for *file cleanup.*

file transfer: the movement of a file from one place or storage medium to another.

file variable: in PL/1, a variable to which file constants can be assigned; it must have both the attributes FILE and VARIABLE. No file-name attributes, other than FILE, can be specified for a file-name variable.

fill: see *character fill, zero fill.*

fill character:

(1) a character used to occupy an area on a human-readable medium; for example, in a business form or a legal document, dashes or asterisks used to fill out a field to ensure that nothing is added to the field once the form or document has been issued.

(2) a character used to fill a field in storage.

filler: one or more characters adjacent to an item of data that serves to bring its representation up to a specified size. (A) (B)

film: see *microfilm.*

film frame: in micrographics, that area of film exposed during each exposure, whether or not the area is filled by an image. Synonymous with *recording area.* (A)

filter: a device or program that separates data, signals, or material in accordance with specified criteria. (A)

final copy: in word processing, the final version of the text. See also *draft copy, edited copy.*

finder: the program that creates the desktop. Can be used to manage documents and programs, and to get information to and from disks.

fine-grained architectures: made up of many comparatively simple processors. See also *coarse-grained parallel computers, grain size, intermediate-grained computer architectures.*

fine sort: usually off-line detail sorting by a sorter; for example, fine sorting could be the function of organizing bank checks and deposits into customer account number order.

firmware (FW): a computer's components that are neither hardware nor software; for example, a unit for storing information used in programming the computer.

firmware circuitry: computer circuitry that performs the functions of program instructions.

firmware ROM: a ROM containing a control program.

first-ended, first-out (FEFO): a queuing scheme whereby messages on a destination queue are sent to the destination on a first-ended, first-out basis within priority groups. That is, higher-priority messages are sent before lower-priority messages; when two messages on a queue have equal priority, the one whose final segment arrived at the queue earliest is sent first.

first-generation computer: a computer utilizing vacuum tube components.

first-in first-out: see *FIFO.* Cf. *first-ended, first-out.*

first-level addressing: see *level of addressing.*

first-level interrupt handler: see *FLIH.*

five-bit byte: synonym for *quintet.* (A) (B)

fix: a correction of an error in a program; usually a temporary correction or bypass of defective code. See also *fixed.*

fixed (F): synonym for *read-only* and *resident.*

fixed area: that portion of main storage occupied by the resident section of the control program.

fixed block (FB): the number of characters in the block is determined by the logic of the computer.

fixed-block architecture (FBA) device: a disk storage device that stores data in blocks of fixed size; these blocks are addressed by block number relative to the beginning of the particular file.

fixed-cycle operation: an operation that is completed in a specified number of regularly timed execution cycles. (A)

fixed disk: at times, synonymous with *hard disk.*

fixed-form: pertaining to entry of data or the coding of statements in a predefined state format. Cf. *free-form.*

fixed-format messages: messages in which line control characters must be inserted upon departure from a terminal and deleted upon arrival at a terminal; fixed-format messages are intended for terminals with dissimilar characteristics. Cf. *variable-format messages.*

fixed-function generator: a function generator in which the function to be generated is set by construction and cannot be altered by the user. (B)

fixed-head disk: a various disk unit that has read/write heads that are fixed in position. In such systems, one head is needed for each track of information recorded on a disk.

fixed-length record: a record having the same length as all other records with which it is logically or physically associated. Cf. *variable-length record.* See also *F format.*

fixed-line number: the line number assigned to a text record and associated with that text record for the duration of the editing work session (unless specifically altered by the user).

fixed media: data storage units that do not depend on mechanical movements for reading and writing data.

fixed partition: a partition have a predefined beginning and ending storage address.

fixed point: the decimal point location technique in which the decimal point is not automatically located by the computer or by a routine; used primarily in contrast with floating point.

fixed-point constant: see *arithmetic constant.*

fixed-point part: in a floating-point representation, the numeral that is multiplied by the exponentiated implicit floating-point base to determine the real number represented; for example, a floating-point representation of the number 0.0001234 is 0.1234-3, where .1234 is the fixed-point part and -3 is the exponent. Synonymous with *mantissa.* (A) (B)

fixed-point representation system: a radix numeration system in which the radix point is implicitly fixed in the series of digit places by some convention upon which agreement has been reached. (A) (B)

fixed program computer: see *wired program computer.*

fixed record length: one of the characteristics of a set of records each of which has the same size, in particular the same number of characters in total, or, in other words, the same total field width including all the record's data elements. Records of this type are useful in financial, accounting, scientific, and similar applications where tabular input-output of limited numeric range is common.

fixed reference phase modulation: a means of phase modulation where the binary digits 0 and 1 are shown by a unit signal element beginning with a phase inversion in a particular direction. Utilizing this method, a reference wave is needed in the demodulator to provide detection of the phase of the data signal.

fixed-size font: synonymous with *bit-mapped font.*

fixed storage: a storage device whose contents are inherently nonerasable, nonerasable by a particular user, or nonerasable when operating under particular conditions; for example, a storage when controlled by a lockout feature, a photographic disk. Synonymous with *nonerasable storage, permanent storage, read-only memory, read-only storage.* Cf. *erasable storage.*

fixed word-length computer: a computer in which data is treated in units of a fixed number of characters or bits.

FL: see *field length.*

flag (F) (FLG):

(1) any of various types of indicators used for identification, for example, a wordmark.

(2) a character that signals the occurrence of some condition, such as the end of a word.

(3) deprecated term for *mark.* (B)

(4) synonym for *switch indicator.* (B)

(5) synonymous with *sentinel.* (A)

flag event: a condition causing a flag to be set; for example, the identification of an error, resulting in an error flag.

flag indicator: a signal that indicates that a specific condition has occurred in a computer.

flag lines: inputs to a microprocessor controlled by input-output units and tested by branch instructions.

flag tests: single bits used to indicate the result of a simple test.

flakey: slang, subject to frequent losses.

flame:

(1) slang, an uninteresting subject.

(2) slang, with all ill-conceived attitude.

flash card: in micrographics, a document introduced during the recording of microfilm to facilitate its indexing.

flat-bed: an optical scanner used in facsimile transmission.

flat panel technology: an alternative to bulky, space eating CRTs. Display technology typically used by laptops includes *liquid crystal* (LCD), *gas plasma, electro-luminescent* (ELD).

FLD: see *field.*

flexibility: the degree to which a computer system can be adapted or tailored to the changing requirements of the user.

flexible disk (FD): synonym for *diskette.*

flexible manufacturing system: utilizing robot-controlled transport of work from one machine to another. Control is provided by numerical control units connected into a computer numerical control system.

flexible membrane keyboard: see *membrane keyboards.*

FLG: see *flag.*

FLIH: first-level interrupt handler. A firmware or software routine that "wakes up" every time an interrupt occurs and determines the relative importance of the interrupt.

flip-flop (FF): a circuit or device containing active elements, capable of assuming either one of two stable states at a given time. Synonymous with *toggle (1).* (A) See also *direct-coupled flip-flop.*

flipping: synonymous with *floppy disk.*

flippy: double-sided floppy disk.

flippy-floppy: see *flippy.*

float: shifting characters into position to the right or left as determined by data structure or programming devices.

floating address: an address easily converted to a machine address by indexing, assembly, or some other method.

floating normalize control: pertaining to a specific bit, in the program status doubleword, that indicates whether (if 0) or not (if 1) the result of floating-point operation is to be normalized.

floating-point base: in a floating-point representation system, the implicit fixed positive integer base, greater than unity, that is raised to the power explicitly denoted by the exponent in the floating-point representation or represented by the characteristic in the floating-point representation and then multiplied by the fixed-point part to determine the real number represented; for example, in the floating-point representation of the number 0.0001234, namely 0.1234-3, the implicit floating-point base is 10. Synonymous with *floating-point radix.* (A) (B)

floating-point BASIC: a version of the language that allows use of decimal fractions. See *integer BASIC.*

floating-point feature: a processing unit feature that provides 4 64-bit floating-point registers to perform floating-point arithmetic calculations.

floating-point literal: a numerical literal whose value is expressed in floating-point notation; that is, as a decimal number followed by an exponent that indicates the actual placement of the decimal point.

floating-point number: a number represented in floating-point notation; the position of the radix point moves, or floats, because all numbers involved in this operation have the same exponent. See also *fixed-point part.*

floating-point operation: an arithmetic operation performed on floating-point numbers where the radix points are shifted permitting addition of numbers with differing exponents. See also *fixed-point part, flop.*

floating-point package: software that permits a computer to perform floating-point arithmetic.

floating-point precision: the maximum number of binary digits used as the mantissa of a single-precision floating-point fraction.

floating-point radix: synonym for *floating-point base.* (A)

floating-point register: a register used to manipulate data in a floating-point representation. (A) (B)

floating-point representation: a representation of a real number in a floating-point representation system; for example, a floating-point representation of the number 0.0001234 is 0.1234-3, where 0.1234 is the fixed-point part and -3 is the exponent. The numerals are expressed in the variable-point decimal numeration system. (B) Cf. *variable-point representation.* (A)

floating symbolic address: a label for identifying a word or other item in a routine independent of the location of the information within the routine.

flop: a floating-point operation per second. See also *floating-point operation.*

floppy: synonymous with *floppy disk.*

floppy disk (FD): a magnetic disk encased in flexible plastic that stores computer data. Usually available in 5¼ in. and 3½ in. formats. These can be single- or double-sided, and are available in a variety of densities. Cf. *microfloppies.*

floppy disk controller: devices that provide control of data transfer to and from a floppy disk.

floppy mini: a smaller floppy that is 5¼ inches square compared to 8 inches for a standard floppy.

flops: the number of floating-point operations per second.

flow: see *normal direction flow, reverse direction flow.* (A)

flow analysis:
(1) in compilers, a technique used to determine the specific interdependence of elements of a computer program.
(2) the detection and recording of the sequencing of instructions in computer programs, for example, as used in monitors and debugging routines. (A)

flowchart: a graphical representation of the definition, analysis, or solution of a problem in which symbols are used to represent such things as operations, data, flow, and equipment. Synonymous with *flow diagram.* Cf. *block diagram.* See *data flowchart, programming flowchart.*

flowcharting: representing a succession of events with lines, showing interconnections, linking symbols, showing events or processes.

flowchart symbol: a symbol used to represent operations, data, flow, or equipment in a flowchart. (A) (B)

flowchart technique: detailed flowcharts showing data and information requirements and actual methods and calculations for processing information.

flowchart text: the descriptive information that is associated with flowchart symbols. (A)

flow control: the procedure for controlling the data-transfer rate.

flow diagram: synonym for *flowchart.*

flow of control: sequence of execution.

flow-process diagram: synonymous with *systems flowchart.*

fluent computers: systems that immediately understand everyday languages making computers accessible to anyone who can write. See also *artificial intelligence.*

fluerics: the area within the field of fluidics in which components and systems perform functions such as sensing, logic, amplification, and control without the use of mechanical parts. (A)

flush:
(1) slang, to delete something, often superfluous.
(2) aligned with a margin.

flutter: the recurring speed variation of relatively low frequency in a moving medium.

flyback: time used by a spot on a terminal screen to pass from the end of a line to the beginning of the next.

flyback periods: time intervals during which a scanning beam is blocked out enabling it to be repositioned to commence the next line or field scanning activity in a television system.

flying spot scanner (FSS): in optical character recognition, a device employing a moving spot of light to scan a sample space, the intensity of the transmitted or reflected light being sensed by a photoelectric transducer. (A)

F-mode records: in COBOL, records of a fixed length, each of which is wholly contained within a block. Blocks may contain more than one record.

FOCH: see *forward channel.*

fold: to compact data by combining parts of the data, for example, to transform a two-word alphabetic key into a one-word numeric key by adding the numeric equivalents of the letters. (A)

folder: a container for documents, programs, and other folders on the desktop or in directory windows.

folding: a technique used with the universal character set (UCS) feature on an impact printer to allow each of the 256 possible character codes to print some character on a chain or train with fewer graphics. For example, folding allows the printing of uppercase graphic characters when lowercase are not available in the character array on the chain or train.

folding ratio: in virtual storage systems, the ratio of the size of real storage to the size of virtual storage.

font:
(1) a collection of letters, numbers, punctuation marks, and other typographical symbols with a consistent appearance, size, and style.
(2) a family or assortment of characters of a given size and style, for example, 9 point Bodoni Modern. See *type font.* (A)

font-change character (FC): a control character that selects and makes effective a change in the specific shape, or size, or shape and size of the graphics for a set of graphemes, the character set remaining unchanged. Synonymous with *face-change character.* (A) (B)

font family: a font in various sizes and styles.

footer: in word processing, a piece of text repeated at the bottom of each page. See *header.*

footprint: slang, desk or floor space needed for accommodating a computer.

forbidden combination: a combination of bits or other representations that is not valid according to some criteria. Cf. *illegal character.* (A)

force: to intervene manually in a routine and change the normal sequence of computer operations.

forced coding: programming requiring minimum waiting time to obtain information out of storage. Synonymous with *minimum-latency programming.*

foreground (FG): in multiprogramming, the environment in which high-priority programs are executed.

foreground area: synonymous with *foreground partition.*

foreground display image: synonym for *dynamic display image.*

foreground initiator: a program that is called into main storage to perform job control functions for foreground programs not executing in batch job mode.

foreground job:
(1) a high-priority job, usually a real-time job.

(2) an interactive or graphic display job that has an indefinite running time during which communication is established with one or more users at local or remote terminals.

foreground partition: in a multiprogramming system, a partition containing a high-priority applications program. Synonymous with *foreground area.*

foreground processing:
(1) the execution of a computer program that preempts the use of computer facilities. (A) (B)
(2) in word processing, a type of system operation that is perceived by the operator to execute immediately at the work station.
(3) cf. *background processing.* (A)

foreground program: in multiprogramming, a high priority program.

foreground region: a region to which a foreground job is assigned.

forgiving system: a user-friendly system all permitting inexperienced users to make mistakes without disastrous consequences.

form: the paper on which output data is printed by a line printer or character printer. See *Backus Naur form, normalized form, precoded form, printed card form.*

FORMAC (formula manipulation compiler): an extension of PL/1 designed for nonnumeric manipulation of mathematical expressions.

formal design review: an evaluation of the documentation of a system by a group of managers, analysts, and programmers to determine completeness, accuracy, and quality of design. Synonymous with *structured walk-through.*

formal logic: the study of the structure and form of a valid argument without regard to the meaning of the terms in the argument. (A) (B)

formal parameter: a variable, declared and used in a procedure or function declaration, that is replaced by an actual parameter when the procedure or function is called.

formal parameter list: the list of formal parameters contained in a procedure or function heading.

format:
(1) the appearance of the text in a document, including all tabs, line and character spacing.
(2) to prepare a disk so information can be stored on it.
(3) see *address format, instruction format.*

format character set: a character set (available in 10-, 12-, and 15-pitch) that provides graphics such as lines, corners, and intersections, that can be used, for example, to print column lines or boxes around data.

format designator: letters and symbols in instruction words for specifying and establishing a given format.

format effector character (FE): any control character used to control the positioning of printed, displayed, or recorded data. Synonymous with *layout character.* (A) (B)

format item: in PL/1, a specification used in edit-directed transmission to describe the representation of a data item in the stream (data format item) or to specify positioning of a data item within the stream (control format item).

format list: in PL/1, a parenthesized list of format items required for an edit-directed data specification.

format statement: in BASIC the PRINT-USING statement is a format statement used to control the graphic quality and the exact location of the printed characters in the output.

formatted display: on a display device, a display in which the attributes of one or more display fields have been defined by the user. Cf. *unformatted display.*

formatted dump: a dump in which certain data areas are isolated and identified.

formatted record: in FORTRAN, a record which is transmitted with the use of a FORMAT statement.

formatted systems services: a facility that provides certain system services as a result of receiving a field-formatted command, such as an INITIATE or TERMINATE command.

formatter: a program or circuit that writes the file marks, track marks, address marks, preambles, postambles, and check characters for floppy disks, disks, or tape drives.

formatting:
(1) determining the order of the information that is input to a computer or peripheral unit.
(2) arranging the layout of data that is output from the computer or a peripheral.

form feed:
(1) paper throw used to bring an assigned part of a form to the printing position.
(2) in word processing, a function that advances the typing position to the same character position on a predetermined line of the next form or page. Synonymous with *page skip.*

form feed character (FF):
(1) a format effector character that causes the print or display position to move to the next predetermined first line on the next form, the next page, or the equivalent. (A) (B)
(2) in word processing, synonym for *page-end character.*

form feed out: a form-positioning feature provided as an option on sprocket feed teleprinters. The automatic positioning of the typing unit to the first line of typing on the next form, at the same time feeding out the form in use so it may be torn off.

form overlay: in computer graphics, a projected pattern such as a report form, grid, or map used as the background for a display image.

form stop: a device that automatically stops a printer when the paper has run out.

formula manipulation: algebraic manipulation of mathematical formulas, primarily used to express computer programs by arithmetic formulas. (A)

for/next loop: the section of code in BASIC that goes through a fixed number of iterations determined by a preset index. See also *DO loop.*

FOR-NEXT statements: in a BASIC program, a pair of statements that automatically executes a specified sequence of instructions a specific number of times. Used to perform looping.

FOR statement: in PASCAL, a looping control structure similar to a WHILE loop but with predefined initial and final values for the loop control variable, as well as automatic incrementing (or decrementing) of the loop control variable.

FORTH: a programming language system characterized by three code and postfix, or reverse Polish, notation.

FORTRAN (formula translation):
(1) a programming language primarily used to express computer programs by arithmetic formulas. (A)
(2) a programming language primarily designed for applications involving numeric computations.

FORTRAN control characters: deprecated term for American National Standard control characters.

fortuitous conductor: any conductor which may provide an unintended path for signals, for example, water pipes, wire or cable, metal structural members, and so on.

40-column display standard: a terminal and the associated transmission system allowing up to 40 columns of characters on a single page of information.

forward-backward counter: a unit capable of adding or subtracting input so that it can count in either an increasing or decreasing direction.

forward bias: a voltage applied to a p-n crystal so that the positive terminal is applied to the p section and the negative terminal to the n section.

forward channel (FOCH): a data-transmission channel in which the direction of transmission coincides with that in which user information is being transferred.

forward error correction: a means of error detection and correction, based upon redundancy checking methods, where a high volume of redundant bits is computed and added to transmitted data. The redundancy is such that the receiving terminal can automatically correct as well as detect errors.

forward file recovery: the reconstruction of a file by updating an earlier version with data recorded in a journal. Cf. *backward file recovery.*

forward scan: an editing function making an output word conform to the control word by comparing positions from right to left and adding punctuations, such as decimals and dollar signs.

forward supervision: the use of supervisory sequences sent from the master to the slave station. Cf. *backward supervision.*

four-address: pertaining to an instruction format containing four address parts. (A)

four-bit binary coded decimal (BCD): a four binary digit computer code that uses unique combinations of zone bits and numeric bits to represent specific characters.

four-bit byte: synonym for *quartet.* (A) (B)

four-plus-one address: pertaining to an instruction that contains four operand addresses and the address of the next instruction to be executed. (A)

fourth-generation computer: a computer generation characterized by physically small, lower-cost microcomputers utilizing microprocessors and memory chips. See also *first-generation computer, second-generation computer, third-generation computer.*

fourth-generation language: computer language that eschews code to more closely mimic human language.

four-wire: the links available in full-duplex mode without requiring additional multiplexing.

FPLA: field-programmable logic array. An array using fusible links for programming the logic configuration.

fractional digit: a digit to the right of a decimal point.

fractional part: synonymous with *fixed-point part.*

fragmentation: occurs when information is placed in the computer's memory in such a way that there are a number of unused portions of memory that, individually, are too small to be useful. To solve this problem, the unused fragments of memory are collected and combined into one large area that can be used to store more information. See *storage fragmentation.*

frame:
(1) that portion of a tape, on a line perpendicular to the reference edge, on which binary characters may be written or read simultaneously. (B)
(2) in high-level data-link control (HDLC), the sequence of contiguous bits bracketed by and including opening and closing flag (01111110) sequences.
(3) in data transmission, the sequence of contiguous bits bracketed by and including beginning and ending flag sequences.
(4) a set of consecutive digit time slots in which the position of each digit time slot can be identified by reference to a frame alignment signal. (C)
(5) in a time division multiplex (TDM) system, a repetitive group of signals resulting from a signal sampling of all channels, including any additional signals for synchronizing and other required system information.
(6) in facsimile systems, a rectangular area, the width of which is the available line and the length of which is determined by the service requirements.
(7) synonym for *tape row*.
(8) see *display frame, film frame, main frame, page frame*.

frame alignment: a procedure where the timing of a receiving terminal is correctly adjusted to the alignment of frames in a received signal.

frame buffer: in computer graphics, a memory device which stores the contents of an image pixel by pixel. Frame buffers are used to refresh a raster image. Sometimes they incorporate local processing ability, and can be used to update the memory. The depth of the frame buffer is the number of bits per pixel, which determines the number of colors or intensities which can be displayed.

frame check sequence (FCS): a sequence of bits attached to a frame providing for the detection and correction of errors in a data link.

frame-creation terminal: a videotex tool designed to produce sophisticated graphics to accompany a text.

frame format: the definition of the structure of an indivisible unit of information transmitted in a data-communication system, including destination address, source address, frame type, the data, and frame check sequence.

frame grabber: a device installed with a visual display unit permitting the storage and continuous display of a frame of information.

frame level functions: the procedures of a packet-switching system for checking the transmission of data, to ensure that line errors have not taken place and for retransmitting frames automatically when errors are found.

frame pitch: in computer graphics, the distance between corresponding points on two successive frames. Synonymous with *pull down*.

frame store: a memory unit capable of storing a display of information for a page of text and graphics. Synonymous with *page store*.

framing: the process of selecting the bit groupings representing one or more characters from a continuous stream of bits.

framing bits: non-information-carrying bits to make possible the separation of characters in a bit stream. Synonymous with *sync bits*.

framing error: an error caused by failure of a receiving unit to identify correctly those bits that constitute a character.

franking: pertaining to devices that stamp or print postage.

free field: a property of information-processing recording media permitting recording of information without regard to a preassigned or fixed field.

free-form: pertaining to entry of data or the coding of statements without regard for predefined formats. Cf. *fixed-form*.

free format: an allowable formatting of program statements characterized by no rules governing the indentation or number of syntax elements that may appear on a line of code.

free storage: storage that is not allocated.

freeware: software given to the customer by a vendor free of charge.

freeze mode: an operational mode where the computer is stopped with all values held as they were when an interrupt took place.

frequency loading: a means for storing the most frequently used records at the beginning of a file so as to minimize access time.

friction feed: in a printer, a means by which paper is moved between the primary roller and the pinch roller.

fried: slang, not working because of hardware failure; burnt out.

FROM: see *fusable read-only memory.*

front end: the preprocessing of data prior to the main task of a program that has commenced.

front panel: a panel containing lights and switches for facilitating debugging by displaying information, and permitting direct control or access to registers or storage. A front panel needs a specific interface in addition to a monitor program.

FRU: see *field replaceable unit.*

fry: see *fried.*

FS: see *file separator character.* (A)

FSP: see *full-screen processing.*

FSS: see *flying spot scanner.*

FU: see *functional unit.*

full duplex (FD) (FDX): synonym for *duplex.* (A)

full-duplex operation: synonym for *duplex operation.*

full-duplex transmission: a method of operating a communications circuit so that each end can simultaneously transmit and receive.

full page display: a terminal displaying at least 80 columns (80 characters across) and 55 lines of copy (the average 8½ × 11 inch page capacity) on the screen at one time.

full-screen editing: a type of editing at a display terminal in which an entire screen of data is displayed at once and in which the user can access data through commands or by using a cursor. Cf. *line editing.*

full-screen processing (FSP): a method of operating a display station that allows the terminal operator to type data into some or all unprotected fields on the display screen before entering the data.

full word: synonym for *computer word.* (A) (B)

fully formed character: a printed character that is a complete image formed by uninterrupted strokes. Cf. *dot matrix character formation.*

fully perforated tape: perforated tape in which the perforations are complete; that is, in which the punch makes a complete hole in the tape (as opposed to chadless tape, where the hole is not completely punched out).

fully populated: a printed circuit board in which all of its capabilities have been implemented and there is no room for adding function by installing chips or other electronic units.

fully qualified name: a qualified name that is complete; that is, one that includes all names in the hierarchical sequence above the structure member to which the name refers, as well as the name of the member itself.

FUNC: see *function.*

function (F) (FCT) (FUNC):
(1) a mathematical entity whose value, that is, the value of the dependent variable, depends in a specified manner on the values of one or more independent variables, not more than one or more independent variables corresponding to each permissible combination of values from the respective ranges of the independent variables. (B)
(2) a specific purpose of an entity, or its characteristic action.
(3) in data communication, a machine action such as carriage return or line feed.
(4) in computer programming, synonym for *procedure.* (A)
(5) in PL/1, a function procedure (programmer-specified or built in); a procedure that is invoked by the appearance of one of its entry names in a function reference and which returns a value to the point of reference.
(6) a subroutine that returns the value of a single variable, and that usually has a single exit; for example, subroutines that

compute mathematical functions, such as sine, cosine, logarithm; or that compute the maximum of a set of numbers.

(7) see *boolean function, distributed function, generating function, recursive function.*

functional design: the specification of the working relationships among the parts of a data-processing system. (A) (B)

functional diagram: a diagram that represents the working relationships among the parts of a system. (A)

functional element: a combination of logical and delay elements that perform an elementary computer function.

functional error recovery: capabilities within an operating system for intervening in some common errors and attempting recovery action for preventing a system crash or program failure.

functional interleaving: the method of having input-output operations and computing activities proceed independently of each other, but sharing the same memory.

functional partitioning: a means of microprocess partitioning directed towards user microprogramming.

functional specification: a document showing the attributes of an item of equipment and/or software system and emphasizing what the equipment does (rather than how it does it). It should also explain how the inputs and outputs are related.

functional test: a test for determining whether a unit or a circuit can operate correctly under working conditions to fulfill the specification for the quality of service outlined in a system.

functional unit (FU): an entity of hardware, software, or both, capable of accomplishing a specified purpose. (A) (B)

function code (FC): the part of a computer instruction that specifies the operation to be carried out.

function digit: a unique computer code digit that describes the arithmetic or logical operation which is to be carried out.

function element: a unit that performs a logic function.

function-evaluation routines: pertaining to a set of commonly used mathematical routines. The initial set of routines include sine, cosine, tangent, arc sine, arc cosine, arc tangent, square root, natural logarithm, and exponential. These routines are written in fixed- and floating-point.

function generator: a functional unit whose output variable is equal to some function of its input variables. (B)

function hole: synonym for *designation hole.* (A)

function key:

(1) in computer graphics, a button or switch that may be operated to send a signal to the computer program controlling the display.

(2) on a terminal, a key, such as an ATTENTION or an ENTER key, that causes the transmission of a signal not associated with a printable or displayable character. Detection of the signal usually causes the system to perform some predefined function for the operator. Synonymous with *soft key.*

function library: subroutines that perform common mathematical functions using floating-point arithmetic (including square roots), exponentiation, and logarithms.

function multiplier: apparatus for altering the values of the product of two varying functions.

function name: in COBOL, a name, that identifies system logical units, printer and card punch control characters, and report codes. When a function name is associated with a mnemonic name in the environment division, the mnemonic name can then be substituted in any format in which substitution is valid.

function part: synonym for *operation part.* (A) (B)

function program: see *object program.*

function punch: synonymous with *designation hole.*

function reference: in PL/1, the appearance of an entry name or built-in function name (or an entry variable) in an expression.

function subprogram: an external function defined by FORTRAN statements and headed by a FUNCTION statement. It returns a value to the calling program unit at the point of reference.

function table:

(1) two or more sets of data so arranged that an entry in one set selects one or more entries in the remaining sets; for example, a tabulation of the values of a function for a set of values of the variable, a dictionary.

(2) a hardware device, or a subroutine that can either decode multiple inputs into a single output or encode a single input into multiple outputs. (A)

fundamental: the frequency under consideration; usually a pure sine wave with no distortion.

fusable read-only memory (FROM): read-only memory that is programmed by the blowing of fuse links. Once fused, FROMs cannot be corrected or altered.

FW: see *firmware*.

G:

(1) see *giga-*.

(2) see *group*.

GAIC: see *gallium arsenide integrated circuit*.

gallium arsenide integrated circuit (GAIC): the super chip of the 1990s. The advantage of gallium arsenide is that it is capable of working at two to three times the speed of silicon, which effectively makes it that much smaller.

game theory: a mathematical process, selecting an optimum strategy in the face of an opponent who has a strategy of his own.

gamut: in computer graphics, the total range of colors which can be displayed on a monitor.

gang punch: to punch identical data into a card deck.

gap: the interval between blocks of data on a magnetic tape needed to enable the medium to be stopped and started between reading or writing. See *interblock gap*.

gap character: a character that is included in a computer word for technical reasons but does not represent data. (A)

gap digit: the digit within a word used for a purpose other than to represent data or instructions, for example, a parity bit.

gapless: a magnetic tape on which raw data is recorded in a continuous fashion without word gaps.

gap scatter: the deviation from correct alignment of the magnetic read/write heads for the parallel tracks on a magnetic tape.

garbage: unwanted and meaningless information in memory or on tape. Synonymous with *hash*.

garbage collection: the rearrangement of the contents of store and the elimination of unwanted data in order to reclaim space for new data. See *garbage*.

garbage in, garbage out: see *GIGO*.

gas plasma display: a display using the glow produced by ionized neon gas for illuminating segments of the characters.

gate:

(1) a combination circuit with only one output channel. (B)

(2) a device having one output channel and one or more input channels, such that the output channel state is completely determined by the input channel states, except during switching transients.

(3) a combinational logic element having at least one input channel.

(4) see *AND gate, OR gate*. (A)

gateway: a computer having access to two networks with a capability of passing traffic between them.

gather write: writing a block of data of logical records from noncontinuous areas of store. See *scatter read*.

Gaussian: in computer graphics, a Gaussian distribution is a frequency distribution for a set of variable data, sometimes called a normal distribution and typically represented by a bell-shaped curve that is symmetrical about the mean. See *normal distribution.*

GDG: see *generation data group.*

GDTM: see *graphical environment operating system.*

GE: greater than or equal to. See *relational operator.*

GEN:
(1) see *generate.*
(2) see *generation.*

generalized mark-up language (GML) tag: see *GML.*

generalized routine: a routine for solving a general class of problems by inserting appropriate values into the program.

generalized sort/merge program: a program that is designed to sort or merge a wide variety of records in a variety of formats.

generalized subroutine: subroutines written for easy and ready use in several programs with only minor adjustments by the programmer.

general program: a program, expressed in computer code, to solve a class of problems or specializing in a specific problem when proper parametric values are supplied. Synonymous with *general routine.*

general-purpose computer (GPC): a computer that is designed to operate upon a wide variety of problems. (A) (B)

general-purpose interface: the registers or portion of memory available to two or more programs.

general-purpose interface bus: see *GPIB.*

general-purpose language: a programming language that is not restricted to a single type of computer, for example, BASIC, FORTRAN.

general-purpose operating system: an operating system designed to handle a wide variety of computing system applications.

general-purpose paper card: a card that meets the specification in applicable ISO standards, except for the printed card form. (A)

general-purpose program: a program performing basic function(s) commonly required in many other programs.

general-purpose register (GPR): a register, usually explicitly addressable within a set of registers, that can be used for different purposes, for example, as an accumulator, as an index register, or as a special handler of data. (A) (B) Cf. *special-purpose register.*

general register (GR): a register used for operations such as binary addition, subtraction, multiplication, and division. General registers are used primarily to compute and modify addresses in a program.

general routine: synonymous with *general program.*

general utility function: an auxiliary operation such as tape searching, tape-file copying, and tape dumps.

generate (GEN):
(1) to produce a computer program by selection of subsets from skeletal code under the control of parameters. (A)
(2) to produce assembler-language statements from the model statements of a macrodefinition when the definition is called by a macroinstruction.

generated address: an address that has been formed during the execution of a computer program. Synonymous with *synthetic address.* (A) (B)

generated error: a complete error made by employing operands that are not accurate, for example, using a rounded number. See *accuracy.*

generating function: in a given series of functions or constants, a mathematical function that, when represented by an infinite series, has those functions or constants as coefficients in the series. (A) (B)

generating program: synonymous with *generator.*

generating routine: synonymous with *generator.*

generation (GEN): in micrographics, a measure of the remoteness of the copy from the original material, the first microfilm representation being the first generation microfilm. (A)

generation data group (GDG): a collection of data sets that are kept in chronological order; each data set is called a *generation data set.*

generation data set: one generation of a generation data group.

generation number: a number forming part of the file label on a reel of magnetic tape. See also *grandfather tape*.

generation of a variable: in PL/1, the allocation of a static variable, a particular allocation of a controlled or automatic variable, or the storage indicated by a particular locator qualification of a based variable or by a defined variable or a parameter.

generator: a controlling routine that performs a generating function, for example, report generator, I/O generator. (A) See *character generator, compiler generator, dot matrix, macrogenerator, stroke character generator, vector generator*.

generator program: a program producing another program or data as output.

generic device type: a component of a data-processing terminal or peripheral unit that other equipment emulate so as to simplify installation.

generic name: in PL/1, the name of a family of entry names. A reference to the name is replaced by the particular entry name whose parameter descriptors match the attributes of the arguments in the argument list at the point of invocation.

get:
(1) to obtain a record from an input file.
(2) in word processing, the act of retrieving a defined block of text from a document and inserting it into the document being created or revised.

GETMAIN: the instruction found in some programming languages found on large-scale computers to request dynamic allocation of further memory.

ghost hyphen: a hyphen that is typed into a word that might eventually have to be hyphenated.

gibberish total: synonymous with *hash total*.

Gibson Mix: a statistically balanced mix of instructions that is typical of general data processing applications; a variation used for benchmark testing.

giga- (G): ten to the ninth power, 1,000,000,000 in decimal notation. When referring to storage capacity, two to the thirtieth power, 1,073,741,824 in decimal notation.

gigabyte: 1,073,741,824 bytes.

gigaflops: 1.2 billion flops. See *flop*.

gigascale integration: a billion components to a chip.

GIGO: garbage in, garbage out; the acronymous expression of the concept that the results produced from unreliable or useless data are equally unreliable or useless.

GJP: see *graphic job processor*.

global: pertaining to that which is defined in one subdivision of a computer program, and used in at least one other subdivision of that computer program. Cf. *local*. (A) See also *global code, global variable symbol*.

global code: that part of an assembler program that includes the body of any macrodefinition called from a source module and the open code portion of the source module. Cf. *local*.

global declaration: synonymous with *manifest constant*.

global identifier: in PASCAL, an identifier declared in the outermost block (main program); an identifier that is not local to a block, but whose scope includes that block.

global variable symbol: in assembler programming, a variable symbol that can be used to communicate values between macrodefinitions and between a macrodefinition and open code. Cf. *local variable symbol*.

glork: slang, anger when one tries to save editing and finds that the system has just crashed.

glossary: a vocabulary with annotations for a particular subject.

glossary function: in word processing, frequently used terms kept in storage which can be inserted at any point in a document by the operator.

GM: see *group mark*.

GML (generalized mark-up language) tag: a high-level formatting expression that, when processed by the DOCUMENT command, expands into one or more SCRIPT control words.

go: start printer.

GOOVOO: a file with a generation data group used for identifying the relative generation and volume numbers of the file.

Gothic character set: a character set (available in 10-, 12-, and 15-pitch) with 63 sans serif graphic characters.

GO TO (GOTO): a branch instruction in a high-level language.

GOTO-less programming: synonymous with *structured programming.*

go to sleep: occurs when a computer halts or a program appears to be doing nothing because it is locked in an endless loop.

GPC: see *general-purpose computer.*

GPIB: general purpose interface bus. A standard interface for connecting various units to a microcomputer. Synonymous with IEEE 488.

gppm: abbreviation for graphics pages per minute, a measure of laser printing speed (non-text).

GPR: see *general-purpose register.*

GR: see *general register.*

graceful exit: a user's ability to exit from a program without having to turn off a unit.

graceful shutdown: the automatic shutdown of a computer system without data loss or another calamity.

grade series: in computer graphics, a scale of colors used in graphics to present change in a variable. A graded series may be composed of progressive change in either lightness or saturation of one hue, in hue steps around the hue circle, or along the gray scale.

grain size: the number and sophistication of processing elements. The ultimate coarse-grained architecture is the von Neumann machine, with one main processor and memory bank. Instructions from the processor and data from memory flow back and forth through the bus, which limits processing speed. See also *coarse-grained parallel computers, fine-grained architectures, intermediate-grained computer architectures.*

gram (G): 0.035 ounces.

grammar: the word order in a communication or a portion of a communication.

grammatical error: a violation of the rules of use of a given computer language. Often such errors will be detected by the compiler as it converts the user's program statements into machine language. Diagnostic messages will then direct the user to the errors.

grandfather cycle: indicating the time for magnetic records to be retained prior to writing to permit records to be reconstructed in the event of losses or errors.

grandfather tape: a copy of a magnetic tape file which, since the copy was generated, has twice undergone an updating cycle. See also *grandparent.*

grandparent: synonymous with *grandfather* when used with files.

graph: a sheet of paper onto which have been placed curves, lines, points, and explanatory alphabetic and numerical information representing numerical data.

grapheme: a written or machine code that represents a single semanteme.

graph follower: a unit that reads data in the form of a graph, usually an optical sensing machine.

graphic: a symbol produced by a process such as handwriting, drawing, or printing. Synonymous with *graphic symbol.* (A) (B)

graphic character: a character, other than a control character, that is normally represented by a graphic. (A) (B)

graphic data reduction: converting graphic material to digital data.

graphic data structure: a logical sequence of digital data representing graphic data used in a graphic display.

graphic display resolution:
(1) the number of lines and characters per line able to be shown on a terminal screen.
(2) the number of pels of a screen. See *pel.*

graphic display unit: a communications terminal that displays data on a screen.

graphic documentation: a process developed for recording data on graphs and film.

graphic file maintenance: a process that updates physical representations, such as microfilm, film prints, output copies, and so on.

graphic information: digitally encoded information representing a description of a drawing.

graphic input device: in computer graphics, a device such as a digitizer which gives the computer the points which make up an image in such a way that the image can be stored, reconstructed, displayed or manipulated. Cf. *graphic output device.*

graphic job processor (GJP): a program that elicits job control information from a user performing job control operations at a display station. It interprets the information entered by the user and converts it into job control language.

graphic language: in computer graphics, any language used to program a display device.

graphic output device: in computer graphics, a device used to display or record an image. A display screen is an output device for soft copy; hard copy output devices produce paper, film, or transparencies of the image. Cf. *graphic input device.*

graphic panel: a display device showing the state of a process control operation in the form of lights, dials, and so forth.

graphic plotter: a plotting device used as a computer output machine.

graphic primitive: synonym for *display element.*

graphical environment operating system: a system that allows the user to run applications and manage disks by clicking and moving icons with a mouse. It provides windows and multitasking.

graphical user interface: program interface to make a program user-friendly. These typically use windows, icons, menus, mice, etc., to bypass coded commands.

graphics:
(1) information presented in the form of pictures or images.
(2) the display of pictures or images on a computer's display screen. Cf. *text.* See *interactive graphics, passive graphics.*

graphics language: see *graphic language.*

graphics mode: a mode in which daisy wheel printers produce lines and drawings, rather than letters and numbers.

graphic solution: a solution to a problem provided by graphs or diagrams replacing printed figures or text.

graphics peripheral: hardware, connected to a computer used to input graphics information such as tablets and light pens, or output graphics information, such as visual displays, plotters, and printers.

graphics plotter: a unit that provides hardcopy output of graphics displayed on a screen. There are two primary types: drum and flat-bed.

graphics tablet: a device for inputting graphics such as diagrams, maps, charts, or free-hand drawings on a computer.

graphic symbol: synonym for *graphic.* (A) (B)

graphic terminal:
(1) a video terminal.
(2) a communication terminal displaying data on a screen or on moving paper.

graph plotter: see *plotter.*

graunch: an unexpectedly damaging error.

gray code: a binary code in which sequential numbers are represented by binary expressions, each of which differs from the preceding expression in one place only. Synonymous with *reflected binary code.* (A)

grid: in optical character recognition, two mutually orthogonal sets of parallel lines used for specifying or measuring character images. (A)

grid chart: a representation of the relation between inputs, files, and outputs in matrix form.

group (G):
(1) a set of related records that have the same value for a particular field in all of the records.
(2) a series of records logically joined together. See also *print data set.*

grouped records: records combined into a unit to conserve storage space or reduce access time.

group indicate: the printing of indicative information from only the first record of a group.

grouping of records: combining of two or more records into one block of information on tape, to decrease the wasted time due to tape acceleration and deceleration and/or to conserve tape space. Synonymous with *blocking of records.*

group item: in COBOL, a data item made up of a series of logically related elementary items. It can be part of a record of a complete record.

group mark (GM): a mark that identifies the beginning or the end of a set of data which may include blocks, characters, or other items. (A) (B)

group marker: synonymous with *group mark.*

group name:

(1) a generic name for a collection of I/O devices, for example, DISK or TAPE. See also *device type, unit address.*

(2) one to eight alphameric characters beginning with an alphabetic #, $, or @ character that identifies a group to RACF.

group printing:

(1) that activity of a machine that does not print data from every card. Instead it summarizes the data held in a group of cards and prints only the summarized totals.

(2) printing one line of information for a specific group.

group separator (GS): the information separator intended to identify a logical boundary between items called groups. (A) (B)

grovel: slang, to work interminably but without progress.

grungy: slang, significantly filthy or grubby, as with a program.

GS: see *group separator.* (A)

GT: greater than. See also *relational operator.*

guard bit: a bit indicating the status of words or groups of words of memory that is used to indicate to hardware units or programs if the contents of a memory location can be altered by a program, or if a core or disk memory words are to be filed or protected.

guard signal: a signal allowing values to be read only when the values are not subject to ambiguity error.

gubbish: nonsense; from garbage and rubbish.

guest: a person that connects to another computer on a network without having to give a name or password.

guest access: a type of access to a computer that permits any network user to connect to the computer for the purpose of file sharing or program linking.

guest computer: a computer performing under the influence of another computer, the host. An operator gives all commands to the host, which decides which ones ought to be passed on to the guest, what functions it should perform, and so on. See *host.*

guidance code: see *operator guidance code.*

guide edge: synonym for *reference edge.* (A) (B)

guide margin: the distance between the guide edge and the center of the closest track of a tape when measuring across a paper tape.

gulp: a small group of binary digits composed of several bytes, and treated as a unit.

gun:

(1) the group of electrodes of the electron beam emitter in a CRT.

(2) slang, to terminate forcibly a program or job.

H:

(1) see *hardware.*

(2) see *head.*

(3) see *hecto.*

(4) see *host.*

HA: see *home address.*

hacker: slang, an individual intensely absorbed with and/or extremely knowledgeable about computer hardware and software. Also used in the pejorative to describe those who break into and corrupt computer systems.

half-add: an instruction that performs bit-by-bit half-adder activities; can be done utilizing an exclusive-OR operation without carries.

half-carry: the carry from bit 3 into bit 4 needed for adding packed binary coded decimal numbers correctly, where two binary coded decimal digits reside in one 8-bit byte.

half-duplex (HD) (HDX): in data communication, pertaining to an alternate, one way at a time, independent transmission. Cf. *duplex.*

half-height floppy disc drives: a design permitting a floppy disc drive to displace approximately one half the physical space needed by the more traditional floppy disc drive.

half-page screen: a screen that can display between 20 and 30 lines of text at a time—about half a normal single-spaced letter page.

half-shift register: a flip-flop used in shift registers requiring two half-shift registers to make one stage of a shift register.

half-spacing: the ability to move down half a line, rather than a whole line, and start typing again.

halftime emitter: a unit that emits synchronous pulses midway between the row pulses of a punched card.

half-word: a contiguous sequence of bits or characters that comprise half a computer word and is capable of being addressed as a unit. (A)

halt (HLT): see *breakpoint halt.* (A)

halt indicator: an indicator on a panel or console that is activated whenever the processor is in the halt mode.

halt instruction: a machine instruction that stops the execution of a program. Synonym for *pause instruction.* (A) (B)

halt switch: a switch on a panel or console that causes the processor to cease executing instructions.

hamming code: a data code that is capable of being corrected automatically. (A)

hamming distance: synonym for *signal distance.* (A)

hand-feed punch: a keypunch into which punch cards or punched cards are manually entered, and removed, one at a time. (A) (B)

hand-held computer: a system small enough to carry in a standard pocket. Cf. *desktop computer, portable computer.*

handler: a portion of the program used to control or communicate with an external unit.

handshaking: the go-ahead signals that control the flow of information sent between two computers when using a communications program.

handshaking protocol: a program sequence that greets and aids the programmer in using procedures or programs of a system.

hands-off operation: synonymous with *closed shop.*

hands-on-background: prior work experience developed by operating the hardware and often used as a criterion of programmer capability.

hands-on operation: synonymous with *open shop.*

handwriting recognition: the capability of a computer having a visual scanning unit to examine handwritten material, verify a signature, or determine information content.

hanger bar: the rack from which magnetic tapes are hung for storage.

hanging: when a program stops, i.e., "crashes," or when a printer freezes.

hang up: an unanticipated stop in a program sequence, caused by a program error.

hangup prevention: creating a program so that no sequence of instructions can cause a halt or a nonterminating situation.

hard card: a hard disk on a circuit board that can be inserted into an expansion slot.

hard copy:

(1) in computer graphics, a permanent copy of a display image that is portable and can be read directly by human beings; for example, a display image that is recorded on paper.

(2) a printed copy of machine output in a visually readable form; for example, printed reports, listings, documents, and summaries. See also *display (1).*

(3) cf. *soft copy.*

hard-copy log: in systems with multiple console support or a graphic console, a permanent record of system activity.

hard copy printer: a printing unit that produces a printout of information from a computer or terminal on paper.

hard-copy video interface: a unit that permits production of hard-copy output on an electrostatic printer/plotter from a video source.

hard disk: a disk made of metal and sealed into a drive or cartridge. A hard disk can store very large amounts of information. It can hold much more information than a floppy disk, and it spins much faster. Cf. *floppy disk.* See *cartridge disk, Winchester disk.*

hard disk pack: a removable set of magnetic disks loaded as a unit on a disk drive.

hard disk storage: a data storage apparatus used to retain files of information in computers, having data recorded on tracks on both sides of a magnetized disk. Cf. *diskette.*

hard error: an error, frequently concerned with a malfunction of hardware that can be readily diagnosed and to some extent predicted. Cf. *soft error.*

hard failure: equipment failure requiring repair before the unit can be placed back into use.

hard patch: a repair to a program file so that it becomes permanent. If the program is reloaded into memory, the fix is still active. Cf. *soft patch.*

hard return: a symbol at the end of a line of text that indicates the end of one line and the beginning of the next. Cf. *soft return.*

hard sector disk: a floppy disk divided into sectors and tracks by physical, nonalterable means such as a hole punched in the disk to designate each sector. See also *soft sector.*

hard sectoring: the physical marking of sector boundaries on a magnetic disk by punching holes in the disk where all available space can be used for data storage.

hard stop: an immediate termination of operation or execution.

hard wait: see *wait state.*

HARDWR: see *hardware.*

hardware (H) (HARDWR) (HDW) (HW): physical equipment used in data processing, as opposed to programs, procedures, rules, and associated documentation. (B) Cf. *software.* (A)

hardware assembler: an assembler consisting of PROMs that are mounted on simulation boards, permitting the prototype unit to assemble its own program.

hardware check: a failure in a hardware unit that halts operation. Synonym for *automatic check.* (A)

hardware configuration: the arrangement and relationship of devices making up a computer system, including the paths that unite them; usually applies to the computer and all its connected peripheral devices.

hardware error: a computer program malfunction, caused by failure of the hardware and not by a bug in the program.

hardware floating point: advanced circuitry in a CPU capable of doing floating-point arithmetic.

hardware interrupt: any interrupt that schedules input-output apparatus permitting operations to be performed simultaneously with processing.

hardware monitor: a device that gathers measurements of electrical events, such as voltage levels, in a digital computer for evaluating its performance. Cf. *software monitor.*

hard wire: to build a program right into the computer, so it cannot be taken out with disassembling the equipment.

hard-wire logic: any system of logic elements using formed or wired connections.

hardwiring: permanently wired electronic components capable of logical decisions, that is, intelligent terminals functioning without software. In a hard-wired computer, the program logic cannot be altered except by replacing the circuit boards or memories.

Hartley: in informational theory, a unit of logarithmic measures of information equal to the decision content of a set of ten mutually exclusive events expressed by the logarithm with the base ten; for example, the decision content of a character set of eight characters equals 0.903 Hartley. Synonymous with *information content decimal unit.* (A) (B)

hash: see *garbage.*

hash index: the first estimate of the location of an entry within a table.

hashing:
(1) the application of an algorithm to the records in a data set to obtain a symmetric grouping of the records. Synonymous with *key folding.*
(2) in an indexed data set, the process of transforming a record key into an index value for storing and retrieving a record.

hash total: the result obtained by applying an algorithm to a set of data for checking purposes; for example, a sum of the numerical values of specified data items. Synonym for *control total, gibberish total.*

HC: see *host computer.*

HD: see *half-duplex.*

HDA: head/disk assembly. The airtight assembly composed of a disk pack and read/write heads; used in a Winchester disk.

HRD: see *header.*

HDW: see *hardware.*

HDX: see *half-duplex.*

head (H): a device that reads, writes, or erases data on a storage medium; for example, a small electromagnet used to read, write, or erase data on a magnetic drum or magnetic tape, or the set of perforating, reading, or marking devices used for punching, reading, or printing on perforated tape. (A) (B) See *magnetic head, read head, read/write head, write head.*

head cleaning kit: material having a dirt solvent for cleaning the read/write head of a tape drive or floppy disk drive.

head crash: damage caused to a magnetic disk surface resulting from impact by the read/write head.

head/disk assembly: see *HDA.*

header (HDR):
(1) system-defined control information that precedes user data.
(2) that portion of a message that contains control information for the message such as one or more destination fields, the name of the originating station, an input sequence number, a character string indicating the type of message, and a priority level for the message. See *block control header.*

header card: a card that contains information related to the data in cards that follow. (A)

header/footer: a word or series of words, and/or page numbers that appear consistently at the top or bottom of all pages of a document, including copyright notices, company logos, and so on.

header record: a record containing common, constant, or identifying information for a group of records that follows. Synonymous with *header table.*

headers and trailers: repetitive words, phrases, or sentences placed at predetermined locations of every page of the document.

header segment: a part of a message that contains any portion of the message header.

header sheet: an instruction sheet for an optical character recognition unit which informs it of the format, and so on, to be expected on follow up sheets.

header table: synonym for *header record.*

head gap: the distance between a read or write head and the surface of the recording medium. See *read/write head.*

heading: in ASCII and data communication, a sequence of characters preceded by the start-of-heading character used as machine sensible address or routing information. Cf. *text.* (A)

heading character: see *start-of-heading character.* (A)

heading record: the record containing an identification or description of the output report for which ensuing records are related to and concerned with the body of a report.

head of string: the first disk drive in a group acting as a group leader by performing certain control activities for the other units.

head-on collision: an event occurring in a two-way data network when two nodes secure the opposite end of a data circuit at the same instant.

head stepping rate: the speed at which a read/write head on the disk drive moves from track to track over the disk surface.

heap: a portion of memory organized as a stack, used by some compilers to store dynamic (pointer) variables during program execution.

hecto (H): hundred.

hectometer (hm): one hundred meters. 109.36 yards.

hello program: a program that is run first in a system when the unit is started, permitting the user to sign on.

HELP: in interactive computers, users type the command *HELP* when they are uncertain about what to do next or how to perform some activities from the keyboard. At that time the computer provides assistance.

hercules graphics card (HGC): a high resolution graphics card for monochrome displays.

hesitation: a short automatic suspension of a main program to carry out a part or all of another operation; for example, a fast transfer of data to or from a peripheral unit.

heterogeneous network: a network of dissimilar host computers, such as those of different manufacturers.

heuristic: pertaining to exploratory methods of problem solving in which solutions are discovered by evaluation of the progress made toward the final result.

heuristic method: any exploratory method of solving problems in which an evaluation is made of the progress toward an acceptable final result using a series of approximate results. (A) (B)

hex: see *sexadecimal.*

hexadecimal: synonym for *sexadecimal.* (A) (B)

hexadecimal constant: in FORTRAN, the character Z followed by a hexadecimal number, formed from the set 0 through 9 and A through F.

hexadecimal notation: notation of numbers in the base 16. Synonymous with *sexadecimal notation.*

hexadecimal number system: a base 16 number system commonly used when printing the contents of main memory to aid programmers in detecting errors.

hexadecimal representation: a notation in which a group of four binary digits is represented by one digit of the hexadecimal (base 16) number system.

hex pad: a keyboard having input to a microprocessor in hexadecimal notation.

HGC: see *hercules graphics card.*

HIC: see *hybrid integrated circuit.*

hidden file: in DOS systems, a file that is not accessible or visible.

hierarchical classification: a designation framework where terms are arranged based on some hierarchical structure.

hierarchical computer network: a computer network consisting of several levels of processing and control computers, each computer specifically designed to perform its particular function.

hierarchical storage management: a time-and-usage sensitive means of handling large quantities of data, where the selection of a storage medium for a specific file depends on how soon or frequently the file is needed.

hierarchy (HIR): see *data hierarchy, hierarchy of operations.*

hierarchy of operations: relative priority assigned to arithmetic or logical operations that must be performed.

high byte: (FFFB) bits 8 through 15 of a 16-bit binary number.

high core: the upper address range of a computer, which in most units is occupied by the operating system.

high density: the provision of a high storage capacity per unit storage space, for example, in bits per inch.

high density disk: a floppy disk that is capable of being formatted to hold more information than the standard low density disks. A 3½-inch high density disk can hold 1.44 M of data, and a 5¼-inch high density disk can hold 1.2 M. A high density disk can also be formatted at low density. Cf. *low density disk.*

high-level compiler: a program capable of translating statements in high-level language into their machine-language equivalents.

high-level index: the first part of a file name, indicating the category of data to which it belongs.

high-level language (HLL): a programming language that does not reflect the structure of any one given computer or that of any given class of computers. (A) (B)

high-level source code: statements or statement lines as original directives that a programmer prepares to direct the movement of a computer when utilizing a high-level language such as BASIC, COBOL, and so on.

high memory: in DOS systems, the first 64K above 1 MB of memory.

high-order digit: a digit occupying a significant or highly valued position in a notational system.

high-order position: the left-most position in a string of characters.

high-overhead: see *overhead.*

high punch: the 12, 11, and zero punch are zone punches, the 12 punch being the highest (vertically) on the standard punched card.

high resolution: the quality of video graphics display systems or printers capable of reproducing images in great detail to a high degree of accuracy. Cf. *low resolution.*

high resolution display: a visual display system that can resolve a picture containing considerable detail.

high resolution graphics: a standard for displaying graphic information permitting fine lines and details to be resolved.

high side: the side of a remote unit facing a computer.

high-speed bus: see *bus.*

high-speed carry: in parallel addition, any procedure for speeding up the processing of carries; for example, standing-on-nines carry. (B) Cf. *cascaded carry.* (A)

high-speed modem: a unit that connects a data terminal apparatus to a communications line and is able to operate at speeds up to 9,600 bits per second. Cf. *modem.*

high-speed printer (HSP): a printer operating at a speed more compatible with the speed of computation and data

processing so that it may function on line.

high-speed reader (HSR): a reading device connected to a computer so as to function on line without seriously holding up the computer.

high-speed read/punch diagnostic: a test for peripherals and controller using a test tape for reading and punching activities.

high-water mark: in computers utilizing a queue, the maximum number of jobs found in the queue awaiting execution during a period of observation.

highway: synonymous with *bus.*

HIPO (hierarchy, input, process, output): a graphics tool for designing, developing, and documenting program function.

HIR: see *hierarchy.*

hi-res: short for *high-resolution graphics.*

histogram: a horizontal bar chart readily printed on a computer printer.

history file: a file in which a record is kept of jobs or transactions.

history run: printing out all transactions of a process for reading or recording purposes.

hit:
(1) a comparison of two items of data that satisfies specified conditions.
(2) a transient disturbance to a data communication medium. (A)
(3) see *light-pen detection.*

hit-on-the-fly printer: synonym for *on-the-fly printer.* (A)

hit ratio: the ratio of the number of successful references to main storage to the total number of references.

HLL: see *high-level language.*

HLT: see *halt.*

hobby computer: a computer not used for profit (or a tax writeoff).

hog: a program requiring large amounts (or the exclusive use) of an available resource, such as a main memory.

HOL: high order languages. See *high-level language.*

hold: to retain data in one storage unit after transferring it to another one or to another location in the same device. Cf. *clear.*

hold button: a button found in analog computer consoles permitting the operation to be temporarily stopped for observation by an operator.

hold facility: the ability to permit interruption of the operation of a computer in such a fashion that the values of the variables at the time of interruption are not altered; thus permitting computation to continue when the interruption stops.

hold instruction: a computer instruction causing data pulled from storage to be simultaneously held in storage after it is called out and transferred to its new location.

hold mode: an operating mode of an analog computer during which computing action is stopped and all variables are held at the value they had when this mode is entered. (B)

hold queue: a queue where jobs already submitted for execution are held until a later period to be run.

hole: the blank left in a card following punching. See also *designation hole.*

hole pattern: synonymous with *pattern* (1).

Hollerith: pertaining to a particular type of code or punched card utilizing 12 rows per column and usually 80 columns per card. (A)

Hollerith card: a punch card characterized by 80 columns and 12 rows of punch positions. (A)

Hollerith code: an alphanumeric punched card code.

home: the beginning position of a cursor on a terminal screen, usually in the top left-hand corner of the screen.

home address (HA): an address written on a direct-access volume, denoting a track's address relative to the beginning of the volume.

homebrew: early systems made by hobbyists (often in basements or garages) which evolved as personal computers and a new business.

home computer: see *personal computer.*

home-grown software: programs written by the user of the computer.

home loop: an operation involving only those input and output units associated with the local terminal.

homeostatis: the dynamic state of a system where input and output are exactly balanced, so that there is no change.

home record: the first record in a chain of records.

hook: a program's modification to hook additional instructions into an existing part of the program. The hook is often a GOTO that points to these instructions, which are found elsewhere.

hopper: see *card hopper.*

horizontal feed: pertaining to the entry of a punch card into a card feed with a long edge first. (A)

horizontal pitch: the number of characters per inch produced on a line by a printer or a display unit.

horizontal positions: see *addressable horizontal positions.* (A)

horizontal raster count: the number of horizontal divisions in a raster.

horizontal scrolling: the ability of a system to shift horizontally blocks of lines of text or data to view more characters than can fit on the screen at one time.

horizontal system: a programming system designed so that instructions are written horizontally, for example, across the page.

horizontal tab: a machine function causing the printing mechanism or cursor to skip to a predetermined position.

horizontal table: in indexing, a table whose entries are stored sequentially; that is, entry one, byte one; entry one, byte two; and so on.

horizontal tabulation character (HT): a formal effector character that causes the print or display position to move forward to the next of a series of predetermined positions along the same line. (A) (B)

horizontal wraparound: on a display device, the continuation of cursor movement from the last character position in a horizontal row to the first character position in the next row, or from the first position in a row to the last position in the preceding row. Cf. *vertical wraparound.*

hosed up: synonymous *dorfed up.*

host (H): an information processor which performs the instruction processing work of the enterprise. A host processor is generally self-sufficient and requires no supervision from other processors. See *data host.* See also *host computer, host interface, host node, host processor, host system.*

host application program: an application program that is executed in the host computer.

host computer (HC):
(1) in a network, a computer that primarily provides services such as computation, data-base access, or special programs or programming languages.
(2) the primary or controlling computer in a multiple computer installation.
(3) a computer used to prepare programs for use on another computer or on another data-processing system; for example, a computer used to compile, link, edit, or test programs to be used on another system.
(4) synonym for *host processor.*

hostile environment: created when applying software to a system for which it was not designed. Utilizes special utilities to make the software and system compatible.

hostile user: a user intending to confuse or interrupt a network. Protections against this happening are usually built into the system.

host interface: the interface between a network and a host computer.

host node: a node at which a host processor is situated.

host processor (HP):
(1) a processor that controls all or part of a user-application network.
(2) in a network, the processing unit in which the access method for the network resides.
(3) a processing unit that executes the access method for attached communication controllers.
(4) synonymous with *host computer.*

host subarea: a subarea that contains a host node.

host system:
(1) a data-processing system that is used to prepare programs and the operating environments for use on another computer or controller.
(2) the data-processing system to which a network is connected and with which the system can communicate.

hot: a terminal or conductor connected, alive, or energized; that is not at ground potential.

hot chassis: a terminal with its chassis connected to one side of a power line, allowing the chassis itself to provide the earth or ground.

hot electron effect: stray alpha particles and vanishing light beams that reduce the efficiency of semiconductor circuits, change a transistor's electrical characteristics, and make them less reliable. See *one-micron memory chips.*

hot I/O: a hardware failure in a peripheral unit.

hot spare: an extra unit such as a modem kept powered on but not active for use in case another similar unit fails. Synonymous with *hot standby.*

hot standby: synonymous with *hot spare.*

hourglass pointer: the symbol that the mouse pointer changes to when the user must wait for the computer to perform an operation.

housekeeping: see *housekeeping operation.*

housekeeping operation: an operation that facilitates the execution of a computer program without making a direct contribution. For example, initialization of storage areas; the execution of a calling sequence. Synonymous with *overhead operation.* (A) (B).

housing: any enclosure or cabinet for storing equipment.

HP: see *host processor.*

HSP: see *high-speed printer.*

HSR: see *high-speed reader.*

HT: see *horizontal tabulation character.* (A)

hub polling: a system of polling where the controller activates the most distant terminal to determine if it wants to send or receive information, and that terminal responds accordingly prior to activating its neighboring terminal directly, and so on until the polling cycle is finished. See also *roll-call polling.*

hue: in computer graphics, subject terms which refers to the objectively measurable dominant wavelength of radiant energy on the visible portion of the electromagnetic spectrum; the most basic attribute of color. Used loosely, also refers to mixtures of different wavelengths, such as purple.

hue circle: in computer graphics, a circle formed from the linear spectral hues of violet, blue, green, yellow, orange, and red. Intermediary colors of red-violet, blue-violet, blue-green, yellow-green, yellow-orange, and red-orange are often included. Synonymous with *color circle* and *color wheel.*

human engineering: method of designing something to aid people, as contrasted with designing for a machine. See also *ergonomics.*

human factors: machine design variables based on limitations of the needs of people.

human-oriented language: a programming language that is more like a human language than a machine language.

HW: see *hardware.*

hybrid circuit: complex circuit which is made by interconnecting individual integrated circuits, semiconductor devices, resistors, and capacitors on thick film or thin film substrates.

hybrid computer: a computer that processes both analog and digital data. See also *analog computer, digital computer.*

hybrid integrated circuit (HIC): a class of integrated circuits wherein the substrate is a passive material such as ceramic and the active chips are attached to its surface.

hybrid interface: the interface between an analog and digital device.

hybrid programming: routines in the hybrid programming library are designed to help engineers and scientists decide which parts of a problem can be solved in digital domain. These routines deal with timing, function-generation integration, and general simulation issues; provide diagnosis of hardware operations; and check on whether the analog device is scaled and wired correctly.

hybrid system: a system having both digital computer and analog computer capability.

HYP: see *required hyphen character.*

HyperCard: programming environment for the Apple Macintosh creating a simple user interface. See also *authoring tool.* See *Hypertext.*

hyperdrives: synonymous with *E-disks.*

hypergroup: synonymous with *15-super-group.*

hypertape: a high-speed tape unit using cartridges to house the supply and takeup reels that permit automatic loading.

Hypertext: a unique database approach, which links various associated data, programs, pictures, etc. Hypertext systems, such as HyperCard, are called authoring systems. See *authoring systems.*

hyphenating: putting in hyphens when a word processor breaks up words at the right margin, to create an even line of text there, as in a printed book.

hysteresis error: the difference in readings obtained in a system with and without hysteresis present.

hysteresis loop: see *magnetic hysteresis loop.* (A)

I:

(1) see *input.*

(2) see *instruction.*

(3) see *interrupt.*

IA: see *instruction address.*

i address: in some devices, the location of the next instruction to be executed based on whether or not a branch operation occurs.

IAL: see *International Algebraic Language.*

I and A: indexing and abstracting.

IAR: see *instruction address register.*

I-beam: a type of pointer shaped like the capital letter "I." Used for entering and editing text.

IBG: see *interblock gap.*

IC:

(1) see *instruction counter.*

(2) see *integrated circuit.*

icand: see *multiplicand.*

icon:

(1) a small pictorial representation of a file, disk, menu, option, or other object or feature.

(2) an image that graphically represents an object, a concept, or a message.

ICU: see *instruction control unit.*

ID:

(1) see *identification.*

(2) see *identifier.*

IDB: see *integrated data base.*

IDE: abbreviation for intelligent drive electronics. A lower priced hard disk drive interface for IBM PC's and compatibles.

idealized system: a theoretical system used as the standard for measuring the performance of other systems.

idea processors: synonymous with *mindmare.*

identification (ID) (IDENT): a label consisting of a coded name showing a unit of data, for example, a file name.

identification division: one of the four main parts of a COBOL program. The identification division identifies the source program and the object program and, in addition, may include such documentation as the author's name, the installation where written, and the date written.

identifier (ID):

(1) a character or group of characters used to identify or name items of data and possible to indicate certain properties of that data. (A) (B)

(2) in COBOL, a data name, unique in itself, or made unique by the syntactically correct combination of qualifiers, subscripts, and indexes.

identifier word: a full-length computer word associated with a search or a search-read function. In a search or search-read

function, the identifier word is stored within a special register in the channel synchronizer and compared with each word read by the peripheral unit.

identify: to assign a label to a file or data or to an item of data held in store.

identity element: a logic element that performs an identity operation. Synonymous with *identity gate.* (A) (B)

identity gate: synonym for *identity element.* (A) (B)

identity operation: the boolean operation, the result of which has the boolean value 1, if and only if all the operands have the same boolean value. An identity operation on two operands is an equivalence operation. (B) Cf. *nonidentity operation.*

idle link: synonym for *inactive link.*

idle time: operable time during which a functional unit is not operated. (B) Cf. *operating time.* (A)

IDP: see *integrated data processing.* (A)

IEEE: Institute of Electrical and Electronics Engineers. A computer society established to advance computer and data-processing technology by promoting cooperation and information exchange among its members and excellence within the field. Synonymous with *I-triple-E.*

IEEE 488: synonymous with *GPIB.*

I/F: see *interface.*

IF-AND-ONLY-IF element: a logic element that performs the boolean operation of equivalence. Synonymous with *IF-AND-ONLY-IF gate.* (A) (B)

IF-AND-ONLY-IF gate: synonym for *IF-AND-ONLY-IF element.* (A) (B)

IF-AND-ONLY-IF operation: synonym for *equivalence operation.* (A) (B)

IFIPS: International Federation of Information Processing Societies. A multinational organization of data-processing societies established to promote and advance worldwide cooperation in the fields of information science and data processing.

IF statement:

(1) a conditional statement that specifies a condition to be tested and the action to be taken if the condition is satisfied.

(2) a statement used for conditional statement execution. IF is always followed by a THEN clause and, optionally, an ELSE clause.

IF-THEN: synonymous with *implication gate.*

IF-THEN element: a logic element that performs the boolean operation of implication. Synonymous with *IF-THEN gate.* (A) (B)

IF-THEN-ELSE: a program statement used in high-level languages. Should a certain logical assertion be true, the statement following the THEN is executed. If the assertion is not true, the statement following the ELSE is executed.

IF-THEN gate: synonym for *IF-THEN element.* (A) (B)

IF-THEN operation: synonym for *implication.* (A) (B)

ignore: provides the ability to ignore certain abnormal conditions which may arise. Synonymous with *ignore character.* See *cancel character.*

ignore character: synonym for *cancel character.* (A) (B)

IIL: see *integrated injection logic.*

illegal character: a character or combination of bits that is not valid according to some criteria; for example, with respect to a specified alphabet, a character that is not a member. Cf. *forbidden combination.*

illegal code: a symbol that is not a true member of any defined code or language.

illegal operation: a process resulting when a computer either cannot perform the instruction part or will perform with invalid and undesired results. The limitation is usually a function of built-in constraints of the computer.

illumination model: synonymous with *reflectance model.*

IM:
(1) see *integrated modem.*
(2) see *interrupt mask.*

image:
(1) a fully processed unit of operational data that is ready to be transmitted to a remote unit; when loaded into control storage in the remote unit the image determines the operations of the unit.

(2) a faithful likeness of the subject matter of the original.
(3) see *card image, cine-oriented image, comic-strip oriented image, core image, display image.*

image area: in micrographics, that part of the film frame reserved for an image. (A)

image dissector: in optical character recognition, a mechanical or electronic transducer that sequentially detects the level of light intensity in different areas of a completely illuminated sample space. (A) Synonymous with *dissector.*

image graphics: in computer graphics, a technique for displaying images without the use of coordinate data, for example, form flash. Synonymous with *noncoded graphics.*

image printer: a printer using optical technology to compose an image of a complete page from digital input.

image processing: processing of images using computer techniques.

image sensor: synonymous with *charge couple device.*

image space: see *display space, image storage space.*

image storage space: in computer graphics, the storage locations occupied by a coded image. Synonymous with *coded-image space.*

IML (IMPL): initial microcode (or microprogram) load. The technique for loading a microprogram into main memory, usually from a diskette.

immediate access: the ability of a computer to enter and retrieve data from memory without delay.

immediate-access storage: a storage device whose access time is negligible in comparison with other operating times. (A)

immediate address: the contents of an address part that contains the value of an operand rather than an address. Synonymous with *zero-level address.* (A) (B)

immediate addressing: a method of addressing in which the address part of an instruction contains an immediate address. (A) (B)

immediate data:
(1) data contained in an instruction rather than in a separate storage location.
(2) data transferred during instruction execution time.

immediate instruction: an instruction that contains within itself an operand for the operation specified, rather than an address of the operand. (A) (B)

immediate processing: synonymous with *demand processing*.

impact paper: a coated paper that may be used to get one or more copies of printed, typed, or handwritten information without the need for a ribbon or other inking device. Each sheet is coated on the front. Pressure on the top of the top sheet causes the character to appear on the front of that sheet and on the front of subsequent sheets underneath the top sheet, thus eliminating the need for carbon paper between sheets.

impact printer (IP): a printer in which printing is the result of mechanical impacts. (A) (B)

imperative macroinstruction: macroinstructions that are converted into object program instructions.

imperative operation: an instruction requiring the manipulating of data by the computer.

imperative statement: a statement that specifies an action to be taken unconditionally. Synonym for *instruction*. (B)

implement: carrying out or giving physical, functional reality to a plan. Some software are tools for implementing usable applications of mathematical, logical, or business concepts.

implementation:
(1) installing a new piece of hardware or software.
(2) the description of how a programming language or other software performs in comparison with others of the same type.

implication: the dyadic boolean operation, the result of which has the boolean value 0, if and only if the first operand has the boolean value 0 and the second has the boolean value 1. Synonymous with *conditional implication operation, IF-THEN operation.* (A) (B)

implication gate: a device or circuit that performs the implication operation. Synonymous with *IF-THEN, inclusion gate.*

implicit address: in assembler programming, an address reference that is specified as one absolute or relocatable expression. An implicit address must be converted into its explicit base-displacement form before it can be assembled into the object code of a machine instruction.

implicit declaration: in PL/1, the establishment of an identifier, which has no explicit or contextual declaration, as a name. A default set of attributes is assumed for the identifier.

implicit differentiation: in analog computers, the technique used where functions are derived implicitly.

implicit opening: in PL/1, the opening of a file as the result of an input or output statement other than the OPEN statement.

implied addressing: a method of addressing in which the operation part of an instruction implicitly addresses operands. (A) (B)

implied decimal point: see *assumed decimal point.*

implied DO: in FORTRAN, the use of an indexing specification similar to a DO statement but without specifying the word *DO* and with a list of data elements, rather than a set of statements, as its range.

import: to include data from a different program or application. Cf. *export.*

imprinter: any device used to produce or impress marks or patterns on a surface, for example, printing presses, typewriters, pens, cash registers, bookkeeping machines, and pressure devices such as those used with credit cards and address plates.

imprinting:
(1) the act of using an imprinter.
(2) the output of any imprinter. (A)

IN: see *input.*

inactive: not operational.

inactive link: a link that is not currently available for transmitting data. Cf. *active link.* Synonymous with *idle link.*

inactive node: in a network, a node that is neither connected to nor available for connection to another node.

INC: see *increment.*

incidental time: synonym for *miscellaneous time.* (A) (B)

incident light: in computer graphics, light falling on an object. The color of an object is perceived as a function of the wavelengths of incident light reflected or absorbed by it.

incipient failure: machine failure that is about to occur.

inclusion: deprecated term for *implication.* (A) (B)

inclusion gate: synonymous with *implication gate.*

inclusive-NOR operation: synonymous with *NOR operation.*

inclusive-OR element: a logic element that performs the boolean operation of disjunction. Synonymous with *inclusive-OR gate.* (A) (B)

inclusive-OR gate: synonym for *inclusive-OR element.* (A) (B)

inclusive-OR operation: synonym for *disjunction.* (A) (B)

inconnector: in flowcharting, a connector that indicates a continuation of a broken flow line. Cf. *outconnector.* (A)

INCR: see *increment.*

INCRE: see *increment.*

increment (INC) (INCR) (INCRE):
(1) a value used to alter a counter or register.
(2) to move a document forward in the read station from one timing mark to the next so that a new line of characters is visible to the scan head.
(3) to move a card from column to column in the punch station so that each column presents itself for punching.
(4) to alter the value of a counter or register by a specified value.
(5) to move a hopper or stacker upward or downward.

incremental: the arrangement of outputs used in rotating sensors, permitting the direction of rotation to be determined.

incremental compiler: a compiler capable of compiling further statements in a program without fully recompiling the program.

incremental computer:
(1) a computer that represents as absolute values the changes to variables instead of the variables themselves.
(2) a computer in which incremental representation of data is mainly used. (B)

incremental integrator: a digital integrator modified so that the output signal is maximum negative, zero, or maximum positive when the value of the input is negative, zero, or positive. (A)

incremental representation: a method of representing variables in which changes in the values of the variable are represented, rather than the values themselves. (B) See *ternary incremental representation.* (A)

incrementer: a hardware component which automatically adds one.

IND: see *indicator.*

indent tab character (IT): a word-processing formatting mode control that requires a device to execute a horizontal tab function after each subsequent appearance of a carrier return character. The number of automatic horizontal tabs performed after each carrier return character is equal to the number of indent tab characters keyed since the last resetting of indent tab mode. Cf. *horizontal tabulation character.*

index:
(1) in programming, a subscript of integer value that identifies the position of an item of data with respect to some other item of data. (B)
(2) a list of the contents of a file or of a document, together with keys or references for locating the contents. (B)
(3) a symbol or a numeral used to identify a particular quantity in an array of similar quantities. For example, the terms of an array represented by X1, X2, ... X100 have the indexes 1, 2, . . 100, respectively. (A)
(4) in micrographics, a guide for locating information in microform using targets, flash cards, lines, bars, or other optical codes.
(5) to prepare a list as in (2). (A)
(6) to move a machine part to a prede-

termined position, or by a predetermined amount, on a quantized scale. (A)

(7) a table used to locate the records of an indexed sequential data set. (A)

(8) in COBOL, a computer storage position or register, the contents of which identify a particular element in a table.

(9) in word processing, to move the paper or display pointer in the direction used during normal printout.

(10) see *code line index*. (A)

index addressing: addressing where the address contained in the second byte of the instruction is added to the index register.

index build: the automatic process of creating an alternate index through the use of access method services.

index character (INX): a word-processing formatting control that moves the printing or display point down to the next line with no horizontal motion. Synonymous with *line feed character*.

index data item: in COBOL, a data item in which the contents of an index can be stored without conversion to subscript form.

indexed address: an address that is modified by the content of an index register prior to or during the execution of a computer instruction. (A)

indexed array: an array where individual entries are accessible by identifying their position using a subscript. Synonymous with *indexed list, subscripted array*.

indexed data name: in COBOL, a data name identifier that is subscripted with one or more index names.

indexed data set: a type of data set in which records are stored and retrieved on the basis of keys that are within each record and are part of the data record itself.

indexed file: a file providing a directory-supported random-access method based on a record identifier whose size is user-specified.

indexed list: synonymous with *indexed array*.

indexed organization: in COBOL, the permanent logical file structure in which each record is identified by the value of one or more keys within that record.

indexed sequential access method (ISAM): a procedure for storing and retrieving data utilizing a set of indexes that describe where records are on disks. Each record has key information, such as a customer name, used to retrieve the whole record.

indexed sequential data set: a data set in which each record contains a key that determines its location. The location of each record is computed through the use of an index.

indexed sequential file: a sequential file ordered on the basis of unique record keys having index stored housing addresses or pointers to show where each record in the file is located; stored on a direct access storage unit and accessed sequentially or randomly.

indexed sequential organization: a file organization in which records are arranged in logical sequence by key. Indexes to these keys permit direct access to individual records.

index entry: the individual line or item of data found in an index, such as an entry in a dictionary.

index file: the table of key fields identifying the specific disk records in another permanent disk file.

index hole: a hole cut in a floppy disk showing the beginning of the first sector.

indexing:

(1) a technique of address modification by means of index registers.

(2) in word processing, a feature that causes the typing position or display pointer to be moved to the corresponding character position of the following typing line. See also *reverse indexing*.

index mark: a record found on a soft-sectored disk indicating the beginning of a sector. See *index hole*.

index name: in COBOL, a name, given by the programmer, for an index of a specific table. An index name must contain at least one alphabetic character. It is one word (four bytes) in length.

index return character (IRT): a word-processing multifunction control used as a formatting control and a device control. As a formatting control, it produces the same effect as a required carrier return in printed or displayed text. As a device control, it is used to delimit a line without ending recording on the current magnetic card track when recording multiple lines on the same track. Cf. *required carrier-return character.*

index sequential file: a file on a random access storage unit in which the address of a record on a physical file is shown on an index containing the record key.

index slot: synonymous with *polarizing slot.*

index term: used to classify a document, or item in a database.

index value: the desired preset value of a controlled quantity, used as the target value for an automatic control system.

index word: an index modifier applied to the address part of a computer instruction. (A) (B)

index word register: a register that stores a word for modifying addresses under the direction of the control section of a computer.

indicator (IND):
(1) a device that may be set into a prescribed state, usually according to the result of a previous process or on the occurrence of a specified condition in the equipment, and that usually gives a visual or other indication of the existence of the prescribed state, and that may in some cases be used to determine the selection among alternative processes, for example, an overflow indicator. (B)
(2) an item of data that may be interrogated to determine whether a particular condition has been satisfied in the execution of a computer program, for example, a switch indicator, an overflow indicator.
(3) see *switch indicator.* (A)

indicator chart: a table or chart used by a programmer for recording items dealing with the indicators in the program.

indirect address: an address that designates the storage location of an item of data to be treated as the address of an operand, but not necessarily as its direct address. Synonymous with *multilevel address.* (B) Cf. *direct address.* (A) See also *level of addressing.*

indirect addressing: a method of addressing in which the address part of an instruction contains an indirect address. (A)

indirect instruction: an instruction that contains the indirect address of an operand for the operation specified. (B) Cf. *direct instruction.* (A)

industrial data processing: data processing for industrial purposes.

industrial robots: industrial machines that are usually controlled by computers, to do simple, repetitive tasks.

industry standard architecture bus (ISA): bus architecture used in the IBM PC/XT and PC/AT.

inferential engine: a computer program used to search a knowledge base and draw judgments when confronted with evidence from a particular case. See also *knowledge base* and *knowledge engineering.*

inferior: synonym for *subscript.*

infinite loop: a loop whose terminating condition is never reached; the loop (theoretically) executes indefinitely and the program never terminates.

infinite pad method: in optical character recognition, a method of measuring reflectance of a paper stock such that doubling the number of backing sheets of the same stock does not change the measured reflectance. (A)

infinity: any number larger than the maximum number that a given computer is able to store in the register.

infix notation: a method of forming mathematical expressions, governed by rules of operator precedence and using parentheses, in which the operators are dispersed among the operands, each operator indicating the operation to be performed on the operands or the intermediate results adjacent to it. If it is desired to distinguish the case in which there are more than two operands for an operation, the term *distributed infix notation* may be used. (B) Cf. *prefix notation, post fix notation.* (A)

infix operator: an operator that appears between two operands.

informal design review: an evaluation of system-designed documentation by selected management, analysts, and programmers prior to the actual coding of program modules to determine necessary additions, deletions, and modifications to the system design.

informatics: see *information science.*

information bits: in data communication, those bits that are generated by the data source and that are not used for error control by the data-transmission system. (A)

information channel: see *data channel.*

information content: in information theory, a measure of information conveyed by the occurrence of an event of definite probability. (B) See *conditional information content, joint information content.* (A)

information content binary unit: synonym for *Shannon.* (A) (B)

information content decimal unit: synonym for *Hartley.* (A) (B)

information content natural unit (NAT): in information theory, a unit of logarithmic measures of information expressed by the neperian logarithm; for example, the decision content of a character set of eight characters equals 2.079 natural units of information. (A) (B)

information costs: costs, including time, expended in securing data.

information feedback system: synonymous with *message feedback system.*

information flow analysis: organizing and analyzing approaches to gather facts and information about an organization, initialization, and flow to final user of reports throughout an organization.

information heading: that part of a message containing control information such as the identification of originating station and message routing information.

information input: data fed into a computer.

information interchange: the process of sending and receiving data in such a manner that the information content or meaning assigned to the data is not altered during the transmission. (A)

information management system: a system established for creating, updating, and maintaining a file or data base.

information measure: in information theory, a suitable function of the frequency of occurrence of a specified event from a set of possible events conventionally taken as a measure of the relative value of the intelligence conveyed by this occurrence. In information theory, the term *event* is to be understood as used in the theory of probability. For instance, the presence of a given element of a set, the occurrence of a specified character or of a specified word in a message. (A) (B)

information processing: synonym for *data processing.* (A) (B)

information rate: see *average information rate.* (A)

information retrieval (IR): actions, methods, and procedures for recovering stored data to provide information on a given subject.

information retrieval system: a computing system application designed to recover specific information from a mass of data.

information revolution: the name given to the present era because of the impact of computer technology on society.

information routing: choosing a path for the transmission of data to a particular destination.

information science: the study of how data are processed and transmitted through digital-processing equipment. Synonymous with *informatics.*

information separator (IS): any control character used to delimit like units of data in a hierarchic arrangement of data. The name of the separator does not necessarily indicate the units of data that it separates. Synonymous with *separating character.* (A) (B)

information sink: see *data sink.*

information source: synonym for *message source.* (B) See *data source.*

information storage and retrieval: utilizing a computer system for storing significant amounts of related data, items of which can rapidly and easily be retrieved and viewed.

information system (IS): the network of all communication approaches used within an organization. Synonymous with *data system.*

information technology: the acquisition, processing, storage and dissemination of various types of information via computers and telecommunications.

information theory: the branch of learning concerned with the study of measures of information and their properties. (A) (B)

information word: an ordered set of characters bearing at least one meaning and handled by the computer as a unit, including separating and spacing.

inherent transparency: data transmission in which there is no need for special control characters.

inherited error: an error carried forward from a previous step in a sequential process.

inhibited (A): pertaining to a state of a processing unit in which certain types of interruptions are not allowed to occur.

in-house: an organization's use of its own personnel or resources to develop programs or other problem-solving systems.

INIT: see *initialize.*

initial address: the address assigned to the initial location of a program. Synonymous with *program origin.*

initial condition mode: an operating mode of an analog computer during which the integrators are inoperative, and the initial conditions are set. Synonymous with *reset mode.* (B)

initial error: an error represented by the difference between the actual value of a data unit and the value used at the beginning of processing.

initial instructions: a routine in memory whose purpose is to aid loading. Synonymous with *initial orders.*

initialization: the process carried out at the commencement of a program to test that all indicators and constants are set to prescribed conditions. See also *initial program load.* See *loop initialization.* (A)

initialize (INIT): to set counters, switches, addresses, or contents of storage to zero or

other starting values at the beginning of, or at prescribed points in, the operation of a computer routine. Cf. *prestore.* (A) See also *initial program load.*

initializer routine: functions such as error checking performed on a message following entry into the system, but prior to the application program beginning its processing.

initial microcode (or microprogram) load: see *IML.*

initial orders: synonymous with *initial instructions.*

initial procedure: an external procedure that is the first procedure invoked in the execution of a PL/1 program.

initial program load (IPL):
(1) the initialization procedure that causes an operating system to commence operation.
(2) the process by which a configuration image is loaded into storage at the beginning of a work day or after a system malfunction.

initial program loader (IPL): the utility routine that loads the initial part of a computer program, such as an operating system or other computer program, so that the computer program can then proceed under its own control. (B) Cf. *bootstrap, bootstrap loader.* (A)

initiating task: the job management task that controls the selection of a job and the preparation of the steps of that job for execution.

initiator: that part of an operating system that performs several jobs simultaneously.

initiator/terminator: the job scheduler function that selects jobs and job steps to be executed, allocates input-output devices for them, places them under task control, and at completion of the job, supplies control information for writing job output on a system output unit.

ink jet printer:
(1) a printing mechanism that produces characters by deflecting drops of ink.
(2) a nonimpact printer that forms characters by the projection of a jet of ink onto paper.

inline code: in a program, instructions that are executed sequentially, without branching to routines, subroutines, or other programs.

in-line package: see *dual in-line package.*

in-line procedure: in COBOL, the set of statements that constitutes the main or controlling flow of the computer program and which excludes statements executed under control of the asynchronous control system.

in-line processing: the processing of data in random order, not subject to preliminary editing or sorting.

in-line subroutine: a subroutine placed directly into a program and which has to be recopied each time it is needed.

inner macroinstruction: a macroinstruction that is nested inside a macrodefinition. Cf. *outer macroinstruction.*

inoperable time: the time during which a functional unit would not yield correct results if it were operated. It is assumed that all environmental conditions for proper operation are met. (A) (B)

INP: see *input.*

input (I) (IN) (INP) (I/P):
(1) one, or a sequence of, input states.
(2) pertaining to a device process, or channel involved in an input process, or to the data or states involved in an input process. In the English language, the adjective *input* may be used in place of such terms as *input data, input signal,* and *input terminal,* when such usage is clear in a given context.
(3) synonymous with *input data, input process.* (A)
(4) see also *input channel, input unit.*
(5) see *manual input, real-time input.* (A)
(6) cf. *output.*

input area: synonym for *input block.*

input block: a block of data received as input. Synonym for *input area.* (A)

input blocking factor (Bi): in a tape sort, the number of data records in each record of the input file.

input bound: a system where speed of performance is limited by capability of the input system.

input buffer register: a device that accepts data from input units or media such as magnetic tape or disks and which then transfers this data to internal storage.

input channel: a channel for impressing a state on a device or logic element. Synonymous with *input (1).* (A)

input converter: an analog-to-digital converter packaged for process control applications.

input data:
(1) data being received or to be received into a device or into a computer program. Synonymous with *input (2).* (B)
(2) data to be processed. Synonymous with *input (1).* (A)

input device: synonym for *input unit.* (A) (B)

input editing: operations on input data for converting the format for more convenient processing and storage. May also review the data for proper format, completeness, and accuracy.

input equipment: apparatus used for transferring data and instruction into a data-processing machine. Includes all peripherals used for gathering or collecting data.

input field: in computer graphics, an unprotected field on a display surface in which data can be entered, modified, or erased.

input file: in COBOL, a file that is opened in the input mode.

input instruction code: an instruction set forming part of an automatic language, usually mnemonic, with operations coded to have some appearance of the actual operation. A type of pseudocode.

input job queue: see *job queue.*

input job stream: synonym for *input stream.*

input limited: descriptive of a program where the overall processing time is limited by the speed of an input unit, delaying processing awaiting the input of additional items.

input line: see *line (1), (2).*

input loading: the amount of load imposed upon the sources supplying signals to the input.

input mode: a mode of operation for a terminal where a file can be created or added to by the repeated entry of lines of a program or data. Cf. *edit mode.*

input module: a package functional unit used for conveying data into another piece of equipment.

input-output (I/O):

(1) pertaining to a device or to a channel that may be involved in an input process, and, at a different time, in an output process. In the English language, *input-output* may be used in place of such terms as *input-output data, input-output signal,* and *input-output terminals,* when such usage is clear in a given context.

(2) pertaining to a device whose parts can be performing an input process and an output process at the same time.

(3) pertaining to either input or output or both. See listings under *I/O.*

(4) synonym for *radial transfer.* (A) (B)

input-output board: on some units, a type of board permitting the computer to be expanded via the back-plane bus to permit further input-output interface channels.

input-output-bound: a situation in which the CPU is slowed down because of I/O operations, which are extremely slow in comparison to CPU internal processing operations.

input-output buffer (IOB): part of memory where data is set on its way to or from a peripheral unit. When a buffer area is used, a number of peripheral units can be operated while the central processor is processing additional data.

input-output bus: see *bus.*

input-output channel (IOC): in a data-processing system, a functional unit, controlled by the processing unit, that handles the transfer of data between main storage and peripheral equipment. (B)

input-output controller (IOC): a functional unit in an automatic data-processing system that controls one or more units of peripheral equipment. Synonymous with *I/O controller, peripheral control unit.* (A) (B)

input-output control system (IOCS): the software and hardware handling transfer of data between a main storage and external storage units.

input-output cycle: a cycle on some system, consisting of inputting (reading data) from or outputting (writing data) into a specified memory location. Timing is for memory-access, read-data, and write-data operations.

input-output device (IOD): synonym for *input-output unit.* (A) (B)

input-output file: in COBOL, a file that is opened in the I/O mode.

input-output generation: see *IOGEN.*

input-output interface: see *I/O interface.*

input-output interruption: see *I/O interruption.*

input-output library: standard routines or programs created to control the operation of peripheral devices.

input-output limited: pertaining to a system or condition where the time for input and output activities exceeds other operations.

input/output management system: a subsystem of the operating system that controls and coordinates the CPU while receiving input from channels, executing instructions of programs in storage, and regulating output.

input-output mode: in COBOL, the state of a file after execution of an OPEN statement, with the I/O phrase specified, for that file and before the execution of a CLOSE statement for that file.

input-output operation: any function in which data can be read from the medium on which it is stored and then transferred to main memory, or where data is transferred from main memory and written on a medium, such as magnetic tape.

input-output orders: see *I/O orders.*

input-output procedure: see *I/O procedure.*

input-output processor: a device that handles normal data input-output control and sequencing.

input-output program system: the input-output control system in a minicomputer.

input-output referencing: the allocation of symbolic names within a program to identify input or output devices, in order that the actual device allocated to the program can be identified at run time.

input-output register (IOR): a register that receives data from input devices and from which data can be transferred to the main memory, arithmetic, or control device; and accepts data from these internal devices to be transferred to output units.

input-output request words: control words used for input-output requests stored in the message reference block until the I/O operation is ended.

input-output routines: standard routines created to simplify the programming of daily operations using input-output devices.

input-output section: in the environment division of a COBOL program, the section that names the files and external media needed by an object program. It also provides information required for the transmission and handling of data during the execution of an object program.

input-output statement: any statement that transfers data between main storage and input-output devices.

input-output (I/O) symbol: a flow charting symbol used to indicate when data are to be entered into the computer or when used to represent I/O.

input-output system: hardware and software required to enter various input-output devices and main memory.

input-output unit (IOU): a device in a data processing system by which data may be entered into the system, received from the system, or both. Synonymous with *input-output device.* (A) (B)

input primitive: in computer graphics, a basic data item from an input device such as a keyboard, locator device, pick device, or valuator device.

input process:
(1) the process of transmitting data from peripheral equipment, or external storage to internal storage.
(2) the process of receiving data by a device. (A)
(3) the process that consists of the reception of data into a data-processing system or into any part of it. Synonymous with *input.* (B)

(4) the entry of information by an end-user into a data-processing system, including the conversion of information from a human language into a language that the system can understand.
(5) see also *output process.*

input program: a utility program that organizes the input process of a computer.

input queue: see *job queue.*

input reader: synonymous with *input routine.* See *reader.* (A) (B)

input register: a register that accepts data from outside the computer at one speed and supplies the information to the computer calculating unit at a different, often higher speed.

input routine: synonymous with *input section.*

input section: the physical area of a store responsible for the reception of input data. Synonymous with *input routine.*

input state: the state occurring on a specified input channel. (A)

INPUT statement: a statement whereby the user of a program assigns data values to variables during the execution of the program. Generally, the computer prints a question mark at the terminal as a signal for the user to type in the value to be assigned to the variable.

input station: see *data-input station.* (A)

input storage: synonymous with *input block.*

input stream: the sequence of job control statements and data submitted to an operating system on an input unit especially activated for this purpose by the operator. Synonymous with *input job stream, job input stream.*

input translator: a portion of some computer programs that converts the incoming programmer's instructions into operators and operands understood by the computer.

input unit (IU): a device in a data-processing system by which data can be entered into the system. Synonymous with *input (2), input device.* (A) (B)

input work queue: a waiting line of job control statements from which jobs and job steps are chosen for processing.

inquiry: a request for information from storage; for example, a request for the number of available airline seats, or a machine statement to initiate a search of library documents.

inquiry and transaction processing: synonymous with *inquiry processing.*

inquiry display terminal: synonymous with *terminal.*

inquiry processing: processing where inquires and records from a number of terminals are used for querying and updating one or more master files maintained by the central system. Synonymous with *inquiry and transaction processing.*

inquiry station:
(1) a user terminal primarily for the interrogation of an automatic data-processing system. (A) (B)
(2) data terminal equipment used for inquiry into a data-processing system.

inquiry transaction: a transaction that does not update a data base.

inquiry unit: synonymous with *inquiry station.*

inscribe: preparing a document to be read by optical character recognition.

insertion cursor: a blinking vertical line that marks the place where the next character typed on the keyboard will be inserted; indicates that the user is in insert mode. Cf. *overtype cursor.*

insertion picture character: in PL/1, a picture specification character that is inserted in the indicated position, on assignment of the associated data to a character string. When used in a P format item for input, an insertion character serves as a checking picture character.

insertion point: the place in a document where typed text is to be added. Set by clicking at the spot where the user wants to make the insertion. The insertion point is marked with a blinking vertical bar.

insertion sort: a sort in which each item in a set is inserted into its proper position in the sorted set according to the specified criteria. (A)

insert mode: the normal mode for entering text. Characters are inserted after the cursor and the existing characters are moved over to make room for the new characters.

INST: see *instruction.*

instability: the measure of the fluctuations in the performance of a variable, circuit, device, or system.

install: to add information to the system file, or to add new system files to the system folder of a startup disk.

installation: a particular computing system, in terms of the work it does and the people who manage it, operate it, apply it to problems, service it, and use the results it produces.

installation processing control: the scheduling of applications and jobs utilizing an automated setup.

installation program: a computer program designed to get the computer or word processor going for the first time—when it is being installed.

installation time: time spent in installing and testing hardware or software. (A)

installed font: a font that is installed with installation software or by dragging it into the system folder.

installer: a program that is used to install or update the system software or to add resources such as networking software.

instantaneous traffic: the average number of concurrent calls in progress within a stated system; expressed in erlangs.

Institute of Electrical and Electronics Engineers: see *IEEE.*

INSTR: see *instruction.*

in-stream procedure: a set of job control statements placed in the input stream that can be used any number of times during a job by naming the procedure in an execute (EXEC) statement.

instruction (I) (INST) (INSTR): in a programming language, a meaningful expression that specifies one operation and identifies its operands, if any. (A) (B) See *absolute instruction, arithmetic instruction, branch instruction, computer instruction, conditional jump instruction, direct instruction, discrimination instruction, dummy instruction, effective instruction, extract instruction, immediate instruction, indirect instruction, jump instruction, logic instruction, macroinstruction, multiaddress instruction, n-address* *instruction, no-operation instruction, n-plus-one address instruction, one-address instruction, one-plus-one address instruction, optional-pause instruction, pause instruction, presumptive instruction, privileged instruction, repetition instruction, restart instruction, stop instruction, three-address instruction, three-plus-one address instruction, two-address instruction, two-plus-one address instruction, unconditional-jump instruction, zero address instruction.* See also *imperative statement.* (A)

instruction address (IA):

(1) the address of an instruction word.

(2) the address that must be used to fetch an instruction.

(3) cf. *address part.* (A)

instruction address register (IAR): a register from whose contents the address of the next instruction is derived. An instruction address register may also be a portion of a storage device specifically designated for the derivation of the address of the next instruction by a translator, compiler, interpreter, language processor, operating system, and so on. Synonymous with *control counter, sequence control register.* (A) (B)

instruction address stop: an instruction address that, when fetched, causes execution to stop.

instruction area: the area of memory where instructions are retained. Synonymous with *instruction storage.*

instruction characters: characters used as code elements for initiating, modifying, and stopping control operations.

instruction code: synonym for *computer instruction code.*

instruction constant: a constant written in the form of an instruction; any instruction which is not intended to be executed as an instruction.

instruction control unit (ICU): in a processing unit, the part that receives instructions in proper sequence, interprets each instruction, and applies the proper signals to the arithmetic and logic unit and other parts in accordance with this interpretation. (A) (B)

instruction counter (IC): a counter that indicates the location of the next computer instruction to be interpreted. (A)

instruction cycle: a sequence of events where an instruction is searched, decoded, and executed. See *execute cycle.*

instruction deck: synonymous with *instruction pack.*

instruction decoder: that portion of the CPU that interprets the program instructions in binary into the needed control signals for the ALU, registers, and control bus.

instruction diagnostic: a unit utilizing hardware and software that completely tests all CPU instructions in all modes, including interrupts.

instruction execution logic: the logic permitting each instruction to be retrieved or fetched from memory, decoded, and executed. May involve program counters, address registers, instruction registers, and the general-purpose register.

instruction format: the layout of an instruction showing its constituent parts. (A) (B)

instruction length: the number of words or bytes necessary for storing an instruction in main memory.

instruction look ahead: searching and decoding one instruction during the execution of another.

instruction mix: computer instructions chosen to complete a specific problem. The optimum mix of instructions determines the speed and accuracy, and programmers attempt to achieve an optimum program or mix.

instruction modifier: a word or part of a word that is used to alter an instruction. (A) (B)

instruction pack: a pack of punched cards maintaining instruction for a program or suite. Synonymous with *instruction deck.*

instruction register (IR): a register that is used to hold an instruction for interpretation. (A) (B)

instruction repertoire:

(1) a complete set of the operators of the statements of computer programming language, together with a description of the

types and meanings that can be attributed to their operands.

(2) loosely, an instruction set. (A)

instruction set: the set of instructions of a computer, of a programming language, or of the programming languages in a programming system. (A) (B)

instruction statement: see *instruction*.

instruction storage: synonymous with *instruction area*.

instruction time (I-time): the time during which an instruction is fetched from the main storage of a computer into an instruction register. See also *execution time*.

instruction word: a word that represents an instruction. (A) (B)

instrumentation: what is required to measure a complex activity, such as the performance level of a computer system, whether hardware or software.

INT:

(1) see *integer*.

(2) see *interrupt*.

integer (INT):

(1) one of the numbers zero, $+1$, -1, $+2$, -2, . . . Synonymous with *integral number*. (A) (B)

(2) in COBOL, a numeric data item or literal that does not include any character positions to the right of the decimal point, actual or assumed. Where the term *integer* appears in formats, *integer* must not be a numeric data item.

integer BASIC: a version of the language that does not use decimal fractions: for example, 1 divided by 3 would yield an answer of 0, not 0.3333. See *floating-point BASIC*.

integer constant: a string of decimal digits containing no decimal point.

integer number: a number without a fractional part; a whole number.

integer programming: in operations research, a class of procedures for locating the maximum or minimum of a function subject constraints, where some or all variables must have integer values. Synonymous with *discrete programming*. (B) Cf. *convex programming, dynamic programming, linear programming, mathematical programming, nonlinear programming, quadratic programming*. (A)

integer variables: in FORTRAN, an integer variable consisting of a series of not more than six alphameric characters (except special characters), of which the first is I, J, K, L, M, or N.

integral boundary: a location in main storage at which a fixed-length field, such as a half-word or double-word, must be positioned. The address of an integral boundary is a multiple of the length of the field, in bytes. See also *boundary alignment*.

integral control action: a control action where the rate or change of output is proportional to the input.

integral modem: a modem built directly into a communicating device. Cf. *stand-alone modem*.

integral number: synonym for *integer*. (A)

integrated:

(1) a computer that can do both word and data processing, and transfer information back and forth from each program.

(2) more specifically, describes any program combining word processing, spreadsheet, database and communications applications.

integrated adapter: an integral part of a processing unit that provides for the direct connection of a particular type of device and uses neither a control unit nor the standard I/O interface. See also *integrated file adapter*.

integrated attachment: an attachment that is an integral part of the basic hardware.

integrated circuit (IC): a combination of interconnected circuit elements inseparably associated on or within a continuous substrate. See *monolithic integrated circuit*. Synonymous with *integrated monolithic circuit*.

integrated component: a single structure with a number of elements that cannot be separated without destroying the function or functions of the unit.

integrated data base (IDB): a data base which has been consolidated to eliminate redundant data.

integrated data processing (IDP): data processing in which the coordination of data acquisition and other stages of data processing are combined in a coherent data-processing system. (A) (B)

integrated disk: in the programmable store system, an integral part of the store controller that is used for magnetically storing files, application programs, controller storage contents, and diagnostics.

integrated drive electronics: see *IDE*.

integrated emulator: an emulator program whose execution is controlled by an operating system in a multiprogramming environment. Cf. *stand-alone emulator.*

integrated file adapter: an integrated adapter that allows connection of multiple disk storage devices to a processing unit.

integrated injection logic (IIL): an integrated circuit logic consisting of the interconnected bipolar transistors of both polarities. Synonymous with *merged transistor logic.*

integrated modem: a modem that is an integral part of the device with which it operates. Cf. *stand-alone modem.*

integrated monolithic circuit: synonymous with *integrated circuit.*

Integrated Services Digital Network (ISDN): the world's telephone companies' operations enabling any telephone line to carry a simultaneous mix of voice, computer, and video signals. ISDN began in September 1985.

integrated software: computer software permitting the user to easily switch between various applications, such as moving from calculating to drawing the results in a graph.

integrated system: the combination of processes that results in the introduction of data that need not be repeated as further allied or related data is also entered.

integration: the sharing of commands and the flow of information from one program to another; a major goal of the software industry.

integrator:
(1) a device whose output variable is the integral of the input variable with respect to time. (B)
(2) a device whose output function is proportional to the integral of the input

function with respect to a specified variable, for example, a watt-hour meter.
(3) see *incremental integrator.* (A)

integrity: see *data integrity.*

Intel: manufacturer of the microprocessors that are the CPUs for IBM PCs and compatibles.

intelligence: processing capability as found in an intelligent terminal. Cf. *artificial intelligence.*

intelligent cable: an interfacing system allowing input and output operations along with word and byte transfer to occur in any mix on all channels concurrently. Such a cable provides a low-cost parallel interface while freeing the creator from expensive development time involved in interfacing the peripherals.

intelligent controller: a unit controlled with local capabilities, such as editing, input validity checking, and complex command decoding.

intelligent copier: a copying unit that uses a microprocessor to control its operations. Such a copier can accept digital information as an input, and use it to yield hard copy.

intelligent disk storage: a disk system that does its own data-base management; only commands from the host computer and data field information need to be passed to the system controller.

intelligent drive electronics: see *IDE.*

intelligent keyboard system: a keyboard system that carries out all alphanumeric and numeric operations for keying, editing, calculating, storing, compressing, and printing.

intelligent peripheral: synonymous with *smart peripheral.*

intelligent terminal: deprecated term for *programmable terminal.* See also *distributed function.*

intelligent time division multiplexor: apparatus that serves as a time division multiplexor and contains a microprocessor control unit for allocating the available bandwidth dynamically, to improve the utilization of the channel. Synonymous with *statistical multiplexor.*

intelligent unit: a machine whose internal functions are directed by a program; usually terminals or peripherals connected to a large computer.

INTEN: see *intensity*.

intensify: to increase the level of brightness of all or part of a display image.

intensity (INTEN): in computer graphics, the amount of light emitted at a display point.

interaction: a basic unit used to record system activity, consisting of the acceptance of a line of terminal input, processing of the line, and a response, if any. See also *interaction time*.

interaction time: in systems with time sharing, the time between acceptance by the system of a line of input from a terminal and the point at which it can accept the next line from the terminal. Cf. *response time*.

interactive: pertaining to an application in which each entry calls forth a response from a system or program, as in an inquiry system or an airline reservation system. An interactive system may also be conversational, implying a continuous dialog between the user and the system.

interactive applications: a data-processing system where users are connected directly, when needed, to a computer, using a terminal and communication lines. The computer program responds to events initiated by users to maintain an accurate up-to-date record of the events or objects being controlled.

interactive compiler: a compiler where every entered statement on a terminal is translated into machine language. Cf. *batch compiler*.

interactive computing: an operating environment where a computer and a person at the keyboard terminal carry out a dialog.

interactive graphics: computer graphics in which a display device is used in the conversational mode. Cf. *passive graphics*.

interactive-keyboard printer: in word processing, a printer that is used in conjunction with a keyboard to print each character as it is keyed.

interactive panel: the screen display sent to a CRT by a computer during a dialog

demanding a user response; reports the results of processing and/or explains an aspect of the system operation.

interactive processing: compiling and executing a program statement when it is entered on a terminal, permitting the programmer to witness the results instantly in order to correct errors when they occur, and to make changes to the program as it is executing. Cf. *batch processing*.

interactive programming: the use of an interactive system to create and compile programs through the use of an editor, compiler, debugger, and other tools.

interactive routine: a programming routine where a series of operations is repeatedly performed, until an earlier specified end-condition is reached.

interactive system: a computer system where the user communicates directly and rapidly with the central processor through a terminal. Synonymous with *user interaction*.

interblock gap (IBG):
(1) an area on a data medium to indicate the end of a block or physical record. (A)
(2) the space between two consecutive blocks on a data medium.
(3) synonymous with *block gap*.

intercycle: the step in the sequence of steps made by the main shaft of a punched card device. At this time, the card feed is stopped, usually because of a control change.

interest worlds: areas of interest that the computer can serve as a tool; for example, art, language, and so on.

interface (I/F): a shared boundary. An interface might be a hardware component to link two devices or it might be a portion of storage or registers accessed by two or more computer programs. (A)

interface bus: a bus providing the interface connections and timing to interconnect differing instruments and either programmable calculators or computers, forming complete instrumentation systems.

interface module: a hardware device providing the interface between a bus and the user's peripheral or instrumentation.

interface processor (IP): a processor that acts as the interface between another processor or terminal and a network, or a processor that controls data flow in a network.

interface routines: linking routines between two systems.

interfix: an approach used in information retrieval systems to describe unambiguously the relation between the keywords in different records to ensure that words which seem related but are not in fact relevant are not retrieved.

interior label: a label placed at the beginning of a magnetic tape to show its contents. Cf. *exterior label.*

interlacing: in computer graphics, scanning technique which sends first the even, then the odd lines of a display in the refresh cycle. This reduces the flickering effect.

interlanguage: the modification of common language, suitable for automatic translation by the unit into machine or computer usable language.

interlayer interface: an exact statement of the procedures and logical structures used for interaction between the different layers of control in a network architecture.

interleaved array: in PL/1, an array whose name refers to a nonconnected storage.

interleaved subscripts: a subscript notation, used with subscripted qualified names, in which not all of the necessary subscripts immediately follow the same component name.

interleaving:
(1) the act of accessing two or more bytes or streams of data from distinct storage units simultaneously.
(2) the alternating of two or more operations or functions through the overlapped use of a computer facility.
(3) the way sectors on a disk are laid out.

interlock: to prevent a machine or device from initiating further operations until the operation in process is completed. See also *deadlock.*

interlude: a small routine that carries out minor preliminary operations prior to entry of the main routine; for example, the

interlude may calculate the values of certain parameters.

intermediate buffer: in word processing, a buffer that saves the original text until a command is made to the system to implement any changes.

intermediate cycle: an unconditional branch instruction that can address itself.

intermediate-grain computer architectures: powerful processor-memory units under the control of a central computer. Each processor can work alone on a job or with other processors. See also *architecture, grain size.*

intermediate language level: a semicompiled program code. A compiler converts the program into a form that does not resemble the original written program, which is not directly executable by the computer. The output (intermediate language level) is then interpreted by another program at run time making it executable.

intermediate pass (sorting): that portion of a merging operation that, because of the number of strings or otherwise, does not reduce the file to a single sequenced string.

intermessage delay: the elapsed time between the receipt at a terminal of a system response, and the time that a new transaction is entered. Synonymous with *think time.*

intermix tape: on some computers, a feature permitting for combinations of different models of tape units to be interconnected to a single computer.

internal arithmetic: computations performed by the arithmetic and logic unit.

internal block: a block that is contained in another block.

internal bus: a bus for transferring data among different registers and between the ALU and control unit.

internal clocking: control by a timing clock of the synchronization of the electronic circuitry of a unit within the unit itself. Cf. *external clocking.*

internal cycle time: see *cycle time.*

internal format: the structure shown by data and instructions when they have been read into the central processor or backing store.

internal fragmentation: disturbance of main memory when data is required to fit into a smaller area than is available.

internal hemorrhage: when the program becomes confused but nevertheless continues to run, yielding questionable results and at times negatively affecting other programs or the performance of the system.

internal interrupt: utilizing an external unit to cause equipment to stop in the normal course of the program and perform a designated subroutine.

internally stored program: a computer program whose instructions are stored in the same locations as the data values so that the instructions themselves can be altered as the computation progresses.

internal memory: the internal parts of an automatic data-processing machine able to hold data.

internal modem: a modem that can be plugged into an expansion slot.

internal name: in PL/1, a name that is not known outside the block in which it is declared.

internal procedure: a procedure that is contained within a block.

internal reader: a facility that transfers jobs to the job entry subsystem.

internals: detailed information on how systems software performs.

internal sort:
(1) a sort performed within internal storage.
(2) a sort program or a sort phase that sorts two or more items within main storage. (A)
(3) a sorting technique that creates sequences of records or keys. Usually, it is a prelude to a merge phase in which the sequences created are reduced to one by an external merge.

internal storage: storage that is accessible by a computer without the use of input-output channels. Deprecated term for *main storage*. Synonym for *primary storage unit*.

internal text: in PL/1, all of the text contained in a block except that text that is contained in another block. Thus the text of an internal block (except its entry names) is not internal to the containing block.

internal timer: an internal clock equipped with multiple registers to monitor the length of external events, or generate a pulse following a fixed time.

internal writer: a facility in the job entry subsystem that allows user written output writers to write data on devices not directly supported by the job control manager.

International Algebraic Language (IAL): an early form of the language that was to evolve as ALGOL.

interpret: to translate and to execute each source language statement of a computer program before translating and executing the next statement. (A) (B)

interpreter (INTERP):
(1) a computer program used to interpret. Synonymous with *interpretive program.* (A) (B)
(2) in punched card operations, a device that prints on a punched card the characters corresponding to hole patterns punched in the card. (B)

interpreter code: an interim, arbitrarily designed code that must be translated to computer coding to function as designed, usually for diagnostic or checking needs.

interpreting:
(1) translating and executing each source language statement of a computer program before translating and executing the next statement.
(2) printing on paper tape or cards the meaning of the holes punched on the same tape or cards. (A)

interpretive code: the instruction repertoire for the source language input to an *interpreter (1).* (A)

interpretive execution: permits retention of all information contained in the user's original source statements.

interpretive language: a programming language needing the support of an interpreter during execution. See *interpreter.*

interpretive program: synonym for *interpreter (1).* (A) (B)

interpretive routine: a routine that decodes instructions written as pseudocodes and immediately executes those instructions. Cf. *compile.*

interpretive trace program: an interpretive program; each symbolic instruction is translated into its equivalent machine code prior to execution, the result is then recorded. See *interpreter (1).*

interpretive translation program: a program for translating each instruction of a source language into computer instructions and permitting each one to be executed before translating the following instruction.

interrecord gap: deprecated term for *interblock gap (2).* (A) (B)

interrobang: see *overprinting.*

interrupt (I) (INT) (INTR):
(1) a suspension of a process, such as the execution of a computer program, caused by an event external to that process, and performed in such a way that the process can be resumed. (A)
(2) to stop a process in such a way that it can be resumed.
(3) synonymous with *interruption.*

interrupt device: an external unit requesting an interrupt, such as a communications unit.

interrupt-driven: a computer system making frequent use of interrupts.

interrupt enable and disable: instructions for setting and resetting an interrupt control flip-flop.

interrupt freeze mode: in analog computers, a situation where all computing action ceases and all values are held as they were when the interrupt took place.

interrupt handler: an I/O routine servicing a specific interrupt.

interruptible: synonym for *enabled.*

interruption: a suspension of a process, such as the execution of a computer program, normally caused by an event external to that process, and performed in such a way that it can be resumed. Synonym for *interrupt (1).* See also *I/O interruption, program-controlled interruption.*

interruption network: a network of circuits in a computing system that continu-

ously monitors its operation. The network detects events that normally require intervention and direction by the supervisor, and initiates interruptions.

interrupt linkage: the technique that causes the computer to switch to the interrupt handling portions of the program as differing interrupts occur.

interrupt mask (IM): ignoring an interrupt by delaying the required action. Synonymous with *interrupt.*

interrupt module: a unit that functions as a monitor for a group of field contacts and informs the computer when an external priority request is generated.

interrupt priorities: different interrupts can be assigned priorities so that if two occur at the same time the interrupt with the higher priority will be handled first.

interrupt request signal: signals to the computer that temporarily suspend the normal sequence of a routine and transfer control to a special routine.

interrupt response time: the elapsed time between an interrupt and the start of the interrupt-handling subroutine.

interrupt-service routine: see *interrupt handler.*

interrupt stacking: delaying action on interrupts by interrupt masking, and, where more than one interrupt occurs during the delay period, forming a queue. Each interrupt is handled in accordance with interrupt priorities.

interrupt trigger signal: a signal that is generated to the CPU, to interrupt the normal sequence of events in the central processor.

interrupt vector: a two-memory location identification assigned to an interrupting unit; contains the starting address and the processor status word for its service routine.

intersection: synonym for *conjunction.* (A) (B)

interstage punching: a mode of card punching such that the odd or even numbered card columns are used. (A)

interval: the time period chosen for a particular purpose.

interval service value: in the system resources manager, a category of information contained in a period definition that specifies the minimum amount of service that an associated job will receive during any interval.

interval timer:
(1) a timer that provides program interruptions on a program-controlled basis.
(2) an electronic counter that counts intervals of time under program control.

interword gap: the time or space permitted between words on a tape, disk, or drum. Permits the medium to be switched and is used for the control of individual words.

intimate: pertaining to software having a close interaction with hardware functions. Synonymous with *machine intimate.*

INTR: see *interrupt.*

intranode address: in a data networking, the addressing information concerned with users connected to the same node.

intranode routing: activities for providing an access path for users connected to the same node in a data network.

intrinsic function: synonymous with *library functions.* Cf. *extrinsic function.*

invalid character: deprecated term for *illegal character.*

invalid exclusive reference: an exclusive reference in which a common segment does not contain a reference to the symbol used in the exclusive reference.

invalid key condition: in COBOL, a condition that may arise at execution time in which the value of a specific key associated with a mass storage file does not result in a correct reference to the file REWRITE, START, and WRITE statements for the specific error conditions involved.

inventory: see *mass storage volume inventory.*

inventory control: a computer program that monitors the products in stock, in a warehouse, and in stores.

inventory master file: pertaining to permanently stored inventory information held for use in the future.

inversion: any procedure for reversing the order of items of data.

invert: to change a physical or logical state to its opposite. (A)

inverted file:
(1) a file whose sequence has been reversed.
(2) in information retrieval, a method of organizing a cross-index file in which a key word identifies a record; the items, numbers, or documents pertinent to that key word are indicated. (A)

inverted structure: a file structure that permits fast, spontaneous searching for previously unspecified information; independent lists are maintained in record keys which are accessible according to the values of specified fields.

inverter: a device whose output variable is of equal magnitude and opposite algebraic sign to its input variable. (B)

invocation: in PL/1, the activation of a procedure.

invoke: in PL/1, to activate a procedure at one of its entry points.

invoked procedure: in PL/1, a procedure that has been activated at one of its entry points.

invoking block: in PL/1, a block containing a statement that activates a procedure.

involuntary interrupt: an interrupt not caused by the object program, but which impacts on the running of the object program.

INX: see *index character.*

I/O: see *input-output.* (A)

I/O appendage: a user-written routine that provides additional control over I/O operations during channel program operations.

I/O area: synonym for *buffer* (3).

IOB: see *input-output buffer.*

I/O bound: processes where the rate of input and/or output of data is the factor determining program speed.

I/O bus: see *bus.*

IOC:
(1) see *input-output channel.*
(2) see *input-output controller.* (A)

I/O channel: see *input-output channel.*

I/O control: in COBOL, the name and the header for an environment division paragraph in which object program requirements for specific input-output techniques are specified. These techniques include rerun checkpoints, sharing of areas by several data files, and multiple file storage on a single tape device.

I/O controller: synonym for *input-output controller*. (B)

IOCS: see *input-output control system*.

IOD: see *input-output unit*.

I/O device: see *input-output unit*.

IOGEN: input-output generation. The activity needed to install an operating system on a large system where the addresses and attributes of all peripheral units controlled by the computer are described in a way that is meaningful to the operating system.

I/O interface: a different unit used to control data transfer between the CPU and input-output devices, such as an input-output channel or an I/O controller.

I/O interruption: an interruption caused by the termination of an I/O operation or by operator intervention at the I/O device.

I/O list: a list of variables in an I/O statement, specifying the storage locations into which data is to be read or from which data is to be written.

I/O orders: instructions executed by an I/O controller for controlling the operations of a particular input-output unit, such as to start and stop a tape drive.

IOP: see *I/O processor*.

I/O path architecture: the basic design of a system's input-output hardware (and, at times, software) that determines the way in which it handles input-output.

I/O port: a data channel or connection to external units used for input and/or output to and from a computer.

I/O procedure: the sequence of instructions required to perform data transfer between the CPU and input-output devices, including input-output instructions of the CPU.

I/O processor: a special-purpose computer to relieve a computer system's primary processor of the time-consuming activity of managing input and output functions.

IOPS: see *input-output program system*.

IOR: see *input-output register*.

I/O test program: a PROM with a program that plugs into and checks input-output circuit boards.

IP:

(1) see *impact printer*.

(2) see *interface processor*.

IPL:

(1) see *initial program load*.

(2) see *initial program loader*. (A)

IR:

(1) see *information retrieval*.

(2) see *instruction register*.

IRG: see *interrecord gap*.

irrational number: a real number that is not a rational number. (A) (B)

irrelevance: in information theory, the conditional entropy of the occurrence of specific messages at a message sink given the occurrences of specific messages at the message source connected to the message sink by a specified channel. (A) (B)

IRT: see *index return character*.

IS:

(1) see *information separator*. (A)

(2) see *information system*.

ISA: see *industry standard architecture bus*.

ISAM: see *indexed sequential access method*.

ISDN: see *Integrated Services Digital Network*.

isochronous: having a regular periodicity.

isochronous transmission: a data-transmission process in which there is always an integral number of unit intervals between any two significant instants. See also *synchronous transmission*.

isolated digital output module: a device providing an output interface along with electrical isolation between the computer and a process control or peripheral unit.

isolated locations: storage locations protected by a hardware unit preventing them from being addressed by a user's program and guarding their contents from accidental alteration.

ISO reference model for open systems architecture: expressed in an architecture providing seven control levels; provides the basis for open systems architecture. Each control level offers a clear definition of the protocols and formats and permits a peer interaction between users who have implemented the architecture with the equivalent level of another user. Two users who have correctly implemented only the first two levels of control are able to exchange information over a network.

ISO Standard: a standard proposed or adopted by the International Standards Organization which in Europe serves similarly as ANSI in the United States. What is known in the U.S. as the ASCII characters set is known in Europe as the ISO character set.

isotropic: describing a medium with physical properties that do not vary with direction.

IT: see *indent tab character.*

ITDM: see *intelligent time division multiplexor.*

item:

(1) one member of a group. A file may consist of a number of items, such as records, which in turn may consist of other items. (B)

(2) a collection of related characters, treated as a unit. (A)

item advance: in grouping of records, a technique for operating successively on different records in memory.

item design: any specification containing the fields making up an item, the order in which the fields are to be recorded, and the number of characters allocated to each field.

item size: the number of characters or digits in a unit of data.

iterate: to execute successively a series of instructions.

iteration: the technique of repeating a group of computer instructions; one repetition of such a group.

iteration factor: in PL/1, an expression that specifies (a) in an INITIAL attribute specification, the number of consecutive elements of an array that are to be initialized with a given constant; (b) in a format list, the number of times a given format item or list of items is to be used in succession.

iteration routine: a routine that repeatedly performs a series of operations until a specified condition is reached.

iterative: a method that repeatedly executes an operation or series of operations until some condition is satisfied.

iterative do-group: in PL/1, a do-group whose DO statement specifies a control variable, a WHILE option, or both.

iterative operation: the repetition of the algorithm for the solution of a set of equations, with successive combinations of initial conditions or other parameters; each successive combination is selected by a subsidiary computation on a predetermined set of iteration rules. (B)

ITF: BASIC: a simple, algebralike language designed for ease of use at a terminal.

ITF: PL/1: a conversation subset of PL/1 designed for ease of use at the terminal.

I-time: see *instruction time.*

I-triple-E: see *IEEE.*

IU: see *input unit.*

Iverson notation: a special set of symbols developed by Kenneth Iverson to described the formal structure of computer languages; used in APL.

jam: a pileup of cards in a card-processing device.

JCL: see *job control language.* (A)

jellybeans: slang, chips used in most computers.

JES (job entry system): the systems software that accepts and schedules jobs for execution and controls the printing of output.

jiffy: slang, an interval of time, usually 1/60 second or 1 millisecond.

JMP: see *jump.*

job:

(1) a set of data that completely defines a unit of work for a computer. A job usually includes all necessary computer programs, linkages, files, and instructions to the operating system. (A)

(2) a collection of related problem programs, identified in the input stream by a JOB statement followed by one or more EXEC and DO statements.

(3) see also *background job, batched job, foreground job, terminal job.*

job batch: a succession of job definitions that are placed one behind another to form a batch. Each job batch is placed on an input device and processed with a minimum of delay between one job or job step and another.

job card: the first job control language statement in a job, indicating the beginning of the job, the user, the name of the job, and so on.

job class: any one of a number of job categories that can be defined. By classifying jobs and directing initiator/terminators to initiate specific classes of jobs, it is possible to control the mixture of jobs that are performed concurrently.

job control: a program that is called into storage to prepare each job or job step to be run. Some of its functions are to assign I/O devices to certain symbolic names, set switches for program use, log (or print) job control statements, and fetch the first program phase of each job step.

job control language (JCL): a problem-oriented language designed to express statements in a job that are used to identify the job or describe its requirements to an operating system. (A)

job-control program: a control program that translates the job-control statements written by a programmer into machine-language instructions that can be executed by the computer.

job control statement: a statement in a job that is used in identifying the job or describing its requirements to the operating system. (A)

job definition: a series of job control statements that define a job.

job entry system: see *JES.*

job-flow control: control over the sequence of jobs being processed, ensuring an efficient use of peripheral devices and central processor.

job input device: a device assigned by the operator to read job definitions and any accompanying input data.

job input file: a data file (or data set) consisting of a series of job definitions and accompanying data.

job input stream: synonym for *input stream.*

JOBLIB: see *job library.*

job library (JOBLIB): a set of user-identified, partitioned data sets used as the primary source of load modules for a given job.

job management: the collective functions of job scheduling and command processing.

job name: the name assigned to a JOB statement; it identifies the job to the system.

job-oriented language: a computer language designed for the specific requirements of a particular type of job.

job-oriented terminal: a terminal designed for a particular application.

job output device: a device assigned by the operator for common use in recording output data for a series of jobs.

job output file: a data file (or data set) consisting of output data produced by a series of jobs.

job output stream: synonym for *output stream.*

job pack area (JPA): an area that contains modules that are not in the link pack area but are needed for the execution of jobs.

job priority: a value assigned to a job that, together with an assigned job class, determines the priority to be used in scheduling the job and allocating resources to it.

job processing: the reading of job control statements and data from an input stream, the initiating of job steps defined in the statements, and the writing of system output messages.

job program mode: a mode where read/write and jump-storage protection exists. As a result, job programs are limited to those areas assigned only. If the job program reads, writes, or jumps to an out-of-limits address, an interrupt will return control to the initiator for remedial action.

job queue: short for input job queue; a queue for storing programs already read into the computer and awaiting execution. Cf. *output job queue.*

job-recovery control file: synonym for *backup file.*

job scheduler: a program in the operating system that chooses the program to be executed next in a sequence based on priority ranking assigned to the programs, the availability of main memory, and so on.

job scheduling: placing new entries into the job queue, usually within a large system. The scheduling is actually prioritizing the order in which jobs are executed. See *job queue.*

job separator pages: separate different jobs being printed and print job names in large block letters at the beginning and end of jobs.

job (JOB) statement: the job control statement that identifies the beginning of a job. It contains such information as the name of the job, an account number, and the class and priority assigned to the job.

job step:
(1) the execution of a computer program explicitly identified by a job control statement. A job may specify that several job steps be executed. (A)
(2) a unit of work associated with one processing program or one cataloged procedure and related data. A job consists of one or more job steps.

job step initiation: the process of selecting a job step for execution and allocating input-output devices for it.

job step restart: synonym for *step restart.*

job stream: the sequence of representations of jobs to be submitted to an operating system. Synonymous with *input stream, run stream.* (B) See *input stream, output stream.*

job support task: a task that reads and interprets job definitions or converts job input and output data from one input-output medium to another.

job swapping: temporarily suspending work on a running job so that a higher priority can be given to another job. The memory workspace of the job and various control information are written to a file, thereby removing the job from the active status. See also *nonswappable.*

job turnaround: the elapsed time from when a job is given to the computer until its printed output arrives at the individual who first submitted the job. Applies only to batch work.

joint denial: a logical operation having a true output only if all inputs are false.

joint information content: in information theory, a measure of information conveyed by the occurrence of two events of definite joint probability. (A) (B)

journal: a chronological record of the changes made to a set of data; the record may be used to reconstruct a previous version of the set. Synonymous with *log.* See *mass storage volume control.*

journaling: recording transactions against a data set so that the data set can be reconstructed by applying transactions in the journal against a previous version of the data set.

joystick: a lever whose movements control a cursor or to write on a visual display unit.

JPA: see *job pack area.*

judder: related to facsimile and identifying a condition where there is a lack of uniformity in the scanning of a picture, resulting in overlapping of elements of the picture.

Julian date: the calendar representation of a computer system, indicating the year and the number of elapsed days in the year; for example, 87.5 is January 5, 1987, the 5th day of 1987.

jump (JMP): in the execution of a computer program, a departure from the implicit or declared order in which instructions are being executed. (B) See *conditional jump, unconditional jump.* (A)

jumper: a short length of electrical conductor used temporarily to complete a circuit or to bypass an existing one. Usually, a plug on top of pins.

jump instruction: an instruction that specfies a jump. See *conditional jump instruction, unconditional jump instruction.* (A) (B)

jumper tester: a device that tests whether or not the assorted options of a device are operating properly.

jump routine: a routine causing the computer to depart from the regular sequence of instruction and shift to another routine.

jump vector: a list of memory addresses where differing modules of a program are placed, with each module performing a separate function.

junctor: a device that links any two half paths in a switching network.

junk: a computer description of a garbled or otherwise unintelligible sequence of signals or other data. Cf. *garbage.*

justification:
(1) the vertical alignment of right or left margins.
(2) the act of adjusting, arranging, or shifting digits to the left or right to fit a prescribed pattern.

justification range: the allowed minimum and maximum space which can be inserted between words within a line.

justified margin: arrangement of data or type printed on pages such that the left- or right-end characters of each horizontal line lie in the same column.

justify:
(1) to control the printing positions of characters on a page so that the left-hand and right-hand margins of the printing are regular. (B)
(2) to shift the contents of a register, if necessary, so that the character at a specified end of the data that has been read or loaded into the register is at a specified position in the register. (B)
(3) to align characters horizontally or vertically to fit the positioning constraints of a required format. (A)
(4) in word processing, to print a document with even right and left margins.
(5) see *left justify, right justify.* (A)

justifying digit: a digit placed into a digit time slot as part of the process of justification and distinguished by the process as not an information bit.

K:
(1) when referring to storage capacity, two to the tenth power; 1024 in decimal notation. (A) See *kilobytes.* See also *file length, megabyte.*
(2) see *key.*

k: an abbreviation for the prefix kilo, that is, 1000 is 1000 in decimal notation. (A)

Karnaugh map: a rectangular diagram of a logic function of variables drawn with overlapping rectangles representing a unique combination of the logic variables and such that an intersection is shown for all combinations. (A) (B)

KB:
(1) see *keyboard.*
(2) kilobyte; 1024 bytes.

KBD: see *keyboard.*

KBS: one kilobyte (1024 bytes) per second.

kernel:
(1) a software product sold with the requirement that it must be modified by the purchaser prior to use on a specific machine.
(2) the central and indispensable part of a computer operating system.

kerning: in word processing, the ability to reduce the amount of space between letters by tightening the text horizontally. See *track kerning.*

key:
(1) one or more characters, within a set of data that contains information about the set, including its identification. (A) (B)
(2) in sorting, synonym for *control word.*
(3) in COBOL, one or more data items, the contents of which identify the type or the location of a record, or the ordering of data.
(4) to enter information from a keyboard.
(5) see *actual key, function key, non-escaping key, primary key, program attention key, program function key, search key, secondary key, sort key.*

KEYBD: see *keyboard.*

keyboard (KB) (KBD) (KEYBD):

(1) a systematic arrangement of keys by which a machine is operated or by which data is entered.

(2) a device for the encoding of data by key depression which causes the generation of the selected code element.

(3) a group of numeric keys, alphabetic keys, or function keys used for entering information into a terminal and into the system.

keyboard buffer: a temporary storage area in a computer, holding characters as they are typed in.

keyboard computer: a computer, the input of which uses a keyboard, possibly an electric typewriter.

keyboard control keys: terminal switches used to control and move the cursor on CRT displays, to change the terminal applications, or to change the communications mode.

keyboard encoder: a unit or circuit for identifying each key function, yielding a word corresponding to that function.

keyboard, enhanced: see *enhanced keyboard.*

keyboard entry: a technique whereby access into the contents of a computer's storage may be initiated at a keyboard.

keyboard equivalent: see *keyboard shortcut.*

keyboard function key: a key that sends out a unique string of characters representing a code, a set of data, or commands to activate peripheral equipment.

keyboard inquiry: interrogation of program progress, storage contents, or other information by keyboard manipulations.

keyboard lockout: property of the keyboard such that it cannot be used to send a message via a network while the required circuit is engaged.

keyboard lockup: where entries typed on a keyboard are ignored.

keyboard perforator: a device for punching alphameric information into tape through the manual depression of a bank of keys.

keyboard processor: a processor found in the keyboard to determine the active key position, to look up a corresponding character code in memory, and to place the appropriate code on the data bus.

keyboard punch: synonym for *keypunch.* (A) (B)

keyboard ROM: a small read-only memory in a keyboard containing standardized character code tables used by the keyboard processor so that the appropriate code can be looked up on the data bus.

keyboard shortcut: a combination of key presses that is used to give a command or set an option. Keyboard shortcuts always involve the use of at least one modifier key.

key bounce: in a keyboard terminal, several repetitions of the same character sent during a keystroke.

keycap:

(1) the actual keyboard button that generates a signal corresponding to a character when depressed.

(2) a desk accessory that shows the characters available for each font in the system.

key-driven: said of any device for translating information into machine-sensible form which requires an operator to depress a key for each character.

keyed direct access: the retrieval or storage of a data record by use of either an index that relates the record's key to its relative location in the file, or data set, or a relative-record number, independent of the record's location relative to the previously retrieved or stored record.

key-encrypting key: a key used in sessions with cryptography to encipher and decipher other keys. Cf. *data-encrypting key.*

key entry: pertaining to the input of data manually by means of a keyboard.

key folding: synonym for *hashing (1).*

keylock: a lock found on some terminals purporting to prevent usage until a key is inserted and turned to the "on" position.

key mat: a prepunched plastic, user-labeled sheet, that fits over keyboard for key identification.

key of reference: in COBOL, the key currently being used to access records within an indexed file.

key pad: a supplementary set of keys, usually numerical and arranged like a calculator; added to a keyboard.

key phrase: in word processing, a single-key abbreviation for often-used phrases. This feature works like block moves, but it involves phrases or sentences instead of paragraphs.

keypunch (KP): a keyboard-actuated punch that punches holes in a data carrier. Synonymous with *keyboard punch*. (B)

keypunch card: see *punch card*.

keypunch operator: a person who uses a keypunch machine to transfer data from source to punched cards.

key sorting: the record file fields which determine, or are used as a basis for determining, the sequence of records retained by a file.

key stations: the number of terminals used for data input on a multiple-user system.

key stroke: the operation of a single key on a keyboard.

key switch: the switch part of a key; the input key on a keyboard.

keytape: a device used to record data directly onto magnetic tape. Consists of a tape drive, keyboard, control and logic circuitry, and occasionally other input devices such as adding machines or paper tape readers.

key-to-address transformations: see *hashing*.

key-to-disk: a data entry strategy where data is sent directly from the keyboard to a disk file.

key-to-diskette: a floppy disk is used instead of the conventional (hard) disk. See also *key-to-disk*.

key-to-tape: a procedure or system where data is typed on a keyboard and recorded directly on a magnetic tape.

key-to-tape machine: apparatus that captures information to be transmitted at a later time period. It consists of a keyboard containing keys for alphanumeric characters. Data entered through the keyboard is encoded on a storage medium, such as magnetic tape or paper tape.

key transformation: a function that maps a set of keys into a set of integers, which can be handled arithmetically to determine the location of the corresponding data elements. (A)

key verification: determining the accuracy of data punched on a punch card utilizing a verifier.

key verifier: synonymous with *verifier*.

key-verify: to make certain that information required in a punched card has truly been properly punched.

key-verify unit: synonymous with *verifier*.

key word:

(1) one of the predefined words of an artificial language. (A)

(2) one of the significant and informative words in a title or document that describe the content of that document.

(3) a symbol that identifies a parameter.

(4) a reserved word whose use is essential to the meaning and structure of a COBOL statement.

(5) deprecated term for *reserved word*.

(6) synonym for *descriptor*. (A)

key word in context (KWIC): a list of available programs arranged alphabetically by the key words in the program titles. Some words are not accepted as indexing words but will be printed as part of the title. This index is prepared by highlighting each key word from a title in the context of words on either side of it and aligning the key words of all titles alphabetically in a vertical column.

key-word parameter: a parameter that consists of a key word, followed by one or more values. See also *positional parameter*.

key-word search: filing and retrieving information by using keywords that describe the contents of individual records.

kilo (k):

(1) thousand. See also *k*.

(2) shortened form of kilogram.

kilobaud: the measure of data transmission speed; a thousand bits per second. See also *baud*.

kilobytes (K): 1024 bytes. See *file length*.

kilomega-: a prefix signifying 10^9. Synonymous with *billi-* and *giga-*.

kiosks: developed in the early 1990s, touch screen computers, often with color graphics and sound. They typically allow consumers to make transactions.

Kipp relay: a circuit having a stable and an unstable state that runs through a full cycle in response to a single triggering action. Synonymous with *electromechanical one-shot, monostable multivibrator*.

kips: kilo instructions per second; a unit of machine speed equalling 1,000 operations per second.

kit: a system assembled by a user.

KLOOJ: see *kludge*.

kludge (KLOOJ): slang, hardware and/or software temporarily improvised from different mismatched parts and consequently unreliable. Synonymous with *kluge*.

kluge: synonym for *kludge*.

knowledge base: a series of interconnected generalized rules used by a knowledge engineer to reduce an expert's wisdom. See also *inferential engine* and *knowledge engineering*.

knowledge-based software: software that permits an executive to tap into compendiums of rules and suggestions for how to handle specific situations. They deal with negotiating skills, training, strategic planning, and other areas that managers cannot delegate.

knowledge engineering: an approach where leading experts in science, medicine, business, and other endeavors are interviewed to find out how they make judgments that are the core of their expertise. The next step is to codify that knowledge so computers can make similar decisions by emulating human inferential reasoning. See also *inferential engine* and *knowledge base*.

KP: see *keypunch*.

KWIC: see *key word in context*.

L:
(1) see *language*.
(2) see *length*.
(3) see *link*.
(4) see *local*.

LA: see *line adapter*.

label (LBL):
(1) one or more characters, within or attached to a set of data, that contains information about the set, including its identification. (B)
(2) in computer programming, an identifier of an instruction. (A) (B)
(3) an identification record for a tape or disk file.
(4) a word or short phrase that can be assigned to an icon by using a label menu.
(5) in PL/1, a name used to identify a statement other than a PROCEDURE or ENTRY statement; a statement label.
(6) see also *entry name, magnetic tape label, name, symbol*.

label constant: in PL/1, an unsubscripted name that appears prefixed to any statement other than a PROCEDURE or ENTRY statement.

labeled common: in PL/1, an expression whose evaluation yields a label value.

label list (of a label variable declaration): in PL/1, a parenthesized list of one or more statement-label constants immediately following the key word LABEL to specify the range of values that the declared variable may have; names in the list are separated by commas. When specified for a label array, it indicates that each element of the array may assume any of the values listed.

label list (of a statement): in PL/1, all of the label prefixes of a statement.

label record: a record used to identify the contents of a file or reel of magnetic tape.

label variable: in PL/1, a variable declared with the LABEL attribute and thus able to assume as its value a label constant.

laced card: a card punched accidentally or intentionally with holes in excess of the hole patterns of the character set used. (A)

lacing: the extra punching in a card for indicating the end of a run.

lag: the delay between two events.

LAN: see *local area network*.

land: synonymous with *real estate*.

landscape: refers to the horizontal orientation of a computer application, either on screen or by a printer. Cf. *portrait*.

language (L): a set of characters, conventions, and rules that is used for conveying information. The three aspects of language are pragmatics, semantics, and syntax. (B) See *algebraic language, algorithmic language, application-oriented language, artificial language, assembly language, command language, computer language, computer-oriented language, high-level language, job control language, linear language, machine language, multidimensional language, natural language, object language, one-dimensional language, problem-oriented language, programming language, source language, stratified language, syntax language, target language, unstratified language*. (A)

language converter: any data-processing unit designed to alter one form of data, that is, microfilm, strip chart, into another, such as punch card, paper tape.

language interpreter: any processor, assembler, or other routine that accepts statements in one language and then produces equivalent statements in another language.

language processor: a computer program that performs such functions as translating, interpreting, and other tasks required for processing a specified programming language. (A) (B)

language statement: a statement that is coded by a programmer, operator, or other user of a computing system, to convey information to a processing program such as a language translator or service program, or to the control program. A language statement may request that an operation

be performed or may contain data that is to be passed to the processing program.

language subset: a part of a language that can be used independently of the rest of the language.

language translator: a general term for any assembler, compiler, or other routine that accepts statements in one language and produces equivalent statements in another language.

language translator program: software that translates the English-like programs written by programmers into machine-executable code.

laptop: a portable computer. Cf. *notebook*. See also *flat-panel technology*.

large scale integration (LSI): the process of integrating large numbers of circuits on a single chip of semiconductor material.

laser printer: a printer that focuses laser beams to form images on photosensitive drums in a fashion similar to that used in Xerographic copiers. They are high speed, high quality, and have relatively high first costs.

last-in, first-out: see *LIFO*.

last-in, last out: see *LILO*.

latching: synonymous with *locking*.

latency: the time interval between the instant at which an instruction control unit initiates a call for data and the instant at which the actual transfer of the data is started. Synonymous with *waiting time, wait state*. (A) (B)

latency delay: a delay in reading or writing data on a storage unit because of mechanical action.

latency time: the time lag between a command for data and its delivery from memory.

lateral reversal: an image reversed left-to-right.

LAU: see *line adapter unit*.

LAWN: see *local area wireless network*.

layer: in open systems architecture, a collection of related functions that comprise one level of a hierarchy of functions. Each layer specifies its own functions and assumes that lower level functions are provided. See *application layer*.

layered architecture: see *layer*.

layout: see *file layout.* (A)

layout character: synonym for *format effector character.* (B)

LB: see *lower bound.*

LBL: see *label.*

LC:

(1) see *line control.*

(2) see *location counter.*

LCB: see *line control block.*

LCD display: a display using liquid crystal diode technology.

LCNTR: see *location counter.*

LDA: see *logical device address.*

LE: less than or equal to. See also *relational operator.*

leader: the blank section of tape at the beginning of a reel of tape. (A)

leader record: a specific record holding the description of information about the group not present in the detail records. Any blank or unused length of tape at the beginning of a tape reel proceding the start of the recorded information.

leaders: dots or dashes used by a printer to fill in a line so as to lead the reader across the page to data at the end of the line.

leading: the vertical spacing between the descending edge of one line of text and the ascending edge of the next line of text. The user can adjust the automatic leading to be a multiple of the font size, or he/she can set manual leading to be a fixed measurement. Cf. *line spacing.*

leading control: a short description or title of a control group of records appearing in front of each such group.

leading decision: a loop control that is executed before the loop body. Cf. *trailing decision.* (A)

leading edge:

(1) the indication that a loop has executed the specified number of times, placed at the beginning of the loop so that the counter is tested before the loop executes.

(2) that part of a pulse during its transition from binary 0 to 1. Cf. *trailing edge.*

leading end: the end of a perforated tape that first enters a perforated-tape reader.

leading pad: characters for filling unused space on the left end of a field of data.

leading zero:

(1) in a positional notation, a zero in a more significant digit place than the digit place of the most significant nonzero digit of a numeral. (A)

(2) a zero, used as a fill character, that appears to the left-most significant digit in a numeric value displayed on a human readable medium.

lead operator: the best person operating a computer or word processor.

leaf: last node of a tree.

leapfrog test: a check routine that copies itself through storage. (A)

learning: see *machine learning.*

learning program: a program that alters itself by making changes based on the experience of the program and results unknown until portions of the program have been run.

leased channel: a point-to-point channel reserved for sole use of a single leasing customer.

least significant bit (LSB): the rightmost bit in a byte, having the lowest numeric place value in binary; for example, the rightmost digit (the 7) has the lowest value in the number 4687.

least significant character: the character in the extreme right-hand position of a group of significant characters in positional notation.

least significant digit: the significant digit contributing the smallest quantity to the value of a numeral.

LED: see *light-emitting diode.*

left justify:

(1) to shift the contents of a register, if necessary, so that the character at the left hand of the data that has been read or loaded into the register is at a specified position in the register.

(2) to control the printing positions of characters on a page so that the left-hand margin of the printing is regular. (A) (B)

left shift: a shift that moves all bits in a register a specific number of positions to the left.

leg: a path found in a routine or a subroutine.

legal: acceptable under software rules of a computer system.

LEN: see *length*.

length (L) (LEN): see *block length, record length, word length*.

length specification: in FORTRAN, an indication, by the use of the form **s*, of the number of storage locations (bytes) to be occupied by a variable or array element.

LET: see *letter*.

LET statement: in BASIC, the fundamental assigning statement. A valid BASIC expression consisting of constants and variables whose numerical values are known together with such operators as +, −, *, /. This is evaluated and the value so determined is assigned to a specific variable. The BASIC expression appears to the right of an equal sign; the variable assigned to the value that has been determined appears to the left.

letter (LET) (LTR): a graphic character that, when used alone or combined with others, represents in a written language one or more sound elements of a spoken language, but excluding diacritical marks used alone and punctuation marks. (A) (B)

letter code: in the Baudot code, the function that leads machines to shift to lower case. The code is used to rub out errors in tape.

letter merge: a function where an address is merged from one list with a form letter, thus personalizing each message.

letter out: synonymous with *erase*.

letter-perfect printer: synonymous with *corresponding printer*.

letter-quality printer: producing the same quality as a typewriter. Synonymous with *correspondence printer*.

LEV: see *level*.

level (LEV): the degree of subordination of an item in a hierarchic arrangement. (A) (B)

level indicator: in COBOL, two alphabetic characters that identify a specific type of file, or the highest position in a hierarchy. The level indicators are FD, SD, RD.

level number:
(1) a reference number that indicates the position of an item in a hierarchic arrangement. Synonymous with *rank*. (A) (B)

(2) in COBOL, a numeric character or two-character set that identifies the properties of a data description entry. Level numbers 01 through 49 define group items; the highest level is identified as 01, and the subordinate data items within the hierarchy are identified with level numbers 02 through 49. Level numbers 66, 77, and 88 identify special properties of a data description entry in the data division.

(3) in PL/1, an unsigned decimal integer constant in a DECLARE or ALLOCATE statement that specifies the position of a name in the hierarchy of a structure. It precedes the name to which it refers and is separated from that name only by one or more blanks. Level numbers appear without the names in a parameter descriptor of an ENTRY attribute specification.

level of access: see *access level, logical access level*.

level of addressing:
(1) *zero level addressing:* the address part of an instruction is the operand; for instance, the addresses of shift instructions, or where the "address" is the data (in interpretive or generating systems).

(2) *first level addressing:* the address of an instruction is the location in memory where the operand may be found or is to be stored.

(3) *second level addressing (indirect addressing):* the address part of an instruction is the location in memory where the address of the operand may be found.

level-one variables: in PL/1, a major structure name; any subscripted variable not contained within a structure.

level set: a revision to a software package replacing most or all of the executable programs with improved software.

levels of nesting: in programming, placing similar constructs one inside the other, as the variously sized dishes of a set are stacked.

lexeme: the written word, particle, or stem that denotes meaning.

lexical analysis: the procedure of a compiler by which various components of a programming statement are identified. Cf. *syntactical analysis*.

lexicon: a vocabulary, not necessarily in alphabetical sequence, with definitions or explanations for terms included.

LF: see *line feed character.* (A)

LFC: see *local forms control.*

LFCB: causes the system to load the buffer image, contained in the core image library, into the forms control buffer of the specified printer.

librarian: a program that creates, maintains, and makes available the total of programs, routines, and data that make up an operating system. Librarian activities include system generation and system editing.

librarian program: the librarian program part of the control function that provides maintenance of library programs used as a portion of the operating system. The library may be stored on a signal secondary storage device, or it may be distributed over several differing storage devices.

library:

(1) a collection of related files. For example, one line of an invoice may form an item, a complete invoice may form a file, the collection of inventory control files may form a library, and the libraries used by an organization are known as its data bank.

(2) a repository for demountable recorded media, such as magnetic disk packs and magnetic tapes.

(3) see *data library, program library.* (A)

(4) see *job library, private library.*

library case: a container, often made of plastic, for storing and protecting floppy disks.

library directory: the library component that contains information, such as the member name and location, about each member in the library.

library facilities: a basic library of general-purpose software to perform common jobs to which the user can add often-used programs and routines.

library file editor: an editor that permits users to combine the compiler or assembler output to form binary libraries resulting in a set of central, updatable program libraries that eliminate program duplication.

library functions: functions that have been built into the BASIC language because many applications require these types of mathematical operations. These functions are included in the BASIC language library. Synonymous with *intrinsic function, stored functions.*

library program: a computer program in or from a program library. (A) (B)

library routine: a proven routine that is maintained in a program library. (A)

library subroutine: a subroutine in a program library.

library tape: a magnetic tape, holding routines used in operating a computer center, available from a library.

library track: a track used for storing static reference data.

licensed documentation: see *licensed publication.*

licensed publication: a publication for a licensed program that contains licensed information and is itself therefore licensed.

LIED: see *linkage editor.*

LIFO (last-in, first-out): a queuing technique in which the next item to be retrieved is the item most recently placed in the queue. (A)

light conduit: a flexible, incoherent bundle of fibers used to transmit light.

light-emitting diode (LED) display: in word processing, a display in which characters are formed from a dot matrix of light-emitting diodes.

light gun: deprecated term for *light pen.*

lightning cutover: synonymous with *big bang implementation.*

light pen (LP): in computer graphics, a light sensitive pick device that is pointed at the display surface. Synonymous with *electronic pen, light gun, selector pen.*

light pen attention: a CRT display device. Synonymous with *selector pen attention.*

light pen detection: in computer graphics, the sensing by a light pen of light generated by a display element in a display space. Synonymous with *light pen hit, light pen strike.*

light pen hit: synonym for *light pen detection.*

light pen strike: synonym for *light pen detection.*

light pen tracking: the process of tracking the movement of a light pen across the screen of a CRT display device.

light stability: in optical character recognition, the resistance to change of color of the image when exposed to radiant energy. (A)

LILO: last in, last out; a sequence followed in data processing.

LIM memory: a form of expanded memory developed by Lotus, Intel and Microsoft.

limited: a word often attached to another term to indicate the machine activity that requires the most time.

limited distance adapter: a modem created to function over short distances, up to perhaps 30 miles.

limiter: a functional unit used to prevent a variable from exceeding specified limits. (B)

line (LN):
(1) on a terminal, one or more characters entered before a return to the first printing or display position.
(2) a string of characters accepted by the system as a single block of input from a terminal; for example, all characters entered before a carriage return or all characters entered before the terminal user hits the attention key.
(3) see *character spacing reference line, delay line, electromagnetic delay line, off-line, on-line, X-datum line, Y-datum line.*

line-access point: the physical point for connection of a terminal to a line.

line adapter (LA): a modem that is a feature of a particular device.

line adapter unit (LAU): one component of a front end which interfaces with a specific communications line to permit communication with a computer.

linear: relating to order in an algebraic equation where all of the variables are present in the first degree only; for example, an equation where none of the variables are raised to powers other than unity or multiplied together.

linear language: a language that is customarily expressed as a linear representation. For example, FORTRAN is a linear language; a flowchart is not. (A)

linear list: synonymous with *dense list.*

linear optimization: in operations research, a procedure for locating the maximum or minimum of a linear function of variables that are subject to linear constraints. Cf. *convex programming, dynamic programming, integer programming, mathematical programming, nonlinear programming, quadratic programming.* Synonymous with *linear programming.* (A) (B)

linear programming: in operations research, a procedure for locating the maximum or minimum of a linear function of variables that are subject to linear constraints. Synonymous with *linear optimization.* Cf. *convex programming, dynamic programming, integer programming, mathematical programming, nonlinear programming, quadratic programming.* (A) (B)

linear representation: an arrangement of graphics in a one-dimensional space. (A)

linear search: a symbol table search that examines every item beginning with the first item and proceeding sequentially.

linear selection: one of the methods of selecting memory or input-output units that dedicates one address line per chip selection, resulting in overlapping memory, noncontiguous memory.

linear structure: a sequential arrangement of data records.

line-at-a-time printer: synonym for *line printer.* (A) (B)

line character: see *new-line character.* (A)

line control block (LCB): a storage area containing control information required for scheduling and managing line operations. One LCB is maintained for each line.

line data set: in systems with time sharing, a data set with logical records that are printable lines.

line drawing display: a cathode ray tube display on which lines are drawn. The lines are either input directly using a graphics tablet or light pen, or indirectly by defining the end points of the lines via a keyboard.

line editing: editing in which data is displayed at a terminal one line at a time and in which the user can access data only through commands. Cf. *full-screen editing.*

line editor: an interactive computer program allowing a terminal user to enter, view, and edit information one line at a time.

line-ending zone:

(1) in word processing, a specifiable number of character positions immediately prior to the right margin at which the machine will automatically start a new line or request operator intervention.

(2) a predetermined amount of printable space immediately to the left or right margin that is used to trigger semiautomatic and automatic line-ending decisions during adjust text mode operations. See also *adjust text mode.*

line feed character (LF):

(1) a format effector that causes the print or display position to move to the corresponding position on the next line. (A) (B) Cf. *line starve character.*

(2) in word processing, synonym for *index character.*

line height: the height of one line of type measured by the number of lines per inch.

line index: see *code line index.* (A)

line misregistration: improper or unacceptable appearance of a line of characters or numerals in optical character recognition, gauged on or with respect to the real or imaginary horizontal base line.

line number:

(1) a number associated with a line in a printout or display.

(2) in systems with time sharing, a number associated with a line in a line data set.

line number editing: in systems with time sharing, a mode of operation under the EDIT command in which lines or records to be entered, modified, or deleted, are referred to by line or record numbers.

line of code: a statement found in a programming language, occupying one line of text.

line pitch: the density of characters on a printed line, expressed characters per inch; for example, five pitch means five characters per inch.

line printer (LP) (LPT): a device that prints a line of characters as a unit. (B) Synonymous with *line-at-a-time printer.* Cf. *character printer, page printer.* (A)

line printing: the printing of a line of characters as a unit.

line quality printer: synonymous with *correspondence printer* and *letter-quality printer.*

line skew: a form of line misregistration, where a string of characters to be read by a OCR appear in a uniformly slanted or skewed condition with respect to a real or imaginary base line.

line spacing: the vertical distance between two lines of type measured baseline to baseline. Cf. *leading.*

lines-per-inch (lpi): on a printer, a measure of the number of lines per vertical inch of paper.

line starve character: the opposite of line feed character.

line trace: the computer program that records and time-stamps all traffic passing between a communications line and a computer.

link (L):

(1) in computer programming, the part of a computer program, in some cases a single instruction or an address, that passes control and parameters between separate portions of the computer program. Synonymous with *linkage.* (B)

(2) in computer programming, to provide a link. (A) (B)

(3) see *data link.*

linkage: synonym for *link (1).* (A) (B)

linkage conventions: standard methods for accomplishing linkage between programs.

linkage editor (LIED): a computer program used to create one load module from one or more independently translated object modules or load modules by resolving cross-references among the modules. Cf. *editor program.*

linkage section: in COBOL, a section of the data division that describes data made available from another program.

link-attached: pertaining to devices that are connected to a controlling unit by a data link. Synonymous with *remote.*

link-attached station: synonymous with *remote terminal.*

link-attached terminal: a terminal whose control unit is connected to a computer by a data link. Synonymous with *remote terminal.*

link bit: a specific one-bit diagnostic register containing an indicator for overflow from the accumulator, and often other registers, and which can be tested under program control.

link connection: synonym for *data circuit.*

link edit: to create a loadable computer program by means of a linkage editor.

linked list: a list where every item includes a forward pointer showing the location of the following item in the list. The pointer eliminates the need to have items stored in contiguous locations in main memory or on a direct-access storage unit.

linked sequential file: a file that has an access interface identical to that used for the various sequential devices (magnetic tape, line printer, etc.). The consistency between sequential device and the disk is achieved with the link sequential file.

linked subroutine: see *closed subroutine.*

linker: a program capable of uniting separately written programs or routines for subsequent loading into memory and execution.

link group: those links that employ the same multiplex devices.

linking loader: a loader used to link compiled/assembled programs, routines, and subroutines, and transform the results into tasks.

linking loader executive: an executive program that connects various program segments so that they can be run in the computer as one unit.

LIOCS: see *logical IOCS.*

LIPID: see *logical page identifier.*

liquid crystal display: see *LCD display.*

LISP: see *list processing.*

list:
(1) an ordered set of items of data. (B)
(2) to print or otherwise display items.
(3) deprecated term for *chained list.* (B)
(4) see *push-down list, push-up list.* (A)

list-directed transmission: in PL/1, the type of stream-oriented transmission in which data in the stream appears as constants separated by blanks or commas and for which formatting is provided automatically.

listening mode: a mode in which a station cannot send or receive messages, but can monitor messages on the line.

listing: a printout, usually prepared by a language translator, that lists the source language statements and contents of a program.

list processing (LISP): a method of processing data in the form of lists. Usually, chained lists are used so that the logical order of items can be changed without altering their physical locations. (A) (B)

list processing languages: specific languages developed by symbol manipulation and used primarily for research rather than for production programming.

list structure: a specific set of data items combined because each element contains the address of the successor item or element. These lists increase in size according to the limits of fixed storage capacity, and can easily insert or delete data items anywhere in a list structure.

LIT: see *literal.*

literal (LIT):
(1) in a source program, an explicit representation of the value of an item, which value must be unaltered during any translation of the source program; for example, the word "FAIL" in the instruction: "if X = 0 print "FAIL"." (A) (B)
(2) a symbol or a quantity in a source program that is itself data, rather than a reference to data. Cf. *figurative constant.*
(3) a character string whose value is implicit in the characters themselves. The numeric literal 7 expresses the value 7, and the numeric literal "CHARACTERS" in expresses the value CHARACTERS.

literal operands: operands, usually in source language statements, that specify the value of a constant rather than the address in which the constant is stored. The coding is more concise than if the constant has been allocated a data name.

literal pool: an area of storage into which an assembler assembles the values of the literals specified in a source program.

literature search: a systematic and exhaustive search for published material on a specified subject, and often the preparation of abstracts or summaries on that material.

live keyboard: a keyboard that allows users to interact with the system while a program is running to examine or change program variables or perform keyboard calculations.

liveware: slang, people involved in operating computers.

LLG: see *logical line group.*

LN: see *line.*

load:
(1) in programming, to enter data into storage or working registers. (A) (B)
(2) to bring a load module from auxiliary storage into main storage for execution.

load-and-go: an operating technique in which there are no stops between the loading and execution phases of a computer program, and which may include assembling or compiling. (A)

load cards: the punched cards which hold the program instructions and the constant values.

loaded origin: the address of the initial storage location of a computer program in main storage at the time the computer program is loaded. (A)

loader: a routine, commonly a computer program, that reads data into main storage. See *absolute loader, bootstrap loader, initial program loader, relocating loader.* (A)

loader program: a program that takes information being entered into the computer or coming from external memory and transfers it into the internal memory of the computer. Such programs also assist in keeping track of where the information is in memory.

loader routine: synonymous with *loading routine.*

loaders and linkage editors: in microprocessors, they perform a number of services for the programmer. They take machine code or object code as input, along with possible programmer commands, and produce the desired memory image. Loaders can be considered a form of translator.

loader types: microcomputer loaders able to complete various coding processes.

load facility: a hardware facility designed to permit program loading.

loading error: an error found in the output of the computer which came about as a result of a change in the value of the load that was supplied.

loading-location misuse errors: a loading-location specification was made but no load or execute was specified; the loading location specified was not within the available range of memory; the loading location is assigned as the first available location.

loading procedure: system, object, and library routines are loaded in a similar fashion. A program can have a fixed origin or can be relocatable. Fixed origin programs are loaded into the specified memory address. Programs are relocated by a base address first set by the executive routine. Following the main program being loaded, any library subroutines or device drivers called will then be loaded. When all the required routines are in memory, the loader returns to the job processor.

loading routine: a routine which, once it is itself in memory, is able to bring other information into memory from input media. Synonymous with *loader routine.*

load leveling: the balancing of work between processing units, channels, or devices.

load map: a map containing the storage addresses of control sections and entry points of a program loaded into storage.

load module: a program unit that is suitable for loading into main storage for execution; it is usually the output of a linkage editor. (B)

load module library: a partitioned data set that is used to store and retrieve load modules. See also *object module library, source module library.*

load-on-call: a function of linkage editor that allows selected segments of the module to be disk resident while other segments are executing. Disk resident segments are loaded for execution and given control when any entry point they contain is called.

load point: the beginning of the recording area on a reel of magnetic tape.

load program: synonymous with *loading routine.*

load sharing: computers placed in tandem (duplexing or triplexing) to share the peak-period load from a system.

LOC:

(1) see *local.*

(2) see *location.*

(3) see *location counter.*

local (L) (LOC): pertaining to that which is defined and used only in subdivision of a computer. (A) See *local code.*

local area network (LAN): a system linking together computers and other electronic office machines to create an inter-office, or intersite network. These networks usually provide access to external networks, for example, public telephone and data transmission networks, information retrieval systems, and so on.

local area wireless network (LAWN): a local area network connected by radio signals.

local code: in assembler programming, that part of a program that is either the body of any macrodefinition called from a source module or the open code portion of the source module.

local forms control (LFC): a system for off-line data-entry operations by diskette storage of fixed formats and data at the locate site.

local identifier: an identifier declared in the block where it is used. See *name precedence.*

local intelligence: in computer graphics, processing power and memory capacity built in to the terminal so it does not need to be connected to a host computer to perform certain tasks.

local mode: the state of a data-terminal device that cannot accept incoming calls or data because it is engaged in some internal activity.

local storage: the collection of general registers in a computer that are available to the central processing unit.

local system: peripherals connected directly to the CPU.

local terminal: a terminal on the same site as the central computer, and which can be directly connected to it.

local variable symbol: in assembler programming, a variable symbol that can be used to communicate values inside a macro definition or in the open code portion of a source module. Cf. *global variable symbol.*

locate: a tape is searched for the first occurrence of specific information.

location (LOC): any place in which data may be stored. (A) Cf. *address.*

location counter (LC) (LCNTR) (LOC): a counter whose value indicates the address of data assembled from a machine instruction or a constant, or the address of an area of reserved storage, relative to the beginning of a control section.

location registers: synonymous with *external registers.*

locator device: in computer graphics, an input device that provides coordinate data; for example, a mouse, a tablet, a thumbwheel. See also *choice device, pick device, valuator device.*

locator qualification: in PL/1, in a reference to a based variable, either a locator variable or function reference connected by an arrow to the left of a based variable to specify the generation of the based variable to which the reference refers, or the implicit connection of a locator variable with the based reference.

locator variable: in PL/1, a variable whose value identifies the location in internal storage of a variable or a buffer.

lock: a means to prevent files or disks from being changed or deleted. They can still be opened or copied.

locked name: in PL/1, a name that is not necessarily available at a given time to all tasks that know the name.

locked page: in virtual storage systems, a page that is not to be paged out.

locked record: in PL/1, a record in an exclusive direct update file that is available to only one task at a time.

locked up:

(1) a processor not having access to a shared resource.

(2) a terminal unable to accept commands because of an error in the entering of an earlier command or because of a malfunction in the terminal.

locking: in code extension characters, having the characteristics that a change interpretation applies to all coded representation following, or to all coded representations of a given class, until the next appropriate code extension character occurs. (A) (B) Cf. *nonlocking.* Synonymous with *latching.*

lockout: to place unaddressed terminals on a multipoint line in control state so that they will not receive transmitted data. See also *blind, polling, selection.*

lock-up table: an approach to control the location to which a jump or transfer is made. It is used primarily when there are numerous alternatives, as with a function evaluation in scientific computations.

log: synonym for *journal.* See *system log.*

logger:

(1) a functional unit that records events and physical conditions, usually with respect to time. (B)

(2) a device that enables a user entity to log in, for example, to identify itself, its purpose, and the time of entry; and to log out with the corresponding data so that the appropriate accounting procedures may be carried out in accordance with the operating system. (A)

logging: the recording of data about specific events. See *data logging.* (A)

logic: see *double rail logic, format logic, symbolic logic.* (A)

logical:

(1) that which is necessary or to be expected because of what has occurred earlier.

(2) having to do with computer logic.

(3) the way a data structure, hardware or software system, is perceived by an individual that may be different from its actual functioning or form.

logical access level: access to a data set by logical records.

logical ADD: synonym for *disjunction.* (A) (B)

logical channel: the identification of each data channel within a network, distinguishing it from other channels sharing the same physical resources. See also *logical channel number.*

logical channel number: unique numbers used to identify channels in a communication control system.

logical chart: synonymous with *logic flowchart.*

logical child segment: in a data base, a pointer segment that establishes an access path between its physical parent segment and its logical parent segment.

logical comparison: a logic operation to determine whether two strings are identical. (A) (B)

logical connectives: operators or words such as AND, OR, OR ELSE, and EXCEPT that make new statements from given statements.

logical constant: in FORTRAN, a constant that specifies a truth value; true or false.

logical data structure: in a data base, a hierarchic structure of segments.

logical decision:

(1) the planning of a computer system prior to its detailed engineering design.

(2) the synthesizing of a network of elements to perform a specified function.

(3) the result of the above, frequently called the logic of the computer.

logical design:

(1) the logic of the system, machine, or network.

(2) computer design from the viewpoint of data flow within the computer without consideration of the hardware utilized.

logical device address (LDA): a number used to represent a terminal or terminal component within a work station.

logical diagram: see *logic diagram.*

logical difference: the members of one set which are not also members of another set.

logical element: the simplest device able to be represented in a system of symbolic logic, for example, flip-flop.

logical error: as distinguished from a grammatical or a data error, a mistake in the problem-solving sequence stated in a computer program. In general, most computer languages and their associated compilers can only protect the user against grammatical errors.

logical expression:

(1) in assembler programming, a conditional assembly expression that is a combination of logical terms, logical operators, and paired parentheses.

(2) in FORTRAN, a combination of logical primaries and logical operators.

logical file: synonym for *file.*

logical flowchart: see *logic flowchart.*

logical group instructions: a group of instructions that usually includes AND, OR, exclusive-OR, compare, and rotate or complement data in registers or in memory.

logical IF: a FORTRAN IV statement will execute when the logical expression is true, or will bypass the statement if found to be false.

logical instruction: an instruction that causes the execution of an operation defined in symbolic logic statements or operators, such as AND & OR. Cf. *arithmetic instruction.*

logical interface: rules governing the way that two units interact, including the identification of signals passing between the equipment and the responses given by one to another under given conditions. Cf. *electrical interface* and *mechanical interface.*

logical IOCS: a comprehensive set of macroinstruction routines provided to handle creation, retrieval, and modification of data files.

logical level (of a structure member): in PL/1, the depth indicated by a level number when all level numbers are in direct sequence, that is, when the increment between successive level numbers is one.

logical line group (LLG): any collection of data links specified by a user as a group at generation of the network control program.

logical multiply: synonym for *AND.* (A) (B)

logical number: a number assigned to a peripheral unit during autoload or system generation time. This number can be changed whenever convenient, in contrast with a physical unit number.

logical operation: synonym for *logic operation.* (A) (B)

logical operator:

(1) in assembler programming, an operator or pair of operators that can be used in a logical expression to indicate the action to be performed on the terms in the expression. The logical operators are AND, OR, NOT, AND NOT, and OR NOT.

(2) a COBOL word that defines the logical connections between relational operators. The three logical operators and their meanings are: OR (logical inclusive—either or both), AND (logical connective—both), and NOT (logical negation).

(3) in FORTRAN, and of the set of three operators. (.NOT., .AND., .OR.).

logical operators: in PL/1, the bit-string operators ¬ (not), & (and), and | (or).

logical page identifier (LIPID): the unique identifier of a specific page.

logical page number (LPN): the relative page number within a logical group. It is added to the logical group number to create a unique LPID.

logical parent segment: in a data base, a segment pointed to by a logical child segment that contains common reference data. The pointer from the logical child segment to the logical parent segment can be symbolic or direct. A logical parent segment can also be a physical parent segment.

logical primary: in FORTRAN an irreducible logical unit: a logical constant, logical variable, logical array element, logical function reference, relational expression, or logical expression enclosed in parentheses, having the value true or false.

logical product: deprecated term for *conjunction.* (A) (B)

logical record (LR):
(1) a record independent of its physical environment. Portions of the same logical record may be located in different physical records, or several logical records or parts of logical records may be located in one physical record. (A) (B)
(2) a record from the standpoint of its content, function, and use rather than its physical attributes; that is, one that is defined in terms of the information it contains.
(3) in COBOL, the most inclusive data item, identified by a level-01 entry. It consists of one or more related data items.

logical relation: in assembler programming, a logical term in which two expressions are separated by a relational operator. The relational operators are EQ, GE, GT, LE, LT, and NE. See also *arithmetic relation, character relation.*

logical shift: a shift that equally affects all of the characters of a computer word. Synonymous with *logic shift.* (A) (B)

logical sum: deprecated term for *disjunction.* (A) (B)

logical symbol: a symbol use to represent any one of the logical operators.

logical term: in assembler programming, a term that can be used only in a logical expression.

logical timer: a software logic element representing the use of a hardware timer.

logical tracing: tracing as performed only on jump or transfer instructions.

logical track: a group of tracks that can be addressed as a single group.

logical volume: a portion of a physical volume which is viewed by the system as a volume.

logic analysis: the delineation or determination of the steps needed to yield the desired computer output or derive the intelligence information from the given or ascertained input data or model.

logic analyzer: a test and diagnostic system equipped with an oscilloscope, able to display bus and other digital states such as 0s and 1s, and perform complex test activities as well.

logic array: an integrated circuit composed of an array of gates that are intercon-
nected as requested by the customer for performing specific functions in the computer. See also *programmable logic.*

logic chart: synonymous with *logic flowchart.*

logic decoder: a logic unit that converts data from one number system to another, for example, an octal-to-decimal decoder. Decoders are also used to recognize unique addresses, such as a device addresses, and bit patterns.

logic design: a functional design that uses formal methods of description, such as symbolic logic. (A)

logic device: a device that performs logic operations. (A)

logic diagram: a graphic representation of a logic design. (A)

logic element: a device that performs an elementary logic function. See *combinational logic element, sequential logic element.* (A)

logic error: a programming error resulting from faulty reasoning on the part of the programmer.

logic file: a data set of one or more logical open records, operating through the use of a file-definition macroinstruction.

logic flowchart:
(1) a chart representing logical elements and their relationships.
(2) the representation of the logical steps in a program using a standard set of symbols.

logic function: deprecated term for *switching function.* (A) (B)

logic instruction: an instruction in which the operation part specifies a logic operation. (A) (B)

logic operation:
(1) an operation that follows the rules of symbolic logic. (B)
(2) an operation in which each character of the result depends on not more than one character of each operand. (B)
(3) synonymous with *logical operation.* (A)

logic product: the result developed from the AND operation as contrasted with product arithmetic.

logic-seeking print head: a bidirectional printing unit for optimizing motion for more efficient printing, where the first line is printed left to right, the second line right to left, and so on.

logic shift: synonym for *logical shift.* (A) (B)

logic signals: synonymous with *logic states.*

logic states: the binary (1 or 0) values at the nodes of logic elements and ICs at a particular time. Synonymous with *logic signals.*

logic symbol: a symbol that represents an operator, a function, or a functional relationship. (A)

logic theory: the science of logical operation which forms the basis of computer activities. Uses simple logic to test hypotheses which are shown to be either true or false by "on" or "off" identifiers in an electronic circuit. See *boolean algebra.*

logic unit: a part of a computer that performs logic operations and related operations. (B) See *arithmetic unit.* (A)

log in: the act of inserting data, usually to a terminal, prior to beginning a dialog or entering a query.

LOGO: a programming language for teaching the basics of computer programming.

log off: to request that a session be terminated.

log on: to initiate a session.

log on request: see *log on.*

log out: synonymous with *log off,* except there is the expectation to receive a printout instead of a manual record.

long instruction format: an instruction occupying more than one standard position or length, such as a two-word instruction.

longitudinal magnetization: a magnetization found in a magnet recording which is in a direction parallel to the line of travel.

longitudinal-mode delay line: a magnetostrictive delay line in which the mode of operation depends on longitudinal vibration in a magnetostrictive material.

longitudinal parity check:
(1) a parity check performed on a group of binary digits in a longitudinal direction for each track.
(2) a system of error checking performed at the receiving station after a block check character has been accumulated.

(3) synonymous with *longitudinal redundancy check.*

longitudinal redundancy check (LRC): synonym for *longitudinal parity check.*

longitudinal redundancy check (LRC) character: on a magnetic tape where each character is represented in a lateral row of bits, a character used for checking the parity of each track in the longitudinal direction. Such a character is usually the last character recorded in each block and is used in some magnetic recording systems to reestablish the initial recording status. (A)

long precision: see *double precision.*

long-term store: a storage medium to hold data that must be retained for a long time.

look ahead: the process of masking an interrupt until the following instruction has been executed.

look up: a program system operation or process in which a table of stored values is searched (or scanned) until a value equal to (or sometimes greater than) a specific value is located.

look-up table: a collection of data in a form suitable for ready reference, frequently as stored-in-sequence machine locations or written in the form of an array of rows and columns for easy entry.

loop:
(1) a set of instructions that may be executed repeatedly while a certain condition prevails. In some implementations, no test is made to discover whether the condition prevails until the loop has been executed once. (A) (B)
(2) in data communication, an electrical path connection—a station and a channel.
(3) see *closed loop, feedback loop, magnetic hysteresis loop.*

loop body:
(1) the part of the loop that accomplishes its primary purpose.
(2) in a counter, a part of the loop control.
(3) cf. *loop control.* (A)

loop box: a register for modifying instructions within a loop.

loop code: coding utilizing a program loop for repetition of a sequence of instructions, resulting in storage savings.

loop computing: performance of the primary function of a loop, by the instructions of the loop itself, as distinguished from loop initialization, modification, and testing, which are housekeeping operations.

loop control: the parts of the loop that modify the loop control variables and determine whether to execute the loop body or exit from the loop. Cf. *loop body.* (A)

loop-control variable: a variable that affects the execution of instructions in the loop body and is modified by a loop control. (A)

loop counter: in assembler programming, a counter used to prevent excessive looping during conditional assembly processing.

looping: repetitive execution of the same statement or statements, usually controlled by a DO statement.

looping execution: the execution of the same set of instructions where for each execution some parameter or sets of parameters have undergone a change.

loop initialization: the parts of a loop that set its starting values. (A)

loop jump: a jump instruction that causes a jump to itself. See also *jump instruction* and *loop.*

loop modification: alteration of instruction addresses, counters, or data by means of instructions of a loop.

loop program: instructions that are repeated until a terminal condition is found.

loop termination: in reading data, the last punched card containing some specific code number which can be tests and thereby used to terminate the loop.

loop testing: determination of when a loop function has been completed by means of instructions of a loop. See also *loop termination.*

loop transfer function: the mathematical function expressing the relationship between the outputs of a properly terminated feedback loop system and the input.

loop transmission frame: the collection of data that is sent around a loop as an entity.

loop update: the process of supplying current parameters associated with a particular loop for use by the control algorithm of that loop in calculating a new control output.

loosely coupled: pertaining to processing units that are connected by means of channel-to-channel adapters that are used to pass control information between the processors. See also *tightly coupled.*

lose: slang, to fail, as with a program.

loser: slang, a very bad situation or program.

lossage: slang, the result of a malfunction. See also *winnage.*

loss of significance: in a register, loss of one or more of the rightmost fractional digits because the result of an operation produced more than seven fractional digits or more than a total of ten whole-number and fractional digits. Cf. *overflow.*

low activity: when a small proportion of total records are processed during an updating run.

low activity data processing: carrying out relatively few transactions on a large database.

low byte: (FFFA) bits 0 through 7 of a 16-bit binary number.

low core: the lowest addresses of the main memory in a computer, beginning at 0.

low delay: the quality desired in a network where there is minimal delay in the delivery of a frame of information at any planned level of offered traffic.

low density disk: a 3½-inch disk that can only hold 720 K of data. It can only be formatted at low density and is not capable of being formatted at high density. Cf. *high density disk.*

lower bound (LB) (LBW): in PL/1, the lower limit of an array dimension.

lower case: noncapitalized alphabetic letters.

lower curtate: the adjacent card rows at the bottom of a punch card. (A)

low-level language (LOWL): a programming language close to machine code and in which each instruction has a one-for-one equivalent in machine code.

low order: the significance given to characters or digits farthest to the right in a number.

low order digit: a digit that occupies a less significant position in a number.

low-order position: the rightmost position in a string of characters.

low resolution: defining a visual display system that cannot be used to present graphic information in fine detail. Cf. *high resolution.*

low side: that part of a remote controller that faces away from the computer with which it communicates.

low speed storage: storage whose access is so slow that it curtails the rate at which data can be processed. This suggests that the access speed is slower than the central processor's calculating speed and/or the speed of peripheral units.

low tape: an indication that the supply of paper tape in a perforator is nearly depleted.

LP:
  (1) see *light pen.*
  (2) see *linear programming.*
  (3) see *line printer.*

lp: lines per inch.

lpi: lines per inch.

LIPD: see *logical page identifier.*

lpm: lines per minute.

LPN: see *logical page number.*

lps: lines per second.

LPT: see *line printer.*

LR: see *logical record.*

LRC: see *longitudinal redundancy check character.*

LSB: see *least significant bit.*

LSD: see *least significant digit.*

LSI: see *large scale integration.*

LT: less than. See *relational operator.*

LTR: see *letter.*

lug: a unit at the end of a conductor used for inserting screws at terminal strips.

luhn scanner: the scanning device invented by H. P. Luhn of IBM, for photoelectrical scanning of punched cards as they are fed through the machine and with some search capabilities.

Lukasiewicz notation: synonym for *prefix notation.* (A)

LWB: see *lower bound.*

M:
  (1) see *machine.*
  (2) see *mantissa.*
  (3) see *master.*
  (4) see *mega.*
  (5) see *memory.*
  (6) see *meter.*
  (7) see *milli.*
  (8) see *mode.*
  (9) see *modem.*
  (10) see *monitor.*
  (11) see *multiplier.*

MAC:
  (1) multiaccess computing. A technique permitting a number of people to hold a conversation with a computer at the same time. See also *time sharing.*
  (2) abbreviation for Apple Macintosh computer.

machine (M): see *accounting machine, electrical accounting machine, Turing machine, universal Turing machine.* (A)

machine address: synonym for *absolute address.* (A) (B)

machine check: an error condition caused by an equipment malfunction.

machine check handler (MCH): a feature that analyzes errors and attempts recovery by retrying the failing instruction if possible. If retry is unsuccessful, it attempts to correct the malfunction or to isolate the affected task.

machine check indicator: a protective unit that is turned on when certain conditions arise within the device, programming the machine to stop, to run a separate correction routine, or to ignore the condition.

machine check interruption (MCI): an interruption that occurs as a result of an equipment malfunction or error.

machine code: the machine language used for entering text and program instructions onto the recording medium or into storage and which is subsequently used for processing and printout. Synonym for *computer instruction code.* (A) (B)

machine-code instruction: symbols stating a basic computer operation to be carried out. It is the combination of bits identifying the machine language operator that becomes a portion of the instruction designating the operation of logic.

machine cognition: the artificial perception in optical machine reading and pattern recognition.

machine cycle:
(1) the identified time interval in which a computer can perform a given number of operations.
(2) the shortest complete process of action that is repeated in order.
(3) the minimum amount of time in which the foregoing can be performed.

machine-dependent: anything which makes use of features unique to a certain computer.

machine equation: see *computer equation.*

machine error: following equipment failure, any deviation from correctness in data results.

machine-independent (MI): pertaining to procedures or programs created without regard for the actual devices that are used to process them.

machine independent language: a programming language having the potential to be understood by a wide range of computers, for example, high level languages such as COBOL, FORTRAN.

machine-independent solution: procedures and/or programs that are organized in terms of the logical nature of the problem rather than in relation to or concerning the various computer devices used to solve them or process them.

machine instruction: synonym for *computer instruction.* (A) (B)

machine instruction code: synonymous with *machine code.*

machine instruction set: synonym for *computer instruction set.* (A)

machine instruction statements: direct counterparts of machine instruction.

machine intimate: synonymous with *intimate.*

machine language (ML):
(1) a language that is used directly by a machine. (A)
(2) in word processing, the language used for entering text and program instructions on to the recording medium or into storage and which is subsequently used for processing and printout.
(3) deprecated term for *computer instruction code.* (A)
(4) synonym for *computer language.* (A) (B)

machine language code: synonymous with *machine code.*

machine learning: the ability of a device to improve its performance based on its past performance. (A) (B)

machine length: the working word length used by a machine.

machine logic:
(1) built-in methods of problem approach and function execution; the way a system is designed to perform, what the activities are, and the type and form of data it can utilize internally.
(2) the capability of an automatic data-processing unit to make decisions based upon the results of tests performed.

machine operation: synonym for *computer operation.* (A)

machine-oriented language (MOL): synonym for *computer-oriented language.* (A)

machine readable: a machine that is capable of being read by an input device.

machine-readable medium: a medium that can convey data to a given sensing device. Synonymous with *automated data medium.* (A)

machine run: the execution of one or more routines that are linked to form one operating unit.

machine-sensible information: information in a form that can be read by a specific machine.

machine spoiled time: down or wasted computer time resulting from computer malfunction during production runs.

machine variable: in an analog computer, the signal that reproduces the variations of the simulated function.

machine word: synonym for *computer word.*

macro: when used as a noun, a single code or command that is used in place of a series of commands or keystrokes. See also *macro assembler, macrodefinition, macroinstruction, macroprototype statement.* (A) (B)

macro assembler: an assembler equipped with a facility for defining and expanding macroinstructions.

macroassembly program: a language processor that accepts statements, words, and phrases to produce instructions for a machine. It is more than an assembly program because it has compiler powers, permitting segmentation of a large program so that portions may be tested separately.

macrocall: synonym for *macroinstruction.*

macrocode: synonymous with *macroinstruction.*

macrocommand: programs that are formed by strings of standard, but related, commands.

macrodeclaration: synonym for *macrodefinition.* (A) (B)

macrodefinition:

(1) a declaration that provides the skeletal code that a macrogenerator uses in replacing a macroinstruction. (A) (B)

(2) a set of statements that defines the name of, format of, and conditions for generating a sequence of assembler language statements from a single source document.

(3) see also *source macrodefinition.* Synonymous with *macrodeclaration.*

macroelement: an order set of data elements that are handled as a unit and provided with a single data-use identifier.

macroexerciser: the repeated operation of supervising programs and other macroinstructions under differing conditions to locate program errors.

macroexpansion: the sequence of statements that result from a macrogeneration operation. Synonym for *macrogeneration.*

macrofacility: the part of an assembly permitting it to yield a sequence of statements from a macrodefinition.

macroflowchart: a chart or table used in the design of the logic of a routine; the seg-

ments and subroutines of the routine are presented by blocks. Synonymous with *modular program flowchart.*

macrogenerating program: synonym for *macrogenerator.* (A) (B)

macrogeneration: an operation in which an assembler produces a sequence of assembler language statements by processing a macrodefinition called by a macroinstruction. Macrogeneration takes place at preassembly time. Synonymous with *macroexpansion.*

macrogenerator (MAG): a computer program that replaces macroinstructions in the source language with the defined sequence of instructions in the source language. Synonymous with *macrogenerating program.* (A) (B)

macroinstruction:

(1) an instruction in a source language that is to be replaced by a defined sequence of instructions in the same source language. The macroinstruction may also specify values for parameters in the instructions that are to replace it. (A) (B)

(2) in assembler programming, an assembler-language statement that causes the assembler to process a predefined set of statements called a macrodefinition. The statements normally produced from the macrodefinition replace the macroinstruction in the program. Synonymous with *macrocall.*

macroinstruction operand: in assembler programming, an operand that supplies a value to be assigned to the corresponding symbolic parameter of the macrodefinition called by the macroinstruction.

MACROL: see *macrolanguage.*

macrolanguage (MACROL): the representations and rules for writing macroinstructions and macrodefinitions.

macrolibrary: a library of macrodefinitions used during macroexpansion.

macroprogramming: writing machine-procedure statements in terms of macroinstructions. (A)

macroprototype: synonym for *macroprototype statement.*

macroprototype statement: an assembler language statement that is used to give a name to a macrodefinition and to provide a model (prototype) for the macroinstruction that is to call the macrodefinition.

macrotrace: an error detection aid such as main memory and file dumps, loggings, and simulators. A macrotrace prints out the record of macros or records them.

MAG: see *macrogenerator.*

magazine slot: see *slot.*

mag card: synonymous with *magnetic card.*

magnetic bias: the steady magnetic field added to the signal field in magnetic recording; may improve the linearity of response during recording.

magnetic card (MC): a card with a magnetizable surface layer on which data can be stored by magnetic recording. Synonymous with *mag card.*

magnetic card reader: a unit used to input information from magnetic cards or transfer information from magnetic cards to another form of storage device.

magnetic cell: a storage cell in which different patterns of magnetization are used to represent characters. Synonymous with *static magnetic cell.* (A) (B)

magnetic character: a character imprinted on a document using magnetic ink.

magnetic code: the way in which data bits are represented on magnetic recording materials.

magnetic core:
(1) a piece of magnetic material, usually toroidal in shape, used for storage. (B)
(2) a configuration of magnetic material that is, or is intended to be, placed in a spatial relationship to current-carrying conductors and whose magnetic properties are essential to its use. It may be used to concentrate an induced magnetic field as in a transformer induction coil, or armature, to retain a magnetic polarization for the purpose of storing data, or for its nonlinear properties as in a logic element. It may be made of such material as iron, iron oxide, or ferrite and in such shapes as wires, tapes, toroids, rods, or thin film. (A)

magnetic core storage: a magnetic storage in which data are stored by the selective polarization of magnetic cores. (A) (B)

magnetic disk (disc):
(1) a flat circular plate with a magnetizable surface layer. Synonymous with *disk.* (B)
(2) in word processing, a recording medium in the form of a flat circular plate on which magnetic recordings can be made on either or both sides.
(3) see also *diskette.*

magnetic disk drive: a secondary storage device that stores magnetically recorded data. A disk resembles a phonograph record; a disk pack resembles several phonograph records stacked one above the other; one or more fixed or movable reading and recording heads can both record and read data. The entire mechanism, the disk pack, the reading and writing heads, the motor to spin the disk pack, and the associated circuitry are collectively referred to as the disk drive.

magnetic disk storage: a magnetic storage in which data are stored by magnetic recording on the flat surface of one or more disks that rotate in use. (B)

magnetic disk store: see *magnetic disk.*

magnetic disk unit: a device containing a disk drive, magnetic heads, and associated controls. (B)

magnetic hand scanner: a hand-held device that reads precoded information from a magnetic stripe.

magnetic head: an electromagnet that can perform one or more functions of reading, writing, and erasing data on a magnetic data medium. See also *read head, read/write head, write head.*

magnetic hysteresis loop: a closed curve showing the relation between the magnetization force and the induction of magnetization in a magnetic substance when the magnetized field (force) is carried through a complete cycle. (A)

magnetic ink: an ink that contains particles of a magnetic substance whose presence can be detected by magnetic sensors. (A)

magnetic ink character recognition (MICR): character recognition of characters printed with ink that contains particles of a magnetic material. Cf. *optical character recognition.* (A)

magnetic ink character sorter: a device capable of reading magnetic characters and then sorting the documents upon which they appear. Used extensively in banks to sort checks.

magnetic ink scanners: machines that read numbers designed in a special type font and printed in a magnetic (iron oxide) ink.

magnetic instability: the property of magnetic material on tape causing variations to take place, due to aging, temperature, and mechanical strain.

magnetic memory: a storage unit that functions using a film of magnetic material for registering or recovering information in the form of bits. Synonymous with *magnetic store*.

magnetic recording: in word processing, a technique of storing data by selectively magnetizing portions of a magnetizable material. (A) (B)

magnetic recording and reading heads: small electrical components, similar to those found in the home tape recorder, but of greater precision, and designed to handle greater recording densities. Computer READ/WRITE heads are employed in most magnetic memories that have moving parts (tape units, card units, disks, drums, etc.).

magnetic slot reader: a device that reads precoded information from a magnetic stripe as it passes through a slot in the reader.

magnetic storage: a storage device that uses the magnetic properties of certain materials. (A) (B)

magnetic store: see *magnetic memory*.

magnetic strip: the line of magnetic ink on the back of a ledger card containing coded data; may or may not be printed on the face of the card.

magnetic strip accounting machine: a unit that records data on the magnetic strip at the rear of the ledger card that can be read by the machine and recorded on a document without manual keyboarding.

magnetic stripe: a strip of magnetic material on which data, usually identification information, can be recorded and from which the data can be read.

magnetic tape (MT):
(1) a tape of magnetic material used as the constituent in some forms of magnetic cores. (A)
(2) in word processing, a recording medium in the form of a ribbon that has one or more tracks along its length on which magnetic recordings can be made on either one or both sides.

magnetic tape cassette: a container holding magnetic tape that can be processed without separating it from the container. A distinction is sometimes made between cassettes and cartridges, based on their physical characteristics.

magnetic tape code: the code (ASCII or EBCDIC) used to read or write data on a magnetic tape.

magnetic tape deck: synonym for *magnetic tape drive*. (B)

magnetic tape drive: a mechanism for moving magnetic tape and controlling its movement. Synonymous with *magnetic tape deck, magnetic tape transport, tape deck, tape transport, tape transport mechanism*. (B)

magnetic tape file: a reel of magnetic tape holding records that are arranged in an ordered sequence.

magnetic tape label: one or more records at the beginning of a magnetic tape that identify and describe the data recorded on the tape and contains other information, such as the serial number of the tape reel.

magnetic tape leader: the portion of magnetic tape that precedes the beginning-of-tape mark. (B)

magnetic tape system: high capacity hardware storage with tape drive and control circuitry. It is useful with large batches of stored information not needing frequent access, and for application where most of the records do not require accessing.

magnetic tape terminal: converts the character pulses from serial-bit form to parallel-bit form while checking for odd parity and translating the code to the desired magnetic-tape code for entry into a buffer storage.

magnetic tape trailer: the portion of magnetic tape that precedes the end-of-tape mark. (B)

magnetic tape transport: synonym for *magnetic tape drive.* (B)

magnetic tape unit: a device containing a tape drive, magnetic heads, and associated controls. (B)

magnetic track: a track on the surface layer of a magnetic storage. (A) (B)

magnetic wire storage: a magnetic storage in which data are stored by selective magnetization of portions of a wire. (B) Deprecated term for *plated wire storage.*

mag tape: deprecated term for *magnetic tape.*

mail box: an area of memory set aside for electronic mail.

mail merge: synonymous with *file merge.*

main control unit: in a computer with more than one instruction control unit, that instruction control unit to which, for a given interval of time, the other instruction control unit may be designated as the main control unit by hardware or by hardware and software. A main control unit at one time may be a subordinate unit at another time. (A) (B)

main file: synonym for *master file.* (A) (B)

main frame: deprecated term for *processor.* Synonym for *central processing unit.*

main logic board: a circuit board that holds RAM, ROM, the microprocessor, custom integrated circuits, and other components that make the computer work.

main memory (MM): usually the fastest storage device of a computer and the one from which instructions are executed. Cf. *auxiliary storage.* See *RAM.*

main-memory mapping: the main memory on some devices is mapped for protection and relocation in four separate maps: system data, system code, user data, and user code. Memory mapping reallocates the user code or the noncritical operating system code to alternate physical memory pages upon detection of a parity or uncorrectable memory error.

main operation: the major application or designed procedure that equipment performs.

main path: the major course or line of direction taken by a computer in the execution of a routine, directed by the logic of the program and the type of data.

main program:
(1) the highest level COBOL program involved in a step. (Programs written in other languages that follow COBOL linkage conventions are considered COBOL programs in this sense.)
(2) in FORTRAN, a program unit not containing a FUNCTION, SUBROUTINE, or BLOCK DATA statement and containing at least one executable statement. A main program is required for program execution.

main storage (MS):
(1) program-addressable storage from which instructions and other data can be loaded directly into registers for subsequent execution or processing.
(2) a storage device whose storage cells can be addressed by a computer program and from which instructions and data can be loaded directly into registers from which the instructions can be executed or from which the data can be operated upon. (B)
(3) cf. *auxiliary storage.*
(4) see also *processor storage, real storage, virtual storage.*
(5) deprecated term for *internal storage.*

main storage unit: synonym for *buffer storage.*

MAINT: see *maintenance.*

maintain: see *maintainability.*

maintainability: the ease with which maintenance of a functional unit can be performed in accordance with prescribed requirements. (A) (B)

maintenance (MAINT):
(1) any activity, such as tests, measurements, replacements, adjustments, and repairs, intended to eliminate faults or to keep a functional unit in a specified state. (A) (B)
(2) those activities intended to keep a machine in, or restore a machine to, good working order.
(3) see *corrective maintenance, deferred maintenance, emergency maintenance,*

file maintenance, preventive maintenance, schedule maintenance. (A)

maintenance pack: a disk drive for keeping copies of computer programs for the purpose of applying and testing maintenance changes.

maintenance panel: a part of a unit of equipment that is used for interaction between the unit of equipment and a maintenance engineer. (A)

maintenance program chain: an instruction set permitting the deletion of records from a file.

maintenance programmer: a programmer responsible for making alterations, corrections, and adjustments to existing programs.

maintenance programming: the act of changing and modifying existing programs to meet changing conditions.

maintenance time: time used for hardware maintenance. It includes preventive maintenance time and corrective maintenance time. Cf. *available time.* See *corrective maintenance time, deferred maintenance time, emergency maintenance time, preventive maintenance time.* (A)

major cycle:
(1) the maximum access time of a recirculating serial-storage element.
(2) a number of minor cycles.

majority: a logic operator having the property that if P is a statement, Q is a statement, R is a statement, ... , then the majority of P, Q, R, ... , is true if more than half the statements are true, false if half or less are true. (A)

majority carrier: the major carrier in a semiconductor; in an n-type semiconductor, having more electrons than holes, electrons are the majority carrier; in a p-type semiconductor, holes outnumber electrons and are the majority carrier.

majority element: a logic element that performs a majority operation. Synonymous with *majority gate.* (A)

majority gate: synonym for *majority element.* (A)

majority operation: a threshold operation in which each of the operands may take only the values zero and one, and that takes the value one if and only if the number of operands having the value one is greater than half the total number of operands. (A) (B)

major key: the primary key in a record.

major sort: the controlling field which determines the overall order in which a group of items is sorted. Cf. *minor sort.*

major state: the control state of a computer, including fetch, defer, execute.

major state logic generator: logic circuits of the CPU utilized for forming the major state for each computer cycle; determines the machine's state as a function of the current instruction, the current state, and the conditions of the peripheral units.

major structure: in PL/1, a structure whose name is declared with level number 1.

major task: the task that has control at the outset of execution of a program. It exists throughout execution of the program.

major total: the result when a summation is terminated by the most significant change of group.

makeup time: that part of available time used for reruns due to faults or mistakes in operating. (B) Cf. *development time, production time.* (A)

malfunction: synonym for *failure.* (A) Cf. *error, fault, mistake.*

malfunction routine: a routine designed to find a hardware fault or to assist in diagnosing an error within a program.

managed extended memory: memory in addition to the first 640 K used by MS-DOS, that is managed by a program.

management: see *computer-assisted management, data management.*

management graphics: synonymous for *business graphics.*

management information system (MIS):
(1) management performed with the aid of automatic data processing. (B)
(2) an information system designed to aid in the performance of management functions. (A)

management science: the formulation of mathematical and statistical models applied to decision making and the practical application of these models through the use of digital computers.

management statistics: a set of information provided by a system, giving basic data required for short- and long-term planning for the operation and enhancement of a network.

mandatory cryptographic session: a cryptographic session in which all outgoing data is enciphered and all incoming data is deciphered. Cf. *selective cryptographic session.*

manifest constant: in a program, the assignment of a value to a symbolic name at the beginning of the program. This value is not subject to change during execution. Synonymous with *global declaration.*

manifolding: the use of numerous sheets of paper and carbon sheets to produce multiple copies at single printings.

manipulated variable: in a process that is sought to control some condition, a quantity or a condition that is changed by the computer to initiate a shift in the value of the regulated condition.

manipulation: see *formula manipulation, symbol manipulation.* (A)

manipulative indexing: indexing where interrelations of terms are shown by coupling individual words.

man-machine simulation: models of systems where humans participate. The model is no longer completely computer-based and requires active participation of a person.

mantissa (M): the positive fractional part of the representation of a logarithm. In the expression, log $643 = 2.808$, the .808 is the mantissa and the 2. is the characteristic. (B) Synonym for *fixed-point part.* Cf. *characteristic.* (A)

manual changeover: an activity performed by a human operator to remove one set of apparatus or lines from operation and make another set available.

manual control: the direction of a computer by means of manually operated switches.

manual entry: a hand insertion of data for some units of a computer.

manual input: the entry of data by hand into a device. (A)

manual input generator: apparatus that accepts manual input data and retains the contents for sensing by the controller or computer.

manual operation: processing of data in a system by direct manual techniques.

manual read: an operation where the computer does the sensing of the contents or settings of manually set registers or switches.

manual storage: storage in the form of manually set switches, arranged in an array or matrix.

manual word generator: a unit that permits a word to be entered directly into memory following a manual operation.

many-for-one languages: languages that take a single functional statement and translate it into a series of subroutines or instructions in machine language, in contrast to a low-level (assembly) language in which statements translate on a one-for-one basis. Examples include FORTRAN, COBOL.

map: to establish a set of values having a defined correspondence with the quantities or values of another set. Synonymous with *map over.* (B) See *Karnaugh map.* (A)

map over: synonym for *map.* (A) (B)

mapped buffer: a display buffer in which each character position has a corresponding character position on the display surface.

mapping: in a data base, the establishing of the correspondences between a given logical structure and a given physical structure.

mapping mode: a computer operation mode where virtual addresses above 15 are transformed through the memory map so that they become references to actual main memory locations.

MAR: see *memory address register.*

margin: the difference between the actual operating point and the point where a wrong operation will take place.

margin-adjust mode: in word processing, the facility to scan forthcoming text as an aid in justifying margins.

marginal check: maintenance in which certain operation conditions, such as voltage or frequency supplied, are varied about their normal values in order to detect and locate components with incipient defective parts. Synonymous with *bias testing, marginal test.*

marginal error: errors that occasionally occur in tapes, and usually disappear simply because the writing is done over a slightly different section of tapes.

marginal test: synonym for *marginal check.*

margin guide: a paper tape device that measures distances across the tape from the guide edge to the center of the nearest track.

margin-punched card: a card punched only on the border, with holes to represent data, thereby leaving the center free for written or printed information.

margin release key: a key that allows movement outside the margins that were previously set.

mark: a symbol or symbols that indicate the beginning or the end of a field, of a word, of an item of data, or of a set of data such as a file, a record, or a block. (B) See *document mark, group mark.* (A)

mark detection: a type of character recognition system that detects from marks placed in areas on paper or cards, called site areas, boxes, or windows, certain intelligence or information.

marker: in computer graphics, a symbol with a recognizable appearance that is used to identify a particular location. See *end-of-tape mark.* (A)

mark matching: a technique in OCR to correlate or match a specimen character with each of a set of masks representing the characters to be recognized. Mask types are holistic masks, peep-hole masks, and weighted-area masks.

Mark I: the first automatic calculator, built at Harvard University in 1943.

Markov chain: a probabilistic model of events, in which the probability of an event is dependent only on the event that precedes it. (A)

mark reader: a reader for detecting pencil marks on documents.

mark scanning: the automatic optical sensing of marks usually recorded manually on a data carrier. (B)

mark sense: to mark a position on a punched card with an electrically conductive pencil for later conversion to machine punching.

mark-sense reader: a data input unit for reading mark-sense documents.

mark sensing: the automatic sensing of conductive marks usually recorded manually on a nonconductive data carrier. Synonymous with *optical-mark recognition.*

mark-sensing card: a card on which mark-sensible fields have been printed. (A)

mark-sensing column: a line of mark-sensible positions, parallel to the Y-datum line of a card. (A)

mark-sensing row: a line of mark-sensible positions parallel to the X-datum line of a card. (A)

mask (MK):
(1) a pattern of characters that is used to control the retention or elimination of portions of another pattern of characters. (B)
(2) to use a pattern of characters to control the retention or elimination of portions of another pattern of characters. (A) (B)

mask bit: a bit used to extract a selected bit from a string.

masked: synonym for *disabled.*

masked ROM: regular ROM whose contents are produced during manufacture by the usual masking process.

masking: extracting certain bits or sensing certain binary conditions, while at the same time ignoring others by inhibition.

mask matching: in character recognition, a method used in character property detection in which a correlation or match is attempted between a specimen character and each of a set of masks representing the characters to be recognized.

mask programmable read-only memory: a PROM that is programmed during the last stages of manufacture, which provides a desired interconnecting pattern.

mask register (MR): a register used for masking.

massaging: manipulating input data to yield a desired format, for example, in word processing.

mass data: a quantity of data larger than the amount storable in a central processing unit of a given computer at any one time.

massively parallel computer: a computer capable of dividing a problem into hundreds of parts and parceling each of them out to a separate microprocessor. The microprocessors used are exactly the kind used in personal computers. See also *vector processors.*

mass memory (MM): large amounts of data stored in a computer's main memory, usually on magnetic tape or disk. Getting data from mass memory is slower than from main memory, but usually the computer does not need to look at this information very often.

mass storage (MS): storage having a very large storage capacity. Synonymous with *bulk storage.* (B)

mass storage device: a device having a large storage capacity, for example, magnetic disk, magnetic drum. (A)

mass storage dump/verify program: a program that permits the user to dump a specified area of memory to a mass storage device such as a magnetic tape, disk, or cassette.

mass storage file: a collection of records assigned to a mass storage device.

mass storage file segment: a part of a mass storage file whose beginning and end are defined by the file limit clause in the environment division.

mass storage on line: the storage of large amounts of data on a device, rendering any item rapidly (i.e., in milliseconds) accessible to the CPU of the computer. Magnetic drums and disks are common types of on-line mass storage devices.

mass storage volume control: synonymous with *journal.*

mass storage volume inventory: a data set that describes mass storage volumes and mass storage volume groups.

mass store: random-access memory.

master (M) (MSTR): a document suitable to the document copying process being used. In some cases it is the original but in others it may need to be specially prepared. Cf. *slave unit.*

master card: a card that contains fixed or indicative information for a group of punched cards. It is usually the first card of the group.

master control program (MCP): a program that controls the operation of a system, either by connecting subroutines and calling segments into memory as needed, or as a program controlling hardware and limiting the amount of intervention required by an operator.

master control routine:
(1) the part of a program that controls linking of other routines and subroutines, or calls selected program segments into memory.
(2) a routine for controlling hardware operations.

master data: a set of data that is rarely changed and supplies basic data for processing operations. The data content of a master file.

master file (MF): a file that is used as an authority in a given job and that is relatively permanent, even though its contents may change. Synonymous with *main file.* (A) (B)

master file inventory: permanently stored inventory information retained for the future.

master instruction tape (MIT): a tape on which all the programs for a system of runs are recorded.

master library tape: a reel of magnetic tape containing all the programs and key subroutines needed in a data-processing installation.

master mode: the mode of a computer operation where all legal basic operations are permissible.

master processor: a main processor in a master/slave configuration.

master program: the controller of all phases of the job setup; directs program compiling and debugging, assigns memory, assigns input-output activity schedules and interweaves multiple programs for simultaneous processing, controls equipment activities and data flow, provides for error detection and correction, and communicates with operators.

master program file: the tape on which all the programs for a system of runs are entered.

master record: the basic updated record used in the next file-processing run; usually it is a magnetic tape item.

master scheduler: a control program routine that responds to operator commands and initiates the requested actions.

master/slave multiprogramming: a system designed to guarantee that one program cannot damage or access another program sharing the same memory.

master/slave system: a system where the central computer has control over, and is connected to, one or more satellite computers.

master station (MST): a station that can select and transmit a message to a slave station.

master tape: a tape having the program or master data file with most of the routines.

master terminal: any terminal in a network that is master, but only one terminal can be master at any one time. As master the terminal can communicate with all other terminals within the network.

master unit: the result of connecting two intelligent devices.

match: a comparison to determine identity of items. Cf. *hit.* (A)

material implication: synonymous with *conditional implication operation.*

math coprocessor: see *coprocessor.*

mathematical check: a programmed check that uses mathematical relationships. Synonymous with *arithmetic check.* (A)

mathematical control mode: the control action or control mode found in a control system, such as proportional, integral, or derivative.

mathematical induction: a method of providing a statement concerning terms based on natural numbers not less than N by showing that the statement is valid for the term based on N and that, if it is valid for an arbitrary value of n that is greater

than N, it is also valid for the term based on $(n + 1)$. (A) (B)

mathematical logic: synonym for *symbolic logic.* (A) (B)

mathematical model: a mathematical representation of a process, device, or concept. (A)

mathematical programming: in operations research, a procedure for locating the maximum or minimum of a function subject to constraints. (B) Cf. *convex programming, dynamic programming, integer programming, linear programming, nonlinear programming, quadratic programming.* (A)

math(s) processing: in word processing software, an ability permitting mathematical computations to be carried out.

matrix:
(1) a rectangular array of elements, arranged in rows and columns, that may be manipulated according to the rules of matrix algebra. (B)
(2) in computers, a logic network in the form of an array in input leads and output leads with logic elements connected at some of their intersections.
(3) by extension, an array of any number of dimensions.
(4) see *dot matrix.* (A)

matrix printer: a printer in which each character is represented by a pattern of dots; for example, a stylus printer, a wire printer. Synonymous with *dot printer.* (A)

matrix storage: storage, the elements of which are arranged so that access to any one location requires the use of two or more coordinates; for example, *cathode-ray storage, magnetic core storage.* (A)

maximize: to expand the active window to fill the whole screen.

MB: megabyte; 1,048,576 bytes.

MBPS: see *mega.*

MBR: see *member.*

MC: .
(1) see *magnetic card.*
(2) see *megacycle.*

MCA: see *microchannel architecture.*

MCGA: multicolor graphics array—a graphics system.

MCP: see *master control program.*

MCU: see *microprogram control unit.*

MDA: monochrome display adapter—a display adapter for IBM PCs.

MDR: see *memory data register.*

mean accuracy: the difference between the "true" value and the arithmetic mean or average of a statistically significant number of readings under specified environmental conditions. It does not include the effect of repeatability.

mean conditional information content: synonym for *conditional entropy.* (A) (B)

mean entropy: see *character mean entropy.* (A)

mean information content: synonym for *entropy.* (A) (B)

mean repair time (MRT): deprecated term for *mean-time-to-repair.* (A) (B)

mean-time-between-failures (MTBF): for a stated period in the life of a function unit, the mean value of the lengths of time between consecutive failures under stated conditions. (A) (B)

mean-time-to-failure: the average time a component or system functions without faulting.

mean-time-to-repair (MTTR): the average time required for corrective maintenance. (A)

mean transinformation content: in information theory, the mean of the transinformation content conveyed by the occurrence of any one of a finite number of mutually exclusive and jointly exhaustive events, given the occurrence of another set of mutually exclusive events. Synonymous with *average transinformation content.* (A) (B)

measurand: a measured physical variable such as pressure, temperature, flow, or distance.

measure of information: see *information measure.* (A)

mechanical dictionary: the language-translating machine component that provides a word-for-word substitution from one language to another. See also *dictionary.*

mechanical differential: a unit in analog computers that provides a mechanical rotation equal to the difference of two input rotations.

mechanical interface: the physical construction of the linkage between two units. Cf. *electrical interface* and *logical interface.*

mechanical translation: the generic term for language translation by computers or similar devices.

media: the plural form of medium, magnetic cards, disks, and cartridges and paper tapes are examples of the various media types devised to carry data or information.

media eraser: an electromagnetic device able to totally erase stored data from any flexible magnetic media, whether it be tape, diskette, cassette, or data cartridge.

media failure: when data are unreadable because of a defect in the magnetic recording surface.

median: the average of a series of values, or that value for which there are an equal number of items with lesser magnitudes and greater magnitudes.

media-resident software: software which is not an integral part of a computer system but is stored on some medium, usually a magnetic disk.

medium: see *empty medium, machine-readable medium, media, virgin medium.*

medium scale integration (MSI): a technology where 10 to 100 gates are produced on a single silicon chip.

meet: synonymous with *AND operation.*

meg: short for *megabyte.*

mega (M) (MBPS): ten to the sixth power, 1,000,000 in decimal notation. When referring to storage capacity, two to the twentieth power, 1,048,576 in decimal notation.

megabit RAM: a chip that can store more than one million characters of information.

megabyte (MB): 1024×1024 bytes, or 1024K; 8 million bits.

megacycle (MC): see *megahertz.*

megaflop realm: measuring speed in millions of floating-point operations (flops) per second. See also *flop.*

megahertz (MHz): a unit of measure of frequency. 1 megahertz = 1,000,000 hertz.

MEM: see *memory.*

member (MBR):
(1) a registered user on a network who belongs to a group.
(2) a partition of a partitioned data set. Synonym for *element*. (A)

membrane keyboards: keyboards with no mechanical linkages on individual keys. The membrane on which characters and other symbols are printed has a conductive back which completes a circuit when moved a few thousandths of an inch. Synonymous with *touch-sensitive keyboards*.

memo posting: a systems technique in which item records are posted to a temporary file before permanent master files are updated.

memory (M) (MEM):
(1) a hardware component of a computer system that can store information for later retrieval.
(2) the high-speed, large-capacity storage of a digital computer. Deprecated term for *main storage*. (A) (B) See also *auxiliary storage, internal storage, mass storage, matrix storage, processor storage, real storage, virtual storage*.

memory address counter: a register for pointing to the next location in memory for an instruction-fetch operation.

memory addressing: the storage locations as identified by their addresses.

memory address register (MAR): a register for holding the address of a data word to be read from or written into memory. MAR can also be used as an internal register for microprogram control during data transfers to and from the memory and peripherals.

memory address space: the range of addressable storage locations in main memory.

memory allocation: a means by which memory is allocated to processes or units.

memory array: memory cells arranged in a rectangular geometric pattern on a chip, organized into rows and columns as in a matrix.

memory bandwidth: the maximum rate, in bytes per second, at which data is transferred to or from main memory in a specific computer system.

memory bank: a block of memory locations responding to contiguous addresses. See also *bank select*.

memory buffer register: a register for storing words as they come from memory, or prior to entering memory.

memory bundling: See *bundling*.

memory cache:
(1) a memory system utilizing a limited but very rapid semiconductor memory, along with a slow but larger capacity memory.
(2) memory that is set aside to increase the efficiency and operating speed of the computer. Cf. *disk cache*.

memory capacity: the number of elementary pieces of data that can be contained in a storage unit.

memory cell: the unit of storage in main memory capable of storing one bit.

memory character format: memory storing approaches of storing one character in each addressable location.

memory core: pertaining to those storage units composed of ferromagnetic cores, or apertured ferrite plates, through which select lines and sense windings are threaded. See *memory*.

memory cycle: operations needed for addressing, reading, writing, and/or reading and writing data in memory.

memory data register (MDR): a register that holds the final data word read from or written into memory location, addressed by the contents of the memory address register.

memory-dependent: a program that must be stored in particular storage locations in main memory for it to execute correctly. Cf. *relocatable*.

memory device: one of many devices, usually constructed to exploit the recording properties of magnetic materials, that stores information for computer processing. Typical are magnetic core, magnetic disk, magnetic card, magnetic drum, and magnetic tape.

memory diagnostic: a routine for checking all memory locations for proper operation with a set of worst-case pattern tests.

memory disks: synonymous with *E-disks*.

memory dump: a listing of the contents of a storage device, or selected parts of it.

memory expansion card: a printed circuit board having additional memory, which can be plugged into a computer to increase the memory capacity.

memory fill: storage in the areas of memory which are not used by a particular routine, of some pattern of characters which will stop the machine if a routine through error tries to execute instructions from areas which were not intended to contain coding. An aid to debugging.

memory guard: electronic or program guard inhibiting or preventing access to a section of the storage device or area especially concerning the main or internal memory of the CPU.

memory hierarchy: a set of memories with differing sizes and speeds, and having different cost-performance ratios.

memory interleaving: a computer system method permitting overlapped accesses to two or more memory modules, thereby increasing the maximum rate at which data can be transferred between main memory and the CPU.

memory latency time: the time needed for memory control hardware to move the memory medium to a position where it can be read.

memory location (ML): a specified location within a computer storage device.

memory management: addressing extension hardware options available for some computers. The memory management option controls the function of user programs in a multiprogram environment.

memory map: a hardware implementation that provides for dynamically relocating, protecting, and executing programs in scattered fragments of memory.

memory-mapped I/O: an addressing strategy where I/O units are addressed as memory locations.

memory-mapped video: a means of CRT information and graphics display where every character or pixel location on a screen corresponds to a unique memory location which the CPU accesses.

memory mapping: a mode of computer operation where the 8 high-order bits of any virtual address greater than 15 are replaced by an alternative value, thus providing for dynamic relocatability of programs.

memory page: the section of memory, typically 256 words.

memory parity: an approach that generates and checks parity on each memory transfer and provides an interrupt if an error is found.

memory pointer registers: special registers that direct (point) the CPU to the location of a word in memory that holds data.

memory port: the connection between main memory and the CPU through which data is transferred.

memory power: a memory hierarchy within some larger computer systems that makes information in core storage available at differing speeds.

memory printout: synonymous with *core dump.*

memory protection: deprecated term for *storage protection.* (A)

memory resident: one that remains in memory after being run, in order that it can be called up at a later time. It can extend the capabilities of the operating system. Many resident programs are often called TSRs. See *TSRs.*

memory refresh: see *dynamic storage.*

memory scan: an option providing a rapid search of any portion of memory for any word.

memory workspace: the quantity of memory needed by a program over and above the amount of memory required to store the program itself. Workspace is often used for input-output device buffer areas and for various other locations required by a program during its execution.

menu: a display of a list of available machine functions for selection by the operator.

menu bar: the white strip across the top of the screen that contains the names of the available menus.

menu-driven: a program relying heavily on menus, thereby providing greater control over the way the program proceeds.

menu name: a word, phrase, or icon in the menu bar or in a dialog box that gives access to the menu. Pressing the menu name opens the menu.

menu selection: making a choice from a menu.

mercury storage: a storage device that utilizes the acoustic properties of mercury to store data. (A)

merge:
(1) to combine the items of two or more sets that are each in the same given order, into one set in that order. (A) (B)
(2) the automatic recording, printing, or sending onto one element of recording medium of selected recorded text, in correct order, from at least two other elements of recording media.
(3) see *balanced merge.* (A)
(4) see also *collate.* (A)

merged transistor logic: synonymous with *integrated injection logic.*

merge order: the number of files or sequences to be combined during a merge operation.

merge pass: in sorting, the processing of records to reduce the number of sequences by a factor equal to the specified merger order.

merge sort: a sort program in which the items in a set are divided into subsets, the items in each subset are sorted, and the resulting sorted items are merged. See *balanced merge sort, unbalanced merge sort.* (A)

merging: see *order-by-merging, sequence by merging.* (A)

MESG: see *message.*

message (MESG) (MSG):
(1) in information theory, an ordered series of characters intended to convey information. (B)
(2) an arbitrary amount of information whose beginning and end are defined or implied. (A)

message buffering: a method of spooling text messages to disk for output with device independence.

message control program: the top-priority program that controls the sending and receiving of messages to and from remote terminals.

message data set: a data set on disk storage that contains queues of messages awaiting transmission to particular terminal operators or to the host system.

message display console: a console device having a cathode-ray tube that allows messages to be displayed. Data stored in memory can be displayed as a page.

message error record: synonym for *error record.*

message exchange: a device placed between a communication line and a computer to handle specific communications activities and thereby free the computer for other work.

message feedback system: a system where the accuracy of data transmission is checked by automatically feeding received signals back to the transmitting terminal for comparison with the original message. Synonymous with *information feedback system.*

message field (MFLD): an area on the screen of a display device where messages are displayed.

message format: the identification and placement of parts of a message, such as its heading, address, text, end of message, and so on.

message handler: a computer program that processes incoming and/or outgoing data-communications messages.

message queue:
(1) a list of messages that are awaiting processing or waiting to be sent to a terminal.
(2) a queue of messages within a message data set waiting to be transmitted to the host system or to a particular terminal operator.

message retrieval: the capacity to retrieve a message after it has entered an information system.

message sink: that part of a communication system in which messages are considered to be received. (B) See *data sink.*

message source: that part of a communication system from which messages are considered to originate. Synonymous with *information source.* (B) See *data source.*

message switch:
(1) a computer that routes printed messages through terminals and other network nodes in the system.
(2) a network node used to route data transactions to other nodes in the system.

message trailer: the last portion of a data-communications message, usually containing control information, but more often signifying the end of the message.

metacompilation: the process of using compilers to compile other compilers used to compile programs for execution.

metal-oxide semiconductor: see *MOS.*

metal-oxide semiconductor memory: a memory utilizing MOS technology.

metamer: in computer graphics, color which is perceived to be the same as another color even though they have different spectral energy distributions. Metamers may look the same under one lighting condition, and show their difference under another condition.

meter (M): 0.9144 yard.

metered unit: a data-processing device for which the user is charged on the basis of usage, rather than a flat rental fee.

metre: see *meter.*

MF: see *master file.*

MFLD: see *message field.*

MFLOP (EM flop): a million floating-point operations per second. A measure of computing power.

MHz: see *megahertz.*

MI:
(1) see *machine-independent.*
(2) see *microinstruction.*

MICR: see *magnetic ink character recognition.* (A)

micro-:
(1) a prefix denoting one millionth (10^{-6}) as in microsecond, one millionth of a second.
(2) more commonly, a prefix denoting small, as in micro-instruction, microprocessor.

microchannel architecture (MCA): the bus in high-end personal computer models allowing multiprocessing to occur within the computer. It permits two or more microprocessors to perform data processing activities at the same time.

Microcobol: a high-level language developed by Computer Analysts and Programmers for business-oriented microprocessor programming. Related to COBOL.

microcode:
(1) one or more microinstructions.
(2) a code, representing the instructions of an instruction set, implemented in a part of storage that is not program-addressable.
(3) to design, write, and test one or more microinstructions.
(4) see also *microprogram.*

microcoding: coding with the use of microinstructions.

microcommand: a command issued in microcode for specifying elementary machine operations that are to be performed within a basic machine cycle.

microcomputer: a computer system whose processing unit is a microprocessor. A basic microcomputer includes a microprocessor, storage, and an input-output facility, which may or may not be on one chip.

microcomputer architecture: designated in bits; for example, 8 bit, 16 bit, and so on, showing the size of the "chunk" of data that can be handled in one execution and the number of memory cells in which data can be stored. The higher the number of bits defined in the microcomputer architecture, the more rapidly the machine will perform most instructions.

microcomputer components: tiny digital computers developed from a few large-scale integrated circuit chips.

microcomputer development system: specially designed systems to utilize software units such as exercisers and emulators to eliminate manual input-output and the need for the user to be fluent in hexadecimal.

microcomputer execution cycle: microcycles needed for a microcomputer to execute an instruction including: (a) fetch instruction from the memory, (b) store in instruction register, (c) decode instruction, and (d) execute operation defined by instruction.

microcomputer kit: hardware or software that permits a user to configure a microcomputer system to a specific product application.

microcomputer kit assembler: a software package for generating object programs from a source program written in symbolic assembly language.

microcomputer POS: a point-of-sale system where the cash register is a special-purpose computer terminal for monitoring and recording transactions directly in the store's data files, performing credit checks, and handling other marketing activities.

microcomputer prototyping system: a kit of hardware and software permitting a user to form a prototype system to his or her own specifications.

microcomputer support units: apparatus for complementing such peripherals as paper-tape readers and punch machines, card readers, printers, and so on.

microcomputer timing modules: circuits used to clock the microcomputer.

microcomputer word processing: microcomputer applications in the office, that is, controlling one or more typewriters that edit text stored on cassettes or floppy disks.

microcontroller:
(1) a microprogrammed machine, a microprocessor, or a microcomputer used in a control operation to alter a process or operation.
(2) any instrument or machine that controls a process with high resolution, usually over a narrow region.

microcycle: a step needed to execute an instruction; used for fetching the instruction. One or two more can be used for data access, and several more for execution.

microdiagnostic: a test routine for exercising a microprocessor and identifying faults.

microfiche: a sheet of microfilm capable of containing microimages in a grid pattern, usually containing a title that can be read without magnification. (A) See also *ultrafiche.*

microfilm:
(1) a high resolution film for recording microimages. (A)

(2) microform whose medium is film, in the form of rolls, that contains microimages arranged sequentially.
(3) to record microimages on film. (A)
(4) see *computer output microfilm.* (A)

microfilmer: see *computer output microfilmer.* (A)

microfloppies: the newest generation of floppy disks. Instead of the typical disk of 5¼ inches in diameter, the new disk used to drive ever-smaller computers, is 3½ inches in diameter.

microflowchart: a flowchart showing detailed program steps, from which coding can be carried out.

microform reader-copier: a device that performs the functions of a reader and a printer to produce hard copy enlargements of selected microimages. Synonymous with *microform reader-printer.*

microform reader-printer: synonym for *microform reader-copier.*

microfunction decoder: medium scale integration arithmetic logic functions that perform lookahead operations for carrying and shifting functions.

micrographics: that branch of science and technology concerned with methods and techniques for converting any form of information to or from microform.

microimage: an image too small to be read with magnification. (A)

microinstruction (MI):
(1) an instruction of a microprogram. (B)
(2) a basic or elementary machine instruction.

microkit: a microcomputer system kit having a CPU, keyboard, CRT display, and cassette tape units.

micromainframe: a microcomputer containing the computing power of a mainframe.

microprocessing unit (MPU): the main constituent of the hardware of a microcomputer, consisting of the microprocessor, the main memory, the input-output interface units, and the clock circuit, in addition to a buffer, driver circuits, and passive circuit elements.

microprocessor (MP): an integrated circuit that accepts coded instructions for execution; the instructions may be entered, integrated, or stored internally. Synonymous with *central processing unit (CPU)*. See also *microcomputer*.

microprocessor analyzer: a digital diagnostic device for testing and debugging of MPU hardware and software.

microprocessor architecture: architectural features including general-purpose registers, stacks, interrupts, interface structure, choice of memories, and so on.

microprocessor assembler simulator: a program that accepts microprocessor assembly language, edits the text, and then permits a user to debug the software on a simulation of the microprocessor; provides 60 to 80 percent assurance that the final storage product will function.

microprocessor cache memory: a storage area used in addition to the main memory.

microprocessor card: a circuit board containing a microprocessor or microprocessing elements.

microprocessor chip: an integrated circuit that holds all necessary elements of a central processor, including the control logic, instruction decoding, and arithmetic-processing circuitry.

microprocessor code assembler: assembler programs for microcodes.

microprocessor compiler: a program that translates the source program into machine language. These compilers, which are usually run on medium- or large-scale computers, are available from several time-sharing services.

microprocessor components: hardware parts of a specific microprocessor configuration, such as ALU, control logic, and register array.

microprocessor controller: a dedicated controller built around a microprocessor. Synonymous with *microcontroller*.

microprocessor debugging program: a program found in microprocessor memory that is used during system development to aid in debugging operations.

microprocessor educator system: a microprocessor-based communications terminal for program development.

microprocessor instruction set: instructions that are a part of the basic software for a given microprocessor.

microprocessor intelligence: the control program for guiding the microprocessor through its various operations.

microprocessor language assembler: a software package for assembling source code on a minicomputer and converting it into binary output for loading into the microprocessor.

microprocessor language editor: a software set, in the form of a binary tape which is loaded into memory utilizing a special program. In memory, the program text can then be altered, deleted, and reformatted.

microprocessor maintenance console: a console for displaying and simulating the contents of any memory location and register.

microprocessor memory interface: memory interface circuits that can generate more address lines and the signals needed to interface with up to 65K or more bytes, of RAM, PROM, or ROM memory.

microprocessor modem: a modulator-demodulator unit under dedicated microprocessor control.

microprocessor ROM programmer: a program to load, verify, and modify programs in a PROM unit.

microprocessor slice: the building-block approach of a 2- or 4-bit microprocessor that builds 8-, 16-, 24-, or 32-bit systems.

microprocessor system analyzer: an instrument for designing, troubleshooting, and testing programs and hardware in microprocessor systems.

microprogram:

(1) a sequence of elementary instructions that corresponds to a specific computer operation, that is maintained in special storage, and whose execution is initiated by the introduction of a computer instruction into an instruction register of a computer. (A) (B)

(2) a group of microinstructions that when executed performs a preplanned function.

microprogram assembly language: computer-dependent machine language using mnemonics for the basic instruction set. In a microprogrammed computer, each assembly language instruction is implemented by a microprogram.

microprogram control logic: devices required to implement machine instructions. A hard-wired computer employs much more control logic than a microprogrammed computer.

microprogram control store: memory, used by the control processor, in which microprograms are stored.

microprogram control unit (MCU): in bipolar microprocessors, a functional unit for maintaining and generating microprogram addresses.

microprogram display: a board for displaying and debugging operations.

microprogram fields: parts of a microinstruction that specify one microoperation. Each of several fields can be independent of any other.

microprogram indexing: a method to locate data within a memory and count the number of times an operation is performed in a microprogram.

microprogram instruction set: repertoire of machine-dependent instruction available to the assembly-language programmer.

microprogrammable instruction: an instruction that does not reference main memory and can have several shift, skip, or transfer commands to be performed.

microprogrammable processor: a processor where the instruction set is not firmly fixed.

microprogrammed microprocessor: in a microprogrammed processor, operations on the fundamental register-transfer level that can be programmed.

microprogrammed processor: a processor whose instruction is not fixed, and can be altered to specific requirements by the programming of ROMs or other memory units.

microprogrammed sequencer: a unit for generating, incrementing, and storing addresses.

microprogram microassembler: a program that translates microprograms in symbolic form into bit patterns that are then loaded into the control store.

microprogram microcode: another name for the microinstructions that make up a microprogram, either in source language or in object-code form.

microprogramming: the preparation or use of microprograms. (A) (B)

microprogramming parameterization: a method of microprogramming using stored parameters to characterize the state of the program. These parameters are stored as program status words which are later tested to determine what actions should occur.

microsecond: one-millionth of a second.

MIDAS: a digital stimulated analog computing program.

middle punch: synonymous with *eleven punch* and *X punch.*

middleware: system software tailored to a particular user's need.

MIDI: musical instrument digital interface; the industry standard for representing sounds digitally.

midicomputers: a computer of intermediate size and computing power, between a minicomputer and mainframe.

migration: see *data migration.*

migration path: a scheme to enhance a computer system's power or hardware while maintaining software compatibility, or vice versa.

milestone: a task or event that cannot be considered completed until all tasks that feed into it are completed.

mill: slang, the *central processing unit.*

milli (M): one thousand or one thousandth.

million floating-point operations: see *mflops.*

mill time: total time spent by the computer in processing one specific job.

millisecond (MS) (MSEC): one-thousandth of a second.

mindmare: programs that promise to help business executives manage their businesses and make decisions. Synonymous with *idea processors.*

MINI: see *minicomputer.*

miniassembler program: a program designed to simplify machine-level programming on various microprocessor systems, by permitting the operator to type mnemonic program symbols on the terminal directly in assembler language, while the program generates the correct object code, placing it in the proper memory location, and printing it out simultaneously on the terminal.

miniaturization: the reduction in size of components and circuits for increasing package density and reducing power dissipation and signal propagation delays.

minicartridge: a magnetic tape holder that is smaller than a cassette, usually 54 percent smaller.

minicomputer (MINI): a computer that does not need the closely controlled environment of main frame computers, and has a richer instruction set than that of a microprocessor.

minicomputer communication processor:
(1) a processor unit containing a minicomputer connected between a central computing facility and a communications network to carry out communications control functions for a full-scale mainframe central computer.
(2) a communication processing unit that interfaces with a minicomputer system.

minicomputer terminal:
(1) a terminal containing a minicomputer for computation, processing, and interface control.
(2) a user-interactive input-output unit for interfacing with a minicomputer system.

minidiskette: a storage medium similar to, but smaller than, the standard flexible disk.

mini-floppy disk: a small floppy disk capable of storing somewhat fewer than 100,000 characters; used primarily in microcomputer systems.

minimal latency coding: programming where the access time for a word depends on its location. Synonymous with *minimum delay coding.*

minimal tree: a tree whose terminal nodes have been so ordered that the tree operates at maximum effectiveness.

minimize: to shrink the active window to an icon on the workspace.

minimum access coding: in machines having non-immediate-access main memory, a technique of coding which minimizes the time wasted by delays in transfer of data and instructions between memory and other machine components. Synonymous with *minimum latency coding.*

minimum access programming: programming directed to minimizing the waiting time needed to obtain information from storage.

minimum access routing: a routine coded so that the actual access time is less than the expected random-access time.

minimum configuration:
(1) hardware systems with no extra-cost options.
(2) the minimum numbers and kinds of hardware and software elements needed to perform a specific processing activity.

minimum delay coding: synonymous with *minimal latency coding.*

minimum delay programming: a method of programming in which storage locations for instructions and data are chosen so that access time is reduced and minimized. (A) (B)

minimum distance code: a binary code in which the signal distance does not fall below a specified minimum value. (A)

minimum latency coding: synonymous with *minimum access coding.*

minimum-latency programming: synonymous with *forced coding.*

miniperipheral: a peripheral device for use with a minicomputer, such as a printer, floppy disk drive, and so on.

minisupercomputer: a computer using multiprocessors providing inexpensive high performance machines.

minor control field: any control field that is of less significance than the major control field in a sorting operation.

minor cycle: the time interval between the appearance of corresponding units of successive words in a storage device that gives serial access to storage positions.

minority carrier: the nondominant carrier in a semiconductor. See *majority carrier.*

minor sort: the field determining the order in which a group of items within a larger group are to be sorted. Cf. *major sort.*

minor structure: in PL/1, a structure that is contained within another structure. The name of a minor structure is declared with a level number greater than one.

minuend: in subtraction, the number of quantity from which another number of quantity is subtracted. (A) (B)

minus zone: the character or digit position that displays the algebraic sign of an operand.

MIPS: million instructions per second; a measure of computer speed.

MIS: see *management information system.* (A)

miscellaneous time: the time during which a computer is used for demonstrations, training, or other such purposes. Synonymous with *incidental time.* (A) (B)

misfeed: when cards, tapes, or other data or storage media fail to pass into or through equipment properly.

misregistration: a character recognition term; the improper state of appearance of a character, line, or document, on site in a character reader, with respect to a real or imaginary horizontal base line.

missing error: subroutines called by the program not found in the library. The names of the missing subroutines are also output.

mistake: a human action that produces an unintended result. Cf. *error, failure, fault, malfunction.* (A)

MIT: see *master instruction tape.*

mix:

(1) a group of varying amounts of differing types of instructions, used to test the processing speed of a computer.

(2) in a multiprogramming environment, the different types of jobs that are executed simultaneously.

mixed-base notation: synonym for *mixed-base numeration system.* (A) (B)

mixed-base numeration system: a numeration system in which a number is represented as the sun of a series of terms, each of which consists of a mantissa and a base, the base of a given term being constant for a given application but the bases being such that there are not necessarily integral ratios between the bases of all the terms; for example, with bases b_3, b_2, b_1 and mantissas 6, 5, and 4, the number represented is given by $6b_3 + 5b_2, + 4b_1$. A mixed-radix numeration system is the particular case of a mixed-base numeration system in which, when the terms are ordered so that their bases are in descending magnitudes, there is an integral ratio between the bases of adjacent terms, but not the same ratio in each case. Synonymous with *mixed-base notation.* (B) Cf. *mixed-radix numeration system.* (A)

mixed-mode expression: synonym for *mixed-type expression.*

mixed number: a number with an integer and fractional part; for example, 9.50.

mixed-radix notation: synonym for *mixed-radix numeration system.* (A) (B)

mixed-radix numeration system: a radix numeration system in which the digit places do not all necessarily have the same radix; for example, the numeration system in which three successive digits represent hours, tens of minutes, and minutes; taking one minute as the unit, the weights of the three digit places are 60, 10, and 1 respectively; the radices of the second and third digit places are 6 and 10 respectively. Synonymous with *mixed-radix notation.* (B) Cf. *mixed-base numeration system.* (A)

mixed-type expression: an arithmetic expression that contains both integer and real arithmetic primaries.

MK: see *mask.*

ML:

(1) see *machine language.*

(2) see *memory location.*

MM:

(1) see *main memory.*

(2) see *mass memory.*

MN: see *mnemonic symbol.*

mnemonic: a combination of keystrokes that quickly chooses a command from a menu without using the mouse.

mnemonic name: a programmer-supplied word associated with a specific function name in the environment division of a COBOL program. It may be written in place of the function name in any format where such a substitution is valid.

mnemonic operation code: an operation code consisting of mnemonic symbols that indicate the nature of the operation to be performed, the type of data used, or the format of the instruction performing the operation.

mnemonic symbol (MN): a symbol chosen to assist the human memory, for example, an abbreviation such as "mpy" for "multiply." (A) (B)

MNP: Microcom Networking Protocol; a communications protocol used by high-speed modems.

MOD:
(1) see *model*.
(2) see *modification*.

mod/demod: modulator-demodulator unit. See also *data set, modem*.

mode (M):
(1) a method of operation; for example, the binary mode, the interpretive mode, the alphanumeric mode.
(2) the most frequent value in the statistical sense.
(3) in PL/1, a characteristic of arithmetic data, real or complex.
(4) see *access mode*.

model (MOD):
(1) a representation in mathematical terms of a process, device, or concept.
(2) a general, often pictorial, representation of a system under study. See *mathematical model*.

model statement: a statement in the body of a macrodefinition or in open code from which an assembler-language statement can be generated at preassembly time. Values can be substituted at one or more points in a model statement; one or more identical or different statements can be generated from the same model statement

under the control of a conditional assembly loop.

modem (M): (modulator-demodulator) a device that modulates and demodulates signals transmitted over data-communication facilities, enabling computers to send data by telephone. (A) See also *line adapter*.

modem chip: a large-scale integration chip used to build a stand-alone modem unit.

modem port: a socket on the computer's back panel marked by a telephone icon, used to connect a modem to the computer.

modes of priority: organization of the flow of work through a computer. The mode depends upon the sophistication of the system and the machine, and will vary from a normal noninterrupt mode to a system in which there are several depths of interrupt. There may also be different modes in different functions such as the input-output mode.

modification (MOD): the process of altering the address portion of an instruction resulting from executing earlier instructions in a program. See *modifier*.

modification level: a distribution of all temporary fixes that were issued since the previous modification level. A new modification level normally does not include new function and does not change the programming support category of the release to which it applies. See also *release, version*.

modification loop: instructions forming a closed path to alter or change instruction addresses or data.

modifier: a word or quantity used to change an instruction causing the execution of an instruction different from the original one. The result is, the same instruction, successively changed by a modifier, can be used repetitively to carry out a different operation each time it is used. See *modify*.

modify: to alter a part of an instruction or routine.

modify instruction: an instruction that will most likely be modified before it is used for the final program.

modular: a degree of standardization of computer system components to allow for combinations and large variety of compatible units.

modular approach: dividing a project into segments and smaller units in order to simplify analysis, design, and programming efforts.

modular compilation: compiling individual portions of a program separately.

modular conversion: synonymous with *pilot conversion.*

modular converter: a data conversion unit interconnected to form data acquisition systems and subsystems.

modular design: a means of designing software or hardware in which a project is divided into smaller units, or modules, each of which may be developed, tested, and completed independently before being combined with the others in the final product. Each unit may be designed to perform a specific function.

modularity: the extent to which a system is composed of modules. (A)

modularization: the design of computers to permit expansion of their capabilities by increasing the central processor's hardware and the number of peripheral devices, as required.

modular program flowchart: synonymous with *macroflowchart.*

modular programming: breaking the writing of a large computer program into several smaller, related units for enhancing the maintainability of programs by making it easier to locate the single point of change.

modulator-demodulator: see *modem.* (A)

module:

(1) a program unit that is discrete and identifiable with respect to compiling, combining with other units, and loading; for example, the input to, or output from, an assembler, compiler, linkage editor, or executive routine.

(2) a packaged functional hardware unit designed for use with other components. (A)

(3) see *disk storage module, load module, object module, programming module, source module.*

(4) synonym for *spindle.*

module boards: interchangeable circuit boards containing a complete or partial functional circuit for building up a system.

module testing: the destructive readoff or use caused by overloading or underloading the computer components, causing failure of substandard units and minimizing nonscheduled downtime.

Moiré pattern: in computer graphics, wavy line distortion of an image which can be caused by sampling error.

MON: see *monitor.*

monadic boolean operator: a boolean operator having only one operand, for example, NOT. (A)

monadic operation: an operation with one and only one operand. Synonymous with *unary operation.* (A) (B)

monadic operator: an operator that represents an operation on one and only one operand. Synonymous with *unary operator.* (A) (B)

monitor (M) (MON) (MTR):

(1) a device that observes and verifies the operations of a data-processing system and indicates any significant departure from the norm. (B)

(2) software or hardware that observes, supervises, controls, or verifies the operations of a system. (A)

(3) see *video monitor.*

monitor console: the system-control terminal.

monitoring program: synonym for *monitor program.* (A) (B)

monitor printer: a device that prints all messages transmitted over the circuit to which it is connected.

monitor program: a computer program that observes, regulates, controls, or verifies the operations of a data-processing system. Synonymous with *monitoring program.* (A) (B)

monitor system: hardware and software utilized in controlling computer system functions that simulates the processor, maintains continuity between jobs, observes and reports on the status of input-output devices, and provides automatic accounting of jobs.

monitor unit: equipment that is supervisory and which is capable of verifying the operation of another unit or group in data-processing system, message routing systems, and so forth.

monochrome display: a visual display unit, based on the principles of the cathode-ray tube, that is capable of displaying information in one basic color such as black and white.

monochrome receiver: see *monochrome display.*

monolithic integrated circuit: a type of integrated circuit wherein the substrate is an active material, such as the semiconductor silicon.

monospaced font: any font in which each character has the same width.

monostable: pertaining to a device that has one stable state. (A)

monostable circuit: a trigger circuit that has one stable state and one unstable state. Synonymous with *monostable trigger circuit.* (A)

monostable multivibrator: synonymous with *Kipp relay.*

monostable trigger circuit: synonym for *monostable circuit.* (A)

Monte Carlo method: a method of obtaining an approximate solution to a numerical problem by the use of random numbers; for example, the random walk method or a procedure using a random number sequence to calculate an integral. (A) (B)

morpheme: a linguistic unit that indicates relationships between words or ideas; a conjunction such as and, with, not.

MOS: metal-oxide semiconductor; a technology that helped make possible new types of complex chips, such as the microprocessor used in personal computers and high-capacity memory. See C MOS.

most-significant bit (MSB): a bit in the left-most position.

most significant character: that character which is in the leftmost position in a number or word.

most significant digit: the digit of a number that contributes the largest quantity to the value of that particular number; for example, in the number 567, the most significant digit is 5. Cf. *least significant digit.*

motherboard: a main circuit board to which additional circuit boards are affixed forming the basis of a microcomputer. The main board contains the CPU, memory, ports, and peripheral device controllers. Synonymous with *back plane* and *chassis.*

motion register: a two-bit register containing a go/stop flip-flop and a forward/reverse flip-flop that controls the motion of the selected tape drive. The register is set under program control.

mountable: disk packs which are interchangeable on any drive.

mount attribute: the attribute assigned to a volume that controls when the volume can be demounted; the mount attributes are permanently resident, reserved, and removable.

mouse: a cigarette-pack size plastic box with at least one button on top and a cable connected to a computer. When moved on the surface of a desk, an arrow shifts on a monitor screen permitting the user to juggle words or statistics around. The "mouse" tells the computer what to do and eliminates clumsy computer commands that have to be typed with a keyboard into some personal machines.

mouse button: see *mouse.*

m-out-of-n code: a form of fixed-weight binary code where m-of-the-n digits are always in the same state.

MOV: see *move.*

movable-head disk: a disk drive where a single read-write head is used to access the tracks on the surface of a disk; the head moves to the specified track, which is then read or written sequentially. Cf. *fixed-head disk.*

move (MOV): in computer programming, to copy from locations in internal storage into locations in the same internal storage. Synonym for *transfer.* (A) (B)

moving-head disk system: a disk instrument which has a read/write head able to move across the surface of the disk to access any one of a number of circular tracks of data.

MP:
(1) see *microprocessor.*
(2) see *multiprocessing.*
(3) see *multiprocessor.*

MPLX: see *multiplexer.*

MPLXR: see *multiplexer.*

MPS:
(1) see *multiprocessing system.*
(2) see *multiprogramming system.*

MPU: see *microprocessing unit.*

MPX: see *multiplexer.*

MPY: see *multiplier.*

MR: see *mask register.*

MRT: see *mean repair time.*

MS:
(1) see *main storage.*
(2) see *mass storage.*
(3) see *millisecond.*

MSB: see *most-significant bit.*

MSBY: most significant byte.

MSD: most significant digit.

MS-DOS: Microsoft Disk Operating System, a commonly used computer operating system. See also DOS.

MSEC: millisecond (1/1000 second).

MSG: see *message.*

MSHP: maintain system history program.

MSI: see *medium scale integration.*

MSS: mass storage system. See *mass storage.*

MSSG: abbreviation for *message.*

MST: see *master station.*

MSX: a standard developed by Microsoft Corporation that allows Japanese computer makers and others to share certain specifications (e.g., computers could use the same program cartridges). Such standardization lowers manufacturing costs and increases the amount of software, or programs, that other companies produce for the machines.

MT: see *magnetic tape.*

MTBF: see *mean-time-between-failures.*

MTL: synonymous with *integrated injection logic.*

MTR: see *monitor.*

MTTF: see *mean-time-to-failure.*

MTTR: see *mean-time-to-repair.*

MUL: see *multiplexer.*

MULT: see *multiplier.*

multiaccess computing: see *MAC.*

multiaccess system: a system permitting a number of people to access a central processor in conventional mode virtually simultaneously.

multiaddress: pertaining to an instruction format containing more than one address part. (A)

multiaddress instruction: an instruction that contains more than one address part. Synonymous with *multiple-address instruction.* (A) (B)

multiaperture core: a magnetic core, usually used for nondestructive reading with two or more holes through which wires may be passed in order to create more than one magnetic path. Synonymous with *multiple-aperture core.* (A) (B)

multiaspect: pertaining to searches or systems that allow more than one aspect or facet of information to be used in combination, one with the other, to effect identifying and selecting operations.

multichip: a circuit consisting of two or more semiconductor wafers, each containing a single element.

multichip IC: an integrated circuit using two or more semiconductor chips in a single package.

multicomputer system: a computer system where two or more computers are operated by the same computer center, forming independent tasks.

multidimensional array: an array of data having more than the usual two dimensions of rows and columns.

multidimensional language: a language whose expressions are assembled in more than one dimension; for example, flowcharts, logic diagrams, block diagrams, and decision tables. Cf. *one-dimensional language.* (A)

multidrop line: synonym for *multipoint link.*

multifile volume: a tape reel on which a number of different files are stored.

multiframe: a group of frames considered as an entity in a system, where the position of each frame is detected by reference to a multiframe alignment signal.

multifrequency board: a computer add-in board that offers more than one function such as added memory, serial/parallel ports, and a clock/calendar.

multifunction system: a computing system capable of performing a host of tasks, for example, a word processor with communication and mathematical potential.

multijob operation: concurrent execution of job steps from two or more jobs.

multilevel address: synonym for *indirect address*. (A) (B)

multipass sort: a sort program that is designed to sort more items than can be in main storage at one time. (A)

multimedia: describes applications which consist of audio and video computer functions.

multiple-address instruction: synonym for *multiaddress instruction*. (A) (B)

multiple-address message: a message to be delivered to more than one destination.

multiple-aperture core: synonym for *multiaperture core*. (A) (B)

multiple declaration: in PL/1, two or more declarations of the same identifier internal to the same block without different qualifications, or two or more external declarations of the same identifier with different attributes in the same program.

multiple device: two or more semiconductor chips in a single package, connected together to function as one unit.

multiple-job processing: controlling the performance of more than one data-processing job at a time.

multiple-length number: an operand that exceeds the capacity of one word.

multiple-length working: a method of fulfilling operations on data so that two or more words are used to represent data items, usually to achieve greater precision.

multiple modulation: a modulation method using a succession of modulation processes where the wave from one stage becomes the modulating wave for the following stage.

multiple operations: the characteristic of being able to perform two or more computer processes concurrently.

multiple precision: pertaining to the use of two or more computer words to represent a number in order to enhance precision. (A) (B)

multiple programming: programming of a computer by permitting two or more arithmetical or logical operations to be executed simultaneously.

multiple system: a computer system containing two or more central processing units with input-output units and other hardware units that are related and interconnected for simultaneous operation.

multiple-task management: managing the performance of more than one data-processing task at a time.

multiple utility: a utility that permits one to three utility operators to be performed simultaneously.

multiplex: to interleave or simultaneously transmit two or more messages on a single channel. (A)

multiplex aggregate bit rate: in a time division multiplexing system, the sum of the bit rates of the separate input channels plus the overhead bits needed by the multiplexing process.

multiplexed operation: a simultaneous operation sharing the use of a common unit of a system so that it can be considered an independent operation.

multiplexer (M) (MPLX) (MPLXR) (MPX) (MUL) (MUX): a device capable of interleaving the events of two or more activities or capable of distributing the events of an interleaved sequence to the respective activities. (A)

multiplexer polling: a technique of polling or voting that permits each remote multiplexer to query the terminals connected to it.

multiplexer simulation: a testing program which simulates the activities of the multiplexer.

multiplex mode: a means of transferring records to or from low-speed I/O devices on the multiplexer channel by interleaving bytes of data. The multiplexer channel sustains simultaneous I/O operations on several subchannels. Bytes of data are interleaved and then routed to or from the selected I/O devices, or to and from the desired locations in main storage. Synonymous with *byte mode.*

multiplex operation: a mode of operation in which the events of two or more activities are interleaved and when required the events in the interleaved sequence are distributed to the respective activities. (A)

multiplexor: see *multiplexer.*

multiplicand: in a multiplication operation, the factor that is multiplied by another number or quantity. (A) (B)

multiplication shift: a shift resulting in multiplication of a number by a positive or negative integral power of the radix.

multiplication time: the time needed for performing a multiply operation.

multiplier (MPY) (MULT): in multiplication, the number or quantity by which the multiplicand is multiplied. Synonym for *multiplier factor.* (B) See *quarter-squares multiplier.* (A)

multiplier factor: in a multiplication operation, the factor by which the multiplicand is multiplied. Synonymous with *multiplier.* (A) (B)

multiplier-quotient register: a register where the multiplier for multiplication is placed, and where the quotient for division is developed.

multiply: see *logical multiply.* (A)

multiply-divide instruction: an instruction allowing multiply and divide operations.

multiply-divide package: subroutines that perform single- and double-precision multiplication and division for signed and unsigned binary numbers.

multiplying punch: synonym for *calculating punch.* (A)

multipoint link: a link or circuit interconnecting several stations. Synonymous with *multidrop line.*

multiport register: a register able to read two locations and write one location at the same time.

multiprecision arithmetic: utilizing more than one word to define the numbers in a

computation where the larger word size allows greater accuracy.

multipriority: a queue of items waiting processing. The queue is composed of items of different priorities and in effect is a queue of queues.

multiprocessing (MP):
(1) a mode of operation that provides for parallel processing by two or more processors of a multiprocessor.
(2) pertaining to the simultaneous execution of two or more computer programs or sequences of instructions by a computer or computer network. (A)
(3) loosely, parallel processing. (A)
(4) simultaneous execution of two or more sequences of instructions by a multiprocessor.

multiprocessing system (MPS): a computing system employing two or more interconnected processing units to execute programs simultaneously.

multiprocessor (MP):
(1) a computer employing two or more processing units under integrated control. (A)
(2) a system consisting of two or more processing units, ALUs, or processors that can communicate without manual intervention.

multiprocessor interleaving: the allocation of memory areas to the different processors of a multiprocessing system to avoid interaction between programs being run at the same time.

multiprogramming:
(1) pertaining to the concurrent execution of two or more computer programs by a computer. (A) Synonymous with *concurrent execution.*
(2) a mode of operation that provides for the interleaved execution of two or more computer programs by a single processor.

multiprogramming executive: a software block providing the operating system for concurrent execution of more than one program including a priority scheduler along with memory allocation and deallocation.

multiprogramming system (MPS): a system that can process two or more programs concurrently by interleaving their execution. Cf. *uniprogramming system.*

multipurpose OCR: an optical character reader than can do more than just read a printed or typed text and translates it into codes that a word processor or computer will recognize. Features include some editing, reformatting, and correcting.

multireel sorting: the automatic sequencing of a file having more than one input tape, without operator intervention.

multirunning: synonymous with *multiprogramming.*

multitasking:

(1) pertaining to the concurrent execution of two or more tasks by a computer. (A)

(2) multiprogramming that provides for the concurrent performance, or interleaved execution, of two or more tasks.

multitasking/multiprogramming: special methods and systems designed to achieve concurrency by separating programs into two or more interrelated tasks that share the same code, buffers, files, and equipment.

multitask operation: multiprogramming called multitask operation to express not only concurrent execution of two or more programs, but also the concurrent execution of a single reenterable program used by many tasks.

multiterminal: a computer or word-processing system with more than one terminal using the same processor.

multithreading: pertaining to the concurrent operation of more than one path of execution within a computer.

multiuser: the ability of a computer to support several interactive terminals at the same time.

multiuser system: a system where computers, terminals, and other peripheral devices are shared in any one of several arrangements.

multiviewports: display capable of simultaneously generating two or more viewing screens that are adjacent and still independent. See *split screen.*

multivolume file: a file too large to be contained on one reel of tape or single disk, so that it spans between two or more such storage media.

mutual exclusion: in a multiprocessor, a means to lock out a processor from a shared resource, such as main memory. This operation is often accomplished using a semaphore.

mutual information: synonym for *transinformation content.* (A) (B)

MUX: see *multiplexer.*

MVT: multiprogramming with a variable number of tasks.

N:

(1) see *nano.*

(2) see *node.*

(3) see *number.*

(4) see *numeric.*

n: in sorting, file size; the number of records to be processed by the sort.

n-address instruction: an instruction that contains n address parts. (A) (B)

n-adic boolean operation: a boolean operation on n and only n operands. (A) (B)

n-adic operation: an operation on n and only n operands. Synonymous with *n-ary operation.* (A) (B)

naive user: someone who wants to use the computer to do something, but does not know much about computers or programming and does not particularly care to.

NAK: see *negative acknowledge character.* (A)

NAM: see *network access machine.*

name:

(1) an alphameric term that identifies a data set, a statement, a program, or a cataloged procedure. The first character of the name must be alphabetic.

(2) in COBOL, a word composed of not more than 30 characters, which defines a COBOL operand.

(3) in FORTRAN, a string of from one through six alphameric characters, the

first of which identify a variable, an array, a function, a subroutine, a common block, or a name list.

(4) see *data name, qualified name.* (A)

(5) see also *entry name, external name, label, name entry.*

named common: a labeled common block.

name entry: n in assembler programming, the entry in the name field of an assembler-language statement.

name precedence: the priority of a local identifier over a more global identifier, where the identifiers have the same name. See *scope.*

names: in COBOL, a record within a file given the level number 01. Data names for elements within a record have lower-level numbers, 02, 03, and so forth.

naming convention: a standard for assigning symbolic names to programs and files by specifying how names are to be structured.

NAND: a logic operation having the property that if P is a statement, Q is a statement, R is a statement, . . . , then the NAND of P, Q, R, . . . T is true if at least one statement is false, false if all statements are true. Synonymous with *NOT-AND, Sheffer stroke.* (A)

NAND element: a logic element that performs the boolean operation of nonconjunction. Synonymous with *NAND gate.* (A)

NAND gate: synonym for *NAND element.* (A)

NAND operation: synonym for *non-conjunction.* (A) (B)

nano-(N): prefix denoting one thousand millionth (10^{-9}), for example, nanosecond, one thousand millionth of a second.

nanoprocessor: a processor operating in the nanosecond cycle range. See *nano-.*

nanosecond (NS) (NSEC): one-thousand-millionth of a second. One billionth of a second.

narrative: the explanatory text added to program instructions. Synonym for *comment.*

n-ary:

(1) pertaining to a selection, choice or condition that has n possible different values or states. (B)

(2) pertaining to a fixed-radix numeration system having a radix of n. (A) (B)

n-ary boolean operation: deprecated term for *n-adic boolean operation.* (A) (B)

n-ary operation: synonym for *n-adic operation.* (A) (B)

NASORD: a programming reference to a file not in sequential order.

NAT: see *information content natural unit.* (A) (B)

native attachment: deprecated term for *integrated attachment.*

native code: machine dependent language, such as an assembly language.

native compiler: a compiler producing code for a processor on which it runs.

native mode: when a unit's activities do not emulate another unit, thereby becoming independent.

natural-function generator: a device that accepts one or more input variables and provides an output variable based on a mathematical function.

natural language: a language whose rules are based on current usage without being specifically prescribed. (B)

natural language system: an information retrieval system where index terms are words actually found within the document. Indexing by natural language is usually less expensive than by ascribing index terms from an authority file or thesaurus.

natural number: one of the numbers 0,1,2 . . . Synonymous with *nonnegative number.* (A) (B)

n-bit byte: a byte composed of binary elements. (A) (B)

NBR: see *number.*

NBS: see *numeric backspace character.*

NC: see *numerical control.* (B)

n-core-per-bit storage: a storage device in which each storage cell uses magnetic cores per binary character. (A) (B)

NDF: no defect found.

NDR: see *nondestructive read.* (A) (B)

NDRO: see *nondestructive readout.* (A) (B)

NE: not equal to. See *relational operator.*

NEAT system (National's Electronic Autocoding Technique): an automatic system for programming used to create an object program in machine language from a source program written by a programmer. One instruction in the object program is created from one instruction in the source program. NEAT will translate and compile source programs that are written in COBOL.

needle: a probe in a manual information retrieval operation that may be passed through holes or notches to assist in sorting or selecting cards. (A)

NEG: negative.

negate:

(1) to perform the operation of negation. (B)

(2) to perform the logic operation NOT. (A)

negated combined condition: in COBOL, the NOT logical operator immediately followed by a parenthesized combined condition.

negated simple condition: in COBOL, the NOT logical operator immediately followed by a simple condition.

negation: the monadic boolean operation the result of which has the boolean value opposite to that of the operand. Synonymous with *NOT operation.* (A) (B)

negative:

(1) less than zero.

(2) having a surplus of negative charges.

(3) the minus terminal of a battery of power supply.

(4) the NOT function.

negative acknowledge character (NAK): a transmission control character transmitted by a station as a negative response to the station with which the connection has been set up. (A) (B)

negative acknowledgment (NAK): in binary synchronous communication, a line control character sent by a receiving terminal to indicate that an error was encountered in the previous transmission and that the receiving terminal is ready to accept another transmission.

negative feedback: the act of returning part of the output to the input in such a way that increased output results in the deduction of a greater quantity from the input.

negator: an element that accepts one binary input signal and has the capability to

yield a single binary output signal of the opposite significance. Synonymous with *NOT element.*

negentropy: deprecated term for *entropy.* (A) (B)

neither-nor operation: synonym for *nondisjunction.* (A) (B)

nest:

(1) to incorporate a structure or structures of some kind into a structure of the same kind. For example, to nest one loop (the nested loop) within another loop (the nesting loop); to nest one subroutine (the nested subroutine) within another subroutine (the nesting subroutine). (B)

(2) to embed subroutines or data in other subroutines or data at a different hierarchical level such that the different levels of routines or data can be executed or accessed recursively. (A)

nested command list: a command list called by another command list.

nested DO: in FORTRAN, a DO loop whose range is entirely contained by the range of another DO loop.

nested logic: a control structure contained within another control structure.

nested macros: the power of a macroinstruction is increased by calling another macro from within the macroinstruction.

nested subroutine: a subroutine called from another subroutine. The first subroutine is called from the main program and executes until it encounters an instruction for transferring control to the second subroutine, which executes until it is finished and then transfers control back to the first subroutine.

nesting:

(1) a routine or block of data included within a larger routine or block of data.

(2) the relationship between the statements held in two perform statements. The statements included in the second or inner perform statement are wholly included in or excluded from the first, or outer, perform statement.

nesting level: in assembler programming, the level at which a term or subexpression appears in an expression, or the level at which a macrodefinition containing an inner macroinstruction is processed by an assembler.

NET: see *network*.

NETBIOS: a Bios program for IBM PC local area networks.

net loss: the sum of gains and losses between two terminals of a unit or system.

network (NET):

(1) an interconnected group of nodes.

(2) the assembly of equipment through which connections are made between data stations.

(3) in data processing, a user-application network.

(4) a collection of devices such as computers and printers that are connected together. A network is a tool for communication that permits users to store and retrieve information, share printers, and exchange information.

(5) see *computer network, heterogeneous network, local area network.*

network access control: tasks related to network administration controls, including monitoring of system operation, ensuring of data integrity, user identification, recording system access and changes, and approaches for granting user access.

network access machine (NAM): a computer programmed to aid a user to interact with a computer network, for example, a network connecting a series of host computers.

network administrator: a person responsible for setting up, maintaining, or troubleshooting a network.

network analog: the expression and solution of mathematical relationships between variables using a circuit or circuits to represent these variables. (A)

network analysis: determining the transfer characteristic and other properties of a passive circuit from its configuration, elements, voltages, and the like.

network analyzer: a device that simulates a network such as an electrical supply network. (A)

network application: the use to which a network is put, such as data collection or inquiry/update.

network architecture: a set of design principles, including the organization of functions and the description of data formats and procedures, used as the basis for design and implementation of a user-application network. See also *open systems architecture.*

network awareness: that condition where a central processor is cognizant of the status of the network.

network buffer: a storage unit for compensating for a difference in the rate of flow of data received and transmitted in a computer communications systems.

network components: in large systems, the host processors, remote computer systems, remote terminals, and transmission paths or channels that connect all the components to each other.

network control: synonymous with *network management.*

network control layer: in a layered network architecture, that layer of logic providing for network control between adjacent network nodes.

network control program generation: the process, performed in a processor, of assembling and link editing a macroinstruction program to produce a network control program.

network drills: the final level of testing in a real-time system where data from all the sites is transmitted and the full complex of equipment, personnel, interfaces, and programs is tested.

network implementation: the realization of a network architecture in hardware and software.

networking: in a multiple-domain network, communication between domains. Synonymous with *cross-domain communication.*

network interface card: an expansion card that connects a computer to a network.

network maintainability: a quality desired in a network permitting its operation under differing conditions, including scheduled and unscheduled maintenance.

network management: those functions that perform control over the operation of a communications network. Synonymous with *network control.*

network management point: the location in a network where information dealing with the loading, utilization, and maintenance of the network is concentrated and analyzed.

network node: synonym for *node*.

network operator: a person or program responsible for controlling the operation of all or part of a network.

network operator console: a system console or terminal in the network from which an operator controls the network.

network operator log on: a log on request issued in behalf of a terminal from the network operator console by using a network operator command.

network path: see *path*.

network service: a multiuser computer service with systematized programs and data bases.

network slowdown: synonym for *system slowdown*.

network stand-alone system: a dedicated network that includes both local and remote data sources. Typical is a system that interconnects branch offices with a headquarters computer or provides communications between several departments within an office complex; for example, inquiry/response processing of a dynamic data base.

network synthesis: formulating a network with particular requirements.

network theory: the use of the physical concept of a network to represent routing problems, flow problems, or project management. Mathematical techniques then operate to find the shortest route, maximum possible flow, or minimum project completion time. PERT, CPM, and other specialized applications of network theory have been developed for project managers.

network user: a person whose computer is connected to a network.

new input queue: a queue of new messages (or a group) within a system that are awaiting processing. The main scheduling routine will scan them along with other queues and order them into processing in order.

new-line character (NL):
(1) a format effector that causes the print or display position to move to the first position on the next line. (B)
(2) cf. *carriage return character*. (A)
(3) in word processing, synonym for *carrier return character*.

new pack: indicates to the system that a change in the current volume on the drive will occur.

next executable sentence: in COBOL, the next sentence to which control will be transferred after execution of the current statement is complete.

next record: in COBOL, the record which logically follows the current record of a file.

next-sequential-instruction feature: the ability of a computer to execute program steps in the order in which they are stored in memory unless branching takes place.

nexus: a point in a system where interconnections occur.

NFF: no fault found.

nibble: a four-bit word.

NIL: a constant in Pascal that can be assigned to a pointer variable, indicating that the pointer points to nothing.

nil pointer: a pointer indicating the end of a chained list.

nine edge: the bottom or lower edge of a punch card. This edge is used for entering the equipment first because of external equipment needs.

nines complement: the diminished radix complement in the decimal numeration system. Synonymous with *complement-on-nine*. (A) (B)

ninety column card: a 90 vertical column punched card, representing 90 characters.

NIP:
(1) see *nonimpact printer*.
(2) see *nucleus initialization program*.

NL: see *new-line character*. (A)

n-level address: an indirect address that specifies n levels of addressing. (A)

n-n junction: a junction between n-type semiconductors with different electrical properties.

NO: see *number*.

no-address instruction: an instruction in which it is not necessary to identify an address in memory.

no-consoles condition: in systems with multiple console support, a condition in which the system is unable to access any full-capability console device.

node (N):

(1) in a network, a point where one or more functional units interconnect transmission lines. The term *node* derives from graph theory, in which a node is a junction point of links, areas, or edges.

(2) the representation of a state or an event by means of a point on a diagram. (A)

(3) in a tree structure, a point at which subordinate items of data originate. (A)

(4) see also *cluster controller node, host node, peripheral node.*

(5) synonymous with *network node.*

node-to-network protocol: a protocol that regulates the interface of a node to the next adjacent node in the network.

noise:

(1) random variations of one or more characteristics of any entity such as voltage, current, or data.

(2) loosely, any disturbance tending to interfere with the normal operation of a device or system. (A)

(3) an unwanted disturbance introduced in a communications circuit. It may partially or completely obscure the information content of a desired signal.

noisy digit: a digit produced during the normalizing of a floating-point number that is inserted during a left shirt operation into the fixed-point part.

noisy mode: a technique of floating-point arithmetic associated with normalization, where digits other than zero are introduced in low-order positions during a left shift. These digits seem to be noise, but, in fact, have been deliberately introduced.

NOMAD language: an algebraic compiler adapted from the MAD (Michigan Algorithmic Decoder) language. It is a high-speed compiler that allows a wide latitude of generality in expressions.

nominal data: data in which each value represents a distinct category, and the value itself acts as a label or name, with no assumption of ordering or distances between categories.

nominal (rated) speed: maximum speed or data rate of a device or facility which makes no allowance for necessary delaying functions, such as checking or tabbing.

nonaddressable: a storage location that cannot be accessed through an instruction.

nonarithmetic shift: synonymous with *logical shift.*

noncoded graphics: synonym for *image graphics.*

noncompat: a malfunction caused by an incompatibility between a tape and a drive.

nonconjunction: the dyadic boolean operation the result of which has the boolean value 0 if and only if each operand has the boolean value 1. Synonymous with *NAND, NAND operation, NOT-BOTH operation.* (B) Cf. *conjunction.* (A)

nonconnected storage: in PL/1, separate locations in storage that contain related items of data that can be referred to by a single name but that are separated by other data items not referred to by that name. Examples are the storage referred to by an unsubscripted elementary name in an array of structures or by a subscripted name referring to an array cross section in which the subscript list contains an asterisk to the left of any element expression.

noncontinguous item: in COBOL, a data item in the working-storage section of the data division which bears no relationship with other data items.

non-data-set clocking: synonym for *business machine clocking.*

nondeletable: a message found on a display screen, which cannot be erased from the screen until a specific command to do so is made.

nondestructive cursor: on a CRT display device, a cursor that can be moved within a display surface without changing or destroying the data displayed on the screen. Cf. *destructive cursor.*

nondestructive read (NDR): reading that does not erase the data in the source location. Synonymous with *nondestructive readout.*

nondestructive readout (NDRO): synonym for *nondestructive read.*

nondisjunction: the dyadic boolean operation the result of which has the boolean value 1 if and only if each operand has the boolean value 0. Synonymous with *neither-nor operation, NOR operation.* (B) Cf. *disjunction.* (A)

non-display-based word-processing equipment: word-processing equipment that does not have an electronic display capability. Cf. *display-based word-processing equipment.*

nonequivalence: synonymous with *exclusive-NOR.*

nonequivalency element: a logic element whose action represents the boolean connective exclusive OR.

nonerasable medium: paper tape units, for example, that are used for punching data that can be used to drive various production machines.

nonerasable storage: deprecated term for *read-only storage.* Synonym for *fixed storage.* (B)

non-escaping key: in word processing, a key that allows a character to be typed without the imprint position being changed.

nonexecutable statement: in FORTRAN, a statement that describes the use or extent of the program unit, the characteristics of the operands, editing information, statement functions, or data management.

nonfile-structured device: a device, such as a paper tape, line printer, or terminal, in which data can not be referenced, as in a file.

nongraphic character: a byte that, when sent to the printer, will not yield a printable character image; used merely for purposes of control (e.g., the carriage return).

nonidentity operation: the boolean operation the result of which has the boolean value 1 if and only if all the operands do not have the same boolean value. A nonidentity operation on two operands is a

nonequivalence operation. (B) Cf. *identity operation.* (A)

nonimpact printer (NIP): a printer in which printing is not the result of mechanical impacts; for example, thermal printers, electrostatic printers, photographic printers. (B)

noninteractive: a program or device that provides no interaction with the operator at executive time.

nonlinear programming: in operations research, a procedure for locating the maximum or minimum of a function of variables that are subject to constraints, or both, as nonlinear. (B) Cf. *convex programming, dynamic programming, integer programming, linear programming, mathematical programming, quadratic programming.* (A)

nonlinear system: a control system model that cannot be represented by linear equations.

nonloadable character set: a character set installed in a device that must be used as is; it cannot be extended or altered.

nonlocking: in code extension characters, having the characteristics that a change in interpretation applies only to a specified number of the coded representations following commonly only one. Cf. *locking.* (A) (B)

nonmapping mode: a mode where virtual addresses are not transformed through a memory map; for example, the virtual address is used as an actual address.

nonnegative number: synonym for *natural number.* (A) (B)

nonnumerical data processing: languages developed by symbol manipulation that are used primarily as research tools rather than for production programming.

nonnumeric item: in COBOL, a data item whose description permits its contents to be composed of any combination of characters taken from the computer's character set. Certain categories of nonnumeric items may be formed from more than restricted character sets.

nonnumeric literal: a character string bounded by quotation marks, which means literally itself. For example,

"CHARACTER" is the literal for the means CHARACTER. The string of characters may include any characters in the computer's set, with the exception of the quotation mark.

nonoperable instruction: an instruction whose only effect is to increment the instruction index counter. Written as CONTINUE.

nonprinting comments: comments inserted into a document onscreen but kept from being printed out.

nonprocedural language: synonym for *non-procedure-oriented language.*

non-procedure-oriented language: a programming language that allows the user to express the solution to a problem in a form other than as an explicit algorithm. Synonymous with *nonprocedural language.*

nonprogrammed halt: a machine stoppage not resulting from a programmed instruction, such as an automatic interrupt, manual intervention, and so on.

non-real-time processing: processing historical data such as batch processing. Used also to describe a failed real-time information-processing system.

nonrecoverable error: deprecated term for *unrecoverable error.*

non-reflective ink: an ink, usually black, with extremely low reflective characteristics to optical character or mark reading devices. This non-reflective ink contrasts greatly with the paper, and enables the scanner to form a recognition pattern to identify the character.

nonresident portion (of a control program): control program routines that are loaded into main storage as they are needed and can be overlaid after their completion.

non-return-to-change recording: a method of recording in which ones are represented by a specified condition of magnetization and zeros are represented by a different condition.

non-return-to-reference recording: the magnetic recording of binary digits such that the patterns of magnetization used to represent zeros and ones occupy the whole storage cell, with no part of the cell

magnetized to the reference condition. Synonymous with *non-return-to-zero recording.*

non-return-to-zero change-on-ones recording (NRZI): non-return-to-reference recording of binary digits such that the ones are represented by a change in the condition of magnetization, and the zeros are represented by the absence of a change. This method is called (mark) recording because only the one or mark signals are explicitly recorded. Synonymous with *non-return-to-zero (mark) recording, NRZ(M).*

non-return-to-zero (change) recording (NRZ(C)): non-return-to-reference recording of binary digits such that the zeros are represented by magnetization to a specified condition, and the ones are represented by magnetization to a specified alternative condition. The two conditions may be saturation and zero magnetization but are more commonly saturation in opposite senses. This method is called change recording because the recording magnet condition is changed when, and only when, the recorded bits change from zero to one or from one to zero.

non-return-to-zero (inverted) recording: deprecated term for *non-return-to-zero change-on-ones recording (NRZ1).*

non-return-to-zero (mark) recording (NRZ(M)): synonym for *non-return-to-zero change-on-ones recording.* (A)

non-return-to-zero recording (NRZ): synonym for *non-return-to-reference recording.*

nonreusable: the attribute that indicates that the same copy of a routine cannot be used by another task.

nonrevertive error checking: a system of error checking where a separate channel is utilized for reporting on errors found at a receiving terminal. The main channel is used continually for message transmission. Cf. *revertive error checking.*

nonrotating disk: synonymous with *semiconductor disk.*

nonscrollable: a message or a part of the screen that will not scroll off the top as new information is written at the bottom of the display; used to advise the computer operator that a major problem has occurred.

nonsimultaneous transmission: usually, transmission in which a device or facility can move data in only one direction at a time. Synonym for *half-duplex.* Cf. *duplex, simultaneous transmission.*

nonspecific volume request: in job control language (JCL) a request that allows the system to select suitable volumes.

nonstorage device: a device not having the ability to retain data.

nonstore through cache: in a processing unit, a store (write) operation, in which data is immediately put into locations in the cache. At some later time, the data is moved from the cache to main storage.

nonswappable: a program whose execution cannot be suspended for an indefinite time period in a system running several programs concurrently. See *job swapping.*

nonswitched point-to-point line: a data set that exists after the job that created it terminates. Cf. *temporary data set.*

nonvolatile memory: a storage medium that holds information when power is removed from the system.

nonvolatile RAM: the use of a RAM for the speedy, minute-by-minute work and then shifting its information to the E²PROM as the power is about to be shut off, thus preserving memory.

nonvolatile storage:
(1) a storage device whose contents are not lost when power is removed.
(2) in word processing, storage that retains text after the electrical power to the machine is switched off.
(3) cf. *volatile storage.*

nonwrap mode: information on a display screen or printer that extends beyond the end of the line and is not carried to the next line.

no-op: see *no-operation instruction.* (A) (B)

no operation: an omitted or absent instruction that has been deliberately left blank, to allow later insertion of data or information without any rewriting, or for the program itself to develop one or more instructions.

no-operation instruction (no-op): an instruction whose execution causes a computer to do nothing other than to proceed to the next instruction to be executed. Synonymous with *do-nothing operation.* (A) (B)

NOP: a mnemonic in assembly languages indicating a do-nothing instruction. See also *no-operation instruction.*

NOR: a logic operator having the property that if P is a statement, Q is a statement, R is a statement, ... , then the NOR of P, Q, R, . . is true if all statements are false, false if at least one statement is true. P NOR Q is often represented by a combination of OR and NOT symbols, such as (PVQ). N NOR Q is called neither P NOR Q. Synonymous with *NOT-OR.* (A)

NOR circuit: a circuit that has an output only when all inputs are down.

NOR element: a logic element that performs the boolean operation of nondisjunction. Synonymous with *NOR gate.* (A)

NOR gate: synonym for *NOR element.* (A)

normal direction flow: a flow direction from left to right or top to bottom on a flowchart. (A) (B)

normal distribution: see *Gaussian.*

normal form (BNF) Backus: a formal language structure for syntax paring, used in design of ALGOL-60.

normalization: the multiplication of a variable by a numerical coefficient so that it will assume a desired value.

normalization routine: a floating-point arithmetic operation related to the normalization of numerals where digits other than zero are developed in the lower order or less significant position during a left shift.

normalize:
(1) to make an adjustment to the fixed-point part and the corresponding adjustment to the exponent in a floating-point representation to ensure that the fixed-point part lies within some prescribed range, the real number represented remaining unchanged. Synonymous with *standardize.* (B)
(2) loosely, to scale.
(3) deprecated term for *scale.* (A) (B)

normalized form: the form taken by a floating-point representation when the fixed-point part lies within some prescribed standard range, so chosen that any given real number will be represented by a unique pair of numerals. Synonymous with *standard form*. (A) (B)

normalized number: a floating-point number converted to normal form.

normalizer: an electronic component of an optical character reader that alters the signal from the scanner to receive a processed rendition of the input character that is more appropriate for detailed or more advanced analysis.

normal restart: synonymous with *warm start*.

normal stage punching: a card punching system where only the even-numbered rows are punched.

normal state: the condition of operation in a computer where the instructions are concerned with conventional aspects of computation such as adding, subtracting, and data transfer.

normative testing: standards of performance that are set for the testing of both quantitative and qualitative system performance.

NOR operation: synonym for *nondisjunction*. (A) (B)

NOT: a logic operator having the property that if P is a statement, then the NOT of P is true if P is false, false if P is true. The NOT of P is often represented by $\bar{P}$, $\sim P$, $\neg P$, P'. (A)

NOT-AND: synonym for *NAND*. (A)

NOT-AND operation: deprecated term for *nonconjunction*. (A) (B)

notation: a set of symbols, and the rules for their use, for the representation of data. (A) (B) See *binary notation, decimal notation, infix notation, mixed-base notation, mixed-radix notation, positional notation, post fix notation, prefix notation.*

NOT-BOTH operation: synonym for *nonconjunction*. (A) (B)

notebook: a portable computer smaller than a laptop.

NOT element: a logic element that performs the boolean operation of negation. Synonymous with *NOT gate*. (A)

note pad: a desk accessory that lets a user enter and edit small amounts of text.

NOT gate: synonym for *NOT element*. (A)

NOT-IF-THEN: synonym for *exclusion*.

NOT-IF-THEN element: a logic element that performs the boolean operation of exclusion. Synonymous with *NOT-IF-THEN gate*. (A) (B)

NOT-IF-THEN gate: synonym for *NOT-IF-THEN element*. (A) (B)

NOT-IF-THEN operation: synonym for *exclusion*. (A)

NOT operation: synonym for *negation*. (A) (B)

NOT-OR: synonym for *NOR*. Deprecated term for *nondisjunction*. (A) (B)

NOT-OR operation: deprecated term for *nondisjunction*. (A) (B)

noughts complement: synonym for *radix complement*. (A) (B)

nought stage: synonymous with *zero condition*.

n-plus-one address instruction: an instruction that contains n + 1 address parts, the plus-one address being that of the instruction that is to be executed next unless otherwise specified. (A) (B)

NRX(C): see *non-return-to-zero (change) recording.*

NRZ: see *non-return-to-zero recording*. (A)

NRZ(C): see *non-return-to-zero (change) recording*. (A)

NRZI: see *non-return-to-zero change-on-ones recording*. (A)

NS: see *nanosecond*.

NSEC: see *nanosecond*.

NSP: see *numeric space character*.

NTF: no trouble found.

nucleus: that part of a control program that is resident in main storage. Synonymous with *resident control program*. (B)

nucleus initialization program (NIP): the program that initializes the resident control program; it allows the operator to request last minute changes to certain options specified during system generation.

NUL: see *null character*. (A)

null:

    (1) empty.

    (2) having no meaning.

    (3) not usable.

null character (NUL): a control character that is used to accomplish media-fill or time-fill, and that may be inserted into or removed from, a sequence of characters without affecting the meaning of the sequence; however, the control of equipment or the format may be affected by this character. (B) See also *space character.* (A)

null character string: synonym for *null string.*

null cycle: the time needed to cycle through a program without introducing data, thereby establishing the lower bound for program processing time.

null file: synonymous with *dummy file.*

null indicator: a unit indicating when a parameter is zero.

null instruction: a program instruction having no functional significance during program execution, but which satisfies a structural requirement, such as breaking a program into segments or reserving memory space for an instruction to be inserted later.

null locator value: in PL/1, a special locator value that cannot identify any location in internal storage; it gives a positive indication that a locator variable does not currently identify any generation of data.

null matrix: a matrix of values where each element is zero. Synonymous with *zero matrix.*

null parameter: synonymous with *dummy parameter.*

null record:
(1) an empty record.
(2) a record containing a null character string.

null set: synonym for *empty set.* (A)

null string:
(1) a string containing no entity. (B)
(2) the notion of a string depleted of its entities, or the notion of a string prior to establishing its entities. Synonymous with *null character string.* (A)

NUM:
(1) see *number.*
(2) see *numeric.*

number (N) (NBR) (NO) (NUM):
(1) a mathematical entity that may indicate quantity or amount of units.
(2) loosely, a numeral.
(3) see *binary number, complex number, Fibonacci number, integral number, irrational number, level number, natural number, random number, rational number, serial number.* (A)

number control: the quantity of a number (value) that is the result of a process or problem in order to prove its accuracy.

number cruncher: deprecated term for a computer that has been designed for arithmetic operations.

number crunching: repetitive or complex arithmetic calculations, as contrasted with moving data within a computer system.

number generator: a set of manual controls onto which a computer operator can set a word for input.

number representation: a representation of a number in a numeration system. Synonymous with *numeration.* (A) (B)

number representation system: synonym for *numeration system.* (A) (B)

number sequence: see *pseudorandom number sequence, random number sequence.* (A)

number system: synonym for *numeration system.* (A) (B)

numeral (NU): a discrete representation of a number. The following are four different numerals that represent the same number, that is, a dozen, in the method shown: twelve, by a word in the English language; 12., in the decimal numeration system; XII by Roman numerals; 1100 in the pure binary numeration system. (B) See *binary numeral, decimal numeral.* (A)

numeralization: the use of digits to represent alphabetic data.

numeral system: a system representing numbers by agreed sets of symbols according to agreed rules.

numeration: synonym for *number representation.* (A) (B)

numeration system: any notation for the representation of numbers. Synonymous with *number representation system, number system.* (B) See *decimal numeration system, mixed-base numeration system, mixed-radix numeration system, pure bi-*

nary numeration system, radix numeration system. (A)

numeric (N) (NUM): pertaining to data or to physical quantities in the form of numerals. Synonymous with *numeral.*

numerical: synonym for *numeric.* (A) (B)

numerical analysis: the study of methods of obtaining useful quantitative solutions to problems that have been expressed mathematically, including the study of the errors and bounds on errors in obtaining such solutions. (A)

numerical code: a restrictive code that has a character set consisting of digits only.

numerical control (NC): automatic control of a process performed by a device that makes use of numeric data usually introduced while the operation is in progress. (A) (B)

numerical control system: a system for controlling industrial machine activities automatically by the insertion of numerical data at a given point.

numerically controlled machine: a device that is controlled by numerical data. See *numerical control.*

numerical data: synonym for *numeric data.*

numerical tape: a punched paper or plastic tape used to feed digital instructions to a numerical control unit.

numeric atomic symbol: for list processing languages, symbols that can be decimal integers, octal integers, or floating-point numbers.

numeric backspace character (NBS): a word processing formatting control that moves the printing or display point to the left by a fixed escapement value equal to the value for numbers in the pitch being used. Cf. *backspace character.*

numeric bit data: see *binary picture data.*

numeric character: synonym for *digit (1).* (A) (B)

numeric character data: see *decimal picture data.*

numeric character set: a character set that contains digits and may contain control characters, special characters, and the space character, but not letters. (A) (B)

numeric character subset: a character subset that contains digits and may contain control characters, special characters, and the space character, but not letters. (A) (B)

numeric code: a code according to which data is represented by a numeric character set. (A) (B)

numeric-coded character set: a coded character set whose character set is a numeric character set. (A) (B)

numeric coding: a system of abbreviation where all information is reduced to numerical quantities.

numeric constant: a constant that is represented by a real number.

numeric control: that field of computer activity that centers around the control of machine tools by mechanical devices; for example, a computer can control assembly-line tools for machining.

numeric data: data in the form of numerals and some special characters; for example, a date represented as 81/01/01. Synonymous with *numerical data.*

numeric-edited character: in COBOL, a numeric character which is in such a form that it may be used in a printed output. It may consist of characters such as the external decimal digits 0 through 9, the decimal point, commas, and the dollar sign.

numeric item: in COBOL, an item whose description restricts its contents to a value represented by characters from the digits 0 through 9. The item may also contain a leading or trailing operational sign represented either as an overpunch or as a separate character.

numeric keypad: a ten-key auxiliary pad, on which numbers are arranged as on a calculator, usually located to the right of the standard typewriter keys on the keyboard.

numeric pad: a keyboard for numeric input to a computer.

numeric processor chip: a processor design created to handle high precision arithmetic and scientific function evaluation.

numeric punch: a hole punched in one of the punch rows designated as zero through nine. A zero punch, and sometimes an eight or nine punch, in combination with another numeric punch, is considered a zone punch. (A)

numeric representation: a discrete representation of data by numerals. (A) (B)

numeric shift: a control for selecting the numeric character set in an alphanumeric keyboard printer.

numeric space character (NSP): a word-processing formatting control used in proportionally spaced printing or display that causes the active position to move to the right a distance equal to the escapement value for numbers in the pitch being used. See also *space character.*

numeric string: a string with no characters. Synonymous with *empty string.*

numeric variable: represents a number that is either supplied to the computer by the programmer or internally calculated by the computer during execution of the program.

numeric word: a word consisting of digits and possibly space characters and special characters. For example, in the Universal Decimal Classification system, the numeric word 61 (03) = 20 is used as an identifier for any medical encyclopedia in English. (A) (B)

nybble: usually four bits, or half a byte.

O:
(1) see *operand.*
(2) see *operation.*
(3) see *operator.*
(4) see *output.*

object code: output from a compiler or assembler which is itself executable machine code or is suitable for processing to produce executable machine code. (A)

object code compatibility: pertaining to a system where changes to the system do not require recompilation or assembly of user programs. Cf. *source code compatibility.*

object computer: in COBOL, the name of an environment division paragraph in which the computer upon which the object program will be run is described.

object deck: synonymous with *object pack.*

object definition:
(1) the set of information required to create and manage an object.
(2) the creation of a control block for an object. It also defines the object as available to the user.

object language: a language that is specified by a metalanguage. Synonym for *target language.* (A) (B)

object library: an area on a direct access storage device used to store object programs and routines.

object machine: the computer on which the object program is to be executed.

object module: a module that is the output of an assembler or a compiler and is input to a linkage editor. (A)

object module library: a partitioned data set that is used to store and retrieve object modules. See also *load module library, source module library.*

object of entry: in COBOL, a set of operands and reserved words, within a data division entry, that immediately follows the subject of the entry.

object-oriented programming: a technology for creating programs, made up of self-sufficient modules containing all of the information required to manipulate a given data structure. These modules are created in class hierarchies, and the methods or code in one class can be passed down the hierarchy or inherited. New and powerful objects can be created rapidly by inheriting their characteristics from existing classes.

object pack: the punched cards where an object program is retained. Synonymous with *object deck.*

object phase: synonymous with *target phase.*

object program: a fully compiled or assembled program that is ready to be loaded into the computer. (B) Synonym for *target program.* Cf. *source program.* (A) cf. *subject program.*

object-program preparation: conversion of programs from one of several easy-to-use source languages, or from certain competitive system languages, to a specific machine code.

object routine: the machine-language routine that is the output following translation from the source language.

object time: the time during which an object program is executed.

occurs: in COBOL, a sequence of data items of the same format. Subscripting is used to refer or designate a specific item in a procedure statement.

OCL:

(1) see *operation control language.*

(2) in office systems, a batch control statement used by an operator to control the printing of a document.

OCR: see *optical character recognition.*

OCT: see *octal.*

octal (OCT): pertaining to a fixed-radix numeration system having a radix of eight. (A) (B)

octal code: a code operating with a base 8. Cf. *binary.*

octal debug method: a debugging and loading program found in an octal system supplied on two preprogrammed PROMs with a supplementary tape.

octal digit: the symbol 0, 1, 2, 3, 4, 5, 6, or 7 used as a digit in the system of notation that uses 8 as the base or radix.

octal number: a number of one or more figures, representing a sum in which the quantity represented by each figure is based on a radix of eight. The figures used are 0, 1, 2, 3, 4, 5, 6, and 7.

octal number system: a number system that expresses values as multiples of powers of eight.

octet: a byte composed of eight binary elements. (A) (B)

octonary: pertaining to the number representation system with a base of eight.

odd-even check: synonym for *parity check.* (A)

odd-even interleaving: dividing memory into several sections and independent paths with the odd and even addresses in alternate sections, permitting further segmenting over normal memory interleaving.

odd parity: a system where the parity bit is added to a word so that the total number of 1s is odd.

odd parity check: a parity check where the number of 1 bits (as opposed to 0 bits) in a group is expected to be odd. Cf. *even parity check.*

OF: see *overflow.*

office automation: utilizing personal computers as word processors and workstations; utilizing local area networks for electronic interoffice mail; other technologies used to upgrade worker productivity and efficiency.

office information system: an electronic system capable of performing a host of office activities, including word processing, information retrieval and telecommunications.

off line: pertaining to the operation of a functional unit without the continual control of a computer.

off-line equipment: machines not in direct communication with the central processing unit. Synonymous with *auxiliary equipment.*

off-line mode: a way of computer operation, meaning that the units are not hooked up together.

off-line processing: processing, not directly associated with or required for main program or real-time communication and control.

off-line storage: storage that is not under control of the processing unit.

off-line unit: input-output unit or auxiliary equipment not under direct control of the CPU.

off premise: in general, standby units, usually a backup or duplicated set of computer equipment, often at another location.

off-punch: a punched hole in a card or tape that does not compare favorably with the proper position for that hole.

offset stacker: a card stacker that can stack cards selectively under machine control so that they protrude from the balance of the deck to give physical identification.

offset variable: in PL/1, a locator variable with the OFFSET attribute, whose value identifies a location in storage, relative to the beginning of an area.

off-the-shelf:
(1) pertaining to production items that are available from current stock and need not be recently purchased or immediately manufactured.
(2) computer software or units that can be used by customers with little or no adaptation.

off time: describing a computer that is not scheduled for use, maintenance, alteration, or repair.

OFL: see *overflow*.

OL: see *on line*.

oligarchic network: a network where most of the clocks that establish timing for events are under the control of a few of the clocks.

OLRT: on-line real time. A system for communicating interactively with users.

OLTEP: see *on-line test executive program*.

OLTS: see *on-line test system*.

OLTT: see *on-line terminal test*.

OMR: see *optical-mark recognition*.

on-board: on a circuit board.

on-chip control logic: logic contained on the microprocessor chip that decodes instructions and coordinates instruction execution with memory and input-output operations that are managed by the system controller.

on condition: an occurrence, within a PL/1 task, that could cause a program interruption. It may be the detection of an unexpected error or of an occurrence that is expected, but at an unpredictable time.

on-demand system: a system from which information or service is available at the time of request.

one address: synonymous with *single address*.

one-address computer: a computer in which every machine instruction contains one address, either that of an operand or of the storage location for the result. Cf. *three-address computer, two-address computer*.

one-address instruction: an instruction that contains one address part. (A) (B)

one-ahead addressing: a method of implied addressing in which the operation part of an instruction implicitly addresses the operands in the location following the location of the operands of the last instruction executed. (A)

one-chip: a unit implemented in a single chip.

one-chip computer: a situation where all the elements of a computer—RAM, ROM, CPU, and input-output interfaces—are implemented on a single chip.

one-core-per-bit storage: a storage device in which each storage cell uses one magnetic core per binary character. (A) (B)

one-digit adder: a binary adding circuit that adds one digit at a time.

one-dimensional language: a language whose expressions are customarily represented as strings of characters, for example, FORTRAN. Cf. *multidimensional language*. (A)

one element: synonymous with *OR element*.

one-for-one: pertaining to an assembly routine where one source-language instruction is converted to one machine-language instruction.

one-for-one translation: conversion of one source language instruction to one machine-language instruction.

one gate: synonymous with *OR element*.

one-level address: synonym for *direct address*. (A) (B)

one-level code: synonymous with *absolute code*.

one-level store: an approach in handling all on-line storage, whatever its physical characteristics, as being of one directly accessible memory.

one-level subroutine: a subroutine that does not itself call a lower level of subroutine during its operation.

one-megabit dynamic RAM: a chip that can store one million bits, or pieces of information, so that the information can be retrieved in any order. The chip has four times the recording ability of the 256-kilobit dynamic RAM.

one-micron memory chips: chips able to store as many as one million units of information. See also *submicron*.

one-pass assembler: an assembler that scans a source program only one time to yield the object program and assembly listing. Cf. *three-pass assembler, two-pass assembler.*

one-pass compiler: a language processor for passing through a source program one time and producing an object module; for example, PASCAL.

one-plus-one address instruction: an instruction that contains two address parts, the plus-one address being that of the instruction that is to be executed next unless otherwise specified. (A) (B)

ones complement: the diminished radix complement in the pure binary numeration system. Synonymous with *complement-on-one.* (A) (B)

one-step operation: manual operation of a central processor, where one instruction is carried out in response to a manual control permitting detailed error diagnosis.

one-way only operation: a simplex mode of operation for a data link. Cf. *two-way alternate communication, two-way simultaneous communication.*

on line (OL):
(1) pertaining to a user's ability to interact with a computer.
(2) pertaining to a user's access to a computer via a terminal. (A)
(3) currently connected to and under the control of the computer. Used to refer to equipment such as printers and disk drives, information storage media such as disks, and the information they contain.
(4) information services the user connects to.

on-line access machine interaction: the interactive procedure for program development and on-line problem solving.

on-line batch processing: the sharing of computer resources between one or more real-time programs and a batch program.

on-line data bases: synonymous with *banks* and *electronic information services.* See *electronic information services.*

on-line data processing: data processing where all changes to records and accounts are carried out at the moment that each transaction occurs; usually requires random-access storage.

on-line data reduction: processing of information as quickly as the information is received by the computing system or as quickly as it is generated by the source.

on-line debugging: the debugging of a program while sharing its execution with an on-line process program.

on-line diagnostics: running of diagnostics on a system while it is on line but off peak to save time and to take corrective action without closing down the entire system.

on-line equipment: processing equipment of compatible computer speed that is directly connected to the main processing devices.

on-line mode: that all equipment within a computer operation is hooked up directly, that is, with the central processing unit.

on-line operation: an operation performed under the CPU's control where data entered from a terminal is immediately processed by the CPU to alter the contents of a record stored on disk.

on-line plotter: a local or remote digital incremental plotter, in either on-line or off-line operation with digital computer, providing a high-speed plotting system of versatility and reliability.

on-line processing: the operation of terminals, files, and other auxiliary units under direct and absolute control of the central processor to eliminate the need for human intervention at any time between initial input and computer output.

on-line program development: a means used in the evolution of computer programs in which programmers are on line to a computer containing compilers, editors, and testing aids, and which allows the programmer to write, check, test, correct, and update programs.

on-line real time: see *OLRT.*

online searching: utilizing a computer-based information retrieval system when there is direct on-line access to a database(s) available on the computer. The computer responds to a series of inquiries from the user.

on-line storage: storage that is under the control of the processing unit.

on-line system: a system in which the input data enters the computer directly from the point of origin or in which output data is transmitted directly to where it is used.

on-line tab setting: a feature in the printer that allows tab stops to be changed and set under commands issued by the computer that controls the printer.

on-line terminal test (OLTT): a diagnostic aid by which a terminal or console may request any of several kinds of tests to be performed upon either the same terminal or console or a different one.

on-line test executive program (OLTEP): a facility that schedules and controls activities on the on-line test system (OLTs) and provides communication with the operator. This program is part of a set of programs that can be used to test I/O devices, control units, and channels concurrently with the execution of a program.

on-line testing: testing of a remote terminal or station that is performed concurrently with execution of the user's programs—that is, while the terminal is still connected to the processing unit—with only minimal effect on the user's normal operation.

on-line test system (OLTS): a system that allows a user to test I/O devices concurrently with execution of programs. Tests may be run to diagnose I/O errors, verify repairs and engineering changes, or to periodically check devices. See also *on-line test executive program.*

on-line unit: input-output device or auxiliary equipment under the direct control of the computer.

on-the-fly printer: an impact printer in which the type slugs do not stop moving during the impression time. Synonymous with *hit-on-the-fly printer.* (A) (B)

on unit: in PL/1, the specified action to be executed upon detection of the on condition named in the containing ON statement. This excludes SYSTEM and SNAP.

OOP: object-oriented programming. See *object oriented programming.*

OP:
(1) see *operand.*
(2) see *operation.*
(3) see *operation part.*
(4) see *operator.*

O/P: see *output.*

op-cod: short for *operating code.*

op code: synonymous with *operating code.*

OPD: see *operand.*

open:
(1) to prepare a data set or file for processing.
(2) in PL/1, to associate a file with a data set and to complete a full set of attributes for the file name.
(3) to make available. Files are opened in order to work with them. Opening an icon usually causes a window to appear, revealing the document or application program the icon represents or showing the contents of a folder or disk.

open architecture: a system whose design is non-proprietary, such as that as the IBM-PC. See also *clone.*

open code: in assembler programming, that portion of a source module that lies outside of and after any source macrodefinitions that may be specified.

open-ended: pertaining to a process or system that can be augmented. (A)

opening a terminal: performing the store and equipment procedures necessary to initiate operations at a point-of-sale terminal. See also *closing a terminal.*

open-loop control: in which the central processing unit does not directly control a process or procedure but instead displays or prints information for the operator to assist in an action-oriented decision.

open-loop system: see *open-loop control.*

open mode: in COBOL, the state of a file after execution of an OPEN statement for that file and before the execution of a CLOSE statement for that file. The particular open mode is specified in the OPEN state as either INPUT, OUTPUT, or I-O.

open routine: a routine able to be inserted directly into a larger routine without the need for a link or calling sequence. Synonymous with *direct insert routine.*

open shop: pertaining to the operation of a computer facility in which most productive problem programming is performed by the problem originator rather than by a group of programming specialists. The use of the computer itself may also be described as open shop if the user/

programmer also serves as the operator. Cf. *closed shop.* (A)

open subroutine: a subroutine of which a replica must be inserted at each place in a computer program at which the subroutine is used. Synonymous with *direct insert subroutine.* (B) Cf. *closed subroutine.* (A)

open system:
(1) a system allowing a variety of computers and terminals to interact together.
(2) a system to which access is publicly available.

open systems architecture (OSA): a model that represents a network as a hierarchical structure of layers of functions; each layer provides a set of functions that can be accessed and that can be used by the layer above it.

open systems interconnection (OSI): the use of standardized procedures to enable the interconnection of data-processing systems in networks.

open systems interface: a specification of a standard means of network interconnection permitting any user to communicate with any other, regardless of the origin of the apparatus and software involved.

open systems interworking: creating links between discrete computers and networks to evolve a freely interacting open system.

operand (O) (OP) (OPD):
(1) an entity to which an operation is applied. (B)
(2) that which is operated upon. An operand is usually identified by an address part of an instruction. (A)
(3) information entered with a command name to define the data on which a command processor operates and to control the execution of the command processor.
(4) an expression to whose value an operator is applied.
(5) see also *key word, key word parameter, positional operand, positional parameter.*

operate mode: synonym for *computer mode.* (B)

operating code: a code with source statements that generate machine code after assembly. Synonymous with *op code.*

operating console: a device containing all controls and indicators needed for the operation of the processor.

operating delay: computer time loss resulting from errors made by operators or others using the system.

operating environment: see *environment, operational environment.*

operating ratio: the ratio of the number of effective hours of computer activities to the total hours of scheduled cooperation.

operating space: synonym for *display space.*

operating system (OS): software that controls the execution of a computer program, and that may provide scheduling, debugging, input-output control, accounting, compilation, storage assignment, data management, and related services. See also *DOS, multiuser, multiprocessing, multitasking, OS/2, real-time UNIX.* (B)

operating system functions: see *operating system.*

operating system supervisor: operating system consists of a supervisory control program, system programs, and system subroutines. A symbolic assembler and macroprocessor, a FORTRAN or other compiler, and debugging aids are also included. A library of general utility programs is provided.

operating system 360 (OS/360): an IBM system that spans a range from computers with sequential scheduling to large multiprogramming computers which can perform task multijobbing. For the smaller units within the 360 series, other types of operating systems exist.

operating time: that part of available time during which the hardware is operating and is assumed to be yielding correct results. It includes program development time, production time, makeup time, and miscellaneous time. Cf. *idle time.* (A)

operation (O) (OP):
(1) a well-defined action that, when applied to any permissible combination of known entities, produces a new entity. (B)
(2) a defined action, namely, the act of obtaining a result from one or more operands in accordance with a rule that com-

pletely specifies the result for any permissible combination of operands.

(3) a program set undertaken or executed by a computer, for example, addition, multiplication, extraction, comparison, shift, transfer. The operation is usually specified by the operator part of an instruction.

(4) the event or specific action performed by a logic element.

(5) see *arithmetic operation, asynchronous operation, auxiliary operation, binary operation, boolean operation, complementary operation, computer operation, concurrent operation, control operation, dual operation, dyadic boolean operation, dyadic operation, equivalence operation, fixed-cycle operation, identity operation, logic operation, majority operation, monadic operation, multiplex operation, n-adic boolean operation, n-adic operation, nonidentity operation, parallel operation, sequential operation, serial operation, simultaneous operation, single-step operation, threshold operation.* (A)

operational address instruction: a computer instruction having no operation part but has the operation implicitly specified by the address parts.

operational amplifier: a high-gain amplifier that is the basic component of analog computing elements; this amplifier performs specified computing operations or provides specified transfer functions. (B)

operational character: a specific character that, when used as a code element, initiates, modifies, or stops a control operation, that is, controlling the carriage return.

operational environment: the physical environment, for example, temperature, humidity, layout, or power requirements, that is needed for proper performance.

operational unit: all equipment or circuitry which performs a computer process.

operational word: a COBOL term used to denote a word that improves readability of the language but need not be on the reserved list.

operation code: a code used to represent the operations of a computer. (B) Synony-

mous with *computer instruction code.* (A) Sometimes shortened to *op-cod.*

operation control language (OCL): a programming language used to code operation control statements.

operation cycle: the series of operations that the CPU goes through. First, it fetches the word containing its next instruction from memory using the address in the program counter. The instruction is loaded into the instruction register and a one (1) is added to the program counter. The CPU decodes the instruction. If necessary, the CPU computes an effective address and places it in the address register. Finally, the CPU executes the instruction and prepares to start the cycle over again.

operation decoder: a device that selects one or more control channels according to the operation part of a machine instruction. (A)

operation expression: an expression containing one or more operators.

operation fields: that portion of the instruction format specifying the process or procedure to be performed.

operation number:

(1) a number designating the position of an operation, or its equivalent subroutine in the sequence of operations comprising a routine.

(2) a number identifying each step in a program given in symbolic code.

operation part (OP): a part of an instruction that usually contains only an explicit specification of the operation to be performed. Synonymous with *function part, operator part.* (A) (B)

operation ratio: the proportion of the total number of hours when devices are actually functioning, including operator time, time for errors, to the total number of hours of scheduled equipment operation.

operation register: a register where the operation code is stored during an operation cycle.

operations analysis: synonym for *operations research.* (A) (B)

operations control: in installation administration and work flow, includes instructions from and to the computer operator, administrative records, logs of system operation, and the control over library programs.

operations multitask: concurrent processing of two or more job steps.

operations research (OR): the application of scientific methods to the solution of complex problems concerning the optimal allocation of available resources. Synonymous with *operations analysis.* (B)

operation table: a table that defines an operation by listing all permissible combinations of values of the operands and indicating the result for each of these combinations. (B) See *boolean operation table.* (A)

operation time: the time needed for an operation to complete the operation cycle.

operator (O) (OP) (OPR):
(1) a symbol that represents the action to be performed in a mathematical operation. (B)
(2) in the description of a process, that which indicates the action to be performed on operands.
(3) a person who operates a machine. (A)
(4) see *arithmetic operator, bit-string operators, boolean operator, complementary operator, dyadic operator, monadic operator, quarternary operator, unary operator.*
(5) see also *concatenation, concatenation character.*

operator command: a statement to a control program, issued via a console device or terminal, that causes the control program to provide requested information, alter normal operations, initiate new operations, or terminate existing operations.

operator console: a functional unit containing devices that are used for communication between a computer operator and an automatic data-processing system. (A) (B)

operator control panel: a part of an operator console of a computer, or of an automatic data-processing system that contains switches used to control the system or part of the system and that may contain indicators giving information on the

functioning of the system or of part of the system. (B)

operator error: an error made by the terminal operator.

operator guidance code: a code displayed on a display device that represents the system's response to certain operating conditions or operator actions.

operator ID: a number entered by an operator during log on that identifies the operator to the system.

operator indicator: a display light for showing conditions on the operator console. These indicators can be set, cleared, and tested under program control.

operator intervention section: the part of the control equipment where operators can intervene in normal programming operations on control.

operator message: a message from the operating system or a problem program directing the operator to perform a specific function, such as mounting a tape reel, or informing the operator of specific conditions within the system, such as an error condition.

operator part: synonym for *operation part.* (A) (B)

operator's console: a console providing capability for manual intervention and the monitoring of computer operations.

opm: operations per minute (equivalent to characters per minute when control functions are included).

OPR:
(1) see *operand.*
(2) see *operator.*

op register: the specific register in which the operation code of the instruction set is kept.

optical bar-code reader: a data station unit that reads coded information from documents, featuring a high-speed printer.

optical character recognition (OCR):
(1) the machine identification of printed characters through use of light-sensitive devices. (A)
(2) character recognition that uses optical means to identify graphic characters.
(3) cf. *magnetic ink character recognition.* (A)

optical characters: special types of characters that can be read by optical character readers.

optical computer: a device using beams of light rather than electrical current to process information, permitting computers to perform far more transactions simultaneously than present electronic versions.

optical disk: a disk whose data is read to and written by lasers. See *CD-ROM*.

optical mark reader: a device for reading forms with pencil marks, punches, and printed marks.

optical-mark recognition (OMR): synonymous with *mark sensing*.

optical reader: a device that reads handwritten or machine-printed symbols into a computing system.

optical scanner:
(1) a scanner that uses light for examining patterns. (B)
(2) a device that scans optically and usually generates an analog or digital signal. (A)

optical scanning: an approach for machine recognition of characters by their images.

optimization: see *linear optimization*.

optimize: a procedure causing a system, process, or operation to take on its most desirable configuration or procedures in the best or most efficient way; for example, when arranging instructions and data in storage so that a minimum of machine time or space is used for storing or accessing them.

optimized code: the compiled code of a program that has been reworked so as to eliminate inefficiencies and unused or unheeded instructions, thereby permitting the program to run faster and requiring less storage space.

optimizer: a utility program for processing executable programs and producing optimized codes.

optimum coding: see *minimum access coding*.

optimum programming: programming to maximize efficiency with regard to a given criterion.

option: a specification in a statement that may be used to influence the execution of the statement. See *default option*.

optional-halt instruction: synonym for *optional-pause instruction*.

optional hyphen: see *soft hyphen*.

optional-pause instruction: an instruction that allows manual suspension of the execution of a computer program. Synonymous with *optional-halt instruction* and *optional-stop instruction*. (A) (B)

optional-stop instruction: synonym for *optional-pause instruction*. (A) (B)

optional word: a reserved word included in a specific format only to improve the readability of a COBOL statement. If the programmer wishes, optional words may be omitted.

option list: in word processing, the display of a list of available machine functions for selection by the operator.

option-switch:
(1) in hardware, a dual in-line package switch or jumper for turning on an optional feature.
(2) in software, a parameter for activating a feature by overriding a default value, thereby emulating the hardware option switch. Synonymous with *option toggle*.

option toggle: synonymous with *option switch (2)*.

OR:
(1) see *operations research*.
(2) see *overrun*.
(3) a logic operator having the property that if P is a statement, Q is a statement, R is a statement, ... , then the OR of P, Q, R, . . . is true if at least one statement is true, false if all statements are false. P OR Q is often represented by P + Q, PVQ. Synonymous with *boolean ADD*, and *logical ADD*. Cf. *exclusive OR*. (A)

OR circuit: synonymous with *OR element*.

ORD: see *order*.

order (ORD):
(1) a specified arrangement used in ordering. An order need not be linear. (B)
(2) an arrangement of items according to any specified set of rules.
(3) to place items in an arrangement in accordance with specified rules.
(4) to arrange items according to any specified set of rules. Synonymous with *sort*.

(5) deprecated term for *instruction, sequence (1)*. (A)

(6) see *merge order*.

order-by-merging: to order by repeated splitting and merging. (A) (B)

order code: deprecated term for *operation code*. (A) (B)

ordered array: the arrangement of data elements into a particular order. The data elements are placed into rows and columns so that each element is individually accessible.

ordered list: a list of data elements in a particular order, utilizing a one-dimensional array.

order entry: a computer program that permits entry of orders into the system, often generating bills, lading bills, and warehouse alert.

ordering bias: the manner and degree by which the order of a set of items departs from random distribution. An ordering bias will make the effort necessary to order a set of items more than or less than the effort that would be required for a similar set with random distribution. (A) (B)

ordering by merge: repeated merging, splitting, and remerging in order to place items in a particular order.

orderly closedown: see *graceful shutdown*.

orderly shutdown: see *graceful shutdown*.

order of the merge: the number of input files to a merge program.

ordinal data: data ranked according to a criterion, with each category having a unique position relative to other categories. Cf. *nominal data*.

ordinal type: in PASCAL, a set of distinct values that are ordered such that each value (except the first) has a unique predecessor, and each value (except the last) has a unique successor; any scalar type except REAL.

ordinary symbol: in assembler programming, a symbol that represents an assembly-time value when used in the name or operand field of an instruction in the assembler language. Ordinary symbols are also used to represent operation codes for assembler-language instructions.

OR element: a logical element operating with binary digits, and providing an output signal from two input signals, as follows:

Input		Output
p	q	r
1	0	1
1	1	1
0	1	1
0	0	0

OR ELSE: a logical operator stating that if P and Q are statements, then P OR ELSE Q is either true or false. Synonymous with *EITHER/OR*.

ORG: see *origin*.

OR gate: a gate that implements the OR operator. (A)

origin (ORG):

(1) the absolute storage address of the beginning of a program or block.

(2) in relative coding, the absolute storage address to which addresses in a region are referenced.

(3) see *assembled origin, computer program origin, loaded origin*.

original language: prior to machine processing, the original form in which a program is prepared.

origination: an approach that determines the type, nature, and origin of a document.

OR operation: synonym for *disjunction*. (A)

OR operator: the logical operator that yields an OR operation.

orphan: a single line or word at the top of a page with the rest of the paragraph on the preceding page.

OR unit: see *OR gate*.

OS: see *operating system*.

OS/2: an operating system for IBM's most powerful, new personal computers. OS/2 is intended to supplant DOS as IBM's state of the art system.

OS/360: see *operating system/360*.

OSA: see *open systems architecture*.

oscillating sort: a merge sort in which the sorts and merges are performed alternately to form one sorted set. (A)

OSI: see *open systems interconnection*.

OUT: see *output.*

outage: an out-of-service condition, usually resulting in the computer being taken out of service for repair.

outage analysis: a report showing the length of time, percentages of time, and reasons why a computer has been taken out of active use. Cf. *operating time.*

outconnector: in flowcharting, a connector that indicates a point at which a flow line is broken for continuation at another point. Cf. *inconnector.* (A)

out device: a unit that translates computer results into usable or final form.

outer macroinstruction: in assembler programming, a macroinstruction that is specified in open code. Cf. *inner macroinstruction.*

outline font: a font that describes each character mathematically as a set of formulas. The mathematical description adjusts itself to render the character in different styles.

out-of-line coding: instructions in a routine stored in a different part of the program storage from the main route; can be added later as a patch.

output (O) (O/P) (OUT):
(1) information transferred from the computer's microprocessor to some external device, such as the screen, a disk, a printer, or a modem. Cf. *input.*
(2) pertaining to a device, process, or channel involved in an output process, or to the data or states involved in an output process. (B) see *input/output, real-time output.* (A) Synonym for *output data, output process.*

output area: an area of storage reserved for output. (A)

output block: a portion of memory held for output data, from which it is transferred to an output unit. Synonymous with *output area.*

output blocking factor (Bo): in a tape sort, the number of data records in each record in the output file.

output bound: a unit limited by the rate at which data can be output from another unit; for example, a computer attached to a slower printer. Cf. *input bound.*

output channel: a channel for conveying data from a device or logic element. (A)

output class: an indicator of the priority of printed output.

output data: data being delivered or to be delivered from a device or from a computer program. (A) (B) Synonymous with *output.*

output device: synonym for *output unit.* (A) (B)

output file: in COBOL, a file that is opened in the output mode.

output formatter: a program for producing punched card or tape versions of assembled microprocessor programs in formats compatible with available storage media.

output job queue: a queue for storing programs that have executed and are waiting to print. Cf. *job queue.*

output job stream: synonymous with *output stream.*

output limited: description of a program where the overall processing time is limited by the speed of an output unit, resulting in a further processing delay until output occurs. See *input limited, processor limited.*

output mode: in COBOL, the state of a file after execution of an OPEN statement, with the OUTPUT phrase specified for that file, and before the execution of a CLOSE statement for that file.

output module: the part of a device that translates the electrical impulses represent data processed by the unit into permanent results such as printed forms, displays, tapes, and so on.

output module valve: a section of a computer that converts output data into analog control signals.

output primitive: synonym for *display element.*

output procedure: in COBOL, a set of statements to which control is given during execution of a SORT statement after the sort function is completed.

output process:
(1) the process that consists of the delivery of data from a data-processing system, or from any part of it.

(2) the return of information from a data-processing system to an end-user, including the translation of data from a machine language to a language that the end-user can understand.

(3) synonymous with *output*.

(4) see also *output data*.

(5) cf. *input process*.

output program: a utility program that organizes the output process of a computer. (A) (B)

output punch:

(1) an output device that transcribes information onto punched paper tape.

(2) an output device that transcribes information onto punched cards.

output queue: see *output work queue*.

output record: the current record stored in the output area prior to being output, or a specific record written to an output unit.

output register buffer: the transfer or buffering unit that receives data from internal storage and transfers it to an output media such as magnetic tape.

output routine: a utility routine that organizes the output process of a computer. (A) (B)

output routine generator: a generator that yields an output routine in accordance with given specifications.

output state: the determination of the condition of that specified set of output channels.

output stream: diagnostic messages and other output data issued by an operating system or a processing system on output devices especially activated for this purpose by the operator. Synonymous with *job output stream, output job stream*.

output table: the bed, or flat surface, of a plotter.

output tape sorting: a tape holding a file in sequences resulting from a specified sort/merge process.

output unit: a device in a data-processing system by which data can be received from the system. Synonymous with *output device*. (A) (B)

output work queue: a queue of control information describing system output data sets, that specifies to an output writer the location and disposition of system output.

output writer: a part of the job scheduler that transcribes specified output data sets onto a system output device independently of the program that produced the data sets.

outside loop: a program loop that executes the control parameters being held constant while the current loop is being carried through possible values.

OV: see *overflow*.

over capacity: values that are not in the range of a quantity are said to be out of range or *over capacity*.

overflow (OF) (OFL) (OV) (OVF):

(1) that portion of a word expressing the result of an operation by which its word length exceeds the storage capacity of the intended storage device.

(2) that portion of the result of an operation that exceeds the capacity of the intended unit of storage.

(3) in a register, loss of one or more of the leftmost whole-number digits because the result of an operation exceeded 10 digits. Cf. *loss of significance*.

(4) see *arithmetic overflow*. (A)

(5) cf. *underflow*.

overflow error: an overflow condition caused by a floating point arithmetic operation.

overflow exception: a condition caused by the result of an arithmetic operation having a magnitude that exceeds the largest possible number.

overflow indicator:

(1) an indicator that signifies when the last line on a page has been printed or passed.

(2) an indicator that is set on if the result of an arithmetic operation exceeds the capacity of the accumulator. The overflow indicator is often used in conjunction with a carry indicator to reflect an unusual or an error condition.

overflow operation: an operation exceeding the capacity of the storage unit, leading to the generation of an overflow situation.

overflow position: an extra position in the register in which the overflow digit is developed.

overflow record: on an indirectly addressed file, a record whose key is randomized to the address of a full track or to the address of a home record.

overhead: the quantity of processing needed to accomplish a goal, as related to the cost and time of computing resources.

overhead bit: a bit other than an information bit, for example, a check bit, or any procedure or format bit.

overhead operation: synonym for *housekeeping operation.* (A) (B)

overlap: to perform an operation at the same time that another operation is being performed; for example, to perform input/output operations while instructions are being executed by the processing unit.

overlapped processing: an approach that permits a computer to work on several programs instead of one.

overlay:
(1) in a computer program, a segment that is not permanently maintained in internal storage. (B)
(2) the technique of repeatedly using the same areas of internal storage during different stages of a program.
(3) in the execution of a computer program, to load a segment of the computer program in a storage area hitherto occupied by parts of the computer program that are not currently needed. (A)
(4) see *form overlay.*

overlay keyboard: a keyboard with narrow key tops that allow an overlay panel to be installed to identify the key functions or fonts.

overlay module: a load module that has been divided into overlay segments, and has been provided by the linkage editor with information that enables the overlay supervisor to implement the desired loading of segments when requested.

overlay path: all of the segments in an overlay tree between a particular segment and the root segment, inclusive.

overlay program: a program in which certain control sections can use the same storage locations at different times during execution.

overlay region: a continuous area of main storage in which segments can be loaded independently of paths in other regions. Only one path within a region can be in main storage at any one time.

overlay segment: a self-contained portion of a computer program that may be executed without the entire computer program necessarily being maintained in internal storage at any one time. (A) (B)

overlay structure: a graphic representation showing the relationships of segments of an overlay program and how the segments are arranged to use the same main storage area at different times.

overlay supervisor: a routine that controls the proper sequencing and positioning of segments of computer programs in limited storage during their execution. (A)

overlay tree: see *overlay structure.*

overload recovery time: the time needed for the output to return to its proper value following the removal of an overload situation.

overload simulator: to test for overload conditions within a system, an artificial condition is created to make the program act as it would during an actual overload or overflow.

overprinting: in word processing, printing one character over another. Used most often with foreign languages, for example, in accenting a word. Also used to create new characters that are referred as an *interrobang.*

overpunch:
(1) to add holes in a card column or in a tape row that already contains holes. Overpunches are often used to represent special characters. (B)
(2) to add holes to perforated tape to change a character, especially to produce a delete character. (A)
(3) synonym for *zone punch.* (A)

overrun (OR): loss of data because a receiving device is unable to accept data at the rate it is transmitted.

overrun error: an error where the previous character in a register has not been totally read by the main processing unit at the time that a new character is present to be loaded in the register.

overstrike: substituting one character for another on a visual display unit, as in word processing, a cursor positioned below the character to be altered, and desired characters substituted via the keyboard.

overtype cursor: a solid block that marks the place where the next character typed on the keyboard will appear; indicates that the user is in an overtype mode. Cf. *insert cursor.*

overtype mode: an alternate method of entering text. Like a typewriter, any character that is typed replaces any existing character under the cursor. Cf. *insert mode.*

overview diagram: a detailed description of a module shown in the visual table of contents.

overwrite: to record into an area of storage so as to destroy the data that was previously stored there.

OVF: see *overflow.*

own coding (sorting): special coding provided by the programmer, that is integrated with the sort/merge coding.

owned: supplied by and belonging to a customer, as opposed to private and public.

owner: the user who creates an entity (or is named the owner of an entity).

P:

(1) see *parallel.*
(2) see *parity.*
(3) see *pico-.*
(4) see *pointer.*
(5) see *power.*
(6) see *procedure.*
(7) see *process.*
(8) see *processor.*
(9) see *program.*
(10) see *punch.*

PA: see *program access key.*

pack: to store data in a compact form in a storage medium by taking advantage of known characteristics of the data and the storage medium, in such a way that the original data can be recovered; for example, to make use of bit or byte locations that would otherwise go unused. (B) See *disk pack.* (A)

package:

(1) the plastic, ceramic, or metal where a completed chip is mounted.

(2) a generalized program written to include the requirements of users. A package is usually less efficient than a purpose-built program designed for the special needs of one user, but does have the advantages of being less costly and quickly available.

packaged: apparatuses that are complete and ready for use, such as modules.

packed decimal: representation of a decimal value by two adjacent digits in a byte. For example, in packed decimal, the decimal value 23 is represented by 00100011. See also *signed packed decimal.* Cf. *unpacked decimal.*

packed file: a data file that has been compressed. See *data compression.*

packed format: a data format in which a byte may contain two decimal digits or one decimal digit and a sign.

packed option: a PASCAL feature allowing more efficient storage of records and arrays.

packing: the usage of storage locations in a file.

packing density: the number of storage cells per unit length, unit area, or unit volume; for example, the number of bits per inch stored on a magnetic tape track or magnetic drum track. (B)

packing factor: the percentage of location on a file that is actually used.

packing sequence: a procedure for loading the upper half of an accumulator with the first data word, shifting this into the lower half, loading the second datum, shift, and so on, so that the three data words are packed in sequence.

pad character: a character introduced to use up time or space while a function (usually mechanical) is being accomplished; for example, carriage return form eject.

padding:

(1) a technique that incorporates fillers in data. (A) (B)

(2) in PL/1, one or more characters or bits concatenated to the right of a string to extend the string to a required length. For character strings, padding is with blanks; for bit strings, it is with zeros.

(3) deprecated term for *filler*. (A) (B)

paddle: a cursor control unit used for computer games.

page (PG):

(1) a block of instructions, or data, or both, that can be located in main storage or in auxiliary storage. Segmentation and loading of these blocks is automatically controlled by a computer. (A)

(2) in a virtual storage system, a fixed-length block that has a virtual address and that can be transferred between real storage and auxiliary storage. (B)

(3) in word processing, a defined section of a document.

(4) to transfer instructions, data, or both, between real storage and external page storage.

pageable memory: that part of a computer's main memory subject to paging under a virtual storage system.

page addressing: addressing where memory is separated into segments in order to make complete usage of addressing capability. See *page.*

page-at-a-time printer: synonym for *page printer.* (A)

page body: in COBOL, that part of the logical page in which lines can be written and/or spaced.

page boundary: the point at which memory addressing progresses from one logical page to the next.

page break: a code indicating where a page will end.

page controls: in word processing, a machine capability to operate by page.

page data set: an extent in auxiliary storage, in which pages are stored.

page-depth control (last line): a control for specifying the maximum number of lines to be printed per page.

page description language (PDL): a language to describe the layout and material on a page to be printed.

page display: in word processing, shows where page breaks will occur when the document is printed.

paged machine: a computer that divides memory addresses into blocks of words, referred to as pages.

page-end character (PE): a word-processing formatting control that denotes the end of a page. Page end may be moved or ignored during text adjust mode operations. Synonymous with *form feed character.* See *required page-end character.*

page fault: an interrupt occurring when a program requires an item of data or an instruction not presently in main memory. This permits the software to transfer the page containing the required data or instruction to main memory from external storage.

page footing: summing of the entries on a particular page, usually at the bottom.

page frame: an area of real storage that can store a page. Synonymous with *frame.* (B)

page heading: the description of a page context from a report, appearing on the top of the page.

page in: the process of transferring a page from the page data set to real storage.

page mode memory: RAM which is divided into discrete pages.

page out: the process of transferring a page from real storage to the page data set.

page pool: the set of all page frames available for paging virtual-mode programs.

page printer: a device that prints one page at a time; for example, xerographic printer, cathode ray tube printer, film printer. Synonymous with *page-at-a-time printer.* Cf. *character printer, line printer.* (A)

page reader: an optical character reader that processes cut-form documents of different sizes that can read information in reel form.

page skip: synonymous with *form feed.*

page stealing: taking away an assigned page frame from a user to make it available for another purpose.

page store: see *frame store.*

page swapping: exchanging pages between main storage and auxiliary storage. (A)

page turning: synonym for *paging.*

pagination: in word processing, the automatic arrangement of text according to a preset number of page layout parameters.

paging:
(1) a time-sharing technique in which pages are transferred between main storage and auxiliary storage. Synonymous with *page turning.* (A)
(2) the transfer of pages between real storage and auxiliary storage. (B)

paging device: a direct-access storage device on which pages and possibly other data are stored.

paging rate: the number of pages moved by a virtual storage system between memory and the page data set per second. The paging rate will progress from an acceptable level to a point where it degrades overall performance of the system.

paging technique: a real storage allocation technique by which real storage is divided into page frames. (B)

paging terminal: a CRT terminal permitting the user to recover buffered information that has been rolled off the screen, both top and bottom, by pressing a button.

paint: in computer graphics, to shade an area of a display image; for example, with crosshatching.

palmtop: a tiny computer used for limited functions.

panel: in computer graphics, a predefined display image that defines the locations and characteristics of display fields on a display surface. Synonymous with *board* and *display panel.* See *control panel, maintenance panel, operator control panel.*

panel data set: a data set that contains predefined display images (called panels) to be displayed at display stations.

panel-definition program: a program written to define one or more field-by-field panels to be stored in a panel data set.

paper-advance unit: a device which drives paper through the printer. Sprockets in the unit engage with holes punched down each side of the paper.

paper feed: the method used when paper is drawn through a printer.

paper jam: a condition in which paper forms have not fed properly during printing and have become wedged in the feeding or printing mechanism, thus preventing the correct forward movement of the forms. A paper jam usually causes one line to be printed over one or more other printed lines.

paper skip: synonym for *paper throw.* (A)

paper tape (PT): deprecated term for *punch tape.*

paper tape automatic development system: a software system composed of loaders and utility programs for paper tape users. The system usually includes programs for debug, binary load, binary dump, verify, and object loader.

paper tape channels: positions across the tape used to represent a character, including parity if any.

paper tape code: deprecated term for *punch tape code.*

paper tape output device: output data received by this unit from the computer.

paper tape punch: an automatic unit that translates and records data from the main memory of a computer onto paper tape.

paper tape reader (PR) (PTR): a device that senses and translates the holes in perforated tape into electrical signals.

paper tape speed: the rate, in characters per second, at which the unit reads or punches paper tape.

paper tape type: indicates the purpose of the unit: reader only (RD), punch only (PN), or read-punch (RP).

paper throw: the movement of paper through a printer at a speed greater than that of a single line spacing. Synonymous with *paper skip.*

paragraph: a set of one or more COBOL sentences, making up a logical processing entity, and preceded by a paragraph name or a paragraph header.

paragraph assembly: process in which a document is assembled on a word processor from paragraphs stored on disks.

paragraph header: in COBOL, a word followed by a period that identifies and precedes all paragraphs in the identification division and environment division.

paragraph indent: a function that automatically indents for a new paragraph.

paragraph key: in word processing, a control used to process text one paragraph at a time.

paragraph name: a programmer-defined word that identifies a paragraph.

parallel (P):

(1) pertaining to the concurrent or simultaneous operation of two or more devices or to the concurrent performance of two or more activities in a single device.

(2) pertaining to the concurrent or simultaneous occurrence of two or more related activities in multiple devices or channels.

(3) pertaining to the simultaneity of two or more processes.

(4) pertaining to the simultaneous processing of the individual parts of a whole, such as the bits of a character and the characters of a word, using separate facilities for the various parts.

(5) cf. *serial.* (A)

parallel access:

(1) simultaneous access to all bits within a storage location comprising a character or word. Equal access time for any bit, character, or word within a storage unit.

(2) the process of obtaining information from or placing information into storage where the time needed for such access is dependent on the simultaneous transfer of all elements of a word from a given storage location. Synonymous with *simultaneous access.*

parallel adder: a digital adder in which addition is performed concurrently on digits in all the digit places of the operands. (A) (B)

parallel addition: addition that is performed concurrently on digits in all the digit places of the operands. (A) (B)

parallel by bit: the handling of all the binary bits or digits of a character simultaneously in different units.

parallel by character: the handling of all the characters of a machine word simultaneously in separate lines, channels, or storage cells.

parallel computer: a computer having multiple arithmetic or logic units that are used to accomplish parallel operations or parallel processing. Cf. *serial computer.* (A)

parallel data controller: a unit providing a flexible programmable interface to external devices or for interfacing multiple family computer devices.

parallel data medium: a medium for entering or recording data and as an input-output media for computers such as cards, disks, and so forth.

parallel digital computer: certain machines that process digits in concurrent procedures as contrasted to serial computing.

parallel interface: interfacing where all bits of data in a given byte (or word) are transferred simultaneously, using a separate data line for each bit.

parallelism: the simultaneous operation of several parts of a computer system.

parallel operation: the concurrent or simultaneous execution of two or more operations in devices such as multiple arithmetic or logic units. Cf. *serial operation.* (A)

parallel port: a port on a PC, usually used to connect a printer. Cf. *serial ports.*

parallel processing (PP): the concurrent or simultaneous execution of two or more processes in a single unit. Implies the use of more than one CPU. Cf. *serial processing.* (A)

parallel processing computers: computers that break a problem into many parts and attack them simultaneously, much as the human brain does. First developed by scientists at MIT and Carnegie-Mellon universities.

parallel processing system evaluation board: the circuit created for system development that contains a CPU, RAM input-output ports, and a clock circuit.

parallel running:

(1) the checking or testing of newly developed systems by running comparatively in conjunction with previously existing systems.

(2) the last step in the debugging of a system.

(3) the running of a newly developed system in a data-processing area in conjunction with the continued operation of the current system.

parallel search storage: a storage device in which one or more parts of all storage locations are queried simultaneously. Cf. *associative storage.* (A)

parallel storage: a storage device in which digits, characters, or words are accessed simultaneously or concurrently. (A)

parallel supercomputer: a computer that can link 1,000 or more microprocessors to reach nearly unfathomable computing speeds of up to 1 trillion calculations a second. See *supercomputer.*

parallel terminal: a data terminal that transmits all components of a data character simultaneously.

parallel test: the comparison of performance between old and new software to verify the accuracy and correctness of the new programs.

parallel-to-serial converter: a device that converts a group of digits, all of which are presented simultaneously, into a corresponding sequence of signal elements. Synonymous with *dynamicizer, serializer.*

parameter (PARM):

(1) a variable that is given a constant value for a specified application and that may denote the application. (A) (B)

(2) a variable that is given a constant value for a specific document processing program instruction; for example, left margin 10.

(3) in word processing, an item in a menu for which the operator specifies a value or for which the system provides a value when the menu is interpreted.

(4) a name in a procedure that is used to refer to an argument passed to that procedure.

(5) see *external-program parameter, keyword parameter, positional parameter, preset parameter, program-generated parameter, symbolic parameter.*

parameter block: a user-created information table that is consequent to each operating system call, usually allowing the operating system to provide requested service accurately.

parameter card: a punched card containing input data that represent special instructions for the specific application of a general routine. Synonym for *control card.*

parameter descriptor: in PL/1, the set of attributes specified for a single parameter in an ENTRY attribute specificator.

parameter descriptor list: in PL/1, the list of all parameter descriptors in an ENTRY attribute specification.

parameter-driven: a software system whose functions are determined primarily by parameters.

parameter list: see *formal parameter list.*

parameter RAM: the portion of Macintosh computer RAM which stores system memory.

parameter testing: tests of sections or subroutines of a program to assure that inputs produce desirable outputs.

parameter word: a word that directly or indirectly provides or designates one or more parameters. (A) (B)

parametric programming: an approach for studying the effect of an optimal linear-programming solution of a sequence of proportionate changes in the elements of a single row or column of the matrix.

parametric subroutine: a subroutine involving parameters where the computer adjusts and generates the subroutine according to the parametric values selected.

parametron: a unique unit composed of two stable states of oscillation, the one is twice the frequency of the other and has the capacity to store one binary digit.

parent: a file whose contents are needed, and at times the only source of information for creating new records. See also *child*.

parent-child relationship: passing of information from one generation of data to the next, for purposes of creating continuity.

parent directory:

(1) for any given directory, the directory in which it is contained.

(2) the directory immediately above the given directory in the hierarchical tree.

parent segment: in a data base, a segment that has one or more dependent segments below it in a hierarchy. See also *child segment*.

parity (P): in computer operations, the maintenance of a sameness of level or count; for example, keeping the same number of binary ones in a computer word to be able to carry out a check based on an even or odd number for all words under examination.

parity check: a check that tests whether the number of ones (or zeros) in an array of binary digits is odd or even. See *longitudinal parity check*. Synonymous with *odd-even check*. (A)

parity error: an error occurring when a unit of data, such as a word or byte, is found to have parity that is inconsistent with the system.

parity generator-checker: a hardware device for generating and checking parity conditions on data words.

parity interrupt: an interrupt occurring because of a parity error.

park: to lock the read/write head of a hard drive for portability.

PARM: see *parameter*.

parmlib: a large number of system control parameters accumulated in a file for establishing the functions of a computer.

parse: in systems with time sharing, to analyze the operands entered with a command and build up a parameter list for the command processor from the information.

parser: a routine in charge of analyzing a program statement and creating its syntactic tree structure based on the specified syntax of the programming language.

parsing: separating a programming statement into the basic units that can be translated into machine instructions.

part: a portion of an instruction word that specifies the address of an operand. Loosely, the operator portion of an instruction.

part failure rate: the number of occasions in a stated time period when a component fails.

partial carry: in parallel addition, a procedure in which some or all of the carries are temporarily stored instead of being immediately transferred. (B) Cf. *complete carry*. (A)

partial RAM: a RAM where some bits fail to perform. In newer 64K chips, as many as half of the bit locations turn out to be unusable.

partial word: a programming unit that allows the selection of a part of a machine word for processing.

partition: subdividing one large block into smaller subunits that can be handled more easily, for example, partition of a matrix. Deprecated term for *segment*. (A) (B)

partitioned access method: see *basic partitioned access method*.

partitioned data base: in a system with a geographically distributed population of users requiring access to update or retrieve information from computer files, a data base in which information relevant to certain regions is updated, maintained, and stored in each region.

partitioned data set (PDS): a data set in direct access storage that is divided into partitions, called members, each of which can contain a program, part of a program, or data. Synonymous with *program library*.

partitioned file: a disk file divided into subdivisions, each of which is a total file unto itself; usually used for storing programs and other control information.

partition sort: a rapid sorting method used by a computer to divide a number of items into groups or subsets.

part operation: that portion of an instruction that specifies the type of arithmetic or logic operations that are to be performed, but not the address of the operands.

parts-on-demand facility: see *smart machines.*

PASCAL: a high-level language; named for Blaise Pascal, who, in 1642, built a digital calculating machine. Based on the language, ALGOL, it emphasizes aspects of structured programming.

pass: one cycle of processing a body of data. See *sort pass.* (A)

passed data set: a data set allocated to a job step that is not deallocated at step termination but that remains available to a subsequent step in the same job.

passing parameters: transferring parameters between a subroutine and a main program.

passive graphics: a mode of operation of a display device that does not allow an on-line user to alter or interact with a display image. Cf. *interactive graphics.*

passive mode: in computer graphics, a mode of operation of a display device that does not allow an on-line user to alter or interact with a display image.

password (PW):
(1) a unique string of characters that a program, computer operator, or user must supply to meet security requirements before gaining access to data.
(2) a code or signal, usually confidential, that enables its user to have full or limited access to a system.
(3) in word processing, a word to be typed in at the work station to identify the operator and permit access to the system or to a specific document. (D)

paste: see *cut and paste.*

patch:
(1) a temporary electrical connection.
(2) to make an improvised modification. (B)
(3) to modify a routine in a rough or expedient way. (A) (B)

path: in a data base, a sequence of segment occurrences from the root segment to an individual segment.

path length:
(1) *in software:* the number of instructions that need to be performed before a task is completed.

(2) *in hardware:* the physical distance a signal traverses to move between two points.

pathname: the complete name of a document beginning with the name of the disk, the names of any subdirectories it may be in, and the name of the document.

pattern:
(1) the punching configuration in a card column representing a single character of a character set. Synonymous with *hole pattern.*
(2) the configuration of printed circuitry on a board or chip.

pattern articulating device: a microprocessor capable of reducing graphic images into data streams and reconstructing images from such data.

pattern recognition: the identification of shapes, forms, or configurations by automatic means. (A) (B)

pattern-sensitive fault: a fault that appears in response to some particular pattern of data. Cf. *program-sensitive fault.* (A)

pause instruction: an instruction that specifies the suspension of the execution of a computer program. A pause instruction is usually not an exit. Synonymous with *halt instruction.* (B) See *optional-pause instruction.* (A)

PC:
(1) see *personal computer.*
(2) see *printed circuit board.*
(3) see *program counter.*

PCB: see *printed circuit board.*

PC board: see *printed circuit board.*

pc board test language: a language in automatic pc board testing that is designed for the needs of testing complex boards containing microprocessors and other large-scale integration components.

PC-DOS: see *DOS.*

PCH: see *punch.*

PCI: see *program-controlled interruption.*

PCI/O: program controlled input-output.

p-code: see *pseudocode.*

PC register: see *program counter.*

PCS: see *print contrast signal.*

PCU: see *program control unit.*

PD: see *procedure division.*

PDAID: see *problem determination aid.*

PDI: see *picture description instruction.*

PDS:

(1) see *partitioned data set.*

(2) see *program data set.*

PE: see *page-end character.*

peak (PK): in OCR, an extraneous mark extending outward from a character past the stroke edge of the character.

peek: a statement in the BASIC programming language that displays the contents of a specific memory location in decimal form.

peek-a-boo: slang, method of verifying the existence or absence of punched holes in identical locations on cards by placing one card on top of another one.

peer-to-peer: a local area network where all computers are connected to each other, not necessarily using a central computer.

peer-to-peer communication: communicating from one user to another user in the network. This implies the ability to initiate the session at the user's discretion.

pel: a picture element of a terminal screen. See *picture element.* Synonym for *PIXEL.*

pel matrix: in computer graphics, a two-dimensional array of encoded points.

pencil: a system for storing, retrieving, and manipulating line drawings.

pen (light) control: a light pen for communication between a processor and the operator. When the penlike device is directed at information displayed on the screen, it detects light from the cathode-ray tube when a beam passes within its field of view.

pending I/O: an input-output operation begun but not yet terminated. The CPU is either idled during this period or else services other programs while the I/O is pending.

penumbral: specific headings that are partially relevant to data being sought.

percolation: in error recovery, the passing of control from a recovery routine to a higher-level recovery routine along a pre-established path.

PERF: see *performance.*

perforated: see *punch.*

perforated tape: a tape on which a pattern of holes or cuts is used to represent data. Synonym for *punched tape.*

perforated tape code: a code used to represent data on perforated tape. Synonymous with *paper tape code, punched tape code.*

perforated-tape reader: synonym for *punched tape reader.*

perforation: a linear series of unconnected cuts in continuous forms paper. The perforation delineates a fold or page boundary. See also *cut-to-tie ratio, tie.*

perforator: a device that punches. See *receiving perforator.*

PERFORM: in the COBOL programming language, a subroutine; a portion of the program that can be executed upon command by other portions of the program.

performance (PERF): together with facility, one of the two major factors on which the total productivity of a system depends. Performance is largely determined by a combination of three other factors: throughput, response time, and availability.

performance degradation:

(1) a condition where the performance of the system is not optimal; for example, when multiple programs compete for necessary resources.

(2) hardware failure of a component.

performance evaluation: the analysis of achievements, employing a data-processing system to provide information on operating experience and to identify any needed corrective actions.

performance group: a class, specified by an installation, which regulates the turnaround time of the user's jobs, job steps, and interactions.

performance monitor: a software package for measuring performance, activities, and events driven.

performance objective: a category of information contained in an installation performance specification. Each performance objective specifies the service rate that an associated job is to receive, for a number of different work-load levels.

perfs: perforation in paper to aid in removing pin-feed edges and bursting continuous paper into separate pages.

PERIF: see *peripheral.*

periodic: repeating a cycle regularly in time and form.

peripheral (PERIF): see *peripheral device.*

peripheral bus: input-output interfaces and peripherals that plug right into the bus slots, creating a simple and powerful method of input-output interfacing.

peripheral controls: controls that regulate the transfer of data between the central processor and peripheral units.

peripheral control transfers: regulates the transfer of data between the central processor and peripheral devices, by reconciling the mechanical speeds of the central processor and minimizing the interruption of activity because of peripheral data transfers.

peripheral control unit: synonym for *input-output controller.* (A)

peripheral conversion program: a program that handles jobs normally done by a separate peripheral processor.

peripheral device: in a data-processing system, any equipment, distinct from the central processing unit, that may provide the system outside communication or additional facilities. Examples include printers, disk drives, monitors, keyboards, mice, modems, etc. (B)

peripheral disk file: a file management system used with floppy disk peripherals; includes complete sets of utility programs for the updating, copying, purging, or addition of files.

peripheral error: an error unable to be corrected and which often causes the termination of execution of the program. Cf. *temporary error.*

peripheral interface adapter (PIA): a device for matching the input-output channels of a computer with peripheral devices. PIA is designed to simplify the task of the user by providing the needed buses for interfacing the peripherals, and the control logic signals for synchronizing the I/O units with the computer.

peripheral interface channel: see *interface.*

peripheral interface module: the optional interface cards used with some peripherals where the modules or cards plug into a common chassis or card frame.

peripheral limited: a system condition occurring when the time taken to end a process is determined by the time taken by peripheral units and not the time taken by the central processor. Cf. *processor limited.*

peripheral node: a node that terminates a path.

peripheral operation: an operation not under the direct computer control, of input-output on other devices. Used to designate the transfer of information between magnetic tapes and other media.

peripherals: the input-output devices and auxiliary storage units of a computer system.

peripheral slots: holding slots with microprocessor devices enabling cards to be added to increase capabilities without hardware modification.

peripheral software driver: programs that permit a user to communicate with and control peripheral units.

peripheral subsystem: consists of one or more peripheral units of the same type connected to an available input-output channel. Each subsystem is controlled by a channel synchronizer/control unit that interprets the control signals and instructions given by the central processor, effects the transfer of data to or from the selected unit and the central processor, indicates to the central processor the status of the available peripheral units, and informs the central processor when faults or mistakes that affect the operation of the subsystem occur.

peripheral support computer: a computer used for auxiliary operations to support a large processing complex; used primarily for card-to-tape, tape-to-card, and tape-to-printer conversions, along with peripheral control operations.

peripheral transfer: the process of transmitting data between two peripheral units. (A) (B)

permanent copy: a message produced on a physical medium, (e.g., a printed message). See also *hard copy.* Cf. *soft copy.*

permanent dynamic storage: dynamic storage where the maintenance of the data stored does not depend on a flow of energy into the storage medium.

permanent error: occurs when a track on a disk pack or floppy disk is modified by writing data over it. The only way to recover from this error is to reinitialize the unit by running a utility program that clears the disk and rewrites all the track and sector marks.

permanent file: a file that is retained from one initial program load until the next. Cf. *temporary file.*

permanently resident volume: a volume that cannot be physically demounted or that cannot be demounted until it is varied off line (i.e., removed from the control of the processing unit).

permanent memory: storage information remaining intact when power is turned off. Synonymous with *nonvolatile storage.*

permanent read/write error: an error that cannot be eliminated by retrying a read/write operation.

permanent storage: a storage device whose content cannot be modified. (B) Cf. *erasable storage.* Synonymous with *fixed storage, read-only storage.*

permutation: an ordered arrangement of a given number of different elements selected from a set. Cf. *combination.* (A) (B)

personal business computer: a microcomputer suitable for handling most of a person's computing needs in a business environment.

personal computer (PC): a relatively inexpensive, general-use computer created for a single user in an office or home.

personality card: a PROM programmer card containing special instructions for interfacing and programming that are unique for that specific PROM or family of PROMs being programmed; provides the proper timing patterns, voltage levels, and other needs for the PROM.

personality module: a module for PROM interlacing and programming. See also *personality card.*

person-machine interface: the protocol that a user must comprehend and operate in order to use a stated unit for its defined purpose.

PERT (Program Evaluation and Review Technique) network: an extensive study of an overall program to list all individual activities, or jobs that must be carried out so as to fulfill the total objective. These efforts are then arranged in a network that displays their relationships.

pessimizing compiler: slang, a compiler that produces object code that is worse than the straightforward or obvious translation.

PF key: see *program function key.*

PG:
(1) see *page.*
(2) see *program generator.*

PGA: pin grid array; a square chip format used by many microprocessors.

PGEC: Professional Group on Electronic Computers; a technical group dedicated to the advancement of computer-related sciences, for example, programming, engineering, storage devices. PGEC is a division of the Institute of Electrical and Electronics Engineers (IEEE).

PGM: see *program.*

PGS: see *program generation system.*

PH: see *phase.* Also known by *Greek letter O.*

phase (PH) (PHSE): a part of a sort/merge program; for example, sort phase, merge phase. See *assembly phase, compile phase, execute phase, translate phase.* (A)

phase-by-phase: a modular buildup or growth of a system according to schedule milestones.

phased conversion: a method of system implementation in which the old system is gradually replaced by the new one; the new system is segmented and gradually applied.

phase encoding: synonym for *phase modulation recording.*

phase library: the ordered set of program phases processed and entered by a linkage editor for execution.

phase logic: instructions for transferring the machine from one operational phase to another.

phase modulation recording: a magnetic recording in which each storage call is divided into two regions which are magnetized in opposite senses; the sequence of these senses indicates whether the binary character represented z is zero or one. Synonymous with *phase encoding.* (B)

photocell matrix: an OCR term for equipment able to project an input on a fixed two-dimensional array of photocells to develop a simultaneous display of the vertical and horizontal components of the character.

photoelectric detection: detecting and reading marks with a photoelectric detector, as in optical character recognition.

PHR: see *physical record.*

phrase: in COBOL, an ordered set of one or more consecutive COBOL character strings that form a portion of a COBOL procedural statement or COBOL clause.

PHSE: see *phase.*

physical-access level: access to a data set by block, which may consist of one or more physical records.

physical block: see *block.*

physical child segment: in a data base, a segment that is dependent on a segment at the next higher level in the data base hierarchy. All segments except the root segment are physical child segments because each is dependent on at least the root. See also *logical child segment.*

physical connection: synonymous with *connection.*

physical design: how data is kept on storage devices and how it is accessed.

physical level interface: in the physical link layer, the specification of the electrical and physical connection at the lowest level of control responsible for actuating, maintaining, and deactivating the links between a network and a terminal. See also *physical link layer.*

physical link: a protocol for making the physical connection between two machines.

physical link layer: in a network architecture, a level of control representing the lowest level in the ISO reference model for open systems architecture. This layer is dependent upon the physical medium for the transmission channel.

physical main storage: deprecated term for *processor storage.*

physical parent segment: in a data base, a segment that has a dependent segment at the next lower level in the physical database hierarchy.

physical record (PHR) (PR): a record whose characteristics depend on the manner or form in which it is stored, retrieved, or moved. A physical record may consist of all or part of a logical record.

physical relationship: in a data base, the description of the relationship between two or more physical segments.

physical resource: any facility of the computer available to do work, such as the processor, main storage, or an I/O device.

physical segment: in a data base, the smallest unit of accessible data.

physical simulation: employing a model of a physical system where computing elements are employed to represent some but not all of the subsystems.

physical unit: an input-output unit identified by its actual label or number.

physical volume: synonym for *volume.*

PI: see *program interruption.*

PIA: see *peripheral interface adapter.*

pianola roll: a roll of paper on which text and program instructions are represented by rows of punched holes.

PIA read-write: the signal generated by a computer to control data transfers on the data bus of the peripheral interface adapter.

pick device: in computer graphics, an input device used to identify a display element or display group. See also *choice device, locator device, valuator device.*

pico- (P): prefix meaning 10^{-12}, as in picosecond, one million millionth of a second. See *picosecond.*

picoprocessor: a self-contained, high-speed miniature digital processor providing controller functions for data transfer, control signaling, status monitoring, and interrupt generation.

picosecond (PS): one trillionth of a second; one thousandth of a nanosecond.

picture:

(1) in a programming language, a description of a character string in which each position has associated with it a symbol representing the properties of the character that may occupy it; for example, in COBOL 9999 is used as a picture of any four-digit numeric word. (A) (B)

(2) the display image of an area on a document.

(3) in a program, a string of characters used in editing to modify the individual characters in a field. There is a one-to-one relationship between the characters in the picture and the characters in the field.

picture description instruction (PDI): the code formed by compressing a high resolution picture definition, enabling detailed and complex graphic images to be transmitted efficiently over a narrow band channel.

picture element (PEL) (PIXEL):

(1) the part of the area of the original document which coincides with the scanning spot at a given instant and which is of one intensity only, with no distinction of the details that may be included.

(2) in computer graphics, the smallest element of a display space that can be independently assigned color and intensity.

(3) the area of the finest detail that can be effectively reproduced on the recording medium.

picture specification: in PL/1, a character-by-character description of the composition and characteristics of binary picture data, decimal picture data, character-string picture data.

picture specification character: in PL/1, any of the characters that can be used in a picture specification. See *binary picture data, decimal picture data.*

piggyback hardware: practice of peripheral equipment manufacturers to "piggyback" on other major computer hardware maker's equipment.

pilot: an original or test program, project, or unit.

pilot conversion: the implementation of a new system into the organization on a piecemeal basis. Synonymous with *modular conversion.*

pin: the leads on a unit such as a chip that plug into a socket and connect it to a system. Each pin provides a function, such as input, output, or ground.

pin board: a perforated board into which pins are manually inserted to control the operation of equipment. Synonym for *plugboard.* (A)

ping-pong buffering: see *double buffering.*

pip: a spot of light on a CRT screen for display pointing or target indicating.

pipelining: commencing one instruction sequence prior to the completion of another.

PIT: see *programmable interval timer.*

pitch:

(1) in word processing, the number of characters per horizontal inch or positioning interval of characters in a line of text; for example, "10 pitch," "12 pitch," proportionally spaced characters.

(2) a unit of type width based on the number of times a character can be set in one linear inch; for example, 10 pitch has 10 characters per inch.

(3) see *feed pitch, row pitch, track pitch.* (A)

PIXEL: see *picture element.* Synonym for *pel.*

pixel pattern: the matrix used in constructing the symbol or character image on a display screen.

PK: see *peak.*

PL:

(1) see *program library.*

(2) see *programming language.*

PLA: see *program logic array.*

plaintext: synonymous with *clear area.*

plain vanilla: free of special modifications or customization.

planar: a semiconductor processing technology where monolithic units extend below the surface of the substrate, but the plane surface remains flat during fabrication. Used for the mother board of IBM PS/2 computers.

plasma: the ionized gaseous discharge within the display unit that makes use of this effect for segment illumination.

plasma-ray device: a flat computer picture screen based on a grid of metallic conductors separated by a thin layer of gas.

When a signal is generated at any intersection along the grid, the gas discharges and causes the transparent screen to glow at this point.

plated wire storage: a magnetic storage in which data are stored by magnetic recording in a film coated on the surface of wire.

platen: a backing, usually cylindrical, against which printing mechanisms strike or otherwise deposit ink to produce an image.

platform: basic hardware and/or software which establishes a computer system.

PLATO: a computer-based educational system consisting of a large, high-speed central computer for servicing up to 1000 terminals in a time-share mode. Good for individual instruction with interactive lessons. Students enter responses through a keyboard or touch answers shown on a screen.

platter: a round flat electromagnetic disk cartridge whose surface is not unlike a dinner plate.

PLIB: see *program library.*

PL/M: a high-level language created for microprocessor systems programming.

PL/M-plus: an extended version of PL/M permitting a user direct access to all bits and fields for manipulation operations. This allows all standard compiler operations on bits, fields, and whole words. Also written as PL/M+.

PL/1 (programming language 1): a programming language designed for numeric scientific computations, business data processing, systems programming, and other applications. PL/1 is capable of handling a large variety of data structures and easily allows variation of precision in numeric computation. (A)

plot: to draw or diagram. To connect the point-by-point coordinate values.

plotter: an output unit that presents data in the form of a two-dimensional graphic representation. (A) (B)

plotting: placing any type of information on a graph.

plotting board: an output device that graphs the curves of one or more variables as a function of its input variables.

plug: a little black box used to change each module's generic number.

plugboard: a perforated board into which plugs or pins may be placed to control the operation of equipment. Synonymous with *board, control panel.* (A) (B)

plugboard chart: a chart that shows, for a given job, where plugs must be inserted into a plugboard. Synonymous with *plugging chart.* (B)

plugboard computer: a computer having a punchboard input and output.

plug compatible: any two units operating from the same socket.

plugging chart: synonym for *plugboard chart.* (A)

plug-in: units where connectors are completed using conductors with pins, plugs, sockets, jacks, or other connectors that are easily removed.

plug PROM: a read-only memory diode array programmed by inserting small plugs into edge connectors. Changing a program only requires removing and replacing the plugs.

PM: see *preventive maintenance.*

PNCH: see *punch.*

pneumatic computer: a computer that stores and transmits information by means of the flow rate or pressure of a gas or a liquid.

pocket: a card stacker in a card sorter.

point (PT): see *branchpoint, breakpoint, checkpoint, decimal point, entry point, radix point, reentry point, rerun point, rescue point, restart point.*

pointer (P) (PTR):

(1) an identifier that indicates the location of an item of data. (A)

(2) in computer graphics, a manually operated functional unit used to specify an addressable point. A pointer may be used to conduct interactive graphic operations such as selection of one member of a predetermined set of display elements, or indication of a position on a display space while generating coordinate data.

(3) a physical or symbolic identifier of a unique target.

(4) an arrow or other symbol on the screen that moves as the mouse or other control device moves.

pointer variable: in PL/1, a locator variable with the POINTER attribute, whose value identifies an absolute location in internal storage.

point of invocation: in PL/1, the point in the invoking block at which the procedure reference to the invoked procedure appears.

point of no return: a first instance in a program in which a rerun is no longer possible since data may no longer be available.

point-of-sale terminal: a terminal device which operates as a cash register in addition to transmitting information.

point size: the height of a printed character in points. There are 12 points to a pica, and 72 points to an inch. Font sizes are given in points.

poke: a statement used in BASIC programming language placing data directly into a particular memory location.

polar:
(1) a logic method where a binary one is represented by current flow in one direction and a zero by current flow in the opposite direction.
(2) having poles, as with a magnet.

polarity:
(1) the orientation of any unit having poles or signed electrodes.
(2) a value created by an ungrounded electrode of any grounded direct-current electrical system.
(3) electrical opposition.

polarizing slot: a slot found in the edge of a printed circuit board that can accept a specific type of connector. Synonymous with *index slot*.

polar operation: a circuit operation where the flow of current is reversed as pulses are transmitted.

polar relay: a relay containing a permanent magnet that centers the armature. The direction of movement of the armature is governed by the direction of current flow.

Polish notation: synonym for *prefix notation*. (A) (B)

poll: a flexible, systematic approach centrally controlled to allow stations on a multipoint circuit to transmit without contending for the line.

polling:
(1) interrogation of devices for purposes such as to avoid contention, to determine operational status, or to determine readiness to send or receive data. (A)
(2) see also *addressing, blind, lockout, selection*.

polling characters: a set of characters peculiar to a terminal and the polling operation; response to these characters indicates to the computer whether the terminal has a message to enter.

polling ID: the unique character or characters associated with a particular station.

polymorphic: the mode of a computer organization or configuration of the primary units so that all components at a specific installation are held in a common pool.

polyphase sort: an unbalanced merge sort in which the distribution of sorted subsets is based on a Fibonacci series. (A)

pool: a group of similar peripherals.

pop: synonymous with *pull*.

population: the electronic components on a printed circuit board.

pop-up menu: a menu (usually in a dialog box) in which the selected options are shown next to a solid triangle and inside a box with a shadow around it. The rest of the menu pops-up when the box is pressed. Cf. *pull-down menu*.

port:
(1) a socket on the back panel of the computer where a user can plug in a cable to connect the computer to another device. See *parallel port* and *serial port*.
(2) an access point for data entry or exit. See *terminal port*. Deprecated term for *adapter*.

portability: the ability to use data sets or files with differing operating systems. Volumes whose data sets or files are cataloged in a user catalog can be demounted from storage devices of one system, moved to another system and mounted on storage devices of that system.

portable compilers: apparatus that edits, enters, and compiles programs in a high-level language that is hand-carried from job to job.

portable computer: a computer that can be easily hand-carried and which has similar dimensions to a typewriter. Cf. *briefcase computer, desktop computer, hand-held computer.*

portable data medium: a data medium easily transportable, independently of the mechanism used in its interpretation.

Port-a-punch card: a trademark for a type of punch card with partially perforated punch positions that can be removed with a pen or stylus.

portrait: vertical orientation or a display of printed matter.

POS: see *position.*

position (POS):

(1) a site on a punched tape or card where holes are to be punched.

(2) a place in a program, set of instructions, or within a context.

(3) see *bit position, punch position, sign position.*

positional notation: synonym for *positional representation system.* (A) (B)

positional operand: in assembler programming, an operand in a macroinstruction that assigns a value to the corresponding positional parameter declared in the prototype statement of the called macrodefinition.

positional parameter: a parameter that must appear in a specified location, relative to other parameters. See also *keyword parameter.*

positional representation: a representation of a real number in a positional representation system. (A) (B)

positional representation system: any numeration system in which a real number is represented by an ordered set of characters in such a way that the value contributed by a character depends upon its position as well as upon its value. Synonymous with *positional notation.* (A) (B)

position code: sites in recording media where data can be entered or recorded to standardize locations for coding information.

positioning time: the time interval required to bring a transducer and the location of the required data on a data medium into the relative physical position necessary for the data to be read; for example, the time required to position a head on a magnetic disk, that is, seek time plus the time required for the data to arrive at the head, that is, rotational delay. (B)

positive justification: in time division multiplexing, the insertion of justifying digits into a stream of information bits to create coincidence with a required series of time slots. See also *justification.*

post:

(1) to enter a unit of information on a record.

(2) to note the occurrence of an event.

postamble: a sequence of binary characters recorded at the end of each block on phase-encoded magnetic tape, for the purpose of synchronization when reading backward. (B)

postedit: to edit the results of a previous computation.

postedit program: a test of the application that has been edited, formatted, and sorted into a test result tape.

post fix notation: a method of forming mathematical expressions in which each operator is preceded by its operands and indicates the operation to be performed on the operands or the intermediate results that precede it. Synonymous with *reverse Polish notation, suffix notation.* (B) Cf. *infix notation, prefix notation.* (A)

posting: see *event posting.* (A)

postinstallation evaluation: the evaluation of a computer configuration to see if it fulfills the objectives established at the time of acquisition.

postmortem: pertaining to the analysis of an operation after its completion.

postmortem dump: dumping that is performed at the end of a run, usually for purposes of debugging, auditing, or documentation. (A) (B)

POSTP: see *postprocessor.*

postprocessor (POSTP): a computer program that effects some final computation or organization. (A) (B)

power (P): one of many software packages available to expand system usages and speed.

power check: the automatic halt of a computer when a large fluctuation in internal electrical power takes place.

power down: steps made by a computer when power fails or is shut off in order to preserve the state of the processor and minimize damage to peripherals.

power dump: an accidental removal of all power.

power-fail: an interrupt that occurs when a loss of primary power is found.

power-fail circuit: a logic circuit that protects an operating program if primary power fails by informing the computer that when power failure is about to occur. This begins a routine that saves all volatile data.

power-fail detect module: a device providing an interrupt or flag at least 500 microseconds before a low-power condition is found and program execution is stopped.

power-fail restart: a device that detects a drop in the input voltage and signals an imminent power failure to the computer.

powerful:
(1) software that is efficient and provides a significant range of options.
(2) in user software, the user's ability to put options into action with little difficulty.
(3) in system software, the ability to generate complex commands with minimal instructions.
(4) hardware that is faster, larger, and more versatile than comparable units.

power supply: a unit that converts the line voltage from a wall socket into the voltages needed by the computer elements.

power up: steps taken by a computer when power is turned on or restored following a power failure.

power up diagnostics: programs, usually in ROM, which evaluate the condition of the CPU and memory on power-up.

PP: see *parallel processing.*

PPM: pages per minute.

PPS: pulses per second.

PPT: see *punched paper tape.*

PR:
(1) see *paper tape reader.*
(2) see *physical record.*
(3) see *prefix.*
(4) see *printer.*
(5) see *program register.*

PRAM: see *parameter RAM.*

pragmatics: the relationship of characters or groups of characters to their interpretation and use. (A) (B)

PRE: see *prefix.*

preamble: a sequence of binary architecture recorded at the beginning of each block on a phase-encoded magnetic tape for the purpose of synchronization. (B)

preanalysis: reviewing the tasks to be accomplished by a computer so as to increase the efficiency of that task.

pre-assembly time: the time at which an assembler processes macrodefinitions and performs conditional assembly operations.

precanned programs: programs that are coded by the manufacturer and supplied to the user in a machine-readable form.

precedence code: a code signifying that characters in the following code(s) will have a different meaning from normal.

precedence prosign: a group of characters that indicate how a message is to be handled.

precedence rules: the order in which operations are performed in an expression.

precision:
(1) a measure of the ability to distinguish between nearly equal values. (B)
(2) the degree of discrimination with which a quantity is stated. For example, a three-digit numeral discriminates among 1000 possibilities.
(3) cf. *accuracy.*
(4) see *double precision, multiple precision, triple-precision.* (A)

precision lasers: see *ultimate wafer.*

precoded form: a form on which certain items of invariant data have been entered prior to the entry of variable data. Synonymous with *prerecorded form.*

precompiled module: a standardized program module, utilized by different programs, which has been independently developed and compiled.

precompiler program: a program designed to locate errors and provide source program correction prior to the computation of the object, deck, or program.

predecessor job: a job whose output becomes the input to another job, and which must run to completion before the other job is begun.

predefined process: in flowcharting, a process that is identified only by name and that is defined elsewhere. (A)

predefined specification: the FORTRAN-defined type and length of a variable, based on the initial character of the variable name in the absence of any specification to the contrary. The characters I-N are typed INTEGER*4; the character A-H, O-Z, and $ are typed REAL*4.

predictive control: a control system using a computer for real-time repetitive comparison of pertinent parameters.

preedit: to edit input data prior to computation.

prefix (PR) (PRE):
(1) in PL/1, a label or a parenthesized list of one or more condition names connected by a colon to the beginning of a statement.
(2) a code at the beginning of a message or record.

prefix multiplier: a scale or conversion factor for increasing a basic unit.

prefix notation: a method of forming mathematical expressions in which each operator precedes its operands and indicates the operation to be performed on the operands or the intermediate results that follow it. Synonymous with *Lukasiewicz notation, Polish notation.* (B) Cf. *infix notation, postfix notation.* (A)

prefix operator: in PL/1, an operator that precedes an operand and applies only to that operand.

prenormalize: normalizing the operands of an arithmetic operation before the operation is performed.

preparatory function: a command that alters the mode of operation of a control system from positioning to contouring, or

which calls for a fixed cycle by the machine.

preprocessor:
(1) a computer program that effects some preliminary computation or organization. (A) (B)
(2) a program that examines the source program for preprocessor statements which are then executed, resulting in the alteration of the source program.

preprocessor statement: in PL/1, a special statement appearing in the source program that specifies how the source program text is to be altered; it is identified by a leading percent sign and is executed as it is encountered by the preprocessor (it appears without the percent sign in preprocessor procedures, which are invoked by a preprocessor function reference).

prerecorded form: synonym for *precoded form.*

prerecorded tracks: a preliminary tape, disk, or drum-recorded routine that simplifies programming and allows block and word addressability.

prescanner: a system program that checks for syntax errors as each line of the program is entered into the system.

preselection: in buffered computers, a technique in which a spare block of information is read into memory from whichever input tape will next be called upon; determined by inspecting the keys of the last records of each block of working storage.

presentation control: elements within a system that are crated within the principles of an open systems architecture, and deal with the data formats and transformations needed by end-users.

presentation graphics: in computer graphics, high quantity graphics intended to visually reinforce points made in the presentation of proposals, plans, budgets, and the like, to top management.

presentation level: a protocol governing the way the system translates from digital codes into English, so that real words can be looked at, not just 1s and 0s.

preset: synonymous with *default.*

preset parameter: a parameter that is bound when the computer program is constructed; for example, when it is flowcharted, coded, or compiled.

presort: the first part of a sort, where records are arranged into strings that equal or exceed a minimum length.

press: to hold down the mouse button. Used in the action of dragging to resize or move objects, or to select objects.

pressure sensitive keyboard: see *membrane keyboards.*

prestore: to store, before a computer program, routine, or subroutine is entered, data that are required by the computer program, the routine, or the subroutine. (B) Cf. *initialize.* (A)

presumptive address: the number that shows as an address in a computer instruction, but which is designed to serve as the base, index, initial, or starting point for subsequent addresses to be modified. Synonymous with *reference address.*

presumptive instruction: an instruction that is not an effective instruction until it has been modified in a prescribed manner. (A) (B)

prevarication: synonym for *irrelevance.*

preventive maintenance (PM): maintenance specifically intended to prevent faults from occurring. Corrective maintenance and preventive maintenance are both performed during maintenance time. Cf. *corrective maintenance.* (A)

preventive maintenance time: time, usually scheduled, used to perform preventive maintenance. (A)

previewing: an optical character recognition term to describe a strategy to try and gain initial or prior information about characters that appear on a source document. Usually describes formatting a document for the printer, and displaying it on screen.

prewired options: optional devices that are closely related to the processor, such as the extended arithmetic element, memory extension control, and one of the analog-to-digital converted options, are prewired in the basic computer so that the time, ef-fort, and cost involved in adding these options at the factory or in the field is a minimum.

PRI: see *priority.*

primary: in high-level data-link control (HDLC), the part of the data station that supports the primary control functions of the data link, generates commands for transmission, and interprets received responses. Specific responsibilities assigned to the primary include initialization of control signal interchange, organization of data flow, and actions regarding error control and error recovery functions. Cf. *secondary.*

primary channel: a channel attached to a unit, such as a modem, as the principal path for communication. Cf. *secondary channel.*

primary colors: in computer graphics, a set of colors from which all other colors can be derived, but which cannot be produced from each other. The additive primaries (light) are red, green, and blue. The subtractive primaries (colorant) are yellow, magenta (a deep pink), and cyan (a blue-green). The psychological primaries (perceived as basic and unmixed) are the pairs red/green, yellow/blue, and black/white.

primary entry point: in PL/1, the entry point identified by any of the names in the label list of the PROCEDURE statement.

primary function: the function that allows a data station to exert overall control of the data link according to the link protocol.

primary key: a portion of the first block of each record in an indexed data set that can be used to find the record in the data set. See also *secondary key.*

primary registers: any general-purpose CPU register with an address in assembly language, where data is loaded from memory, acted upon, and written back to memory utilizing program instructions.

primary space allocation: an area of direct-access storage space initially allocated to a particular data set or file when the data set or file is defined.

primary storage unit: synonymous with *internal storage.*

primary store: the main storage method in a computer.

primary track: on a direct-access device, the original track on which data is stored.

prime record key: in COBOL, a key whose contents uniquely identify a record within an indexed file.

primitive element: in computer graphics, a graphic element such as a point or line segment which can be readily called up and extrapolated or combined with other primitive elements to form more complex objects or images in two or three dimensions.

print: synonym for *copy*.

printable item: in COBOL, a data item, the extent and contents of which are specified by an elementary report entry. This elementary report entry contains a COLUMN NUMBER clause, a PICTURE clause, and a SOURCE, SUM, or VALUE clause.

print area: the upper part of the 96-column punched card.

print bar: synonym for *type bar*. (B)

print barrel: synonym for *print drum*. (B)

print contrast ratio: in optical character recognition, the ratio obtained by subtracting the reflectance at an inspection area from the maximum reflectance found within a specified distance from that area, and dividing the result by that maximum reflectance. Cf. *print contrast signal*. (A)

print contrast signal (PCS): in optical character recognition, a measure of the contrast between a printed character and the paper on which the character is printed. Cf. *print contrast ratio*. (A)

print control character: a control character for print operations such as line spacing, page ejection, or carriage return. (A)

print data set: a data set in which programs store data to be printed.

print density: the number of printed characters per unit of measurement on a page.

print drum: a rotating cylinder that presents characters at more than one print position. Synonymous with *print barrel*. (B)

printed card form: the layout or format of the printed matter on a card. The printed matter usually describes the purpose of the card and designates the precise location of card fields. (A)

printed circuit board (PCB) (PC board): an insulating board onto which a circuit has been printed or etched. Synonym for *card, chassis, PC board.*

printer (PR) (PRN) (PRNTR) (PRT) (PRTR) (PTR):
(1) an output device that produces a durable record of data in the form of a sequence of discrete graphic characters belonging to a predetermined character set.
(2) a device that writes output data from a system on paper or other media.
(3) see *bar printer, chain printer, character printer, daisywheel printer, dot matrix, drum printer, fully formed character, ink jet printer, laser printer, line printer, matrix printer, nonimpact printer, on-the-fly printer, page printer, thermal printer.* (A)

printer controller: a high-speed line printer controller that contains the circuitry needed to interface a high volume printing device to a microcomputer.

printer driver: a program that translates the file that is printed into the language the printer understands. A printer cannot be used unless the correct driver is installed on the current start-up disk.

printerfacing: the provision of an interface between microcomputers and output printing terminals.

printer limited: the relatively slow speed of a printer reducing the rate at which processing can occur.

printer operating speed: the rate at which print-out occurs, expressed in characters per second or in words of five recorded characters, including space, per minute.

printer plotter: a printer capable of graphics reproduction in addition to character printing.

printer port: a socket on the computer's back panel marked with a printer icon.

printer skipping: the rate a unit advances a form through its carriage without printing.

printer software: the software that controls the interaction of the computer and the printer. This includes the printer driver and the font software.

printer spacing chart: a form utilized in deciding the format of printed output.

printer speed: the rate at which a unit operates when it is actually printing data.

printer spooler: a program that tracks all of the documents printed, and feeds them to the printer.

print format: a representation of the manner by which data is printed, illustrating column widths, position of page numbers, headings, and so on.

printhead: the device that does the actual printing on some printers.

printing counter: a counter on a magnetic-tape terminal that advances by one for each tape block transmitted or received. Following transmission, the total number of blocks is automatically printed.

printing pitch: see *pitch.*

print line: the normal set of printed characters and spaces placed in a horizontal row as a unit.

print mechanism: any mechanical unit used for printing information from a computer or data terminal.

print-only ticket: a ticket that contains only printed information and does not have a magnetic stripe.

print-out:
(1) in computer technology, the printed output of a computer.
(2) in word processing, the printing or typing of recorded text.

print pool: the area where all printers are placed together.

print position: one of the many positions on a form where a character can be printed.

print queue: a prioritized list maintained by the operating system of all printed output waiting on a spool for output.

print record: a record in a print data set. See also *group (3).*

print record header: identification and control information at the beginning of the first block of a print record.

print speed: the number of characters printed per unit of time.

print through: an undesired transfer of a recorded signal from one part to another part of a recording medium when these parts are brought into contact. (B)

print wheel:
(1) a rotating disk that presents characters at a single print position. Synonymous with *type wheel.* (B)
(2) in word processing an interchangeable printing element, used in some impact printers.

PRIO: see *priority.*

priority (PRI) (PRIO) (PRTY): a rank assigned to a task that determines its precedence in receiving system resources. See also *job priority, time-sharing priority.*

priority number: in COBOL, a number, ranging in value from 0 to 99, which classifies source program sections in the procedure division.

priority polling: in data communications, a polling plan where high-activity nodes are polled more frequently than those with only occasional traffic. Cf. *circular polling.*

priority processing: a method of operating a computer in which computer programs are processed in such a way that the order of operations to be performed is fully determined by a system of priorities. (A)

priority queuing: arranging in sequence according to relative importance.

priority routine: in an interrupt, the leaving of one program by the processor to work on the program connected with the interrupt or the priority routine.

priority scheduler: a form of job scheduler that uses input and output work queues to improve system performance.

priority scheduling system: a job scheduler, in larger systems, that have a resultant improved system performance attained by means of input/output queues.

priority structure: the organization of a system for processing.

private address space: an address space assigned to a particular user.

private library: a user-owned library that is separate and distinct from the system library.

private network: a network formed and operated for the total use of a specific organization or group of users.

privilege: see *access privileges.*

privilege class: authorization to a specific program to use privileged instructions.

privileged instruction:
(1) an instruction that may be used only by a supervisory program. (A) (B)
(2) an instruction that can be executed only when the processing unit is in the supervisor state.

privileged mode: a mode of operation in which privileged instructions can be executed. Should a privileged instruction be encountered when the computer is not in a privileged mode, an interrupt can occur or the instruction can be ignored.

PRN: see *printer.*

PRNTR: see *printer.*

probability of failure: the measure of the reliability of equipment that is expressed as the probability of the apparatus failing over a stated time period.

probability theory: the mathematical characterization of uncertainty. As most real world decisions involve elements of uncertainty (about future events or uncontrollable influences) such uncertainties need to be explicitly incorporated into decision analyses.

problem data: in PL/1, a string or arithmetic data that is processed by a PL/1 program.

problem definition: the presentation of a problem for computer solution in a structured, logical fashion.

problem description: a statement of problem, perhaps including a description of the method of solving it, procedures, and algorithms. (A) (B)

problem determination: the process of identifying the source of a problem; for example, a program component, a machine failure, telecommunication facilities, user- or contractor-installed programs or equipment, an environment failure such as a power loss, or a user error.

problem determination aid (PDAID): a program that traces a specified event when it occurs during the operation of a program.

problem diagnosis: analysis that results in identifying the precise cause of a hardware, software, or system failure.

problem file: all the material required to document a program to be run on a computer.

problem identification: determining the source of an error within a program or a malfunction in hardware.

problem input tape: an input tape, either punched paper tape or magnetic tape, that contains problem data for checking out a given computer system.

problem language: a language used by a programmer in stating the definition of the problem.

problem-oriented language: a programming language that is especially suitable for a given class of problems. Procedure-oriented languages such as FORTRAN, ALGOL; simulation languages such as GPSS, SIMSCRIPT; list processing languages such as LISP, IPL-V; information retrieval languages. (B) Synonym for *application-oriented language.*

problem program: any program that is executed when the processing unit is in the problem state; that is, any program that does not contain privileged instructions.

problem state: a state during which the processing unit cannot execute input/output and other privileged instructions.

problem statement: a statement describing a problem to be solved by an algorithm.

problem time: in simulation, the duration of a process, or the length of time between two specified events of a process. (A)

PROC:
(1) see *procedure.*
(2) see *processing.*
(3) see *processor.*

procedural language: synonym for *procedure-oriented language.* (A) (B)

procedural statement: synonym for *instruction.*

procedure (P) (PROC):
(1) the course of action taken for the solution of a problem. (B)

(2) the description of the course of action taken for the solution of a problem. (A)

(3) a sequenced set of statements that may be used at one or more points in one or more computer programs, and that usually has one or more input parameters and yields one or more output parameters.

(4) the actions taken to implement protocols.

(5) in PL/1, a collection of statements, headed by a PROCEDURE statement and ended by an END statement, that is part of a program, that delimits the scope of names, and that is activated by a reference to one of its entry names.

(5) see *cataloged procedure, in-line procedure.*

procedure division (PD): one of the four main component parts of a COBOL program. The procedure division contains instructions for solving a problem. The procedure division may contain imperative statements, conditional statements, paragraphs, procedures, and sections.

procedure library (PROCLIB): a program library in direct-access storage containing job definitions. The reader/interpreter can be directed to read and interpret a particular job definition by an execute statement in the input stream.

procedure model: the functions provided in a given system and the needed behavior of elements within the system.

procedure name: in COBOL, a word that precedes and identifies a procedure, used by the programmer to transfer control from one point of the program to another.

procedure-oriented language: a programming language that allows the user to express the solution to a problem as an explicit algorithm; for example, FORTRAN, ALGOL, COBOL, PL/1. Synonymous with *procedural language.*

procedure reference: in PL/1, an entry constant or variable or a built-in function name followed by none or more argument lists. It may appear in a CALL statement or CALL option or as a function reference.

procedures analysis: see *systems analysis.*

procedure statement: a declaration used to assign a name to a procedure. Synonymous with *subroutine statement.*

procedure step: a unit of work associated with one processing program and related data within a cataloged or in-stream procedure. A cataloged procedure consists of one or more procedure steps.

procedure subprogram: a function or subroutine subprogram.

process (P):

(1) a systematic sequence of operations to produce a specified result. (A)

(2) in a computer system, a unique, finite course of events defined by its purpose or by its effect, achieved under given conditions.

(3) an executing function, or a function that is waiting to be executed.

(4) to perform operations on data in a process. (B)

(5) see *input process, output process, predefined process.*

processable scored card: a scored card including at least one separable part that can be processed after separation. (A)

process-bound: a condition that occurs when a program monopolizes the processing facilities of the computer, making it impossible for other programs to be executed.

process chart: synonymous with *systems flowchart.*

process check: synonym for *program execption.*

process control compiler: a compiler for programming PROMs using a process control language or machine language. The compiler accepts keyboard entry of data, displays it for editing, compiles the program, and loads it into the PROM chips.

process control language (PCL): a language, similar to FORTRAN that permits a control program to be created in English, which is then entered using a keyboard and converted into machine language for storage in a PROM.

process controller: a computer that controls the process to which it is connected and executes machine language programs to fulfill this control.

process control loop: a complete process control system where computers are used for the automatic control and regulation of processes and operations.

process exception: synonym for *program exception.*

processing (PROC): the performance of logical operations and calculations on data, including the temporary retention of data in processor storage while it is being operated upon. See *administrative data processing, automatic data processing, background processing, batch processing, business data processing, data processing, distributed data processing, electronic data processing, foreground processing, industrial data processing, integrated data processing, list processing, multiprocessing, parallel processing, priority processing, real-time processing, remote-access data processing, remote batch processing, sequential batch processing, serial processing.*

processing capacity: pertaining to a calculation that is usually the maximum limitation of places of a number that can be processed at any one time, for example, a 12-place number.

processing logic: rules designed for operation of a stated application or system function and realized by hardware, software, or a combination of both.

processing multithread: a sequence of events in programs needed for the computer processing of a message known as a thread. In multithread processing, message threads are handled in parallel.

processing program: a program that performs such functions as compiling, assembling, or translating for a particular programming language.

processing section: the part of a computer that changes input data into output data.

processing symbol: a rectangular figure used in flowcharts to indicate a processing operation (e.g., a calculation).

processing system: see *data-processing system.* (A)

process interrupt card: a card that provides a means by which a user, or processes that the user specifies, can generate interrupts and request service on a priority basis.

process loop test: a check to determine if there is a need for loop operations.

process optimization: an extensive process-controller program, based on the model of the process, directs the data acquisition and control system. Processed data is continuously collected and analyzed for computation of optimum operating instructions, which are given to the process operator via an on-line typewriter.

processor (P) (PROC):

(1) in a computer, a functional unit that interprets and executes instructions. (B)

(2) a functional unit, part of another unit such as a terminal or a processing unit, that interprets and executes instructions.

(3) deprecated term for *processing program.*

(4) the computer hardware component that performs the computations directed by software commands. In microcomputers, the processor is a single integrated circuit called a microprocessor.

(5) see *central processor, data processor, host processor, language processor, multiprocessor.*

(6) see also *processing.*

processor basic instructions: processor modules that execute basic instructions grouped into categories—register operations, accumulator operations, program counter and stack control operations, input-output operations, machine operations.

processor bound: computation where the internal processor speed is the limiting resource for programs.

processor complex: when multiple central processors work together within a single housing.

processor error interrupt: occurs if a word accessed in any portion of the system is found to contain incorrect check bits, or if an error occurs in the addressing of a memory location.

processor evaluation module: a circuit card containing all the needed components of a computer.

processor front-end: a small computer that serves as a line controller for a larger processor.

processor interface: the transfer of data between a processor and the standard communication subsystem. The transfer takes place through input data leads, connected to the processor input channel, and output data leads, connected to the processor output channel.

processor limited: a system condition occurring when the time taken to finish a process is dictated by the time taken by the central processor rather than the time taken by peripheral units. Cf. *peripheral limited.*

processor module: the circuit card containing the microprocessor along with the logic and control circuitry needed to operate as a processing unit.

processor organization: the three main sections of a computer—arithmetic and control, input-output, and memory.

processor status word: synonymous with *program status word.*

processor storage:
(1) the storage provided by one or more processing units.
(2) in virtual storage systems, synonymous with *real storage.*

processor transfer time: the time needed for data transfer.

processor verbs: verbs that specify to the processor the procedures by which a source program is to be translated into an object program. These verbs do not cause action at object time.

process time: time used for translating a source program into an object program through the action of a processor program and the computer.

PROCLIB: see *procedure library.*

product: the number or quantity that results from a multiplication. (A) (B)

product area: an area in main storage that stores results of multiplication operations specifically.

production control: in computers, a data acquisition system from the floor of a product in line or process for the speed up and simplification of the flow of production information for management.

production program: a program executed at regular intervals, such as a payroll program.

production routine: a routine that produces the results of the problem or program as it was designed, as contrasted with the routines which are designed for support, housekeeping, or to compile, assemble, translate, and so on.

production run: an operational run of a fully tested and proven system.

production time: that part of operating time that is neither development time nor makeup time. (A)

productive time: fault-free time of uninterrupted production runs.

productivity: see *system productivity.*

PROG:
(1) see *program.*
(2) see *programmer.*

program (P) (PGM) (PROG):
(1) to design, write, and test programs.
(2) in word processing, a set of instructions incorporated into the design of the equipment, read in from a recording medium, or entered by an operator, that enables the equipment to perform tasks without further intervention by the operator.
(3) a set of actions or instructions that a machine is capable of interpreting and executing.
(4) a set of instructions describing actions for a computer to perform to accomplish a task, conforming to the rules and conventions of a particular programming language. Computer programs are collectively referred to as software. See *application program.*
(5) see *assembly program, checking program, computer program, control program, diagnostic program, editor program, input program, library program, monitor program, object program, output program, relocatable program, reusable program, self-adapting program, snapshot program,*

sort program, source program, supervisory program, target program, trace program, translating program, utility program.
(6) deprecated term for *routine.* (B)

program access (PA) key: on a display device keyboard, a key that produces a call to a program that performs display operations. See also *program function (PF) key.*

program address counter: synonymous with *instruction register.*

program address register: a register holding the instruction location to be transmitted to the control ROM.

program area block: synonymous with *program block.*

programatics: pertaining to the study that deals with the techniques of programming and programming languages.

program attention key: on a display device keyboard, a key that produces an interruption to solicit program action. See also *program access (PA) key, program function (PF) key.*

program block: in problem-oriented languages, a computer program subdivision that serves to group related statements, delimit routines, specify storage allocation, delineate the applicability of labels, or segment parts of the computer program for other purposes. (A) Synonym for *program area block.*

program breakpoint: a location where the execution of a program is halted to allow visual check, printing out, or other performance analysis.

program cards: punched cards with program instructions; usually with one instruction per card.

program chaining: a method for permitting programs to be run that are larger than main memory, by sequential loading and executing of successive modules of that program.

program check: a condition that occurs when programming errors are detected by an I/O channel.

program check interruption: caused by a condition encountered in a program, such as incorrect operands.

program checkout: a run-through of a program to determine if all designs and results of a program are as anticipated.

program compatibility: the result of portability, when a program is run on two different computers.

program compilation: the process of employing a compiler.

program control: pertaining to the act of organizing the activities of a device on line to a central processor.

program control data: data used in a PL/1 program to effect the execution of the program, that is, any data that is not string or arithmetic data.

program-controlled interruption (PCI): an interruption that occurs when an I/O channel fetches a CCW with the program-controlled interruption flag on.

program controller: the central processor unit that organizes the execution of instructions. Synonymous with *program control unit.*

program control unit (PCU): synonymous with *program controller.*

program counter (PC): a specific CPU register that holds the address value of the memory location where the following CPU directive is to be obtained.

program crash: occurs when a computer program in attempting to execute an impossible instruction has no means of recognizing the impossibility and stopping.

program data set (PDS): the data set on disk storage that contains user programs to be executed.

program development: the preparation of computer programs for carrying out a host of applications.

program development time: that part of operating time that is used for debugging. (A)

program documentation: a vital part of programming, an approach used by machine operators for changing programs, training people how to run programs and handle problems should they occur.

program drum: a revolving cylinder on which a program card is attached.

program error: a mistake found in the program code.

Program Evaluation and Review Technique: see *PERT.*

program event recording (PER): a hardware feature used to assist in debugging programs by detecting and recording program events.

program exception: the condition recognized by a processor that results from execution of a program that improperly specifies or uses instructions, operands, or control information. Synonymous with *process check, process exception.*

program execution time: the interval during which the instructions of an object program are executed. (A)

program fetch time: the time at which a program in the form of load modules or phases is loaded into main storage for execution.

program file: a system that is easily updated and flexible and used for the maintenance of the entire software library.

program flowchart: a visual representation of a computer problem where machine instructions or groups of instructions are shown by symbols.

program function (PF) key: on a display device keyboard, a key that passes a signal to a program to call for a particular display operation. See also *program access (PA) key.*

program-generated parameter: a parameter that is bound during the execution of a computer program. Synonymous with *dynamic parameter.* (A) (B)

program generation system (PGS): a system allowing the user to output selected areas of memory in object-program format and load programs into memory.

program generator (PG): a program that allows a computer to write other programs automatically.

program halt: a halt in a program that occurs when the program meets a halt instruction. Synonymous with *coded stop.*

program-independent modularity: the property of a system that permits it to accept changes and adjust processing to yield maximum usage of all modules without reprogramming.

program instruction:

(1) in word processing, an instruction code which, when read, causes one or more functions to operate automatically.

(2) control codes stored on the recording media or in the processing device, causing the machine to respond as desired.

program interruption (PI): the suspension of the execution of a program because of a program exception.

program level: in the network control program, an order of operational priorities established by the communication controller hardware; the five levels operate similarly to subroutines, are responsible for particular phases of system operation, and become active by interruptions to the individual levels.

program library (PL) (PLIB):

(1) a collection of available computer programs and routines. (A)

(2) an organized collection of computer programs that are sufficiently documented to allow them to be used by persons other than their authors. (B)

(3) synonym for *partitioned data set.*

program line: a single instruction written on a standard coding form and stored as a single entity.

program linking:

(1) the ability of an application program to exchange information directly with another program over a network. To use program linking, both programs must have the capability.

(2) when a program is too large to be stored in memory, it can be divided into links by means of a FORTRAN link statement. During run time, routines in the monitory system automatically handle the execution of the segments of the linked program.

program loader: see *initial program loader, loader.*

program loading routine: a procedure for inserting instructions and the constant values of the program into the computer.

program logic array (PLA): the area of a chip responsible for implementing the decoding of instructions and the logic control activities.

programmable communications interface: synonymous with *universal syn-*

chronous-asynchronous receiver/trans-mitter.

programmable communications processor: a device that relieves the CPU of the task of monitoring data transmissions.

programmable data control unit: front-end systems that are FORTRAN-written application software-control communication systems. These systems preformat messages to a format of the host processor and maintain disk files for message queuing and system backup.

programmable function key: a feature allowing a user to key in a program and assign it to a function key and also display the program and edit it using normal terminal functions.

programmable input-output chip: an input-output chip, often an eight-bit interface chip that multiplexes one connection to the data bus into two or more eight-bit ports.

programmable interval time: a chip with a separate clock and several registers used to count time independently of the microprocessor, for real-time applications. At the end of a time period, it sets a flag or generates an interrupt, or merely stores the time elapsed.

programmable key: a key that is programmed, so that when pressed, the word processor carries out a function that otherwise might require a sequence of three or four keys.

programmable logic: systems that provide logic functions that can be changed by a user. See *logic array.*

programmable logic array: a general-purpose logic circuit that contains an array of logic gates that are connected to perform various functions. Synonymous with *re-programmable associative ROM.*

programmable memory: memory with locations that are addressable by the program counter.

programmable point-of-sale terminal: a terminal that has a read-only microprogram memory.

programmable read-only memory (PROM): an integrated circuit of read-only memory that can be programmed by a user; for example, following manufacture, by means of a hardware device known as a PROM programmer. See *programmer unit.* See *EPROM.*

programmable read-only memory blaster: a device for changing the protected read-only memory section found in some PROMs, allowing the entire PROM to be changed by the user.

programmable remote display terminal: a typical programmable display terminal with a microprocessor to function as an intelligent remote terminal station or as a cluster of stations. It is used for the entry of data, data processing, control and monitoring, conversational interaction and off-line operation.

programmable storage:
(1) storage that can be addressed by an application programmer.
(2) the portion of internal storage in a communication controller in which user-written programs are executed. Cf. *control storage.*

programmable terminal (PT): a user terminal that has computational capability. Synonymous with *intelligent terminal.*

programmable unit: hardware that operates under the influence of a storage program, whose programs can be changed or replaced by the user.

program maintenance: keeping programs up to date by correcting errors, making alterations as requirements change and changing the programs to take advantage of new units.

programmed check: a check procedure that is part of a computer program. Cf. *automatic check.* (A)

programmed computer: synonym for *stored program computer.* (A) (B)

programmed dump: a library subroutine called by object programs at run time, returning control to the calling program or to the monitor following completion.

programmed instructions: subroutines used as if they were single commands by using one of the programmed instructions of the system repertoire, allowing a programmer's own special commands to be self-defined through the use of subroutines that can be altered by the operating routine if desired.

programmed operators system (SYS-POP): a function making monitor mode service routines available to user mode programs without loss of system control or use of user memory space.

programmer (PROGR): a person who designs, writes, and tests computer programs. (A)

programmer analyst: a computer specialist who defines problems by performing limited systems analysis as well as writing the programs.

programmer control panel: a panel that supplies access to the CPU registers and memory.

programmer-defined macro: a macroinstruction used in a program and is defined by a programmer at the commencement of a specific program.

programmer/duplicator: a typical device contains a master control unit and a plug in PROM personality module. When connected it can be commanded to program, list, duplicate, and verify PROMs.

programmer's template: a pattern guide having flowchart, logic, and other symbols used in programming.

programmer unit: a hardware unit that provides the means for programming PROM, using a control program that permits instructions to be blown and verified.

programming: the designing, writing, and testing of programs. (B) See *automatic programming, convex programming, dynamic programming, integer programming, linear programming, macroprogramming, mathematical programming, minimum delay programming, multiprogramming, non-linear programming, quadratic programming.* Synonymous with *software engineering.* (A)

programming audit: a program enabling the employment of a computer as an auditing tool.

programming compatibility: systems that can be augmented and increased in power as required.

programming flowchart: a flowchart representing the sequence of operation in a computer program. Synonymous with *programming flow diagram.* (A)

programming flow diagram: synonym for *programming flowchart.* (A) (B)

programming language (PL):
(1) an artificial language established for expressing computer programs. Each language has a vocabulary of keywords, and a syntax for programming instructions. (B)
(2) a set of characters and rules, with meanings assigned prior to their use, for writing computer programs.

Programming Language: see *PL/1.*

programming manager: a person responsible for planning, scheduling, and supervising program development and maintenance work.

programming module: a discrete identifiable set of instructions, usually handled as a unit by an assembler, a compiler, a linkage editor, a loading routine, or other type of routine or subroutine. (A)

programming statement: one of a set of symbolic expressions used to write programs. (A)

programming system (PS): one or more programming languages and the necessary software for using these languages with particular automatic data-processing equipment.

program mode: a program that is active at a given terminal, where the terminal is now in the program mode. In this mode the user enters program statements that make up the substance of his program.

program module: programming instructions that are treated as a unit by an assembler, compiler, loader, or translator.

program-name: in COBOL, a user-defined word that identifies a COBOL source program.

program origin: see *computer program origin.* (A)

program package: a group or collection of logically related operational program segments; that is, all those having to do with the processing of a certain type of inquiry.

program parameter: see *external-program parameter.* (A)

program postedit: a test of the application or operational program that is edited, formatted, and sorted into a test result tape.

program preparation: conversion of programs from one of several easy-to-use source languages, or from certain competitive system languages, to a machine code.

program product: a copyrighted (or otherwise protected) program supplied by a vendor for a change.

program read-in: the procedure and means of developing, by either hardware or software approaches, programs that do not normally reside in main memory and that must be read in from auxiliary storage when required for processing. Such techniques are needed in systems that cannot retain all computer instructions in main memory at one time.

program reference table (PRT): an area of memory for storage of operands or references to arrays, files, or segments of the program, permitting programs to be independent of the actual memory locations occupied by data and parts of the program.

program register (PR): synonymous with *instruction register.*

program relocation: the execution of a program in a location that is different from the location for which the program was originally assembled.

program runs: the actual running of a program. Programs and runs are synonymous except to show the time and action being performed. Cf. *program.*

program scheduler: a scheduler used to determine which program in memory is to be run, dumped, terminated, and so forth.

program segment: computer instructions set in groups of an artificially fixed size to fit into standard-sized areas of main storage to aid memory allocation and program read-in.

program segmenting: programs that do not fit into memory are segmented by using a source-language linking statement, allowing sections of the program to be loaded and executed independently.

program selection:

(1) selection of a particular program for operation.

(2) a function that identifies and actuates a particular program for operation.

program selector: in word processing, a control by means of which a particular machine program is selected for operation.

program-sensitive fault: a fault that occurs as a result of some particular sequence of program steps. Cf. *pattern-sensitive fault.* (A)

program sensitive malfunction: a malfunction that occurs only during some unusual combination of program steps.

program specification: a full definition of the processes and steps carried out by a program, acting as the basis of work for a programmer.

program stack: a dedicated memory portion for providing multiple-level nesting capability.

program statement: the basic unit used for constructing programs.

program status word (PSW): an area in storage used to indicate the order in which instructions are executed, and to hold and indicate the status of the computer system. Synonymous with *processor status word.*

program step: a single operation within a program; frequently an instruction.

program stop: a stop instruction within a machine that automatically stops the machine upon reaching the end of processing, completing a solution, or under another condition.

program storage: where a program is secured within main memory.

program tape: a tape containing the sequence of instruction needed for solving a problem, and which is read into the computer prior to running a program.

program test: running of a sample problem with a given answer so as to uncover errors in a program.

program testing: running a program with test data so as to verify that it is properly performing expected operations.

program testing time: machine time expanded for program testing, debugging, and volume and compatibility testing.

program trace: a report that identifies the flow of execution through a computer program, to show each statement that was executed and the order in which it occurred.

program translation: translation from a source language program to a target program; for example, from FORTRAN to machine language.

program unit: in FORTRAN, a main program or a subprogram.

program verbs: verbs that cause the processor to generate machine instructions that are executed by the object program.

progressive overflow: on a direct-access storage device, the writing of overflow records on the next consecutive track. Cf. *chaining overflow.*

prolog: in PL/1, the processes that occur automatically on a block activation.

PROM: see *programmable read-only memory.*

PROM blower: see *blow, programmer unit.*

PROM burner: synonymous with *PROM blower.* See *blow, programmer unit.*

PROM monitor: a program stored in PROM allowing the computer to be programmed using a simple keyboard.

PROM programmer: a device capable of programming PROMs, usually with a teletypewriter or keypad.

PROM programmer card: a card permitting blocks of memory to be automatically programmed into PROM.

prompt: any message presented to an operator by an operating system, indicating that particular information is needed before a program can proceed.

prompt character: a character displayed by the computer to solicit a response from the user. Generally used as a request for input.

prompt facility: a facility that assists a terminal operator by displaying messages that describe required input or giving operational information.

PROM simulator: a unit using RAM for testing and debugging operations prior to PROM programming.

proof copy mode: a printer's ability to make a proof copy with notations, highlighting, or symbols to mark revisions.

proof list: a printout giving instructions and narrative as originally prepared and the object code resulting from them.

proofreader: synonymous with *dictionary.*

propagate: passing through a system from one component to another.

propagated error: an error that takes place in a single operation as a result of a propagating error in another operation.

propagating error: an error that takes place in a single operation and results in other operations.

proper subset: a subset that does not include all the elements of the set. (A) (B)

property detector: pertaining to a component of a character reader that has the normalized signal for the use in extracting a set of characteristic properties or characteristics on the basis of which a character can be identified as it comes along.

proportionally spaced font: any font in which different characters have different widths; thus the space taken up by words having the same number of letters varies. For example, the letter M is wider than the letter I, so that MMMMM produces a wider string than IIIII. Cf. *monospaced font.*

proportional pitch: see *proportionally spaced font.*

proprietary program: the development of a program, controlled by an owner through the legal right of possession and title.

proprietary software: the programming software, libraries, and other nonhardware operating aids in a computer system, not furnished by the manufacturer, but originated by the user or firms engaged in the development and sales of software systems.

prosthetic: a computer's use as a versatile tool, providing access to a large variety of inaccessible spaces and activities.

protected field:

(1) in word processing, preset data or an area that cannot be modified or overridden by the operator without altering the program.

(2) on a display device, a display field in which the user cannot enter, modify, or erase data. Cf. *unprotected field.*

protected formatting: a strategy that allows a computer to write protected data on the screen. The operator fills in the blank (unprotected) areas but cannot alter the protected data, format, or programming.

protected free storage: see *free storage.*

protected mode: in IBM PCs and compatibles, encompasses the following memory features: *protection, extended memory, virtual memory, multitasking.*

protected storage: storage that cannot be accessed without certain specified keys.

protection: an arrangement for restricting access to or use of all, or part of, a data-processing system. Synonymous with *lockout.* See *storage protection.*

protection key: an indicator that appears in the current program status word whenever an associated task has control of the system; this indicator must match the storage keys of all main storage blocks that the task is to use. Synonymous with *storage protection key.*

protective ground: a pin on an interface for a modem, used to ground the modem.

protocol: a specification for the format and relative timing of information exchanged between communicating parties. Synonymous with *line control discipline, line discipline.*

protocol converter: a device for translating the data transmission code of one computer or peripheral to the data transmission code of another computer or peripheral, enabling equipment with different data formats to communicate with one another.

prototype statement: synonym for *macroprototype statement.*

proving: testing a machine to show that it is free from faults, frequently following corrective maintenance.

PRT: see *program reference table.*

PRTY: see *priority.*

PS:
(1) see *picosecond.*
(2) see *programming system.*

PS/2: IBM's Personal System/2 generation of PC's.

psec: see *picosecond.*

pseudoapplication program: an operational program that is written to test supervisory programs.

pseudoclock: a main storage location used by timer supervision routines to calculate timer intervals and time of day.

pseudocode: a code that requires translation prior to execution. (A)

pseudocolors: in computer graphics, color arbitrarily assigned to an image to represent data values, rather than natural likeness. Often used in satellite imagery. Synonymous with *false colors.*

pseudocursor: in computer graphics, a symbol that simulates the operation of a cursor on a display.

pseudodrives: synonymous with *E-disks.*

pseudofile address: using a false address by an application program to obtain a record from file. The pseudoaddress is converted by the supervisory program into an actual machine address.

pseudoinstruction: deprecated term for *declaration.* (A) (B)

pseudolanguage: an artificial, uniquely designed to perform a distinct activity, that is, a special set of rules is devised with particular meanings assigned to chosen expressions.

pseudo-OP: short for *pseudooperation.*

pseudooperation: an operation controlling the action of an assembler. Often shortened to *pseudo-OP.*

pseudopaging: a way of viewing memory locations where programmers refer to memory address as being organized into blocks of words referred to as "pages" for reference purposes only.

pseudorandom number sequence: an ordered set of numbers that has been determined by some defined arithmetic process but is effectively a random number sequence for the purpose for which it is required. (A) (B)

pseudovariable: in PL/1, any of the built-in function names that can be used to specify a target variable.

PSW: see *program status word.*

p-system: a software system that translates p-code into the machine language appropriate to a particular CPU.

PT:

(1) see *paper tape.*

(2) see *point.*

(3) see *programmable terminal.*

PTR:

(1) see *paper tape reader.*

(2) see *pointer.*

(3) see *printer.*

public domain software: software not copyrighted, and freely exchanged and copied.

puffer: in computer statistics, to invent or manipulate data to prove one's theory or to give one advantage over another.

pull: removing an element from a stack. Cf. *push.* Synonymous with *pop.*

pull down: in micrographics, the length of film advanced after each exposure.

pull-down menu: a menu (usually in the menu bar) whose name or icon is shown. The menu is pulled down by pressing the name or icon. Cf. *pop-up menu.*

pull operation: an operation where operands are taken from the top of a pushdown stack in memory and placed in general registers.

pulse: a variation in the value of a quantity, short in relation to the time schedule of interest, the final value being the same as the initial value. See *clock pulse, synchronization pulses.* (A)

pulse code: a code where digits are represented by means of sets of pulses.

pulse digit: a drive pulse corresponding to a logical 1-digit position in some or all of the words within a storage unit.

pulse-double recording: a specific method for magnetic recording of bits in which each storage cell comprises two regions magnetized in opposite senses with unmagnetized regions on each side.

pulse stretcher: a circuit that can extend the length of a pulse.

PUN: see *punch.*

punch (P) (PUN) (PCH) (PNCH):

(1) a perforation, as in a punched card or paper tape. (A)

(2) a device for making holes in a data carrier.

(3) a device that interprets coded electrical signals so as to produce the holes in cards or tapes.

(4) see *automatic-feed punch, calculating punch, card punch, digit punch, eleven punch, gang punch, hand-feed punch, keyboard punch, keypunch, numeric punch, reproducing punch, spot punch, summary punch, twelve punch, zone punch.* (A)

punch area: the lower part of the 96-column punched card.

punch card: a card into which hole patterns can be punched. See *Hollerith card.* (A)

punch column:

(1) a line of punch positions parallel to the Y-datum line of a card.

(2) a line of punch positions along a card column. (A)

punched card:

(1) a card punched with hole patterns. (A)

(2) in word processing, a card on which text and program instructions are represented by rows of punched holes.

(3) see *Hollerith card.* (A)

punched card reader: synonym for *card reader.* (A)

punched-card verifier: equipment that ensures that data punched into cards is the same as the data on original documents from which it was drawn.

punched paper tape (PPT): a strip of paper on which characters are represented by combinations of holes punched across the strip.

punched tape:

(1) a tape punched with hole patterns. Synonymous with *perforated tape.*

(2) in word processing, a tape, usually of paper, on which text and program instructions are represented by rows of punched holes.

punched tape code: a code used to represent data on punched tape. Synonymous with *paper tape code, perforated tape code.*

punched tape machine: any tape punch that automatically converts coded electrical signals into perforations in tape.

punched tape reader: a device that reads or senses the hole patterns in a punched tape, transforming the data from the hole patterns to electrical signals. Synonymous with *perforated-tape reader.*

punching: see *interstage punching.*

punching position: synonym for *punch position.* (A) (B)

punching station: the place in a card track where a punch card is punched. (A) Synonymous with *punch station.*

punch path: in a punch, a path that has a punch station. (B)

punch position: a defined location on a data carrier where a hole may be punched to record data. Synonymous with *code position, punching position.* (B)

punch row: a line of punch positions along a card row. (A)

punch station: synonym for *punching station.*

punch tape: a tape in which hole patterns can be punched. (B)

punch tape code: a code used to represent data on punch tape. (B)

punctuation character: in COBOL, a comma, semicolon, period, quotation mark, left or right parenthesis, or space.

punctuation symbol: synonym for *delimiter.* (A)

pure binary numeration system: the fixed-radix numeration system that uses the binary digits and the radix 2; for example, in this numeration system, the numeral 110.01 represents the number "six and one quarter," that is, $1 \times 2^2 + 1 \times 2^1 + 1 \times 2^{-2}$. Synonymous with *binary numeration system.* (A) (B)

pure generator: a routine able to write another routine. The pure generator can be a section of a program in an assembler on a library tape and can then be called by the assembler to perform.

pure machine-aided translation: where the lexicons of two or more languages are computerized to supply a human translator with target language equivalents of source language lexical items.

pure machine translation: a machine translation system where the computer attempts the total translation itself.

purge date: a date written to a data medium on or following when the file is released and the data may be overwritten by more recent data.

push: adding an element to a stock. Cf. *pull.* Synonymous with *put.*

push-down: a last-in, first-out method of queuing where the last item attached to the queue is the first to be withdrawn.

push-down list: a list that is constructed and maintained so that the next item to be retrieved and removed is the most recently stored item still in the list, that is, last-in, first-out. (B) Synonymous with *stack.* (A)

push-down queue: a last-in, first-out (LIFO) method of queuing in which the last item attached to the queue is the first to be withdrawn. See *LIFO.*

push-down stack: synonym for *push-down list.*

push-down storage: a storage device that handles data in such a way that the next item to be retrieved is the most recently stored item still in the storage device, that is, last-in, first-out (LIFO). Synonymous with *push-down store.* (A) (B)

push-down store: synonym with *push-down storage.* (A) (B)

pushing: see *stack architecture.*

push-pin: an item at the top of a menu that allows the menu to be pinned, so it stays open and can be moved around the workspace.

push-up list: a list that is constructed and maintained so that the next item to be retrieved is the earliest stored item still in the list, that is, first-in, first-out (FIFO). (A) (B)

push-up storage: a storage device that handles data in such a way that the next item to be retrieved is the earliest stored item still in the storage device, that is, first-in, first-out (FIFO). Synonymous with *push-up store.* (A) (B)

push-up store: synonym for *push-up storage.* (A) (B)

put: to place a single data record into an output file.

put-away: a memory location in which the processor stores specific information.

PW: see *password.*

PWR: abbreviation for *power.* See *power.*

Q:
(1) see *query.*
(2) see *queue.*
(3) see *quotient.*
(4) a register used as an accumulator extension, needed for efficient multiply-divide programming.

QA: see *quality assurance.*

Q address: a source location in internal storage in some devices from which data is transferred.

QBE: see *query by example.*

QCB: see *queue control block.*

QEL: see *quality element.*

QIC: quarter-inch cartridge.

QISAM: see *queued indexed sequential access method.*

Q output: the reference output of a flip-flop.

QR: see *quotient.*

QSAM: see *queued sequential access method.*

QT: see *quotient.*

Q test: a test or comparison of two or more units of quantitative data for nonequality or equality.

quad capacity: a floppy disk with double-density, double-sided recording characteristics to achieve greater storage per disk.

quad density: the storage density of a disk medium; storing four times the amount of information per disk as single density.

quadratic programming: in operations research, a particular case of nonlinear programming in which the function to be maximized or minimized is a quadratic function and the constraints are linear functions. (B) Cf. *convex programming, dynamic programming, integer programming, linear programming, mathematical programming, minimum delay programming, nonlinear programming.* (A)

quadrature: expresses the phase relationship between two periodic quantities of the same period when the phase difference between them is one fourth of a period.

quadripuntal: pertaining to four punches, specifically, having four random punches on a punched card; used in determinative documentation.

quadruple-length register: four registers that function as a single register. Each register may be individually accessed. Synonymous with *quadruple register.* (A) (B)

quadruple register: synonym for *quadruple-length register.* (A) (B)

qualification: in COBOL, the making a name unique by adding IN or OF and another name, according to defined rules and procedures.

qualification testing: the testing of programs, equipment, or systems before delivery to a customer.

qualified name:
(1) a data name explicitly accompanied by a specification of the class to which it belongs in a specified classification system. (A) (B)
(2) in PL/1, a hierarchical sequence of names of structure members, connected by periods, used to identify a component of a structure. Any of the names may be subscripted. See also *locator qualification.*

qualifier:
(1) all names in a qualified name other than the rightmost, which is called the simple name.
(2) in COBOL, a group data name that is used to refer to a nonunique data name at a lower level in the same hierarchy, or a section name at a lower level in the same hierarchy, or a section name that is used to refer to a nonunique paragraph. In this way, the data name or the paragraph name can be made unique.

quality assurance (QA): a system of measurement and planning approaches purporting to improve the performance of data-processing operations.

quality control: where systematic and regular reviews of the timeliness, accuracy, completeness of data entry is accomplished.

quality diagnostic: software that verifies the proper operation of the CPU, memories, and input-output functions. Checks instructions, memory, real-time clock, printer and associated keyboard, power fail restart, automatic loader, and so on.

quantity: a positive or negative number specifying a value. It can be a whole number, a fraction, or a combination of both.

quantization: the subdivision of the range of values of a variable into a finite number of nonoverlapping, and not necessarily equal subranges or intervals, each of which is represented by an assigned value within the subrange. For example, a person's age is quantized for most purposes with a quantum of one year. (A)

quantization interval: an interval between two adjacent values in quantization.

quantize: to divide the range of a variable into a finite number of nonoverlapping intervals that are not necessarily equal, and to designate each interval by an assigned value within that interval. (A)

quantizing error: distortion created by analog to digital conversion. This error occurs when analog signals fall between the possible digital values.

quantum: a subrange in quantization. (A)

quantum clock: a device that allocates an interval or quantum of processing time to a program established by priorities used in computing systems that have time-sharing procedures.

quarter-micron chips: chip containing tens of millions of transistors.

quarternary operator: an operator that requires exactly four operands. (A) (B)

quarter-squares multiplier: an analog multiplier whose operation is based on the identity $xy = .25 \ [(x + y)^2 - (x - y)^2]$ incorporating inverters, analog adders, and square-law function generators. (B)

quartet: a byte composed of four binary elements. Synonymous with *four-bit byte*.

quasi instruction: synonymous with *pseudoinstruction*.

query (Q):
(1) the process by which a master station asks a slave station to identify itself and to give its status.

(2) in interactive systems, an operation at a terminal that elicits a response from the system.

query by example (QBE): a method and programming language for searching sizeable quantities of data for information that satisfies user-specified formats or ranges of values.

query language: a class of English-like language that permits non-programmers to inquire about the contents of a data base and receive fast responses. Synonymous with *search language*.

query station: a unit of equipment that introduces requests or queries for data, states of processing, information, and so forth, while the machine is computing or processing or communicating.

queue (Q):
(1) a line or list formed by items in a system waiting for service; for example, tasks to be performed or messages to be transmitted in a message routing system.

(2) to arrange in, or form, a queue.

(3) see *doubled-ended queue*. (A)

queue control block (QCB): a control block that is used to regulate the sequential use of a programmer-defined facility among requesting tasks.

queued access method: any access method that synchronizes the transfer of data between the computer program using the access method and input-output devices, thereby minimizing delays for input-output operations. (A)

queue data set: a data set on a direct-access device used to contain one or more queues.

queued driven task: a task whose unit or work is represented by an element in a queue.

queued indexed sequential access method (QISAM): an extended version of the sequential form of the basic indexed sequential access method (BISAM). When this method is used, a queue is formed of input data blocks that are awaiting processing or output data blocks that have been processed and are awaiting transfer to auxiliary storage or to an output device.

queued sequential access method (QSAM): an extended version of the basic sequential access method (BSAM). When this method is used, a queue is formed of input data blocks that are awaiting processing or output data blocks that have been processed and are awaiting transfer to auxiliary storage or to an output device.

queue element (QEL):
(1) a block of data in a queue.
(2) one item in a queue.

queue link word: see *chaining.*

queue management: the network control program supervisor code controlling the manipulation of block control units and queue control blocks; it manages input, pseudoinput, and work queues.

queuing: the programming technique used to handle messages that are awaiting transmission.

queuing analysis: the study of the nature and time concerning the discrete units needed to pass through channels.

queuing list: a list used for scheduling actions in real time on a time–priority basis.

queuing theory: a probability theory useful in examining delays or lineups at servicing points.

quibinary code: a binary-coded decimal code for representing decimal numbers where each decimal digit is represented by seven binary digits that are coefficients of 8, 6, 4, 2, 0, 1, 0, respectively.

quick-access memory: a portion of memory having short access time, as compared to the main memory of the central processing unit.

quick cell facility: a high performance storage allocation technique using a fixed-block size.

quick copy: to quickly copy a text selection by positioning the pointer over the selection, holding down the right mouse button, moving the pointer to the location where the user wishes to insert the text, and releasing the mouse button.

quick start: synonym for *system restart (2).*

quiesce: to reject new jobs in a multiprogramming system, while at the same time continuing to process jobs already entered.

quiescing: the process of bringing a device or a system to a halt by rejection of new requests for work. (A)

QUIKTRAN: a subset of FORTRAN including built-in functions augmented by versatile operating statements for complete control maintenance.

quinary: see *biquinary code.* (A)

quintet: a byte composed of five binary elements. Synonymous with *five-bit byte.* (A) (B)

quoted string: in assembler programming, a character string enclosed by apostrophes that is used in a macroinstruction operand to represent a value that can include blanks. The enclosed apostrophes are part of the value represented. Cf. *character expression.*

quotient (Q) (QR) (QT): the number or quantity that is the value of the dividend divided by the value of the divisor and that is one of the results of a division operation. (B) Cf. *remainder.* (A)

qwerty: a typical typewriter keyboard that begins with these six letters, left-to-right, in the top row below the numerals.

R:
(1) see *read.*
(2) see *reader.*
(3) see *record.*
(4) see *register.*
(5) see *relation.*
(6) see *request.*
(7) see *reset.*
(8) see *ring.*

RA: see *return address.*

RACE: random access computer equipment.

rack: a frame or chassis on which a microprocessor is mounted.

radial transfer: the process of transmitting data between a peripheral unit and a unit of equipment that is more central than the peripheral unit. (B) Synonymous with *input-output, input process (2), output process*. (A)

radio button: a small diamond button or a small round button used to turn options on and off in menus and in dialog boxes.

radix: in a radix numeration system, the positive integer by which the weight of the digit place is multiplied to obtain the weight of the digit place with the next higher weight; for example, in the decimal numeration system that radix of each digit place is 10, in a biquinary code the radix of each fives position is 2. (B) Deprecated term for *base*. See *floating-point radix, mixed-radix notation*. (A)

radix complement (RC): a complement obtained by subtracting each digit of the given number from the number that is one less than the radix of that digit place, then adding one to the least significant digit of the result and executing any carries required; for example, 830 is the tens complement, that is, the radix complement of 170 in the decimal numeration system using three digits. Synonymous with *noughts complement, true complement*. (B) See *diminished radix complement*. (A)

radix-minus-one complement: synonym for *diminished radix complement*. (A) (B)

radix mixed: a numeration system that uses more than one radix, such as the biprimary system.

radix notation: synonym for *radix numeration system*. (A) (B)

radix numeration system: a positional representation system in which the ratio of the weight of any one digit place to the weight of the digit place with the next lower weight is a positive integer. The permissible values of the character in any digit place range from zero to one less than the radix of that digit place. Synonymous with *radix notation*. (A) (B)

radix point: in a representation of a number expressed in a radix numeration system, the location of the separation of the characters associated with the integral part from those associated with the fractional part. (A) (B)

RALU: see *register and arithmetic logic unit*.

RAM (Random Access Memory): the part of a computer's memory available for programs and documents. RAM usually means the part of memory available for programs from a disk. A computer with 512K of RAM has 512 kilobytes available for the user to run programs. The contents of RAM are lost when the computer is turned off. Cf. *read-only memory*. See *dynamic random access memory; static RAM, 64K RAM*.

RAM address register: a register containing the address location to be accessed in RAM.

RAM card system: a complete RAM with control logic on a single circuit board or card.

RAM disks: synonymous with *E-disks*.

RAM dump: copying the contents of all or a portion of a storage, usually from an internal storage such as a RAM, into an external storage such as a printout.

RAM enable: a RAM control line permitting new data to be written into the address field.

RAM loader: a program that reads a program from an input unit, and usually in a type of random-access memory.

RAM mail box: a set of locations in a common RAM storage area, reserved for data addressed to specific peripheral units as well as other microprocessors in the immediate environment.

rampage through core: when a program error results in the program to write data in the wrong places, or alters memory locations improperly.

RAM print-on-alarm: data system condition where continuous scanning of data channels occurs, but output of data is imitated only when an alarm condition as interpreted by the CPU in a RAM is encountered.

RAMPS: see *resource allocation in multipleproject schedule*.

RAM refresh: dynamic random-access memory units need an occasional refresh operation to guarantee that data is retained, since bits are represented by a capacitive charge.

RAM refresh cycle: the period needed for dynamic RAM refresh.

RAM resident-programs: multitasking programs making it possible to run several different programs at the same time, allowing one to switch effortlessly back and forth between a spreadsheet, data base, word-processing program, and the like, transferring data between these applications as needed. Once loaded they remain in the computer's memory and can be called up at any time by means of a couple of keystrokes.

RAM save: an option preventing data in ROMs from being lost because of power outages.

RAM register simulator: a program that simulates execution of computer programs. It is interpretive and provides bit-for-bit duplication of instruction execution timing, register contents, and other functions.

RAM/ROM pattern processor: a test system used to check RAM and ROM patterns.

RAM test program: a program using a PROM that plugs into prototyping boards for a thorough checkout.

random:

(1) with any particular order or sequence.

(2) a file organization where each record is read or written directly, regardless of where they are in the file, without searching through other records.

random access:

(1) a method of providing or achieving access where the time to retrieve data is constant and independent of the location of the item addressed earlier.

(2) in COBOL, an access mode in which specific logical records are obtained from or placed into a mass storage file in a non-sequential manner. (A)

(3) deprecated term for *direct access.*

random-access input-output: an input-output control capability that allows efficient random processing of records stored on a direct-access drive. An efficiency is achieved by issuing seeks in an order that minimizes the average seek time, and seeks are overlapped with other processing.

random-access I/O routines: direct, serial, and random processing of drum and disk files provided by these routines.

random-access memory: see *RAM.*

random-access programming: programming without concern for the time needed for access to the storage positions called for in the program.

random-access software: an array of programming and operating aids that includes a loader/monitor, a program for updating program files, a special sort, input-output routines, and utility routines.

random-access sorts: separate program furnished by manufacturers to sort data stored on random-access disks and drums.

random-access storage: deprecated term for *direct-access storage.*

random-access system: a method of filing data in a manner which approximates equal time to the processing of data, that is, usually that type of core storage or auxiliary storage which is ultrafast.

random-access time: the average time frame between the end of readout of a word from storage at a randomly chosen address, and the end of readout of another word from any different randomly chosen address.

random-data set: see *direct data set.*

random failure: failure whose occurrence at a given time is unpredictable. Synonymous with *chance failure.*

randomizing: a technique by which the range of keys for an indirectly addressed file is reduced to smaller ranges of addresses by some method of computation until the desired address is found.

random number:

(1) a number selected from a known set of numbers in such a way that the probability of occurrence of each number in the set is predetermined. (B)

(2) a number obtained by chance.

(3) one of a sequence of numbers considered appropriate for satisfying certain statistical tests.

(4) one of a sequence of numbers believed to be free from conditions that might bias the result of a calculation.

(5) see *pseudorandom number sequence.*

random number generator: a special machine routine or hardware unit designed to yield a random number or a series of such numbers according to specified limitations.

random number sequence: an ordered set of numbers, each of which may not be predicted only from a knowledge of its predecessors. (B) See *pseudorandom number* sequence. (A)

random processing: the treatment of data without respect to its location in external storage, and in an arbitrary sequence governed by the input against which it is to be processed.

random scan: deprecated term for *directed-beam scan.*

random sequence: a sequence not arranged by ascending or descending keys, but instead in an organized fashion in bulk storage, by locations.

random variable: the result of a random experiment.

random-walk method: in operations research, a variance-reducing method of problem analysis in which experimentation with probabilistic variables is traced to determine results of a significant nature. (A)

range:

(1) the set of values that a quantity or function may take. (B)

(2) in spreadsheets, more than one contiguous cells.

(3) the difference between the highest and lowest value that a quantity or function may assume.

(4) deprecated term for *span.* (B)

(5) see *error range.* (A)

range (of a default specification): in PL/1, a set of identifiers, constants, or parameter descriptors to which the attributes in a default specification of a DEFAULT statement apply.

range (of a DO loop): the statements that physically follow a DO statement, up to and including the statement specified by

the DO statement as being the last to be executed in the DO loop.

range (of a DO statement): in FORTRAN, those statements which physically follow a DO statement, up to and including the statement specified by the DO statement as being the last to be executed in the DO loop.

rank: synonym for *level number.* (A) (B)

RAP: see *remote-access point.*

rape: slang, fouling up; making a serious mistake, as with describing file-system damage.

rapid access: see *random access storage.*

rapid access loop: in drum computers, a small section of memory which has much faster access than the remainder of memory. Synonymous with *recirculating loop, revolver.*

rapid access memory: in computers with memories with different access times, the section that has faster access than the remainder of the memory.

RAS: reliability, availability, serviceability.

raster display device: in computer graphics, a display device in which display images are generated on a display space by raster graphics. See also *stair stepping.*

raster graphics: computer graphics in which display images, composed of an array of picture elements arranged in rows and columns, are generated on a display space.

rated speed: synonym for *nominal speed.*

rated thruput: the maximum amount of data that can be "put through" per unit of time. See also *nominal speed.*

rating: the value that determines the limiting capacity or limiting conditions for a unit.

ratio: see *error ratio, print contrast ratio, read-around ratio.* (A)

ratio control: a specific limitation in the relation between two quantities as expressed in direct or percentage comparison.

rational number: a real number that is the quotient of an integer divided by an integer other than zero. (A) (B)

raw data: data that has not been processed or reduced.

RB: see *return to bias.*
RBA: see *relative byte address.*
RCD: see *record.*
RCR: see *required carrier-return character.*
RD: see *read.*
RDB: see *relational database.*
RDR: see *reader.*

read (R) (RD): to acquire or interpret data from a storage device, from a data medium, or from another source. (B) See *destructive read, nondestructive read.* (A)

read after write verify: a function for determining that information currently being written is accurate as compared to the information source.

read-around ratio: the number of times a specific spot, digit, or location in electrostatic storage may be consulted before spillover of electrons causes a loss of data stored in surrounding spots. The surrounding data must be restored before the deterioration results in any loss of data. (A)

read back and printout: retrieving from computer storage or registering that which was read into a data-processing machine and to present this data on a printed page.

read-back check: a check for accuracy of transmission in which the information transmitted to an output unit is returned to the information source and compared with the original information, to ensure correctness of output.

read cycle time: the minimum time interval between the start of successive read cycles of a device that has separate reading and writing cycles. (A) (B)

READ DATA statements: a pair of statements used to assign values to variable names. READ DATA statements are used primarily when large sets of data are needed and the interactive capabilities of the computer are not needed.

reader (R) (RDR):
(1) in micrographics, a device that enlarges microimages for viewing. (A)
(2) in word processing, a device that accesses the coded information on recording media for further processing.

(3) a device that converts information in one form of storage to information in another form of storage.
(4) a part of the scheduler that reads an input stream into the system.
(5) see *card reader, character reader, perforated-tape reader.* (A)

reader-copier: see *microform reader-copier.*

reader-interpreter: a part of job management that reads and interprets a series of job definitions from an input stream.

reader-printer (RP): in micrographics, a device that performs the functions of a reader and a printer to produce hard copy enlargements of selected microimages. (A)

reader-sorter: a unit of punch card equipment that senses and transmits input while sorting documents.

read head: a magnetic head capable of reading only. (B)

reading: the acquisition or interpretation of data from a storage device, from a data medium, or from another source. (A) (B)

reading access time: the elapsed time before data is read or used in the computer during the equipment read cycle.

reading head: synonymous with *read head.*

reading rate: the number of characters, words, or items that are sensed by an input unit in a stated time period.

reading station: synonym for *read station.* (A) (B)

read-mostly memory: a type of ROM that is programmed while on the computer and is used to control the operation of the computer. It is used primarily for reading its program and is written on only when a change is required in the controlling program.

read-only memory (ROM): memory whose contents the computer can read, but not change. Information is placed into read-only memory only once, during manufacturing. The contents of ROM are not erased when the computer's power is turned off. Cf. *random-access memory.* Synonym for *fixed storage.* Deprecated term for *read-only storage,* but now more popular. See *CD-ROM.*

read-only: a type of access to data that allows it to be read but not copied, printed, or modified. Synonymous with *fixed.*

readme file: a text file placed onto software distributions disks that hold last-minute updates or corrections that have not been printed in the documentation manual.

read-only storage (ROS): a storage device whose contents cannot be modified, except by a particular user, or when operating under particular conditions; for example, a storage device in which writing is prevented by a lockout. Synonymous with *fixed storage, permanent storage.* (B)

readout: display of processed information on a terminal screen. Cf. *print-out.*

readout device: synonym for *character display device.* (A) (B)

read-process-write: the process of reading in one block of data, while simultaneously processing the preceding block and writing out the results of the previously processed block.

read protection: restriction of reading of the contents of a data set, file, or storage area by a user or program not authorized to do so.

read punch: a unit of input-output apparatus that punches coded holes into cards, reads input data into the system, and segregates output cards.

read rate: the number of units of data; for example, words and blocks capable of being read by an input unit within a given time span.

read release: a feature of some units that allows more computer processing time by releasing the read mechanism.

read reverse: where the device can read tape under program control in either direction.

read scatter: the ability of a computer to distribute or scatter data into several memory areas as it is being entered into the system on magnetic tape.

read screen: a transparent screen through which documents are read in optical character recognition.

READ statement: in a BASIC program, a statement for assigning data values to variables.

read station: the location in a reader where the data on a data carrier are read. Synonymous with *reading station, sensing station.* (B)

read time: the interval between the beginning of transcription from a storage unit and the completion of transcription.

read while writing: the reading of a record or set of records into storage from a tape at the same time another record or group of records is written from storage onto tape.

read/write: the nature of an operation, such as the direction of data flow.

read/write channel: a channel separating a peripheral unit and the central processor.

read/write check indicator: a unit that shows upon interrogation whether or not an error was made in reading or writing.

read/write counter: a unit for storing the starting and current addresses being transferred by a read-write channel between the main memory and peripheral units.

read/write cycle: the sequence of operations needed to read and write; for example, restore memory data.

read/write head: a magnetic head capable of reading and writing. Synonym for *magnetic head.* (B)

read/write memory: information in a storage that can be changed at will and read as frequently as needed. Cf. *read-only memory.*

read/write privilege: authority given to a program permitting it to read from a file or write or alter data in a file. Cf. *read-only, write-only.*

read/write storage: see *read/write memory.*

ready condition: the condition of a task that is in contention for the processing unit.

ready line: a line on some processors created to interface the processor to a slow memory or to a slow input-output unit.

ready state: a state in which a task is ready to be activated and is contending for processor execution time.

ready status word: a status word indicating that the remote computing system is waiting for entry from the terminal.

real address: the address of an actual storage location in real storage. (A) (B)

real constant: a string of decimal digits which must have either a decimal point or a decimal exponent, and may have both.

real estate: on a printed circuit board or semiconductor chip, the area available for electronic circuitry. Synonymous with *land.*

real number: a number that may be represented by a finite or infinite numeral in a fixed-radix numeration system. (A) (B)

real storage (RS): the main storage in a virtual storage system. Physically, real storage and main storage are identical. Conceptually, however, real storage represents only part of the range of addresses available to the user of a virtual storage system. Traditionally, the total range of addresses available to the user was that provided by main storage. (B)

real storage management (RSM): routines that control the allocation of pages in real storage.

real time (RT):

(1) pertaining to the processing of data by a computer in connection with another process outside the computer according to time requirements imposed by the outside printing in conversational mode and processes that can be influenced by human intervention while they are in progress. (B)

(2) pertaining to an application in which response to input is fast enough to affect subsequent input, such as a process control system or a computer-assisted instruction system.

real-time channel: units of equipment that offer interface between the end of communication and the computer memory.

real-time clock: develops readable digits or periodic signals for the computer to permit computation of elapsed time between events, and to initiate the performance of time-initiated processing.

real-time control: the control of a process by real-time processing. (A) (B)

real-time debug routine: a program permitting a user to test, examine, and modify a program task while the real-time application program is running.

real-time executive (RTE): a program providing a multiprogramming foreground-background system with priority scheduling, interrupt handling, and load-and-go capabilities.

real-time executive system: a multiprogramming foreground-background system with priority handling, interrupt capability, and program load-and-go capabilities.

real-time guard: a mode resulting in an interrupt to an address in central store when any attempt is made to perform a restricted operation. The guard mode is terminated by the occurrence of an interrupt.

real-time image generation: in computer graphics, performance of the computations necessary to update the image is completed within the refresh rate, so the sequence appears correctly to the viewer. An example is flight simulation, in which thousands of computations must be performed to present an animated image, all within the 30-60 cycles per second rate at which the frames change.

real-time information system: a system providing information fast enough for the process to be controlled by the operator utilizing this information.

real-time input: input data received into a data-processing system within time limits that are determined by the requirements of some other system or at instants that are so determined. (A) (B)

real-time mode: a mode of operation where data needed for the control or execution of a transaction are affected by the result of processing; eliminates slow information-gathering techniques and slow communication.

real-time monitor: an operating and programming system created to monitor the construction and execution of programs.

real-time operating system: a comprehensive software operating system for supporting the computer in dedicated real-time applications. The system includes a system generation program, input-output routines, and analog-to-digital conversion routines.

real-time operation: synonym for *real-time processing (1).* (A) (B)

real-time output: output data delivered from a data-processing system within time limits that are determined by the requirements of some other system or at instants that are so determined. (A) (B)

real-time processing:

(1) a mode of operation of a data-processing system when performing real-time jobs. Synonymous with *real-time operation.* (B)

(2) the manipulation of data that are required or generated by some process while the process is in operation; usually the results are used to influence the process, and perhaps related processes, while it is occurring. (A) (B)

real-time remote inquiry: an on-line inquiry station that permits users to interrogate computer files and receive immediate responses.

real-time satellite computer: a computer that relieves the larger computer of time consuming input and output functions in addition to performing pre- and postprocessing activities such as validity editing and formatting for print.

real-time simulation: the operation of a simulator such that the time-scale factor is equal to corresponding computer time of the simulator. (A)

real-time system (RTS): a system that processes data in a rapid fashion so that the results are available in time to influence the process being monitored or controlled.

real-time working: deprecated term for *real-time processing.* (A) (B)

reboot: reloading the system software, enabling the machine to begin as if first used.

REC: see *record.*

receiver register: a register used to input received data into a system at a clock rate set by the control register.

receiving perforator: a punch that converts coded electrical pulse patterns into hole patterns or cuts in perforated tape. Synonymous with *tape punch.* (A)

RECFM: see *record format.*

recirculating loop: see *rapid access loop.*

RECNUM: see *record number.*

recognition: see *character recognition, magnetic ink character recognition, optical character recognition, pattern recognition.* (A)

recognition logic: software in an optical character recognition reader permitting it to translate printed text into digital form.

recompile: to compile a program again, often following a debugging process or when the program needs to be run on a different computer.

recomplementation: an internal procedure that performs nines or tens complementation, as needed on the result of an arithmetic operation.

reconfiguration:

(1) a change made to a given configuration of a computer system; for example, isolating and bypassing a defective functional unit, connecting two functional units by an alternative path. Reconfiguration is effected automatically or manually and can be used to maintain system integrity.

(2) the process of placing a processing unit, main storage, and channels off line for maintenance, and adding or removing components.

reconfigure: to alter the components of a computer system and the interconnection of the components.

reconstitute: restoring a file to the condition that existed at an earlier processing period.

reconstitution: synonym for *reconstruction.*

reconstruction: the restoration of data to a previously known or defined state. Synonymous with *reconstitution.*

record (R) (RCD) (REC): a collection of related data or words, treated as a unit; for example, in stock control each invoice could constitute one record. (B) See *logical record, variable-length record.* (A) See also *records.*

record blocking: grouping of records by blocks that can be read and/or written to magnetic tape in a single operation, thereby increasing the efficiency with which the tape is used.

record check time: elapsed time needed to verify a record transfer on tape.

record control schedule: a schedule showing all functions involved regarding disposition of business records, that is, transfers, retention, and so forth.

record count: the number of records within a file, for purposes of control.

record description: in COBOL, the total set of data description entries associated with a particular logical record.

recorded voice announcement (RVA) unit: a device capable of continuous playback.

recorder on demand: see *ROD*.

record format: the contents and layout of a record. *(RECFM)*

record format descriptor:
(1) a file in a store controller that can be used to describe the record format. Descriptors are used by the data maintenance/inquiry function to process records in the keyed files.
(2) a record within this file.

record gap: deprecated term for *interblock gap*. (A) (B)

record group: several records, when placed together identify with a single key located in one of the records.

record head: synonymous with *write head*.

recording: see *double-pulse recording, electron beam recording, magnetic recording, non-return-to-reference recording, non-return-to-zero change-on-ones recording, non-return-to-zero (change) recording, non-return-to-zero recording, return-to-reference recording.* (A)

recording area: synonym for *film frame*. (A) (B)

recording density: the number of bits in a single linear track measured per unit of length of the recording medium. (A)

recording head: a head for transferring data to a storage unit, such as a drum, disk, tape, or magnetic card.

recording mode: in the COBOL system, the representation in external media of data associated with a data-processing system.

record layout: the arrangement and structure of data or words in a record, including the order and size of the components of the record. (A) (B)

record length (RL): the number of words or characters forming a record. (A) (B)

record mark: a special character to limit the number of characters in a data transfer, or to separate blocked or grouped records in tape.

record name: in COBOL, a data name that identifies a logical record.

record number (RECNUM): see *relative record number, transaction record number.*

record ready: a signal from a file-access unit to the computer that a record whose address was earlier given by a seek command has now been found and may be read into memory.

records: any unit of information that is to be transferred between the main memory and a peripheral unit; can be of any length. See *record.*

record separator character (RS): the information separator intended to identify a logical boundary between records. (A) (B)

record sorting: the basic element of a file such that the sorting of file constitutes the reordering of file records. Synonymous with *item.*

record storage mark: a character appearing only in the record storage unit of the card reader to limit the length of the record read into processor storage.

record type: a data structure defined to contain the information describing the entities being racked by a data base, and their associated attributes.

RECOV: see *recovery.*

recoverable ABEND: an error condition in which control is passed to a specified routine that allows continued execution of the program. Cf. *unrecoverable ABEND.* See also *STAE, STAI.*

recoverable error: an error condition that allows continued execution of a program.

recovery (RECOV): a process in which a specified data station resolves conflicting or erroneous conditions arising during the transfer of data. See *backward file recovery, forward file recovery.*

recovery from fallback: restoration of a system to complete operation from a fallback mode of operation following the removal of the cause for the fallback.

recovery management support (RMS): the facilities that gather information about hardware reliability and allow retry of operations that fail because of processing unit, I/O device, or channel errors. See also *machine check handler.*

recovery program: a program that permits a computer system to continue operating when certain apparatus fail.

recovery routine: a routine that is entered when an error occurs during the performance of an associated operation. It isolates the error, assesses the extent of the error, indicates subsequent action, and attempts to correct the error and resume operation.

recovery system: a computer program which records the progress of processing activities, allowing reconstruction of a run in the event of a computer crash. See *program crash.*

recovery termination manager: a program that handles all normal and abnormal termination of tasks by passing control to a recovery routine associated with the terminated function.

recursion: in PL/1, the reactivation of an active procedure.

recursive: pertaining to a process in which each step makes use of the results of earlier steps.

recursive function: a function whose values are natural numbers that are derived from natural numbers by substitution formulae in which the function is an operand. (A) (B)

recursively defined sequence: a series of terms in which each term after the first is determined by an operation in which the operands are some or all of the preceding terms. (A) (B)

recursive process: a method of computing values of functions where each state of processing contains all subsequent signs, that is the first stage is not completed until all other stages are ended.

recursive routine: a routine that may be used as a routine of itself, calling itself directly or being called by another routine, one that itself has called. The use of a recursive routine or computer program usu-

ally requires the keeping of records of the status of its unfinished uses in, for example, a push-down list. (A) (B)

recursive subroutine: a subroutine that may be used as a subroutine of itself, calling itself directly or being called by another subroutine, one that it itself has called. The use of a recursive subroutine or computer program usually requires the keeping of records of the status of its unfinished uses in, for example, a push-down list. (A) (B)

RED: see *reduction.*

redact: to edit or revise input data.

redaction: a new or recently revised edition of input data.

redefine: in COBOL, to reuse the same storage area for different data items during program execution by employing proper instructions in the data program.

redirected I/O: the simplification of input-output alternatives of a program where the assumption is made that all I/O units are the same, that is, in PASCAL, the printer, keyboard, and display are treated as files.

redirection: reading or writing from a file or device that is different from the one that is usually the target for the source.

red tape: see *housekeeping.*

reduced instruction set computing (RISC): a microprocessor design focusing on rapid and efficient processing of a relatively small set of instructions. RISC is founded on the premise that most of the instructions a computer decodes and then executes are rather simple.

reduction (RED): in micrographics, a measure of the number of times the linear dimensions of an object are reduced when photographed. The reduction is generally expressed as 1:16, 1:24. See *data reduction.*

redundancy:
(1) in information theory, the amount R by which the decision content H_0 exceeds the entropy H; in mathematical notation: $R = H_0 - H$. Usually, messages can be represented with fewer characters by using suitable codes; the redundancy may be considered as a measure of the

decrease of length of the messages thus achieved. (A)

(2) in the transmission of information, that fraction of the gross information content of a message that can be eliminated without loss of essential information. (B)

(3) see *relative redundancy*. (A)

redundancy check: a check that depends on extra characters attached to data for the detection of errors. See *cyclic redundancy check*.

redundancy check bit: a check bit that is derived from a character and appended to the character. (A)

redundancy check character: a check character that is derived from a record and appended to the record. See *cyclic redundancy check character, longitudinal redundancy check character*. (A)

redundant character: see *check character*.

reel: a cylinder with flanges on which tape or film may be wound. (A) (B)

reel-to-reel: a type of ribbon or tape feed found on some printers.

reenterable: synonym for *reentrant*.

reenterable program: synonym for *reentrant program*. (A) (B)

reenterable routine: synonym for *reentrant routine*. (A) (B)

reenterable subroutine: synonym for *reentrant subroutine*. (A) (B)

reentrant: the attribute of a program or routine that allows the same copy of the program or routine to be used concurrently by two or more tasks.

reentrant code: a set of instructions that forms a single copy of a program that is shared by two or more programs. These routines have instructions and constants that are not subject to modification during execution.

reentrant program: a computer program that may be entered repeatedly and may be entered before prior executions of the same computer program have been completed, subject to the requirement that neither its external program parameters nor any instructions are modified during its execution. A reentrant program may be used by more than one computer pro-

gram simultaneously. Synonymous with *reenterable program*. (A) (B)

reentrant routine: a routine that may be entered repeatedly and may be entered before prior executions of the same routine have been completed, subject to the requirement that neither its external program parameters nor any instructions are modified during its execution. A reentrant routine may be used by more than one computer program simultaneously. Synonymous with *reenterable routine*. (A) (B)

reentrant subroutine: a subroutine that may be entered repeatedly and may be entered before prior executions of the same subroutine have been completed, subject to the requirement that neither its external program parameters nor any instructions are modified during its execution. A reentrant subroutine may be used by more than one computer program simultaneously. Synonymous with *reenterable subroutine*. (A) (B)

reentry point: the address or the label of the instruction at which the computer program that called a subroutine is reentered from the subroutine. (A) (B)

reentry system: a character recognition concept for a system where the input data to be read are printed by the computer with which the reader is associated.

REF: see *reference*.

reference (REF): in PL/1, the appearance of a name, except in a context that causes explicit declaration.

reference address: synonymous with *base address*.

referenced variable: a variable accessed not by name but through a pointer variable; a dynamic variable; a variable created by the procedure NEW in Pascal.

reference edge: that edge of a data carrier used to establish specification or measurements in or on the data carrier. Synonymous with *guide edge*. See *document reference edge*.

reference format: in COBOL, a format that provides a standard method for describing COBOL source programs.

reference instruction: an instruction that permits reference to systematically arranged or stored data.

reference language: the set of characters and formation rules used to define a programming language. (B)

reference list: the printout produced by a compiler to show instructions as they appear at the end of a run, indicating their locations.

reference program table: a portion of storage used as an index for operations, variables, and subroutines.

reference record: a computer output that lists the operations and their positions in the last routine.

REFER expression: in PL/1, the expression preceding the keyword REFER, from which an original bound, length, or size is taken when a based variable containing a REFER option is allocated, either by an ALLOCATE or LOCATE statement.

REFER object: in PL/1, the unsubscripted element variable appearing in a REFER option that specifies a current bound, length, or size for a member of a based structure. It must be a member of the structure, and it must precede the member declared with the REFER option.

reflectance: in OCR, the diffuse reflectivity of ink-free areas of the substrate on which printing exists.

reflectance model: in computer graphics, the function which describes light on a surface by making assumptions concerning light sources, angles, surface texture, and the like. Synonymous with *illumination model.*

reflected binary code: synonym for *gray code.* (A)

reformat: to alter the representation of data from one format to another.

refresh (RFRSH) (RFSH): in computer graphics, the process of repeatedly producing a display image on a display space so that the image remains visible.

refreshable: the attribute of a load module that prevents it from being modified by itself or by another module during execution. A refreshable load module can be replaced by a new copy during execution by

a recovery management routine without changing either the sequence or results of processing.

refresh rate:
(1) in computer graphics, the rate per unit time at which a display image is refreshed.
(2) in word processing, the rate at which a display image is renewed in order to appear stable.

REG: see *register.*

regenerate: synonymous with *refresh.*

regeneration:
(1) in computer graphics, the sequence of events needed to generate a display image.
(2) the restoration of stored information.
(3) see *signal regeneration.* (A)

regenerative feedback: an approach that returns part of the output of a unit, system, or process to the input in a way that causes a greater feedback.

regenerative memory: a memory unit whose contents gradually disappear if not periodically refreshed.

regenerative reading: a read operation involving the automatic writing of data back into the positions from which it is extracted.

regenerative storage: storage requiring a periodic refreshing.

regenerative track: part of a track on a magnetic drum or magnetic disk used in conjunction with a read head and a write head that are connected to function as a circulating storage. Synonymous with *revolver track.* (A)

region: see *overlay region.*

REGIS: see *register.*

register (R) (REG) (REGIS): a storage device, having a specified storage capacity such as a bit, a byte, or a computer word, and usually intended for a special purpose. (B) See *address register, base address register, base register, circulating register, double-length register, floating-point register, general-purpose register, instruction address register, instruction register, quadruple-length register, return code register, sequence control register, shift register, triple-length register.* (A)

register address: an address where the operand lies in one of the general registers.

register address field: that part of an instruction word containing a register address.

register and arithmetic logic unit (RALU): a collection of logic elements (such as accumulators, stack, and arithmetic logic unit) that provides data storage and processing functions.

register capacity: the upper and lower limits of the numbers that can be processed in a register.

register file: a bank of multiple-bit registers used as temporary storage locations for data or instructions and referred to as a *stack*.

register input-buffer: a unit that accepts data from input units or media such as magnetic tapes or disks and then transfers this data to internal storage.

register length: the storage capacity of a register. (B)

register pointer: the part of the program status double-word that points to a set of 16 general registers used as the current register block.

register select: lines utilized to choose one register out of a given number with a unit. Pins are usually connected to the address bus.

register-to-register instruction: a programming action for moving information from one CPU register to another.

register-to-storage instruction: a programming action for moving information from a CPU register to a location within memory.

register transfer module (RTM): a functional register device created for the construction of register logic systems.

registered group: a group of registered users that is listed on a computer on a network.

registered user: a network user whose name and password are listed on a computer on the network. Usually, registered users have greater access privileges to shared folders and disks than do guest users.

registration: the accurate positioning of an entity relative to a reference. (A)

rejection: synonymous with *NOR operation*.

REL:
(1) see *release*.
(2) see *relocatable*.

relation (R): in assembler programming, the comparison of two expressions to see if the value of one is equal to, less than, or greater than the value of the other.

relational database (RBD): a data base in which relationships between data items are explicitly specified as equally accessible attributes.

relational expressions: an expression that consists of an arithmetic expression, followed by a relational operator, followed by another arithmetic expression, and that can be reduced to a value that is true or false.

relational operator:
(1) an operator that operates on at least two operands and yields a truth value.
(2) in assembler programming, an operator that can be used in an arithmetic or character relation to indicate the comparison to be performed between the terms in the relation. The relational operators are EQ (equal to), GE (greater than or equal to), GT (greater than), LE (less than or equal to), LT (less than), and NE (not equal to).
(3) in COBOL, a reserved word, or a group of reserved words, or a group of reserved words and relational characters. A relational operator plus programmer-defined operands make up a relational expression.

relational symbols: symbols such as $>$ (greater than), $<$ (less than), or $=$ (equal to) that are used to compare two values in a conditional branching situation.

relation character: in COBOL, a character that expresses a relationship between two operands. The following are COBOL relation characters:

character	meaning
$>$	greater than
$<$	less than
$=$	equal to

relation condition: in COBOL, a statement that the value of an arithmetic expression or data item has a specific relationship to another arithmetic expression or data item. The statement may be true or false.

relative address: an address expressed as a difference with respect to a base address. (A) (B)

relative addressing: a method of addressing in which the address part of an instruction contains a relative address. (A)

relative addressing mode: an addressing mode that specifies a memory location in a program counter or another register for reference.

relative address label: a label for identifying the location of data by reference to its position with regard to another location in the program.

relative block number: a number that identifies the location of a block expressed as a difference with respect to a base address. The relative block number is used to retrieve that block from the data set.

relative byte address (RBA): a relative address expressed in terms by bytes as an offset from a point of reference.

relative code: a code where all addresses are written with respect to an arbitrarily chosen position, or in which all addresses are represented symbolically in machine language.

relative coding: coding that uses machine instructions with relative addresses. (A)

relative data: in computer graphics, values in a computer program that specify displacements from the actual coordinates in a display space or image space. Cf. *absolute data.*

relative data set: a data set in which each record is assigned a record number according to its relative position within the data set storage space; the record number must be used to retrieve the record from the data set. See also *indexed data set.*

relative error: the ratio of an absolute error to the true, specified, or theoretically correct value of the quantity that is in error. (A) (B)

relative file: in COBOL, a file with relative organization.

relative organization: in COBOL, the permanent logical file structure in which each record is uniquely identified by an integer value greater than zero, which specifies the record's logical ordinal position in the file.

relative record number (RRN): a number that indicates the location of a logical record, expressed as a difference with respect to a base address. The relative record number is used to retrieve the logical record from the data set.

relative redundancy: in information theory, the ratio r of the redundancy R to the decision content H (so)s. (A) (B)

relative time clock (RTC): a clock system permitting the executive to maintain track of time and service interrupts.

relaxation oscillator: an oscillator that operates by being driven to a regenerative state rapidly and repetitively.

release (REL): synonymous with *disconnect.*

release read: a feature permitting greater processing time by releasing the read mechanism.

relevance ratio: an information retrieval term expressing the ratio of the number of pertinent documents retrieved by a specific query to the total number of documents retrieved by the query criteria.

reliability: the ability of a functional unit to perform its intended function under stated conditions, for a stated period of time. (A) (B)

reliability theory: a descriptive mathematical model of the probability that the system components and the total system will function satisfactorily during the performance of a mission.

relink: see *linkage editor.*

reloadable control storage: the area of main memory held for storing microprograms that permits a microprogram to be loaded for execution.

relocatability: the ability to situate a program or data in an area of memory at differing times without modification to a program.

relocatable (REL): the attribute of a set of codes whose address constants can be modified to compensate for a change in origin.

relocatable address: an address that is adjusted when the computer program containing it is relocated. (A) (B)

relocatable assembler: an assembler for generating an object program with memory addresses entered as displacements from a relative program origin or as external references.

relocatable code: a computer program where addresses found within the instruction's care change if the origin (its starting point) of the program is altered, thereby allowing the program to be relocated to any point in memory, without impacting on the operation.

relocatable expression: in assembler programming, an assembly-time expression whose value is affected by program relocation. A relocatable expression can represent a relocatable address.

relocatable linking loader: allows users to combine multiple independent binary modules into an executable program, with capabilities for automatic library search, conditional load, comprehensive load map listings, and origin definition flexibility.

relocatable phase: output of the linkage editor containing relocation information. The relocation loader in the supervisor uses this information to relocate the phase into any partition the user selects at execution time.

relocatable program: a computer program that is in such a form that it may be relocated. (A) (B)

relocatable routine: a routine with instructions written in relative code so that they can be traced and acted on throughout memory. See *relative coding.*

relocatable subroutine: a subroutine located physically and independently in the memory, its object-time location determined by the processor.

relocatable term: in assembler programming, a term whose value is affected by program relocation.

relocate: to move a computer program or part of a computer program, and to adjust the necessary address references so that the computer program can be executed after being moved. (A) (B)

relocating loader: a loader that adjusts addresses, relative to the assembled origin, by the relocation factor. (A)

relocation: the modification of address constants to compensate for a change in origin of a module, program, or control section. See *dynamic relocation.* (A)

relocation dictionary (RLD): the part of an object module or load module that identifies all addresses that must be adjusted when a relocation occurs. (A)

relocation factor: the algebraic difference between the assembled origin and the loaded origin of a computer program. (A)

remainder: in a division operation, the number or quantity that is the undivided part of the dividend, having an absolute value less than the absolute value of the divisor, and that is one of the results of a division operation. (B) Cf. *quotient.* (A)

remark: synonymous with *comment.*

remote (RMT): equipment located at a distance. Synonym for *link-attached.*

remote access: pertaining to communication with a data-processing facility through a data link. (A)

remote-access data processing: data processing in which certain portions of input-output functions are situated in different places and connected by transmission facilities. Synonymous with *teleprocessing.* See also *distributed data processing.*

remote-access data-processing network: a network in which input-output devices are connected by data links to a central computer. Synonymous with *teleprocessing network.*

remote-access point (RAP): a multiplexor or concentrator found in a given location that provides access to a network in areas not directly covered by nodes having full network facilities.

remote batch entry: submission of batches of jobs through an input-output unit that has access to a computer through a data link. (A) (B)

remote batch printer (RBP): a printer connected as a remote terminal under a central computer's control that is used for print information in batches after the information has been prepared by a computer.

remote batch processing: batch processing in which input-output units have access to a computer through a data link. (A) (B)

remote batch terminal: a terminal used in remote batch processing.

remote command submission: a program's ability to transfer a batch command file to a remote system and cause it to be executed.

remote console: a terminal unit in a remote computing system.

remote control: a system of control performed from a distance.

remote data concentration: the multiplexing of a number of low-activity or low-speed lines or terminals on to one high-speed line between a remote terminal and a central processor.

remote debugging: using remote terminals for the testing of programs.

remote format item: in PL/1, the letter R specified in a format list together with the label of a separate FORMAT statement.

remote host: an information processor which is logically fully compatible with the host system, but configured at a remote location within the system.

remote input: input that must be sent to a central computer for processing.

remote inquiry: the interrogation of the contents of a data-processing storage unit from a device displaced from the storage unit site; permits the computer to be interrogated from various locations for immediate answers to inquiries.

remote job entry (RJE): submission of jobs through an input unit that has access to a computer through a data link. (A) (B)

remote printer: apparatus for printing information at a location remote from the center at which the information is stored.

remote printing: producing hard copy output from a printer from a distant location from the processor which provides the printer's electronic input.

remote program loader (RPL): a feature that includes a read-only storage unit and a small auxiliary-storage device installed in a remote controller to allow the controller to be loaded and dumped over the data link.

remote station (RST): data terminal equipment for communication with a data-processing system through a data link. Synonym for *link-attached station.*

remote subsets: input and output units located at points other than the central computer site.

remote system: a system where terminals are connected to a central computer by a communication channel.

remote terminal (RT): synonym for *link-attached terminal.*

remote terminal operator: a person who uses a remote terminal to enter data into a computer.

removable disk: a disk or disk pack that is removed from a disk drive, permitting the drive to be used by other disks.

removable media: a data storage media that is removed from a drive that reads/writes it, such as magnetic tape and floppy disks.

removable random access: pertaining to disk packs, tape strips, or card strips that can be physically deleted and replaced by another, permitting for a theoretically unlimited storage capacity.

REM statement: stands for REMARK. A REM statement is nonexecutable. REMs are inserted at appropriate places in a program along with comments that should enable future users to understand the intent of the various sections of the program.

reorder: deprecated term for *order (1).* (A) (B)

repagination: in word processing, the process in which a word processor adjusts a multipage document as it is revised in order to ensure uniform page length and appearance.

repair time: time consumed to diagnose, clear, or repair machines or systems, including fault location, detection, correction, and consequent tests.

repeatability: the measure of the difference between the mean value and some maximum expected value for a particular data reading.

repeat-action key: a key that, when held fully depressed, causes an action (such as typing a character) to be repeated until the key is released; for example, a typematic key.

repeat character (RPT): a word-processing device control that causes a storage location pointer to reset to a designated buffer beginning point for the device. See also *page-end character, switch character.*

repeat counter: a software counter that records the number of times an event occurs in a program, for later comparison.

repeated selection sort: a selection sort in which the set of items is divided into subsets and one item, that fits specified criteria, from each subset is selected to form a second level subset. A selection sort is applied to this second level subset, the selected item in this second level subset is appended to the sorted set and is replaced by the next eligible item in the original subset, and the process repeated until all items are in the sorted set. See also *tournament sort.* (A)

repeating last command: a function that occurs when a button on the keyboard is pressed telling the device to do again what it had previously done when depressed. This saves keystrokes.

repeat key:
(1) a key held down to make contact repeatedly without any need for further depression.
(2) a key pressed at the same time as another one to make the second key repeat for the duration of the time that the repeat key is held down.

repeat statement: in PASCAL, a looping control structure similar to a WHILE loop, except that there will always be at least one execution of the loop, since the loop condition is tested after the body of the loop.

reperforator: see *receiving perforator.* (A)

repertoire: see *instruction repertoire.* (A)

repertory: the numerous sets of operations that are represented in a given operation code.

repetition factor: in PL/1, a parenthesized unsigned decimal integer constant that specifies (a) the number of occurrences of a string configuration that make up a string constant, and (b) the number of occurrences of a picture specification character in a picture specification.

repetition instruction: an instruction that causes one or more instructions to be executed an indicated number of times. (A)

repetitive addressing: a method of implied addressing, applicable only to zero-address instructions, in which the operation part of an instruction implicitly addresses the operands of the last instruction executed. (A) (B)

repetitive operation: the automatic repetition of the solution of a set of equations with fixed combinations of initial conditions and other parameters. (B)

repetitive specification: in PL/1, an element of a data list that specifies controlled iteration to transmit one or more data items, generally used in conjunction with arrays.

replacement: the substitution of different machines for other devices that perform the same or similar operations.

report: an output document prepared by a data-processing system.

report clause: in COBOL, a clause in the report section of the data division that appears in a report description entry or a report group description entry.

report description entry: in COBOL, an entry in the report section of the data division that is composed of the level indicator RD, followed by a report name, followed by a set of report clauses as required.

report file: in COBOL, an output file whose file description entry contains a REPORT clause. The contents of a report file consist of records that are written under control of the report writer control system.

report footing: in COBOL, a report group that is presented only at the end of a report.

report generation: a technique for producing complete machine reports from information that describes the input file and the format and content of the output report. See *RPGII.*

report generator: a general-purpose program designed to print out information from files on presentation to it of parameters specifying the format of the files concerned plus the format and content of the printed report, and procedures and regulations for establishing totals, page numbering, and so forth. Synonymous with *program generator.*

report group: in COBOL, in the report section of the data division, an 01 level-number entry and its subordinate entries.

report heading: in COBOL, a report group that is presented only at the beginning of a report.

report line: a division of a page representing one row of horizontal character positions. Each character position of a report line is aligned vertically beneath the corresponding character position of the report line above it. Report lines are numbered from 1, by 1, starting at the top of the page.

report name: in COBOL, a user-defined word that names a report described in a report description entry within the report section of the data division.

report program generator (RPG): synonymous with *report generator.*

report section: in COBOL, the section of the data division that contains one or more report description entries and their associated report group description entries.

report writer control system (RWCS): in COBOL, a record that consists of the report writer print line and associated control information, necessary for its selection and vertical positioning.

REPR: see *representation.*

representation (REPR): see *analog representation, coded representation, digital representation, discrete representation, floating-point representation, incremental representation, linear representation, number representation, numeric representation, variable-point representation.* (A)

representational error: an arithmetic error that occurs when the precision of the result of an arithmetic operation is greater than the precision of a given machine.

representation system: see *fixed-point representation system, number representation system, positional representation system, variable-point representation system.* (A)

reproduce: synonym for *duplicate.* (A)

reproducer: synonym for *reproducing punch.* See also *tape reproducer.* (A) (B)

reproducing punch: a punched card device that prepares one punched card from another punched card, copying all or part of the data from the punched card that is read. Synonymous with *reproducer.* (A)

reproduction codes: function codes in a master tape that are carried through the data operations and appear in the produced tape.

reprogrammable associative ROM: synonymous with *programmable logic array.*

reprographics: a technique of producing output whereby the computer is connected to a typesetting machine and the output is film repro paper.

REQ: see *request.*

request (R) (REQ): a directive (by means of a basic transmission unit) from an access method that causes the network control program to perform a data-transfer operation or auxiliary operation.

request for price quotation: see *RPQ.*

required carrier-return character (RCR): a word processing formatting control that moves the printing or display point to the first position of the next line and resets indent tab mode. Required carrier return must be executed wherever it occurs in the character string. See also *carrier return character.* Synonymous with *required new-line character.* Cf. *index return character.*

required cryptographic session: deprecated term for *mandatory cryptographic session.*

required hyphen character (HYP): a word processing formatting graphic used whenever the graphic hyphen must not be changed during formatting operations. Cf. *syllable hyphen (character).*

required new-line character: synonym for *required carrier-return character.*

required page-end character (RPE): a word-processing formatting control that initiates the procedure for terminating a page. Required page end must be honored as a page delimiter wherever it occurs in a character string. See also *page-end character.*

required space character (RSP): a word processing formatting graphic that causes the printing or display point to move right to the next active position. Required space is treated as a graphic character (not as an interword space or information separator) in implementing formatting operations; for example, to concatenate words in a phrase which is to be underscored using the word underscore character. See also *space character.*

rerun:
(1) a repeat of a machine run from its beginning, usually made desirable or necessary by a false start, by an interruption, or by a change. (B)
(2) to perform a rerun. (A) (B)

rerun mode: use of a terminal to have previously entered data printed or displayed at the terminal. This mode allows the terminal operator to visually check the data, get a clean copy of the data, or correct the data.

rerun point: that location in the sequence of instructions in a computer program at which all information pertinent to the rerunning of the program is available. (A)

rerun routine: a routine using rerun points for restarting.

RES:
(1) see *reset.*
(2) see *restore.*

rescue dump: recording on magnetic tape of the entire memory information, which includes the status of the computer system at the time the dump is carried out.

rescue point: synonym for *restart point.* (A) (B)

reserve: allocating a memory area and/or peripheral devices to a program functioning in a multiprogramming system.

reserved word:
(1) a word of a source language whose meaning is fixed by the particular rules of that language and cannot be altered for the convenience of any one computer program expressed in the source language; computer programs expressed in the source language may also be prohibited from using such words in other contexts in the computer program. For example, SINE may be a reserved word to call a subroutine for computing the sine function; in COBOL, the COBOL words. (B)
(2) a word that is defined in a programming language for a special purpose, and that must not appear as a user-declared identifier.

reset (R) (RES) (RST):
(1) to cause a counter to take the state corresponding to a specified initial number. (A) (B)
(2) to put all or part of a data-processing device back into a prescribed state. (B)
(3) to restore a storage device to a prescribed initial state, not necessarily that denoting zero. (B)
(4) cf. *set.* (A)

reset button: resets the settings in a dialog box to their original values without closing the box.

reset cycle: the return of a cycle index to its initial or some preselected condition.

reset key: the switch or computer console used for resetting the error-detection system and for restarting the program after the detection of an error.

reset mode: synonym for *initial condition mode.* (B)

reset rate: the number of corrections, per unit of time, made by the control system.

reset switch: a switch used for either an error reset or a master reset.

reset to n: a procedure setting a device as a register, counter, and so on, for storing or displaying a value, say n, by returning a counting device to its initial state, thus representing n, that is, some number as it was predetermined or desired.

reset to zero (RZ): to start from the beginning; returning to point of origin for reconsideration or redesign of a project.

reside: to be stored permanently, or actively, at a particular place.

residence: the data storage device on which the file referred to is stored.

resident: that which exists permanently in memory; for example, a resident compiler. See *memory resident.*

resident compiler: a compiler that utilizes the computer itself to generate programs.

resident control program: synonym for *nucleus.*

residential error ratio: the error ratio remaining after attempts at correction. (A)

resident font: a font built into a printer.

resident loader: a loader permanently stored in main memory.

resident modules: keeps track of program execution status and which overlay modules are needed.

resident program: a program that remains in a particular area of storage.

resident program select list: a list of programs that are in, or that are scheduled to be copied into, resident program storage.

resident routines: the most frequently used components of the supervisor which are initially loaded into main storage.

residential terminal: a home terminal.

residual value: the value of a piece of equipment at the end of a lease term.

resistor-transistor logic (RTL): logic carried out by the use of resistors, with transistors producing an inverted output.

resolution: the degree of precision with which an object is represented. A printer's resolution is determined by the number of dots per inch.

resolution error: an error caused by the inability of a computing device to show changes of a variable smaller than a given increment.

resolver: a functional unit whose input variables are the polar coordinates of a point and whose output variables are the Cartesian coordinates of the same point, or vice versa. (B)

resolver differential: a unit for obtaining zero shift or offset in control systems using resolver feedback.

resource: any facility of the computing system or operating system required by a job

or task, and including main storage, input-output devices, the processing unit, data sets, and control or processing programs.

resource allocation: the assignment of the facilities of a data-processing system for the accomplishment of jobs; for example, the assignment of main storage, input-output devices, files. (B)

resource allocation in multiproject schedules (RAMPS): any part of the total computer system; machinery, programs, and people who operate it are considered a resource. See also *resource.*

resource management: the function that protects serially accessed resources from concurrent access by competing tasks.

resource manager (RM): a general term for any control program function responsible for the allocation of a resource.

resource sharing: the function of allocating the processing load of an enterprise to the available processing facilities when multiple facilities exist.

resource sharing control: the tying together of multiple computers in distributed processing systems so that several systems can function together sharing the work load.

response: an answer to an inquiry. See *spectral response.* (A) Cf. *command (2).*

response/throughput bias (RTB): in the system resources manager, a category of information contained in a period definition, that indicates how the work-load manager is to weigh trade offs between satisfying a system throughput objective and the IPS-specified service rate.

response time: the elapsed time between the end of an inquiry or demand on a data-processing system and the beginning of the response; for example, the length of time between an indication of the end of an inquiry and the display of the first character of the response at a user terminal. (A) (B) See also *interaction time, turnaround time.*

RESRT: see *restart.*

restart (RESRT):

(1) the resumption of the execution of a computer program using the data recorded at a checkpoint. (B)

(2) to perform a restart. (A) (B)

(3) see *checkpoint restart.*

(4) see also *checkpoint records.*

restart condition: in the execution of a computer program, a condition that can be reestablished and that permits a restart of the computer program. (A) (B)

restart instruction: an instruction in a computer program at which the computer program may be restarted. (A) (B)

restart point: a place in a computer program at which its execution may be restarted; in particular, the address of a restart instruction. Synonymous with *rescue point.* Deprecated term for *restart condition.* (A) (B)

restart procedure: the procedure permitting processing to continue from the last checkpoint, rather than the beginning of the run.

restore (RES): to return the active window to its previous size after having been enlarged to fill the whole screen. See *reset.*

RESTORE statement: a statement that returns the data pointer to the first data item in the first DATA statement in the program.

result: an entity produced by the performance of an operation. (A) (B)

RET: see *return.*

retention period check: synonym for *expiration check.*

retina: in optical character recognition, a major component of a scanning unit.

retrieval: see *information retrieval.* (A)

retrieval code: in micrographics, a code for manual or automatic retrieval of microimages. (A) (B)

retrieve: to carry out retrieval. Synonym for *fetch.*

retrieving: searching of storage to locate the data needed, and choosing or removing the required data from storage.

retrofit: to alter an existing routine or system to accommodate a new section or an alteration to an existing section, and to evolve changes in related routines or systems.

retrofit testing: testing to assure system operation after having replaced some units and/or programs.

retry: to resend the current block of data (from the last EOB or ETB) a prescribed number of times, or until it is entered correctly or accepted.

return (RET):

(1) within a subroutine, to bind a variable in the computer program that called the subroutine. (B)

(2) within a subroutine, to effect a link to the computer program that called the subroutine. (B)

(3) see *carriage return.* (A)

return address (RA): synonymous with *link.*

return character: see *carriage return character.* (A)

return code: a code used to influence the execution of succeeding instructions. (A)

return code register: a register used to store a return code. (A)

return instruction: an instruction that returns control of the main routine following the execution of a subroutine.

return key:

(1) a key on a terminal used as an enter key.

(2) a key on a terminal used to return the cursor to the first position of the next line.

return to bias (RB): a mode or recording in which the state of the medium changes from a bias state to another state, and then returns to record a binary one or zero.

return-to-reference recording: the magnetic recording of binary characters in which the patterns of magnetization used to represent zeros and ones occupy only part of the storage cell, the remainder of the cell being magnetized to a reference condition. (A) (B)

return-to-zero recording: return-to-reference recording in which the reference condition is the absence of magnetization. (B)

returned value: in PL/1, the value returned by a function procedure to the point of invocation.

reusable: the attribute of a routine that allows the same copy of the routine to be used by two or more tasks. See also *reenterable, serially reusable.*

reusable program: a computer program that may be loaded once and executed repeatedly, subject to the requirements that any instructions that are modified during its execution are returned to their initial states and that its external program parameters are preserved unchanged. (A) (B)

reusable routine: a routine that may be loaded once and executed repeatedly, subject to the requirements that any instructions that are modified during its execution are returned to their initial states and that its external program parameters are preserved unchanged. (A) (B)

reverse clipping: synonym for *shielding*.

reverse-code dictionary: an alphabetic code or numeric-alphabet code arrangement associated with their corresponding English words or terms. See also *dictionary*.

reverse direction flow: in flowcharting, a flow in a direction other than left to right or top to bottom. (A)

reverse indexing: in word processing, the feature that causes the typing position or display pointer to be moved to the corresponding character position of the preceding typing line.

reverse Polish notation: synonym for *postfix notation*. (A) (B)

reverse video: a form of highlighting a character, field, or cursor by reversing the color of the character, field, or cursor with is background; for example, changing a red character on a black background to a black character on a red background.

reversible counter: a device with a finite number of states, each of which represents a number that can be increased or decreased by unity or by a given constant on receipt of an appropriate signal; the device is usually capable of bringing the number represented to a specific value, for example, zero. (B)

revert: a command that permits the user to drop all the changes made to a document but haven't yet saved.

revertive error checking: a technique of error checking where the transmitting terminal generates a sequence of check digits derived from an algorithm performed on the content of a frame about to be transmitted. Cf. *nonrevertive error checking*.

revise: any proof produced following corrections.

revolver: synonymous with *rapid access loop*.

revolver track: synonym for *regenerative track*. (A)

rewind (RWND): to return a magnetic or paper tape to its beginning.

rewind time: the measurement of elapsed time needed to transfer tape to the supply reel.

rewrite: to regenerate data in storage units where the process of reading data results in its destruction.

rewrite dual gap head: a character written on tape is immediately read by a read head so the accuracy of recorded data can be ensured.

RFRSH: see *refresh*.

RFSH: see *refresh*.

RGB monitor: a type of color monitor that receives separate signals for each primary color (red, green, and blue) and uses these signals to display color images.

ribbon cartridge: the inked printer ribbon within a housing that is snapped in place within the print unit.

right justified: when the right-hand digit or character occupies its allotted right-hand position, data is said to be right justified.

right justify:
(1) to shift the contents of a register, if necessary, so that the character at the right-hand end of the data that have been read or loaded into the register is at a specified position in the register. (B)
(2) to control the positions of characters on a page so that the right-hand margin of the printing is regular. (B)
(3) to align characters horizontally so that the rightmost character of a string is in a specified position. (A)

right shift: to displace digits in a word to the right, having the result of division in arithmetic shift.

rigid disk: a disk memory in which the magnetic medium is coated on to a rigid substrate.

ring (network) (R): a network in which each node is connected to two adjacent nodes.

ripple counter: a counting circuit where flip-flops are connected in series, with one flip-flop affecting the next in sequence until the last flip-flop is triggered. See also *T flip-flop.*

ripple-through carry: synonymous with *high-speed carry.*

rivers: the undesirable alignment of spaces found in a text.

RJE: see *remote job entry.* (A) (B)

RL: see *record length.*

RLD: see *relocation dictionary.*

RM: see *resource manager.*

RMS: see *recovery management support.*

RMT: see *remote.*

RO: see *read-only.*

ROD: recorder on demand. Displays percentages of errors recorded.

role indicator: in information retrieval, a code assigned to a word, that is, a descriptor, indicating the role which the word plays in the text where it occurs.

roll: in computer graphics, to scroll in an upward or downward direction.

rollback: a programmed return to a prior checkpoint. (A)

rollback snapshot: the recording of data taken at periodic intervals in a program to permit the program to begin again at the last recording following a system failure.

roll-call polling: a technique of polling where each terminal unit is addressed in strict sequence by the controller to determine which, if any, unit is ready to send or receive a frame of information, beginning at the nearest terminal and working out towards the most distant. See *hub polling.*

roll in: to restore in main storage data or one or more computer programs that were previously rolled out. (A)

roll on: locating a reel, and placing it on a tape drive that is plugged directly into the computer for on-line use.

roll out: to transfer data or one or more computer programs from main storage to auxiliary storage for the purpose of freeing main storage for another use. (A)

roll out/roll in: a procedure for managing storage whereby certain programs are temporarily taken out of main storage, placed on disk storage, and returned when an operation is complete. See also *roll in, roll out.*

rollover: a keyboard encoding mechanism permitting a number of keys to be depressed at the same time free from error.

roll paper: printer paper in continuous form found on a spool.

roll your own: a program created by a user for fitting specific needs as a substitute for purchasing a generalized package for the purpose.

ROM: see *read-only memory.*

ROMable: a code designed to be placed in ROM memory.

ROM address lines: lines or pins used to choose a specific word in ROM.

ROM assimilator: a self-contained computer system with assembly and utility programs that can develop, debug, and simulate proposed ROM programs.

ROM loader: a loader program that is implemented in ROM.

ROM-oriented architecture: a system where a microprocessor instruction set is executed completely from ROM without the need for external RAM.

ROM/RAM: a circuit containing a mask programmable MOS ROM in addition to RAM; designed for applications requiring only a small amount of ROM and RAM.

ROM/RAM/CPU: a chip for low cost applications which contains a processor along with RAM and ROM memories.

ROM simulator: a device created to replace ROM or PROM during program development and debugging; simulates PROM or ROM configurations and provides an inexpensive means of altering microprograms.

ROM terminal: a terminal using a ROM for storing instructions.

root directory: the first-level directory of any disk. It is created when the user first formats a disk and then is able to create files and subdirectories in it.

root node: in PASCAL, the external pointer to a tree data structure; the top or base node of a tree.

root segment:

(1) in overlay program, the segment that remains in storage during the execution of the overlay program; the first segment in an overlay program.

(2) in a database, the highest segment in the hierarchy.

ROS: see *read-only storage.*

rotate: a computer instruction that causes the bits in a word to shift a certain number of places to the left or to the right.

rotational delay: the amount of time taken for the recording surface of a direct-access storage unit to rotate the proper position under the read/write head; used in estimating access time and expressed in milliseconds.

rotational position sensing (RPS): a feature that permits a disk storage device to disconnect from a block multiplexer channel (or its equivalent), allowing the channel to service other devices on the channel during positional delay.

RO terminal: a communicating machine able to receive but not transmit. Most printers are RO terminals.

round: to delete or omit one or more of the least significant digits in a positional representation and to adjust the part retained in accordance with some specified rule. The purpose of rounding is usually to limit the precision of the numeral or to reduce the number of characters in the numeral, or to do both. The most common forms of rounding are rounding down, rounding up, and rounding off. (B) Cf. *truncation.* (A)

round down: to round, making no adjustment to the part of the numeral that is retained. If a numeral is rounded down, its absolute value is not increased. Rounding down is a form of truncation. (A) (B)

rounding error: an error due to roundoff. (B) Cf. *truncation error.*

round off: to round, adjusting the part of the numeral retained by adding 1 to the least significant of its digits, and executing any necessary carries, if (a) the most significant of the digits deleted was greater than half the radix of that digit place, or (b) the most significant of the digits deleted was equal to half the radix and one or more of the following digits were greater than zero, or (c) the most significant of the digits deleted was equal to zero, and the least significant of the digits retained was odd. In (c) even may be substituted for odd. (A) (B)

round robin: a cyclical multiplexing technique, allocating resources in fixed-time slices.

round up: to round, adjusting the part of the numeral that is retained by adding 1 to the least significant of its digits, and executing any necessary carries if and only if one or more nonzero digits have been deleted. If a numeral is rounded up, its absolute value is not decreased. (A) (B)

route: see *virtual route.* See also *routing.*

routine (RTN): part of a program, or a sequence of instructions called by a program, that may have some general or frequent use. See *dump routine, input routine, library routine, output routine, recursive routine, reusable routine, subroutine, supervisory routine, tracing routine, utility routine.*

routing: the assignment of the path by which a message will reach its destination.

routing affinity: a temporary relationship between a source and a destination.

routing code: a combination of one or more digits used to route a call to a predetermined area.

routing indicator: an address, or group of characters, in the header of a message defining the final circuit or terminal to which the message has to be delivered.

routing key: see *key.*

row: a horizontal arrangement of characters or other expressions. Cf. *column.* See *card row, mark-sensing row, punch row.* (A)

row binary: pertaining to the binary representation of data on cards on which the significances of punch positions are assigned along card rows. For example, each row in an 80-column card may be used to represent 80 consecutive binary digits. Cf. *column binary.* (A)

row matrix: a matrix of one row and n columns. A row vector.

row pitch: the distance between corresponding points of adjacent rows, measured along a track. Synonymous with *array pitch.* (A) (B)

row scanning: an approach in decoding which key of a keyboard was pressed. Each row is scanned in turn by outputting a 1. The output on the columns when examined, results in identification of the key.

RP: see *reader-printer.*

RPE: see *required page-end character.*

RPG: see *report program generator.* (A)

RPGII: a commercially oriented programming language specifically designed for writing application programs that meet common business data-processing requirements.

RPL: see *remote program loader.*

RPN: see *reverse Polish notation.*

RPQ: request for price quotation. A customer request for a cost estimate for programming support and/or alterations or additions to a computer system.

RPROM: reprogrammable read only memory.

RPS: see *rotational position sensing.*

RPT: see *repeat character.*

RRN: see *relative record number.*

RS:

(1) see *real storage.*

(2) see *record separator character.*

R-S flip flop: a flip-flop using two cross-coupled NAND gates.

RSM: see *real storage management.*

RSP: see *required space character.*

RST:

(1) see *remote station.*

(2) see *reset.*

R-S-T flip-flop: synonymous with *binary pair.*

RS-422-423: Electronics Industries Association standards for serial transmission that extends the distances and speeds beyond RS-232 standard. Both interfaces may be implemented with a variety of other connectors. See *RS-232C.*

RS-232C: the industry standard for a 25-pin interface that connects computers and various forms of peripheral equipment, for example, modems, printers, and so on.

RS-232 compatible controller: a module created for interfacing a microcomputer system to most asynchronous modems.

RT:

(1) see *real time.*

(2) see *remote terminal.*

(3) see *response/throughput bias.*

(4) see *real-time clock.*

(5) see *real-time executive.*

(6) see *resistor-transistor logic.*

(7) see *register transfer module.*

(8) see *routine.*

(9) see *real-time system.*

rub-out character: synonym for *delete character.*

rude: slang, a badly written program.

ruler: a line on which margins and tabs are set, usually in word processing. A format line.

run:

(1) a single performance of one or more jobs. (B)

(2) a single, continuous performance of a computer program or routine. (A)

runaway: the condition which arises when an input to a physical system is subject to a sudden, negative increase or decrease.

runaway tape: resulting from hardware error or malfunction, when a tape reel spins out of control, resulting often in the tape ripping.

run book: all material needed to document a computer application, including problem statement, flowcharts, coding, and operating instructions.

run chart: a flowchart of one or more computer runs in terms of input and output.

run diagram: files, transactions, information, and data in a graphic representation that are handled under the program control to yield the newly updated files, list of alterations, or specific reports.

run documentation: detailed instructions written for an operator, outlining how to run a particular computer program.

run duration: synonym for *running time.* (A) (B)

run indicator: an indicator for showing that the processor is in a run mode.

run locator: a routine which locates the correct run on a program tape, whether initiated by another routine or manually.

run mode: a mode where the computer is considered to be functioning when it is automatically executing instructions held in its memory cards and cells.

running dry: examination of the logic and coding of a program from a flowchart and written instructions, and recording of the results of each step of the operation before running the program on the computer.

running time: the elapsed time taken for the execution of a computer program. Synonymous with *run duration*. (A) (B)

run phase: synonymous with *target phase*.

run schedule: a listing of work to be performed under time needed to carry out such work.

run stream: synonym for *job stream*.

run-time: the phase of program execution during which program instructions are performed.

run-time error: a program error not detected during translation, that causes a processing error to occur during execution.

run-time error handler: a systems software facility for intercepting, diagnosing, and issuing error messages pertaining to run-time error.

run-time library: a set of utility routines from a language translator for interfacing the program with a specific operating system.

run unit: in COBOL, a set of one or more object programs that function at object time as a unit to provide problem solutions.

RVA: see *recorded voice announcement*.

RW: see *read/write*.

RWCS: see *report writer control system*.

RWM: see *read/write memory*.

RWND: see *rewind*.

rx: abbreviation for receive.

RZ: see *reset to zero*.

S:
(1) see *scalar*.
(2) see *set*.
(3) see *sign*.
(4) see *software*.
(5) see *source*.
(6) see *stack*.
(7) see *state*.
(8) see *storage*.
(9) see *synchronous*.
(10) see *system*.

SA:
(1) see *system administrator*.
(2) see *systems analyst*.

SAM: see *sequential-access method*.

sample (SMPL):
(1) to obtain the values of a function for regularly or irregularly spaced distinct values of an independent variable. (B)
(2) in statistics, obtaining a sample from a population. (A)

sampling:
(1) a random method of checking and controlling the use of data by obtaining the values of a function for regularly or irregularly spaced, discrete values.
(2) a method of communication control in which messages are selected by a computer that chooses only those for which processing is needed.
(3) in statistics, obtaining a sample from a population.

sampling rate: in computer graphics, the frequency at which points are recorded in digitizing an image. Sampling errors can cause aliasing effects.

SAS: statistical analysis system. An integrated system of programs written in PL/1, contained in one package program and used in data analysis, including modification and programming of data, file handling, and report writing.

satellite computer (SC):
(1) a computer that is under the control

of another computer and performs subsidiary operations.

(2) an off-line auxiliary computer.

satellite processor (SP): an information processor which is arbitrarily assigned a subsidiary role in a system, communicating with (and perhaps depending upon to some degree) a host for support services and/or guidance. See *satellite computer.*

save:

(1) to record permanently and store a program or data on a storage unit such as a floppy disk.

(2) to preserve something that has been typed onscreen.

(3) to save information by transferring it from main memory (RAM) to a disk. Work that is not saved disappears when the computer is turned off or if the power is interrupted.

save area: an area of main storage in which the contents of registers are saved. (A)

save as: a command that lets the user save the current version of a document under a different name. This new document is kept open so the user can continue editing.

SB: see *standby.*

SBA: see *shared batch area.*

SBC: see *single board computer.*

SBS: see *subscript character.*

SC:

(1) see *satellite computer.*

(2) see *semiconductor.*

(3) see *session control.*

scalar (S): a quantity characterized by a single number. (B) Cf. *vector.* (A)

scalar data type: a set of distinct values (constants) that are ordered.

scalar item: in PL/1, a single item of data; an element.

scalar multiplication: the product of a real number and a matrix.

scalar variable: in PL/1, a variable that can represent only a single data item; an element variable.

scale:

(1) to change the representation of a quantity, expressing it in other units, so that its range is brought within a specified range. (B)

(2) to adjust the representation of a quantity by a factor in order to bring its range within prescribed limits. (A)

(3) in computer graphics, to enlarge or reduce all or part of a display image by multiplying their coordinate by constant values.

(4) a system of mathematical notation: fixed-point or floating-point scale of an arithmetic value.

scale factor (SF):

(1) a number used as a multiplier in scaling. (A) (B)

(2) in FORTRAN, a specification in a FORMAT statement whereby the location of the decimal point in a real number (and, if there is no exponent, the magnitude of the number) can be changed.

(3) in PL/1, a specification of the number of fractional digits in a fixed-point number.

(4) see *time scale factor.* (A)

scaler:

(1) a device that generates an output equal to the input multiplied by a constant.

(2) a converter used at the input of a unit, bringing the quantity being measured within the range of measurement or the instrument.

scaling:

(1) in computer graphics, enlarging or reducing all or part of a display image by multiplying the coordinates of the image by a constant value.

(2) in assembler programming, indicating the number of digit positions in object code to be occupied by the fractional portion of a fixed-point or floating-point constant.

scamp: a small, cost-effective microprocessor where addresses are produced by four 16-bit pointer registers with processor timing generated on the chip.

scan:

(1) to examine sequentially, part by part. (A)

(2) in word processing, rapid view of displayed text by vertical scrolling.

(3) see *directed-beam scan.*

scanned interrupt: an interrupt system where each peripheral unit is polled in a predetermined order so that the one with the highest priority is serviced first.

scanner (SCN): a device that examines a spatial pattern one part after another, and generates analog or digital signals corresponding to the pattern. Scanners are often used in mark sensing, pattern recognition, or character recognition. (B) See *optical scanner.* (A)

scanning: the sequential examination or exposure of a set of characters or image.

scanning machine: a device that automatically reads printed data and converts it into machine language. Two types of this machine are optical scanners and magnetic-ink scanners.

scanning order: the order in which the computer searches the disk drives for a startup disk. See *start-up disk.*

scanning rate: the rate at which a scanner samples.

scanning unit: any attachment to a microform reader permitting the user to bring any section of the microform to a position in which it can be more easily read. Synonymous with *scanner.*

scatter diagram: synonymous with *scatter plot.*

scatter gap: the alignment deviation of magnetic recording head gaps, for groups of heads for racks of a magnetic tape handler.

scatter loading: placing the control sections of a load module into nonadjoining positions of main storage. Cf. *block loading.*

scatter plot: in computer graphics, shows a two-variable frequency distribution by plotting a dot or symbol at each data point. Sometimes a line or curve is added to show the correlation (if there is one) between the variables represented on the two axes. Synonymous with *dot chart* and *scatter diagram.*

scatter read: locating data in noncontiguous memory areas as it is being read into the computer system.

SCERT: Systems and Computers Evaluation and Review Technique. Mechanized routines for creating a model of a computer system by evaluating various hardware configurations. Used widely in data-processing planning and hardware selection.

SCH:
(1) see *schedule.*
(2) see *scheduler.*

schedule (SCH): to select jobs or tasks that are to be dispatched. (B)

scheduled downtime: the needed idle time required for normal servicing of computer devices when such equipment is unavailable for functioning. Usually expressed as a percent of the total available time.

scheduled operation: the time periods when a user plans to utilize specific devices, excluding hours rescheduled for equipment failure.

schedule job: a control program that is used to examine the input work queue and to select a next job to be processed.

schedule maintenance: maintenance carried out in accordance with an established schedule. (A) (B)

scheduler (SCH): a computer program designed to perform functions such as scheduling, initiation, and termination of jobs. (A) See *master scheduler.*

scheduler work area (SWA): an area in virtual storage that contains most of the job management control blocks (such as the JCT, JFCB, SCT, and SIOT). There is one scheduler work area for each initiator.

scheduling: allocating the time of a module.

scheduling theory: a prescriptive theory dealing with the sequencing of events; for example, orders processed through a job shop or time sharing in a computer system, so as to optimize some output measure like minimum time to accomplish all jobs or maximize the number of jobs completed on time.

schematic diagram: a diagram showing the scheme of a circuit or system utilizing graphic symbols; allows for continuous circuit and flow paths.

schematic symbols: stylized line drawing representing various elements and used universally (e.g., AND gate, NOR gate).

scholar's work station: a computer uniquely designed to tie into data networks far more complex than anything in place today. Synonymous with *3-M machine.*

scientific data processing: the use of electronic data processing for scientific research. Cf. *administrative data processing.*

scientific instruction set (SIS): a set of instructions that includes the instructions of both the standard instruction set and the floating-point feature.

scientific notation: the expression of quantities as a fractional part (mantissa) and a power of ten (characteristics). See *mantissa.*

scissoring: in computer graphics, removing parts of a display image that lies outside a window. Synonymous with *clipping.* Cf. *shielding.*

SCN: see *scanner.*

scope: in assembler programming, that part of a source program in which a variable symbol can communicate its value. See also *global, local.*

scope (of a condition prefix): in PL/1, the portion of a program throughout which a particular condition prefix applies.

scope (of a declaration): in PL/1, the portion of a program throughout which a particular declaration is a source of attributes for a particular name.

scope (of a name): in PL/1, the portion of a program throughout which the meaning of a particular name does not change.

scored card: a special card that contains one or more scored lines to facilitate precise folding or separation of certain parts of the card. (A)

SCP: see *system control program.*

SCPD: see *scratch pad.*

scrapbook: a desk accessory in which frequently used pictures or passages of text can be saved. The scrapbook can store multiple images. Cut or copy images from the scrapbook can be copied into documents created with most application programs. Cf. *clipboard.*

scratch: to erase data on a volume or delete its identification so that it can be used for another purpose.

scratch file: a file used as a work area.

scratch pad (SCPD) (SP): synonymous with *temporary storage area.*

scratch tape: a tape that contains information not intended to be retained.

screen: an illuminated display surface; for example, the display surface of a CRT or plasma panel.

screen attribute byte: a character position on the screen of a display terminal that defines the characteristics of the next field displayed on the screen such as protected, not protected, displayable, nondisplayable.

screen dump: transferring images or data from a terminal display to storage or a peripheral unit in order to have it printed.

screen fonts: fonts found on a screen.

screen format: the way information is shown on a display.

screen generator: a program to aid in the definition of CRT screen forms, which are a particular pattern of symbols on a CRT screen for data entry and display.

screen image: in computer graphics, a pattern of points, lines, and characters displayed on an illuminated display surface of a display device. See also *display image.*

screen image buffer: the area within memory holding an image of the information shown on the display. A program writes information into the screen image buffer and then relays this buffer as a message to the display, thereby changing the viewed output.

screenload: the maximum number of characters that can appear on a screen at any given time.

screen-oriented programs: in word processing, displays on a video screen exactly as it will appear on the printed page.

screen read: permitting a message displayed on a terminal screen to be retransmitted to a microprocessor or peripheral device, in order that data can be formatted for storage or for editing.

screen refresh: see *refresh.*

screen saver: a program that automatically darkens the computer screen following a period of inactivity so as to save the picture tube from phosphor burn-in caused by having the same image on the screen for too long a time period.

scroll: to move all or part of the display image vertically to display data that cannot be observed within a single display image.

scroll bars: the bars that appear at the right and bottom edges of a window. A scroll bar contains scroll arrows that the user can clock to scroll the view up or down in small steps, and a slider against a gray paging area to represent where the user is in relation to the entire document.

scrolling:
(1) in computer graphics, moving vertically or horizontally a display image in a manner such that new data appear at one edge as old data disappears at the opposite edge.
(2) in word processing, the functions of scroll up, scroll down, scroll right, or scroll left.
(3) see also *translating*.

scrub: to pass through a significant amount of data, avoiding duplication or unwanted items of information.

SCSI: Small Computer System Interface. A specification of mechanical, electrical, and functional standards for connecting peripheral devices such as hard disks, printers, and optical disks to small computers.

SCSI cable terminator: a device used in a SCSI chain to maintain the integrity of the signals going through the chain. With some devices, the terminator is built in.

SCSI chain: a group of SCSI devices linked to one another through SCSI peripheral cables and linked to the SCSI port on the computer through a SCSI system cable.

SCSI port: the socket on the back panel of the computer to which SCSI devices can be connected.

SDA: source-data automation, the various approaches for recording data in coded forms on paper tapes, punched cards, or tags that can be reused to yield many other records without rewriting.

SDI: selective dissemination of information, pertaining to a literature search notification and hard copy supply system that serves clients with internal or external documents.

SDL: see *system directory list*.

SDLC (synchronous data link control): a communications line discipline associated with the IBM system network architecture SNA and offers a number of advantages to users of data networks.

SE: see *system engineer*.

search:
(1) the examination of a set of items for one or more having a given property. (B)
(2) to examine a set of items for one or more having a given property. (A) (B)
(3) see *binary search, chaining search, dichotomizing search, Fibonacci search*. (A)

search and replace: in word processing, changing the word or character in the document, or changing the word or character to any other word or character.

search cycle: the part of a search that is repeated for each item, normally consisting of locating the item and carrying out a comparison. (A) (B)

searching storage: synonymous with *associative storage*.

search key: in the conduct of a search, the data to be compared to specified parts of each item. (A) (B) Synonym for *seek key*.

search language: synonymous with *command language* and *query language*.

search terms: words or groups of words used in on-line searching when specifying a request for information. Search terms correspond to headings under which items in a database are indexed.

search time: time needed to find a particular field of data in storage.

secondary: in a high-level data-link control (HDLC), the part of a data station that executes data-link control functions as instructed by the primary. Cf. *primary*.

secondary allocation: a data storage area for a disk file when the major space allocation is insufficient to hold the total file.

secondary channel: a channel that is part of a device such as a modem, which enables tests and diagnostic information to be obtained about the performance of the modem without interrupting the primary channel, which is used for data transmission. Cf. *primary channel*.

secondary console: in a system with multiple consoles, any console except the master console. The secondary console handles one or more assigned functions on the multiple console system.

secondary destination: any of the destinations specified for a message except the first destination.

secondary entry point: in PL/1, an entry point identified by any of the names in the label list of an ENTRY statement.

secondary key: a portion of the first block of each record in an indexed data set that may be used to find the record in the data set. The secondary key is valid only when so defined in the data set control block (DSCB). See also *primary key.*

secondary level address: the part of an instruction indicating a location where the address of the referenced operand is found.

secondary logical unit (SLU) key: a key-encrypting key used to protect a session cryptography key during its transmission to the secondary half-session.

secondary memory: memory used for transferring large blocks of data into main storage, having a large capacity and a long access time.

secondary station: a data station that can perform the secondary function, but not the primary function.

secondary storage: synonym for *auxiliary storage.*

secondary store: synonymous with *backing store.*

second computer age: the coming of artificial intelligence by computers. See *artificial intelligence.*

second-generation computer: a computer utilizing solid state components.

second-level addressing: see *level of addressing.*

second source: an alternative supplier of an item of hardware or software. The availability of a second source is usually a major consideration when purchasing devices.

section:
(1) in COBOL, a logically related sequence of one or more paragraphs. A section must always be named.

(2) in computer graphics, to construct the bounded or unbounded intersecting plane with respect to one or more displayed objects and then to display the intersection.
(3) deprecated term for *segment.* (A) (B)
(4) see also *control section.*

section header: in COBOL, a combination of words that precedes and identifies each section in the environment, data, and procedure divisions.

section name: in COBOL, a word specified by the programmer that precedes and identifies a section in the procedure division.

section number: the number that identifies a specific section in a series of sections that make up a file.

section text: part of a load module with computer instructions in final form and data defined with specified initial values.

sector: that part of a track or band on a magnetic drum, a magnetic disk, or a disk pack that can be accessed by the magnetic heads in the course of a predetermined rotational displacement of the particular device. (B) See *disk sector.*

security: see *data-processing system security, data security.*

seek: to selectively position the access mechanism of a direct-access device. Deprecated term for *search (1), search (2), search cycle.* (A)

seek area: synonymous with *cylinder.*

seek key: in word processing, a control used to locate an address on the recording medium. Synonymous with *search key.*

seek time: the time that is needed to position the access mechanism of a direct-access storage device at a specified position. See also *access time.*

SEG: see *segment.*

segment (SEG):
(1) a self-contained portion of a computer program that may be executed without the entire computer program necessarily being maintained in internal storage at any one time. (B)
(2) to divide a computer program into segments. (A) (B)
(3) see *child segment, dependent segment, logical child segment, logical parent seg-*

ment, overlay segment, parent segment, physical child segment, physical parent segment, physical segment, root segment.

segmentation: a programmer-defined and monitor-implemented approach of separating a program into self-contained segments so that only certain parts need be in memory at any one time.

segmenting: dividing information into unique units that can be handled at once.

segment mark: a special character written on tape to separate each section of a tape file.

segment number: the part of a virtual storage address needed to refer to a segment.

segregating unit: a device that pulls and/or separates individual cards from a group. The device is equipped with two feeding magazines and four receivers that interfile or segregate the cards into various sequences, at the speed of hundreds of cards per minute from each feeding magazine.

seize: to gain control of a line in order to transmit data. Cf. *bid.*

select:
(1) to choose one of several alternate subroutines from a file of subroutines.
(2) to activate the control and data channels to and from an input-output unit, preparatory to reading from or writing on the machine.
(3) to take alternative A if the report on a condition is of one state, and alternative B if the report on the condition is of another state.

selectable unit (SU): a collection of new and changed modules and macros that provide added program function or hardware support. Selectable units are shipped independently of a release and are installed singly or in groups at the option of the user.

selecting: the process of requesting one or more data stations on a multipoint connection to receive data.

selecting data: extracting specific or relevant information from a large body of data or the removal of certain records from the file.

selection:
(1) addressing a terminal or a component on a selective calling circuit.
(2) the process by which a computer contacts a station to send it a message.
(3) see also *blind, lockout, polling.*

selection check: a check that verifies the choice of devices, such as registers, in the execution of an instruction. (A)

selection-replacement approach: an approach used in the internal part of a sort program. The results of the comparisons between groups of records are stored for use later.

selection sort: a sort in which the items in a set are examined to find an item that fits specified criteria; this item is appended to the sorted set and removed from further consideration, and the process repeated until all items are in the sorted set. See *repeated selection sort.* (A)

selective assembly: run tapes that have programs chosen by the programmer from both an input deck of new programs and a tape file of previously processed symbolic programs.

selective cryptographic session: a cryptographic session in which an application program is allowed to specify the request units to be enciphered. Cf. *mandatory cryptographic session.*

selective dissemination of information: see *SDI.*

selective dump: the dumping of the contents of one or more specified storage areas. (A) (B)

selective erase: a feature that allows the operator to revise any portion of an image on a display by removing only the offending part instead of having to redraw the entire picture less that part to be altered.

selective listing: the output printing of data that meets various sets of predetermined criteria.

selective trace: a tracing routine that uses only specified criteria. Typical criteria include: instruction tape (arithmetic jump), instruction location (specific region), and data location (specific region).

selector mode: one of the two modes in which a block multiplexer channel can operate.

selector pen: a penlike instrument that can be attached to a display station. When a program using full-screen processing is assigned to the display station, the pen can be used to select items on the screen or to generate an attention. Synonym for *light pen.*

selector pen attention: synonym for *light pen attention.*

self-adapting computer: a computer that has the ability to change its performance characteristics in response to its environment. (A) (B)

self-adapting program: a computer program that has the ability to change its performance characteristics in response to its environment. (A) (B)

self-checking code: synonym for *error-detecting code.* (A)

self-checking number: a number with a suffix figure related to the figure(s) of the number, used to verify the number after it has been transferred from one medium or unit to another.

self-complementing code: a machine language where the code of the complement of a digit is the complement of the code of the digit.

self-defining term: in assembler programming, an absolute term whose value is implicit in the specification of the term itself.

self-demarking code: synonym for *self-checking code.* See *error-detecting code.*

self-documenting code: in PASCAL, a program containing meaningful identifier names, as well as judicious clarifying comments.

self-learning: a capability of a computer to improve its capability so that it can make decisions as programmed with instructions and based on information received, new instructions received, results of calculations, or environmental changes.

self-organizing computer: a computer that has the ability to make rearrangements in its internal structure. (A) (B)

self-organizing program: a computer program that has the ability to make rearrangements in its internal structure. (A) (B)

self-relative address: a relative address that uses as a base the address of the instruction in which it appears. (A) (B)

self-relative addressing: a method of addressing in which the address part of an instruction contains a self-relative address. (A) (B)

self-relocating program: a program that can be loaded into any area of main storage, and that contains an initialization routine to adjust its address constants so that it can be executed at that location.

self-resetting loop: synonymous with *self-restoring loop.*

self-restoring loop: a loop that has instructions causing all locations addressed during the loop to be restored to the condition that was obtained when the loop was entered. Synonymous with *self-resetting loop.*

semanteme: an element of language that expresses a definite image or idea; for example, the word *tree.*

semantic error: an error concerned with the meaning or intent of the programmer that is his/her responsibility. The programmer is then provided with an extensive set of debugging aids for manipulating and referencing a program when in search of errors in the logic and analysis.

semantics:

(1) the relationships of characters or groups of characters to their meanings, independent of the manner of their interpretation and use. (B)

(2) the relationships between symbols and their meanings. (A)

semicompiled: converted by a compiler from a source language into an object code, though not including subroutines needed by the source language program.

semiconductor (SC): a material with an electrical conductivity that is between that of a metal and an insulator. Silicon is a common semiconductor used in the manufacture of computer chips. See *hole pattern.*

semiconductor disk: a significant memory for emulating a disk drive where action occurs more quickly and thereby upgrades performance. Synonymous with *nonrotating disk.*

semiconductor memory: a type of main memory on a semiconductor where bits are stored as on or off states, or in which the elements are magnetized in either of two directions. Cf. *bubble memory, core memory.*

semirandom access: a method for locating information in memory that combines in the search for the desired item some form of direct access, usually followed by a limited sequential search.

sense:
(1) the study of data relative to a set of criteria.
(2) to determine the arrangement of hardware, in particular a manually set switch.
(3) to read holes in cards or paper and magnetic spots on tape, drums, and so forth.

sensing: see *mark sensing.* (A)

sensing element: the part of a unit that is directly responsive to the value of the measured quantity.

sensing station: synonym for *read station.* (A) (B)

sensitivity analysis: the interdependence of output values by a test of a range of input values.

sensitivity control: synonymous with *conference control.*

sensor: a device that converts measurable elements of a physical process into data meaningful to a computer.

sensor-based: pertaining to the use of sensing devices, such as transducers or sensors, to monitor a physical process.

sensor-based computer: a computer designed and programmed to receive real-time data (analog or digital) from transducers, sensors, and other data sources that monitor a physical process. The computer may also generate signals to elements that control the process. For example, the computer might receive data from a gauge or flow meter, compare the data with a predetermined standard, and then produce a signal that operates a relay, valve, or other control mechanism.

sensor-based system: an organization of components, including a computer whose primary source of input is data from sensors and whose output can be used to control the related physical process.

sentence: in COBOL, a sequence of one or more statements, the last ending with a period followed by a space.

sentinel: synonym for *flag.* (A)

separating character: synonym for *information separator.* (A) (B)

separator: synonym for *delimiter.* See *group separator, information separator.* See also *file separator character, record separator character, unit separator character.* (A)

separator page: in a printout, the page preceding and following an actual report, indicating the name of the job that produced it, the time and date, and other pertinent information for identifying the output.

septet: a byte composed of seven binary elements. Synonymous with *seven-bit byte.* (A) (B)

SEQ:
(1) see *sequence.*
(2) see *sequential.*

sequence (SEQ):
(1) a series of items that have been sequenced. (B)
(2) an arrangement of items according to a specified set of rules; for example, items arranged alphabetically, numerically, or chronologically.
(3) deprecated term for *order.* (B)
(4) synonym for *collating sequence.* (B)
(5) see *collating sequence, consecutive sequence computer, pseudorandom number sequence, random number sequence, recursively defined sequence.* (A)

sequence by merging: to sequence by repeated splitting and merging. (A) (B)

sequence checking: used to prove that a set of data is arranged in either ascending or descending order prior to processing.

sequence checking routine: a routine that verifies each instruction executed and prints out certain data; for example, to print out the coded instructions with addresses, and the contents of each of several registers, or it can be designed to print out only selected data, such as transfer instructions and the quantity actually transferred.

sequence computer: see *arbitrary sequence computer, consecutive sequence computer.*

sequence control register: deprecated term for *instruction address register.* (B)

sequence control tape: a tape that contains the sequence of instructions needed for solving a problem.

sequence counter: synonymous with *sequence control register.*

sequence error: an error caused when a card is not in sequence within an object program.

sequence numbering: the numbering of records in a file, of messages, of source program statements, and other such entities in processing to indicate their order. The purpose is only to indicate order, not to count items.

sequence packing: the procedure for loading the upper half of an accumulator with the first data word, shifting this into the lower half, loading the second datum, shifting, and so on, so that the three data words are packed in sequence.

sequencer: a device that puts items of information into a particular order; for example, it will determine whether A is greater than, equal to, or less than B, and sort or order accordingly.

sequence register: a register that, when activated, designates the address of the following instruction to be performed by the computer.

sequence symbol: in assembler programming, a symbol used as a branching label for conditional assembly instructions. It consists of a period, followed by one to seven alphanumeric characters, the first of which must be alphabetic.

sequencing by merging: a technique of repeated merging, splitting, and remerging to place items into an organized arrangement.

sequencing criteria: the fields in a record that determine, or are used as the basis for determining, the sequence of records in a file.

sequencing key: synonym for *sort key.* (A)

sequential (SEQ): pertaining to the occurrence of events in time sequence, with no simultaneity or overlap of events. Cf. *concurrent, consecutive, simultaneous.* (A)

sequential access:

(1) the facility to obtain data from a storage device or to enter data into a storage device in such a way that the process depends on the location of that data and on a reference to data previously accessed. (A) (B)

(2) an access mode in which records are obtained from, or placed into, a file in such a way that each successive access to the file refers to the next record in the file. The order of the records is established by the programmer when creating the file.

(3) cf. *direct access.*

sequential-access method (SAM): see *basic sequential access method.*

sequential-access storage: a storage device in which the access time depends upon the location of the data and on a reference to data previously accessed. (B)

sequential batch processing: a mode of operating a computer in which a run must be completed before another run can be started. (A)

sequential circuit: a logic device whose output values, at a given instant, depend upon its input values and internal state at that instant, and whose internal state depends upon the immediately preceding input values and the preceding internal state. A sequential circuit can assume a finite number of internal states and may therefore be regarded, from an abstract point of view, as a finite automaton. (A) (B)

sequential collating: sequencing a group of records by comparing the key of one record with another record until equality, greater than, or less than, is determined.

sequential computer: a computer in which events occur in time sequence, with little or no simultaneity or overlap of events. (A)

sequential control: a mode of computer operation in which instructions are executed in an implicitly defined sequence until a different sequence is explicitly initiated by a jump instruction. (A) (B)

sequential data set: a data set whose records are organized on the basis of their successive physical positions, such as on magnetic tape. Cf. *direct data set.*

sequential file organization: the arrangement of data records in a predetermined order, for example, alphabetically or numerically; the records can be accessed only serially by examining each record in turn until the desired one is located. Either serial or random access storage devices may be used.

sequential logic element: a device having at least one output channel and one or more input channels, all characterized by discrete states, such that the state of each output channel is determined by the previous states of the input channels. Cf. *combinational logic element.* (A)

sequential operation: a mode of operation in which two or more operations are performed one after another. Synonymous with *consecutive operation.* (A) (B)

sequential organization: records of a sequential file are arranged in the order in which they will be processed.

sequential processing (sp): the processing of records in the order in which records are accessed.

sequential queue: the first-in, first-out method of queuing items waiting for the processor.

sequential sampling: a sampling inspection where the decision to accept, reject, or inspect another unit is made following the sampling of each unit.

sequential scheduling system: a form of the job scheduler that reads one input stream and executes only one job step at a time from that input stream.

sequential search: a search strategy where each record key of an ordered file is compared to the desired key until a proper match is determined, with the records compared in the order in which they appear within the file. Cf. *binary search.*

sequential storage device: a storage unit, that is, a magnetic tape, providing sequential access to data stored on it, and pos-

sessing an access time dependent upon the location of the data, as an item can be accessed only by first reading through the preceding data.

SER: see *serial.*

SERDES: serializer/deserializer. A device that serializes output from, and deserializes input to, a business machine.

SEREP: see *system error recording editing program.*

serial (SER):

(1) pertaining to the sequential performance of two or more activities in a single device. In English, the modifiers *serial* and *parallel* usually refer to devices, as opposed to *sequential* and *consecutive,* which refer to processes. (B)

(2) pertaining to the sequential processing of the individual parts of a whole, such as the bits of a character or the characters of a word, using the same facilities for successive parts.

(3) cf. *parallel.* (A)

serial access: the facility to obtain data from a storage device or to enter data into a storage device in such a way that the process depends on the location of that data and on a reference to data previously accessed. (B) Cf. *direct access.* Synonym for *sequential access.* (B)

serial-access storage: a storage device in which the access time depends upon the location of the data and on a reference to data previously accessed. (B)

serial adder: a digital adder in which addition is performed by adding, digit place after digit place, the corresponding digits of the operands. (A) (B)

serial addition: addition that is performed by adding, digit place after digit place, the corresponding digits of the operands. (A) (B)

serial attribute coding: coding where the attributes of a character to be displayed are stored as nondisplayable codes in the page store serially with characters to be displayed.

serial bit-stream: binary digits found in sequence one following the other, where the pattern of bits within a specific sequence can have a particular meaning.

serial bit transmission: a data transmission system where the bits representing a character are consecutively transmitted.

serial-by-bit: the handling of character bits in a fashion of one following another; either serially or in parallel.

serial computer:

(1) a computer having a single arithmetic and logic unit.

(2) a computer, some specified characteristic of which is serial; for example, a computer that manipulates all bits of a word serially.

(3) cf. *parallel computer.* (A)

serial data: data transmitted sequentially, a bit at a time.

serial data controller: a digital receiver-transmitter that interfaces specific microcomputers to a serial communications channel.

serial file: a file where items are sequentially entered requiring that they also be searched sequentially.

serial flow: activities for each operation are performed singly and not at the same time other tasks are being completed.

serial input-output: a method of data transfer between a computer and a peripheral unit where data are transmitted for input to the computer or output to the unit bit by bit over a single circuit.

serialize: to change from parallel-by-byte to serial-by-bit. Cf. *deserialize.*

serializer: a device that converts a space distribution of simultaneous states representing the data into a corresponding time sequence of states. Synonymous with *dynamicizer.* (B) Synonym for *parallel-to-serial converter.*

serially reusable: the attribute of a routine that allows the same copy of the routine to be used by another task after the current use has been concluded.

serially reusable load module: a module that cannot be used by a second task until the first task has finished using it.

serially reusable resource (SRR): a logical resource or an object that can be accessed by one task at a time.

serial memory: memory where items are stored and obtained sequentially, one at a time.

serial mouse: a mouse that can be connected to a serial port.

serial number: an integer denoting the position of an item in a series. (A) (B)

serial operation: pertaining to the sequential or consecutive execution of two or more operations in a single device such as an arithmetic or logic unit. Deprecated term for *sequential operation.* Cf. *parallel operation.* (A)

serial-parallel: a combination of serial and parallel; for example, serial by character, parallel by bits comprising the character.

serial-parallel converter: apparatus created for altering data in serial format to parallel format.

serial-parallel register: a shift register used for performing serial-to-parallel data conversion.

serial ports: the connectors for peripheral devices that receive data in a serial format (that is, one bit at a time).

serial printer: synonymous with *character printer.*

serial processing: pertaining to the sequential or consecutive execution of two or more processes in a single device such as a channel or processing unit. Cf. *parallel processing.* (A)

serial programming: programming of a computer where only one arithmetical or logical operation can be executed at a time, for example, a sequential operation.

serial sort: a sort that requires only sequential access to the items in a set. A serial sort can be performed using only serial access storage devices. (A)

serial storage: see *sequential-access storage.*

serial-to-parallel converter: a device that converts a sequence of signal elements into a corresponding group of digits, all of which are presented simultaneously. Synonymous with *deserializer, staticizer.*

serial transfer: a transfer of data in which elements are transferred in succession over a single line.

serial word operation: a feature of some handling units in which words are read, one following another, in groups.

serial work flow: a system of operations where each operation is performed singly, and not simultaneously with other tasks.

series:

(1) a set of related mathematical expression terms.

(2) appearing in a string of individual but related items.

server: a computer or device that administers network functions and applications. See *dedicated server.*

serviceability: the capability to perform effective problem determination, diagnosis, and repair on a data-processing system.

service bit: a bit used in data transmission dealing with the process and not the data itself.

service bureau: an organization that packages its services so that all users have to do is to supply the input data and pay for the results.

service program: a computer program that performs utility functions in support of the system. Synonym for *utility program.*

service rate: in the system resource manager, a measure of the rate at which system resources (services) are provided to individual jobs. It is used by the installation to specify performance objectives, and used by the work-load manager to track the progress of individual jobs. Service is a linear combination of processing unit, I/O, and main storage measures that can be adjusted by the installation.

service request interrupts: interrupts used for servicing buffer channel requests. They are an internal machine function and are not directly under the control of the programmer.

service routine: synonymous with *utility routine.* (A) (B)

servomotor controller: a computer-based device capable of running multiaxis DC servomotor-controlled machines.

servomultiplier: an analog computer device that has a position control and is able to multiply each of several different variables by a single variable, represented by analog voltages. The multiplier is used as an input signal to a mechanism that turns shafts.

session:

(1) a connection between two stations that allows them to communicate.

(2) the period of time during which a user of a terminal can communicate with an interactive system; usually, the elapsed time between log on and log off.

(3) see *batch session, work session.*

session control (SC): an RU category used for requests and responses exchanged between the session control components of a session and for session activation/ deactivation requests and responses.

session logic: a protocol setting up ways to log on to the system, to hold a session with the computer, and to log off.

set (S):

(1) a finite or infinite number of objects of any kind, of entities, or of concepts, that have a given property or properties in common. (B)

(2) to cause a counter to take the state corresponding to a specified number. Cf. *reset (1).* (A) (B)

(3) to put all or part of a data-processing device into a specified state, usually other than that denoting zero. (B)

(4) see *alphabetic character set, alphabetic-coded character set, alphanumeric character set, alphanumeric-coded character set, card set, character set, coded character set, code set, empty set, instruction set, machine instruction set, numeric character set, numeric-coded character set, universal set.* (A)

(5) see *data set.*

set breakpoint: a user debug command designed to create the setting of a breakpoint in a memory location. At program execution, this breakpoint, when encountered, causes a temporary program suspension and a transfer of control to the system debug routine.

set-point control: a control system operating from commands or information from variable set points in the system.

set symbol: in assembler programming, a variable symbol used to communicate values during conditional assembly processing.

settling time: time needed for a dot to move to a new point on the screen and stay still without vascillating. It is an important specification for displays made from dots. Dot writing time and settling time, together, determine the maximum rate at which one can produce a clean, stored display using binary data.

setup:

(1) in a computer that consists of an assembly of individual computing units, the arrangement of interconnections between the units, and the adjustments needed for the computer to operate upon a particular problem. (B)

(2) an arrangement of data or devices to solve a particular problem. (A) (B)

(3) the preparation of a computing system to perform a job or job step. Setup is usually performed by an operator and often involves performing routine functions, such as mounting tape reels and loading card decks.

setup diagram: a diagram specifying a given computer setup. (A) (B)

setup time: the time required by an operator preparing a computing system to perform a job or job step.

seven-bit byte: synonym for *septet.* (A) (B)

several-for-one: a transaction considered to mean the creation of a number of machine instructions from one program instruction. This is an indication of the various types of software.

severity code: a code assigned to an error detected in a source module.

sexadecimal:

(1) pertaining to a selection, choice, or condition that has sixteen possible different values or states. (B)

(2) pertaining to a fixed-radix numeration system having a radix of sixteen. Synonymous with *hexadecimal.* (A) (B)

sexadecimal notation: synonymous with *hexadecimal notation.*

sextet: a byte composed of six binary elements. Synonymous with *six-bit byte.* (A) (B)

SF: see *scale factor.*

SFT: see *shift.*

shadow: to increase computer speed by switching tasks to RAM memory from ROM memory.

Shannon: in information theory, a unit of logarithmic measures of information equal to the decision content of a set of two mutually exclusive events expressed by the logarithm to base two; for example, the decision content of a character set of eight characters equals three Shannons. Synonymous with *information content binary unit.* (A) (B)

shared batch area (SBA): a temporary storage area in the store controller where all data received from, or transmitted to, the host processor is stored while waiting to be operated upon.

shared DASD: disk drives and/or drum storage shared by two or more independent, adjacent computers.

shared data base: a database used in a computer networking environment that can be updated and accessed simultaneously by users in differing locations, applying programs that provide updating and control means operating independently of the location of the data.

shared disk:

(1) a magnetic disc that may be used for information storage by two or more systems at the same time.

(2) a hard disk, CD-ROM disc, or other medium whose contents can be retrieved over the network. A disk can be shared by a file server or a computer that has file sharing turned on.

shared file: a direct-access device that may be used by two systems at the same time; a shared file may link two systems.

shared folder: a folder that is available to some or all network users over the network.

shared main storage multiprocessing: a mode of operation in which two processing units have access to all of main storage.

shared read-only system residence disk: a system residence disk that is tailored so that most of the system residence information is read only and accessible to all relevant virtual machines, leaving a relatively smaller private read/write system disk that must be dedicated to each virtual machine. This technique can substantially reduce the disk requirements of an installation by avoiding needless duplication of disk packs by virtual machines that use the same operating system.

shared storage: the ability to share core storage between two computers, where either machine can insert information into storage, and either device can access the data and use it.

shared system: see *shared read-only system residence disk.*

shared virtual area (SVA): an area located in the highest addresses of virtual storage. It can contain a system directory list (SDL) of frequently used phases, resident programs that can be shared between partitions.

shareware: software that can be tried without purchasing. The user is honor-bound to pay for the software if he or she continues to use it.

sharing: interleaved time use of a device; a method of activity where a computer facility is shared by several users concurrently.

Sheffer stroke: synonym for *NAND*. (A)

shelf life: the length of time a document, or unit, will remain serviceable to users.

shell:
(1) a program that connects and interprets commands written by users for the underlying operating system. A shell interprets user requests, calls programs from memory, and executes them one at a time.
(2) a synonym for *user interface.*

SHF: see *shift.*

shielding: in computer graphics, blanking of all portions of display elements falling within some specified region. Synonymous with *reverse clipping.* Cf. *scissoring.*

shift (SFT) (SHF):
(1) the converted movement of some or all of the characters of a word each by the same number of character places in the direction of a specified end of the word. (A) (B)
(2) to move data to the right or left.

(3) see *arithmetic shift, end-around shift, logical shift.* (A)

shift character: a control character that determines the alphabetic/numeric shift of character codes in a message.

shift down modem: a modem which yields a change from a higher to a lower bit rate.

shift-in character (SI): a code extension character, used to terminate a sequence that has been introduced by the shift-out character, that makes effective the graphic characters of the standard character set. (A) (B)

shifting register: a register created or adapted to perform shifts.

shift instruction: a computer instruction causing the contents of an accumulator register to shift to the right or to the left.

shift-out character (SO): a code extension character that substitutes for the graphic characters of the standard character set an alternative set of graphic characters upon which agreement has been reached or that has been designated using code extension procedures. (A) (B)

shift register (SB): a register in which shifts are performed. (A) (B)

shop: see *closed shop, open shop.*

short card: a special-purpose paper card that is shorter in length than a general-purpose paper card; for example, a 51 column card. (A)

shortest word: a word of the shortest length that a computer can utilize, and which is most often half of the full length word.

short instruction: the use of an index specification in a FORTRAN READ or WRITE statement.

short instruction format: a standard length, that is, one word, instruction as opposed to a long instruction. Most instructions are of this type.

short-line seeking: when a line ready for printing does not cover the full page, the printer performs a carriage return at the end of the short line and commences to print a new line, speeding up printer efficiency.

short stack: a stack of only a few bytes, which are used to permit the monitor program to store flags temporarily when interrupts occur. The short stack improves the interrupt handling capability of the computer at low cost.

short-term storage: data stored in core memory for a brief time period.

short word: a fixed word of lesser length within a system that is capable of handling words of two different lengths. Often referred to as a half-word because the length is exactly the half-length of a full word.

shoulder tap: a technique that enables one processing unit to communicate with another processing unit.

show: a console command giving the status of a system function.

show D: indicate disks currently up on specific spindles.

show P: display which jobs are running and in which partition at a given time.

show T: indicate tapes being held by specific jobs.

SHY: see *syllable hyphen character.*

SI:

(1) see *shift-in character.* (A) (B)

(2) single instruction.

(3) see *swap-in.*

SIB: see *screen image buffer.*

sieve of Erasosthenes: see *Erasosthenes' sieve.*

sift: extracting desired items of information from a large amount of data.

sifting sort: synonym for *bubble sort.* (A)

SIG:

(1) see *signal.*

(2) see *special interest group.*

SIGGRAPH: special interest group for graphics. A nonprofit organization dedicated to the advancement of computer graphics.

sight check: a check performed by sighting through the holes of two or more aligned punched cards toward a source of light to verify the punching; for example, to determine if a hole has been punched in a corresponding punch position on all cards in a card deck. (A)

sign (S): the symbol which distinguishes positive from negative numbers.

signal (SIG):

(1) a variation of a physical quantity, used to convey data.

(2) see *start signal.*

signal distance: the number of digit positions in which the corresponding digits of two binary words of the same length are different. Synonymous with *hamming distance.* (A)

signal-enabling: a means of permitting an operation to occur.

signaling rate: see *data signaling rate.*

signal inhibiting: a way of preventing an operation from occurring.

signal level: an OCR term that relates to the amplitude of the electronic response which occurs from the contrast ratio between the area of a printed character and the area of a document background.

signal quality detector: a pin on an interface for a modem showing if there is a probability that an error has taken place in data received by the modem.

signal regeneration: signal transformation that restores a signal so that it conforms to its original specification. (A) (B)

signal tracing: the following of a signal path in hardware or on diagrams to locate faults.

sign and currency symbol characters: in PL/1, the picture specification character S, +, -, and $. These can be used (a) as static characters, in which case they are specified only once in a picture specification and appear in the associated data item in the position in which they have been specified, or (b) as drifting characters, in which case they are specified more than once (as a string in a picture specification) but appear in the associated data item at most once, immediately to the left of the significant portion of the data item.

signature analysis: a way of isolating digital logic faults at the component level. Although considered most useful in servicing microprocessor-based products, the technique is applicable to all digital systems. It involves the tracing of signals and the conversion of lengthy bit streams into four-digit hexadecimal signatures.

signature testing: the comparison of the actual output digital signatures, such as transition counts, with the expected correct signatures recorded from a known-good unit.

sign bit: a bit or a binary element that occupies a sign position and indicates the algebraic sign of the number represented by the numeral with which it is associated. (A) (B)

sign character: a character that occupies a sign position and indicates the algebraic sign of the number represented by the numeral with which it is associated. (A) (B)

sign check indicator: an indicator set, according to specification, on a change of sign or when a sign is either positive or negative.

sign condition: in COBOL, a statement that the algebraic value of a data item is less than, equal to, or greater than zero. It may be true or false.

sign digit: a digit that occupies a sign position and indicates the algebraic sign of the number represented by the numeral with which it is associated. (A) (B)

signed binary: a binary representation of signed integer numbers setting aside one bit, often the high-order or leftmost bit, to show the sign of the number.

signed decimal: a type of packed decimal numeric representation where the low-order nibble of the last byte contains a value showing whether the number is positive or negative.

signed field: a field that has a character in it to designate its algebraic sign.

signed number: the number preceded by a negative or positive sign.

signed packed decimal: representation of a decimal value by two adjacent digits in a byte. The rightmost four bits of the field contain a sign. See also *packed decimal.*

sign flag: a CPU flag status byte showing the sign (positive or negative) of the result of an arithmetic action.

significance: synonym for *weight.* (A) (B)

significant digit: in a numeral, a digit that is needed for a given purpose; in particular, a digit that must be kept to preserve a given accuracy or a given precision. (A) (B)

significant digit arithmetic: a method of making calculations using a modified form of a floating-point representation system in which the number of significant digits in the result is determined with reference to the number of significant digits in the operands, the operation performed, and the degree of precision available. (A) (B)

significant figure: deprecated term for *significant digit.* (A) (B)

sign magnitude: a scheme for binary representation where the most critical bit is used for the sign and the rest of the number represents the absolute value.

sign-off: the closing instruction to the computer, which terminates communication with the system.

sign-on: the opening instruction to the computer, which begins communications with the system.

sign position: a position, normally located at one end of a numeral, that contains an indicator denoting the algebraic sign of the number represented by the numeral.

silicon chip: a wafer of silicon providing a semiconductor base for a number of electrical circuits. See also *chip, steppers.*

Silicon Valley: the area near Sunnyvale, in the Santa Clara Valley of California where numerous semiconductor manufacturers are located.

SIM: see *simulator.*

SIMM: Single In-line Memory Module, a circuit board that contains eight RAM chips (as well as a ninth to check parity). SIMMs are connected to SIMM sockets on the computer's main circuit board.

simple buffering: a technique for controlling buffers in such a way that the buffers are assigned to a single data control block and remain so assigned until the data control block is closed.

simple condition: in COBOL, an expression that can have two values, and causes the object program to select between alternate paths of control, depending on the value found. The expression can be either true or false.

simple parameter: in PL/1, a parameter for which no storage-class attribute is specified; it may represent an argument of any storage class, but only the current generation of a controlled argument.

simple sequence: program logic where one statement after another is executed in order, as stored.

simple type: a scalar type; a type that is not structured; any of the PASCAL types; INTEGER, REAL, BOOLEAN, CHAR, or any user-defined (ordinal) type.

SIMUL: see *simultaneous.*

simulate:

(1) to represent certain features of the behavior of a physical or abstract system by the behavior of another system; for example, to represent a physical phenomenon by means of operations performed by a computer or to represent the operations of a computer by those of another computer. (B)

(2) to imitate one system with another, primarily by software, so that the imitating system accepts the same data, executes the same computer programs, and achieves the same results as the imitated system.

(3) cf. *emulate.* (A)

simulated attention: a function that allows terminals without attention keys to interrupt processing. The terminal is queried periodically for a specified character string. See also *attention interruption.*

simulation: the representation of selected characteristics of the behavior of one physical or abstract system by another system; for example, the representation of physical phenomena by means of operations performed by a computer system, the representation of operations of a computer system by those of another computer system. Cf. *emulation.* See *real-time simulation.* (A)

simulation language: a language created to simulate systems utilizing computers.

simulation modeling: representing reality with mathematical models to show the impact of changes on the values of specific reality factors.

simulator (SIM): a device, data-processing system, or computer program that represents certain features of the behavior of a physical or abstract system. (B) See *computer simulator.* (A)

simultaneity: to permit central processor functions to occur at the same time as input-output activities.

simultaneous (SIMUL): pertaining to the occurrence of two or more events at the same instant of time. (B) See also *consecutive, sequential.* Cf. *concurrent.* (A)

simultaneous access: synonymous with *parallel access.*

simultaneous computer: a computer that contains a separate unit to perform each portion of the entire computation concurrently, the units being interconnected in a way determined by the computation; at different times in a run, a given interconnection carries signals representing different values of the same variable; for example, a differential analyzer.(A) (B)

simultaneous contrast: in computer graphics, changes in the appearance of a color relative to its background or adjacent colors.

simultaneous input-output: in word processing, the process in which some word processors allow a new document to be typed (or an old document to be revised) while another document is being printed. Sometimes called *background printing.*

simultaneous operation: a mode of operation in which two or more events occur at the same instant of time. (A) (B)

simultaneous peripheral operations online: see *spooling.*

simultaneous processing: the performance of two or more data-processing tasks at the same instant of time. Cf. *concurrent processing.*

simultaneous transmission: transmission of control characters of data in one direction while information is being received in the other direction. Cf. *nonsimultaneous transmission.*

single address: pertaining to an instruction format containing one address part. Synonymous with *one address.* (A)

single-address code: synonymous with *single-address instruction.*

single-address instruction: an instruction format containing one operand address only. Synonymous with *single-address code.*

single bit error: an error found in a data-transmission sequence where a single bit is inverted. For example, a 0 becomes a 1 or a 1 becomes a 0.

single board computer (SBC): a complete computer, including ROM, RAM<, CPU, and I/O interface, implemented on a single printed circuit board.

single-cycle key: a push button on printers that when pressed, causes an additional line to be printed despite an end-of-form indication.

single error: an erroneous bit, preceded and followed by at least one correct bit.

Single In-line Memory Module: see *SIMM.*

single-length working: representing binary numbers so that the value of each number will be contained in a single word.

single-operand addressing: where one portion of the instruction word specifies a register; the second portion provides information for locating the operand, that is, clear, increment, test, and so on.

single-operand instruction: an instruction that contains a reference to a single register, memory location, or machine.

single operation: see *half-duplex.*

single-pass program: a program that results in the production of the solution to a problem or following one run, of one computer word to represent a number in accordance with the required precision.

single precision: pertaining to the use of one computer word to represent a number in accordance with the required position. (A) (B)

single quote mark: a special FORTRAN character used to enclose literal messages.

single setup: a method of operating a computer where each step is performed in response to a single manual operation.

single-sheet feeding: feeding of separate sheets of paper rather than roll or fan-folded form.

single sided: a method of disk storage utilizing one side of a disk.

single-sided double-density: see *SSDD.*

single-sided single-density: see *SSSD.*

single-step: pertaining to a method of operating a computer in which each step is performed in response to a single manual operation. (A) See also *single stepping.*

single-step debug: a debugging technique using short routines to set up system states for checking the response of a microprocessor.

single-step operation: a mode of operating a computer in which a single computer instruction or part of a computer instruction is executed in response to an external signal. Synonymous with *step-by-step operation.* (A) (B)

single stepping:
(1) working through a program by hand, one step at a time.
(2) a troubleshooting strategy where the computer is slowed down so that a technician can directly obtain information at specified processing steps.

single thread: the potential for doing one and only one thing at a time.

single-user system: a computer or word processor designed for one person only.

single vertical key: a push button on a printer that produces an additional printed line for indication.

single-word instruction: an instruction format requiring only one memory location.

sink: see *data sink, message sink.* (A)

SIO: see *serial input-output.*

SIS: see *scientific instruction set.*

site: the physical or geographical location of a system such as a room, building, or building complex. Colocated systems are typically interconnected by local privately owned communications facilities.

six-bit BCD: a six-bit digit computer code using unique combinations of zone bits and numeric bits to represent specific characters.

six-bit byte: synonym for *sextet.* (A) (B)

16K RAM: see *64K RAM.*

64K RAM: random-access memory that stores more than 64,000 bits of computer data on a tiny slice of silicon, four times as much as the 16K RAM—the previous generation chip. See also *RAM.*

SK: see *skip.*

skeletal code: a set of instructions in which some parts such as addresses must be completed or specified in detail each time the set is used. (A) (B)

skew: the angular deviation of recorded binary characters from a line perpendicular to the reference edge of a data medium. (B)

skew character: a form of incorrect registration in optical character recognition.

skip (SK):

(1) to ignore one or more instructions in a sequence of instructions.

(2) to pass over one or more positions on a data medium; for example, to perform one or more line feed operations. (A)

(3) see also *paper throw.* (A)

skip code: a functional code that instructs the machine to skip certain predetermined fields in memory.

skip flag: a one bit, in a specific position, that causes bytes to be skipped until the count equals zero, thus permitting the computer to ignore portions of the input record to the memory.

skip instruction: an instruction having no impact other than directing the processor to proceed to another instruction designated in the storage portion.

skip key: in word processing, a control that initiates the skip process. Synonymous with *access button.*

skipping: advancing paper through a printer without printing on it.

skipping print zones: in BASIC, a technique that involves enclosing a space (i.e., the character blank) in quotation marks.

skip test: a microinstruction for conditional operations based on the state of readiness of units in a register.

slack bytes: in COBOL, bytes inserted between data items or records to ensure correct alignment of some numeric items. Slack bytes contain no meaningful data. In some cases, they are inserted by the compiler; in others, it is the responsibility of the programmer to insert them. The "synchronized" clause instructs the compiler to insert slack bytes when they are needed for proper alignment. Slack bytes between records are inserted by the programmer.

slate PC: a notebook computer with an electronic pen interface. See *notebook.*

slave computer: a backup system consisting of a second computer that performs the same steps of the same programs executed by the master computer. If the master computer fails or malfunctions, the slave computer takes over without interruption of operation. See *failsafe system, volatile memory.* Cf. *rescue dump, satellite processor.*

slave mode: the mode of computer operation where most of the basic controls affecting the computer's condition are protected from the program.

slave tube: a cathode-ray tube connected to another CRT so that both units will perform in the same way.

slave unit: a unit submitting to the control of another external machine, the master. Cf. *master.*

SLDR: see *system loader.*

sleep: a machine's apparent inactivity when an error causes an endless loop.

SLIB: see *source library.*

slice architecture: a microcomputer architecture using a section of the register file and arithmetic and logic unit in one package. Each end of each 2- or 4-bit register is accessible through the chip's edge, to permit registers to be cascaded together forming larger word lengths.

slot: see *expansion slot.*

slow storage: a device or storage modem with access time more lengthy in relation to the speeds of arithmetic activities of the computer and more lengthy when compared to other faster access peripheral devices.

slow-time scale: synonym for *extended-time scale.* (A)

SLSI: super large-scale integration; more than 100,000 transistors for each chip.

SLT: see *solid logic technology.*

SLU: see *secondary logic unit.*

slurp: slang, to read a large data file entirely into core before working on it.

small-business computer: a computer used for small business data processing that usually comes with software and is relatively easy to operate.

Small Computer System Interface: see *SCSI.*

small scale integration (SSI): the technology holding one to ten gates per unit.

smart machines: computers that assist plant managers to optimize scheduling by turning out different products on different days or even different hours, thus evolving a parts-on-demand facility.

smart peripheral: a peripheral unit having its own processor and memory, so as to relieve the host system of many functions normally associated with the functioning of that peripheral. Synonymous with *intelligent peripheral.*

smart-power integrated circuit: a chip combining on a single bit of silicon the logic of a computer and the electric-power handling capabilities usually assigned to a collection of power transistors and other components.

smart terminal: a terminal with processing potential that functions without the power of the computer to which it is attached.

smash: a destruction of an area of program or memory by overwriting with another segment of program or memory.

S-mod records: in COBOL, records that span physical blocks. Records may be fixed or variable in length. Blocks may contain one or more segments. A segment may contain one record or a portion of a record. Each segment contains a segment-length field control field indicating whether or not it is the first, last, only, or an intermediate segment of the record. Each block contains a block-length field.

smoke test: the moment when a unit is turned on for the first time. If there is no smoke it is assumed the device is functioning properly.

smooth: to apply procedures that decrease or eliminate rapid fluctuations in data. (A)

SMPL: see *sample.*

smudge: in OCR, the displacement of ink under shear beyond the edges of a printed character.

SNA: systems network architecture. A comprehensive product of hardware and software for integrated data-communications/data-processing systems.

snapshot debug: a debugging approach where the programmer specifies the beginning and end points of segments needed for a snapshot dump.

snapshot dump:
(1) a dynamic dump of the contents of one or more specified storage areas. (B)
(2) a selective dynamic dump performed at various points in a machine run. (A)

snapshot program: a trace program that produces output data only for selected instruction or for selected conditions. (A) (B)

snapshots: the capture of the total state of a machine (real or simulated)—the memory contents, registers, flags, and so on.

sniffing: an error detection and correction method in computing.

SNOBOL: see *string-oriented symbolic language.*

SO: see *shift-out character.* (A) (B)

socket: the end of a circuit, able to receive a plug to complete the circuit.

SOF: see *start-of-format control.*

SOFT: see *software.*

soft computer programs: see *soft software.*

soft copy: in computer graphics, a nonpermanent display image that cannot be separated from a display device; for example, data displayed on a CRT display device. Synonymous with *transient copy.*

soft error: deprecated term for *transient error.*

soft fail: synonymous with *fail soft.*

soft font: erasable fonts sent from a computer to a printer. Cf. *resident font.*

soft hyphen: a special hyphen character that prints only if it breaks a word at the end of a line; otherwise, it is invisible.

soft key: synonymous with *function key.*

soft keyboard: the display represented on a terminal screen that has been arranged in the form of a keyboard.

soft patch: a change made to a program's machine language code while the program is still in memory, lasting only as long as the program remains in memory. Cf. *hard patch.*

soft return: automatic returns inserted by a word-processing program. Cf. *hard return.*

soft sector: the portion of a disk marked by information written on the disk; used by the disk controller to locate particular areas of the disk.

soft-sectored disk system: a disk format in which the beginning of every sector is decided by the user and is recorded on the disk.

soft-sector formatting: the standard diskette, designed for use with a format where the sector information is prerecorded on the diskette during the initialize operation. In this case, a single hole on the diskette acts as a reference point. The format in which the sector information is prerecorded on the diskette is referred to as the *soft-sectored format.*

soft software: as contrasted with software that takes a general purpose computer and adapts it to a particular task, soft software takes a standard software product and adapts it to a particular user.

software (S) (SOFT) (SW):
(1) programs, procedures, rules, and any associated documentation pertaining to the operation of a computer system.
(2) in word processing, computer programs, procedures, rules, and any associated documentation concerned with the operation of a word-processing system.
(3) cf. *hardware.*

software bundling: see *bundling.*

software-compatible: pertaining to a computer that can accept and run programs prepared for other computers.

software configuration: the types of, and the relationships among, system control programs installed on a system.

software cross assembler: a software system for translating a symbolic representation of instructions and data into a form that can be loaded and executed by the computer.

software development process: a systematic technique for developing the software for any system.

software development system: all hardware that is used for the quick development of software.

software documentation: program listings and/or documentation consisting of technical manuals describing the operation and use of programs.

software driver: a series of instruction, followed by the computer to reformat data for transfer to and from a specific peripheral unit.

software emulation: software programs found in microprograms that allow one computer to execute the machine-language code of another computer, to minimize reprogramming during conversion of one system to another or for use in a development system.

software engineering: synonymous with *programming.*

software evaluation and development modules: a software system of modules that permit a means of building up and testing a proposed computer system prior to hardware production.

software floating point: routines built into high-level programming languages enabling them to perform floating-point arithmetic on computer hardware designed for integer arithmetic.

software house: a company that offers software support service to users.

software integrity: the reliability of software.

software interface: the rules permitting two computer programs to interact with each other, and ensuring the accurate and efficient transfer of information between the programs.

software library: the collection of programs used by an operating system.

software maintenance: the task of keeping software up-to-date and working properly.

software monitor: a software package, usually stored on PROMs that allows the computer to operate with a fundamental interactive intelligence.

software network components: software components available through a time-sharing service.

software package: the subroutine programs that are sold by the computer manufacturer, or from software firms, or individuals who write software programs.

software path length: the number of machine language instructions that need to be performed for a given task; the more instructions, the longer the path length, and the more time needed to complete the task.

software prototyping: software development providing program assembly, on-line execution, and debugging.

software stack: an area in read/write memory set aside under program control. An on-chip hardware stack provides increased performance.

software support system: executes the object program as a microprocessor. The programmer can check to determine if the original source program performs the functions accurately.

software system: the entire set of programs and software development aids in a computer system.

software tools: computer programs able to write other programs.

software trace mode: a mode where the program stops and the internal status of the microprocessor is made available to the outside world wherever breakpoint conditions are met. In addition to the mnemonic instructions and the memory addresses, the user views register contents, program counter location, stack pointer, and condition codes or flags. Breakpoints can be set at each instruction if so desired. The major advantage of this mode is the depth of insight it gives into program operation; it is fully interactive, enabling the user to alter register contents, make source code changes to correct program errors, reassemble programs, and rerun to test corrections.

SOH: see *start-of-heading character.* (A) (B)

solid error: an error that always occurs when a particular device is used.

solid logic technology (SLT): miniaturized modules used in computers, that re-

sult in faster circuitry because of reduced distance for current to travel.

solid state (SS): see *solid state component.*

solid state (SS) component: a component whose operation depends on the control of electric or magnetic phenomena in solids; for example, a transistor, crystal diode, ferrite code. (A)

solid state computer: a computer that uses solid state, or semiconductor, components. Synonymous with *second-generation computer.*

solid-state disk: see *semiconductor disk.*

solution check: a solution to a problem obtained by independent means to verify a computer solution.

sort (sorting):

(1) to segregate items into groups according to specified criteria. Sorting involves ordering, but need not involve sequencing, for the groups may be arranged in an arbitrary order. (B)

(2) the operation of sorting.

(3) to arrange a set of items according to keys which are used as a basis for determining the sequence of the items; for example, to arrange the records of a personnel file into alphabetical sequence by using the employee names as sort keys.

(4) in word processing, rearrangement of blocks of text in groups according to specific instructions.

(5) synonym for *order.*

(6) see *balanced merge sort, bubble sort, exchange sort, external sort, insertion sort, internal sort, merge sort, multipass sort, oscillating sort, polyphase sort, repeated selection sort, selection sort, serial sort, sifting sort, tournament sort, unbalanced merge sort.*

sort algorithm: the means for sorting data, that is, the internal procedure followed by the computer according to program instructions.

sort blocking factor: in sorting, the number of data records to be placed in each block.

sorter:

(1) a device that deposits punched cards in pockets selected according to the hole patterns in the cards. (B)

(2) a person, device, or computer routine that sorts.

(3) deprecated term for *sort program.* (A) (B)

sort field: a specified field in a record, used to sort the records of the file.

sort file: in COBOL, a collection of records to be sorted by a SORT statement. The sort file is created and can be used by the sort function only.

sorting: see *sort.*

sorting control field: a continuous group of characters within a record that forms all or a portion of the control word.

sorting item: the basic element of a file where the sorting of the file constitutes the reordering of file records.

sorting program: synonym for *sort program.* (A) (B)

sorting rewind time: elapsed time used by a sort/merge program for restoring intermediate and final tape to its original position.

sorting scratch tape: tape or tapes used to store intermediate-pass data during a sort program.

sorting sequencing key: the field in a record that determines, or is used as a basis for determining, the sequence of records in a file.

sorting string: a group of sequential records, normally stored in auxiliary computer storage, that is, disk, tape.

sorting variable-length records: denumerable file elements for which the number of words, characters, bits, fields, is not constant.

sorting work tape: a tape used to store intermediate-pass data during a sort program.

sort key:

(1) a key used as a basis for determining the sequence of items in a set.

(2) one or more keys within an item, used as a basis for determining the sequencing of items in a set. Synonymous with *sequencing key.* (A)

sort/merge file description entry: in COBOL, an entry in the file section of the data division that is composed of the level indicator SD, followed by a file name, and

then followed by a set of file clauses as required.

sort/merge generator: custom programs for sorting files of data.

sort/merge program: a processing program that can be used to sort or merge records in a prescribed sequence.

sort pass: during the execution of a sort program, a single processing of all items of a set for the purpose of reducing the number of strings of items and increasing the number of items per string. (A)

sort program: a computer program that sorts items of data. Synonymous with *sorting program.* (A) (B)

sort selection: in word processing, selection of storage addresses by means of predetermined codes.

sort utility: the activity performed by a program, often a utility package, in which items in a data file are arranged or rearranged in a logical or specifically defined sequence as designated by a key word or field in each item in the file.

sortworker: a temporary file established by a sort program for holding intermediate results when the amount of data for sorting is larger than the available memory workspace.

sound output port: a socket on the back panel of a computer marked with a speaker icon, used to connect headphones or speakers to the computer.

source (S) (SRC): the disk or folder that holds the original of a file to be copied or translated. See *data source, message source.* (A)

source address: in systems with source-destination architecture, the address of the unit or memory location from which data is being transferred.

source code: the program in a language prepared by a programmer. This code cannot be directly executed but first must be compiled into object code.

source code compatibility: pertaining to a system where changes to the system do not require changes to a user's source code, but may require a recompile or assembly of the source code. Cf. *object code compatibility.*

source-code instruction: an instruction used as a pointer in a microprogrammed system, emulating a specific instruction set being executed.

source computer: in COBOL, the name of the environment division paragraph where the computer upon which the source program is to be compiled is described.

source data:
(1) the data provided by the user of a data-processing system.
(2) the data contained in a source program or source module.

source data acquisition: direct entry of data into a computer at the point where the data originates.

source data automation: see *SDA*.

source data card: a card that contains manually or mechanically recorded data that is to be subsequently punched into the same card. (A)

source deck: synonymous with *source pack*.

source document: a form containing data that are eventually processed by a computer.

source editor: a program that facilitates the entry and modification of the source code into a computer system for later translation, on-line storage, off-line storage, or listing on a printer for later reference.

source file: a CRAM (Card Random-Access Memory) deck, disk, drum, or magnetic tape that holds the information file used as input to a computer run.

source item: in COBOL, an identifier designated by a SOURCE clause that provides the value of a printable item.

source key: in PL/1, a key referred to in a record-oriented transmission statement that identifies a particular record within a direct-access data set.

source language: a language from which statements are translated. (A) (B)

source language debugging: debugging information requested by the user and displayed by the system in a form consistent with the source programming language.

source language translation: the translation of a program to a target program to machine language the instructions

being equivalent in the source program and to the automatic or problem-oriented language, the translating process completed by the device under the control of a translator program or compiler.

source library (SLIB):
(1) a means for specifying computer processing; translated into object language by a compiler or assembler.
(2) a compiler language, for example, FORTRAN, from which machine-language instructions flow by the use of translation routines or compilers.
(3) the language in which the input to the FORTRAN processor is prepared.

source listing: a printout of a source program processed by a compiler and showing compiler messages, including any syntax errors in the program.

source machine: a device able to carry out the compilation of source code. Cf. *object-computer*.

source macrodefinition: in assembler programming, a macrodefinition included in a source module. A source macrodefinition can be entered into a program library; it then becomes a library macrodefinition.

source module: the source statements that constitute the input to a language translator for a particular translation.

source module library: a partitioned data set that is used to store and retrieve source modules. See also *load module library, object module library*.

source operand register: a register in some systems that contains the last source operand of a double operand instruction. The high byte may not be correct if the source is a forbidden mode.

source pack: a stack of punched cards with instructions in source code. Synonymous with *source deck*.

source program: a computer program expressed in a source language. (B) Cf. *object program*. (A)

source recording: the recording of data in machine-readable documents, such as punched cards, punched paper tape, or magnetic tape. Once in this form, the data may be transmitted, processed, or reused without manual processing.

source/sink (S/S):   see *data sink, data source.*

source statement: a statement in symbols of a programming language.

source statement library (SSL): a collection of books (such as macrodefinitions) cataloged in the system by the librarian program.

source table: in a program, a table containing predefined data elements from which the program can select an element to be moved automatically into the source area.

source tape: a tape that holds the source program.

source tape preparation: a program for preparing and editing symbolic source tapes, permitting the tape to be edited by typing commands on the keyboard which generate corrections and yield a new source tape.

source utility: facilitates the preparation and modification of symbolic assembly language source tapes.

SOUT: see *swap-out.*

SP:
(1) see *satellite processor.*
(2) see *scratch pad.*
(3) see *space.*
(4) see *space character.*
(5) see *stack pointer.*
(6) see *structured programming.*

space (SP):
(1) a site intended for the storage of data; for example, a site on a printed page or a location in a storage medium.
(2) a basic unit of area, usually the size of a single character.
(3) one or more space characters.
(4) to advance the reading or display position according to a prescribed format; for example, to advance the printing or display position horizontally to the right or vertically down. (A)
(5) see *display space, image storage space, virtual space, working space.*
(6) cf. *backspace.*

space allocation: the amount of data storage space assigned to a file on a disk drive.

space character (SP): a graphic character that is usually represented by a blank site in a series of graphics. The space charac-

ter, though not a control character, has a function equivalent to that of a format effector that causes the print or display position to move one position forward without producing the printing or display of any graphic. Similarly, the space character may have a function equivalent to that of an information separator. (A) (B) See also *numeric space character, required space character.* See also *null character.*

space code: similar to skip code, but restricted to one space only at a time.

space request: a parameter accompanying the establishment of a new file, stating the amount of disk storage space assigned to the file. If the space request cannot be satisfied, the system halts the job before commencing execution of the program that requires the file space.

space suppression: preventing a normal movement of paper in a printer following the printing of a line of characters.

span: the difference between the highest and the lowest values that a quantity or function may take. (B) See *error span.* (A)

spanned record: a record that is contained in more than one block.

sparse array: an array where zero is the predominant character.

spatial data: in computer graphics, locational data. Usually refers to distribution of variables or the relationships between variables in a geographic region. Demographic features, marketing distributions, energy resource data, and topographic data are examples of information readily represented spatially, that is, on a map.

SPEC: see *specification.*

special character:
(1) a graphic character in a character set that is not a letter, not a digit, and not a space character. (A) (B)
(2) in COBOL, a character that is neither numeric nor alphabetic. Special characters in COBOL include the space ( ), the period (.), as well as the following: $+ - *$ / $= \$, ; "$) (.

special interest group (SIG): individuals who gather and share information about a particular computer-oriented interest such as word processing, business applications, privacy and rights, and so on.

special interest group for graphics: see *SIGGRAPH.*

specialized application language: synonymous with *special-purpose language.*

SPECIAL-NAME: in COBOL, the name of an environment division paragraph in which implementor names are related to user-specified mnemonic names.

special-purpose computer: a computer that is designed to operate upon a restricted class of problems. (A) (B)

special-purpose language: a programming language designed for use in relatively narrow aspects of broader application areas; for example, COGO for civil engineering, CDL for logical design, GPSS for simulation. Synonymous with *specialized application language.*

special-purpose register: a CPU register dedicated to a specific function and available for that purpose only. Cf. *general-purpose register.*

special register (SR): in COBOL, compiler-generated storage areas primarily used to store information produced with the use of specific COBOL features.

special symbol (or character): a character other than a standard letter or number, such as #, &, or *.

specific address: synonym for *absolute address.* (A)

specification (SPEC): a precise definition of the records and programs needed to carry out a particular processing function.

specification statement: in FORTRAN, one of the set of statements which provide the compiler with information about the data used in the source program. In addition, the statement supplies support information required to allocate storage for this data.

specification subprogram: in FORTRAN, a subprogram headed by a BLOCK DATA statement and used to initialize variables in labeled (named) common blocks.

specific code: synonymous with *absolute code.*

specific coding: synonymous with *absolute coding.* (A)

specific polling: a polling technique that sends invitation characters to a device to find out whether the device is ready to enter data.

specific program: a program for solving a specific problem only.

specific routine: a routine for a particular data-handling problem where each address refers to explicitly stated registers and locations.

specific volume request: a request for volumes that inform the system of the volume serial numbers.

spectral response: the variation in sensitivity of a device to light of different wavelengths. (A)

spell check: synonymous with *dictionary.*

spelling: the order of signs as they appear within printed or written words.

spelling checker: software that proofreads by comparing every word in a text file to a dictionary, then marks and/or indicates misspelled words.

spider configuration: a type of distributed system in which a central computer is used to monitor the activities of several network computers.

spindle: synonym for *module.*

spin lock: a lock that prevents a processing unit from doing work until the lock is cleared. Cf. *suspend lock.*

split: the formation of two ordered files from one regular file.

split catalog: a library catalog where the different varieties of entry are filed separately, for example, subject entry, author entry.

split screen: the division into sections of a display surface in a manner that allows two or more programs to use the display surface concurrently.

splitting: the partitioning of the capacity of a storage device into independent sections.

spool: see *spooling.* (A)

spooler: software permitting input and output units to be shared by a large number of users in an orderly way and free of interference. Spoolers can also control input or output sequences in accord with a pre-programmed specification of priorities.

spooler/despooler: a system control program for controlling the spooling and printing of reports.

spooling (simultaneous peripheral operation on line):
(1) the use of auxiliary storage as a buffer storage to reduce processing delays when transferring data between peripheral equipment and the processors of a computer. (B)
(2) the reading of input data streams and the writing of output data streams on auxiliary storage devices, concurrently with job execution, in a format convenient for later processing or output operations. (B)
(3) synonymous with *concurrent peripheral operations.*

spot carbon: carbonizing on some areas so that only certain entries are reproduced on the copy.

spot punch: a device for punching one hole at a time in a data carrier. (B)

spread: synonym for *irrelevance.* (A) (B)

spreadsheet: a screen-oriented, interactive program enabling a terminal user to lay out financial or other numeric data on the screen. Rows and columns are totalled.

sprocket hole: synonym for *feed hole.* (A)

sprocket track: synonym for *feed track.*

SPS:
(1) see *string process system.*
(2) see *symbolic program system.*

SPSS: statistical package for the social sciences. An integrated system of programs within one package program; used to analyze social science data and written in FORTRAN.

SQ: see *squeezed files.*

square matrix: a matrix having the same number of rows and columns.

squeal: pertaining to magnetic tape, subaudible tape vibrations, primarily in the longitudinal mode, caused by frictional excitation at heads and guides.

squeezed files (SQ): normal data or program files placed in a more efficient fashion utilizing squeeze and unsqueeze (USQ) utilities to reduce wasted space and transfer time.

squeezeout ink: a means of printing to assist in optical character recognition re-

sulting in the outline of each character to be printed darker than its center.

squish: synonymous with *compaction.*

SR:
(1) see *shift register.*
(2) see *special register.*
(3) see *status register.*
(4) see *storage register.*

SRAM: see *static RAM.*

SRC: source.

SRM: see *system resources manager.*

SRR: see *serially reusable resource.*

SS:
(1) see *solid state.*
(2) see *start-stop character.*

S/S:
(1) see *source/sink.*
(2) see *start-stop character.*

SSD: solid state disk. See *semiconductor disk.*

SSDD: single-sided double-density. A data-recording format on floppy disk storage.

SSI: see *small scale integration.*

SSL: see *source statement library.*

SSSD: single-sided single-density. A data-recording format on floppy disk storage; the base format, to which other formats are compared (e.g., SSDD).

ST: see *start signal.*

ST-506: standard interface for connecting IBM-PC hard drives.

STA: see *station.*

stability: see *computational stability, light stability.* (A)

stable state: in a trigger circuit, a state in which the circuit remains until the application of a suitable pulse. (A) (B)

stable trigger: synonymous with *binary pair.*

stack (S) (STK): synonym for *push-down list, push-down storage.* (B)

stack architecture: a computer using a stack for part of its internal memory; reduces the number of registers needed for temporary storage and decreases the number of steps needed in a program.

stacked graph: a graph with two or three x scales and the same number of y scales plotted so that there are discrete plotting grids placed one above the other.

stacked job: synonym for *batched job (2).*

stacked job processing: a technique that permits multiple job definitions to be grouped (stacked) for presentation to the system, which automatically recognizes the jobs, one after the other. More advanced systems allow job definitions to be added to the group (stack) at any time and from any source, and also honor priorities. See also *batch processing.*

stacker: see *card stacker.*

stack indicator: synonym for *stack pointer.* (B)

stack manipulation: a system having instruction addressing modes that permit temporary data storage structures for the handling of data that is often processed.

stack pointer (SP): the address of the storage location holding the item of data most recently stored in push-down storage. Synonymous with *stack indicator.* (B)

STAE (specify task asynchronous exit): a macroinstruction that specifies a routine to receive control in the event of the issuing task's abnormal termination.

staging: the moving of data from an office or low-priority device back to an on-line or higher-priority device, usually on demand of the system or on request of the user. Cf. *data migration.*

STAI (subtask ABEND intercept): a keyword of the ATTACH macroinstruction that specifies a routine to receive control after the abnormal termination of a subtask.

stair stepping: the discontinuous nature of a line drawn by a raster display at any angle other than vertical, horizontal, or 45 degrees. A raster display approximates the line because of limitations of technology and resolution. See also *raster display device.*

stand-alone:
(1) pertaining to an operation that is independent of another device, program, or system.
(2) in word processing, a single, self-contained word processor, as opposed to a word-processing terminal that is connected to and dependent upon a remote memory and processing unit.

stand-alone data-processing system: a data-processing system that is not served by telecommunication facilities.

stand-alone emulator: an emulator whose execution is not controlled by a control program; it does not share system resources with other programs and excludes all other jobs from the computing system while it is being executed.

stand-alone key-to-tape device: a self-contained unit that takes the place of a keypunch device.

stand-alone modem: a modem that is separate from the unit with which it operates. Synonymous with *external modem.*

standard code sets: a set of internationally accepted codes and their approved significance within an approved data-communication code.

standard component: a component produced by one or more manufacturers.

standard data format: in COBOL, the concept of actual physical or logical record size in storage. The length in the standard data format is expressed in the number of bytes a record occupies and not necessarily the number of characters, since some characters take up one full byte of storage and others take up less.

standard file: in PL/1, a file assumed by the processor in the absence of a FILE or STRING option in a GET or PUT statement; SYSIN is the standard input file and SYSPRINT is the standard output file.

standard form: synonym for *normalized form.* (A) (B)

standard function: synonymous with *built-in function.*

standard interface: the interface form designed so that two or more devices, systems, or programs can easily be associated or joined.

standardize: synonym for *normalize.* (A) (B)

standard label (SL): a fixed-format identification record for a tape or disk file.

standard operating procedure: the regular or common mode of operation of a computer.

standard program: a computer program that meets certain criteria, such as being written in a standard machine language (FORTRAN, COBOL, ALGOL), and bringing forth an approved solution to a problem.

standard system action: in PL/1, action specified by the language to be taken in the absence of an on unit for an on condition.

standby (SB):
(1) a condition of equipment that permits complete resumption of stable operation with a short span of time.
(2) a duplicate set of equipment to be used if the primary unit becomes unusable because of malfunction.

standby application: an application where two or more computers are tied together as part of a single overall system, whereas with an inquiry application, stand ready for immediate activation and necessary action.

standby block: a technique in which spare input-output blocks of information are always in memory to make more efficient use of buffers.

standby computer: a computer used in a dual or duplex system that is ready to take over the real-time processing problems when needed.

standby equipment: automatic data-processing machines, not in use, but ready for emergencies caused by breakdowns and/or overload.

standby register: a register in which verified and or accepted information is stored for a future rerun in case a mistake is made during processing, or computer malfunction.

standby time:
(1) the elapsed time between inquiries when devices are operating on an inquiry application.
(2) the time when two or more computers are tied together and available to answer inquiries or process intermittent actions on stored data.

standby unattended time: time when the equipment is in an unknown condition and not in use working on problems.

Stanford mouse: a computer input device that looks like a mouse on roller skates. Rolling the plastic unit on a table top controls the movement of the cursor on the video display screen. See *mouse.*

standing-on-nines carry: in the parallel addition of numbers represented by decimal numerals, a procedure in which a carry to a given digit place is bypassed to the next digit place. If the current sum in the given digit place is nine, the nine is changed to zero. (A) (B)

star program: synonymous with *blue ribbon program.*

start bit: synonym for *start signal.*

start code:
(1) a bit at the beginning of a series of bits representing a single character. This code indicates the beginning of a character to maintain synchronization between the transmitting and receiving terminals.
(2) any bit sequence or character sequence used for signifying the beginning of a unit of information in a transmission sequence.

started task: a program, though not a part of the operating system, that is made resident and treated as though it were.

start element: synonym for *start signal.*

starting-dialing signal: in semiautomatic or automatic working, a signal transmitted from the incoming end of a circuit, after the receipt of a seizing signal, showing that the needed circuit conditions have been established for receiving the numerical routine information.

starting point: on a CRT display device, same as *current beam position.*

start key: in word processing, the control used to initiate certain preset functions of the equipment. Synonymous with *enter key, execute key.*

start-of-format control (SOF): a unique word-processing control grouping of characters used as a leading delimiter for a format parameter list embedded in a character string. Start-of-format delimits parameters that control tab stop settings, right margin, choice of single or double index, and text adjust mode operation.

start-of-heading character (SOH): a transmission control character used as the first character of a message heading. (A) (B)

start-of-text character (STX): a transmission control character that precedes a text and may be used to terminate the message heading. (A) (B)

start signal (ST):
(1) a signal to a receiving mechanism to get ready to receive data or perform a function. (A)
(2) in a start-stop system, a signal preceding a character or block that prepares the receiving device for the reception of the code elements. A start signal is limited to one signal element generally having the duration of a unit interval. Synonymous with *start bit, start element.*

start-stop (SS) (S/S) character: a character including one start signal at the beginning and one or two stop signals at the end.

start-stop time: see *acceleration time.*

start time: pertaining to the time between the interpretation of the tape instructions to read or write and the transfer of information to or from the tape into storage, or from storage into tape. Synonymous with *acceleration time.*

start up: to get a system running. Starting up is the process of first reading the operating system program from a disk and then running an application program.

start-up disk: a disk with all the necessary program files to set the computer into operation.

start-up drive: the disk drive that will start up the computer system.

STAT: see *status.*

state (S): see *input state, stable state, unstable state.*

state code: a coded indication of the state of the CPU, such as responding to an interrupt, executing an input-output instruction, and so on.

statement (STMT):
(1) in a programming language, a meaningful expression that may describe or specify operations and is usually complete in the context of that programming language. (B)

(2) in computer programming, a symbol string or other arrangement of symbols. (A)

(3) in COBOL, a syntactically valid combination of words and symbols written in the procedure division. A statement combines COBOL reserved words and programmer-defined operands.

(4) in FORTRAN, the basic unit of a program, composed of a line or lines containing some combination of names, operators, constants, or words whose meaning is predefined to the FORTRAN compiler. Statements fall into two broad classes: executable and nonexecutable.

(5) a basic element of a PL/1 program that is used to delimit a portion of the program, to describe names used in the program, or to specify action to be taken. A statement can consist of a condition list, a label list, a statement identifier, and a statement body that is terminated by a semicolon.

(6) deprecated term for *instruction.* (A) (B)

(7) see *assignment statement, conditional statement, job control statement.*

statement body: in PL/1, that part of a statement that follows the statement identifier, if any, and is terminated by the semicolon. It includes the statement options.

statement function: in FORTRAN, a function defined by a function definition within the program unit in which it is referred to.

statement function definition: in FORTRAN, a name, followed by a list of dummy arguments, followed by an equal sign (=), followed by an arithmetic or logical expression.

statement function reference: in FORTRAN, a reference in an arithmetic or logical expression to a previously defined statement function.

statement identifier: the PL/1 keyword that indicates the purpose of the statement.

statement label: a symbolic name or line number of a statement in a program, translated into a memory address.

statement-label constant: see *label constant.*

statement-label variable: see *label variable.*

statement number: in FORTRAN, a number of from one through five decimal digits placed within columns 1 through 5 of the initial line of a statement. It is used to identify a statement uniquely, for the purpose of transferring control, defining a DO loop range, or referring to a FORMAT statement.

statement separator: a symbol used to tell the compiler where one instruction ends and another begins in a program, such as the semicolon in PASCAL.

statement verb: the key word that describes the function to be performed when a statement is presented to a computer program.

state-of-the-art: the most current research and up-to-date technology in a specific field of endeavor.

static allocation: the allocation of resources to a program prior to execution. They remain assigned to the program until it completes execution. Cf. *dynamic allocation.*

static buffer allocation: synonym for *static buffering.*

static buffering: assigning a buffer to a job, program, or routing at the beginning of execution, rather than at the time it is needed. Synonymous with *static buffer allocation.* Cf. *dynamic buffering.*

static data structure: a data structure fixed in size at compile time. See *static allocation.*

static display image: in computer graphics, that part of a display image, such as a form overlay, that is infrequently changed by the user during a particular application. Synonymous with *background display image.* Cf. *dynamic display image.*

static dump: a dump that is performed at a particular point in time with respect to a machine run, frequently at the end of a run, and usually under the control of a supervisory program. (A) (B)

static error: an error that is independent of the time variable.

static file: a file that has a low rate of additions and deletions of records. Cf. *volatile file.*

static gain: the gain of a unit under steady-state conditions.

static handling: handling, completely done by the compiler program.

staticize:
(1) to convert serial or time-dependent parallel data into static form.
(2) loosely, to retrieve an instruction, and its operands from storage prior to its execution. (A)

staticizer: synonym for *serial-to-parallel converter.*

static magnetic cell: synonym for *magnetic cell.* (A)

static magnetic storage: the storage of information bits on a medium that retains the data in place so that it is available at any time.

static memory: memory that is nonvolatile and does not need to be refreshed as long as power is presented.

static RAM (SRAM): unlike ordinary, volatile memory, static memory retains its contents even when the main current is turned off. The trickle of electricity from a battery is enough to refresh it. Cf. *dynamic RAM.*

static relocation: in a multiprogramming system, the assignment of a set of storage locations in main memory to a program prior to being executed; those locations are then used by the program for all subsequent execution. Cf. *dynamic relocation.*

static storage: storage other than dynamic storage. (A)

static storage allocation: the allocation of storage for static variables.

static subroutine: a subroutine that involves no parameters other than the addresses of the operands.

static test mode: a setup mode of an analog computer during which special initial conditions are set in order to check the patching and the proper operation of the computing devices except the integrators. (B)

static turtle: in LOGO language, a cursor with a fixed spatial position and heading that responds to commands such as LEFT, FORWARD, and so on.

static variable: a variable that is allocated before execution of the program begins and that remains allocated for the duration of execution of the program.

station (STA):
(1) one of the input or output points of a system that uses telecommunication facilities; for example, the telephone set in the telephone system or the point where the business machine interfaces with the channel on a leased private line.
(2) one or more computers, terminals, devices, and associated programs at a particular location.
(3) see *control station, inquiry station, link-attached station, master station, read station, remote station, secondary station, work station.*
(4) see also *terminal.*

stationary information source: synonym for *stationary message source.* (A) (B)

stationary message source: a message source each message of which has a probability of occurrence independent of the time of its occurrence. Synonymous with *stationary information source.* (A) (B)

stationary: a document that serves as a template. When opening a stationary document, a copy of the document is created and opened. The original remains unchanged.

statistical analysis system: see *SAS.*

statistical multiplexor: synonymous with *intelligent time division multiplexor.*

statistical package for the social sciences: see *SPSS.*

statmux: statistical multiplexor. Synonymous with *intelligent time division multiplexor.*

status: the current condition of a device or machine; usually indicates the flag flip-flops or special registers.

status bit handshaking: delegating certain bits of a parallel I/O port to coordinate information transfer with a peripheral unit, signifying device read, buffer full, printer out of paper, and so on.

status byte: a byte of storage containing neither data nor a machine instruction, but showing one or more alternative conditions used to control execution of a program.

status lights: lights on the front of a printer that indicate the status of the printer— on, paper jam, processing a job, etc.

status register (SR) (STR): a register containing information about the condition of a functional unit or peripheral device.

status scan: a key or command that causes scans of all modems, on a selected line, and displays the status of modem/terminal power, and so on.

status word: information needed to resume processing after the handling of interruption of operations.

steady-state: a condition where all values remain essentially constant or recur in a cyclic fashion.

step:
(1) one operation in a computer routine.
(2) to cause a computer to execute one operation.
(3) see *job step, single-step.* (A)

step-by-step operation: synonym for *single-step operation.* (A) (B)

step change: the change from one value to another in a single increment and in negligible time.

step counter: a counter in the arithmetic unit for counting the steps in a process such as multiplication, division, or shift operations.

step function: a function which is zero preceding time zero, and then has a constant value after time zero.

steppers: ultrasophisticated machines that print integrated circuits on silicon. A stepper fabricates tiny chips with millions of transistors. The silicon wafer is moved one step ahead, therefore the word stepper, to print the next group of chips.

step restart: a restart that begins at the beginning of a job step. The restart may be automatic or deferred, where deferral involves resubmitting the job. See also *checkpoint restart.*

step-wise refinement: in PASCAL, a design method in which an algorithm is specified at an abstract level and additional levels of detail are added in successive iterations throughout the design process. See *top-down testing*.

STK: see *stack*.

STMT: see *statement*.

stochastic: containing an element of chance.

STOP: a console command. Allows the operator to stop the partition in which the operation is given.

stop bit: synonym for stop signal.

stop character (STP): a word processing control that interrupts the sequence of output processing and provides a means for the operator or machine to make changes in text-processing parameters or data. See also *repeat character, switch character*.

stop instruction: an exit that specifies the termination of the execution of a computer program. (A) (B)

stop loop: a small closed loop used for operator convenience, that is, to show an error, improper usage, or special result.

stopper: the highest memory location in any given system.

STOP statement: the BASIC statement that halts the execution of a program.

stop time: the elapse of time between completion of reading or writing of a tape record and the time when the tape ceases to move.

STOR:

(1) see *storage*.

(2) see *store*.

storage (S) (STOR):

(1) the retention of data in a storage device.

(2) a storage device. (A)

(3) the action of placing data into a storage device. (B)

(4) in word processing, a unit into which recorded text can be entered, in which it can be retained and processed, and from which it can be retrieved.

(5) a device, or part of a device, that can retain data.

(6) see *associative storage, auxiliary storage, buffer storage, capacitor storage, cathode-ray storage, circulating storage, core storage, cryogenic storage, delay line storage, direct-access storage, dynamic storage, electrostatic storage, erasable storage, external storage, fixed storage, free storage, immediate-access storage, internal storage, magnetic core storage, magnetic disk storage, magnetic storage, magnetic wire storage, main storage, mass storage, matrix storage, mercury storage, n-core-per-bit storage, nonvolatile storage, one-core-per-bit storage, parallel search storage, parallel storage, permanent storage, push-down storage, push-up storage, real storage, secondary storage, serial-access storage, static storage, temporary storage, unprotected dynamic storage, virtual storage, volatile storage, word-organized storage*.

storage allocation: the assignment of storage areas to specified data. (B) See *dynamic storage allocation*. (A)

storage area: pertaining to the designated location in various storage units; for example, for programs, constants, input-output buffer storage.

storage block: a continuous area of main storage, consisting of 2048 bytes, to which a storage key can be assigned.

storage capacity: the amount of data that can be contained in a storage device, measured in binary digits, bytes, characters, words, or other units of data. (B)

storage cell: one or more storage elements, considered as a unit. (B)

storage compacting: a hardware feature allowing the dynamic relocating of programs residing in the central storage, to provide an efficient multiprogramming environment.

storage cycle: the periodic sequence of events that occurs when information is transferred to or from main storage.

storage cycle time: the time needed for a complete storage cycle.

storage density: the number of units of data that can be stored in a unit length or area of a storage medium.

storage device:

(1) a functional unit into which data can be entered, in which they can be retained,

and from which they can be retrieved. (A) (B)

(2) a facility in which data can be retained.

storage drum: a random-access storage device that can hold 4 million alphanumeric characters or up to 8 million digits, which can be retrieved at a rate of 1.2 million characters per second.

storage dump: the copying of all, or a portion of a storage.

storage element: a basic unit of a storage device. (B)

storage exchange: the interchange of the total contents of two storage devices or locations, such as two registers.

storage fill: storing of characters in storage areas not used for data storage or the program for a specific machine run.

storage flip-flop: a bistable storage unit that stores binary data as states of flip-flop elements.

storage fragmentation: inability to assign real storage locations to virtual addresses because the available spaces are smaller than the page size.

storage integrator: in an analog computer, used to store a voltage in the hold condition for future usage while the rest of the computer assumes another computer control state.

storage interference: in a system with shared storage, the referencing of the same block of storage by two or more processing units.

storage key: an indicator associated with one or more storage blocks, that requires that tasks have a matching protection key to use the blocks.

storage light: a control console panel light showing that a parity-check error has occurred on a character as it was read into storage.

storage location: an area in a storage device, usually one that can be explicitly and uniquely specified by means of an address. (A) (B)

storage location selection: in word processing, selection of a group or groups of text by preselecting a particular storage address or addresses.

storage map: a listing or diagram of storage locations in main memory used by a program and/or data to determine the amount of storage used and the location of various items of data.

storage media: type of medium utilized (i.e., disk, tape).

storage medium: any surface for reading and/or writing information in a machine-readable form (e.g., disk, punched cards, tape, etc.).

storage overlay: see *overlay segment.*

storage pool: a group of similar data storage units; the tape drives in a computer installation are collectively called the tape pool.

storage protection: a facility that limits access to a storage device, or to one or more storage locations by preventing writing or reading or both. (B) See also *fetch protection, store protection.*

storage protection key: see *protection key, storage key.*

storage region: see *overlay region.*

storage register (SR): a device for holding a unit of information.

storage resolver: a small section of storage, in the drum, tape, or disk storage units, that has faster access than the remainder of the storage.

storage stack: synonym for *push-down list.*

storage-to-storage instruction: a machine language instruction that moves a word of data from one place within memory to another.

storage unit: a register in the memory or storage of the computer.

storage volatility: the inability of a storage unit to retain data when power is eliminated.

store (STOR):

(1) to place data into a storage device.

(2) to retain data in a storage device. (B)

(3) in computer programming, to copy data from registers into internal storage. (B)

(4) deprecated term for *storage.*

store and forward mode: a manner of operating a data network in which packets or messages are stored before transmission toward the ultimate destination.

store controller:

(1) a programmable unit in a network used to collect data, to direct inquiries, and to control communication within a system.

(2) in PSS, the primary link between terminals attached to it and the host processor. Synonymous with *subsystem controller.*

store controller disk: an integral part of a programmable store system controller that is used for auxiliary storage of store controller data, user files, and application programs.

store controller storage: in SPPS II, that portion of store controller working storage that is available to the user for executing application programs.

store controller storage save: the automatic writing of the critical areas of store controller storage onto the integrated disk when power is turned off or when a power failure is detected.

stored functions: synonymous with *library functions.*

stored program: a program that is completely contained in memory, capable of being altered in memory, and can be stored along with the data on which it is to function. Synonymous with *stored routine.*

stored program computer: a computer controlled by internally stored instructions that can synthesize and store instructions, and that can subsequently execute these instructions. Synonymous with *programmed computer.* (A) (B)

stored response chain (SRC): a fixed sequence of responses to prompts issued by an interactive program, stored in a file to save the terminal user the trouble of keying the same commands for often repeated functions.

stored routine: synonymous with *stored program.*

store loop driver: a hardware component to connect the store controller to the store loop.

store protection: a storage protection feature that determines right of access to main storage by matching a protection key, associated with a store reference to main storage, with a storage key, associated with each block of main storage. See also *fetch protection.*

store support procedure: a procedure that assists personnel in administrative, operational, and managerial operations, apart from customer checkout.

store-through cache: in a processing unit, a store (write) operation, in which data is immediately put into both cache and main storage locations.

STP: see *stop character.*

STR: see *status register.*

straight line coding:

(1) a set of instructions in which there are no loops. (B)

(2) a programming technique in which loops are avoided by unwinding. (A) (B)

strapping option: a means of enabling or disabling hardware features by rearranging jumpers on a printed circuit board.

stratified language: a language that cannot be used as its own metalanguage; for example, FORTRAN. (B) Cf. *unstratified language.* (A)

stream: see *data stream.*

streaming: the condition of a modem or terminal that has locked into a constant carrier signal, preventing normal transmission of data.

streaming tape: a hard disk back-up system. A magnetic tape, in a cassette, that fits into a special recorder and makes a copy of everything on the hard disk in a matter of minutes.

STRESS: see *structural engineering system solver.*

strikeover: a character with a line through it. Used in legal documents to indicate what the attorney has omitted—so the other attorney can see what would otherwise be deleted.

string: a linear sequence of entities such as characters or physical elements. (B) See *alphabetic string, binary element string, bit string, character string, null string, symbol string, unit string.* (A)

string break: in sorting, a situation that occurs when there are no records with keys higher than the highest key thus far written.

string file: tape, wire, or string used to arrange documents for easy reference and usage.

string length: in sorting, the number of records in a string.

string manipulation: the manipulation of groups of contiguous characters in memory, treating them as units of data.

string operation: an operation carried out on a string, such as concatenating, copying, or rearranging it, or identifying different substrings within it.

string-oriented symbolic language (SNOBOL): a high-level programming language, oriented toward the maneuvering of character strings.

string process system (SPS): a package of subroutines that perform basic operations on strings of characters. SPS performs string reading and writing, hash-code string look-up, and string comparisons.

string sorting: a group of sequenced records normally stored in auxiliary computer storage, that is, disk, tape, or drum.

string variable: in PL/1, a variable declared with the BIT or CHARACTER attribute, whose values can be either bit strings or character strings.

stringy floppy: an endless loop of recording tape in a cartridge used as external memory.

stripe recording: a magnetic recording where a stripe of magnetic material is deposited on a document or card.

striping: in flowcharting, the use of a line across the upper part of a flowchart symbol to signify that a detailed representation of a function is located elsewhere in the same set of flowcharts. (A)

strip off: extracting selected information from a larger collection of data.

stroke:
(1) in character recognition, a straight line or arc used as a segment of a graphic character. (A)
(2) in computer graphics, a straight line or arc used as a segment of a display element.
(3) see *Sheffer stroke.*

stroke center line: in character recognition, a line midway between the two stroke edges. (A)

stroke edge: in character recognition, the line of discontinuity between a side of a stroke and the background, obtained by averaging, over the length of the stroke, the irregularities resulting from the printing and detecting processes. (A)

stroke edge irregularity: deviation of the edge of a character from its stroke edge in optical character recognition.

stroke generator: see *stroke character generator.*

stroke width: in character recognition, the distance measured perpendicularly to the stroke center line between the two stroke edges. (A)

STRUC: see *structure.*

structural design language (STRUDL): an extension of the STRESS language for the analysis and design of structures. See also *structural engineering system solver.*

structural engineering system solver (STRESS): a language used in civil engineering for solving structural analysis problems. See also *structural design language.*

structure (STRUC): in PL/1, a hierarchical set of names that refers to an aggregate of data items that may have different attributes. See *block structure.*

structure chart: a graphic representation of top-down programming, displaying modules of the problem solution and relationship between modules; there are two types—system and process.

structure design: a design methodology incorporating a high degree of modularity, and employing generic control structures having only one entry and one exit. See *top-down programming.*

structured language: a computer language to aid or enforce structured programming, for example, PASCAL, ALGOL.

structure program: a program broken into modules, each of which is self-contained. This modular approach eases design and maintenance of complex computer programs. See *top-down programming.*

structured programming (SP): a technique for organizing and coding programs that reduces complexity, improves clarity, and makes them easier to debug and modify. Typically, a structured program is a hierarchy of modules that each have a single entry point and a single exit point; control is passed downward through the structure without unconditional branches to higher levels of the structure. Synonymous with *GOTO-less programming*.

structured type: a type composed of more than one element, which at its lowest level is a simple type; any of the PASCAL types ARRAY, RECORD, SET, and FILE.

structured walk-through: synonymous with *formal design review*.

structure expression: in PL/1, an expression whose evaluation yields a structure value.

structure flowcharts: flowcharts indicating input, processing, files, and output without indicating the exact techniques of processing.

structure member: in PL/1, any of the minor structures of elementary names in a structure.

structure of arrays: in PL/1, a structure containing arrays specified by declaring individual member names with the dimension attribute.

structuring: in PL/1, the makeup of a structure, in terms of the number of members, the order in which they appear, their attributes, and their logical levels (but not necessarily their names or declared level numbers).

STRUDL: see *structural design language*.

stub card: a special-purpose card that has a separable stub attached to a general-purpose paper card. A stub card may be a scored card. (A)

STX: see *start-of-text character*. (A) (B)

style: a set of stylistic variations applied to text. Styles include bold, italic, underline, and other variations. More than one style can be applied to a single selection of text.

stylus: in computer graphics, a pointer that is operated by placing it in a display space or a tablet; for example, a light pen, a sonic pen, a voltage pencil.

stylus printer: a matrix printer that uses a stylus to produce patterns of dots. Synonym for *matrix printer*. (B)

SU: see *selectable unit*.

SUB:
(1) see *subroutine*.
(2) see *substitute character*.

subaddress: an order code permitting access to an input-output unit. In the disk system, the subaddress can be the module number.

subalphabet: an alphabet subset; for example, any group of less than 26 letters.

subcommand: a request for an operation that is within the scope of work requested by a previously issued command.

subdirectory: a directory contained within another directory.

subfield:
(1) a subdivision of a field; a field within a field.
(2) in PL/1, that portion of a picture specification field that appears before or after a V picture specification character.

subgeneration: in PL/1, the portion of a generation represented by a qualified reference, a subscripted reference, or both.

subject or entry: in COBOL, a data name or reserved word that appears immediately after a level indicator or level number in a data division entry. It serves to reference the entry.

subject program: one written by the user, usually in a high-level language such as BASIC, to perform a given job, as opposed to the object program, which is the result of intermediate translation into machine code which may be directly processed. See *object program*.

subjob: a machine run or routine.

submicron: units able to store four-million-unit chips. See also *hot electron effect, one-micron memory chips*.

submicron era: the time when superchips with circuit lines thinner than 1 micron will be used, enabling chips to be crammed with incredible amounts of storage capacity and processing power.

submit: entering a batch job into a system for execution.

submodular phase: a phase made up of selected control sections from one or more modules as compared with a phase that is made up of all control sections from one or more modules.

subparameter: one of the variable items of information that follows a key-word parameter and can be either positional or identified by a key word.

subpool: all of the storage blocks allocated under a subpool number for a particular task.

subprogram:
(1) a program that is invoked by another program.
(2) in FORTRAN, a program unit headed by a FUNCTION, SUBROUTINE, or BLOCK DATA statement.

subrange type: a data type composed of a specified range of any standard or user-defined ordinal type.

subroutine (SUB):
(1) a sequenced set of statements that may be used in one or more computer programs and at one or more points in a computer program.
(2) a routine that can be part of another routine. (A)
(3) in PL/1, a procedure that is invoked by a CALL statement or CALL option. A subroutine cannot return a value to the invoking block, but it can alter the value of variables.
(4) see *closed subroutine, dynamic subroutine, open subroutine, recursive subroutine, reentrant subroutine.* (A)

subroutine address stack: a stack register for saving the program return address for subroutines.

subroutine call: the subroutine, in object coding, that performs the call function. (A)

subroutine library (SLIB): a standard proven subroutine set that is retained on file for use at a future time.

subroutine statement: synonym for *procedure statement.*

subroutine subprogram: in FORTRAN, a subroutine consisting of FORTRAN statements, the first of which is a SUBROUTINE statement. It optionally returns one or more parameters to the calling program unit.

subroutine table: the routine for maintaining a listing of the subroutines in core and for bringing from file the subroutines as required by the application program.

subscript:
(1) a symbol that is associated with the name of a set to identify a particular subset or element. (A) (B)
(2) in COBOL, an integer or a variable whose value refers to a particular element in a table.
(3) in FORTRAN, a subscript quantity or set of subscript quantities, enclosed in parentheses and used in conjunction with an array name to identify a particular array element.
(4) in PL/1, an element expression that specifies a position within a dimension of an array. A subscript can also be an asterisk, in which case it specifies the entire extent of the dimension.
(5) synonymous with *inferior.*

subscript character (SBS): a word-processing formatting control that causes the printing or display point to move down approximately one-half the normal single line space increment with no horizontal motion. The subscript character is a latching control that requires a superscript character to cause the printing or display point to return to the previous horizontal alignment. Cf. *superscript character.*

subscripted array: synonymous with *indexed array.*

subscripted data name: in COBOL, an identifier that is composed of a data name followed by one or more subscripts enclosed in parentheses.

subscripted variable: a variable that is followed by one or more subscripts enclosed in parentheses.

subscript list: in PL/1, a parenthesized list of one or more subscripts, one for each dimension of an array, which together uniquely identify either a single element or cross section of the array.

subscript quantity: in FORTRAN, a component of a subscript; a positive integer variable, or expression that evaluates to a positive integer constant. If there is more than one subscript quantity in a subscript, the quantities must be separated by commas.

subsegment: a part of a segment.

subsequent counter: an instruction counter created to step through or count microoperations or parts of larger programs.

subset:

(1) a set, each element of which is an element of a specified other set. (A) (B)

(2) a set contained within a set.

(3) a modulation and demodulation device.

(4) see *alphabetic character subset, alphanumeric character subset, character subset, numeric character subset, proper subset.* (A)

subset (of a programming language): a variant form of a programming language that has fewer features or more restrictions than the original language. See *subset.*

substantive input: the transferal of data from an external storage unit to an internal storage unit, usually from a mass storage device and off line, but not always so.

substitute: to replace an element of information by some other element of information.

substitute character (SUB): a control character used in the place of a character that is recognized to be invalid or in error, or that cannot be represented on a given device. (A) (B)

substitution statement: in BASIC, a program instruction that evaluates the numeric value of a valid BASIC expression appearing to the right of the equal sign and assigns that value to the single variable named to the left of the equal sign. For example, LET Z = X + Y; the numeric values assigned to X and Y are added and the result assigned to Z. See *assignment statement.*

substitution table: a layout chart for keyboard. In word processing used to show which standard character keys can be used as special character keys.

substrate: in a microcircuit, the supporting material upon which or within which an integrated circuit is fabricated, or to which an integrated circuit is attached. Synonymous for *base.*

substring:

(1) a sequence of consecutive characters that is part of a character string (e.g., "Base" as a substring of "Baseball").

(2) an operation in which such a sequence is identified.

subsystem: a secondary or subordinate system, usually capable of operating independently of, or asynchronously with, a controlling system.

subsystem controller: synonym for *store controller.*

subsystem definition: synonym for *subsystem generation.*

subsystem definition statement: one of the statements that is used to define either the configuration of terminals attached to a subsystem controller or the processing options for data within the subsystem.

subsystem generation: the process of creating a programmable store system operational environment and storing it in a library. Subsystem generation includes selection of the desired functions by coding the required programmable store system macroinstructions, assembling the macros, and processing the assembler output with the controller configuration facility or the terminal configuration facility. See also *operational environment.* Synonymous with *subsystem definition.*

subsystem store controller: see *store controller.*

subsystem support program: any program that is part of the subsystem support services. A subsystem support program is executed in the host system.

sub task: a task that is initiated and terminated by a higher order task.

subtracter: a device whose output data are a representation of the difference between the numbers represented by its input data. (B) See *adder subtracter.* (A)

subtrahend: in a subtraction, the number or quantity subtracted from the minuend. (A) (B)

successive approximation: a trial and error method for solving equations where the computer guesses the solution to an equation.

successor job: a job that accepts as input the output of an earlier job, so that it cannot be started until the predecessor has finished properly.

sudden death: any abrupt failure of a working unit or system.

suffix notation: synonym for *post fix notation.* (A) (B)

suite: a number of programs related to each other and run in sequence to enable a processing job to be terminated.

sum: the number or quantity that is the result of the addition of two or more numbers or quantities. (A) (B)

sum check: in a summary tag-along sort, a data field designated for accumulated totals. Synonym for *summation check.*

sum counter: in COBOL, a signed numeric data item established by a SUM clause in the report section of the data division. The sum counter is used by the report writer control system to contain the result of designated summing operations that take place during production of a report.

summarize: to reduce large amounts of data to a more concise and usable form.

summary punch: a card punch that may be connected to another device, such as a tabulator, to enter data that was calculated or summarized by the other device. (A) (B)

summation check: a comparison of check sums, computed on the same data on different occasions, to verify data integrity. Synonymous with *sum check.*

summer: synonym for *analog adder.* (B)

summing integrator: a device whose output variable is the integral of a weighted sum of the input variables with respect to time. (B)

superchip: a computer chip able to do the work of existing mainframes.

supercomputer:
(1) material capable of carrying current without the resistance that usually wastes energy in the form of heat.
(2) presently, any machine that will perform at peak speeds greater than 20 million operations per second. See *parallel supercomputer.*

supermini: a computer that is an extension of a minicomputer, with a word length of (usually) 32 bits and main storage of one million bytes or more.

superscript character (SPS): a word-processing formatting control that causes the printing or display point to move up approximately one-half the normal single line space increment with no horizontal motion. The superscript character is a latching control that requires a subscript character to cause the printing or display point to return to the previous horizontal alignment. Cf. *subscript character.*

supervisor: the part of a control program that coordinates the use of resources and maintains the flow of processing unit operations. See also *system supervisor.* Synonym for *supervisory program, supervisory routine.* (A) (B) See *overlay supervisor.* (A)

supervisor call instruction (SVC): an instruction that interrupts the program being executed and passes control to the supervisor so that it can perform a specific service indicated by the instruction. Synonymous with *system call.* (A) (B)

supervisor mode: a mode of operation where only certain operations, such as memory-protection modification instructions and input-output operations are allowed.

supervisor overlay: a routine for controlling fetching of overlay segments, utilizing information recorded in the overlay module by the linkage editor.

supervisor state: a state during which the processing unit can execute input-output and other privileged instructions. Cf. *problem state.*

supervisory console: a system console containing the operator control panel and operator input-output units for system control.

supervisory program: a computer program, usually part of an operating system, that controls the execution of other computer programs and regulates the flow of work in a data-processing system. Synonymous with *executive program, supervisor*. (A) (B)

supervisory routine: a routine, usually part of an operating system, that controls the execution of other routines and regulates the flow of work in a data-processing system. Synonymous with *executive routine, supervisor*. (A) (B)

supervisory services: a general term for all functions in the supervisor that are available to the user.

supervisory software: specialized programs that usually reside permanently in the computer's main memory and control the flow and processing of users' application programs. Synonymous with *systems software*.

supervisory system: all of the supervisory programs used by a given system.

super VGA: a graphics standard offering better resolution than VGA. See *video-graphics adapter*.

support chip: a component in a system required for operation, but additional to the main central processor.

support programs: programs that aid the supervisory programs and the application programs, and include diagnostics, testing, data generators, and so forth.

support system: programs, hardware, and skills used to develop, operate, and maintain a data-processing unit.

suppress: preventing printing.

suppression: see *zero suppression*.

SUPV: see *supervisor*.

surface analysis: a program that writes a known series of characters onto a magnetic data storage medium and reads them back to determine if and where flaws occur.

surge: an unexpected voltage or current change in an electrical circuit, causing devices to supply wrong results or even to stop running.

surge protector: a unit that plugs into a wall socket to protect computers from alternating current line surges.

suspended state: a software state in which a task is not dispatched by the system and is not contending for the processor.

suspend lock: a lock that prevents requesters doing work on a processing unit but allows the processing unit to continue doing other work. Cf. *spin lock*.

SVA: see *shared virtual area*.

SVC: see *supervisor call instruction*.

SVC interruption: an interruption caused by the execution of a supervisor call instruction, causing control to be passed to the supervisor.

SVC routine: a control program routine that performs or begins a control program service specified by a supervisor call instruction.

SVGA: see *Super VGA*.

SW: see *software*.

SWA: see *scheduler work area*.

swap: in systems with time sharing, to write the main storage image of a job to auxiliary storage and to read the image of another job into main storage.

swap-in (SI): in system with time sharing, the process of reading a terminal job's main storage image from auxiliary storage into main storage.

swap-out (SOUT): in system with time sharing, the process of writing a terminal job's main storage image from main storage to auxiliary storage.

swapping: a process that interchanges the contents of an area of main storage with the contents of an area in auxiliary storage. (B) See *page swapping*. (A)

SWCH: see *switch*.

switch (S) (SW) (SWCH):
(1) in a computer program, a parameter that controls branching and is bound prior to the branch point being reached. Synonymous with *switch point*. (B)
(2) a device or programming technique for making a selection; for example, a toggle, a conditional jump. (A)

switch character (SW): a word-processing device control that causes reading of a character string to switch from one character string source to another without operator intervention. See also *repeat character, stop character*.

switch code: in word processing, a program instruction for switching that causes control to transfer to one of a number of possible statements, depending on existing or prior conditions; for example, the switch in ALGOL 60; the computed GOTO in FORTRAN.

switch control computer: a computer designed to handle data transmission to and from remote computers and terminals.

switch core: a core in which the magnetic material generally has a high residual flux density and a high ratio of residual to saturated flux density with a threshold value of magnetizing force below which switching does not occur. (A) (B)

switch indicator: in computer programming, an indicator that determines or shows the setting of a switch. Synonymous with *flag.* (A) (B)

switching element: deprecated term for *logic element.* (B)

switching function: a function that has only a finite number of possible values and the independent variables of which have only a finite number of possible values. (A) (B)

switch insertion: placing data or instructions by means of manually operated switches.

switchover: transferring the real-time processing work load from one specific or multiplexer program to another within a duplex system.

switch point: synonym for *switch (1).* (A) (B)

SY: see *system.*

syllable: a character string or a binary element string in a word. (A) (B)

syllable hyphen (character) (SHY): a word-processing formatting graphic that prints in the same way as a required hyphen character. It prints only at syllable boundaries at line endings to indicate continuation of a word on the next line. A syllable hyphen may be ignored or dropped if words are repositioned during text adjust mode operations. Synonymous with *discretionary hyphen.* Cf. *required hyphen character.*

SYM:
(1) see *symbol.*
(2) see *system.*

symbiont control: symbionts, besides being routines from main programs, perform off-line operations, such as tape-to-printer, independent of the main program. These operations may be suspended, terminated, or reinstated.

symbionts: small routines that run concurrently with the series of main programs. See also *symbiont control.*

symbol (SYM):
(1) a conventional representation of a concept or a representation of something by reason of relationship, association, or convention. (B)
(2) a representation of something by reason of relationship, association, or convention. (A)
(3) in assembler language, a character or character string that represents addresses or arbitrary values. A symbol may consist of no more than eight characters, the first character being a letter (A through Z, $, @, or #) and the other characters being either letters or digits. No blanks or special characters are allowed.
(4) see *abstract symbol, flowchart symbol, logic symbol, mnemonic symbol, ordinary symbol, sequence symbol, set symbol, variable symbol.*

symbolic: using characters or character strings in a defined syntax to stand for machine-related constructs such as instructions or data.

symbolic address: an address expressed in a form convenient for computer programming. (A) (B)

symbolic addressing: a method of addressing in which the address part of an instruction contains a symbolic address. (A) (B)

symbolic assembler: an assembler that allows the programmer to code instructions in a symbolic language.

symbolic assembly system: using an assembler to translate mnemonic instruction into machine format, providing the means of entering linkages, mapping common data, and using address modifiers.

symbolic code: a code expressing programs in source language, permitting the programmer to refer to storage locations and operations by symbolic names and addresses that are independent of their hardware-determined labels and addresses.

symbolic coding: the preparation of routines and computer programs in a symbolic language. (A)

symbolic concordance: a program that yields a cross-referenced list of all the symbolic names in a program.

symbolic debugging: symbolic commands utilized to aid in the debugging procedure.

symbolic deck: a deck of punched cards containing programs written in symbolic language.

symbolic editor: permits the editing of source-language programs by adding or deleting lines of text.

symbolic instruction: an instruction in a source language. Synonymous with *symbolic coding.*

symbolic I/O assignment: a means by which a problem program can refer to an I/O device by a specific I/O symbolic name. Before the program is executed, a device is assigned to the symbolic name.

symbolic language: a programming language whose instructions are expressed in symbols convenient to humans rather than in machine language.

symbolic logic: the discipline in which valid arguments and operations are dealt with using an artificial language designed to avoid the ambiguities and logical inadequacies of natural languages. Synonymous with *mathematical logic.* (A) (B)

symbolic names: names assigned by programmers to represent addresses or locations within a program.

symbolic notation: the method of representing a storage location by one or more figures.

symbolic number: a numeral, used in writing routines, for referring to a specific storage location; such numerals are converted to actual storage addresses in the final assembling of a program.

symbolic parameter:
(1) in assembler programming, a variable symbol declared in the prototype statement of a macrodefinition. A symbolic parameter is usually assigned a value from the corresponding operand in the macroinstruction that calls the macrodefinition. See also *key-word parameter, positional parameter.*
(2) in job control language, a symbol preceded by an ampersand that represents a parameter or the value assigned to a parameter or subparameter in a cataloged or in-stream procedure. Values are assigned to symbolic parameters when the procedure in which they appear is called.

symbolic placeholder: a symbol in a command list that is replaced by an actual value when the command list is executed.

symbolic programming: writing a program in a source language.

symbolic program system: a computer system which accepts high level programming languages.

symbolic unit: an external storage area or input-output unit during coding.

symbol-manipulating language: see *LISP.*

symbol manipulation: the processing of symbols that have no explicit numerical values. (A)

symbol rank: synonym for *digit place.* (A) (B)

symbols: see *editing symbol.*

symbol string: a string consisting solely of symbols. (A) (B)

symbol table: a table created by a compiler or assembler to relate symbolic addresses to their absolute addresses.

symbol variable: a symbol in macroassembly processing that assumes any of a given set of values.

symmetrical channel: a channel pair in which the send and receive directions of transmission have the same data signaling rate. See also *binary symmetric channel.* (A)

symmetrical I/O unit: in multiprocessing, a unit that is attached to two processors; it appears as the same I/O unit to each processor, and can be accessed in the same manner by each processor.

symmetric channel: see *binary symmetric channel.*

symmetric list processor: a high-level list processing language.

symmetric processors: processors with identical configurations.

symmetric storage configurations: machine configurations with identical storage units.

SYN:

(1) see *synchronous.*

(2) see *synchronous idle character.* (A) (B)

SYNC: see *synchronous.*

sync bits: synonym for *framing bits.*

sync character: a character transmitted to establish appropriate character synchronization in synchronous communication.

synchro: a rotary position indicator made up of two systems, devices, or functions.

synchro-duplexing: the scheme of producing a document on a printing unit through the synchronous running of a program tape and a master tape or a pure data tape.

synchronization pulses: pulses introduced by transmission equipment into the receiving equipment to keep the two equipments operating in step. (A)

synchronize: locking the elements of a system into step with one another.

synchronizer: a unit that serves as a buffer, and maintains synchronization by counteracting the effects of transmitting data between units that operate at differing rates.

synchronizing pilot: a reference signal to maintain the synchronization of the oscillators of a carrier system.

synchronizing signal: a signal accompanying data transmission to ensure that the data are transmitted and received in synchronism with a clock. See *clock.*

synchronous (S) (SYN) (SYNC):

(1) pertaining to two or more processes that depend upon the occurrences of specific events such as common timing signals. (B)

(2) occurring with a regular or predictable time relationship.

synchronous clock: a system where events are controlled by signals from a clock generator at a desired rate or frequency.

synchronous communication: the method of transferring serial binary data between computer systems or between a computer system and a peripheral device.

synchronous computer: a computer in which each event, or the performance of any basic operation, is constrained to start on signals from a clock and usually to keep in step with them. (B) Cf. *asynchronous computer.* (A)

synchronous data link control: see *SDLC.*

synchronous idle character (SYN): a transmission control character used by synchronous data-transmission systems to provide a signal from which synchronism or synchronous correction may be achieved between data terminal equipment, particularly when no other character is being transmitted. (A) (B)

synchronous input: an input permitting data to be entered only when a clock pulse is present.

synchronous mode comparator: a comparator used to compare the assembled contents of registers in the synchronous mode.

synchronous node: any communication utilizing synchronous data transmission.

synchronous operation:

(1) a mode of operation in which each action is started by a clock.

(2) an operation that occurs regularly or predictably with respect to the occurrence of a specified event in another process; for example, the calling of an input-output routine that receives control at a precoded location in a computer program. (A)

(3) cf. *asynchronous operation.*

synchronous preprocessor: apparatus used for interfacing synchronous lines to computers to minimize the overhead for the computer by handling most of the interrupt processing and character manipulation.

synchronous receiver: a receiver for assembling characters from serial communications lines and asserting a flag as each character is received.

synchronous serial data adapter: a unit for converting parallel data to serial or serial data to parallel in a synchronous system.

synchronous transfer: an input-output transfer that takes place in a certain amount of time without regard to feedback from the receiving device.

synchronous transmission:

(1) data transmission in which the time of occurrence of each signal representing a bit is related to a fixed time frame. Synonymous with *isochronous transmission.*

(2) data transmission in which the sending and receiving instruments are operating contiguously at substantially the same frequency and are maintained, by means of correction, in a desired phase relationship.

synchronous unit: a unit that transmits signals at regular, timed intervals to the system with which it communicates. Cf. *asynchronous device.*

synchronous working: performing a sequence of operations under the control of equally spaced signals from a clock. Cf. *asynchronous working.*

syndetic:

(1) having connections or interconnections.

(2) pertaining to a document or catalog with cross-references.

synergetic: combining each unit of a system, but one which when combined or added, develops a total larger than their arithmetic sum.

synonym: in an indirectly addressed file, a record whose key randomizes to the address of a home record.

SYN register: a register that holds the synchronous character code used for receiver character synchronization.

syntactical analysis: an activity of a compiler to ensure that the rules of the programming language have been followed properly. Cf. *lexical analysis.*

syntactic error: synonymous with *syntax error.*

syntax:

(1) the relationship among characters or groups of characters, independent of their meanings or the manner of their interpretation and use. (B)

(2) the structure of expressions in a language.

(3) the rules governing the structure of a language.

(4) the relationships among symbols. (A)

syntax checker: a program that tests source statements in a programming language for violations of the syntax of that language.

syntax diagram: a pictorial definition of the syntax rules of a programming language.

syntax-directed compiler: a compiler based on the syntactical relation of the character string.

syntax error: a mistake in the formulation of an instruction to a computer. Synonymous with *syntactic error.*

syntax language: a metalanguage used to specify or describe the syntax of another language. (A)

syntax scanner: the subprogram performing the first phase of the translation of a program into executable form by a compiler or interpreter.

synthetic address: synonymous with *generated address.* (A) (B)

synthetic language: synonymous with *source language.*

SYS: see *system.*

SYSADMIN: see *system administrator.*

SYSGEN: see *system generation.*

SYSIN: a system input stream; also, the name used as the data-definition name of a data set in the input stream.

SYSLOG: see *system log.*

SYSOPOs: see *System Programmed Operators.*

sysops: system operators. See *system operator.*

SYSOUT: a system output stream; also, an indicator used in data-definition statements to signify that a data set is to be written on a system output unit.

SYSRES: the disk pack which contains the supervisor.

SYST: see *system.*

system (S) (SY) (SYM) (SYS) (SYST):

(1) in data processing, a collection of men, machines, and methods organized to accomplish a set of specific functions. (A)

(2) an assembly of components united

by some form of regulated interaction to form an organized whole.

(3) the operations and procedures through which a business activity is accomplished.

(4) a coordinated collection of interrelated and interacting parts organized to perform some function or achieve some purpose—for example, a computer system comprising a processor, a keyboard, a monitor, and a disk drive.

(5) see *data-processing system, decimal numeration system, fixed-point representation system, information feedback system, management information system, mixed-base numeration system, mixed-radix numeration system, number representation system, numeration system, operating system, positional representation system, programming system, pure binary numeration system, radix numeration system, variable-point representation system.*

system activity measurement facility (MF/1): a facility that collects information such as paging activity and the use of the processing unit, channels, and I/O devices, to produce trace records and reports.

system administrator (SA) (SYSADMIN): the person at a computer installation who designs, controls, and manages the use of the computer system.

system analysis report: a report given to top management after the system analysis phase has been completed, to report the findings of the system study; includes a statement of objectives, constraints, and possible alternatives.

system boundary: the physical limits of a specific system, excluding the users at the transmitting and receiving stations, but including terminals and the transmission channel.

system bus: the bus carrying data between various units in a computer; consisting of the data bus, address bus, and control bus.

system calendar: a date-and-year calendar automatically maintained by a system, where programs determine today's date by a supervisor call to the operating system, thereby returning the calendar setting.

system call: synonymous with *supervisor call instruction.*

system catalog: the master index of all files under the control of a large computer's operating system, indicating the name of each file, its date of creation, last access date, location, and attributes.

system chart: synonymous with *systems flowchart.*

system check: a check on the overall performance of a system, usually not made by built-in computer check circuits; for example, control totals, hash totals, and record counts.

system check module: a unit that monitors system operability as power fails or deviations from expected computer activities develop. It initiates necessary emergency actions by the computer.

system clock:

(1) an electronic circuit in the CPU that issues a steady high-frequency pulse signal by which all internal components are synchronized.

(2) the time-of-day clock of a computer system.

system command:

(1) a user's instruction, not part of the program, that calls for action by the computer's executive program.

(2) in BASIC, a system command distinguished from a program statement by the absence of a line number.

system command executive: an executive program that accepts and interprets commands by a user.

system communication processing: the transmission of data to a central computer for processing from a remote terminal as opposed to a terminal connected directly to the central computer.

system constants: permanent locations within the monitor (control unit), containing data used by system programs.

system controller: regulates and coordinates all communications between major computer-system components, input-output controller, and real-time units.

system controller and bus driver: a single-chip unit that produces all signals needed to interface RAM, ROM, and input-output units to the computer system.

system control program (SCP): any piece of systems software that will give overall direction and control to the computer.

system data bus: a bus created for communication between all external units and the CPU.

system definition: in industry systems, the time, before a system is put into use, when desired functions and operations of the system are first selected from various available options. Synonymous with *system generation*.

system description: a broad outline of a system, outlining its goals and the operational procedures for its use.

system design: the specification of the working relations between all parts within a system in terms of their characteristic actions.

system design aids: hardware and software support items found in the design of equipment used in computer applications.

system diagnostic: a program used for detecting overall system malfunctions, rather than isolating errors or faults.

system directory list (SDL): a list containing directory entries of highly used phases and of all phases resident in the shared virtual area. This list is contained in the shared virtual area.

system engineer: an adequately trained data-processing professional, often employed by the vendor, whose task is to provide technical assistance to customers.

system error: an instruction that is either not recognized by an operating system or is in violation of the procedural rules.

system error recording editing program (SEREP): a stand-alone program used to edit and print hardware error condition log-out data from main storage.

system extension: a program that expands the capabilities of system software, for example, device drivers.

system file: a file that some computers use to start up and to provide systemwide information.

system flowchart: the group of symbols to represent the general information flow; focuses on inputs and outputs rather than on internal computer operations.

system generation (SYSGEN): the process of selecting optional parts of an operating system and of creating a particular operating system tailored to the requirements of a data-processing installation.

system implementation: the final phase in the development of a new or revised system; the goal of implementation is to ensure that the system is completely debugged and operational and is accepted by the users.

system-improvement time: machine downtime required for the installation and testing of new devices, and machine downtime required for modification of existing components, including all programming tests to check out the modified units.

system input device: a device specified as a source of an input stream.

system interface: any unit that connects support hardware to a processor.

system interface module: a circuit board or card providing the interface for external units to the system.

system interrupts: programmed requests from a processing program to the control program for some action; for example, initiation of an input-output operation.

system key: a key that protects system data from damage or modification by unauthorized users.

system-level timer: a timer of the operating system, used for setting deadlines for events, reminding itself to take an action following a specified interval, and for other such alarm clock needs. It has the highest priority of any timer.

system library: a collection of data sets or files in which the various parts of an operating system are stored.

system loader (SLDR): see *loader*.

system log (SYSLOG): a data set or file in which job-related information, operational data, descriptions of unusual occurrences, commands, and messages to or from the operator may be stored.

system monitor: a program that permits the user to load and execute programs stored on paper tape or other external units.

system noise:

(1) extra bits or words that should be removed from data prior to its use.

(2) any disturbance tending to interfere with the normal operation of the system, by creating signals that are read as pulses.

system nucleus: see *nucleus*.

system operator: an operator responsible for performing system-oriented procedures.

system-oriented: applications using a common bus system for all data and communications within the computer system itself.

system output device: a device assigned to record output data for a series of jobs.

system output writer: a job scheduler function that transcribes specified output data sets onto a system output unit, independently of the program that produced the data sets.

system overhead: the percentage of time a computer system functions as a supervisor rather than in the performance of a specific program.

system packages: sets of programs that make it possible to operate computers more conveniently and efficiently.

system productivity: a measure of the work performed by a system productivity largely depends on a combination of two other factors: the facility (ease of use) of the system and the performance (throughput, response time, and availability) of the system.

system program: a sequence of instructions written to coordinate the operation of all computer circuitry and help the computer run quickly and efficiently.

System Programmed Operators (SYSOPOs): a facility on some computers permitting user programs to directly access a set of public subroutines. These are not replicated for each user but are used in common.

system programmer:

(1) a programmer who plans, generates, maintains, extends, and controls the use of an operating system with the aim of improving the overall productivity of an installation.

(2) a programmer who designs programming systems and other applications.

system programming: creating and maintaining system software.

system programming language: a language developed for wiring system-oriented software packages.

system quiesce: a procedure that allows an authorized operator to start an orderly shutdown of store system activity before changing from one application program to another, turning power off to the store controller, or using terminal resources to perform additional jobs.

system reliability: the probability that equipment will perform accurately all tasks under stated tactical and environmental conditions.

system residence device: an auxiliary storage device (disk, tape, or drum) on which operating-system programs are stored and from which they are loaded into main storage.

system residence volume: the volume on which the nucleus of the operating system and the highest level index of the catalog are located.

system-resident: with software, indicating the instructions and data forming an integral portion of the computer system. Cf. *media-resident software*.

system resource: any facility of the computing system that may be allocated to a task.

system resources manager (SRM): a group of programs that controls the use of system resources in order to satisfy the installation's performance objectives.

system response field: the portion of a basic transmission unit (BTU) containing the network control program status response to a request issued by the host.

system restart:

(1) a restart that allows reuse of previously initialized input and output work queues. Synonymous with *warm start*.

(2) a restart that allows reuse of a previously initialized link pack area. Synonymous with *quick start*.

systems analysis: the analysis of an activity to determine precisely what must be accomplished and how to accomplish it.

systems analyst (SA): an individual trained to undertake the tasks of systems analysis.

Systems and Computers Evaluation and Review Technique: see *SCERT.*

systems and programming (S & P): the department in the organization responsible for applications programming.

systems approach: looking at the overall situation rather than the narrow implications of the task at hand; particularly, looking for interrelationships between the task at hand and other functions which relate to it.

systems definition: a complete description, totally documented, of a problem and its solution or proposed solution.

systems design: a design that graphically illustrates the nature and content of input, files, procedures, and output in order to show the needed connection processes and procedures.

systems disk: a disk reserved for storage of programs and data used by an operating system and programs, such as loaders and assemblers.

systems flowchart: a visual representation of the system through which data provided by the source documents are converted into final documents.

systems generation: a systems disk generated by a user, who specifies the configuration, file protected area, error handling, and so forth.

systems house: a company that puts together systems, often using other people's equipment and computer programs, mildly modified.

systems integration: combining of products from several vendors (both software and hardware) to form a turnkey system designed for a particular task or customer.

systems library: a collection of programs used by the operating system and various assemblers, loaders, and the like.

system slowdown: a network control program mode of reduced operation invoked when buffer availability drops below a threshold level; the network control program limits the amount of new data it accepts while continuing normal output activity.

systems network architecture: see *SNA.*

system software: software components that support application programs by managing system resources, such as memory, and input and output devices.

systems program: a program that controls the operation of the computer system.

systems programmer: an individual responsible for writing, installing, maintaining, repairing, troubleshooting, and modifying systems software.

systems software: synonymous with *supervisory software.* See also *applications software.*

systems standard: a specified characteristic needed to allow system activity.

systems subroutines: pertaining to various input-output format controls that provide for various format statements found in FORTRAN language.

system supervisor (SS): the network control program code that provides the functional interface between the line scheduler and message processing tasks in the background, and the I/O interrupt handlers. It is composed of four services: task, queue, and buffer management, and supervisor services.

system support program: a program contributing directly to the use and control of a system and the production of end results, including linkage editors, job control processors, and utility packages.

system task: a control program function that is performed under the control of a task control block.

system test: the running of the total connected set of units within the system to collect test data and check the adequacy of the design.

system tester: a test unit for checking modules in modular industrial control systems.

system utility device: a device that is assigned for the temporary storage of intermediate data for a series of job steps.

system utility programs: a collection of problem state programs designed for use by a system programmer in performing such functions as changing or extending the indexing structure of the catalog.

system variable symbol: in assembler programming, a variable symbol that does not have to be declared because the assembler assigns it a read-only value.

T:
(1) see *terminal.*
(2) see *test.*
(3) see *time.*
(4) see *timer.*
(5) see *track.*
(6) see *transaction.*
(7) see *transmit.*

tab:
(1) a label, marker, or indicator, found at either or both ends of a medium, as tapes, to allow rapid awareness of its message.
(2) an automatic stop that the user sets in a word processing application to create columns for tables. There are four types of tabs: right justify, left justify, center justify, and decimal.

tabbing: a means of shifting a cathode ray tube cursor or printer head to a prespecified column on the screen or paper.

tab command: a command that shifts the cursor to the next tab stop.

TAB function: an intrinsic BASIC function used to position output in a desired format.

table:
(1) an array of data each item of which may be unambiguously identified by means of one or more arguments. (B)
(2) a collection of data in which each item is uniquely identified by a label, by its position relative to the other items, or by some other means. Synonymous with *dictionary.*

(3) see *boolean operation table, decision table, function table, operation table, truth table.* (A)

table-driven: a program for making use of tables found in memory.

table element: in COBOL, a data item that belongs to the set of repeated items comprising a table. An argument together with its corresponding functions makes up a table element.

table function: any item of data in a table obtained when a search argument matches a table argument.

table look-at: see *table.*

table look-up (TLU): a procedure for obtaining the value corresponding to an argument from a table of values. (A) (B)

table look-up instruction: an instruction that initiates a table look-up. (A) (B)

table simulator: a computer program able to compute the values in a table rather than simply looking them up as stored.

tab stop: the column position to which a printing device advances on receipt of an appropriate command.

tabular language: a means for stating programming requirements as decision tables. Synonymous with *tab.*

tabulate:
(1) to format data into a table.
(2) to print totals. (A)

tabulating equipment: machines and equipment that use punched cards. Synonymous with *electronic accounting machines.*

tabulation character: see *horizontal tabulation character, vertical tabulation character.* (A)

tabulator: a device that reads data from a data carrier such as punched cards or punched tape, and produces lists, tables, or totals. (B)

tag: one or more characters, attached to a set of data, that contains information about the set, including its identification. (A) (B)

tag converting device: equipment that performs automatic reproduction of information from perforated price tags to punched cards.

tag file: tags stored as a file and used within a program to access directly all records stored in another file.

tag sort: a sort in which addresses of records (tags), and not the records themselves, are moved during the comparison procedures.

tail: a flag indicating the termination of a list.

take-up reel: a specific reel on which tape is wound or can be wound during processing.

talk: transferring data between two units (e.g., a computer and a terminal).

tally: an account of the number of times something has happened.

tandem system: a system network where data proceeds through one central processor into another. This is the system of multiplexers and master-slave arrangements.

tape: see *carriage control tape, chadless tape, magnetic tape, perforated tape.* (A)

tape alternation: a selection, controlled by the program, of first one tape unit followed by another, normally during input or output operations, permitting successive reels of a file to be mounted and removed without interrupting the program.

tape beginning control: a special perforation, reflective spot, or transparent part of the first portion of a magnetic tape to show its start.

tape cartridge: a self-contained continuous loop of magnetic tape in a plug-in package typically storing over two million 8-bit bytes.

tape character: information consisting of bits stored across the several longitudinal channels of a tape.

tape code: see *perforated tape code.* (A)

tape comparator: a device that compares two tapes which are expected to be identical. Comparison is made row by row and the device stops when any discrepancy occurs.

tape conditioning: running a tape forward to the end of the tape, reversing it, and running the tape backward to the beginning of the tape.

tape-controlled carriage: an automatic paperfeeding carriage controlled by a punched paper tape.

tape control unit: a device, including associated buffering, for controlling the activities of the magnetic tape transport.

tape conversion program (TCP): a program for duplicating paper tapes and converting from one tape format to another.

tape crease: the fold or wrinkle in a magnetic tape leading to an error in the reading or writing of data at that point.

tape deck: deprecated term for *magnetic tape unit.* Synonym for *magnetic tape drive.* (A) (B)

tape drive (TD): a mechanism for controlling the movement of magnetic tape. This mechanism is commonly used to move magnetic tape past a read head or write head, or to allow automatic rewinding. Synonymous with *tape deck, tape transport.* See *magnetic tape drive.* (B) Deprecated term for *tape unit.* (B)

tape-drive controller: a device for interfacing one or more tape drive units to a computer providing error checking and buffering.

tape dump: the transfer of complete contents of information recorded on tape to the computer or another storage medium.

tape erasure: where a signal recorded on a tape is removed and the tape is then made ready for rerecording.

tape feed: a device that feeds tape to be read or sensed by the machine.

tape feed switch: a switch that actuates the reperforator to meter a predetermined length of tape.

tape file:
(1) a record file consisting of a magnetic or punched paper tape.
(2) a set of magnetic tapes in a tape library.

tape input: pertaining to the introduction of data to machines using tapes.

tape input tape output: see *TIP TOP.*

tape label (TPLAB): a record at the beginning and end of a reel of magnetic tape showing information about the file stored on the tape. See *trailer label.*

tape leader: the part at the beginning of a reel of magnetic or punched tape that is often left blank to permit for initial threading or to hold some sort of marker or code to show the nature of the data stored on the tape. Holes, notches, other magnetization, and so on, are used for such purposes.

tape library: the area in a computer room for storing magnetic tapes.

tape limited: the processing speed time limited by the speed of the magnetic or paper tape devices.

tape load point: the position on a piece of magnetic tape where reading or writing may commence.

tape mark (TM): a character on a magnetic tape file that divides the file into a new section. Synonymous with *control mark*.

tape operating system (TOS): a software package designed for computers having at least 16,000 words of memory with no random-access storage and at least four magnetic tape systems.

tape perforator: an off-line, keyboard-operated unit for punching code holes in paper tape.

tape perforator interface: a circuit providing the buffering and matching needed to drive a tape perforator.

tape pool: a collective name for a group of tape drives. See also *storage pool.*

tape punch: a computer-actuated punch that punches holes in punch tape or punched tape. Synonym for *receiving perforator.* (B)

tape punch control keys: keys that control activities, such as power on, feeding tape at the beginning and end of reel, tape error, and punch on and off.

tape rack: a rack for holding reels of magnetic tape.

tape reader: synonym for *punched tape reader.*

tape reader-punch: see *punched tape reader.*

tape reader-punch controller: a unit for interfacing paper tape units to a computer system.

tape reel: magnetic tape wound around a spool; used with industry standard magnetic tape storage systems.

tape reproducer: a device that prepares one tape from another tape by copying all or part of the data from the tape that is read. (B)

tape resident system: an operating system that uses magnetic tapes for on-line storage of system routines.

tape row: that portion of a tape, on a line perpendicular to the reference edge, on which all binary characters may be either recorded or sensed simultaneously. Synonymous with *frame.* (B)

tape speed: the speed at which tapes are transported from feed to take-up reels during normal recording or reproduction.

tape spool:
(1) a cylinder without flanges, on which tapes may be wound. (B)
(2) a coiled length of perforated tape. (A)

tape station: deprecated term for *magnetic tape unit.* (A) (B)

tape-to-card: pertaining to equipment or methods that transmit data from either magnetic tape or punched tape to punched cards.

tape-to-print program: transfers data from magnetic tape to printer.

tape-to-tape converter: a machine that changes one form of input-output medium or code to another.

tape transport: deprecated term for *magnetic tape unit.* Synonym for *magnetic tape drive.* (A) (B)

tape transport mechanism: synonym for *magnetic tape drive.* (B)

tape unit (TU): a device containing a tape drive, together with read heads and write heads and associated controls. See *magnetic tape unit.* (A)

tape volume: a single reel of magnetic tape.

target computer: a computer that has not been designed to use a particular program, but has another computer translate such a program for its use. Synonymous with *object computer.*

target CPU: a type of central processing unit for which a language processor yields machine language output. All language processors have a target CPU.

target language: a language into which statements are translated. Synonymous with *object language.* (A) (B)

target market: the industry or application for which a product has been specifically created.

target pack: a disk pack used to maintain systems software. When any change is made to a system control program, the program is copied to the target pack and changes are made there and tested using that copy.

target phase: the time when the target program is run. Synonymous with *object phase, run phase.*

target program: a computer program in a target language that has been translated from a source language. Synonymous with *object program.* (A) (B)

target variable: in PL/1, a variable to which a value is assigned.

task (TSK):
(1) a basic unit of work to be accomplished by a computer. The task is usually specified to a control program in a multiprogramming or multiprocessing environment. (B)
(2) in word processing, a basic unit of work to be accomplished by the operator.
(3) in a multiprogramming or multiprocessing environment, a computer program, or portion thereof, capable of being specified to the control program as a unit of work. Tasks compete for system resources.

task control block (TCB): the consolidation of control information related to a task.

task dispatcher: provides a capability to initiate parallel tasks and to synchronize their execution.

tasking: see *multitasking.* (A)

task management: those functions of the control program that regulate the use by tasks of the processing unit and other resources, except for input-output devices.

task name: in PL/1, an identifier used to refer to a task variable.

task queue: a queue of all the task control blocks present in the system at any one time.

task scheduler: in real-time operating systems, organizes and schedules the processing of events not directly connected to user interrupts and provides multiple execution paths through a program.

task start: the creation of a new task in the system.

task states: the states of execution status of a task relative to the processor-active state, ready state, suspended state, and wait state.

task switch:
(1) allocation of the processor to another task; for example, a ready or active task of higher priority than the current task in execution.
(2) a change in the task that is in control of the processor. The new task's state changes from ready to active and the current task is placed in a state other than active.

task-to-task communication: where a user program on a node of a computer network exchanges messages or data with a user program of another node.

task variable: in PL/1, a variable with the TASK attribute whose value gives the relative priority of a task.

taste: slang, the quality found in programs.

TC: see *transmission control character.*

TCB: see *task control block.*

TCF: see *terminal configuration facility.*

TCP: see *tape conversion program.*

TCS: see *terminal control system.*

TD: see *tape drive.*

teaching machine: any machine which performs computer-aided instruction.

technical services: synonymous with *tech support.*

technical support: synonymous with *tech support.*

technique: the method used to collect, process, convert, transfer, and retrieve data to prepare reports.

technique flowcharts: flowcharts showing data and information needs and the methods used for processing this information.

tech support: a computer systems firm that performs systems programming and provides other technical consultation to a data-processing department or organization. Synonymous with *technical services, technical support.*

TELEC: see *telecommunication.*

TELECC: see *telecommunication.*

telecommunication (TELEC) (TELECC):
(1) communication over a distance, as by telegraph or telephone.

(2) any transmission, emission, or reception of signs, signals, writing, images, and sounds or intelligence of any nature by wire, radio, optical, or other electromagnetic systems.
(3) the transmission of signals over long distances, such as by telegraph, radio, or television. (B)

teleprocessing (TP): synonym for *remote-access data processing.* Deprecated term for *distributed data processing.* See also *distributed function.*

teleprocessing monitor (TPM): a software system created to ease the development of on-line or real-time computer applications. TPM is the interface between user applications and the general-purpose operating system of a main frame or mini-computer.

teleprocessing network: synonym for *remote-access data-processing network.*

teleprocessing terminal: used for on-line data transmission between remote process locations and a central computer system. Connection to the computer system is achieved by a data-adapter device or a transmission control.

temporary data set: a data set that is created and deleted in the same job.

temporary error: an error recovered by correcting data or reattempting the read or write operation. Cf. *peripheral error, permanent error.*

temporary file: a file that can be erased or overwritten when it is no longer needed. Cf. *permanent file.*

temporary read/write error: an error that is eliminated by retrying a read/write operation.

temporary storage: in computer programming, storage locations reserved for immediate results. Synonymous with *working storage.* (A)

temporary storage area: the area of memory reserved for data in process or in an intermediate state of computation. Synonymous with *scratch pad.*

ten (10)-key pad: in word processing, a separate set of keys numbered 0 through 9 on a word processor's keyboard that allows easy entry of numbers, aligning them automatically on the decimal point; similar to a calculator key pad.

tens complement: the radix complement in the decimal numeration system. Synonymous with *complement-on-ten.* (A) (B)

tense: slang, describing very clear and efficient programs.

TERM: see *terminal.*

term: the smallest part of an expression that can be assigned a value. See *absolute term, arithmetic term, logical term, relocatable term.*

terminal (T) (TERM) (TML):
(1) a point in a system or network at which data can either enter or leave. (A)
(2) a device, usually equipped with a keyboard and a display device, capable of sending and receiving information over a link. See also *job-oriented terminal, remote terminal.*

terminal cluster: a group of two or more terminals controlled by one computer.

terminal component: a separately addressable part of a terminal that performs an input or output function, such as the display component of a keyboard-display device or a printer component of a keyboard-printer device.

terminal configuration facility (TCF): a set of macrostatements to be coded by the user and modules in programmable store system host support that are used to define and create the terminal operational environment.

terminal controller: a hard-wired or intelligent (programmable) device which provides detailed control for one or more terminal devices.

terminal control system (TCS): a control program for handling multiterminal operations in a computer. Schedules the use of hardware and all input-output processing.

terminal cursor: a movable mark that locates a character on a CRT screen.

terminal digit posting: the arranging and recording of serial numbers of documents on the basis of the last configuration of the digits of the serial number.

terminal display mode: the way in which points are displayed on the CRT screen.

terminal distributed system: an arrangement of computers within an organization where the computer complex has separate computing facilities all functioning in a cooperative fashion, rather than the conventional single computer at a single location.

terminal edit operation: an operation such as clear entire screen, clear unprotected positions, character typeover, character insert/delete, line insert/delete, erase to end of page, and erase line/field.

terminal entry: any input operation on a terminal.

terminal I/O wait: the condition of a task in which the task cannot continue processing until a message is received from a terminal.

terminal job: in systems with time sharing, the processing done on behalf of one terminal user from log on to log off.

terminal keyboard: a keyboard that is part of a communications terminal that is used for manual input of data or control signals.

terminal/light pen system: a system of a specially designed terminal and light pen. By pointing the pen to the desired character position and pressing its tip to the screen, a selection of data for action by the system is made.

terminal mode: a mode of operation of a general purpose computer such that its cathode ray tube and/or printer is used as a terminal for another computer.

terminal modem eliminator: a unit that allows direct terminal to terminal or terminal to computer connection and eliminates the need for two modems operating back to back.

terminal node (TN): the last node of a tree, with no following nodes.

terminal port:
(1) in a network, the functional unit of a node through which data can enter or leave the network.
(2) that part of a processor that is dedicated to a single data channel for the purpose of receiving data from or transferring data to one or more external or remote devices.

terminal quiesce: an orderly shutdown of all terminal activity.

terminate and stay resident: see *TSRs*.

termination (of a block): in PL/1, cessation of execution of a block, and the return of control to the activating block by means of a RETURN or END statement, or the transfer of control to the activating block or to some other active block by means of a GO TO statement.

termination (of a task): cessation of the execution of a task. See also *closedown*.

termination symbol: a symbol on the tape showing the end of a block of information.

terminator: see *SCSI cable terminator*.

terminator/initiator: a program that makes a job step ready to run in some computers and performs regular housekeeping functions following the end of a job.

terminology bank: in machine-aided translation systems a computer-based glossary of terms providing translations for all entries.

ternary:
(1) pertaining to a selection, choice, or condition that has three possible different values or states. (B)
(2) pertaining to a fixed-radix numeration system having a radix of three.

ternary code: a code in which only three states are considered.

ternary incremental representation: incremental representation in which the value of an increment is rounded to one of three values, plus or minus one quantum or zero. (A) (B)

test (T) (TST): the examination of a criterion, to determine the present arrangement of some element of computer hardware; for example, a manually set switch.

test alphabetic: a validity check developed to ensure that input is properly alphabetic.

test bed: a software package used for program testing.

test card: the card used for testing all input-output functions and simulating regular and direct-memory access controllers. The card includes special-purpose test logic for a complete test of each input-output bus signal.

test case: a set of input data which is intended to determine the correctness of a routine.

test condition: in COBOL, a statement that, taken as a whole, may be either true or false, depending on the circumstances existing at the time the expression is evaluated.

test data: the data used in a check problem. Synonymous with *test deck*.

test deck: synonym for test data.

test file: a file of data for testing a computer program throughout its development. It contains a smaller amount of data than a corresponding production file, but data in a test file are ordinarily carefully structured to show the entire range of possibilities that would ever be encountered in live data for exercising the program thoroughly.

test for blanks: a validity check developed to ensure that appropriate fields are blank.

testing: the running of a system or a program against a predetermined series of data to arrive at a predictable result for the purpose of establishing the acceptability of the system or program.

testing nominative: the standard of performance established for quantitative and qualitative testing.

test macro: the ordered set of software and hardware created for testing of large scale integration units. The system includes a conditioning module, a memory, and a programmable clock generator with the associated software package.

test numeric: a validity check developed to ensure that input is appropriately numeric.

test problem: a problem selected to determine whether a computer or a program is operating properly.

test program: a program developed to use and check the differing hardware units of a computer.

test program system: a checking system utilized before running a problem where a sample problem of the same type with a known solution is run.

testrad: a group of four pulses or bits, used to express a decimal or hexadecimal (base sixteen) number in binary form.

test record: a record in a test file.

test routine: a routine designed to show whether a computer is functioning correctly.

test run: a run used to check that a program is functioning correctly.

test tape program: a tape containing both program instructions and preapproved test data or coding to be used for analysis diagnostics or checkout runs.

test under mask: a test for checking the status of selected bits in a byte by comparing the byte as a whole with another byte in which the tested bits are set to 1 and all other bits are reset to 0. If any of the selected bits is set to 1, this fact is sensed and a status flag is set.

text (TXT):
(1) in ASCII and data communication, a sequence of characters treated as an entity if preceded and terminated by one STX and one ETX transmission control character, respectively. (A)
(2) in word processing, information for human comprehension that is intended for presentation in a two-dimensional form; for example, printed on paper or displayed on a screen. Text consists of symbols, phrases, or sentences in natural or artificial languages, picture, diagrams, and tables.
(3) the control sections of an object module or load module.
(4) that part of a message that is of concern to the party ultimately receiving the message; that is, the message exclusive of the header or control information.
(5) cf. *heading*. (A)

text cursor: a marker indicating where the next character is typed on the keyboard that will appear in the text.

text editing: in word processing, the process of making simple additions, deletions, and changes to a stored document.

text editor: software providing a user with a source text-generation system that allows the stored text statements to be altered at any time, including inserting, deleting, or replacing lines in the text buffer.

text field: an area in which the user can enter and edit text. In dialog boxes, the small boxes typed in are text fields.

text file: a file of characters that is also divided into lines. Cf. binary file.

text function: in a graphics system, a function that permits text to be entered into a drawing.

text processing: using a terminal connected to a computer to create, alter, and yield text, that often needs revision and numerous copies.

text section: that portion of a load module with computer instructions in final form and data defined and with specified initial values.

text segment: a portion of a message that contains no part of the message header.

T flip-flop: a flip-flop having only one input electrode causing a unit to be triggered; used in ripple counter applications. See also *ripple counter.*

then: see *IF-THEN element.* (A)

thermal light: a display signal that is visible to a computer operator when the temperature in a device is higher than it is supposed to be.

thermal printer: a small-format, non-impact printer producing characters by applying heat to special heat-sensitive papers. These printers are of slow speed, poor quality reproduction, and require high paper costs. Their advantages are that they are less expensive to purchase than other printers and are able to combine graphic and alphanumeric output readily.

thin film: loosely, magnetic thin film. (A)

think time: synonym for *intermessage delay.*

thin window display: in word processing, an electronic display containing as many as 96 characters, and often a single line only.

third-generation computer: a computer that uses logic technology components. The class of computers introduced in the mid-1960s which use integrated circuits as their principal components and whose speed is measured in nanoseconds. These computers feature on-line multiprocessing, multiprogramming, and database management systems, as well as increased mass storage capacity and telecommunications input. See *first-generation computer, second-generation computer.*

thirty-nine feature code: pertaining to a code designed for punched cards to represent numerals only from 0 to 39 but with no more than two punches in any column.

thrashing: in a virtual storage system, a condition in which the system can do little useful work because of excessive paging.

threaded language: a high-level programming language where a part of a program is compiled into executable form as it is entered, and other parts are interpreted as the program runs.

tree-address computer: a computer where each machine instruction contains three addresses, those of both operands and the address where the result should be stored. The address of the following instruction is stored in a register rather than in the instruction. Cf. *one-address computer, two-address computer.*

three-address instruction: an instruction that contains three address parts. (A) (B)

three-bit byte: synonym for *triplet.* (A)

three-bit error: an error found in a data-transmission sequence where three consecutive bits are incorrectly received. Cf. *two-bit error.*

3-M machine: synonymous with *scholar's work station.*

three-pass assembler: an assembler that scans a source program three times; the first pass constructs a symbol table, the second yields the assembly listing, and the third produces the object program. Cf. *one-pass assembler, two-pass assembler.*

three-plus-one address instruction: an instruction that contains three address parts, the plus-one address being that of the instruction that is to be executed next, unless otherwise specified. (A) (B)

3.5-inch disk: a flexible, plastic disk measuring 3.5 inches in diameter encased in a rigid plastic shell. These disks come in three types: high-density (1.4 MB capacity), double-sided (800K), and single-sided (400K). See *floppy disk.*

threshold:

(1) a logic operator having the property that if P is a statement, Q is a statement, R is a statement, . . . then the threshold of P, Q, R, . . . is true if at least N statements are true, false if less than N statements are true, where N is a specified nonnegative integer called the threshold condition.

(2) the threshold condition as in (1). (A)

threshold element:

(1) a logic element that performs a threshold operation. Synonymous with *threshold gate.* (B)

(2) a device that performs the logic threshold operation but in which the truth of each input statement contributes, to the output determination, a weight associated with that statement. (A)

threshold gate: synonym for *threshold element.* (A) (B)

threshold operation: an operation performed on operands to obtain a value of a threshold function. (A) (B)

threshold quantity: the number of items that must be purchased to qualify for a reduced price.

throughput: a measure of the amount of work performed by a computer system over a given period of time, for example, jobs per day. (A) (B) Synonymous with *thruput.*

throw-away unit: an electronic device that is not serviceable. When it fails, it is discarded and often replaced.

thruput: synonymous with *throughput.*

tick: slang, an interval of time; the basic clock time on the computer.

ticking: in OCR, the marks caused by the bottom of the upper case character while typing in lower case, or vice versa.

tie: in perforated continuous forms paper, the interval between cuts.

tiers: three equal, 32-column, horizontal sections into which the punch area of a card has been divided.

tightly coupled: pertaining to processing units that share real storage, that are

controlled by the same control program, and that can communicate directly with each other. See also *loosely coupled.*

time (T): see *access time, available time, compiling time, computer time, corrective maintenance time, cycle time, deferred maintenance time, development time, downtime, emergency maintenance time, idle time, installation time, maintenance time, makeup time, operating time, preventive maintenance time, problem time, production time, program development time, program execution time, real time, translating time, word time.* (A)

time-derived channel: any channel obtained by the time-division multiplexing of a channel.

time-division system: a communication system using methods and principles associated with time division multiplexing (TDM).

time out (TMO) (TO):

(1) a parameter related to an enforced event designed to occur at the conclusion of a predetermined elapsed time. A time-out condition can be cancelled by the receipt of an appropriate time-out cancellation signal.

(2) a time interval allotted for certain operations to occur; for example, response to polling or addressing before a system operation is interrupted and must be restarted.

(3) a terminal feature that logs off a user if an entry is not made within a specified period of time.

time quantum: the time given to a user in a time-sharing system.

timer (T): a register whose content is changed at regular intervals in such a manner as to measure time. Synonymous with *time register.* (A) (B)

time register: synonym for *timer.* (A) (B)

time scale: see *extended-time scale, fast-time scale, variable time scale.* (A)

time scale factor: in simulation, the ratio of computer time to the corresponding problem time. (A)

time schedule controller: a specific controller in which the reference input signal (or the set point) adheres automatically to a predetermined time schedule.

time share: to use a device for two or more interleaved c purposes. (A)

time-share BASIC: an enhancement of BASIC utilized as a conversational language providing access to a computer system for a maximum number of users.

time-shared computer: a computer system permitting usage by a significant number of subscribers, usually through data-communication subsystems.

time sharing (TS):
(1) pertaining to the interleaved use of time on a computer system that enables two or more users to execute computer programs concurrently. (A)
(2) a mode of operation of a data-processing system that provides for the interleaving in time of two or more processes in one processor. (B)
(3) a method of using a computing system that allows a number of users to execute programs concurrently and to interact with the programs during execution.

time-sharing interchange: allows the interactive user to issue commands that cause batch programs to be executed under various programs by transferring data and other required input, either entered at the interactive terminal or stored in files, from offices to a batch-processing system operating within the time-sharing network.

time-sharing link: a communication channel where several subscribers share the same physical line by occupying the line momentarily in bursts of activity, occupying a specific time slot. Each user is unaware of the others sharing the same resource.

time-sharing monitor system: a collection of programs remaining permanently in memory to provide overall coordination and control of the total operating system.

time-sharing option (TSO): an optional configuration of the operating system that provides conversational time sharing from remote stations.

time-sharing priority: in systems with time sharing, a ranking within the group

of tasks associated with a single user, used to determine their precedence in receiving system resources.

time-sharing system (TSS): a combination of hardware and software in a computer system that allocated central processor time and other computer services to multiple users at different locations so that the computer, in effect, processes a number of programs simultaneously.

time-sharing user modes: at any moment, a user is in one of the following execution modes, (1) inactive; (2) command; (3) ready; (4) running; (5) waiting (a) for input-output completion, (b) for console action, (c) for task completion, (d) to be loaded.

time shifting: a function in time-division multiplexing systems for adjusting the time slot of an incoming channel to the required time slots for an outgoing channel.

time slice:
(1) an interval of time on the processing unit allocated for use in performing a task. After the interval has expired, processing unit time is allocated to another task; thus a task cannot monopolize processing unit time beyond a fixed limit.
(2) in systems with time sharing, a segment of time allocated to a terminal job.

time slicing:
(1) a mode of operation in which two or more processes are assigned quantity of time on the same processor. (B)
(2) a feature that can be used to prevent a task from monopolizing the processing unit and thereby delaying the assignment of processing unit time to other tasks.
(3) in systems with time sharing, the allocation of time slices to terminal jobs.

time slot: the brief time period during which a specific unit is able to obtain access to another to deliver or accept digital signals.

time stamp: information added to a message, record, or other form of data showing the date and time it was processed by a computer.

time switch: apparatus for controlling the usage of a resource by competing processes, by allocating a time slot of a few milliseconds or microseconds to each process.

time utilization: arranging a program to permit processing to continue while records needed for processing are located in a file and read into core and working storage.

timing error: error generated when a program is unable to keep pace with the tape-transfer rate, or a new motion or select command is released prior to the earlier command being fully completed.

timing loop: a set of instructions in a program that does nothing, but whose execution is known. When an action requires deferral for a short period of time, the loop is executed an appropriate number of times to cause the appropriate delay.

timing master: the primary source of timing signals in a computer.

timing meter: a unit that measures the time duration of a function by sampling the state of a memory element or elements associated with that activity. One type of timing meter is a binary counter driven by a clock derived either from the basic CPU clock or from a special generator.

tiny BASIC: a high-level programming language, specially created for microcomputers, that is a subset of BASIC.

TIP TOP: tape input tape output. Designating a computer system able to both read data from and write data on magnetic tape.

title bar: the bar at the top of a window that shows the name of the window. When the window is active, the title bar is highlighted with horizontal lines.

TK: see *track.*

TLU: see *table look-up.*

TM:
(1) see *tape mark.*
(2) see *Turing machine.*

TML: see *terminal.*

TMO: see *time out.*

TN: see *terminal node.*

TO: see *time out.*

TOC: table of contents.

TOD: time of day.

TOD clock: time-of-day clock.

TOF:
(1) in an editor, the top of file; the start of data.
(2) on a printer, the switch that positions the page at the top; the top of form.

toggle:
(1) pertaining to any device having two stable states. Synonym for *flip-flop.* (A)
(2) to switch settings.

token: a distinguishable unit in a sequence of characters.

token passing: a way of passing control from terminal to terminal, on a local area network in the shape of a ring.

token ring: where an electronic vehicle carries data from computer to computer along a ring-shaped layout. See also *token passing.*

top-down programming: the design and coding of computer programs using a hierarchical structure in which related functions are performed at each level of the structure.

top-down testing: a technique for testing the modules (procedures and functions) of a program, as they are written, by calling them with actual parameters and providing stub (dummy) modules for those modules not yet written but referenced in the program. See *step-wise refinement.*

top of file: see *TOF.*

top of form: see *TOF.*

TOS: see *tape operating system.*

total system: a strategy to place critical operational components of an organization under the complete or partial control of computers. Synonymous with *integrated system.*

touch screen terminal: a terminal with a screen that is sensitive to touch, consequently, data can be input easily. See *light pen, mouse, soft keyboard.*

touch-sensitive keyboards: synonymous with *membrane keyboards.*

touch terminal: a terminal with which a user physically interacts by touching the screen with a finger to select an input, instead of more traditional input units such as keyboards or light pens.

tournament sort: a repeated selection sort in which each subset consists of no more than two items. (A)

tower configuration: a floor-standing cabinet that is taller than it is wide. Desktop computers are sometimes turned on their side and placed onto a set of feet that creates a tower configuration.

tpi: see *tracks per inch.*

TPLAB: see *tape label.*

TR: see *track.*

TRA: see *transfer.*

trace:

(1) a record of the execution of a computer program; it exhibits the sequences in which the instructions were executed. (A)

(2) to record a series of events as they occur.

trace debug: a debugging program that displays a set of registers and/or memory locations as they are encountered throughout the execution of a program, usually without interrupting the program execution.

trace flow: a debugging unit that prints out contents of various registers and memory locations in a particular program segment specified by a user.

trace program: a computer program that performs a check on another computer program by exhibiting the sequence in which the instructions are executed and usually the results of executing the instructions. (A) (B)

trace routine: a routine for providing a time history of machine registers and controls during the execution of an object routine, providing the status of all registers and locations affected by each instruction every time the instruction is executed.

trace table: a storage area in which trace information is placed.

tracing routine: a routine that provides an historical record of specified events in the execution of a computer program. (A)

track (T) (TK) (TR) (TRK):

(1) the path or one of the set of paths, parallel to the reference edge on a data medium, associated with a single reading or writing component as the data

medium moves past the component. (B)

(2) the portion of a moving data medium, such as a drum, tape, or disk, that is accessible to a given reading head position. (A)

(3) in word processing, an area on magnetic recording media along which a series of signals may be recorded.

(4) see *address track, card track, clock track, feed track, magnetic track, regenerative track.* (A)

track access time: in disk and floppy disk storage, the time needed for the read/write head to shift mechanically from its present position to a desired track and to settle.

trackball: an input device on a video terminal where the trackball is moved with the palm of the hand and, correspondingly moves the cursor on the screen. Trackballs are used in various graphic applications as well as in games. Variations of trackballs are made to replace mice, since the trackball is stationary and takes up less desktop room than a mouse.

track density: the number of adjacent tracks per unit of distance on a storage unit, such as magnetic tape or disk.

track hold: a facility that protects a track while it is being accessed. When data on a track is being modified by a task in one partition, that track cannot be accessed at the same time by a task or subtask in another partition.

track kerning: adjusts the character and word spacing uniformly over a range of text.

track pitch: the distance between corresponding points of adjacent tracks. (A) (B)

tracks: see *track.* See also *sector.*

tracks density: the number of bits written in a single position across the width of a tape, including parity bits.

tracks per inch (tpi): a unit of measurement for track density on a floppy disk.

tractor feed: a means for accurately positioning and transporting fan-fold paper in printers.

tractor holes: synonym for *carrier holes.*

tractors: grippers to guide paper through the printer.

trailer:
(1) a record that follows a group of detail records and provides information about a group not present in the detail records.
(2) a record that follows a header.

trailer card: a card that contains information related to the data on the preceding cards. Synonymous with *detail card.* (A)

trailer label: a file or data set label that follows the data records on a unit of recording media.

trailer record: a record which follows one or more records and contains data related to those records.

trailing decision: a loop control that is executed after the loop body. Cf. *leading decision.* (A)

trailing edge:
(1) an indicator as to whether or not a loop has executed the specified number of times, placed at the end of the loop so that the loop is executed prior to the testing of the counter.
(2) that part of a pulse during its transition from binary 1 to 0. Cf. *leading edge.*

trailing end: the end of a perforated tape that last enters a perforated-tape reader. (A)

trailing pad: filler characters inserted after information in order to fulfill length requirements for cosmetic desires.

trailing zero: in positional notation, a zero in a less significant digit place than the digit place of the least significant nonzero digit of a numeral. (A)

trail printer: in word processing, a printer that is not uniquely associated with a particular keyboard or display-based workstation and that is used for automatic printout of text already recorded onto a recording medium or in electronic storage within associated word processing equipment. Printing follows or "trials the next generation."

train printer: an impact printer that prints fully formed characters one line at a time by striking type bars suspended from a constantly rotating train of carriers against an inked ribbon and paper. See *line printer.*

TRAN:
(1) see *transaction.*
(2) see *transmit.*

TRAN-PRO: see *transaction processing.*

TRANS: see *translator.*

transaction (T) (TRAN) (TRX):
(1) in batch or remote batch entry, a job or job step.
(2) in systems with time sharing, an exchange between a terminal and another device that accomplishes a particular action or result; for example, the entry of a customer's deposit and the updating of the customer's balance.

transaction data: data describing a particular event in a data-processing application area, such as job number, quantity, price, and so on.

transaction file: a file containing relatively transient data that, for a given application, is processed together with the appropriate master file. Synonymous with *detail file.*

transaction listing: see *audit trail, system log.*

transaction log: in the programmable store system, a record of transactions performed at the point-of-sale terminal. This log is magnetically recorded and stored on the store controller integrated disks.

transaction-oriented system: a specialized type of on-line system that handles interactive-type applications that revolve around entering, retrieving, updating, and/or manipulating information utilizing one or more user-written programs.

transaction processing (TRAN-PRO): the ability of a computer to enter and process a collection of several related actions; the ability to handle multiple transactions from one or more terminals in a network. A transaction may be a single entry or a series of entries that would initiate a series of automatic actions within the computer system.

transaction record: a record in a transaction data set, created by one or more executions of a program that is coded to generate transaction records.

transaction record header: identification and control information at the beginning of the first block of a transaction record.

transaction record number: a number assigned to a transaction record when its generation is initiated and within the range of numbers available for the defined group.

transaction tape: a magnetic tape with transactions or change records. Synonymous with *change tape.*

transborder data flow: the flow of information or data across national boundaries.

transceiver: a terminal that can transmit and receive traffic.

transcribe: to transfer data from one data medium to another, converting them as necessary for acceptance by the receiving medium. (A) (B)

transcriber: machines associated with a computer used for transferring the input or output data from a record of information in a stated language to the computer medium and language, or from a computer to a record of information.

transcription: the conversion of data from one language, code, or medium to another, including reading, translating, and recording functions.

transcription break: a flowchart symbol or unit that shows the relationship between two files. The symbol is directional and suggests the flow of information from one file to another that is impacted upon by the information.

transducer: a device for converting energy from one form to another. (A)

transfer (TRA) (XFER):
(1) to send data from one place and to receive the data at another place. Synonymous with *move.* (A) (B)
(2) in word processing, the movement of selected recorded text from one element of recording medium to another.
(3) deprecated term for *jump.* (A) (B)
(4) see *block transfer, peripheral transfer, radial transfer.* (A)

transfer check: a check on the accuracy of a data transfer. (A)

transfer command: an instruction changing control from one part of a program to another by indicating a remote instruction.

transfer control: action from a branch instruction as it transfers control from one portion of a program to another.

transfer instruction: deprecated term for *jump instruction.* (A) (B)

transfer interpreter: a device that prints on a punched card characters corresponding to hole patterns punched in another card. (B)

transfer key: in word processing, a control that initiates the transfer process.

transfer of control: see *jump.*

transfer of control card: see *transition card.*

transfer operation: moves information from a storage location or one storage medium to another; often refers to movement between different storage media.

transfer rate: see *data-transfer rate.*

transferred information: synonym for *transinformation content.* (A) (B)

transfer table: a table containing a list of all transfer instructions of programs in main memory, permitting the transfer of control between programs.

transfer time: the time interval between the instant at which a transfer of data starts and the instant at which the transfer is completed. (B)

transform:
(1) to change the form of data according to specific rules, without significantly changing the meaning of the data. (B)
(2) in computer graphics, to change a display image, for example, by scaling, rotating, or translating.
(3) synonymous with *convert.* (A)

transformation (T): see *key transformation.* (A)

transient: pertaining to a program that does not reside in main storage or to a temporary storage area for such programs.

transient area: a storage area used for temporary storage of transient programs or routines.

transient copy: synonymous with *soft copy.*

transient error: an error that occurs once or at unpredictable intervals.

transient state: the condition of a station when it is setting up to transmit.

transinformation: see *transinformation content.*

transinformation content: in information theory, the difference between the information content conveyed by the occurrence of an event and the conditional information content conveyed by the occurrence of the same event, given the occurrence of another event. Synonymous with *mutual information, transferred information, transmitted information.* See *mean transinformation content.* (A) (B)

transistor: a small solid-state, semi-conducting device, ordinarily using germanium, that performs nearly all the functions of an electronic tube, especially amplification.

transit field: the section of a check, preprinted with magnetic ink, that includes the bank number.

transition card: in the loading of a deck of program cards, the card that causes the termination of loading, then initiates the execution of the program.

translate: to transform data from one language to another. (A) (B)

translate duration: synonym for *translating time.* (A) (B)

translate phase: the logical subdivision of a run that includes the execution of the translator. Synonymous with *translating phase.* (A) (B)

translater: see *translator.*

translating: in computer graphics, moving all or part of a display image on the display space from one location to another without rotating the image.

translating phase: synonym for *translate phase.* (A) (B)

translating program: synonym for *translator.* (A) (B)

translating time: the elapsed time taken for the execution of a translator. Synonymous with *translate duration.* (A) (B)

translation: pertaining to the conversion of data from one expression in one particular form to an expression in another without a significant change in meaning or value.

translator (TRANS): a computer program that translates from one language into another language and in particular from one programming language into another programming language. Synonymous with *translating program.* (A) (B)

translator routine: a routine that compiles a source program expressed in problem-oriented language to an object program in machine code.

transliterate:
(1) to convert data, character by character. (B)
(2) to convert characters of one alphabet to the corresponding characters of another alphabet. (A)

transmission (X):
(1) the sending of data from one place for reception elsewhere.
(2) in ASCII and data communication, a series of characters including headings and texts. (A)
(3) synonymous with *data transmission.* (A)
(4) see *duplex transmission, half-duplex transmission, synchronous transmission.*
(5) see also *data communication.*

transmission-block character: see *end-of-transmission-block character.* (A)

transmission control (TC) character: any control character used to control or facilitate transmission of data between data-terminal equipment (DTEs). (A) (B)

transmission preprocessor: apparatus for removing a portion of the processing overhead from the CPU.

transmission speed: the number of information elements sent per unit of time, expressed as bits, characters, word groups, or records per second or per minute.

transmission system code: a way of using a character parity check plus a block check to find errors.

transmit (T) (TRAN) (XMIT) (XMT):
(1) to send data from one place for reception elsewhere. (A)
(2) to move an entity from one place to another; for example, to broadcast radio waves, to dispatch data via a transmission medium, or to transfer data from one data station to another via a line.
(3) see also *transfer.*

transmit data set: a data set on diskette storage that is generated by packing data from one or more transaction data set groups.

transmittal mode: the method by which the contents of an input buffer are made available to the program, and the method by which a program makes records available for output.

transmitted information: synonym for *transinformation content.* (A) (B)

transmitter card: a card that converts parallel digital data into asynchronous serial data in ASCII format.

transmitter holding register: a register for holding parallel-transmitted data, transferred from the data-access lines by a write operation.

transmitter-receiver serial/parallel module: a device for converting parallel data for serial transmission and for receiving serial data into a parallel format.

transmitter register: a register that serializes data and presents it to the transmitted data output.

transmitter (or receiver) signal element timing: a pin on an interface for a modem, providing the transmitting (or receiving) section of the modem with timing information.

transparency: in data communications, a characteristic of transmitted data with bit patterns similar to particular control characters; often causing the receiving unit to interpret the bit pattern falsely.

transparent: in data transmission, pertaining to information that is not recognized by the receiving program or device as transmission control characters. See *inherent transparency.*

transparent data:
(1) data that is not recognized as containing transmission control characters.
(2) data in a transmit data set that is not interpreted as containing control characters. Transparent data is preceded by a control byte and a count of the amount of data following.

transparent information: information that is not recognized as transmission control characters by a receiving program or device.

transparent transmission: transmission where the transmission medium does not recognize control characters or initiates any control activity.

transport: see *tape transport.* (A)

transport level: a protocol for sending messages from one network to another.

transport unit: peripheral devices or media handling unit, such as a card feed.

transverse check: a system of error control based on a preset rule for formation of characters.

transverse scanning: scanning where the head moves across, rather than along, the recording tape.

trap (TRP): an unprogrammed, or conditional, jump to a specified address that is automatically activated by hardware, a recording being made of the location from which the jump occurred. (A) (B)

trap/breakpoint: halts that are inserted in object code to cause a branch to a debug program at proper times and places.

trapped instruction: an instruction executed by a software routine when hardware is unavailable.

trapping mode: used in program-diagnostic procedures. If the trapping mode flip-flop is set and the program includes any one of specific instructions, the instruction is not performed but the following instruction is taken from location 0. Program-counter contents are saved in order to resume the program following executing the diagnostic procedure.

trash: an icon on the Apple Macintosh display that can be used to discard programs, documents, and folders.

trash heap: a memory area owned by a program, where the values are no longer useful, thereby wasting memory space.

traverse: the area through which a punched card is transported through the unit.

tray: the flat file drawer used to store punched cards.

tree sort: a sort that exchanges data items treated as nodes of a tree.

tree structure: a hierarchical calling sequence, consisting of a root segment and one or more levels of segments called via the root segment.

trend: to print or record variable values.

triad: a group of three characters or bits.

trial run: a means for checking the accuracy of methods. A sample card deck or part of the actual run data can be used for such a check.

trigger: to cause the immediate execution of a computer program, often by intervention from the external environment, by means of a manually controlled jump to an entry point. (A) (B)

trigger circuit: a circuit that has a number of stable states or unstable states, at least one being stable, and designed so that a desired transition can be initiated by the application of a suitable pulse. (A)

trigger pair: synonymous with *binary pair.*

trip computer: a small computer used in a vehicle to obtain current information on fuel consumption, driving range on remaining fuel, number of miles to destination, and other desired information.

triple diffusion: a semiconductor method where three impurity depositions are prepared on the substrate.

triple-length register: three registers that function as a single register. Synonymous with *triple register.* (B)

triple-length working: arithmetic operations performed on numbers requiring three words in order to yield proper precision.

triple-precision: pertaining to the use of three computer words to represent a number in accordance with the required precision. (A) (B)

triple register: synonym for *triple-length register.* (A) (B)

triplet: a byte composed of three binary elements. Synonymous with *three-bit byte.* (A) (B)

TRK: see *track.*

trouble location problem: a test problem when incorrectly solved, gives information on the location of the faulty device; used after a check problem has shown that a fault exists.

troubleshoot: to detect, locate, and eliminate errors in computer programs or faults in hardware.

TRP: see *trap.*

true complement: deprecated term for *radix complement.* (A) (B)

true form: the representation of a number stored as it is written, with positive numbers stored in true form, and negative numbers stored in complement form. Cf. *complement form.*

truncate:
(1) to terminate a computational process in accordance with some rule; for example, to end the evaluation of a power series at a specified term. (A)
(2) to remove the beginning or ending elements of a string.

truncation:
(1) the deletion or omission of a leading or of a trailing portion of a string in accordance with specified criteria. (B)
(2) the termination of a computation process before its final conclusion or natural termination, if any, in accordance with specified rules. (B)
(3) cf. *round.* (A)

truncation error: an error due to truncation. (A) (B)

truth table:
(1) an operation table for a logic operation. (B)
(2) a table that describes a logic function by listing all possible combinations of input values and indicating, for each combination, the true output values. (A)

truth table generator: a method using a microprocessor for developing a truth table from a diagnostic written in the microprocessor machine code or assembly language.

truth value: the input and output quantities in a truth table.

TRX: see *transaction.*

TS: see *time sharing.*

TSK: see *task.*

TSO: see *time-sharing option.*

TSRs (terminate and stay resident): programs that remain in memory at all times so that at all times they can be instantly activated. Often, they have instant access to a calculator or calendar. TSR programs often conflict with each other, each one fighting for the right to exist within the computer, and various combinations of programs will not function together. See *memory resident.*

TSS: see *time-sharing system.*

TST: see *test.*

TU: see *tape unit.*

tube: synonymous with *screen.*

Turing machine (TM): a mathematical model of a device that changes its internal state and reads from, writes on, and moves, a potentially infinite tape, all in accordance with its present state, thereby constituting a model for computerlike behavior. See *universal Turing machine.*

turnaround document: a computer-readable form, such as a punch card, produced by a computer and often marked with preliminary information that is later used as data to a program following an event occurring.

turnaround time: the elapsed time between submission of a job and the return of the complete output. (B) See also *response time.*

turnkey: installation or system that is complete, self-contained, and able to function without additional modification.

turnkey console: in personal computers, the low cost switch control panel for operator control of power, initialize, and execution.

turnkey system: a system that is supplied to the user in a ready-to-run condition; preparatory procedures such as installation, setup, and testing are usually done by the supplier.

turnpike effect: a phenomenon occurring on highways, networks, and other traffic-oriented situations. When traffic increases, bottlenecks and delays increase until everything eventually locks up.

turtle: the small triangular pointer on a display screen used with the logo language to implement turtle graphics. See also *dynaturtle.*

turtlegraphics: a method of forming graphic images on a display or output unit by sending commands to a "turtle" represented by a cursor on a CRT screen or plotter pen, and so on.

tutorial:

(1) any class or demonstration on a topic.

(2) instruction pertaining to the running of hardware and/or software, found usually in a manual or program form.

tutorial lights: on "intelligent" terminals, programmable indicator lights interlaced with the transaction sequence providing tutorial lead-through to an operator and/or providing a pictorial history of keyboard activity during a transaction.

tweaking parameters: making minor adjustments in the performance of systems software for improving throughput.

twelve edge: synonymous with *twelve punch.*

twelve punch: a punch in the top row of a Hollerith card. Synonymous with *twelve edge, Y punch.* (A)

twenty-nine feature code: a code designed for punched cards to represent numerals only from 0 to 29 but with no more than two punches in any one column.

twin check: a continuous duplication check achieved by the duplication of hardware and/or an automatic comparison of data.

two-address: see *two-address instruction.*

two-address code: a specific instruction code containing two operand addresses.

two-address computer: a computer where each machine instruction contains two addresses, the address of each operand. The result is placed in the location earlier taken by one of the operands. Cf. *one-address computer, three-address computer.*

two-address instruction: an instruction that contains two address parts. (A) (B)

two-bit byte: synonym for *doublet.* (A) (B)

two-bit error: an error in a data-transmission sequence where two consecutive bits are incorrectly received. Cf. *three-bit error.*

two-channel switch: a hardware feature that allows an input-output device to be attached to two channels.

two-chip microprocessor: a microprocessor whose total architecture is developed utilizing only two integrated-circuit chips.

two condition code: a code for representing binary information consisting of the values of 0 and 1.

two-dimensional array: where data elements are arranged into a conceptualized grid having rows and columns. Individual elements are identified by specifying their row and column numbers (subscripts).

two-level address: an indirect address that specifies two levels of addressing. (A)

two-level subroutine: a subroutine with another subroutine.

two-out-of-five code:
(1) a binary-coded decimal notation in which each decimal digit is represented by a binary numeral consisting of five bits of which two are of one kind, conventionally ones, and three are of the other kind, conventionally zeros. The usual weights are 0-1-2-3-6 except for the representation of zero which is then 01100. (B)
(2) a positional notation in which each decimal digit is represented by five binary digits of which two are one kind, for example, ones, and three are the other kind, for example, zeros. (A)

two-pass assembler: an assembler requiring scanning of the source program twice, where the first pass constructs a symbol table and the second pass carries out the translation. Cf. *one pass-assembler, three-pass assembler.*

two-pass compiler: a design of language processors. On the first pass through the program, the compiler checks the syntax of statements and builds a table of all symbols, showing whether they are computational variables or labels requiring the assignment of memory addresses. On the second pass, the compiler translates program statements into executable machine language, utilizing the symbol table for forming the instructions involving variables and addresses.

two-plus-one address instruction: an instruction that contains three address parts, the plus-one address being that of the instruction that is to be executed next unless otherwise specified. (A) (B)

twos complement: the radix complement in the pure binary numeration system. Synonymous with *complement-on-two.*

two-way alternate communication: communication in which information is transferred in both directions, one direction at a time. Synonymous with *either-way communication.*

two-way simultaneous communication: communication in which information is transferred in both directions at the same time. Synonymous with *both-way communication.*

TXT: see *text.*

typamatic key: on a keyboard, the key which, when depressed, keeps repeating the character or function until released.

TYPE: in programming, a general classification of data to which a given element belongs, that is, text, integer, real. The TYPE constrains the kinds of things that can be done to an element of data.

typeahead buffer: a buffer in a keyboard or a microcomputer for holding information keyed before the CPU is ready to accept it.

type bar: a bar, usually mounted vertically on an impact printer, that holds type slugs. Synonymous with *print bar.* (A) (B)

type declaration: in FORTRAN, the explicit specification of the type, and, optionally, length of a variable or function by use of an explicit specification statement.

type definition: a definition of a data type in PASCAL in the type declaration of a block, with the type identifier on the left of the equal sign and the definition on the right.

type face:
(1) the design, or style, of characters produced by a specific printer.
(2) the printing surface of a piece of type which bears the character about to be printed.

type font: type of a given size and style, for example, 10-point Bodoni Modern. (A)

type-out key respond: a specific push button on a console inquiry keyboard that locks the typewriter keyboard and allows the automatic processing to continue.

typeover: in word processing, the ability to replace text simply and quickly by typing new information "over" the old.

type wheel: synonymous with *print wheel.*
(A) (B)

U:

(1) see *unit.*

(2) see *update.*

(3) see *user.*

UA: see *user area.*

UB: see *upper bound.*

UBS: see *unit backspace character.*

UCS: see *universal character set.*

U format: a data set format in which blocks are of unknown length.

UG: see *user group.*

ULSI: ultra large scale integration. See *large scale integration.*

ultimate wafer: a computer wafer having its entire surface covered with working circuit. Precision circuits lasers permit the direct etching and correcting of tiny circuits and wires one by one. Perfection of these wafers will lead to the development of much smaller computers by allowing the complex circuitry of hundreds of silicon chips to be etched onto a single, thin wafer.

ultrafiche: in micrographics, microfiche with images reduced by a very high reduction factor.

ultra large-scale integration: see *large scale integration.*

umacro: a subroutine of either the system adapter, the I/O adapter, or the text processor of access method services that provide a common service for other access method services processor and programmable store system host support.

umbral: a heading that is totally relevant to the data being sought.

U-mode records: in COBOL, records of undefined length. They may be fixed or variable in length; there is only one record per block.

unallowable digit: a character or combination of bits that are not accepted as a valid representation by the computer, machine design, or by a specific routine, and suggests malfunction.

unambiguous name: the name of a file identified exactly as it is known to a computer system. Cf. *ambiguous name.*

unary operation: synonym for *monadic operation.* (A) (B)

unary operator:

(1) an arithmetic operator having only one term. The unary operators that can be used in absolute, relocatable, and arithmetic expressions are: positive (+) and negative (−).

(2) in COBOL, an arithmetic operator (+ or −) that can precede a single variable, a literal or a left parenthesis in an arithmetic expression. The plus sign multiplies the value by +1; the minus sign multiplies the value by −1.

(3) synonym for *monadic operator.* (A)

unbalanced merge sort: a merge sort, which is an external sort, such that the sorted subsets created by the internal sorts are unequally distributed among some of the available auxiliary storage devices. The subsets are merged onto the remaining auxiliary storage devices and the process repeated until all items are in one sorted set. Cf. *balanced merge sort.* (A)

unblank: in computer graphics, to turn the beam on.

unblind (blind): a procedure to control a transmission printer or reperforator.

unblock: deprecated term for *deblock.*

unbundling: separating hardware and software pricing.

uncatalog: to remove an entry from the system catalog, resulting in the system no longer knowing of the file's existence.

uncommitted storage list: blocks of storage that are chained together and not allocated at any specific moment.

unconditional:

(1) subject to a specific instruction only.

(2) free of any condition.

unconditional branch: a program command that always alters the serial execution of program statements by jumping the sequence of execution either forward or backward in the order of progression. The imperative GO TO is most frequently associated with such statements.

unconditional branch instruction: deprecated term for *unconditional jump instruction.* (A) (B)

unconditional control transfer instruction: deprecated term for *unconditional jump instruction.* (A) (B)

unconditional jump: a jump that takes place whenever the instruction that specified it is executed. (A) (B) Synonymous with *unconditional transfer of control.*

unconditional jump instruction: an instruction that specifies an unconditional jump. (A) (B)

unconditional transfer instruction: deprecated term for *unconditional jump instruction.* (A) (B)

unconditional transfer of control: synonymous with *unconditional jump.*

uncorrectable error: an error where the intent of a programmer cannot be determined. The CPU rejects the statement and continues processing.

undefined: a variable or constant not yet assigned a particular length or data type before it is used in a program.

undefined record: a record having an unspecified or unknown length. See also *U format.*

underflow: a result whose value is too small for the range of the number representation being used. Cf. *overflow.*

underpunch: a locational punch in one of the lower rows, 1-9, of an 80-column 12-row punch card.

underscore: a line under an individual character.

under-the-cover modem: deprecated term for *integrated modem.*

undetected error rate: the ratio of the number of bits incorrectly received but undetected or uncorrected by the error-control device, to the total number of bits, unit elements, characters, and blocks that are sent.

undo: to abandon a change just made, before the machine adopts it as final.

unformatted diskette: a diskette that contains no data and no track or sector format information.

unformatted display: a display screen on which no display field has been defined by the user. Cf. *formatted display.* See also *protected field.*

unformatted file: a data file that does not follow some consistent organization in terms of record length, order of data elements, and so on. Text files are usually unformatted.

unformatted record: in FORTRAN, a record for which no FORMAT statement exists, and which is transmitted with a one-to-one correspondence between internal storage locations and external positions in the record.

unichassis: a memory chassis for mounting memory and control cards in a rack panel.

uniformly accessible storage: storage that purports to lessen the effect of variation of access time for an arbitrary sequence of addresses.

uninterruptible power supply (UPS): a power conditioning device situated between commercial power and a computer facility. The commercial power is used for charging batteries and is converted to alternating current by electronic circuitry for use with the computer system.

union: synonymous with *OR operation.*

union catalog: a compiled list of the contents of two or more tape libraries.

uniprocessing (UP): sequential execution of instructions by a processing unit or independent use of a processing unit in a multiprocessing system.

uniprogramming system: a computer system where jobs are brought into main memory and totally executed, one following another. Cf. *multiprogramming system.*

unit (U):
(1) a device having a special function.
(2) a basic element. (A)
(3) see *arithmetic and logic unit, arithmetic unit, delay unit, functional unit, information content natural unit, input-output unit, input unit, logic unit,magnetic tape unit, main control unit, main storage*

unit, output unit, peripheral control unit, tape unit.

unit address: the three-character address of a particular device, specified at the time a system is installed; for example, 191 or 293. See also *device type, group name.*

unitary code: a code having only one digit; the number of times it is repeated determines the quantity it represents.

unit backspace character (UBS): a word processing formatting control that moves the printing or display point to the left one escapement unit as defined to provide character alignment in proportionally spaced text. See also *backspace character.*

unit diagnostics: a program used to detect malfunctions in such units as the input-output and the arithmetic circuitry.

uniterm: a word, symbol, or number used as a descriptor for retrieval of information from a collection, especially in a coordinate indexing system.

uniterm indexing: an indexing system using uniterm descriptors.

uniterming: pertaining to an information-retrieval system involving word selection considered important and descriptive of the contents of a document for later retrieval of the material.

unit record (UR): a card containing one complete record; a punched card.

unit record devices: punch card units such as collators and tabulating machines.

unit separator character (US): the information separator intended to identify a logical boundary between units. (A) (B)

unit string: a string consisting of only one entity. (A) (B)

unit testing: the testing of a single module or a related group of modules.

unity: contained as one.

UNIVAC I: universal automatic computer, the first commercial electronic computer; became available in 1951.

universal access: the default access authority that applies to a data set if the user or group is not specifically permitted access to the data set. Universal access can be any of the access authorities.

universal automatic computer: see *UNIVAC I.*

universal button box: a set of buttons whose operation are determined by the computer program.

universal character set (UCS): a printer feature that permits the use of a variety of character arrays.

universal controller: see *basic controller.*

universal instruction set: a set of instructions that includes those for floating-point arithmetic, fixed-point binary arithmetic and logic, decimal arithmetic, and protection feature.

universal PROM programmer: a device permitting users to program and verify PROMs utilizing commands from the system console.

universal set: the set that includes all of the element of concern in a given study. (A) (B)

universal synchronous-asynchronous receiver/transmitter (USART): a chip established as a peripheral unit for data communications and operating in a desired serial data mode. The chip accepts data from the CPU in parallel and converts the data into a continuous serial stream for transmission. It also converts received serial data into parallel format for the CPU. USART signals the CPU when it can accept new characters for transmission, or when it has new data for the CPU. Synonymous with *programmable communications interface.*

universal synchronous receiver/transmitter (USRT): a high-speed transmission converter that provides serial-to-parallel and parallel-to-serial conversion to interface a parallel controller or terminal with a serial synchronous communication network. Upon receiving serial bits, USRT converts the serial data into parallel words. USRT is dependent on a timing system rather than on the start and stop bits used in USART. Cf. *universal synchronous-asynchronous receiver/transmitter (USART).*

universal Turing machine: a Turing machine that can simulate any other Turing machine. (A)

UNIX: a powerful operating system program, originally developed by Bell Labs engineers, making it possible for applications programs that perform specific tasks to be transferred easily from one brand of system to another. UNIX can also readily handle several tasks at once, an important feature in an office where many people use a computer at the same time.

unlike device types: data storage units different in their operation or characteristics; for example, tape and disk drives. When a file is concatenated across unlike device types, the operating system adapts and reformats the data so that they can be treated consistently by the program.

unload: removing information in large quantities as in unloading the storage contents onto a magnetic tape.

unlock: to allow a locked disk or document to be changed, deleted, or renamed. See *lock.*

unmodified instruction: deprecated term for *presumptive instruction.* (A) (B)

unpack: to recover the original form of the data from packed data. (A) (B)

unpacked decimal: representation of a decimal value by a single digit in one byte. For example, in unpacked decimal, the decimal value 23 is represented by xxxx0010 xxxx0011, where xxxx in each case represents a zone. Cf. *packed decimal.*

unprotect: removing constraints on access to a file so that any program may read and modify the data it holds.

unprotected dynamic storage: synonym for *dynamic storage.*

unprotected field: on a display device, a display field in which the user can enter, modify, or erase data. Cf. *protected field.*

unrecoverable ABEND: an error condition that results in abnormal termination of a program. Cf. *recoverable ABEND.*

unsigned integer: an integer value without a sign (+ or −), and therefore assumed to be positive.

unsigned real number: a real value without a sign (+ or −), and therefore assumed to be positive.

unsolicited message: a warning or error message from a program indicating that something is wrong. Synonymous with *unsolicited status.*

unsolicited status: synonymous with *unsolicited message.*

unsqueeze: see *squeezed files.*

unstable state: in a trigger circuit, a state in which the circuit remains for a finite period of time at the end of which it returns to a stable state without the application of a pulse. (A)

unstack: removing from the top of a stack.

unstratified language: a language that can be used as its own metalanguage; for example, most natural languages. (B) Cf. *stratified language.* (A)

unused time: time available for machine activities that is left unused and frequently unattended by any computer system personnel.

unwind: to state explicitly and in full, without the use of modifiers, all the instructions that are involved in the execution of a loop. (A) (B)

UP: see *uniprocessing.*

up: in computing, an operation system. Cf. *down.*

up and running: a computer system or piece of equipment that has just been put into operation and is working properly.

UPB: see *upper bound.*

update (U): to modify a master file with current information according to a specified procedure.

up-down counter: a binary counting device that changes its counting mode from up to down (or vice versa) without disturbing the count stored up to that time.

up-down counter module: a module providing event counting for a computer system. It is capable of detecting count overflows and setting up flags for this situation.

upgrade: an improvement in a device or a version of software, often seen as taking the user into a new level of performance.

upper bound (UB) (UPB): in PL/1, the upper limit of an array dimension.

upper case: capital letters.

upper curtate: the adjacent card rows at the top of a punch card. (A)

UPS: see *uninterruptible power supply.*

up stop:
(1) a mechanical device limiting upward motion of a moveable part.
(2) a physical part (usually nonmovable) used to limit or stop the upward travel of the armature in an electromechanical device such as a relay.

up time: deprecated term for *available time.* Synonym for *operating time.* (A) (B)

upward compatibility: the capability of a computer to execute programs written for another computer without major alteration, but not vice versa.

UR: see *unit record.*

US: see *unit separator character.* (A)

USART: see *universal synchronous-asynchronous receiver/transmitter.*

USASCII: United States of America Standard Code for Information Exchange. A code using eight bits per character (one being a parity bit), the character set consisting of graphic characters and control characters, used for the interchange of information between data-processing systems and communications systems, and between the machines associated with systems of both types. Deprecated term for *ASCII.* (A)

USASI: United States of America Standards Institute; a former name of the American National Standards Institute. Deprecated term for *ANSI.*

usec: microsecond; 1/1,000,000 of a second.

user (U):
(1) anyone who requires the services of a computing system. See also *end user.*
(2) a person who requires the services of a computing system.

user area (UA): pertaining to the area of a magnetic disk where semipermanent data is kept.

user data signaling rate: the rate at which a terminal receives information, usually given in bits per second. It may not be the same rate as information received by any modem associated with the terminal since, in some forms of data transmission, envelopes of control information pass between distant modems, but only higher-level user information within the envelopes is passed to and from the terminals.

user-definable keys: keyboard keys able to initiate specific operations in a program; the user defines the functions of the keys.

user-defined function: as distinguished from a stored or library function, one specified by a user in a program. After it has been specified, a user-defined function may be used by reference to its name, often following the same rules in most languages as for a stored function. The exact rules of specification follow the rules of a given computer language.

user-defined (enumerated) type: the ordered set of distinct values (constants) defined as a data type in a program. See *ordinal type.*

user-defined word: a COBOL word that must be supplied by a user to satisfy the format of a clause or statement.

user exit: a do-nothing instruction built into a software product where the customer can install a hook to activate a custom feature. Should the exit not be used, execution simply proceeds past it.

user facility: a set of functions available on demand to a user, and provided as part of a data network transmission service. Synonymous with *user service.*

user-friendly: a system which relatively untrained users can interact with easily. Usually, suggests the use of a high level programming language.

user group (UG): an organization utilizing a variety of computing systems sharing knowledge and programs that each have used and developed.

USERID: see *user identification.*

user identification (USERID):
(1) a symbol identifying a system user.
(2) a code that uniquely identifies a user to the system.

user input area: on a display device, the lines of the screen where the user is required to key in command or data lines.

user interaction: synonymous with *interactive system.*

user interface:
(1) an organizational unit within a data-processing department that coordinates

activities between the computer operators and the system users.

(2) the portion of an interactive computer program that issues messages to and receives commands from a terminal user.

(3) the entire set of rules and convention by which a computer system communicates with the user. May change with different software.

user label: an identification record for a tape or disk file; the format and contents are defined by the user, who must also write the necessary processing routines.

user library: a library stored within a computer, for either private or general usage.

user memory: CPU memory accessed and altered by a user. It is the part of the random access memory usually used by application programs.

username: the name chosen by a computer owner or network administrator to identify a user. After this identification is complete, the user is a registered user and can connect to that computer as such.

user-oriented language: a programming language whose vocabulary and grammar rules mimic those of a discipline. Programs written in such a language employ the jargon of the discipline and parallel the solution processes to it.

user profile table: in systems with time sharing, a table of user attributes built for each active user from information gathered during log on.

user program: a program written specifically for or by a particular user. Cf. *utility program.*

user-programmable keys: special function keys on a terminal whose functions vary with the program in use.

user relations: synonymous with *user interface (1).*

user service: any set of data-processing functions made available to the user. Synonym for *user facility.*

user's group: see *user group.*

user space: storage that is not system space.

user terminal (UT): an input-output unit by which a user communicates with a data-processing system. (B)

user-written code:

(1) a program written by an individual or organization that actually uses it.

(2) a modification to a package that is invoked by a user exit.

USQ: see *squeezed files.*

USRT: see *universal synchronous receiver/ transmitter.*

UT: see *user terminal.*

utilities: software utilized for routine activities; designed to aid the operation and use of the computer. Examples include an editor, a debugger, a file handler.

utility: software for routine tasks or for assisting programmers.

utility bug: a design-aid program for the testing and debugging of utility functions, punching and loading of paper tapes, selecting breakpoints, and searching memory.

utility control console: a computer console used primarily to control utility and maintenance programs.

utility functions: pertaining to auxiliary operations such as tape searching, media conversion, and tape dumps.

utility program:

(1) a computer program in general support of the processes of a computer; for instance, a diagnostic program, a trace program, a sort program. Synonymous with *service program.* (A) (B)

(2) a program designed to perform an everyday task such as copying data from one storage device to another.

utility routine: a routine in general support of the processes of a computer; for instance, in input routine. Synonymous with *service routine.* (A) (B)

utility system: a program or system or set of systems developed to perform miscellaneous or utility functions such as card-to-tape, tape-to-printer, and other operations or suboperations.

utilization loggers system: a program or a unit that collects statistical information about how a system is performing.

UV PROM eraser: a device for erasing the contents of erasable programmable read-only memory (EPROM) chips by exposing them to ultraviolet light, permitting other data to be "burned" into them.

V:
(1) see *variable.*
(2) see *vector.*
(3) see *verification.*
(4) see *verify.*
(5) see *virtual.*

VA: see *virtual address.*

vacuum servo: a peripheral unit that maintains a magnetic tape reservoir, maintained by the absence of air pressure on one side of the tape.

VAL: see *value.*

validate: see *validation.*

validation: the checking of data for correctness, or compliance with applicable standards, rules, and conventions. (A)

validity check: a check that a code group is actually a character of the particular code in use.

validity checking: a screening method where data records are checked for range, valid coding, illogical bit combinations or storage addresses, and other related factors.

valley: in OCR, an indentation in a stroke.

valuator device: in computer graphics, an input device that provides a scalar value. See also *choice device, locator device, pick device.*

value (VAL):
(1) a specific occurrence of an attribute, for example, "blue" for the attribute "color."
(2) a quantity assigned to a constant, a variable, parameter, or a symbol. See also *argument.*

value-added firms: dealers and resellers, third parties, that buy hardware, write software for specific industries, and sell the entire system. See also *comprehensive distribution channels.*

VAR: see *variable.*

VARBLK: see *variable block.*

variable (V) (VAR):
(1) in computer programming, a character or group of characters that refers to a value and, in the execution of a computer program, corresponds to an address. (B)
(2) a quantity that can assume any of a given set of values. (A)
(3) in COBOL, a data item whose value may be changed during execution of the object program.
(4) in FORTRAN, a data item that is not an array or array element, identified by a symbolic name.
(5) in PL/1, a named entity that is used to refer to data and to which values can be assigned. Its attributes remain constant, but it can refer to different values at different times. Variables fall into three categories, applicable to any data type: element, array, and structure. Variables may be subscripted, qualified, or both, or may be pointer-qualified.
(6) see *loop-control variable.*

variable address: an address that is to be modified or has already been modified by an index register or similar unit.

variable block (VB): the number of characters in the block is determined by the programmer (usually between some practical limits).

variable-cycle operation: a characteristic of asynchronous units; computer activity where any cycle or operation can be of a different time length.

variable declaration: the creation of a variable in PASCAL in the variable declaration section of a block with the variable identifier on the left of the colon and the type definition or identifier on the right.

variable field length: a data field that has a variable number of characters; requiring item separators to indicate the end of each item.

variable field storage: an indefinite limit of length for the storage field.

variable-format messages: messages in which line control characters are not to be deleted upon arrival nor inserted upon departure; variable-format messages are intended for terminals with similar characteristics. Cf. *fixed-format messages.*

variable function generator: a function generator in which the function to be generated may be set by the user before or during computation. (B)

variable information processing (VIP): a generalized proprietary program for information storage and retrieval system that provides for retrieval approaches without programming.

variable-instruction length: a CPU having the ability to recognize different types of instructions with varying lengths.

variable-length character encoding: using a variable number of bits to represent characters, so that the most often used ones are represented with the least number of bits, thereby reducing the amount of storage space needed.

variable-length record:
(1) a record having a length independent of the length of other records with which it is logically or physically associated. Cf. *fixed-length record.*
(2) pertaining to a file in which the records are not uniform in length. (A)

variable-length word: a computer word where the number of characters is not fixed but is variable and subject to the discretion of the programmer.

variable name: an alphanumeric title given to represent a particular program variable.

variable pitch: the ability to set characters up close together, or farther apart.

variable point: within a number system, the location of the point indicated by a special character at that location.

variable-point representation: a positional representation in which the position of the radix point is explicitly indicated by a special character at that position. Cf. *floating-point representation.* (A)

variable-point representation system: a radix numeration system in which the radix point is explicitly indicated by a special character at that position. (A) (B)

variable record length: implies a set of records, all of which are not of the same length, character count, or field format specification. Typical of business ap-

plication; for example, a file of names and addresses, in which each name or address may be of differing length.

variable symbol: in assembler programming, a symbol used in macro and conditional assembly processing that can assume any of a given set of values.

variable time scale: in simulation, the time scale used in data processing when the time scale factor is not constant during a run. (A)

variable word: the specific feature where the number of characters handled in a device is not constant.

variable word length: refers to a machine in which the number of characters comprising a computer word is almost completely under the control of the coder. Not usually applied to machines in which there is a very limited form of control, such as half-words or double-length words. Cf. *fixed word-length computer.*

variable word length storage: synonymous with *character-addressable storage devices.*

vary:
(1) to turn on or turn off.
(2) to activate or deactivate.

vary off line:
(1) to change the status of a device from on line to off line. When a device is off line, no data set may be opened on that device.
(2) to place a device in a state where it is not available for use by the system; however, it is still available for executing I/O.

vary on line: to restore a device to a state where it is available for use by the system.

VDT: see *video display terminal.*

VDU: see *visual display unit.*

vector (V):
(1) a quantity usually represented by an ordered set of numbers. (A) (B)
(2) in computer graphics, a directed line segment.
(3) cf. *scalar.* (A)

vectored interrupt: an interrupt that carries a branch address or a peripheral unit identifier.

vectored priority interrupts: maskable products used with time counters for external inputs or dedicated external inputs, where each vector jumps the program to a specific memory address.

vectored restart: the automatic ability to clear the system during restart, saving program steps.

vector generator (VG): in computer graphics, a functional unit that generates directed line segments.

vector graphics: the most common class of graphics; where all vector output consists of lines and curves drawn point-to-point by the output unit as ordered by the computer.

vectoring: automatic branching to a specified address.

vector instruction: an instruction that accepts an interrupt and branches to the correct routine or unit.

vector graphics: the use of geometric formulas to translate images. See *object oriented programming, raster graphics.*

vector processors: a supercomputer designed to bring rigid order to unruly problems. They achieve tremendous speeds, (upward of 800 million floating point instructions per second) by dividing their problems into similar mathematical operations. See also *massively parallel computer.*

vector transfer: pertaining to communication linkage between two programs.

Veitch diagram: a means of representing boolean functions in which the number of variables determines the number of squares in the diagram; the number of squares needed is the number of possible states, that is, two raised to a power determined by the number of variables. (B) See also *Venn diagram.* (A)

vendor management: the technique for evaluating and managing the effectiveness of a vendor in data processing.

Venn diagram: a diagram in which sets are represented by regions drawn on a surface. (B) See also *Veitch diagram.* (A)

VER: see *verify.*

verb: a COBOL reserved word that expresses an action to be taken by a COBOL compiler or an object program.

verge-punched card: synonym for *edge-punched card.* (A)

verification (V): the act of determining whether an operation has been accomplished correctly.

verification mode: in systems with time sharing, a mode of operation under the EDIT command in which all subcommands are acknowledged and any textual changes are displayed as they are made.

verifier: a device that checks the correctness of transcribed data, usually by comparing with a second transcription of the same data or by comparing a retranscription with the original data. (A) (B) Synonymous with *key verifier, key-verify unit.*

verify (V) (VER):
(1) to determine whether a transcription of data or other operation has been accomplished accurately.
(2) to check the results of keypunching. (A)

vernier: in machinery, an auxiliary device for giving a piece of apparatus higher adjustment accuracy.

version:
(1) a number indicating a program's chronological position relative to previous and subsequent releases of the program.
(2) a separate program product, based on an existing program product, that usually has significant new code or new function. Each version has its own license, terms, conditions, product type number, monthly charge, documentation, test allowance (if applicable), and programming support category. See also *modification level, release.*

vertical: up and down. Some display screens show only a few lines vertically, but others show 40 or more.

vertical feed: pertaining to the entry of a punch card into a card feed with a short edge first. (A)

vertical parity check: a check in which the binary digits of a character column are added and the sum checked against an earlier computed parity digit to test whether the number of ones is odd or even.

vertical pitch: the number of lines per inch vertically measured on a particular printed page.

vertical positions: see *addressable vertical positions*. (A)

vertical processor: a microprogrammed computer using a narrow microinstruction word, thereby restricting the number of microorders per microinstruction, but making microprogramming easier.

vertical raster count: the number of vertical divisions in a raster.

vertical redundancy check (VRC): an odd parity check performed on each character of a block contrast with ASCII-coded data as the block is received. See also *cyclic redundancy check, longitudinal redundancy check*.

vertical resolution: the number of discrete picture elements that can be resolved along a vertical line drawn upon a display screen.

vertical scrolling: the ability of a system to move up and down through a page or more of data that is displayed on a terminal screen.

vertical table: a table where the bytes of each entry are sequentially stored, that is, entry one, byte one, entry two, byte two, and so on. FORTRAN stores arrays this way.

vertical tabulation character (VT) (VTAB): a format effector that causes the print or display position to move to the corresponding position on the next of a series of predetermined lines. (A) (B)

vertical wrapararound: on a display device, the continuation of cursor movement from the bottom character position in a vertical column to the top character position in the next column, or from the top position in a column to the bottom position in the preceding column. Cf. *horizontal wraparound*.

very large scale integration (VLSI): over 10,000 transistors per chip.

VG: see *vector generator*.

VGA: see *video graphics adapter*.

VID: see *video*.

video (VID): brightness and color data fed to a terminal. Synonymous with *terminal*.

video computer: a computer created for running cartridges that contain rote learning programs and games.

video display terminal (VDT): synonymous with *cathode-ray tube*.

video generator: a unit that accepts commands from a keyboard and drives the TV monitor.

videograph: high-speed cathode-ray printer.

video graphics adapter (VGA): a graphics card that works with either a color monitor or a black-and-white gray-scale monitor. See *super VGA*.

videographic display: computers that can draw pictures using dots or lines; computers that can rotate objects, showing them in perspective, moving them around, stretching, or shrinking them.

video monitor: a display device that can receive video signals by direct connection.

video-scan optical character reader: a unit that combines optical character reader with mark sense and card read. It can read printing and marks in the same pass as well as read holes in cards.

video terminal (VT): a terminal having a keyboard for sending information to the computer and a picture tube like a TV for displaying information. The video terminal is fast, silent, and has no moving parts. Its chief drawback is that it does not make a permanent record of the information displayed.

VIO: see *virtual I/O*.

VIP: see *variable information processing*.

virgin medium: a data medium in or on which data have never been recorded; for example, paper that is unmarked, punch tape that has no holes. (B)

virtual (V): pertaining to a conceptual, not physical, presence.

virtual address (VA): the address of a notational storage location in virtual storage. (A) (B)

virtual address space: in virtual storage system, the virtual storage assigned to a batched or terminal job, a system task, or a task initiated by a command.

virtual computing system: synonym for *virtual machine*.

virtual console function: a CP command that is executed via the diagnose interface.

virtual copy: the production of an exact duplicate of the contents of locations in the memory of a computer onto an external bulk storage unit, including reproducing the information regarding the exact memory addresses in which the data being stored resides.

virtual image: in computer graphics, the complete visual representation of an encoded image that could be displayed if a display surface of sufficient size were available.

virtual I/O (VIO): a facility that pages data into and out of external page storage; to the problem program, the data to be read from or written to direct-access storage devices.

virtual machine (VM): a functional simulation of a computer and its associated devices.

virtual memory (VM): deprecated term for *virtual storage*. (A) (B)

virtual memory printer: a pointer for keeping track of the parts of programs and data scattered between main memory and auxiliary storage in a virtual memory system.

virtual memory technique (VMT): a memory system operating as if all instructions and data were on main memory when they are actually segmented between main memory and secondary storage. The method locates the instruction and operands, and if not in main storage, transfers them from secondary storage sites which serve as the virtual memory sites.

virtual point picture character: in PL/1, the picture specification character V, which is used in picture specifications to indicate the position of an assumed decimal or binary point.

virtual processing time: the time required to execute the instructions of a virtual machine.

virtual route (VR): a path between a data source and a data sink that may be created by various circuit configurations during the transmission of packets or messages.

virtual space: in computer graphics, a space in which the coordinates of the display elements are expressed in terms of user coordinates.

virtual storage (VS): the notion of storage space that may be regarded as addressable main storage by the user of a computer system in which virtual addresses are mapped into real addresses. The size of virtual storage is limited by the addressing scheme of the computer system and by the amount of auxiliary storage available, and not by the actual number of main storage locations. (B)

virtual storage access method (VSAM): an access method for direct or sequential processing of fixed and variable-length records on direct-access devices. The records in a VSAM data set or file can be organized in logical sequence by a key field (key sequence), in the physical sequence in which they are written on the data set or file (entry sequence), or by relative-record number.

virtual storage management (VSM): routines that allocate address spaces and virtual storage areas within address spaces and keep a record of free and allocated storage within each address space.

virtual terminal network: a network permitting the user to choose the type of terminal to be used at each location independently.

virus: a program designed with malicious intent to damage files. Virus programs can be spread through networks and bulletin board services as well as on disks. Virus-detection and virus-elimination programs are available through dealers and user groups.

virus-detection: see *virus*.

virus-elimination: see *virus*.

visible file: the systematic arrangement of forms, cards, or documents so that data placed on the margin can serve as an index for the user to rapidly see without the need to withdraw each item.

VisiCalc: the first electronic spreadsheet software written for a personal computer.

visual display: in word processing, a device for electronically displaying text. Depending on the equipment, the display may be full page, partial page, single line, or partial line.

visual display station: an input-output unit permitting the inquiry of a CPU using a CRT or similar display.

visual display unit: synonymous with *terminal.*

visual inquiry station: an input-output unit that allows the interrogation of an automatic data-processing system by the immediate processing of data from a person or terminal source, together with the display of the results of the processing; often on a cathode-ray tube.

visual scanner:
(1) a unit that scans optically and usually generates an analog or digital signal.
(2) a unit that optically scans printed or written data and generates their representation.

visual terminal: a device permitting the inquiry of a processor along with the input of data, using a visual display technology.

VLSI: see *very large scale integration.*

VM:
(1) see *virtual machine.*
(2) see *virtual memory.*

V-mode records: in COBOL, records of variable length, each of which is wholly contained within a block. Blocks may contain more than one record. Each record contains a record length field, and each block contains a block length field.

VMT: see *virtual memory technique.*

VOCAB: see *vocabulary.*

vocabulary (VOCAB): a list of operations or instructions, available to a computer programmer, to use in writing the program for a given problem on a specific computer. Synonymous with *character.*

voice-data work stations: desktop machines for managers that combine a personal computer and an advanced telephone in a single, compact unit.

void:
(1) in character recognition, the inadvertent absence of ink within a character outline. (A)
(2) in OCR, a light spot in a character that is surrounded by ink.

VOL: see *volume.*

volatile: becoming lost or erased when power is removed.

volatile dynamic storage: a dynamic storage that relies upon a supply of power along with refresh circuitry for maintaining stored information.

volatile file: a temporary or rapidly changing program or file.

volatile memory: a storage medium in which information is destroyed when power is removed from the system. See also *volatile storage.*

volatile storage:
(1) a storage device whose contents are lost when power is removed. (B)
(2) in word processing, storage from which recorded text is lost when power to the machine is switched off.
(3) cf. *nonvolatile storage.*

volatility: the percentage of records on a file that are added or deleted in a run. See also *activity.*

volatility of storage: the tendency of a storage unit to lose data when power is removed. Storage media can be classed as volatile or nonvolatile.

VOLSER: volume/serial. A complete unit of storage space, such as a reel of tape, that is identified to the computer by a *volume serial number.*

voltage pencil: synonym for *stylus.*

volume (VOL):
(1) a certain portion of data, together with its data carrier, that can be handled conveniently as a unit. (B)
(2) a data carrier that is mounted and demounted as a unit; for example, a reel of magnetic tape, a disk pack. (B)
(3) that portion of a single unit of storage that is accessible to a single read/write mechanism; for example, a drum, a disk pack, or part of a disk storage module.
(4) space on a hard disk or a file server that's defined and named as a place to store files. A hard disk is usually a single volume, but it can be partitioned into several volumes.
(5) see *base volume, duplicate volume.*

volume label: the name given a disk to identify it.

volume serial number: see *VOLSER.*

volume switch procedures: standard procedures executed automatically when the end of a unit or reel has been reached before the end of file has been reached.

volume table of contents (VTOC): a table on a direct-access volume that describes each data set on the volume.

volume test: the processing of a volume of actual data to check for program malfunctions. See *debug*. Cf. *redundancy check*.

voluntary interrupt: an interrupt to a processor or system caused by an object program's deliberate use of a function known to cause an interrupt that is under program control.

von Neumann bottleneck: the single channel along which data and instructions must flow between a conventional computer's central processor and its memory. It can limit the pace of production.

von Neumann sort: in a sort program, merging strings of sequenced data. The power of the merge is equal to T/2.

V picture specification character: see *virtual point picture character*.

VR: see *virtual route*.

VS: see *virtual storage*.

VSAM: see *virtual storage access method*.

VSM: see *virtual storage management*.

VT:
(1) see *vertical tabulation character*. (A)
(2) see *video terminal*.

VTAB: see *vertical tabulation character*.

VTOC: see *volume table of contents*.

V-type address constant: in the assembler language, an address constant used for branching to another module. See also *A-type address constant*.

W:
(1) see *waiting time*.
(2) see *wait time*.
(3) see *word*.
(4) see *write*.

wafer: a thin slice from a silicon ingot that is the basis of the chip. See *steppers*.

wafer-scale integration: see *ultimate wafer*.

waiting list: see *wait list*.

waiting state: see *wait state*.

waiting time (W):
(1) the condition of a task that depends on one or more events in order to enter the ready condition.
(2) the condition of a processing unit when all operations are suspended.
(3) synonym for *latency*. (A)

wait list: synonymous with *queue*.

wait state: synonym for *latency*. (B)

wait time (WT): see *waiting time*.

walkthrough: an administrative procedure for reviewing the design and operation of a new program or job.

wallpaper: slang, a file containing a listing or transcript, especially a file containing a transcript of all or part of a session.

wand: a device used to read information encoded on merchandise tickets, credit cards, and employee badges.

warm boot: reloading or reinitializing systems software in such a way that programs presently in execution are unaffected. Cf. *cold boot*.

warm start: a restart that allows reuse of previously initialized input and output work queues. Synonym for *normal restart, system restart*.

warm-up time: the interval between the energizing of a unit and the commencement of the applications of its output characteristics.

warning message: an indication that a possible error has been detected. Cf. *error message*.

watchdog: devices used to discern whether some prescribed condition is present, usually within a predetermined time period.

watchdog timer: a timer set by a program to prevent the system from looping endlessly or becoming idle because of program or equipment malfunction.

watermark magnetics: a system for encoding information into a magnetic stripe; used in banking as the encoded information is not erased or altered when the stripe passes through a strong magnetic field.

WD: see *word*.

WE: see *write enable.*

weak external reference (WXTRN): an external reference that does not have to be resolved during linkage editing. If it is not resolved, it appears as though its value was resolved to zero.

wearout failure: failure due to normal deterioration or mechanical wear, the probability of which increases with usage.

weight: in a positional representation, the factor by which the value represented by a character in the digit place is multiplied to obtain its additive contribution in the representation of a real number. Synonymous with *significance.* (A) (B)

weighted average: a moving average performed on data where some of the values are more heavily valued than are others.

what you see is what you get: see *WYSIWYG.*

whirley bird: deprecated term designating some type of disk pack equipment.

whiteboards: see *electronic whiteboards.*

wide area network: a network encompassing a large geographic area. Cf. *local area network.*

wild card: in word processing, a card that allows the user to search for text strings in which certain parts of the string don't matter.

Winchester disk: a type of hard disk, usually not interchangeable.

window: a rectangular area that displays information on the desktop. Documents are created and viewed through windows as well as the contents of disks.

windows: deprecated term for Microsoft Windows; a popular operating environment for DOS systems.

window editor: an interactive editing program that treats the viewing area of a video display as if it were a window with a view of the computer's memory. This window can then be shifted around by commands to look at different areas of memory, while other commands effect changes in what is seen.

windowing: the ability to display simultaneously a collage of material, that is, graphics or different parts of text from the same document, on a computer screen.

winnage: slang, when a lossage is corrected. See *lossage.*

wire board: synonymous with *board.*

wired program computer: a computer in which the instructions that specify the operations to be performed are specified by the placement and interconnection of wires; the wires are usually held by a removable control panel, allowing flexibility of operation, but the term is also applied to permanently wired machines which are then called fixed program computers.

wireless terminal: a portable, or handheld terminal that communicates with a computer by radio.

wire matrix printer: a type of impact printer that creates characters through the use of dot-matrix patterns. Synonymous with *dot matrix printer.* See also *wire printer.* (B)

wire storage: see *magnetic wire storage.* (A)

wire wrap (WW) board: a circuit board using wires that are wrapped numerous times around a square pin to make contact.

wirewrapped panel: a panel for accommodating a random-access memory system along with the read-only memory and processor needed for a computer system.

wiring board: see *control panel.*

word (W) (WD):
(1) a character string or a binary element string that is convenient for some purpose to consider as an entity. (B)
(2) a character string or a bit string considered as an entity. (A)
(3) in COBOL, a string of not more than 30 characters, chosen from the following: the letters A through Z, the digits 0 through 9, and the hyphen (-). The hyphen may not appear as either the first or last character.
(4) synonymous with *full word.*
(5) see *alphabetic word, computer word, double-word, half-word, index word, instruction word, numeric word, parameter word, reserved word.* (A)

word-addressable: a computer where each word has a unique address used in a program for accessing data. Cf. *byte-addressable.*

word address format: the order of appearance of the character information within a word.

word boundary: a memory address that is evenly divisible by the word length of a computer.

word capacity: the selection of one of the word lengths of the devices as a datum and thus to classify different operations as partial or multiples of these lengths for working.

word count: the number of words in a record or other data item.

word counter: a register holding the transfer word count during block transfer operations.

word counter register: a register for keeping track of input-output transfer.

word-half: a group of characters representing half of a computer word for addressing purposes as a unit found in storage.

word index: the contents of a storage position or register that can be used to automatically alter the effective address of any given instruction.

word length: the number of characters or binary elements in a word. (A) (B)

word mark: an indicator that signals the beginning or the end of a word.

word-organized storage: a storage device into which or from which data can be entered or retrieved only in units of a computer word. (B)

word-oriented: pertaining to an early memory system where "words," each of which had a location number and contained bits of binary digits to hold about 10 numeric positions.

word pattern: the smallest meaningful language unit recognized by a machine.

word processing (WP):
(1) a means for improving the efficiency and effectiveness of business communications.
(2) pertaining to machines, systems, or processes, that provide: (a) efficient text entry techniques (either manual keying or machine reading), (b) serial processing of text and control character strings, (c)

final format text presentation (printed or displayed) for business communications.

word-processing center: a central location handling word processing for many people throughout a company.

word-processing equipment: equipment used to prepare business correspondence by keying and temporarily storing text for subsequent revision and editing the stored text in groups of characters such as words, lines, paragraphs, or pages, as distinguished from equipment that permits only character-by-character editing. Text may be printed out immediately upon keying or at a later time automatically or semi-automatically from internal storage or from a recording medium such as magnetic cards or tape made by the text originating machine or by a print-only machine.

word processor (WP): a text editing unit designed for preparation, storage, and dissemination of text initiated on typewriterlike devices.

word-processor networks: a system where word processors are interconnected by communications facilities providing for the distribution of information recorded as documents within a word-processing environment.

word size: a fixed number of bits, dependent upon the hardware architecture, serving as the basic logical unit of information. The CPU processes and transfers each word as a separate entity.

word space: the actual area or space occupied by a word in serial digital units such as drums, disks, tapes, and serial lines.

word time: in a storage device that provides serial access to storage locations, the time interval between the appearance of corresponding parts of successive words. (A)

word time comparator: the circuitry that compares the word time counter with the specified word time at the moment of coincident pulse. This is done to verify that the correct word has been read.

word underscore character (WUS): a word-processing control that causes the word immediately preceding it to be graphically underscored.

word wrap: in word processing, the capability to move automatically the last word on a line to a new line if otherwise it would overrun the right margin. (D)

word wraparound: see *wraparound.*

work area: an area of memory used for temporary storage of data during processing. Synonymous with *working storage, work space.*

work file:

(1) a file used to provide storage space for data that is needed only for the duration of a job.

(2) in sorting, an intermediate file used for temporary storage of data between phases.

(3) see also *work volume.*

workgroup: a group of users, usually on a local area network.

working area: synonym for *working space.* (A) (B)

working equipment: the basic set of machines for modules in which more than one set is available and the other sets are standby equipment in the event of a failure of the working units.

working memory: the internal memory that stores information for processing.

working register: a register reserved for data on which operations are performed.

working routine: produces the results of the problem or program as it was designed, as contrasted with the routines designed for support, housekeeping, or to compile, assemble, translate, and so on.

working set:

(1) the set of a user's pages that must be active in order to avoid excessive paging.

(2) the amount of real storage required for paging in order to avoid a thrashing condition.

working space (WS): that portion of main storage that is used by a computer program to temporarily hold data. Synonymous with *working area, working storage.* (A) (B)

working storage: synonym for *temporary storage, working space.* (A)

working storage section: in COBOL, section name (and the section itself) in the data division. The section describes records and noncontiguous data items that are not part of external files, but are developed and processed internally. It also defines data items whose values are assigned in the source program.

work-in-process queue: items that have had some processing and are queued by and for the computer to finish the required processing.

work output queue: a list of data which is output, but is stored temporarily in an auxiliary medium until a printer or other output unit becomes available.

work process schedule: sets operating time of the overall data-processing activity to ensure that the equipment is effectively used.

work queue entry: the control blocks and tables created from one job in an input stream and placed in the job's input work queue or in one of the output work queues.

work session: a session initiated by an operator when the log on sequence has been successfully completed and ending when the operator logs off. An inquiry session may be included as part of the work session. See also *session.*

work space (WS): synonymous with *work area.*

work stack:

(1) a list that is constructed and maintained so that the next information to be retrieved is the most recently stored information in the list, that is, a last-in, first-out (LIFO) or push-down list.

(2) an area of unprotected main storage allocated to each task and used by the programs executed by that task.

work station (WS): a configuration of input-output equipment at which an operator works. (D)

work volume: a volume made available to the system to provide storage space for temporary files or data sets at peak loads.

wormwhole: slang, a location in a monitor containing the address of a routine, with the intent of making it easier to substitute a different routine.

worst case: where maximum stress is placed on a system as in making it purposely error-prone, or inefficient for testing.

WP:

(1) see *word processing.*

(2) see *word processor.*

(3) see *write protection.*

WPRT: see *write protection.*

WR: see *write.*

wraparound:

(1) in computer graphics, the display at some point on the display space of the display elements whose coordinates lie outside of the display space.

(2) the continuation of an operation from the maximum addressable location in storage to the first addressable location.

(3) the continuation of register addresses from the highest register address to the lowest.

wrap capability: the ability to directly connect the input and output lines of a modem.

wrap mode: a means of display management on a video screen where a portion of a line exceeding the width of the screen wraps around to the start of the following line so that it can be seen.

write (W) (WR): to make a permanent or transient recording of data in a storage device or on a data medium. (A) (B)

writable control storage: a read/write memory found in the control part of a system. The read/write memory replaces a ROM and gives the designer additional capability to alter the characteristics of the computer system.

writable control store: the control part of read/write memory permitting a user to microcode a specialized instruction set for system application.

write addressing: to direct or control a write operation in a unit where the first location address contains all zeros and each successive address is incremented by one bit, as with a binary counter.

write after read: restoring earlier read data into a memory unit following completion of the read cycle.

write cycle time: the minimum time interval between the start of successive write cycles of a storage device that has separate reading and writing cycles. (B)

write enable (WE): to install in a tape reel a write-enable ring. Such a reel is write-enabled. A reel with the ring removed is protected.

write-enable ring: a device that is installed in a tape reel to permit writing on the tape. If a tape is mounted without the ring in position, writing cannot occur; the file is protected.

write head: a magnetic head capable of writing only. (B)

write interval: the determination of the interval during machine activity when output data is available for an output operation, that is, the net time exclusive of transmission which it takes to perform an output operation such as printing or writing on tape.

write key: a code in the program status double-word used in conjunction with a memory lock to determine whether or not a program can write into a specific page of actual addresses.

write key field: that part of the program status double-word that contains the write key.

write memory lock: a 2-bit write-project field optionally provided for each 512-word page of core memory addresses.

write-only: transferring information from logic unit or files.

write-process-read: reading in one block of data, while simultaneously processing the preceding block and writing out the results of the previously processed block.

write protection (WP) (WPRT): restriction of writing into a data set, file, disk, or storage area by a user or program not authorized to do so.

writer: see *output writer.*

write ring: a "ring" used to allow data to be written on a scratch tape. No ring, no write.

write time: the interval between the beginning of transcription to a storage unit and the end of transcription.

write-to-operator (WTO): an optional user-coded service whereby a message may be written to the system console operator informing him of errors and unusual system conditions that may need correcting.

write-to-operator with reply (WTOR): an optional user-coded service whereby a message may be written to the system console operator informing him of errors and unusual conditions that may need correcting. The operator must key in a response to this message.

writing: the action of making a permanent or transient recording of data in a storage device or on a data medium. (A) (B)

writing head: see *write head.*

writing-while read: reading a record(s) into storage from a tape at the same time another record(s) is written from storage onto tape.

WS:

(1) see *working storage.*

(2) see *work space.*

(3) see *work station.*

WTO: see *write-to-operator.*

WTOR: see *write-to-operator with reply.*

WUS: see *word underscore character.*

WW: see *wire wrap board.*

WXTRN: see *weak external reference.*

WYSIWYG: what you see is what you get. The ability to view on a screen exactly what will be printed, including different typefaces, the placement of graphics and scanned images, column layouts, and headers/footers.

X:

(1) see *index.*

(2) see *transmission.*

x-axis: the horizontal axis, as on a CRT screen, graph, printer, or plotter.

X-datum line: an imaginary line, used as a reference edge, along the top edge of a punch card, that is, a line along the edge nearest the 12-punch row of a Hollerith card. (A)

XEC: an instruction to execute register contents. See *execute.*

XEQ: see *execute.*

xerographic printer: a printer with paper that is electrically charged on the areas that are to represent characters, and dusted with dry ink particles which adhere to the charged areas.

XFER: see *transfer.*

X-height: the height of a lower-case letter when ascenders and descenders are excluded.

Xmas-tree sorting: a technique utilized in the internal portion of a sort program. The results of the comparisons between groups of records are stored for later use.

XMIT: see *transmit.*

XMODEM: a file transfer protocol used to send and receive files in discrete packets. XMODEM checks for transmission errors after each packet is sent and received.

XMT: see *transmit.*

X-off: transmitter off.

X-on: transmitter on.

XON/XOFF: a communications protocol that tells a computer to start or stop sending data by sending either an XON or an XOFF, which are ASCII characters.

XOR: see *exclusive-OR.*

XOR gate: a gate producing a signal of binary 0 when both input signals are 1 or both input signals are 0; otherwise the output signal is 1.

X punch: synonym for *eleven punch.* (A)

XREF: see *cross-reference listing.*

Xs-3: excess three (code).

X.25: an international standard method of connection between computers or terminals and a public network which operates using packet switching.

xy address: the intersection of xy coordinates.

xy coordinates: the specification of a location (an address) by the use of graphing. These coordinates are often used as cursor addresses on a display screen, as subscripts of an array element, and for other such indexing.

X-Y plotter: synonymous with *data plotter.*

xyz space: in computer graphics, a three-dimensional coordinate system based on the 1931 chromaticity diagram which plotted X, Y, and Z as the tristimulus values of a color.

y-axis: the vertical axis, as on a CRT screen, graph, printer, or plotter.

Y-datum line: an imaginary line, used as a reference edge, passing along the right edge of a punch card at right angles to the X-datum line. (A)

yield: the usable chips in a production batch.

yoke: a group of read/write heads attached that can be moved together.

yoyo mode: slang, the condition of a system when it rapidly alternates several times between being up and being down.

Y punch: synonym for *twelve punch.* (A)

Z: see *zero bit.*

zap: to erase. Cf. *blow.*

Zapf Dingbat: see *dingbat.*

zatacoding: a system of superimposing codes by edge-notched cards.

Z80: a microprocessor chip; an 8-bit CPU used in microcomputers.

zero: in data processing, the number that, when added to or subtracted from another number, does not alter the value of that other number. (B) See *leading zero, trailing zero.* (A)

zero access storage: storage for which the latency (waiting time) is small.

zero address: synonym for *immediate address.*

zero address code: an instruction code containing no instruction code for the following address.

zero address instruction: an instruction that contains no address part, and is used when the address is implicit or when no address is required. (A) (B)

zero bit: the two high-order bits of the program counter that are labeled the Z (zero) and L (link) bits.

zero compression: that process that eliminates the storage of insignificant leading zeros to the left of the most significant digits. See also *zero suppression.*

zero condition: the state of a magnetic cell when it represents zero. Synonymous with *cleared condition, nought state, zero state.*

zero elimination: synonymous with *zero suppression.*

zero-error reference: a constant ratio of incremental cause and effect.

zero fill: a character fill with the representation of the character zero. Synonymous with *zeroize.* (A) (B)

zero flag: an indicator set to a logic 1 condition if a register that is tested contains all 0s in its cell positions. It is set to a logic 0 state if any cell in the register is in a 1 condition.

zeroize: synonym for *zero fill.* (A) (B)

zero kill: a feature on some sorters determining that only zeros remain in the high order positions of documents while the documents are being sorted in lower order positions.

zero-level address: synonym for *immediate address.* (B) See *level of addressing.*

zero matrix: synonymous with *null matrix.*

zero-page addressing: where the zero page instructions permit for shorter code and execution times by only fetching the second byte of the instruction and assuming a zero high address byte.

zero proof: a procedure of checking computations by adding positive and negative values so that if all computations are accurate the total of such proof would be zero.

zero-punch: a punch in the third row from the top of a Hollerith card. (A)

zero state: synonymous with *zero condition.*

zero suppression: the elimination from a numeral of zeros that have no significance in the numeral. Zeros that have no significance include those to the left of the nonzero digits in the integral part of a numeral and those to the right of the nonzero digits in the fractional part.

zero-suppression characters: in PL/1, the picture specification characters Z, Y, and *, which are used to suppress zeros in the corresponding digit positions.

zero wait state: describes microprocessors that do not need to wait for slower chips.

Z-fold: synonymous with *fan-fold paper.*

ZMODEM: a file transfer protocol that is faster than *XMODEM.*

zone:

(1) that part of a character code used with the numeric codings to represent nonnumeric information.

(2) a part of internal storage allocated for a particular purpose.

(3) zones are set up by a network administrator and are used to group the devices on the network for easier access.

zone bits: the bits other than the four used to represent the digits in a dense binary code.

zone decimal: the representation of a decimal number in one or more eight-bit bytes, where the rightmost four bits of each byte represent a digit and the leftmost four bits represent the zone bits.

zoned format: a binary-coded decimal format where one decimal digit consists of zone bits and numeric bits and occupies an entire byte of storage.

zone digit: a digit utilized as a key to a section of code; can be used independently of other markings for control significance within a system.

zone punch:

(1) a hole punched in one of the upper 3 card rows of a 12-row punch card. (B)

(2) a hole punched in one of the punch rows designated as 12, 11, or 0, and sometimes 8 or 9. A 0 punch, and sometimes a 9 punch, by itself, is considered a numeric punch.

(3) a zero punch in combination with a numeric punch.

(4) cf. *digit punch.* (A)

zone rows: the upper three rows (numbered 12, 11, and 0) found on an 80-column punched card.

zoom box: a small box in the top-right corner of the title bar of the active window. Clicking the zoom box resizes the window so that the user can see all of its contents (if possible). Clicking it again returns the window to its previous size.